**Information Technology
Research and Development**
Critical Trends and Issues

Pergamon Titles of Related Interest
Published in Conjunction with OTA

COMMERCIAL BIOTECHNOLOGY: AN INTERNATIONAL ANALYSIS
FEDERAL POLICIES AND THE MEDICAL DEVICES INDUSTRY

Related Titles

Bell / DATABASE PERFORMANCE
Blunden / INFORMATION TECHNOLOGY AND THE PRINT AND PUBLISHING INDUSTRIES
Bytheway / STRUCTURED METHODS
Cluff / THE COMPUTER USER
English / DATA COMMUNICATIONS
Fox / EXPERT SYSTEMS
Gvishiani / SYSTEMS RESEARCH
Rijnsdorp / TRAINING FOR TOMORROW: EDUCATIONAL ASPECTS OF COMPUTERIZED AUTOMATION
Rushby / COMPUTER BASED LEARNING
Wallis / SOFTWARE ENGINEERING DEVELOPMENTS

Related Journals*

COMPUTER STATE OF THE ART REPORTS
COMPUTERS AND EDUCATION
COMPUTERS AND OPERATIONS RESEARCH
INFORMATION PROCESSING & MANAGEMENT
INFORMATION SYSTEMS
SYSTEMS RESEARCH

*Sample copies available on request

Information Technology Research and Development
Critical Trends and Issues

Office of Technology Assessment
Congress of the United States
Washington, DC

Pergamon Press
New York • Oxford • Toronto • Sydney • Frankfurt

Pergamon Press Offices:

U.S.A.	Pergamon Press Inc., Maxwell House, Fairview Park, Elmsford, New York 10523, U.S.A.
U.K.	Pergamon Press Ltd., Headington Hill Hall, Oxford OX3 0BW, England
CANADA	Pergamon Press Canada Ltd., Suite 104, 150 Consumers Road, Willowdale, Ontario M2J 1P9, Canada
AUSTRALIA	Pergamon Press (Aust.) Pty. Ltd., P.O. Box 544, Potts Point, NSW 2011, Australia
FEDERAL REPUBLIC OF GERMANY	Pergamon Press GmbH, Hammerweg 6, D-6242 Kronberg-Taunus, Federal Republic of Germany

Library of Congress Cataloging in Publication Data

```
Main entry under title:

Information technology research and development.

   Includes index.
   1. Electronic data processing--Research.
2. Telecommunication--Research.   I. United States.
Congress.  Office of Technology Assessment.
QA76.27.I535  1985    004    85-26026
ISBN 0-08-033648-5
```

Published in cooperation with the Office of Technology Assessment, Congress of the United States, 1985

All rights reserved. No part of this publication may be reproduced, stored in a retrieval system or transmitted in any form or by any means: electronic, electrostatic, magnetic tape, mechanical, photocopying, recording or otherwise, without permission in writing from the publishers.

Printed in Great Britain by A. Wheaton & Co. Ltd., Exeter

Contents

Chapter	Page
1. Introduction and Summary	3
2. The Environment for R&D in Information Technology in the United States	25
3. Selected Case Studies in Information Technology Research and Development	55
4. Effects of Deregulation and Divestiture on Research	111
5. Education and Human Resources for Research and Development	139
6. New Roles for Universities in Information Technology R&D	169
7. Foreign Information Technology Research and Development	201
8. Information Technology R&D in the Context of U.S. Science and Technology Policy	279
9. Technology and Industry	307
Index	339

Office of Technology Assessment

Congressional Board of the 99th Congress

TED STEVENS, *Alaska, Chairman*

MORRIS K. UDALL, *Arizona, Vice Chairman*

Senate	House
ORRIN G. HATCH *Utah*	GEORGE E. BROWN, JR. *California*
CHARLES McC. MATHIAS, JR. *Maryland*	JOHN D. DINGELL *Michigan*
EDWARD M. KENNEDY *Massachusetts*	CLARENCE E. MILLER *Ohio*
ERNEST F. HOLLINGS *South Carolina*	COOPER EVANS *Iowa*
CLAIBORNE PELL *Rhode Island*	Vacant

JOHN H. GIBBONS
(Nonvoting)

Advisory Council

WILLIAM J. PERRY, *Chairman* *Hambrecht & Quist*	CLAIRE T. DEDRICK *California Land Commission*	CARL N. HODGES *University of Arizona*
DAVID S. POTTER, *Vice Chairman* *General Motors Corp.*	JAMES C. FLETCHER *University of Pittsburgh*	CHARLES N. KIMBALL *Midwest Research Institute*
EARL BEISTLINE *University of Alaska*	S. DAVID FREEMAN *Consultant*	RACHEL McCULLOUCH *University of Wisconsin*
CHARLES A. BOWSHER *General Accounting Office*	GILBERT GUDE *Congressional Research Service*	LEWIS THOMAS *Memorial Sloan-Kettering Cancer Center*

Director

JOHN H. GIBBONS

The Technology Assessment Board approves the release of this report. The views expressed in this report are not necessarily those of the Board, OTA Advisory Council, or of individual members thereof.

Foreword

New computer and communications technologies are obviously transforming American life. They are the basis of many of the changes in our telecommunications system and also a new wave of automation on the farm, in manufacturing and transportation, and in the office. They are changing the form and delivery of government services such as education and the judicial system. Information products and services have become a major and still rapidly growing component of our economy.

A strong U.S. research and development effort has, in the past, been the source of much of this new technology. However, recent events, such as the restructuring of the U.S. telecommunications industry and the emergence of strong foreign competition for some technologies, have changed the environment for R&D. Consequently, the House Committee on Science and Technology, the House Committee on Energy and Commerce, and its Subcommittee on Telecommunications, Consumer Protection, and Finance asked OTA to conduct an assessment of the current state of R&D in these critical areas.

In this report, OTA examines four specific areas of research as case studies: computer architecture, artificial intelligence, fiber optics, and software engineering. It discusses the structure and orientation of some selected foreign programs. Finally, it examines a set of issues that have been raised in the course of the study: manpower, institutional change, the new research organizations that grew out of Bell Laboratories, and implications of trends in overall science and technology policy.

Information technology research and development in the United States is a remarkably adaptable system—important changes may already be taking place in funding patterns, institutional structures, manpower development, and government policies. Hence, the policy issues for Congress are not so much to stimulate change as to remove barriers to productive change, and to monitor and maintain the health of the R&D enterprise in a time of rapid change in an industry so central to our national economy and security.

OTA gratefully acknowledges the contributions of the many experts, within and outside the Government, who served as panelists, consultants, contractors, and reviewers of this document. As with all OTA reports, however, the content is the responsibility of OTA and does not necessarily constitute the consensus or endorsement of the advisory panel or the Technology Assessment Board.

JOHN H. GIBBONS
Director

OTA Information Technology Research and Development Project Staff

John Andelin, *Assistant Director, OTA*
Science, Information and Natural Resources Division

Fred W. Weingarten, *Communication and Information Technologies Program Manager*

Project Staff

Donna L. Valtri, *Project Director*[1]

Fred W. Weingarten, *Project Director*[2]

Chuck Wilk, *Senior Analyst*

Linda G. Roberts, *Senior Analyst*

Linda Garcia, *Analyst*

M. Karen Gamble, *Analyst*

Prudence S. Adler, *Analyst*

Jim Dray, *Research Analyst*

Earl Dowdy, *Research Analyst*

Lauren Ackerman, *Research Analyst*

John Williams[3]

Peg Kay[4]

Administrative Staff

Elizabeth A. Emanuel, *Administrative Assistant*

Shirley Gayheart, *Secretary*

Jennifer Nelson, *Secretary*

Marsha Williams, *Secretary*

Renee S. Lloyd, *Secretary*

Contractors

Myles Boylan	J. F. Coates, Inc.	Barbara Davies
Russell Drew	Sidney Fernbach	Michael Goetz
Stan Liebowitz	Abbe Mowshowitz	Larry Olson
	Bruce Owen	John Young

---

[1] Project Director from November 1982 to December 1983.
[2] Acting Project Director from December 1983.
[3] Detailee from the Federal Communications Commission from October 1982 to October 1983.
[4] Detailee from the National Bureau of Standards, May 1984.

Information Technology Research and Development Advisory Panel

Roger G. Noll, *Chairman*
Professor of Economics, Stanford University

Geneva Belford
  Department of Computer Science
  University of Illinois

Steven Bisset
  President
  Megatest, Inc.

John E. Bryson
  Morrison & Foerster

NandiKishore M. Chitre
  Director
  Systems Planning Division
  INTELSAT

Ralph E. Gomory
  Vice President and Director of Research
  IBM Corp.
  Thomas J. Watson Research Center

John V. Harrington
  Director
  COMSAT Laboratories

William C. Hittinger
  Executive Vice President
  RCA/David Sarnoff Research Center

Bruce Lusignan
  Director
  Communication Satellite Planning Center
  Stanford University

Donald McCoy
  Vice President and General Manager
  CBS Technology Center

Ithiel de sola Pool*
  Professor of Political Science
  Massachusetts Institute of Technology

Paul E. Ritt, Jr.
  Vice President and Director of Research
  GTE Laboratories, Inc.

Larry W. Sumney
  Executive Director
  Semiconductor Research Corp.

Victor Vyssotsky
  Executive Director
  Research, Information Sciences
  AT&T Bell Laboratories

Robert E. Wesslund
  Vice President for Technology Exchange
  Control Data Corp.

George R. White
  Senior Research Fellow
  The Harvard Business School

Advanced Computer Architecture Workshop

Duane Adams
  Consultant
  Defense Advanced Research Project Agency

James C. Browne
  Department of Computer Science
  University of Texas

Alan Charlesworth
  Senior Staff Engineer
  Floating Point Systems, Inc.

Kent K. Curtis
  Section Head, Computer Science
  Division of Mathematical and Computer
    Sciences
  National Science Foundation

Sidney Fernbach
  Consultant
  Control Data Corp.

Dennis Gannon
  Assistant Professor
  Department of Computer Science
  Purdue University

Robert G. Gillespie
  Vice Provost for Computing
  University of Washington

David Kuck
  Department of Computer Sciences
  University of Illinois

---

*Deceased Mar. 11, 1984.

Neil Lincoln
  Vice President and Chief Architect
  ETA Systems, Inc.

Roger G. Noll
  Professor of Economics
  Stanford University

Paul Ritt, Jr.
  Vice President and Director of Research
  GTE Laboratories, Inc.

Paul Schneck
  Leader, Information Sciences Division
  Office of Naval Research

Jacob Schwartz
  Director
  Division of Computer Sciences
  Courant Institute of Mathematical Sciences

Burton J. Smith
  Vice President
  Research and Development Department
  Denelcor, Inc.

Harold Stone
  Professor
  Department of Electrical and Computer
    Engineering
  University of Massachusetts

Jim Thornton
  Chief Executive Officer
  Network System Corp.

Kenneth G. Wilson
  James A. Weeks Professor of Physical
    Science
  Newman Laboratory
  Cornell University

Fiber Optics Workshop

Thomas Giallorenzi, *Chairman*
  Superintendent, Optical Sciences Division
  Naval Research Laboratory

Michael Barnoski
  Consultant
  Pacific Palisades, CA

Melvin Cohen
  Director, Interconnection Technology
    Laboratory
  AT&T Bell Laboratories

Anthony J. DeMaria
  Assistant Director of Research for Electrical
    and Electrooptics Technology
  United Technology Research Center

Charles W. Deneka
  Director, Optical Waveguide Technology
  Corning Glass Works

Charles Kao
  ITT Executive Scientist
  ITT Corp.

Herwig Kogelnick
  Director
  Electronics Research Laboratory
  AT&T Bell Laboratories

Henry Kressel
  Senior Vice President
  E. M. Warburg, Pincus & Co.

William Streifer
  Senior Research Fellow
  Xerox Corp.

John Whinnery
  Department of Electrical Engineering and
    Computer Science
  University of California, Berkeley

Amnon Yariv
  Professor of Electrical Engineering and
    Applied Physics
  California Institute of Technology

Software Engineering Workshop

Richard A. DeMillo
  Professor of Information and Computer
    Science
  Georgia Institute of Technology

George Dodd
  Department Head
  Computer Science Department
  General Motors Research Laboratories

Capers Jones
  Manager of Programming Technology
    Analysis
  ITT Corp.

Brian Kernighan
  Head, Computing Structures Research
  AT&T Bell Laboratories

Ann Marmor-Squires
  Chief Technologist
  TRW Defense Systems Group

Robert Mathis
  Director
  Ada Joint Program Office
  Department of Defense

Harlan Mills
  IBM Fellow
  IBM Corp.

Leon J. Osterwell
  Chairman
  Computer Science Department
  University of Colorado

C. V. Ramamoorthy
  Professor of Electrical Engineering and
    Computer Science
  University of California, Berkeley

Paul Schneck
  Leader, Information Sciences Division
  Office of Naval Research

Ben Shneiderman
  Professor of Computer Science
  University of Maryland

Steve Squires
  Software Technology Programming Manager
  Defense Advanced Research Projects Agency

Terry A. Straeter
  Vice President and Program Director
  General Dynamics Electronics

Raymond Yeh
  Professor of Computer Science
  University of Maryland

Artificial Intelligence Workshop

Bruce Bullock
  Vice President
  Teknowledge Federal Systems

Marvin Denicoff
  Executive
  Thinking Machines Corp.

Ewald Heer
  Program Manager
  Autonomous Systems and Space Mechanics
  Jet Propulsion Laboratory

Thomas F. Knight
  Assistant Professor of Electrical Engineering
    and Computer Science
  Artificial Intelligence Laboratory
  Massachusetts Institute of Technology

Mitchell Marcus
  Member of the Technical Staff
  Linguistics and Artificial Intelligence
    Research Department
  AT&T Bell Laboratories

Ronald Ohlander
  Program Manager
  Defense Advanced Research Projects Agency

Kamron Parsaye
  President
  Silogic, Inc.

Stephen Polit
  Manager of Advanced Development
  Artificial Intelligence Group
  Digital Equipment Co.

Azriel Rosenfeld
  Director
  Center for Automation Research
  Computer Science Center
  University of Maryland

David Waltz
  Professor of Electrical Engineering and
    Research Professor
  Coordinated Science Laboratory
  University of Illinois

Patrick H. Winston
  Professor of Computer Science and Electrical
    Engineering and Director
  Artificial Intelligence Laboratory
  Massachusetts Institute of Technology

Information Technology Research and Development Federal Workshop

Charles Brownstein
  Head
  Information Science Division
  National Science Foundation

Douglas Crombie
  Chief Scientist
  National Telecommunications and
    Information Administration

John A. Daly
  Special Assistant
  Agency for International Development

Craig Fields
  Assistant Director for Systems Services
  Defense Advanced Research Projects Agency

Clinton W. Kelly, III
  Assistant Director, Systems Science Division
  Defense Advanced Research Projects Agency

Robert Lovell
  Director of Communications
  National Aeronautics and Space
    Administration

Robert Powers
  Chief Scientist
  Office of Science and Technology
  Federal Communications Commission

John Riganati
  Division Chief
  System Components Division
  National Bureau of Standards

Paul Schneck
  Leader, Information Science Division
  Office of Naval Research

Elias Schutzman
  Program Director
  Electrical Optical Communications Program
  National Science Foundation

Reviewers and Other Contributors

Robert Ayres
  Carnegie-Mellon University

Richard Baxter
  British Embassy

Donald S. Beilman
  Microelectronics Center of North
    Carolina

John Biddle
  Computer and Communications
    Industry Association

Marlan Blissett
  University of Texas

Erich Bloch
  Semiconductor Research Corp.
  IBM Corp.

Justin Bloom
  Technology International, Inc.

Bill Boesman
  Congressional Research Service

Jane Bortnick
  Congressional Research Service

Paul Bortz
  Brown, Bortz & Covington

Martha Branstad
  National Bureau of Standards

Kenneth Brown
  American Enterprise Institute for
    Public Policy Research

Glen Chaney
  AT&T Bell Laboratories

Gary Coleman
  Department of Education

Arthur Cordell
  Science Council of Canada

Matthew Crugnale
  Gnostic Concepts, Inc.

Beverly Daniel
  General Accounting Office

George Dummer
  Massachusetts Institute of
    Technology

Lauren Erling
  ADAPSO

Frank Fisher
  Urban Institute

Penny Foster
  National Science Foundation

Donald R. Fowler
  California Institute of Technology

Peter Fuchs
  Harvard University

Osmund Fundingsland
  General Accounting Office

Robert Gallawa
  National Bureau of Standards

Howard Gobstein
  General Accounting Office

Robert A. Gross
  Columbia University

Walter Hahn
  George Washington University

Glen Hansen
  Department of Commerce

Richard Hersh
  University of Oregon

Christopher Hill
  Congressional Research Service

Joseph Hull
  Department of Commerce

B. R. Inman
  Microelectronics & Computer
    Technology Corp.

Charles L. Jackson
 Shooshan & Jackson, Inc.
Don Kash
 University of Oklahoma
Todd LaPorte
 University of California-Berkeley
Christopher LeMaistre
 Rensselaer Polytechnic Institute
Jean-Pierre Letouzey
 French Embassy
Thomas Linney
 Council of Graduate Schools
Harold Linstone
 Portland State University
John G. Linvill
 Stanford University
John Logsdon
 George Washington University
Albert Lumbroso
 French Embassy
Enrique Marcatili
 AT&T Bell Laboratories
Michael Marcus
 Federal Communications Commission
Nick Metropolis
 Los Alamos National Laboratory
Charles H. Miller
 AT&T
Robert Miller
 University of Houston
Robert Morgan
 Washington University

Joel Moses
 Massachusetts Institute of Technology
Jane Myers
 Patent and Trademark Office
Tom Nardone
 Bureau of Labor Statistics
Dorothy Nelkin
 Cornell University
William F. Nelson
 GTE Laboratories, Inc.
Arnie Packer
 Manpower Economist
Paul Penfield
 Massachusetts Institute of Technology
Robert Pepper
 Department of Commerce
Paul Polishuk
 Information Gatekeepers, Inc.
John M. Richardson
 National Research Council
Michel Robin
 French Embassy
Martha G. Russell
 University of Minnesota
Grant Saveers
 Digital Equipment Corp.
Wendy Schacht
 Congressional Research Service
Jurgen Schmandt
 University of Texas

Dan Slotnick
 University of Illinois
Ollie Smoot
 Computer and Business Equipment Manufacturers Association
Bill Stotesbery
 Microelectronics & Computer Technology Corp.
Gregory Tassey
 National Bureau of Standards
Henry Taylor
 Naval Research Laboratory
Al Teich
 American Association for Advancement of Science
William Wells
 George Washington University
Irwin White
 New York State Energy R&D Agency
Robert Willard
 Information Industries Association
John G. Williams
 Carruthers, Deutsch, Garrison & Williams
Paul Wilson
 AT&T
Paul Zurkowski
 Information Industries Association

In-House Reviewers

Audrey Buyrn, *Program Manager*
Martha Harris, *Project Director*
Paul Phelps, *Project Director*
Henry Kelly, *Project Director*
John Alic, *Project Director*
Barry Holt, *Analyst*
Eric Bazques, *Analyst*

Information Technology Research and Development
Critical Trends and Issues

Chapter 1
Introduction and Summary

Contents

	Page
Goals for Federal R&D Policy	3
Principal Findings	5
The Nature of Information Technology R&D	6
Software as Technology	7
Multidisciplinary Nature	7
Close Boundary Between Theory and Application	8
Complexity	8
Case Studies	9
Advanced Computer Architecture	9
Software Engineering	11
Fiber Optics	12
Artificial Intelligence	13
Issues and Strategies	14
Impacts of Telecommunications Deregulation	14
Scientific and Technological Manpower	16
Changing Roles of Universities	17
Foreign Programs	18
Science Policy	19
Summary	21

Chapter 1
Introduction and Summary

American society is becoming increasingly reliant on the use of electronic information technology, principally computer and communication systems. Economists and social scientists point out that information is a basic resource for society and an important factor of production for the economy. Information technology provides business, governments, and citizens with the basic tools necessary to communicate and use information. Furthermore, the information industry, itself, including both those that produce electronic hardware and those that offer information services, is an increasingly important part of U.S. industrial strength.

Because of this reliance on information technology, public attention has been drawn to the process of innovation in that field, developing new technological products and bringing them to the marketplace. Since research and development (R&D) is generally considered to be a key element driving innovation (although not the only one), Congress is concerned with the general health of R&D in information technologies. Concerns include the effects that changes in the structure of the U.S. telecommunications industry are having on industrial R&D, and the implications of new foreign programs intended to challenge traditional U.S. market leadership in some areas of computers and communications. OTA examined these and related questions at the request of the House Committee on Science and Technology, the House Committee on Energy and Commerce, and its Subcommittee on Telecommunications, Consumer Protection, and Finance.

Goals for Federal R&D Policy

Currently, public concern with information technology is focused on its role in promoting economic competitiveness. However, Federal interest in promoting R&D and technological innovation, dating back to the writing of the Constitution, has always been motivated by several distinct goals, only one of which has been economic growth. These goals, which may for any specific technology or program either complement or compete with one another, are applicable to information technology.

- *Support National Defense:* A modern military force is dependent on communications and computer technologies for many purposes, including intelligence, missile guidance, command and control, and logistics. Projected future applications include battlefield management, fully automated weapons, and computer-based artificial intelligence advisors for pilots. The military importance of information technology is demonstrated by the predominant role the Department of Defense plays in support of R&D in that field (nearly 80 percent of direct government funding in this area is supplied by DOD).

- *Provide for Social Needs:* Government has always treated the telecommunications system as a basic social infrastructure. One major goal of communication policymakers is "universal service." New services such as cable television and information services delivered over telecommunication channels can potentially improve the quality of life for American citizens. For example, OTA, in a recent report, pointed out the role information technology could play in improving the quality of and access to education and also stressed the need for additional R&D focused on educational technology. Another recent OTA report has described the po-

tential benefits of information technology to handicapped individuals.
- *Promote Economic Growth:* The information technology industry (those who make and sell or provide access to communications media) and the information industry (those who use the new technologies to produce and sell new information services and products) are a growing part of the U.S. economy. Their economic importance is felt both domestically and internationally. These industries also have an important indirect effect, in that the technologies and services they produce contribute materially to the economy in such forms as productivity growth, better quality of products, and improved managerial decisionmaking. The health of the information industries depends in part on their ability to bring forth new products and develop new applications; this ability, in turn, depends on R&D.
- *Advance Basic Understanding of the World:* Research in computer and communication science has contributed to basic understanding in fields that transcend pure information technology. For example, research in artificial intelligence has led to insights into brain functions and human thinking and problem solving. Communications researchers have made a Nobel Prize-winning contribution to our understanding of the origins of the universe. The study of computer languages has both benefited from and contributed to theories of the evolution and structure of natural human languages. Similarly, information technology researchers have contributed to knowledge in such other fields as fundamental mathematics, logic, and the theory of genetic coding.

Moreover, computers have become indispensable research tools in many areas of science ranging from physics and astronomy to biology and social science. Some scientists now speak of "computational research" as a new, wholly different form as important to the progress of knowledge as is experimental and theoretical research.

- *Enhance National Prestige:* The United States has always been a world leader in computer and communication technologies, both in the discovery of new basic knowledge and in its development into commercial products. In certain areas of marketable technology, such as supercomputers (very powerful computers, the largest and fastest available on the market) or communication satellites, U.S. firms have in the past held an undisputed technological lead. Although such technological dominance has nearly disappeared in most cases and could not have been expected to continue as other nations developed research capability and industrial strength in information technology, preserving U.S. technological competitiveness and leadership is still an important public policy goal with implications that extend beyond purely economic advantage.
- *Support Civilian Agency Missions:* Many civilian Federal agencies need to use advanced information systems to perform their missions more efficiently or effectively. For example, computers and communication systems underlie the space exploration programs of the National Aeronautics and Space Administration (NASA). Weather researchers working for the National Oceanic and Atmospheric Administration (NOAA) and fusion researchers for the Department of Energy need access to the most advanced supercomputers. Although the support of mission agencies for basic research is limited, they have funded development and, often, applied research directed to meeting their specific needs.

Over the years, these Federal interests have led to a wide array of policies, programs, and agencies designed to promote the conduct of research and development in the United States and to appropriate its benefits to American society. Many of them have helped stimulate the development of computers and communication technologies.

The principal issue examined in this study is whether those policies, programs, and agencies

are now adequate and appropriate for advancing information technologies in light of the emerging needs of society for these technologies, their particular characteristics, and the rapidly escalating world competition in producing and selling products and services based on them.

Principal Findings

In summary, OTA's study of information technology research and development reached the following conclusions:

- *Information technology is an area in which the United States has historically shown great strength, both in basic science and marketed technology; and this strength has benefited the Nation in several ways.* It has contributed to the growth of a strong economic sector, the information industry. It has contributed to national security. It has stimulated the evolution of basic science.
- *Most areas of information technology examined in this study, including microelectronics, fiber optics, artificial intelligence, computer design, and software engineering, are still in the early stages as technologies.* Much improvement in technological capability remains to be developed, and that improvement will depend on both fundamental research and technological development. Hence, R&D will be an important factor in stimulating continuing innovation.
- *By most measures, U.S. research and development in information technology is strong and viable; however, those traditional measures may not be realistic guides to the future needs of the United States for R&D in these areas.* In particular, increasing competition from foreign nations (in particular, Japan) as well as the growing intrinsic importance of information technology to the United States, suggest that more attention should be paid by policymakers to the needs for R&D in information technology. Many of these nations, motivated both by economic concerns and broader social goals, have developed national programs designed to foster information technology.
- *In response to these new pressures, industry support is growing rapidly for short-term applied research and developmental work, both within industrial labs and through support of university work.* Industry has generally looked, and still looks, to the academic community to perform and the Federal Government to fund the long-term basic research that will underlie future technological advances.
- *Universities, traditionally viewed as centers for basic research, are reexamining their roles with respect to applied research and are forming new types of relationships with industry and government.* State governments, in particular, looking for stimuli to economic development see new high-technology industry, including the information industry, as interested in being located near strong university basic research programs. Many states have formed new organizations within their universities in order to strengthen research, focus it toward problems of interest to industry, and facilitate the transfer of technology from the research laboratory to industrial application. With most of these experiments, it is too early to tell whether they will be successful in stimulating industrial development and whether they will have beneficial or negative effects on the universities.
- *The Department of Defense is the predominant source of Federal support of information technology research and development, providing nearly 80 percent of the funding.* Although some spillover to the civilian sector from DOD research can

be expected, its work is predominately focused on military requirements and cannot be relied on to provide for all civilian needs. An important issue for consideration by Congress is whether increased funding by nondefense agencies of long-term research in information technology is needed to focus more work on civilian needs.

- *There is substantial concern that technical and scientific information flows between the United States and other countries are unbalanced outward.* Proposals to redress that balance focus both on increasing access to foreign information and on restricting outflows of U.S. information. Policies that would enhance the access of U.S. information scientists to the work of foreign researchers (through such vehicles as translation services, travel grants, and foreign science exchange programs) would help their own work. Such programs would also help science policy experts to evaluate the state of foreign technology more accurately.

  Steps have also been taken to tighten controls over the export of technical information on national security grounds. In considering such controls, Congress needs to balance national security considerations against both first amendment rights and the possible negative impacts on domestic R&D.

- *Instruments for scientific research are growing more sophisticated and are becoming obsolete at an increasingly rapid pace.* As a result, they are more expensive and yet must be replaced more frequently if researchers are to keep at the forefronts of knowledge. In particular, computer software researchers need access to sophisticated computational facilities and data communication networks, and those working on microelectronics need access to chip processing facilities and computer-aided-design tools.

- *Policies designed to stimulate information technology R&D need to be evaluated for possibly significant tradeoffs and external costs in other areas.* Some costs are clear. For example, R&D tax incentives are a short-term loss of Federal revenues. Policies designed to draw more highly trained people into information technology may create manpower shortages in other areas of research. Devoting educational resources to information technology education and training draws them away from other areas of need, at a time when overall resources are not growing.

The Nature of Information Technology R&D

For purposes of this study, OTA defines the term "information technology" to refer to electronic hardware that is used to create, communicate, store, modify, or display information and to programming or "software" that is developed to control the operation of that hardware. Modern information technology is based on the microelectronic chip, the large-scale integrated circuit that over the last decade has transformed the computer and communications industries through steady and rapid increase of performance and decrease in price. This high rate of technological improvement in microelectronics will continue into the 1990s and probably beyond. Changes in the information technology products and services available in the marketplace will likely be as revolutionary in the next decade as they have been over the last one that has seen the appearance and growth of such technologies as the personal computer, fiber optics, satellite communications, the video cassette recorder, and two-way cable television. Industry will compete worldwide to bring these new prod-

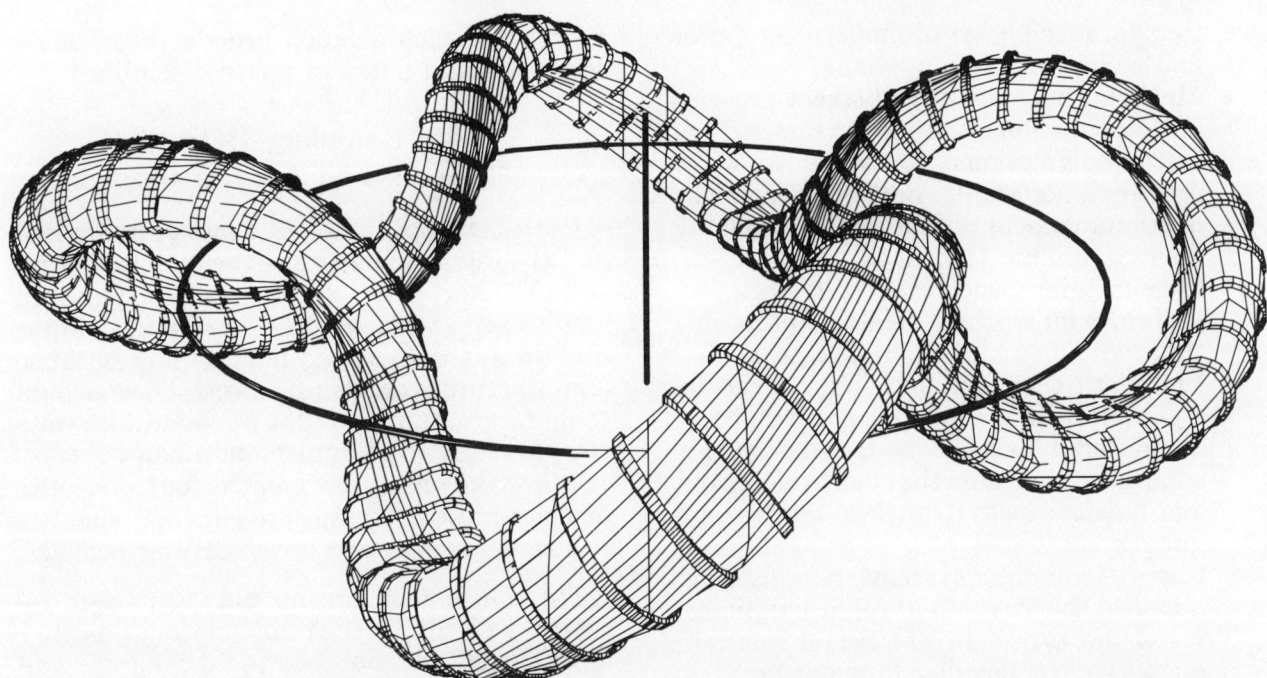

Photo credit: Arthur A. Merin, National Magnetic Fusion Energy Computer Center, Lawrence Livermore National Laboratory

The use of computer modeling and graphics to study fusion energy. Outer magnetic surface of four-period helical axis stellarator (HELIAC)

ucts and services to use, and an important element of that competition will be research and development.

Information technology has characteristics that distinguish it from many other areas of R&D and that affect policies designed to stimulate and direct it.

Software as Technology

"Software," or programs, are sets of instructions that direct a computer in its tasks. The term can also refer to information; for example, computer data bases, the information content transmitted over communication lines, or that contained on a video disk. Because software often can be the most complex part of an information system, research and development on software is considered to be of equal importance to research on hardware technology. Yet, to some people, software does not "look" like technology. The concepts and techniques that underlie programs are intangible, and their embodiment is usually in a form such as a list of instructions on paper or a sequence of images on a video screen. Research in information technology includes research on both hardware and software technology, and on the boundaries between them, for many computational techniques may appear in either hardware or software.

Software as an area of research presents Federal R&D support with some unusual problems. For example, intellectual property as expressed in software is difficult to protect. It can also be hard to distinguish between R&D in computer programming, work which advances the state of software technology, and using existing techniques to write new programs and maintain old ones—a distinction that drew particular attention in the debate over R&D tax credits, for example.

Multidisciplinary Nature

R&D in information technology spans a wide variety of disparate fields of work. For example:

- Solid-state physicists work to improve the performance of the semiconductor devices

that form the heart of modern computer and communication systems.
- Mathematicians study abstract theories of computation, looking for methods of faster calculations, for ways to write error-free software, and to transmit the maximum amount of information reliably over communication lines.
- Psychologists and brain physiologists find clues for writing "smarter" programs that can solve more complex problems.
- Linguistic theorists contribute to the design of new languages for programming computers and build the foundations for computer programs that can understand and automatically translate human languages.
- Users of computer systems, ranging from physical scientists to graphic artists, develop new types of software for their applications. In this development process, they make fundamental contributions to software technology.
- Sociologists, psychologists, and the management scientists search for the most effective ways to design office automation and decision support systems. Their research ranges from human factors, which examines direct human-machine interaction, to investigations of organizational decisionmaking.
- A few computer scientists, sociologists, historians of science, and experts in other fields, examine the broader questions of the interactions of information technology with society.

As a result of this breadth of subject area, relevant Federal programs of R&D support are distributed among many Government agencies and among many organizational parts of those agencies. The National Science Foundation (NSF), for example, has at least four divisions, each in a different directorate, that support research directly related to computers and communications systems. Another important implication is that manpower programs must be concerned not just with the supply of "core" computer scientists and engineers, but with a much broader base of researchers and users in many disciplines.

Close Boundary Between Theory and Application

Both the rapid pace of commercialization and the intrinsic nature of the technology result in a short time lag between basic research results and commercialization. Because information systems are so flexible and because manufacturers are using powerful new design tools to create new types of computers, less time is required to implement a new concept. It may take only a few months for the results of a basic research project in pure mathematics to be realized in a commercial software package.

This close relationship between basic research and commercial application, possibly most closely paralleled by biotechnology, creates unusual and difficult issues for institutions, such as universities, that are traditionally concerned only with basic research published in the public domain. These issues include publication policies, intellectual property rights, faculty conflicts of interest, competition with the private sector, and research priorities. Federal agencies that fund basic research, such as NSF, also find themselves dealing with these issues more frequently.

Complexity

Modern computer/communications systems are among the most complex technologies ever assembled by human beings. Computers consist of millions of logical subunits. Computer programs can contain millions of instructions. These complex machines, running complex programs, are then interlinked through communications networks. To be able to understand, predict, and control the behavior of these technologies requires a powerful theory of complex processes. No such theory yet exists, although it remains a major goal of computer science.

It is because of this complexity that, even though computers and communication systems are artificial devices—technologies created and built by human beings—there is basic science devoted to understanding their behavior. This science has a strong experimental component to it. Many computer scientists and engineers need access to large-scale computers. Writing large, complex programs to do unusual tasks is a common research methodology aimed at understanding basic principals underlying the structure of problems and software.

Case Studies

Information technology is a broad subject area. To better understand and describe R&D issues, four specific areas of technology were examined in more detail. These case studies covered both software and hardware and both computer and communications technologies. In addition, all four technologies have raised policy issues in the last few years.

Advanced Computer Architecture

Although computers have increased in sophistication over the years, and individual models differ from one another in detail, the higher level logical design, called the "architecture," of most commercially available computers is based on concepts that date back a few decades.

New concepts of computer architecture now being explored in the laboratory will underlie two types of innovation: 1) the development of highly specialized, low-cost computer modules that do specific types of tasks at extremely high speeds; and 2) the future generations of supercomputers.

Low-cost specialized computers are designed to perform specific types of computational tasks very efficiently. When hardware is expensive, as computer hardware has been in the past, users usually try to allocate its cost over a variety of applications. Hence, the so-called *general-purpose computer,* which performs a wide variety of computations relatively well, has been and continues to be the mainstay of the computer industry. However, most types of computational tasks have unique characteristics. Since hardware costs have dropped significantly, new market possibilities have appeared for inexpensive special purpose hardware that takes advantage of these characteristics. The general purpose computer system of the future may serve mainly as a routing switch, sending a computing task to the appropriate one of several different specialized processors attached to it.

Supercomputers, the label given to the most powerful machines on the market at any time, have received significant press attention lately. Until recently, U.S. firms have been the only significant marketers of supercomputers. However, Japanese firms have now brought out supercomputers that, by some measures, seem to perform comparably to U.S. machines. In addition, Japan has embarked on two major supercomputer projects. One is designed to develop the next generation of high-speed numerical calculating machines; the other, the Fifth-Generation Computer Project based on artificial intelligence theories, is intended to produce a machine that performs reasoning functions similar to human thinking processes.

The Federal Government is considering several responses to maintain leadership in this technology. For example, the Defense Advanced Research Projects Agency (DARPA) is beginning a "Strategic Computing Program" to develop artificial intelligence capabilities for the needs of the Department of Defense. The National Science Foundation has embarked on a program intended both to increase their support of computer architecture research and to put more supercomputer capability in the hands of scientific users. Both

Photo credit: AT&T

A microprocessor on a chip. This chip contains an entire computer, as powerful as some minicomputers

NASA and the Department of Energy have developed similar plans to increase the advanced supercomputing capability available to their researchers.

If they were fully implemented, these Federal plans would constitute an important response to the growing need for access to advanced computing resources. Over the last decade, computing resources available to basic researchers, particularly in universities, have steadily fallen behind the state of the art. Although the U.S. computer industry has traditionally led the market in the supercomputer field, basic researchers in other countries such as West Germany and Japan may have more and easier access to supercomputers from the United States than their counterparts at American universities.

In addition to providing access to supercomputers for agency supported researchers, such Federal procurements would also stimulate the market for the next generation machine, a market that has traditionally been small and, hence, unattractive to computer manufacturers. As the principal user of them, the Federal Government has always had a major influence on the supercomputer market. This Federal stimulus may be particularly important for experimental machines that are based on new architectural concepts. Markets and applications for these machines are particularly unpredictable.

Should Congress decide that additional Federal emphasis on computer design is in the national interest, support of basic research should also be expanded to provide the scientific base for succeeding generations of advanced architecture computers, large and small. Although R&D on the next generation supercomputers and other specialized architectures is underway in a few industrial laboratories, firms participating in this specialized market tend to be small. Longer term basic research is usually left to be performed in academic laboratories and receives little industrial support. Hence, Federal support of basic research can have significant effect.

In the past, responding to funding limitations as well as the complexity of implementing computer hardware in a laboratory, agencies have usually kept basic research in machine architecture at the theoretical, or "paper and pencil" stage. This restriction has not allowed new concepts to be tested as hardware. To allow such testing, some of these conceptual level basic research projects need to be funded at a level that allows them to be carried to experimental and even prototype stages. Microelectronics allows such hardware experimentation to be done more easily and cheaply than in the past, because prototypes can now be assembled from chips that form large logical modules containing thousands of functions.

Software has also been and continues to be a major problem area. Taking full advantage of a supercomputer's speed and power requires the design of specialized programs. Significantly more research needs to be done on numerical computational techniques and programming theory for new computer architectures.

Software Engineering

The computer industry has transformed over the few decades of its existence from being hardware dominant to being software dominant. In the early years, hardware was the most expensive component of a computer system. Software was often given away free by computer manufacturers, and the costs of developing custom programs were much less than the costs of purchasing and maintaining the machines. The situation is now reversed. In most cases, costs of developing and maintaining software are now the dominant costs of creating and operating large computer applications. Although developments in microelectronics have steadily and rapidly reduced the cost and increased the performance of computer hardware, improvements in the productivity of programmers has come much more slowly.

Since the limits of cost, reliability, and time required to create new applications are increasingly dictated by software instead of hardware considerations, research directed toward improving the productivity of programmers and designers will have high leverage. "Software engineering" is the term used to describe this area of research.

Research in software engineering ranges widely in content and approach. At one extreme is highly theoretical work directed at developing a fundamental understanding of the nature of programs and "proving" in some mathematical sense that they act as intended. At the other end of the spectrum are behavioral and management scientists concerned with understanding how people interact with computer systems and how to manage programming projects. Not all research related to understanding programming and program behavior is called "software engineering"; many fields of computer science and engineering contribute.

The Department of Defense, faced with an annual software expense estimated at $4-$8 billion, supports a large effort in software engineering. DOD has funded the design of a new programming language, *ADA,* and a "programming environment" called *STARS* that provides a set of automated tools for use by the program designer. These tools are intended to be standards, required to be used in the development of DOD software.

Because the economic stakes are so high, researchers at industry centers such as the Bell

Laboratories and IBM's T. J. Watson Research Laboratories have also been active in software engineering research. University researchers in software engineering, supported by Federal agencies, have concentrated on understanding better the theoretical underpinnings of computer programs.

Other countries have also recognized the importance of software engineering. It has been made an explicit part of the British information technology research program. The Japanese, realizing that software has been a major weakness in their attempts to be competitive in the worldwide computer market, are experimenting with what they call "software factories." The French have always had strength in the area of programming, particularly the theory of programming languages. The Department of Defense language, ADA, was developed in a French laboratory.

Although the potential benefits to the Nation of advances in software engineering are high, the implications for Federal support are less clear. Some experts, arguing that lack of fundamental research is not the key bottleneck, point to the failure of designers to apply existing basic theories and research methodologies to the development of large-scale systems. To do so would require closer industry-university researcher interaction and might be helped by the establishment of some large laboratory facilities to study design problems on a realistic scale.

Other experts, pointing out that we still lack the fundamental theoretical breakthrough necessary to develop a true discipline of software engineering, argue that the problems will persist until such a theory is established. Expanded long-term Federal support of a broad range of fundamental research on software is necessary to develop a sound theoretical basis to programming.

Fiber Optics

The last decade has seen the rapid development of a new communications medium, information transmitted by pulses of laser light through thin glass fibers. These optical fibers can transmit far more information than can copper wires or coaxial cables of the same size. Since information is transmitted as light, fiber optics are resistant to both electrical interference and eavesdropping. The potential capacity and economy of optical fiber is such that it not only will help keep communications costs down, but, over the long term, it will relieve the growing congestion of the radio spectrum and may ease some of the demands for satellite communications.

Optical fiber is already used for communication lines between some major cities in the United States, and a transatlantic cable using optical transmission will be laid in the late 1980s. By the end of the 1980s optical fiber will be used heavily in nearly every stage of the telecommunication systems, from local intraoffice networks to long-distance lines.

Although European firms are also developing capability in fiber optics, the principal foreign competition has been from the Japanese, whose technology is roughly at a par with that available from U.S. firms. Since a large world market for fiber optical hardware is growing, innovation in this technology is critical to U.S. competitiveness in telecommunications.

The technology of the fibers, themselves, is still advancing rapidly along three general lines: 1) techniques to increase the information capacity of the fibers; 2) improvements to the transparency of the glass, which allow longer distances between "repeaters," devices that detect the signals and retransmit them on down the line; and 3) improved process technologies for manufacturing fibers. Hence, even though fiber optics is now in the commercial marketplace, the need for basic research continues and the current state-of-the-art is a long way from any fundamental limits to this technology.

Applied research and development on fiber optics, because it is expensive and capital-intensive, is concentrated in a few large laboratories; and, since the economic reward for technological advance is clear, it is done primarily by industry. However, long-term development of fiber optics will depend on funda-

include the ability to recognize and translate human speech, to prove the truth of mathematical statements, and to win at chess.

For two reasons public attention has recently focused on an area of AI called *expert systems*. First, expert systems are seen to be the first significant commercialization of 25 years of research in artificial intelligence; and, secondly, they form the basis of the Japanese Fifth Generation Computer Project.

An expert system is an "intelligent" computer information retrieval system designed for use in a specific decisionmaking task, say medical diagnosis. It stores not only data, itself, but the rules of inference that describe how an expert uses the data to make decisions. By asking questions and suggesting courses of action, the expert system interacts with a decisionmaker to help solve a problem. AI researchers now understand this process well enough to be able to build profitable commercial systems for applications in very narrow areas of specialization, for example, advising on repair of telephone cable or diagnosing pulmonary disease.

Although few computer scientists doubt that sometime in the next century, people will interact with computers differently than they do now and that computers will show behavior that we would now call "intelligent," they differ over the nearer term significance of expert systems. Some maintain that expert systems represent an interesting and profitable, yet small, application area. In their view, AI continues to move slowly and is a long way from realizing the potential predicted for it. Others argue that expert systems are a model of how most computing will be done within a decade; and, hence, that future U.S. leadership in computer science will depend on an aggressive program of research in this field.

The Department of Defense has always been a dominant supporter of AI research, including work on expert systems. It has funded this work by establishing and funding large-scale laboratories at a few academic and nonprofit research centers. Civilian support is limited.

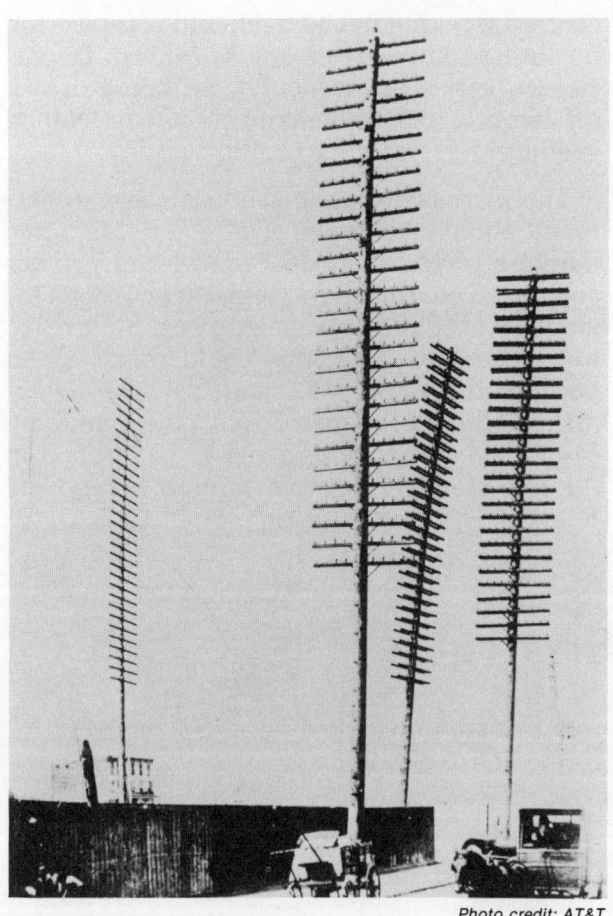

Photo credit: AT&T

Telephone lines circa 1887. Fiber optics is only the most recent of many technological developments that have increased the capacity and shrunk the physical size of communication lines

mental research in materials and solid-state electronics. Increased Federal funding of research in universities would achieve the dual objectives of stimulating fundamental research and training people at the Ph.D. level in fiber optics technology. A current lack of trained research personnel has been pointed out to be a handicap to progress in this field.

Artificial Intelligence

"Artificial Intelligence (AI)" is a term that has historically been applied to a wide variety of research areas that, roughly speaking, are concerned with extending the ability of the computer to do tasks that resemble those performed by human beings. These capabilities

NSF has steadily supported basic research in AI, but has done so at a relatively low funding level, and NASA has funded work supporting applications to autonomous spacecraft. DOD experience suggests that AI research is best performed in large laboratories with access to large-scale computing facilities and collections of specialized software. Some areas of research will begin to require access to specialized hardware and the facilities to design and build new systems.

This field in particular is experiencing an acute faculty shortage. The new commercial excitement in A/I comes after a long period of relative disinterest by funding agencies. As a result, there are few researchers and research centers working in the field, and competition for limited human resources is sharp. In particular, experienced faculty are being drawn off campus just as demand for newly trained graduates is growing rapidly.

The increased public attention and excitement about the promise of AI holds some dangers to the field. If Federal and private support is contingent on high expectations for significant short-term advances, failure to meet those expectations could result in an abrupt withdrawal of funding. Yet AI is a very difficult field of research, just in its infancy. Much basic science remains to be learned in AI, and steady long-term support is required for that learning.

Issues and Strategies

The level and nature of R&D in all fields, including information technology, is influenced by many social, economic, and political factors beyond those specifically related to science and technology. For example, the overall cost of capital and the general health of the national economy will affect management's ability and incentives to invest in R&D. Trade and export policies that affect the access of domestic firms to foreign markets or vice versa will influence the willingness of U.S. firms to invest in innovation.

Some observers have suggested that senior corporate managers in many firms have downplayed investment in R&D, which promises risky and long-term payoffs, in favor of short-term gains. According to this view, although these managers may have been reacting rationally in terms of immediate economic incentives and the desires of stockholders, the result of their decisions has been a low rate of innovation and a long-term loss of competitiveness.

Although these broad factors set an overall environment for R&D decisions, Congress also deals with several specific policy issues that directly relate to science and technology. In this study, OTA concentrated on those direct issues, particularly as they relate to information technology.

Impacts of Telecommunications Deregulation

During the last few years, the fundamental structure of the telecommunications industry has changed. AT&T has been subdivided into several smaller (although still very large) independent firms. Many telecommunication products and services traditionally provided by regulated monopolies are now provided through a competitive marketplace. Improved innovation and international competitiveness in the telecommunications industry is one of the benefits intended by proponents of deregulation, and OTA expects such increased innovation will occur over the next decade. The open question is whether that burst of innovation will be at the expense of basic research that would lay the foundation for future innovation.

However, although technological development should increase, many science policy experts have worried about the impact of deregulation on basic research. In particular, they view Bell Laboratories as a national scientific resource and have expressed concern that a new, competitive AT&T will have decreased

Ch. 1—Introduction and Summary • 15

Photo credit: AT&T

Alexander Graham Bell opening the first telephone line to Chicago

commitment to the basic research that has traditionally marked at least part of the Laboratories' activities.

OTA found that, although laboratory management will be admittedly more interested in the contribution of research programs to AT&T business, short-term effects on basic research will likely be small. In the first place, most large firms in historically competitive information technology areas, such as computers, have a history of supporting long-term research. Furthermore, AT&T senior management has a strong appreciation for the contribution that research at the Laboratories has made to the growth of the telephone system. They are unlikely to make a sudden shift in policy in the foreseeable future. Finally, most of the areas in which AT&T Bell Laboratories has particular scientific strength are those that, although fundamental, are clearly related to information technology—e.g., solid-state physics and computer science. Since the line between basic and applied research in these fields tends to be particularly hazy, fundamental work is likely to continue to be supported even were management to adopt a short time horizon for results.

Long-term prospects for basic research at AT&T Bell Laboratories will depend, in part, on AT&T's success as a competitor in the computer and telecommunications industry. This long-term success will depend on many factors including the regulatory environment, the economic climate, the skill of AT&T management in operating under new rules, and the contributions made by the Laboratories to innovation.

The divestiture has also introduced a new and potentially important organization, Bell Communication Research (Bellcore), to the information technology R&D arena. Bellcore serves the seven Bell operating companies, which hold it jointly. It commands the resources of a significant number of researchers from the pre-divestiture Bell Laboratories. Bellcore's relationships with the operating companies and its research activities are in the genesis stage at present; thus, some time will be required to determine its overall contribution to the national R&D effort.

At the same time, the former Bell Laboratories was a major performer of information technology research in the United States, and the divestiture in the telecommunications industry is a structural and regulatory change unprecedented in scale. The impact of this change on industrywide research including that done at AT&T Bell Laboratories and Bellcore should be closely monitored by Congress.

Scientific and Technological Manpower

The Federal Government has historically assumed a role in stimulating the production of technical manpower in areas of national interest. Policy has focused on increasing both the quantity and quality of technical graduates, but it has also played an important role in equity. Federal scholarship and fellowship programs are vital mechanisms to eliminate financial barriers to entry into technological careers.

Information technology is a fast-growing field of national importance, and Federal policies for developing R&D manpower in information technology may be deemed warranted by Congress. However, those policies should be broadly focused rather than aimed at narrow fields of specialization, and they should be consistent and steady over the long term.

Any policy designed to increase technical manpower will not take full effect for several years. The delays are inherent in the education system. They represent both the time it takes educational institutions to respond by developing new instructional programs and hiring staff, and the time it takes for a student to pass through the system. Hence, these policies should be directed, not to short-term, but to long-term needs. If addressed to current shortages, Federal programs run the risk of overproduction by the time they take effect, for needs may have changed or labor market forces such as high wages may have already encouraged adequate new entrants in the field.

Detailed long-term needs for technical manpower are hard to assess in a field changing as rapidly as information technology. Hence, projections of future requirements differ significantly from one to another. They do not account well for the appearance of new fields of specialization, such as the recent emerging area of fiber optics, nor the sudden growth in importance of older fields of research such as artificial intelligence. Thus, policies that deal broadly with science and engineering manpower in all fields are most likely to be successful.

OTA found that, although some shortages exist in specific fields, the long-term outlook is promising. Enrollments at university programs, both at the undergraduate and graduate level have been increasing rapidly, and educators from some institutions have expressed concern that in a few years there may be an overabundance of computer scientists and engineers, at least at the bachelor's degree level. Similarly, as competition for admission to undergraduate and graduate programs grows, so should the quality of the graduates.

Science education policy also addresses equity issues. Undergraduate and graduate technological education is increasingly expensive. Access barriers to high-paying careers in information technology could become formidable for some parts of society, due both to cost and poor preparation at the precollege level. To help offset these barriers, Federal policy may need to address scholarships, fellowships, traineeships, and other forms of direct assistance to students, as well as the improvement of precollege science education.

Changing Roles of Universities

The United States has traditionally looked to its university system whenever national needs called for improved technological innovation and the development of new expertise. This dependence on the education system, probably unparalleled in the world, has often resulted in experiments in institutional structures associated with higher education. The Morrow Act established the land grant colleges to develop a scientific basis for agriculture and to train farmers in modern techniques. During World War II and after, major federally funded research laboratories were established in association with universities. Examples include the Lincoln laboratories at the Massachusetts Institute of Technology, the Lawrence Radiation Laboratory at the University of California, Berkeley, and the Jet Propulsion Laboratory at the California Institute of Technology.

Once again, in response to some of the concerns raised earlier in this chapter, many universities are experimenting with new structures designed with the dual objectives of improving the quality of technical education on campus and improving the flow of research results into industrial innovation. In contrast to many past experiments, these new structures are, by and large, not in response to Federal programs. Rather, many of them respond to initiatives both from industry looking for closer ties with academic programs and from States who see strong academic technical programs as attracting high-technology industry and, thus, serving as stimuli for economic development.

Some potential issues have arisen, but to date problems appear to have been or are being resolved to mutual satisfaction by negotiation between the academic institutions and the industrial sponsors. They include the following:

- How intellectual property rights are distributed among researchers, their institutions, and the industrial sponsors.
- When and under what circumstances research results may be published.
- Who establishes research priorities and standards of scientific quality.

Over the longer term, other issues will also become important, such as the overall influence on the directions of academic basic research. Another long term concern is the potential imbalance of campus resources and attention between science and technology on the one hand and other important scholarly fields such as foreign studies, social science, the arts, or the humanities.

Another question of equity concerns the balance between institutions, themselves. In the first place, are these programs "zero-sum games" in which the gains of a few institutions are mainly at the expense of all the others? Secondly, although the top research institutions have been able to negotiate arrangements that, in their view, do not threaten their other academic roles, less influential schools will have far less bargaining power.

Since many of these institutional experiments are new, it is too early to tell whether they will be successful in meeting their sponsor's expectations or whether the negotiated solutions to the major issues will work. However, it is important that Federal science agencies watch these developments carefully for two reasons:

- Many of these new research institutions will be performers of federally funded research or will be cosponsors of federally funded research.
- Many of the issues under negotiation between universities and industry, such as ownership of intellectual property rights and restrictions on publication are currently echoed as problems in government/university relationships.

Foreign Programs

Programs in other countries designed to promote innovation in information technology have received attention in the United States. These programs have raised both concern about increased competition in technologies in which the United States has traditionally been a world leader, and they have provided models to those who suggest that the United States also needs to develop more coherent programs to foster innovation by domestic industries. Some examples of such programs are the following:

- The Japanese *Fifth Generation Computer Project* is an attempt to move beyond current concepts of computer design to develop an entirely different type of machine based on artificial intelligence concepts.
- The French *La Filiere Electronique Program* is a five-year national information technology R&D program with long-term goals of strengthening the French electronics industry and developing technology for social applications.
- *ESPRIT,* is a pan-European program intended to draw together the technical resources of Europe to focus on R&D in information technology.
- The British *Alvey* program, constituted in part as a British response to the Japanese Fifth Generation Computer Project, is a program of government support for research and development in semiconductors and computer software.

Regardless of assessments of the specific prospects for any one program or its implications for U.S. policy, they demonstrate in total the new competitive world that is developing in information technology. No longer can the United States expect to maintain unquestioned technological leadership and unchallenged domination of world markets in information technology. Other nations now see it in their own interests to build scientific and industrial strength in these areas and are taking steps to do so. U.S. science and technology policy will need to adapt to take this new reality into account.

However, the foreign programs being established do not necessarily constitute useful models for U.S. policies, for several reasons. In the first place, many of them are too new to determine success. Secondly, each is tailored to the unique patterns of government/industry/academic relationships as they exist in country of origin and may not be workable in the country. Finally, many of these programs are designed to address particular bottlenecks to innovation that may exist in the specific country. U.S. science and technology has a different balance of strengths and weaknesses. For example, some countries have a lack of venture capital, others a shortage of scientific manpower, and still others have strong cultural barriers between business and academic institutions that impede technology transfer.

Information technology R&D is, in many respects, an international activity. For example, some domestic firms are owned or partially owned by foreign firms (and vice versa). Many large computer and communications companies are multinationals that operate laboratories in several nations; and many companies have agreements to exchange and cross-license technology with foreign counterparts. Scientists have always viewed basic research as an international activity. Thus, international conferences, scientific journals, and exchange of researchers are common.

Programs designed to strengthen and protect technology as a purely domestic resource need to balance this goal against the natural limitations posed by this international character. For example, the managers of ESPRIT, a program designed to stimulate European technology, must decide whether and on what basis to admit or deny the participation of multinationals based, at least partly, outside of Europe. Companies concerned about what they may view as stringent controls over technology in one country can simply move their R&D efforts to their laboratories in other countries.

Science Policy

Federal programs designed to stimulate information technology R&D exist in the much broader context of Federal science and technology policy.

Congress needs to ask whether existing science and technology policy serves the needs of information technology R&D both in terms of its unique characteristics and the potential importance of the technology to the nation. Similarly, it is important to ask whether policies designed specifically to support information technology R&D are consonant with the broader scope of science and technology policy.

OTA identified three major sets of policy issues that, although applicable to a broad range of science and technology, seem particularly important in the context of information technology.

Institutional Focus.—The Federal Government has traditionally and purposefully supported research and development through several programs administered by different agencies. Despite occasional calls for centralizing R&D support within a single science and technology agency, this historical approach was accepted for two basic reasons. In the first place, agencies with specific technological needs were considered to be best suited to support R&D focused on their needs. Secondly, multiple sources have been considered healthy for the support of science, since diversity and redundancy are both important attributes of scientific research.

The issue of government organization is being reexamined, in the case of information technology. Arguments in favor of a more centralized and/or coordinated approach are based both on the changing nature of R&D and on the challenges posed by new foreign programs stressing R&D in fields such as microelectronics, computer systems, and communications technology.

Research is becoming increasingly expensive. Research equipment such as a microelectronic fabrication facility or a supercomputer can cost several million dollars in capital costs, plus several hundred thousands of dollars a year to maintain and operate. Salaries of research-level technologists are escalating, and much research in information technology now requires large teams of different specialists and technicians. This cost and complexity of R&D not only may make redundancy and duplication of effort a luxury, but may even make some types of research impossible to initiate without coordination of Federal programs.

Some foreign research programs targeted at specific technologies have claimed successes in the sense of capturing a world market—the most notable being the Japanese program for the so-called "64k" computer memory chip for computers that stores about 64,000 characters of information on a microchip. While Japanese success in this market may be attributed to many factors, the existence of a specific government program may have been a major influence. Seeing such programs targeted at selected technologies in Japan and Europe has led some experts to call for the United States to respond with a similar approach to domestic R&D.

A communication satellite being launched from a space shuttle. Satellite communication technology was stimulated by both Federal military and civilian R&D programs

Photo credit: NASA

Such programs, if initiated, would not likely be restricted to information technology alone, but would be focused on a wide range of technologies deemed critical. It would be a significant departure from the past approach that featured multiple government programs of support for basic research, agency-by-agency support of applied research based on mission needs, and, with a few exceptions, private sector support for innovation and product development.

Military and Domestic R&D.—Military funding tends to dominate the Federal R&D budget, particularly in the case of information technology. Such a high level of DOD involvement is not surprising considering the importance of information technology to its mission. The policy issue is whether the high level of defense support provides adequate underpinnings for the broad development of civilian technology or whether a case exists for strong civilian agency support of R&D.

There is no doubt that past DOD and Department of Energy support of R&D in such areas as microelectronics and computer design has been a spur to the entire information technology industry. However, there is evidence that, as the technology becomes more mature, military requirements have begun to diverge from civilian interests. For example, in the area of supercomputers and very high speed integrated circuits, there is a significant doubt that the DOD Strategic Computing and very high speed integrated circuit programs, although responsive to DOD needs, will also serve civilian needs. Hence, there may be a need to boost civilian support in information R&D.

Influence of International Competitiveness.—The growing concern over economic issues, in particular, international competitiveness has led to issues in which attempts to treat technology as a national resource that can be held and protected conflict with traditional approaches to science policy.

For example, concern about the international flow of scientific and technical information conflict with the historical science policy goal of establishing international cooperation in science and technology. Open publication of some scientific material has been challenged on the grounds that the information should be restricted to the United States. Some have suggested that the practice of admitting foreign science students, who comprise a significant percentage of degree candidates in information technology, conflicts with U.S. economic interests. Restrictions have been imposed on foreign scholars attempting to attend U.S. conferences and seminars.

Other policies assume that the United States does not need to draw on foreign science. Hence, research project support typically gives little attention to the potential benefits of travel by U.S. scientists to foreign research laboratories and conferences. Unlike the practices of other countries, little support is provided to provide translations and analyses of foreign research papers and monographs. Yet U.S. scientists, in general, do not have facility in some of the significant scientific languages of today, particularly Japanese. Due to the weakening of foreign language requirements in some graduate programs, many U.S. information scientists do not even have facility with traditional scientific languages like French and German.

Summary

During the past decade, information technology has grown to major economic and social importance in the United States and abroad. The desire to maintain a competitive posture in worldwide markets as well as the urge to realize potential social benefits of new computer and communications systems has focused public attention on the process of innovation, in particular, on R&D. OTA has found that, in response to these pressures, the system has been remarkably adaptable. Federal programs are changing rapidly in response to new perceived needs; science and engineering enrollments are increasing in response to an anticipated need for more technological manpower; and universities and industry are changing their traditional patterns of research and relationships. The policy problem will be to monitor and manage this change. In particular, Congress will need to:

- determine and maintain an appropriate level and balance of R&D support for information technology (including research on the social impacts of these technologies),
- remove unintended barriers to government and private sector R&D efforts,
- assure that these changes in the R&D system do not have unintentional side effects on other sectors or goals of the U.S. system of science and technology, and
- assure access by researchers in all disciplines to powerful new computational and data communication technologies.

Chapter 2
The Environment for R&D in Information Technology in the United States

Contents

	Page
Introduction	25
Concepts for R&D	27
The Roles of the Participants and the R&D Environment	28
Federal Government Role in R&D	28
Industrial R&D	34
Universities' Role in R&D	37
Conflicts in Perspectives, Goals, and Policies	42
Measures of the Health of U.S. R&D in Information Technology	43
Information Industry Profile	43
U.S. Patent Activity	45
A Synthesis: The Changing U.S. R&D Environment	51
Observations	52

Tables

Table No.

		Page
1.	Federal Obligations for Total Research and Development: Fiscal Year 1984	28
2.	Federal Obligations for Basic Research in Information Technology-Related Fields	29
3.	Federal Obligations for Applied Research in Information Technology-Related Fields	29
4.	The Top 15 in R&D Spending	44
5.	Federal and Department of Defense Obligations for Basic Research, Applied Research, and Development, 1983	45
6.	Federal and Department of Defense Obligations for Basic and Applied Research by Field, 1983	46
7.	Technology Distribution of the Top 50 U.S. Patent Electrical Categories 1978-80	46
8.	Percentages of U.S. Patents Granted in Information Technology and in All Technologies, 1981	49
9.	Foreign-Origin U.S. Patents in Some Components of Information Technology	49
10.	Foreign-Owned U.S. Patents in Selected Telecommunications Classes, 1982	49

Figures

Figure No.

		Page
1.	Interrelationships in the R&D Process	26
2.	Science, Engineering, and Technician Employment Within High-Technology Industries, 1980	35
3.	Federal Obligations to Universities and Colleges for R&D Plant	39
4.	Estimated Ratio of Civilian R&D Expenditures to Gross National Product for Selected Countries	45
5.	U.S. Patents in Information Technology, SIC Codes 357, 365, 366, 367	48
6.	Share of Foreign Patenting in the United States for the Three Most Active Countries in Selected Product Fields: 1981	50
7.	U.S. Patent Activity of 10 Foreign Multinational Corporations, 1969-80	50

Chapter 2
The Environment for R&D in Information Technology in the United States

Introduction

"Information technology" is a generic term for a cluster of technologies (discussed in detail in ch. 9) that provide automated capabilities for

- data collection;
- data input;
- information storage and retrieval;
- information processing;
- communication; and
- information presentation.

The information technology industry has become an integral component of U.S. industrial strength. In common with other high-technology[1] industries, the robustness of information technology depends in part on a base of research and development (R&D). However, several interacting factors are straining long-established U.S. policies vis-a-vis research and development:

- rising costs and complexity of R&D;
- intensive competition for both domestic and foreign markets;
- limited resources; and
- accelerating technological advances.

This report describes those factors and examines their effects on the information technology industry and its R&D base, raising questions both about current policies and about proposals for improving the competitive position of the United States in international information technology markets.

The world's major countries are coming to view the development of high technology—and particularly information technology—as a key to economic gains, important social objectives, and national defense and prestige. These countries have adopted national industrial policies in information technology, investing hundreds of millions of dollars in the hope of achieving preeminence, both in R&D and in commercial markets. This growth of foreign competition[2]—especially from Japan—has stimulated a concomitant growth of R&D in the United States.

The trend toward internationalizing R&D, manufacturing, and distribution is increasing. American companies are deciding that technological strength can also be improved by licensing technology from other domestic and foreign businesses, by acquiring equity positions in firms with needed technology, and by establishing R&D and manufacturing operations in foreign countries in order to obtain access to rapidly changing commercial applications.

Figure 1 shows some important components of the R&D process and diagrams their interrelationships. The remainder of this report will focus on those components.

- This chapter describes some of the key players in the process and discusses some measures of health of the information technology industry.
- Chapter 3 presents four case studies, each dealing with an important element in the cluster of technologies that comprise information technology.

---

[1]The term high technology is used throughout this chapter to refer to those industries characterized by a high proportion of R&D expenditures per employee, or a significantly larger proportion of skilled workers than the industry average, and a rapidly evolving underlying technological base. Thus computers and electronics are within the scope of this meaning; auto and steel manufacturing are not, in spite of the recent trend to modernize and automate.

[2]See also *International Competitiveness in Electronics* (Washington, DC: U.S. Congress, Office of Technology Assessment, OTA-ISC-200, November 1983).

Figure 1.—Interrelationships in the R&D Process

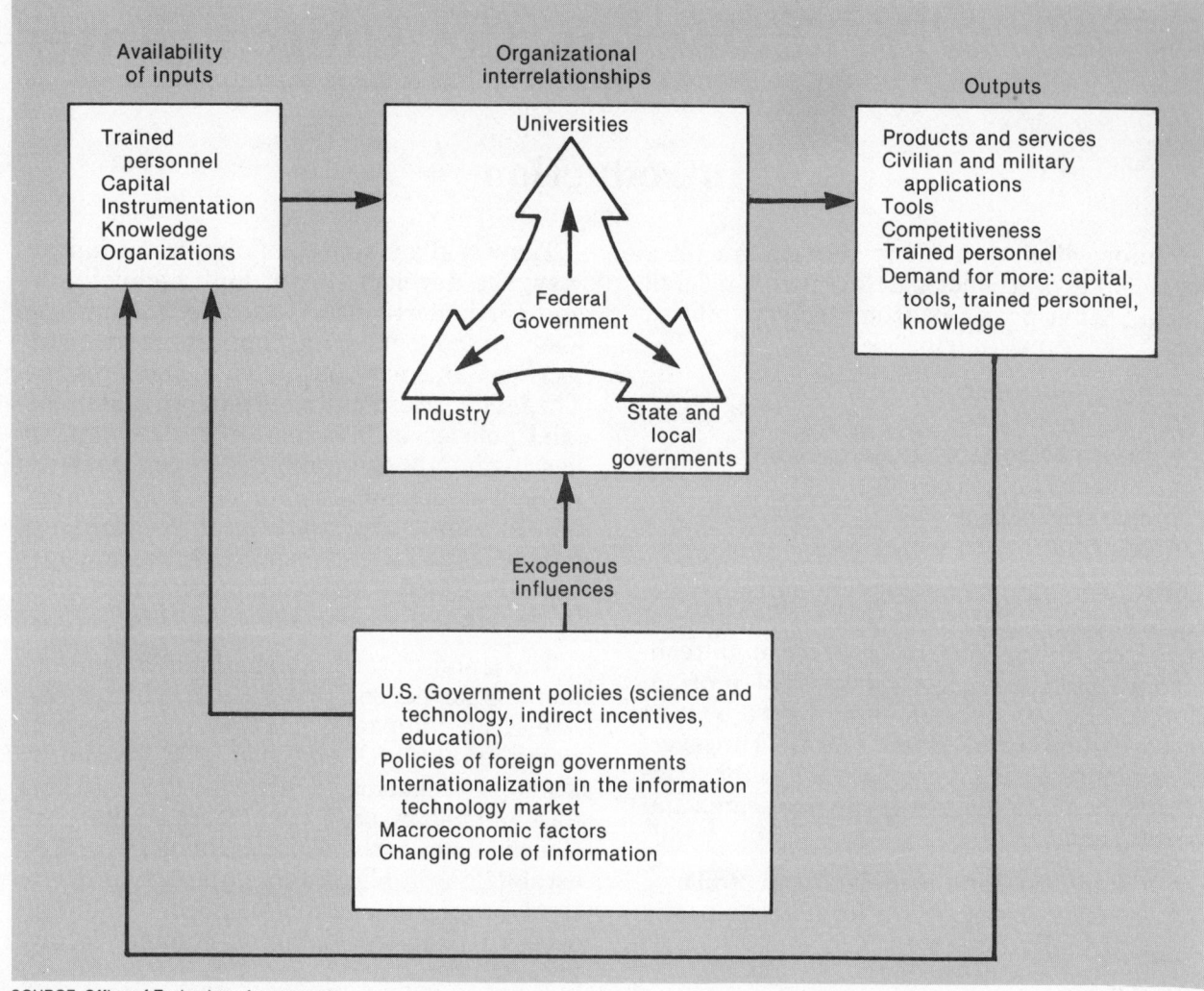

SOURCE: Office of Technology Assessment.

- Chapter 4 discusses the recent divestiture of AT&T in the context of its potential effect on the R&D activities of Bell Laboratories.
- Chapter 5 considers the availability of trained personnel to the R&D process.
- Chapter 6 examines new university-industry institutional relationships and their changing roles in the R&D environment.
- Chapters 7 and 8 focus on some of the exogenous elements: the science and technology policies of foreign governments in chapter 7; the science and technology policies of the United States in chapter 8.
- Chapter 9 describes the technological underpinnings of information technology, the directions of key research areas, and the characteristics of the information technology industry.

Concepts for R&D

R&D includes a wide variety of activities—ranging from investigations in pure science to product development. Because segments of information technology draw on so many science, engineering and other disciplines—computer science, manufacturing, electrical, mechanical and industrial engineering, physics, chemistry, mathematics, psychology, linguistics—it is difficult to assign particular efforts to the general category of information technology.

As defined by the National Science Foundation (NSF), R&D is categorized as follows:[3]

- *Research* is systematic study directed toward fuller scientific knowledge or understanding of the subject studied.
- In *basic research* the objective is to gain fuller knowledge or understanding of the fundamental aspects of phenomena and of observable facts without specific applications toward processes or products in mind.
- In *applied research* the objective is to gain knowledge or understanding necessary for determining the means by which a recognized and specific need may be met.
- *Development* is the systematic use of the knowledge or understanding gained from research directed toward the production of useful materials, devices, systems, or methods, including design and development of prototypes and processes.

The definitions of "applied" and "basic" research are especially troublesome in a field as dynamic as information technology, in which laboratory concepts evolve into marketable products very rapidly. In the area of artificial intelligence, for example, the work is often basic in the sense that it seeks new ways of understanding complex symbolic processes, and applied in the sense that much of the work is directed at prototype applications. This fuzziness has led to differing judgments as to which projects are applied and which are basic, and to confusion in data collection, because the terms are not applied uniformly by Federal agencies, industry, or academia.

Apart from the difficulty in drawing a clean line between basic and applied research, there is an additional problem in identifying the set of industries that collectively comprise the information industry. For purposes of this report, we use the term to include electronics, computer, and telecommunications equipment manufacturers, providers of computer-based services, and commercial software developers.

There are, then, two major areas of ambiguity in any discussion of information technology R&D: ambiguities inherent in designating an effort as "information technology" and ambiguities arising from the overlap of basic and applied research. Because of this, *quantification of R&D efforts in information technology is necessarily approximate and the numbers cited in this report should be regarded as estimates, not as "hard" data.*

One further term, "innovation," should also be clarified. As used in this report, innovation is a process that includes research and development, manufacturing or production, and distribution.[4] The Nation's innovative capacity depends on the effective functioning of all parts of the process. Success in the marketplace requires proficiency in some—not well understood—combination of those parts. There are other factors that influence marketplace success, such as the timing of the introduction of commercial products, the influence of entrepreneurs, and a variety of government policies. Thus, while excellence in research and development provides no assurance of leadership in the commercial marketplace, it may very well be a necessary (if not sufficient) ingredient of success.

---

[3]National Science Foundation, *Federal Funds for Research and Development Fiscal Years 1981, 1982, and 1983*, Volume XXXI Detailed Statistical Tables, NSF 82-326 (Washington, DC, U.S. Government Printing Office, 1982), p. 1.

[4]*International Competition in Advanced Technology: Decisions for America,* Office of International Affairs, National Research Council, 1983, pp. 21-22.

The Roles of the Participants and the R&D Environment

Industry, universities, and Government (State, local, and Federal) are the three key contributors to R&D in the United States. The effectiveness of the Nation's R&D is dependent on the vitality of each of the participants and on their interrelationships. Federal support of R&D and Federal policies that maintain a healthy economy encourage industrial investment in R&D.[5] A vigorous industry, in turn, provides a large Federal and State tax base, making possible added support for academic institutions. For their part, well-financed academic institutions generate well-trained personnel as well as the dynamic knowledge base necessary to fruitful R&D efforts.

In addition to describing the roles of each of the participants and the environment for R&D, this section identifies some of the diverse changes taking place in the R&D environment—those already in place, and others in transition—that may profoundly modify some longstanding institutional patterns.

Federal Government Role in R&D

The Federal Government plays several key roles in information technology R&D. As a major *user* of information technology products (about 6 percent of the total automated data processing market and most of the market for supercomputers), its requirements are of considerable interest to the industry. As a *sponsor* of research, the Federal Government funds roughly half of the total R&D carried out in the United States[6] and about two-fifths of the research by the electrical machinery/communications industry (a key component of the information technology complex). In addition, the Federal Government itself *performs* about $11 billion of R&D[7] (table 1) in its own and contract laboratories.

Beyond that, the Government helps to shape the environment in which private firms make their R&D decisions. In some cases, this is a result of deliberate Government policy intended to stimulate (or suppress) industry investment. At other times, the environment is affected by uncoordinated actions—intended to serve other purposes—taken by a variety of Federal entities including the Federal Reserve Board, the courts, regulatory bodies and a plethora of executive branch agencies including the Departments of Justice, Commerce, State, and Defense, the National Security Council, and the Environmental Protection Agency.

Government Funding of R&D in Information Technology

The Federal Government provided about 65 percent of the funding in 1982 for R&D in science and engineering fields in the Nation's

---

[5] David M. Levy and Nestor E. Terleckyj, *Effects of Government R&D on Private Investment and Productivity: A Macroeconomic Analysis,* National Planning Association, revised Jan. 5, 1983, pp. 17-19.

[6] *Federal Support for R&D and Innovation,* Congressional Budget Office, April 1984, p. iii.

[7] *Probable Levels of R&D Expenditures in 1984: Forecast and Analysis,* Columbus Division of Battelle Memorial Institute, December 1983, p. 1.

Table 1.—Federal Obligations for Total Research and Development: Fiscal Year 1984 (Estimated)
(millions of dollars)

				Extramural[a]						
				United States and Territories						
	Total	Intramural[b]	Industrial firms	FFRDCs[c] administered by industrial firms	Universities and colleges	FFRDCs[c] administered by universities and colleges	Other nonprofit institutions	FFRDCs[c] administered by nonprofit institutions	State and local governments	U.S. supported Foreign[d]
Total all agencies...	$45,497.0	$10,969.9	$22,957.4	$1,614.4	$5,270.7	$2,291.9	$1,335.5	$683.2	$189.1	$184.8

NOTES: [a] All organizations outside the Federal Government that perform with Federal funds.
[b] Agencies of the Federal Government.
[c] Federally funded R&D centers.
[d] Foreign citizens, organizations, or governments, or international organizations, such as NATO, UNESCO, WHO, performing work abroad financed by the Federal Government.

SOURCE: "Federal Funds for Research and Development, Fiscal Years 1982, 1983, 1984," vol. XXXII, Detailed Statistical Tables NSF 83-319, p. 30.

universities and colleges.[8] Data collected by the National Science Foundation (see tables 2 and 3) indicate that Federal obligations for basic research in fields related to information technology included $103.7 million for computer science and $115.4 million for electrical engineering in fiscal year 1984. For applied research, funding levels are $145.8 million for computer science and $568.3 million for electrical engineering. These categories alone amount to $933 million in basic and applied R&D funding. In addition, there are other R&D areas related to information technology —e.g., mathematics, physics, and materials sciences.

The Department of Defense (DOD), which has the largest of the Federal agency R&D budgets, is becoming increasingly dependent on electronics and computer science. By 1985, those fields will absorb nearly 25 percent of the total DOD R&D spending.[9] Within DOD, the Defense Advanced Research Projects Agency (DARPA) has heavily funded efforts in artificial intelligence, microelectronics, networking and advanced computer architecture.

No other agency compares with DOD, which accounts for about 60 percent of the Federal R&D budget.[10] NSF, for example, accounts for about 3 percent of the Federal total, with a fiscal year 1983 appropriations of just over $1 billion[11] and $1.32 billion and $1.5 billion in fiscal years 1984 and 1985 respectively.[12] NSF funding, which is heavily weighted toward the "basic" end of the R&D scale, supports research through grants, scholarships, university laboratory modernization, the establishment of university-based "centers of excellence," and similar programs. Many of the information technology-related disciplines are funded through NSF programs: communications, electrical engineering, optoelectronics, mathematics, physics, materials research, information sciences, and so on. These information technology-related fields accounted for over $90 million in fiscal year 1984.

Since 1972, NSF has been the primary Government force in creating university-industry cooperative research centers, providing some of their startup funds, planning grants, and advice during their first years of opera-

[8]National Science Foundation, Early Release of Summary Statistics on Academic Science/Engineering Resources, Division of Science Resources Studies, December 1983. Also see *Federal R&D Funding: The 1975-85 Decade,* National Science Foundation, March 1984, p. 11.

Table 2.—Federal Obligations for Basic Research in Information Technology-Related Fields
(millions of dollars)

Year	Computer science	Electrical engineering	Total
1974	NA	$38.45	NA
1975	NA	47.76	NA
1976	$26.59	53.08	$79.67
1977	31.02	55.14	86.16
1978	40.28	57.41	97.70
1979	42.96	62.03	104.98
1980	46.22	70.59	116.80
1981	52.21	78.51	130.71
1982	67.45	93.63	161.07
1983[a]	80.25	91.89	172.14
1984[a]	$103.66	$115.38	$219.04

[a]National Science Foundation estimates.
NA—Not available.
SOURCE: National Science Foundation, "Federal Funds for Research and Development, Detailed Historical Tables: Fiscal Years 1955-84," p. 275.

Table 3.—Federal Obligations for Applied Research in Information Technology-Related Fields
(millions of dollars)

Year	Computer science	Electrical engineering	Total
1974	NA	$230.79	NA
1975	NA	239.20	NA
1976	$46.99	244.61	$291.60
1977	58.34	327.59	385.93
1978	66.97	375.22	442.19
1979	63.31	355.84	418.15
1980	82.38	446.56	528.93
1981	69.32	478.17	547.48
1982	103.49	518.56	622.05
1983	121.18	525.75	646.92
1984[a]	$145.85	$568.33	$714.18

[a]National Science Foundation estimates.
NA—Not available.
SOURCE: National Science Foundation, "Federal Funds for Research and Development, Detailed Historical Tables: Fiscal Years 1955-84," p. 327.

[9]Cited in a speech by Dr. Leo Young, Office of the Under Secretary of Defense for Research and Engineering, DOD, at the IEEE 1984 Conference on U.S. Technology Policy, Feb. 22, 1984, Washington, DC.
[10]*Probable Levels of R&D Expenditures in 1984,* op. cit.
[11]*Federal Funds for Research and Development, Fiscal Years, 1981, 1982, and 1983,* op. cit., p. 25.
[12]Fiscal Year 1985 National Science Foundation Budget Estimate to Congress.

tion. The centers are expected to become self-supporting.[13] By the end of fiscal year 1984, NSF was involved with 20 of these centers and expects to make awards to at least 10 new centers in 1985.

A number of the centers are involved with information technology-related research. For example:

- Rensselaer Polytechnic Institute's Center for Interactive Computer Graphics is doing applied research in computer-aided design (CAD).
- North Carolina State University's Communications and Signal Processing Laboratory is primarily engaged in basic research.
- Both basic and applied research is being performed at the University of Rhode Island's Robotics Center.
- Ohio State University is doing basic and applied research in robotic welding.
- Georgia Institute of Technology's Center for Material Handling is engaged in applied research.

The National Science Board has recommended broadened NSF support for engineering research, an area long neglected in favor of the agency's traditional emphasis on basic scientific research. Congress approved about $150 million for NSF grants for engineering research in fiscal 1985, about 10 percent of the agency's total research budget.[14] The President's budget request for fiscal year 1985 calls for more funding for this purpose, as well as for establishment of cross-disciplinary engineering centers at universities which would, among other effects, promote research on computers and manufacturing processes.[15] Government funding of engineering equipment and facilities at universities decreased from $42 million to $17 million per year between 1974 and 1981,[16] but has been rising since then.

The Pattern of Government Funding of R&D in Information Technology

The Federal Government has had a long history of funding R&D in information technology-related fields. It is currently the major sponsor of those types of information technology R&D in which it has special interests. These include artificial intelligence, supercomputers, software engineering, and very large scale integrated circuits (VLSI), all areas in their technological infancy and with enormous potential for military as well as commercial applications. There is a long list of related technologies that have been stimulated by Government—often defense or other mission agencies—sponsorship of R&D including radar, guidance systems, satellite communications, and many others.

There are some historic examples of intensive Government sponsorship of technological development in areas where the potential benefit was expected to be great, but the risks and costs of research were high and therefore unattractive to industry—e.g., computers, aviation and communications satellites. One of the classic illustrations of a successful, major Government contribution to information technology R&D is in the field of satellite communications. The National Aeronautics and Space Administration (NASA) (which currently accounts for about 7 percent of the Federal R&D budget) had the leading role in pioneering technological progress toward commercial development, accelerating the time frame for the introduction of this technology, influencing the structure of the U.S. domestic and international telecommunications common carrier industries, and effecting significant cost savings over the long run.[17]

In these cases, the Government, through the undertaking of a number of risky and expensive R&D programs and with extensive private sector involvement, developed a large pool of baseline technology that served to prove the feasibility of geostationary satellite

---

[13]DOD is also supporting this program through an $8 million grant, primarily for laboratory equipment.

[14]"National Science Foundation Starts to Broaden Support of Engineering Research," *The Chronicle of Higher Education*, Jan. 18, 1984, p. 17, and interviews with NSF officials, January 1985.

[15]Ibid.

[16]*Probable Levels of R&D Expenditures in 1984*, op. cit.

[17]Morris Teubal and Edward Steinmuller, *Government Policy, Innovation and Economic Growth: Lessons From a Study of Satellite Communications*, Research Policy 11 (1982) 27-287, North Holland Publishing Co.

communications. These R&D programs were for the purposes of proving the feasibility of various technological advances such as geostationary orbiting satellites, electromagnetic propagation of signals from outer space, traveling wave tubes, automatic station keeping, and aircraft communications. The NASA programs initiated to undertake the extensive R&D included the SCORE, ECHO, and RELAY programs, the SYNCOM series of launches that paved the way for Intelsat I, the first commercial communications satellite, and the Applications Technology Satellites series. The costs for the RELAY, ECHO, and SYNCOM Programs alone through 1965 were over $128 million—an amount that few companies could—or would—commit, particularly considering that the feasibility of synchronous satellite operation was seriously questioned.[18]

It is also interesting to note that these NASA programs likely had some important side-effects on the structure of the U.S. international satellite communications industry. Because AT&T was the only private company to have heavily invested its own funds for satellite communications R&D—with focus on the nonsynchronous TELSTAR system—it is likely that AT&T would have dominated the new international and domestic satellite communications services industry. Instead, the NASA programs, through continuous transfer of technology to, and close interaction with, commercial firms stimulated the competition that followed the 1972 Federal Communication Commission's decision allowing open entry into the domestic satellite communications services industry.

The market for the supply of satellite communications equipment was also open to competition due to the expertise gained by NASA contractors. In addition, the international satellite network that evolved is owned and operated by INTELSAT, an international consortium, with the U.S. portion owned and operated by COMSAT, a broadly based private/public corporation.

Other Federal Government Policies

The Federal Government has many other means for promoting (or suppressing) private sector R&D activities including antitrust policy, patent policy, tax credits, technology transfer from Federal laboratories and federally funded R&D centers, and the promotion of Research and Development Limited Partnerships (RDLP). Export controls, whether for national security or political purposes, serve as a negative influence in promoting private sector R&D. A major source of corporate funding for R&D, international sales, is lessened, and the open exchange of technical data is limited. Six policies intended to promote private sector R&D are reviewed below.

PATENT POLICY

Previous policies assigning Federal ownership of patents based on Government-funded R&D have been modified in recent years with the intent to stimulate patenting and commercialization of invention. Public Law 96-517 (1980), which permits small businesses, not-for-profit institutions, and universities to obtain patents based on Government-sponsored R&D, is intended to encourage university-industry collaboration and patenting. The Government's right to patent ownership was further reduced by Presidential Memorandum (February 1983). This memorandum modified the Federal Acquisition Regulations by extending the concepts of the current law to allow all Government contractors to retain patent rights.

There are obvious tensions in this situation, since it is sometimes argued that the public should own patents derived from research it has funded. The counter-argument is that Government-owned patents tend not to become commercialized and the public reaps no real benefit from them. For example, Federal efforts to license its patents have resulted in a meager 4 percent being licensed, in contrast with 33 percent for university-owned patents.[19]

---

[18]Ibid., p. 277.

[19]Lansing Felker, U.S. Department of Commerce, Office of Productivity, Technology, and Innovation, during interviews with OTA staff, January 1984.

Allowing universities and businesses to retain ownership stimulates commercialization, but may also have the effect of distorting the university's traditional role as a developer of fundamental knowledge.

TECHNOLOGY TRANSFER

The Stevenson-Wydler Technology Innovation Act of 1980[20] was an attempt "to improve the economic, environmental, and social well-being of the United States," through such means as: establishing organizations in the executive branch to study and stimulate technology; promoting technology development through the establishment of centers for industrial technology; stimulating improved utilization of federally funded technology development by State and local governments and the private sector; and by other activities.[21] The act has been selectively implemented. Most of the Federal Laboratories have established Offices of Research and Technology Applications (ORTAs) which collect and disseminate the results of their respective Laboratory's research. The Center for the Utilization of Federal Technology, in the National Technical Information Service of the Department of Commerce, serves as a central clearinghouse.

However, the heart of the act, the Cooperative Generic Technology Program, has never been implemented. In February 1984, the Secretary of Commerce issued the first report to the President and the Congress on the progress of Federal activities conducted pursuant to the Act.[22] It appears that much of the work cited in the Report as "Stevenson-Wydler" activities would have been performed even if the act had not existed. For instance, the new patent policies discussed above and the R&D Limited Partnership (RDLP) discussed below were both cited as "Stevenson-Wydler" initiatives.[23]

The Act has probably had an effect on the activities of the Federal Laboratory Consortium (FLC). In 1984, the FLC established an award for excellence in technology transfer and issued 26 such awards. The Federal Laboratories, however, are mission-oriented; and no Federal Laboratory has a mission emphasizing the development of commercial technologies.[24] Thus, the concept of cooperative generic research laboratories envisioned by the Act has not been tested.

TAX CREDITS

Tax credits for businesses performing R&D have been expanded through the Economic Recovery Tax Act (ERTA) of 1981, which will expire in 1986 unless extended.[25] A key provision of ERTA allows companies to claim 25 percent tax credits for their qualified R&D costs above their average expenditures for the prior 3-year period. The law also allows for increased deductions for manufacturer's donations of new R&D equipment to universities, and provides a new capital cost recovery system for R&D equipment (modified later by the Tax Equity and Fiscal Responsibility Act of 1982—TEFRA).

Opinion is mixed as to whether this tax credit is effective in stimulating R&D investment. One study,[26] based on the limited available data, observes that the tax credit may well be helpful in encouraging increased R&D budgets. However, a current study finds very little effect on increased R&D spending due to the tax credit.[27] Battelle Memorial Institute attributes at least part of the increased industry investment in R&D to the tax credits.[28]

---

[20]Public Law 96-480.
[21]For more details see the Stevenson-Wydler Technology Innovation Act of 1980, Report to the President and the Congress from the Secretary of Commerce. February 1984.
[22]Ibid.
[23]Ibid., p. 4.

[24]OTA Memorandum, "Development and Diffusion of Commercial Technologies: Does the Federal Government Need to Redefine Its Role?" March 1984, p. 26.
[25]Public Law 97-34, August 1981.
[26]Eileen L. Collins, *An Early Assessment of Three R&D Incentives Provided by the Economic Recovery Tax Act of 1981*, National Science Foundation, PRA Report 8307, April 1983.
[27]Preliminary findings of an ongoing study by Edwin Mansfield, financed by the National Science Foundation.
[28]*Probable Levels of R&D Expenditures in 1984*, pp. 2, 11-12, op. cit.

R&D LIMITED PARTNERSHIPS

The Department of Commerce has been promoting wider use of R&D Limited Partnerships (RDLPs), and offers advisory assistance to businesses in their use. RDLPs are intended to attract venture capital to commercial R&D by limiting the potential losses to the venture capitalists while still permitting them to retain patent rights, if any, and to have prospects for receiving royalties or a subsequent buy-out by the company. RDLPs are sometimes used for conducting R&D with relatively short-term payoffs—e.g., 3 to 4 years. The use of RDLPs primarily affects the segments of the innovation sequence from prototype through product development.

During 1982, $275 million is estimated to have been invested in RDLPs, mainly through large brokerage houses. In 1983, the amount is estimated at $490 million; in 1984, it was $220 million.[29] Although these investments have tended to go for biotechnology, some have been allocated to information technology projects in fields such as computers, software, microelectronics, telecommunications, robotics, and artificial intelligence. The drop in funding in 1984 is believed by investment bankers to be due to two trends. First, there is a general drop in investor interest in high technology. Second, some investors appear to be concerned about possible changes in tax laws that may give less favorable treatment of R&D tax deductions and capital gains.

ANTITRUST POLICY

There have been administrative proposals and congressional bills that would limit the use of the treble damage penalty against companies found guilty of antitrust violations and establish clearer guidelines for companies considering cooperative research activities.

There have been arguments noting that the antitrust laws have not had a chilling effect on cooperative research since they are rarely used. However, until recently businesses have been exceptionally cautious about such ventures because of concern over litigation.

Some of the questions that arise in considering more liberalized interpretation of antitrust legislation concerning joint research are:

- Will U.S. companies, long accustomed to performing much of their R&D individually, be able to adapt swiftly to a different mode of operation? What will be the real commitment to shared research? How will intellectual property issues be resolved?
- Will there be new opportunities for collusion among joint R&D partners that recreate historical antitrust problems?
- Will joint R&D dilute the benefits of competition even in basic research? Will small firms be disadvantaged?

In the closing days of the 98th Congress, the National Cooperative Research Act of 1984 was passed. The Act eliminates the treble damage penalties in antitrust cases involving joint R&D ventures when those ventures meet the conditions of the Act, in particular, by providing prior notification to the Federal Trade Commission and the Justice Department.

INDUSTRIAL POLICY

An important topic debated in Congress concerns industrial policy and the appropriate role of Government in strengthening industry. One approach would provide an environment generally conducive to industry reinvestment, productivity improvements, and increased competitiveness through tax, antitrust, patent, and other policies. A different approach would assist selected industries, create a high-level industry-labor-Government advisory council, and provide loans and loan guarantees.

Among the issues that surround the debates are whether the Government could be effective in selecting industries for support; whether businesses, without further encouragement, would invest their resources in areas most beneficial to the Nation's competitiveness; and whether foreign national industrial policies pose insuperable problems for U.S. businesses.

---

[29]Data based on interviews by OTA staff with officials from the Office of Productivity, Technology, and Innovation, U.S. Department of Commerce, and key sources in the investment banking community, Jan. 29, 1985.

There may also be important lessons from the various foreign experiences with targeted industrial policies, many of which may not be suitable as models for the United States (see Ch. 7: Foreign Information Technology R&D).

Industrial R&D

The corporate motivation for performing R&D centers about the need to maintain or improve market share and profitability for both the short and long term. For high-technology businesses in general, R&D plays a critical—although not singular—role in helping the firm to sustain or improve its competitive position.

Funding and Licensing of Research

The information technology industry in the United States spent about $10.8 billion for R&D in 1983. As is typical of a high-technology industry, the firms in information technology often spend a large proportion of their sales revenue on R&D—for supercomputer manufacturers the ratio was nearly 20 percent in 1982, and it is believed to have been comparable in 1983. In 1983, overall R&D spending by computer manufacturers rose by 19.5 percent; spending by computer software and service vendors rose by 38.9 percent; and telecommunications R&D rose by 31 percent. The importance of R&D to these firms can be seen from the fact that even during the recent economic recession they continued to make substantial R&D investments.

While information technology companies perform much of their R&D in-house, they also make use of research originating in universities, other companies, and the Federal Government through licensing and other arrangements for technology transfer. Licensing and cross-licensing are often used as means of acquiring technology quickly and for recovering R&D expenses.

Protection of Research Results

Leadtimes in research and product development are very important for capturing markets, recovering R&D expenses, and contributing to profitability and further R&D investment. A 6-month leadtime in getting products into commercial markets can make the difference between market dominance and substantial losses. The information technology industry's significant investments in R&D, the high mobility of technical personnel, and the increasing internationalization of R&D, encourage rapid diffusion of technical data and frequent introduction of new products. These characteristics intensify the need for legal protection of new ideas and products.

Certain areas of information technology are especially vulnerable to "borrowing" and the degree of legal protection available is uncertain. Software, for instance, can be copywrited but cannot be patented except in certain instances. Policy is being made in the courts, virtually on a case-by-case basis, and the resultant ambiguities satisfy no one. The entire problem of intellectual property rights has become a matter for national attention.

Industry-University Links

Chapter 6 of this report describes in detail the relationship of the information technology industry and the universities. International competition is causing U.S. industry to become increasingly sensitive to the importance of academia both as a performer of information technology-relevant basic research and as a supplier of trained personnel.

The information technology industry is a major "consumer" of technically trained personnel. As shown in figure 2, the office/computing and communications industries are rivaled only by the aircraft and parts industry in terms of overall employment of scientists, engineers, and technicians. According to statistics compiled by the National Center for Education Statistics,[30] some 21,400 electrical, electronic, and communications engineering and 25,500 computer and information science majors graduated in 1982. Within those disciplines, less than 2 percent are unemployed.[31] There is some controversy surrounding the putative shortage of future manpower for information technology research (discussed at

---

[30]National Center for Education Statistics, Survey of Earned Degrees Conferred, reported to OTA by Dr. Vance Grant, Jan. 3, 1984.

[31]Congressional Budget Office, *Defense Spending and the Economy*, Table A-7, p. 59, February 1983.

Figure 2.—Science, Engineering, and Technician Employment Within High-Technology Industries, 1980

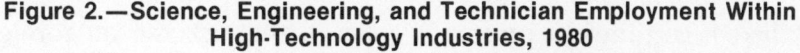

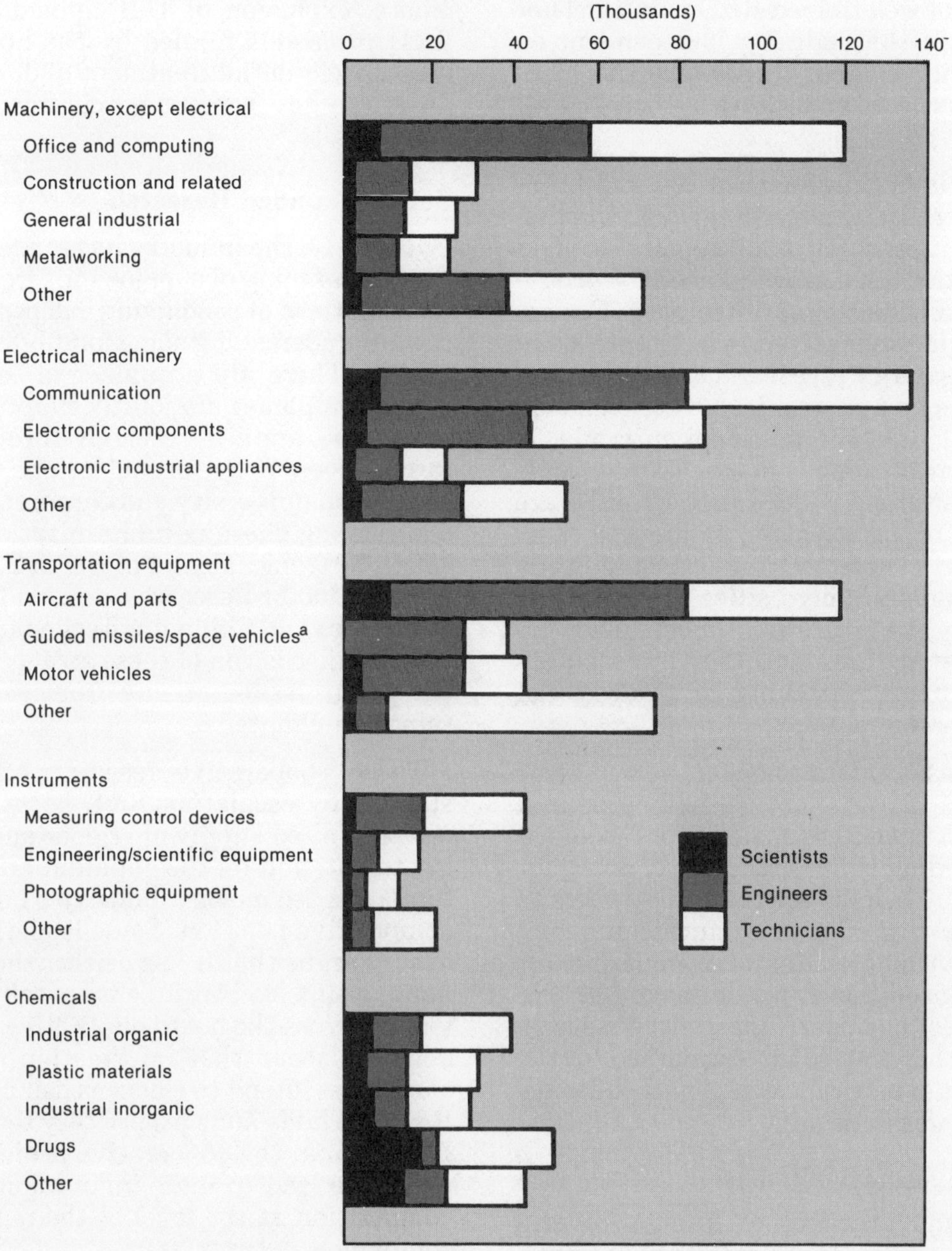

aScientific employment was not reported because confidentiality rules and/or statistical reliability prohibit data release.

SOURCE: National Science Foundation, *Changing Employment Patterns of Scientists, Engineers, and Technicians in Manufacturing Industries: 1977-80.*

length in ch. 7) but there is certainly no present oversupply of well-trained R&D personnel nor is there doubt that industry is dependent on the university system to produce the manpower necessary to maintain a sufficient level of R&D.

Industry is both influenced by, and influences, university training programs. In addition to its needs for traditionally trained graduates, there is a growing need for graduates with multidisciplinary training. For example, companies involved in fiber optic communications require researchers trained in both physics and electronics—a combination which is not part of traditional curricula. A similar situation applies in the "expert" systems field, where a wider range of skills are needed and broad scientific training is especially valued. These shifting industry needs place demands on universities to alter their curricula and to create multidisciplinary institutional structures, and they increasingly require frequent retraining of professional technical personnel.

In some cases, information technology firms requiring special skills not normally produced by academia have compensated for the shortfall by providing additional cross-training for employees, by helping selected universities to develop new curricula, or by furnishing supplemental teaching staff. For example, in 1983 IBM announced that it would make $10 million available to support university researchers and another $40 million earmarked for the development of curricula in computer-aided design and manufacturing.

Foreign Government Policies

Policies and practices of foreign governments and companies can influence the profitability of U.S. companies or deny them markets, and thus effectively restrict their ability to invest in R&D. These policies and practices include pricing exports at below cost in order to capture larger market share and the advantage of scale, targeting specific advanced technology markets through government-sponsored industrial strategies, creating nontariff barriers (e.g., discriminatory certification practices), restrictions on foreign direct investments, exclusion of U.S. subsidiaries from R&D programs funded by the host government, preferential treatment of domestic producers in government procurement, and export credits.[32]

Jointly Funded Research

Recently, the industry has made what may be the beginning of a major shift from its traditional pattern of conducting independent R&D, toward undertaking some joint or cooperative efforts. There are a number of examples in which companies are jointly supporting basic and some applied research through newly formed cooperative organizations, which rely heavily on university and corporate researchers. Among these new organizations are the Microelectronics Center of North Carolina, the Semiconductor Research Corp., and the Microelectronics and Computer Technology Corp. A detailed discussion of these arrangements and the policy issues arising from them is contained in chapter 6.

These cooperative research efforts were spurred by escalating R&D costs, by a perceived limited supply of science and engineering talent, and by the apparent erosion of information technology industry's international competitive position. Some leaders in the industry argue that it has neither the resources nor the time to continue its established pattern of across-the-board duplicative R&D. This does not mean that information technology companies intend to slacken their competitive R&D work vis-à-vis proprietary technologies. If anything, the cooperative projects are expected to lead to more innovation and more competition at the level of the participating companies.

Cooperative research programs require a careful distinction between proprietory and nonproprietory technology. Nonproprietary technology is made up of:

- generic technology, consisting of scientific and engineering principles that form

---

[32] For more details, see *International Competition in Advanced Technology: Decisions for America*, op. cit., pp. 28-37.

a competitively neutral technology base that can be shared by all firms without reducing the potential benefits for any one firm; and
- infratechnology, consisting of the knowledge base necessary to implement product and process design concepts. It includes such things as basic data characterizing materials, test methods, and standards. Like generic technology, the infratechnology is competitively neutral.

The various cooperative arrangements are concerned with the nonproprietary technologies.

Cooperative Government-industry development of nonproprietary technical standards is a related area important to industry. A recent example is the cooperative effort of the National Bureau of Standard's Institute for Computer Sciences and Technology (ICST) and 12 information technology firms in developing and demonstrating networking technology for office systems. A similar cooperative project is aimed at developing networking technology for the factory floor. These efforts are based on the development of nonproprietary standards. The programs, which began joint demonstrations in 1984, permit the products of different manufacturers to work together compatibly and therefore expand the market for them.

In the long term, continued expansion of U.S. cooperative research activities could have policy implications for the appropriate amounts and focus of Federal funds for R&D, for universities' needs for outside support, and for invigorating segments of the university research environment—and the potential for altering the status of U.S. R&D relative to other nations.

Universities' Role in R&D

The exceptionally broad nature of the underpinnings of information technology, and the escalating complexity associated with continued advances based on research, indicate an increasing role for universities. Major advances in fundamental knowledge are often the result of decades of dedicated and expensive research—efforts which few commercial firms would be willing to undertake. In each of the four areas of information technologies selected for the chapter 3 case studies (advanced computer architecture, fiber optics, software engineering, and artificial intelligence), universities have made and are continuing to make valuable research contributions in technologies that the private sector commercializes.

The intensity and breadth of university research is dependent on a wide variety of factors, ranging from the prestige of the institution, graduate enrollment, ability to retain qualified faculty and researchers, adequacy of funding for researchers, adequacy of facilities and laboratory equipment, affiliations with major companies, and increasingly on interactions with other researchers domestically and internationally. It is also dependent on a large proportion of foreign graduate students—as many as 50 percent in some universities—particularly in disciplines such as engineering.

The intensity of university R&D is also dependent on the level of funding for research provided by the Federal and State governments, as well as by industry. About 85 percent of the funding for university and college R&D came from external sources.[33] Federal and State governments as well as industry provide funding for research, for scholarships, for laboratory equipment, and for real estate. The universities accounted for about one-half of all basic research expenditures in 1984, with 70 percent of their funding provided by the Federal Government.

Laboratory Research Instrumentation and Facilities

During the past few years, problems concerning the obsolescence of university laboratory research instrumentation and facilities, and a lack of access to supercomputer equipment, have been recognized in many academic disciplines. This problem is not specific to in-

---
[33]National Science Foundation, *Early Release of Summary Statistics, etc.*, table 1, December 1983.

formation technology, but this field is among those affected. A decline in university research capabilities could result in a significant decline in the overall rate of the Nation's scientific advance.

One study notes that when the appropriate instrumentation needed to conduct specific research is unavailable, then research objectives are altered to match that which is available.[34] This source also reports that leaders within the scientific community have estimated the cost of updating university research equipment to lie between $1 billion and $4 billion. In particular, instrumentation with costs between $100,000 and $1 million at U.S. research universities is reported as becoming obsolete.[35] One estimate stated that selected instrument costs have increased fourfold since 1970.[36]

Compounding the problem is the fact that the most up-to-date research equipment has a short lifetime—only 3 to 8 years.[37] Another study which compared university laboratory equipment with that of industrial laboratories found that the median age of university laboratory equipment was twice that of the equipment found in the laboratories of companies performing high-quality research.[38]

The same study also noted that until recently, not a single top-line supercomputer was installed in service at a U.S. university. A number of foreign universities, however, are equipped with supercomputers.[39] In part as a response, the Federal Government is increasingly sharing its supercomputers with its contractors, many of which are universities. During fiscal year 1984, $6 million was authorized for NSF to buy access to the equivalent of one supercomputer for scientific use. This amount was increased to $40 million in fiscal year 1985 and will contribute to the establishment of six or seven supercomputing centers nationwide over the next 5 years. In addition, four U.S. universities have recently acquired supercomputers.

Further acquisitions of supercomputers by universities may be curtailed both by financial limitations and by the difficulty of assembling the expert staff needed to maintain the facilities. Consequences of obsolescence are likely to include foregone opportunities to perform frontier university research, less-than-optimal training for graduate students, a continuation of the migration of faculty and new graduates to industrial laboratories, and a deterioration in the quality of U.S. instrumentation, because university researchers traditionally provide valuable feedback and innovative improvements to the instrument manufacturing community.

A number of factors have contributed to the obsolescence of university laboratory equipment. Among these are the long-term decrease in Federal funding for R&D plant in universities and colleges since 1965[40] (fig. 3); an approximately four- to six-fold increase between 1970-80 in the costs of state-of-the-art instru-

---

[34]Testimony of Charles A. Bowsher, Comptroller General, GAO, before the Senate Committee on Commerce, Science, and Transportation, Subcommittee on Science, Technology, and Space, Research Instrumentation Needs of Universities, May 27, 1982.

[35]*Obsolescence of Scientific Instrumentation in Research Universities,* Emerging Issues in Science and Technology, 1981, A Compendium of Working Papers for the National Science Foundation, National Science Board, p. 49.

[36]*Science,* vol. 204 (1979), p. 1365, as reported in *Obsolescence of Scientific Instrumentation in Research Universities.*

[37]*International Competition in Advanced Technology: Decisions for America,* op. cit., pp. 47-48.

[38]L. Berlowitz, R. A. Zdanis, J. C. Crowley, and J. C. Vaughn, "Instrumentation Needs of U.S. Universities," *Science,* vol. 211, Mar. 6, 1981, p. 1017, as reported in *Obsolescence of Scientific Instrumentation in Research Universities.*

[39]Among these are: West Germany's Max Planck Institute and the Universities of Karlsruhe, Stuttgart, Berlin, and KFA; Japan's Universities of Tokyo and Nagoya; England's Universities of London and Manchester; France's Ecole Polytechnique; and in Sweden, one-half time access by universities to a major auto manufacturer's supercomputer.

[40]"The Nation's Deteriorating University Research Facilities, A Survey of Recent Expenditures and Projected Needs in Fifteen Universities," prepared for the Committee on Science and Research of the Association of American Universities, July 1981, p. 4. This survey covered 15 leading universities and six academic disciplines.

Figure 3.—Federal Obligations to Universities and Colleges for R&D Plant

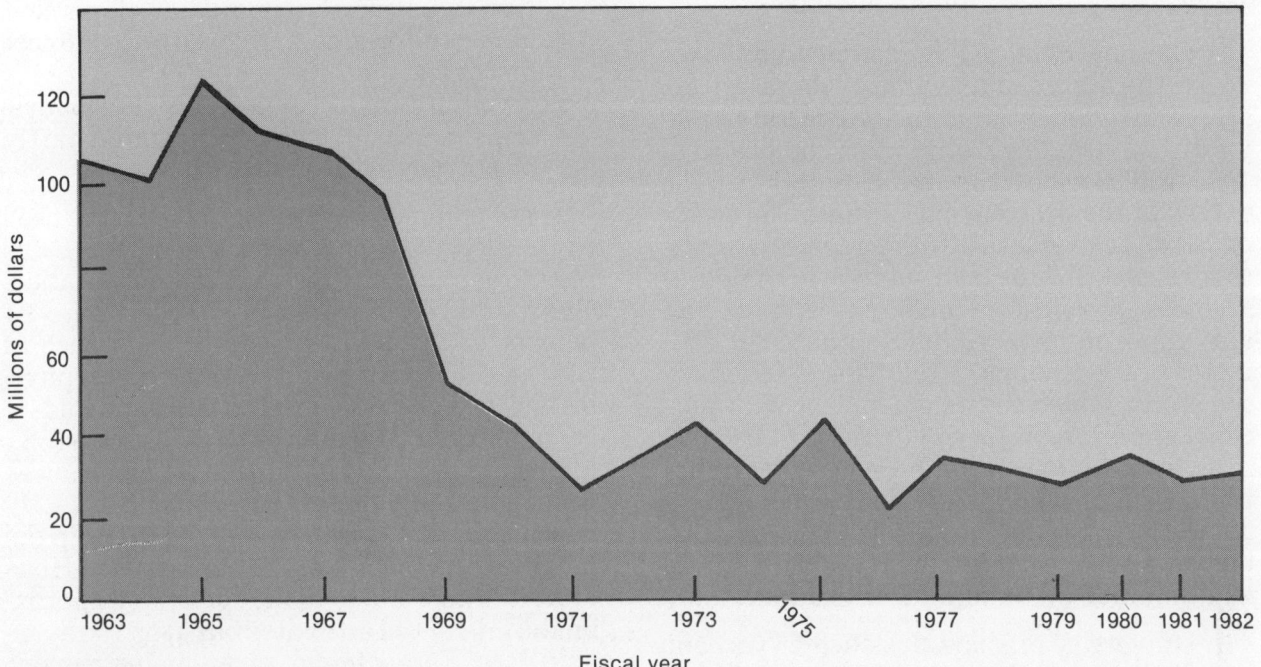

SOURCE: National Science Foundation.

mentation[41]; and the short lifetime of state-of-the-art equipment and high maintenance costs. In addition, during periods of decreased funding, university laboratory administrators tend to forego instrumentation purchases rather than reduce project staffs.[42] Further, until recently, Federal funding for research projects did not allow for purchase of instrumentation if it was to be shared with other projects.

Quantification of the Problem

Until recently, much of the information concerning the extent of the obsolescence problem has been anecdotal. However, there are now a number of initiatives to provide statistical data quantifying its scope and the effect on specific disciplines. In addition to the need for suitable data collection, there is a need to identify critical areas affected, the trends or rate of change, and likely influence of new initiatives to relieve the problems.

A GAO investigation into the instrumentation of obsolescence issue found "a tremendous lack of information": an absence of trend data on nationwide research equipment expenditures by universities, a lack of consensus on university laboratory needs, and no comprehensive indexes that would measure changes in the price of equipment[43][44] or the costs to maintain it. GAO also found that the rapidly increasing costs for instrumentation in conjunction with relatively level funding of basic research (in constant 1972 dollars) at universities and colleges for the period 1968-81 combined to have a "large effect on re-

---

[41]"Revitalizing Laboratory Instrumentation, The Report of a Workshop of the Ad Hoc Working Group on Scientific Instrumentation," National Research Council, March 1982, p. 1. This source estimates a sixfold increase in costs, while others estimate a fourfold increase.

[42]Testimony of Charles A. Bowsher, Comptroller General, GAO, op. cit.

[43]Ibid [GAO testimony].

[44]An illustration of cost escalation is the $100,000 premier electron microscope of the 1960s, which could distinguish objects smaller than one-millionth of a meter. By 1970, the scanning transmission electron microscopes had improved the resolution by a factor of 1,000, and cost more than $1 million. (Testimony of Dr. Edward A. Knapp, Director, NSF before the House Subcommittee on Science, Research, and Technology, Feb., 1984.)

searchers' acquisition and maintenance of research equipment."

A National Science Foundation study[45] surveyed the status of university laboratory research instrumentation in 1982 in three major disciplines. The study, when completed in 1985, will provide some useful insights into the extent of the problem nationwide. The study polled 43 academic institutions concerning the condition of their instrumentation in computer sciences, physical sciences, and engineering disciplines in order to develop national estimates of the findings. Preliminary data from the study, which covers equipment with purchase prices ranging from $10,000 to $1,000,000 in use in 1982, may not either confirm or refute the notion of a serious problem with instrumentation obsolescence in these three fields, but does seem to demonstrate that the problem may not be uniform. For example:

- University officials classified 26 percent of the research equipment listed in these fields in 1982 as "not in current use." Some portion of this undoubtedly is obsolete. Seventeen percent of the laboratory equipment associated with computer science research was obsolete; 24 percent of the physical sciences and engineering equipment was obsolete.
- One-half of all of the academic research instruments in the fields surveyed that were still in use in 1982 were purchased during the 1978-82 period. Only 12 percent of the computer science instrumentation was purchased prior to 1972, and 78 percent was purchased during 1978-82.
- Concerning state-of-the-art equipment, 98 percent of the computer science equipment in this category had been acquired since 1978, compared with 80 percent of the engineering research equipment. Eighty-four percent of all of the state-of-the-art equipment surveyed was listed as in excellent condition, as compared with 42 percent of all equipment covered by the survey.
- The replacement value of all instrumentation in use was estimated at 42 percent above the original purchase price (almost matching the inflation rate).
- Two-thirds of all research instrument systems in use in 1982 were acquired partly or entirely with Federal funds.

These preliminary findings indicate the need to develop data providing a comprehensive picture of university research instrumentation. The 43 universities surveyed account for 94 percent of the R&D expenditures in each of the three disciplines (computer sciences, physical sciences, engineering) covered and had instrumentation inventories that cost nearly $1 billion—a significant portion of which was funded by the Federal Government. Exactly how much total funding is needed to equip the laboratories adequately is not known. However, it is possible to make some very approximate, inferential estimates based on the available data. For example: given an instrument inventory of $1 billion and assuming that the equipment has a 4-year lifespan, one-quarter of the equipment ($250 million current dollars) would be needed annually to upgrade the equipment assigned to those three disciplines in the 43 universities.

Remedial Activities

Federal agencies, State governments, and industry have begun to address the instrumentation problem. For example, the Department of Defense initiated a $150 million 5-year program in fiscal year 1983 to fund instrumentation in areas of research in support of its mission. DOD's University Research Instrumentation Program is based in part on a 1980 study[46] of the instrumentation needs of U.S. university laboratories to conduct defense-related research. The pervasiveness of the problem is illustrated by the estimated 2,500 responses from the academic research community to an initial DOD invitation for proposals for funding.

---

[45]"One Fourth of Academic Research Equipment Classified Obsolete," Science Resources Studies Highlights, NSF, 1984.

[46]American Association of Universities Report to the National Science Foundation, Scientific Instrumentation Needs of Research Universities, June 1980. See also Berlowitz, et. al., op. cit.

In addition, NSF's appropriation increased from $195 million in fiscal year 1984 to about $234 million in fiscal year 1985 for support of advanced instrumentation. Some $122 million in fiscal year 1985 (up from $104 million in fiscal year 1984) will be allocated to research instrumentation for individual project grants, and the remainder for instrumentation for multi-user regional instrumentation centers and major equipment in national centers.

The universities are also concerned about obsolete or inadequate research facilities, or buildings—which Federal agencies have not funded since the 1960s. One preliminary estimate of the funds needed to fully upgrade facilities at the Nation's major research universities is between $990 million and $1.3 billion per year.[47] NSF is leading the interagency Steering Committee on Academic Research Facilities (which includes representation from DOD, DOE, the National Institutes of Health, and U.S. Department of Agriculture) to address this issue. The committee is expected to recommend that a study be initiated to clarify requirements for additional buildings or modernization programs for the Nation's academic research institutions. In addition, the National Science Board addressed this issue during its June 1984 session and recommended that funding for facilities become a component of the fiscal year 1986 NSF budget. It recommended that NSF conduct pilot programs for R&D facilities construction in three areas of priority research (large-scale computing, engineering research centers, and biotechnology), and that NSF support the Committee by obtaining improved data on the condition of university facilities. The House Authorization bill for the fiscal year 1984 budget of the Department of Defense directed that agency to determine the need to modernize university science and engineering laboratories for national security purposes. Congress has requested NIH to make a similar determination with respect to its mission.

State Government and Industry Initiatives

Among the various State government initiatives to improve university research capabilities are those of North Carolina, Massachusetts, New York, California, and Minnesota (see ch. 6).

Industry is also contributing at a significant level to academic information technology research and education. For example, seven computer vendors alone have made recent commitments to contribute some $180 million in cash and equipment to universities. One source "conservatively" estimates the level of donations of computer equipment to higher institutions of education to exceed $100 million in 1982. Among the major contributors were IBM, Digital Equipment Corp., Apple Computer, Inc., Hewlett-Packard Co., Wang Laboratories, Inc., NCR Corp., and Honeywell, Inc.

Two other recent examples further illustrate the trend: Brown University built a $1.5 million computer science facility based on contributions from IBM, Xerox Corp., Gould, Inc., and others; the University of California at Berkeley has commitments of $18 million in cash and equipment from firms such as Fairchild Camera & Instrument Corp., Advanced Micro Devices, Bell Laboratories, Digital Equipment Corp., GE, Harris, Hewlett-Packard, Hughes Aircraft, IBM, Intel, National Semiconductor, Semiconductor Research Corp., Tektronix, Texas Instruments, and Xerox.[48]

Changing University Role

The role of university research may be at the threshold of significant change. Faced with the increasing expense and risks associated with research, a limited supply of trained personnel (especially in needed multidisciplinary skills), and intensifying competition, U.S. industry is taking steps to bolster the universities' role in the performance of research in information

---

[47]Adequacy of Academic Research Facilities, A Brief Report of a Survey of Recent Expenditures and Projected Needs in Twenty-Five Academic Institutions, National Science Foundation, April 1984.

[48]These donations are seen as motivated by business strategies, and to some extent, by the 1981 changes in the Federal tax regulations which provide tax advantages for donations of new equipment to schools.

technology. State governments are promoting their universities' research capabilities to attract technology-intensive industry.

The National Science Foundation's support of engineering research at universities is also contributing to the change. With a $150 million appropriation for fiscal year 1985, NSF will increase the range of engineering projects supported and will help to establish more university engineering centers to promote research on computers, manufacturing processes,[49] and other nationally important technologies. Many of these joint activities are emphasizing strengthened linkages among the ties, promoting entrepreneurship, and improving the overall scientific and technological base of State and local communities.[50] They are also serving to add to both the supply and the quality of degreed professionals, and to modernize the tools available in participating university laboratories.

The universities may find themselves in a position in which they are looked to as critical to U.S. competitiveness in domestic and world markets, to our ability to maintain technological prominence and to remain reasonably self-sufficient in critical areas for national security purposes. Undoubtedly, for these and other reasons—such as the growing need for life-long education for many professionals—there will be forces for change in the role of universities.

Conflicts in Perspectives, Goals, and Policies

These various participants—academia, industry, and Federal and State governments—work together in a sort of dynamic balance, despite some differing perspectives among participants, and some discords in goals and policies. For example:

1. National economic goals for improving productivity and competitiveness in international markets are supportive of a healthy information technology industry. However, productivity improvements are viewed by some as possibly resulting in fewer employment opportunities, and lower job skill requirements and pay levels.
2. National science endeavors are fostered by measures that increase fundamental knowledge, consistent with university and scientists' objectives—including the sharing of research results internationally—but may be contrary to national security objectives of controlling technology transfer and industry concerns for protecting research data.
3. Universities' and scientists' interests in conducting undirected (basic) research may be in conflict with industry's and mission agencies' need for achieving specific results. The current trend toward increased university-industry collaboration and toward university patenting may result in more directed university research and less independence of universities.
4. U.S. policies toward opening university admission to foreign students have been enormously successful, but other regulations encourage emigration of aliens after graduation, thus depriving U.S. firms and academic institutions of needed talent.

The most striking observation concerning the roles of the various participants is that they are in a state of flux. To date, the directions of the changes appear to be: 1) modified interrelations among the participants in the R&D process, 2) a significantly larger role in research for participating universities, and 3) a potential strengthening of national capabilities to conduct R&D in information technology.

---

[49]National Science Foundation starts to broaden support of engineering research, *The Chronicle of Higher Education*, Jan. 18, 1984, p. 17, and updated by NSF officials, January 1985.

[50]For more detailed information, see Technology, Innovation, and Regional Economic Development, Background Paper No. 2, Encouraging High Technology Development, Office of Technology Assessment, February 1984.

Measures of the Health of U.S. R&D in Information Technology

There is no single indicator of the health of R&D in information technology. However, a combination of indirect indicators can provide an impression of its overall vigor in the United States. Indicators of industry growth include the level of funding for R&D, the availability of trained personnel, trade balances for information technology exports and imports, and patent trends. Although the indicators used are not comprehensive, taken together they portray a robust industry with significant growth in sales and investment in R&D. They also show that these industries account for the employment of a high proportion of the Nation's technically trained work force as well as a substantial proportion of its industry- and government-funded R&D. Paradoxically, they provide a varying contribution to the U.S. trade balance, and a declining proportion of the total number of information technology patents granted in the United States.

These indicators, while generally promising in themselves, provide far less than a complete picture of the state of health of U.S. R&D in the information technology industry. International competition in both information technology markets and in R&D is intensifying and U.S. leadership in many of these areas is being seriously challenged. Also, as described previously, aspects of the R&D process are in flux and it is too early to tell whether the changes are for better or for worse. In addition, while this report focuses on information technology R&D, several other factors play critical roles in U.S. competitiveness. These include marketing strategies, manufacturing capabilities, and global macroeconomic and trade conditions.

Beyond that, as noted earlier in this chapter, the "information technology industry" is an ill-defined entity and the available statistics are often noncomparable. Much of our information is based on statistics pertaining to a small subset of the Standard Industrial Code (SIC) for manufacturing companies without accounting for the significant revenues from services. One statistical comparison will serve to illustrate the problem of noncomparability: In 1982, shipments of *all* electronic computing equipment establishments totaled $34.1 billion; in the same year, data processing revenues of the top 100 information technology companies totaled $79.4 billion.[51]

Because of these data inconsistencies the information presented is skewed by the noncomparable databases; and, for that reason, quantifications can only be regarded as approximate.

Information Industry Profile

The review presented in chapter 9 of business statistics for the U.S. information technology industry indicates that this industry is generally robust as measured in a variety of ways, and in comparison with U.S. industry as a whole. For example, for the 1978-82 period: sales revenue grew by 66 percent compared with 40 percent for the composite U.S. industry; profits grew by 36 percent compared with 6 percent for the composite. Profits-to-sales ratios were about 9 percent v. 5 percent; and the growth in the number of employees averaged 12 percent v. a negative 8 percent.[52]

Concerning R&D, the information technology industry is also vigorous. R&D expenditures compare very favorably to the composite industry when measured as a percentage increase over the period, as a percentage of sales, or in terms of R&D expenditures per employee. This industry accounted for 28 percent of the total R&D spending by all industries.

---
[51]Based on a draft report, *The Computer Industry and International Trade: A Summary of the U.S. Role,* by Robert G. Atkins, Information Processes Group, Institute for Computer Sciences and Technology, 1984.

[52]These data primarily represent large firms. See table 52 (ch. 9) for limitations.

In fact, a listing of the 15 U.S. companies that spend the most on R&D—as a percentage of sales, and in dollars spent per employee—is almost completely populated with information technology companies such as Cray Research, Telesciences, Advanced Micro Devices, LTX, Amdahl, Computer Consoles, and Convergent Technologies[53] (table 4).

The electrical and communications industry increased R&D budgets by approximately 13 percent in 1984 and 1985. These increases resulted in large part from R&D on semiconductors and telecommunications. During 1984 and 1985, electrical and electronics companies plan to accelerate their investment in communications R&D, including work on integrated power semiconductors and cellular radio.[54] Thus, the industry viewed broadly is committed to well-funded R&D.

Comparison of R&D Funding by Selected Countries

Funding levels for R&D are generally recognized as important to the innovation process, as noted earlier. The United States has fallen behind two of its major competitors, as measured in terms of total outlays for R&D as a percentage of Gross National Product (excluding expenditures for defense and space).[55] Figure 4 shows that both Japan and West Germany have been outpacing the United States (as well as France and the United Kingdom) by this measure for more than a decade. Both of these countries have relatively small R&D expenditures for defense and space purposes as a percentage of GNP—e.g., 2.5 and 5.6 percent in 1981 for Japan and West Germany, respectively, in contrast with 31 percent for the United States, 29 percent for France, and 30 percent (in 1975) for the United Kingdom.

The Influence of DOD Funding of R&D in Information Technology

DOD funding for R&D in information technology reflects its growing dependence on this technology and its reluctance to be dependent on foreign sources for technology critical to national security. Defense spending for R&D generally has ranged from a high of 90 percent of Federal R&D spending in 1953 to a low of 50 percent during 1976-80, and is expected to rise to 70 percent in 1985.[56]

Table 5 shows the distribution of DOD funding for 1983 among basic and applied research,

---

[53]*Business Week*, R&D Scoreboard 1982, June 20, 1983, pp. 122-153.
[54]Science Resource Studies, Highlights, National Science Foundation, NSF 83-327, Dec. 15, 1983, p. 2, and NSF 84-329, Oct. 15, 1984.

[55]See William C. Boesman, U.S. Civilian and Defense R&D Funding: Some Trends and Comparisons with Selected Industrialized Nations, Congressional Research Service, Library of Congress, Aug. 26, 1983.
[56]Ibid.

Table 4.—The Top 15 in R&D Spending

In percent of sales		In dollars per employee	
1. TeleSciences	31.6%	1. Ultimate	$37,089
2. Policy Management Systems	26.6	2. Fortune Systems	19,390
3. Fortune Systems	22.3	3. TeleSciences	18,797
4. Management Science America	20.8	4. Convergent Technologies	18,721
5. King Radio	20.0	5. Activision	16,667
6. Dysan	19.4	6. Cray Research	16,467
7. Advanced Micro Devices	19.4	7. Management Science America	15,563
8. Modular Computer Systems	17.6	8. Amdahl	15,413
9. ISC Systems	16.6	9. Digital Switch	15,017
10. Computer Consoles	16.6	10. Policy Management Systems	14,677
11. LTX	16.4	11. Applied Materials	14,545
12. Ramtek	15.6	12. Auto-trol Technology	14,413
13. Applied Materials	15.6	13. Computer Consoles	13,816
14. Auto-trol Technology	15.4	14. Network Systems	13,292
15. Kulicke & Soffa Industries	15.3	15. LTX	13,229

SOURCE: Standard & Poor's Compustat, Inc., as cited in *Business Week*, "A Deepening Commitment to R&D," July 9, 1984, p. 64; and "The U.S. Still Leads the World in R&D Spending," June 20, 1983, p. 122.

Figure 4.—Estimated Ratio of Civilian R&D Expenditures to Gross National Product for Selected Countries

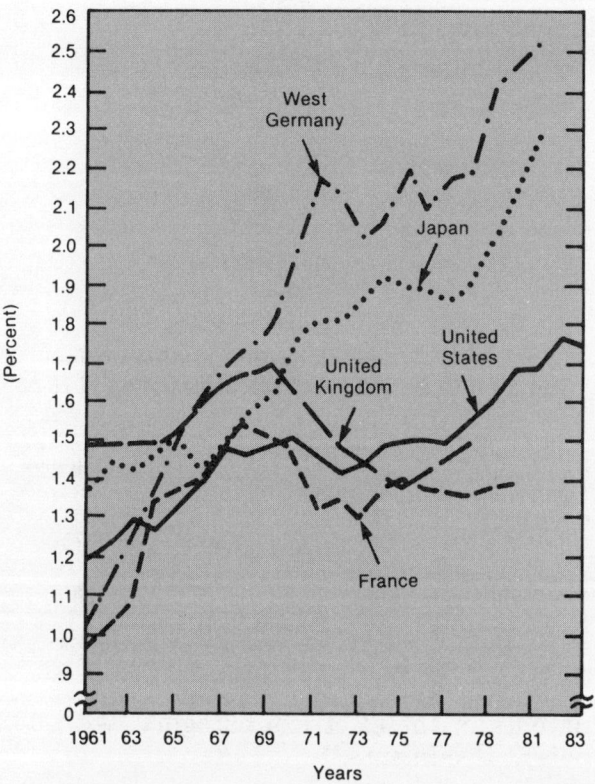

and development. DOD spending for basic research accounts for some 13.6 percent of the total Federal obligations, while applied research accounts for 33.9 percent, and development accounts for 71.3 percent.

Table 6 shows that the DOD R&D budget dominates some fields of Government R&D spending for basic and applied research. For example, in funding for basic research in electrical engineering, DOD accounts for some 69 percent; in computer sciences, 55 percent; and in mathematics 42 percent. In applied research, the DOD is a major Federal funder for electrical engineering (90 percent), computer sciences (87 percent), and mathematics (29 percent). These, as well as others, are disciplines supported primarily by the DOD R&D budget and that have a central influence on advances in information technology for the Nation.[67]

There have been many commercially applicable advances in information technology that have their origin in, or had strong early support from, DOD funded R&D. These include very high speed integrated circuits (VHSIC), digital telecommunications, and new high-performance materials. However, there are some major disadvantages for the commercial sector to DOD funded R&D. Among these are: security classifications which tend to slow advancements in technology; rigid technical specifications for military procurements which have limited utility for commercial applications; and the "consumption" of limited, valuable scientific and engineering resources for military purposes, which may inhibit commercial developments. This issue is discussed in more detail in chapter 8.

U.S. Patent Activity

It is generally accepted that patenting is a measure, even if imperfect, of the effectiveness of R&D activities. A key observation is that patenting in information technology is among

---
[57]Ibid.

Table 5.—Federal and Department of Defense Obligations for Basic Research, Applied Research, and Development, 1983 (Estimated) (millions of dollars)

	Total R&D		Basic research		Applied research		Development	
Total Federal Government	$42,973.8	100%	$5,765.2	100.0%	$7,499.7	100.0%	$29,708.9	100.0%
Department of Defense	$24,519.6	57.1%	$ 782.1	13.6%	$2,543.9	33.9%	$21,193.6	71.3%

SOURCE: National Science Foundation, "Federal Funds for Research and Development Fiscal Years 1981, 1982, and 1983," vol. XXXI, Detailed Statistical Tables (NSF 82-326) (Washington, DC: U.S. Government Printing Office, 1982), pp. 174, 179, 181, 183. Percentages calculated from data in the table. As cited in Boesman, "U.S. Civilian and Defense R&D Funding; Some Trends and Comparisons With Selected Industrialized Nations," Congressional Research Service, Library of Congress, Aug. 26, 1983.

Table 6.—Federal and Department of Defense Obligations for Basic and Applied Research by Field, 1983 (Estimated) (millions of dollars)

	Total Federal funds	DOD funds	DOD as a percentage of total Federal funds
Basic research:			
Electrical engineering	$103.8	$71.8	69.1%
Computer sciences	73.0	40.0	54.8
Mathematics	100.7	42.6	42.3
Applied research:			
Electrical engineering	$520.5	$471.2	90.5%
Computer sciences	91.5	79.4	86.7
Mathematics	48.5	13.9	28.6

SOURCE: National Science Foundation, "Federal Funds for Research and Development, Fiscal Years 1981, 1982, and 1983," vol. XXXI Detailed Statistical Tables (NSF 82-326) (Washington, DC: U.S. Government Printing Office, 1982), pp. 73, 75, 79, 82, 98, 101, 104, 109. Percentages calculated from data in the table. As cited in Boesman.

the most intensive of all technologies. U.S. patenting of foreign origin[58] in all technologies has doubled in the past two decades to 41 percent—indicating escalating world competition for U.S. patents in general. A small number of foreign multinational corporations have a dominant (but perhaps somewhat diminishing) role in the proportion of foreign-origin U.S. patents. These "multinationals" emphasize information technology patents. The overall picture derived from this review of patent data confirms the finding reported in chapter 3 that foreign competition in information technology is increasing.

U.S. Patent Data

The top 50 electrical patent categories (ranked by actual numeric growth in the number of patents) received 8,139 patents during 1978-80 time period (table 7). Within these categories, semiconductors and circuits accounted for 48 percent and computers 15 percent, respectively. In the computer category, General Purpose Programmable Digital Computer Systems was the most active, as in previous years, receiving 632 patent documents. Miscellaneous Digital Data Processing Systems received the second largest number of patents in the electrical category, with 548 patent documents.[59]

Table 7.—Technology Distribution of the Top 50 U.S. Patent Electrical Categories 1978-80

Ranked by actual file growth	Percent of categories
Semiconductors and circuits	48%
Computers	15%
Other	37%
Total number of patents in the 50 patent categories	8,139

SOURCE: Tenth Report, Technology Assessment and Forecast, U.S. Patent and Trademark Office, U.S. Department of Commerce, November 1981, pp. 16, 24.

Solid-state devices, integrated circuits, and transistor categories together account for 24 of the 50 categories in the total ranked by *actual* growth from 1978 to 1980.[60] The percent growth in the number of these patents generally ranges from about 40 percent to 59 percent.[61] Solid-state devices account for 8 of the 11 highest growth entries. Lasers, laminagraphy, and fiber optics are also among the information technology segments included in the high patent growth entries. The two subclasses of fiber optics inventions show patent

---

[58]The country origin of a patent is determined by the country of residence of the first named inventor.

[59]Tenth Report, Technology Assessment and Forecast, Patent and Trademark Office, U.S. Department of Commerce, November 1981, pp. 14-18.

[60]Actual growth is the numeric increase resulting from additions to the patent copies (including cross-reference copies) to the file in the 3-year period 1978-80, Ibid. p. 11.

[61]Percent growth, as used by the U.S. Patent and Trademark Office, is computed by dividing the actual growth for the 3-year period examined (1978-80) by actual growth for the 6-year period (1975-80), and multiplying by 100. Ibid., p. 11.

growth rates of over 70 percent. The listing, in fact, is composed almost exclusively of information technology inventions. Computer technology patents showed growth rates of over 70 percent for the 1978-80 period, well above the average of 46 percent for all technologies during the same time period.[62]

There are reasons for caution against generalizations concerning the use of patent statistics—e.g., variations in the importance and the degree of "invention" of different patents; the propensity (or absence of it) of some companies, and perhaps countries, to patent as opposed to using other alternatives—e.g., trade secrets, or lead times in the market place; the cost factor as a disincentive to patenting, as well as concern for antitrust allegations based on patent dominance; rapid technological change (making patents of limited value); differences in the scope of patent categories that may give a misleading impression of substantial amount of patenting activity in a broadly scoped subcategory or vice versa.

Nevertheless, the evidence shown above clearly seems to support the observation that the level of patenting for information technology in the United States is vigorous and may be indicative of extensive R&D in this field.

Foreign-Origin U.S. Patents

In 1973 the U.S. Patent and Trademark Office (USPTO), began detailed documentation of foreign-origin patent activity through its Office of Technology Assessment and Forecast (OTAF). One of OTAF's reports,[63] which is cited extensively in this section, provides useful background and many important findings on foreign patenting in the United States. Among the findings are:

1. Because patents obtained in the United States convey no protection in other countries and vice versa, inventors tend to patent in more than one country, and especially in countries that represent large potential markets. As a consequence, U.S. patent statistics tend to mirror trends in technological activity worldwide.
2. Although foreign-origin patenting in all technologies averaged only 20 percent of the total U.S. patenting for the years 1963-66, the percentage share has continued to increase, reaching 40 percent of the total for the year 1980, and 41 percent for the 1981 to mid-1983 period.

Figure 5 illustrates the long-term decline in the number of U.S.-origin information technology patents granted in the United States between 1968 and 1981, and the relative leadership position of Japan compared to France, West Germany, and the United Kingdom. It is not clear as to why the total number of U.S. patents has declined steeply between 1971 and 1980, but the U.S. Patent and Trademark Office advises that except for Japan, the trend was worldwide during that period. (Note that in 1979 a shortage of funds at the Patent Office limited the number of U.S. patents granted, artificially lowering the total for that year).

As shown by table 8, the share of U.S.-origin patents decreased from 79 to 58 percent of the total during 1968-81, while the share of Japanese-origin information technology patents granted in the United States increased from 3 to 19 percent.

The two "top 50" electrical category lists noted earlier reveal a significant proportion of foreign-origin U.S. patents in the high patent-growth categories. Fifty-four of the entries in both lists show the percentage of foreign origin to exceed the average of 38.5 percent for all technologies for 1978-80. This is not surprising, since the high-growth patent subclasses are pursued by companies in all of the developed countries.

Table 9 shows the percentage of foreign-origin U.S. patenting in patent category groupings dealing with some components of information technology. Three of the five category groupings examined (two in fiber optics and one in television) show foreign-origin patenting

---
[62]Ibid., p. 22-26.
[63]Ibid., see for example, Section I, Part IV—"Most Foreign Active Patent Technologies," pp. 27-32, and Section II, Patent Trends: Foreign Multinational Corporations Patenting Trends in the United States, pp. 33-46.

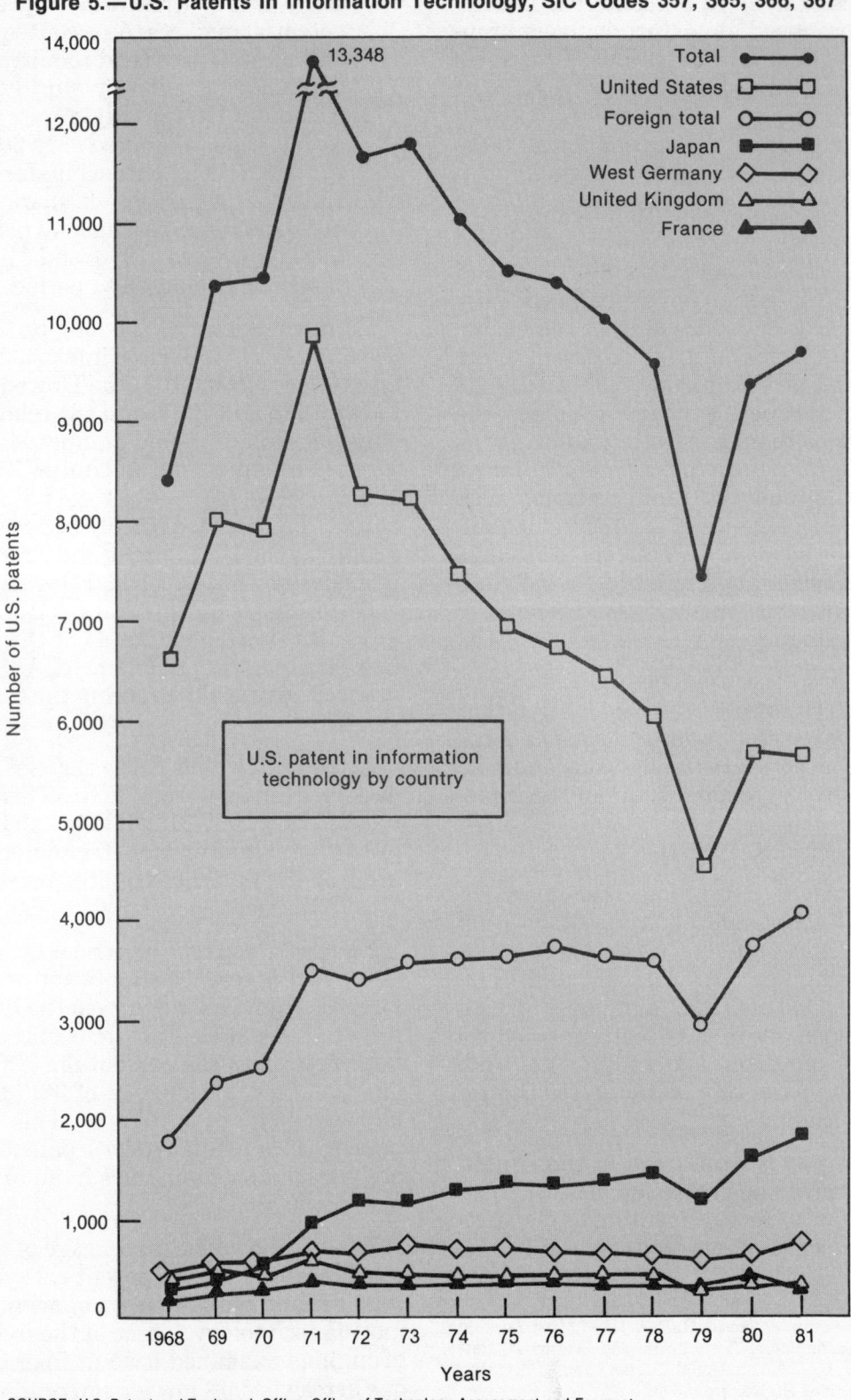

Figure 5.—U.S. Patents in Information Technology, SIC Codes 357, 365, 366, 367

SOURCE: U.S. Patent and Trademark Office, Office of Technology Assessment and Forecast.

Table 8.—Percentages of U.S. Patents Granted in Information Technology (IT) and in All Technologies (ALL), 1981

Year	United States		Japan		West Germany		United Kingdom		France	
	IT	ALL	IT	ALL	IT	ALL	IT	ALL	IT	ALL
1968	79	77	3	2	5	6	4	4	3	2
1981	58	60	19	13	8	10	4	4	4	3
1982	NA	59	NA	14	NA	9	NA	4	NA	3

NA—Not available.

aInformation Technology (IT) here includes SIC Codes 357, Office Computing and Accounting Machines; and 365-367, Communication Equipment and Electronic Components.

SOURCES: The Office of Technology Assessment and Forecast, U.S. Patent and Trademark Office, All Technologies Report, 1963-June 1983, and Indicators of the Patent Output of U.S. Industries (1963-81). IT numbers were calculated from data developed with assistance from the National Science Foundation, Science Indicators Unit.

Table 9.—Foreign-Origin U.S. Patents in Some Components of Information Technology

Title	Percent foreign origin 1/81-6/83
Light transmitting fiber, waveguide, or rod	48.2%
Laser light sources and detectors	50.6%
Color and pseudo color television	52.8%
Active solid-state devices, e.g., transistors, solid-state diodes	40.8%
General-purpose programmable digital computer systems and miscellaneous digital data processing systems	34.9%

NOTE: The percent foreign origin is determined by dividing the total number of U.S. patents granted between January 1981 and June 1983 to foreign-resident inventors by the total patents granted in the same time period, and multiplying by 100.

SOURCE: Office of Technology Assessment and Forecast, Patent and Trademark Office, U.S. Department of Commerce.

to be significantly higher than the average of 41 percent.

Table 10 shows that in selected telecommunications categories, the Japanese share of foreign-owned U.S. patents ranges from 38 to 56 percent. For all categories of telecommunications, Japanese residents received 45 percent of the foreign origin U.S. patents from 1980-83.[64] Figure 6 depicts the shares of U.S. patents for commmunications equipment and electronic components among Japan, West Germany, and the United Kingdom.

These findings are consistent with comments from OTA workshop participants concerning the growing intensity of foreign competition in R&D. The statistics no doubt understate the level of foreign ownership of U.S. patents, since they do not take into account patents of U.S. origin that are controlled by foreign interests, e.g., patents issued to U.S. residents or companies that are foreign-owned or foreign-controlled, or the inclination of foreign multinational corporations to patent in other countries (see section below on Foreign Multinational Companies). Even understated, however, the intensity of foreign influence over U.S.-patented technology[65] is clearly significant. By way of providing perspective, it

---
[64]*Patent Profiles: Telecommunications*, Patent and Trademark Office, Office of Technology Assessment and Forecast, U.S. Department of Commerce, August 1984, p. 15.
[65]Ibid., p. 4.

Table 10.—Foreign-Owned U.S. Patents in Selected Telecommunications Classes, 1982

	Percent foreign of total	Percent Japanese of total	Percent Japanese of foreign
Telephony	43%	17%	39%
Light wave communication	53%	20%	38%
Analog carrier wave communications	43%	24%	56%
Digital and pulse communications	40%	16%	38%

Telephony—Class 179/1R-1AA; 1AT-1FS, 1H-1MF, 1MN-1SS, 1SW-106, 108R-190.
Light wave communications—372/43-59 & 75; 357/17 & 19; 455/600-619; 370/1-4; 350/96.1-96.34.
Analog carrier wave communications—455/1-355.
Digital and pulse communication (excludes light wave, includes error detection and A/D & D/A conversion)—375/all subclasses; 371/1-6 & 30-71; 178/all subclasses; 340/347, AD-347, AD-347 SY; 332/9R-15; 329/104-109.

SOURCE: Reports prepared by Office of Technology Assessment and Forecast for publication in late 1984.

Figure 6.—Share of Foreign Patenting in the United States for the Three Most Active Countries in Selected Product Fields: 1981

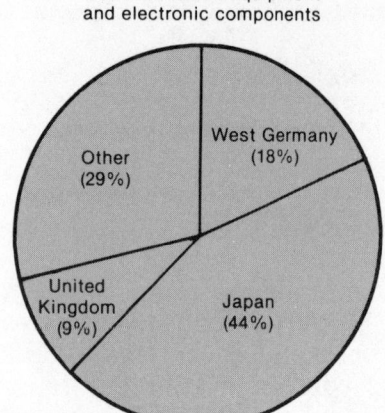

SOURCE: National Science Board, National Science Foundation, *Science Indicators—1982*, 1983.

should be noted that some other countries have an even higher percentage of foreign-origin patents, e.g., Canada, 93.4 percent; the United Kingdom, 84.2 percent; France, 67.6 percent. Japan has 16.6 percent.[66]

---
[66]Industrial Patent Statistics, WIPO, 1982.

Foreign Multinational Corporations

Another important OTAF finding concerns the role of foreign multinational corporations (FMNCs) in patenting. Taking into account the relative annual sales of the 10 major FMNCs and their ranking among the "Fortune 500" companies, OTAF has found a strong correlation between ranking by patents and sales level.[67] A comparison of the 10 FMNCs' patenting with total U.S. patenting for 1969-80 is shown in figure 7.

In addition to noting that the FMNCs' ownership of U.S. patents has recently (1980) leveled off to about 5.5 percent, the OTAF study observes that:

- The 10 FMNCs own or control, on the average, 4.7 percent of all U.S. patents granted each year.
- The extent of the 10 FMNCs' ownership of U.S. patents doubled from 1969 to 1976—although the rate of increase had diminished to near zero by 1980.

---
[67]*Patent Profiles*, op. cit., p. 38.

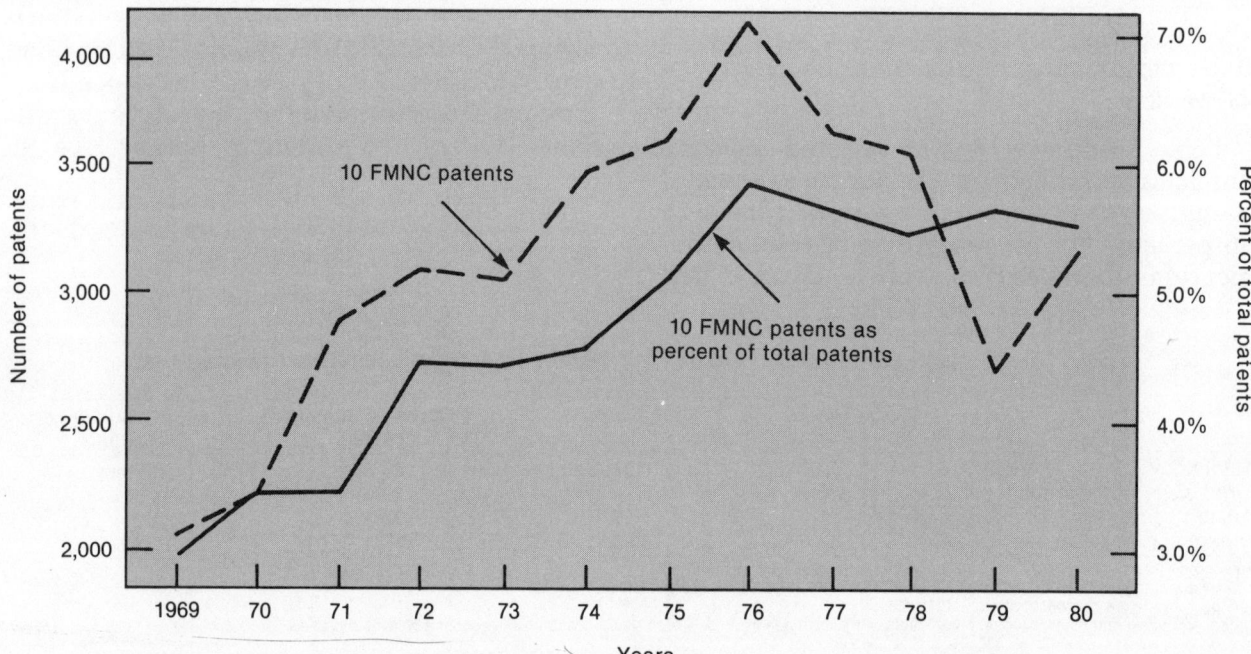

Figure 7.—U.S. Patent Activity of 10 Foreign Multinational Corporations, 1969-80

SOURCE: Tenth Report, Technology Assessment and Forecast, Patent and Trademark Office, U.S. Department of Commerce, November 1981, p. 38.

- More recently, (1979-80) the percentage of U.S. patents granted to the 10 FMNCs has begun to decline in proportion to total foreign origin U.S. patents suggesting a diminished role in ownership of U.S. patents for these particular FMNCs.

The trend, while changing, shows that about one in every eight U.S. patents of foreign origin is owned or controlled by only 10 FMNCs[68]—an indication of the concentration of foreign-owned U.S. patents by a few multinational firms.

These statistics further confirm the testimony of OTA workshop participants concerning growing foreign competition in information technology R&D, and the observation that other countries have developed national policies and programs that target information technology.

[68]Ibid. (OTAF Study), p. 40.

A Synthesis: The Changing U.S. R&D Environment

Some measures, such as investment in R&D and growth in profits, indicate that R&D in U.S. information technology is vigorous. Other measures, such as competition in advanced-technology products and foreign ownership of U.S. patents, indicate a less robust situation. Thus, although information technology research and development is making marked advances, it is—at the same time—undergoing pressure from foreign competition. In response to the pressure, the participants in the R&D process are initiating a variety of changes. These changes are discussed in later chapters of this report.

Industry continues to invest heavily in information technology R&D—an indication of its belief in R&D's importance to competitiveness. The increasing costs of R&D are making new institutional arrangements such as joint research ventures and closer ties with universities more attractive. However, industry experts recognize that although R&D is necessary to competitiveness it is not sufficient to ensure it; other components of the innovation process are also important to maintaining competitiveness in international trade.

Universities are encouraging new institutional arrangements with industry, and the importance of their role in the R&D process (particularly in performing basic research) may be growing. There are widespread problems relating to both the quantity and quality of university equipment and facilities for conducting information technology R&D, although these conditions may be improving. Some *State Governments* have become active in helping their universities to improve research capabilities and in encouraging university-industry pairings (see ch. 6).

Finally, the *Federal Government* has adopted policies intended to encourage private sector investment in R&D and to facilitate the transfer of technology from Government to industry. The Federal Government's (especially DOD's) expenditures for information technology R&D are growing rapidly and continue to have a strong influence on the direction of technological development in some information technology areas.

Observations

Some useful observations can be made based on the changes taking place in the U.S. R&D environment. First, the growth in foreign competition—whatever its effect on U.S. jobs and trade balances for the long term—is stimulating R&D investment, as shown in chapter 9. There has probably not been a time since the turn of the century when new products and product improvements have been marketed in such rapid succession as has been the case with information technology, nor a peacetime era when R&D had such a central role in the affairs of nations.

Second, the U.S. information technology industry is facing a "new world" of foreign competition. The intensive level of targeted and well-funded foreign competition is not likely to decline in the foreseeable future. Each of our major competitors' governments believe in the central importance of information technology as an essential ingredient for achieving economic, social, or national security goals, as well as the penalties—in terms of worsening trade balances and job losses—associated with falling by the wayside in the competitive race. As a consequence, they have established national policies and programs to enhance their domestic industrial position.

Third, as foreign competition has inexorably strengthened in the post-World War II era, the broad margin of error that the United States once enjoyed has essentially vanished.

The long-term effects of several factors—national industrial policies, nontariff trade barriers (e.g., prohibiting the import of certain products or services), incentives for industrial innovation, interest rates, export controls—will determine the winners and losers, as nations maneuver to remain competitive. The United States will need to find ways to monitor its position relative to international competitors and to refine its policies as needed to keep in step with the changing global R&D environment.

Chapter 3
Selected Case Studies in Information Technology Research and Development

Contents

	Page
Introduction	55
Case Study 1: Advanced Computer Architecture	55
Findings	55
Changing Computer Architecture	56
Computer Architecture R&D	57
Critical Areas of Research	63
Manpower	65
International Efforts	65
Case Study 2: Fiber Optic Communications	67
Findings	67
Advantages	67
Commercialization Trends	69
United States R&D	71
Directions of U.S. Research	73
Research in Japan	74
Case Study 3: Software Engineering	75
Findings	75
Introduction	75
Software R&D Environments	76
Content and Conduct of Software Engineering R&D	79
International Efforts in Software Engineering R&D	85
Case Study 4: Artificial Intelligence	87
Findings	87
Introduction	87
Artificial Intelligence R&D Environments	89
Content and Conduct of Artificial Intelligence R&D	96
Foreign National Efforts in Artificial Intelligence R&D	105

Tables

Table No.		Page
11.	Major Federal Advanced Computer Architecture R&D Projects	57
12.	Milestones in the History of Computer Architecture	57
13.	1982 Federal Spending for Computer Architecture R&D	58
14.	Federal Open Access Supercomputer Facilities	58
15.	Summary of Current and Planned Government Open Access Advanced Computer Architecture Software Development Facilities	59
16.	NSF Plans for Computer Research	60
17.	Summary of New Commercial Supercomputer Systems Under Development	61
18.	1983 DARPA, DOE, and NSF University Funding of Advanced Computer Architecture	62
19.	Major Government Sources of Artificial Intelligence R&D Funding	94
20.	NSF Grant Awards in Artificial Intelligence	94
21.	Strategic Computing Cost Summary	94
22.	Representative Expert Systems	104

Figures

Figure No.		Page
8.	Computer Architecture Functional Elements	56
9.	Optical Fibers Are Small, Lightweight and Versatile	68
10.	The Software Life Cycle	80
11.	Artificial Intelligence	90
12.	Artificial Intelligence Science and Engineering	92
13.	Strategic Computing Program Structure and Goals	95
14.	A Semantic Network	98
15.	Markets for Artificial Intelligence	101

Chapter 3
Selected Case Studies in Information Technology Research and Development

Introduction

These case studies present a microcosm of the R&D process in information technology. The diversity of research and development efforts in information technology make it virtually impossible to examine in detail all of the many fields and disciplines. Therefore, four fields have been selected for detailed analysis. They are: Advanced Computer Architecture (ACA), Fiber Optics (FO), Software Engineering (SE), and Artificial Intelligence (AI).

These fields were selected for several reasons. They depict the wide range, diversity and inter-relatedness of the fields and applications of information technology. An analysis of them provides a broad overview of the scientific, technical and institutional issues in information technology R&D. These fields were chosen to include both hardware and software and both computer and communications technologies. They also illustrate the mix of long-term goals and near-term capabilities, thus reflecting the importance of these different perspectives in the R&D process. These four areas, moreover, are among those considered to be critical in determining the direction and pace of advance of information technology as a whole. The importance of advances in the four fields is exemplified by the development of government funded national R&D programs in Japan, Britain and the European Economic Community.

Case Study 1: Advanced Computer Architecture

Findings

- The technology of advanced computer design is critically important for the expansion of information technology in many fields. There is extensive R&D activity underway in universities, in industry, and in the National Laboratories aimed at producing and exploiting new computer designs; but there is considerable uncertainty over which new designs will be viable.
- Since their invention, electronic computers have been based on one architectural model, the von Neumann sequential processing architecture. The limits of computational speed achievable with this design are being reached; significant further increases in computer performance will require *parallel processing architectures*, which are inherently more complex to design and to use.
- VLSI (Very-Large-Scale Integrated Circuit) design facilities, based on powerful computers, are now being used to develop and test computer architectural designs, including parallel processors and special designs for certain dedicated operations, such as communications signal processing, image processing, and graphics.
- Software has been difficult to produce for computers of advanced, high-performance design. As the variety and complexity of architectural types increases, the difficulty of developing and integrating software will increase. Therefore, research in software development for novel computer designs will be critical.

- The Federal Government has been a major driver of advanced computer architecture because of its scientific and national security applications. The Government has influenced the evolution of computer design through the funding of R&D and the procurement of state-of-the-art systems. This leverage, though still important, is diminishing as commercial applications for advanced computers grow and as Federal requirements become a smaller fraction of sales.
- National programs in Japan, Great Britain, France, Germany, and the European Community have been established to pursue advanced computer R&D. The Japanese have recently demonstrated an ability to produce advanced architecture computers of competitive performance to American products.
- American companies and universities pursuing R&D in computer design face difficulties:

    Universities cannot afford design and testing facilities for developing an architectural idea to the point where its performance can be assessed.

    Companies face large, risky investments in the design of new high-performance computer systems. Markets for novel machines are initially small and expand only slowly as new applications are exploited and software becomes available.

Changing Computer Architecture

Computer architecture is the internal structure of a computer, the arrangement of the functional elements that carry out calculations and information manipulations. (see fig. 8).

Since the early 1950s, all electronic computers (with a few exceptions) have been designed around one basic architectural model, the von Neumann machine, invented by mathematician John von Neumann. In this architecture, *instructions and data* are stored in memory, fetched one by one in sequential fashion, and acted on by the processor. Computer design is now changing, encouraged by two factors.

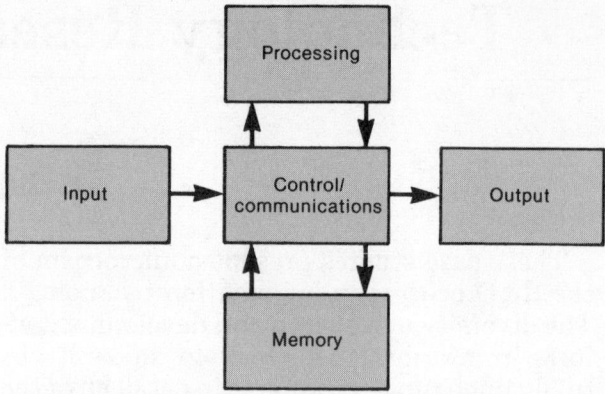

Figure 8.—Computer Architecture Functional Elements

SOURCE: Office of Technology Assessment.

First, the limits imposed by physical laws on the computational speed attainable with traditional computer design are being approached. Science and engineering demand continual advances in computational speed to increase the precision of calculations and to improve accuracy in models and simulations.[1] Sequential processing constitutes a severe restriction on the precision and completeness that these calculations and models can achieve in a reasonable amount of time. Therefore, computer designers are studying architectures that can make possible decomposition of large calculations into pieces for simultaneous processing by a number of computational units *in parallel*.

Second, as information technology is applied in more and more areas, special problems are encountered that impose unique demands on computer capabilities. Until recently, system designers have relied on software to apply the capability of von Neumann processors to problems. Now, it is possible to create special integrated circuits to address specific problems.

---

[1] These are the applications normally associated with so-called "supercomputers." Major current applications are in, for example, weather modeling and the simulation of nuclear weapons explosions. The reader is referred, for a discussion of the applications of and policy issues surrounding supercomputers, to *Supercomputers: Foreign Competition and Federal Funding* by Nancy Miller, Congressional Research Service, Issue Brief 83102, latest update July 12, 1984.

Computer architecture R&D is making possible the economical design of custom computer architectures for specialized applications including telecommunications and data acquisition *signal processors, image* and *graphics processors,* and *symbol processors* for the manipulation of nonnumerical information.

The impending changes in computer architecture promise cost-effective solutions to many problems, but they also challenge the designers, suppliers and buyers of computer systems. Designers will need to have more detailed appreciation of applications; computer vendors will be faced with more complexly segmented markets; and buyers will need to be more sophisticated in defining their needs and in choosing among a wider offering of products.

Computer Architecture R&D

Federal Government Involvement

The Government has had considerable involvement in advanced computer architecture R&D (see table 11), both as a funder and a performer of work. Major elements of the software development work for each generation of these systems have been done by the National Laboratories, especially Los Alamos (LANL) and Lawrence Livermore (LLNL).[2] Moreover, the impetus for the development of each successive generation of advanced architecture scientific computers has come predominantly from government demand for faster, higher capacity, and more sophisticated systems for weapons, intelligence, energy, and aerospace applications (see table 12). The National Labs still constitute the greatest concentration of users of supercomputers (see table 15).

The Federal Government has provided between $15 and $20 million in annual funding for advanced computer architecture R&D in recent years (see table 13). In addition to sponsoring research in universities and in industry, the Government has performed computer research at the National Labs.

---
[2]The first Cray-1 computer was placed in Los Alamos National Lab *without any software.*

Table 11.—Major Federal Advanced Computer Architecture R&D Projects

Machine	Year delivered	Agency	Contractor	Major use
ENIAC	1945	Army	University of Pennsylvania	Ballistics calculations
NORC	1950	Navy	IBM	Ordinance research
—	1950	NSA	Sperry	Classified
CDC 1604	1959	NSA	Control Data	Classified
LARC	1961	AEC	Sperry	Nuclear weapons design
STRETCH	1961	AEC	IBM	Nuclear weapons design
CDC 6600	1964	LLNL	Control Data	Nuclear weapons
ILLIAC IV	1972	DARPA/NASA	Burroughs/University of Illinois	Aerodynamics
MPP	1983	NASA	Goodyear Aerospace	Image processing
S-1	—	LLNL/Navy	—	Signal processing

SOURCE: Office of Technology Assessment.

Table 12.—Milestones in the History of Computer Architecture

Class	Date	Typical machines	Major innovation
I	1953	IBM 701	Vaccuum tubes
II	1960	CDC 1604	Transistors
III	1964	IBM 360	I/O processing
		CDC 6600	Freon cooling
IV	1970	IBM 370	Integrated circuits
		CDC 7600	
V	1972	Illiac IV	Parallel processing
		TI ASC	Pipeline architecture
VI	1976	Cray-1	Vector processing

SOURCE: Office of Technology Assessment.

Table 13.—1982 Federal Spending for Computer Architecture R&D (millions of dollars)

Department of Defense	$12.0[a]
Department of Energy	2.9[a]
National Aeronautics and Space Administration	1.5[a]
National Science Foundation	1.2
Total	$17.6

[a]Estimates.

SOURCE: Department of Defense and Department of Energy numbers from the Office of Technology Assessment Workshop on Advanced Computer Architecture; NASA number from personal communication with Paul Schneck; NSF number from *Summary of Awards, FY 1982*, NSF Directorate for Mathematical and Physical Sciences, Computer Sciences Section.

DOE spent $645,000 at Los Alamos and $500,000 at Lawrence Livermore National Labs in fiscal year 1983 on two experimental research projects on advanced computer architecture hardware.[3] In addition, Los Alamos is leasing a Denelcor HEP-1 to experiment with parallel processing software concepts. The Navy, in conjunction with Lawrence Livermore, has been involved with the design and construction of an advanced architecture computer, termed the S-1 Project. The design is intended to handle signal processing tasks for Navy missions. Approximately $20 million has been spent over the last 4 years on the S-1 Project.[4]

Facilities and help in advanced computer applications development are provided to researchers in science and engineering fields to support the missions of several Government departments (DOD, DOE, NASA), and to further basic research (NSF). Seven Federal facilities provide limited open access to certain groups of researchers (see table 14).

The National Laboratories plan to add more supercomputers over the next few years, so it can be expected that Government scientists and engineers and contractors on mission agency work will have access to state-of-the-art large-scale computing facilities (see table 15). Academic researchers will have limited access to these facilities for work in fields related to agency missions (e.g., fusion energy, atmospheric and ocean sciences, and aerodynamics). These facilities also provide support for software development.

The Department of Defense, through the Defense Advanced Research Projects Agency (DARPA), has formulated ambitious plans for research and development in advanced computer-based systems. Included will be efforts to develop high speed signal processor architectures and to integrate numeric and symbolic processing in advanced computer architectures for use in intelligent weapons systems.[5]

In April 1983, the National Science Foundation organized a working group to study

---

[3]Edward Oliver at the OTA workshop on Advanced Computer Architecture, July 14, 1983.

[4]Personal communication from Sidney Fernbach, Consultant, Control Data Corp.

[5]This program, called "Strategic Computing," is covered in some detail in the Artificial Intelligence Case Study later in this chapter.

Table 14.—Federal Open Access Supercomputer Facilities

Facility	Major system	Research users	Charges
NCAR	2 CRAY 1-As	Atmospheric and ocean sciences	No charge to NSF users. $2,200 per prime CPU hour for others
MFECC	2 CRAY 1 1 CDC 7600	Magnetic fusion energy community	No charge
LANL	Open 1 CRAY 3 CDC 7600s 1 CYBER 825	Government agencies, labs, and nonprofit institutions	$636 per prime CPU hour
NASA-Ames	CRAY 1-S CDC 7600	Computational fluid and aerodynamics	No charges to NASA grantees. $2,000 per CPU hour for CRAY
NASA-Goddard	CYBER 205	NASA-funded and NASA-project related	No charge to NASA grantees. $1,000 per CPU for others
NASA-Langley	CYBER 203	NASA and NASA-funded scientists	$1,300 per CPU hour
NASA-Lewis	CRAY 1-S	Principally aerodynamics related	No charge for NASA supported

SOURCE: *A National Computing Environment for Academic Research*, National Science Foundation, October 1983.

Photo credit: U.S. Department of Energy, Los Alamos National Laboratory

View of a part of the main computing facility at Los Alamos National Laboratory. CRAY 1 in foreground

Table 15.—Summary of Current and Planned Government Open Access Advanced Computer Architecture Software Development Facilities

Agency	Current systems	Number of users	Planned additions fiscal years 1984-88
National Science Foundation	2 Class VI	850	1 Class VII
Department of Energy	3 Class VI	6,400[a]	1 Class VI, 5 Class VII
National Aeronautics and Space Administration	3 Class VI, 1 special	3,000	1 VI, 1 VII, 1 special
Totals	8 Class VI, 1 special	10,250	2 VI, 7 VII, 1 special

[a]Includes researchers performing classified work.

SOURCE: *A National Computing Environment for Academic Research,* National Science Foundation.

what was recognized as a critical scientific imperative. The report of that group stated:[6]

> Computing facilities have a decisive effect on the kind of research which is done by academic scientists and engineers. During the 1950s and 1960s the Government encouraged the growth of computing in research, research methods were transformed in discipline after discipline, and the United States enjoyed a large, ever-widening lead in quantitative research and modeling complex phenomena. In the 1970s Government support slackened and academic computing facilities no longer kept pace with advancing technology... Science has passed a watershed in using computers for research. Computers are no longer just tools for measurement and analysis but have become the means for making new discoveries... Academic research in computer architecture, computational mathematics, algorithms, and software for parallel computers should be encouraged to increase computing capability.

In response to this imperative, the NSF working group recommended an expansion in spending for academic research in advanced computers, and improved access to computing facilities including 10 new supercomputer facilities and special networks to make these systems widely available (see table 16).

The House Committee on Science and Technology considered R&D in advanced computers and access to powerful computer systems by scientists and engineers in many fields to be crucial elements in the advancement of science and technology. Accordingly, they approved a budget of $40 million in fiscal year 1985 for NSF's Advanced Scientific Computing initiative, thus doubling the administration's request for this program.[7]

Industry's Role

Three U.S. companies are developing next generation (Class VII) supercomputer systems. In addition, two Japanese companies (Fujitsu and Hitachi) have introduced new systems and a third (Nippon Electric-NEC) is developing a new supercomputer, planned for delivery in 1985 (see table 17).

Cray will introduce the Cray-2 in 1985. This will be a four processor vector machine.[8] The Cray-3 is scheduled for introduction in 1986. It will be an 8 to 16 processor vector machine with Galium Arsenide (GaAs) (see ch. 9) circuitry. Cray sees integrated circuit technology as critical. The Japanese are the major suppliers of state-of-the-art fast bi-polar memory chips, and one-half of the integrated circuits in current Cray machines are Japanese made.[9]

Control Data (CDC) spun off development work for its next generation advanced architecture machine to a new company, ETA Systems, which CDC capitalizes with $40 million for 40 percent ownership. This approach is being taken by CDC because small groups with dedication, entrepreneurial spirit, and a personal stake in the success of the project are considered important.[10] ETA Systems will spend $4 million to $6 million the first year on direct R&D costs. Plans are for the first demonstration machines to be available late

---

[6] *A National Computing Environment for Academic Computing,* prepared under the direction of Marcel Bardon by the Working Group on Computers for Research, Kent K. Curtis, Chairman, July 1983, pp. 1-2.

Table 16.—NSF Plans for Computer Research
(million of dollars)

	Fiscal years		
	1984	1985	1986
Local facilities	$45.5	$ 90.9	$106.7
Supercomputers	14.4	70.0	110.0
Networks	2.1	7.3	11.5
Advanced computer systems and computational mathematics	8.0	20.0	33.0
Total	$69.9	$188.1	$261.2

SOURCE: *A National Computing Environment for Academic Research,* National Science Foundation.

[7] Authorizing Appropriations to the National Science Foundation, House Committee on Science and Technology, Report 98-642, Mar. 30, 1984, pp. 8-9.

[8] *Vector computers* have specialized architectures that achieve high speed calculation of mathematical formulas by treating entire arrays of data (vectors) as processable by single instructions, saving time on certain calculations that can be arranged as a series of vectors.

[9] L. T. Davis, "Advanced Computer Projects," presentation at the *Frontiers of Supercomputing Conference,* Los Alamos, Aug. 15, 1983.

[10] W. Norris, "A Conducive Environment for Supercomputers," banquet address at the *Frontiers of Supercomputing Conference,* Los Alamos, Aug. 18, 1983.

Table 17.—Summary of New Commercial Supercomputer Systems Under Development

Company	Model	Maximum speed (MFLOPS[a])	Available
Cray Research	Cray-2	1,000	mid 1985
	Cray-3	NA	1985-86
ETA Systems	GF-10	10,000	1986-87[b]
	GF-30	30,000	NA
Denelcor	HEP-2	4,000	1985-86
NEC	SX-2	1,300	March 1985

NA—Not announced.
[a]MFLOPS (million floating point operations per second): a measure of computer performance on high precision calculations.
[b]L. M. Thorndyke at the *Frontiers of Supercomputing Conference*, Los Alamos, August 1983.
SOURCE: *The IEEE Committee on Super Scientific Computers.*

in 1986, and volume production of two machines per month is planned for 1987. The design will employ two to eight vector processors with the maximum eight processor version to sell in the range of $20 million.[11]

Denelcor, a former maker of analog computers, developed a parallel processing computer design (HEP-Heterogeneous Element Processor). Since 1982, this design has been available for sale or lease. Considered to be an experimental machine by users at facilities such as Los Alamos, this design is a step toward a new generation of computer architectures. Work is currently underway on the HEP-2, which should be competitive with Cray and CDC machines if component and software problems can be overcome. Moreover, the viability of Denelcor efforts will require higher sales than have so far occurred with the HEP-1.[12]

In addition, other U.S. firms including computer companies (Digital Equipment, Hewlett-Packard, Honeywell, IBM, NCR and Sperry), telecommunications companies (Harris), semiconductor companies (Advanced Micro Devices, Intel, Monolithic Memories, Mostek, Motorola and National Semiconductor), electronics companies (Allied, Eaton, General Electric, RCA and Westinghouse) and aerospace companies (Martin-Marietta) are involved to some extent in research on parallel processing, data-flow or multiprocessor architectures.[13]

Industry representatives characterize the advanced computer architecture business as risky. The market is small: approximately 100 Class VI supercomputers have been installed worldwide as compared to tens of thousands of less powerful computers. Development costs are high: design tools include other advanced architecture machines for hardware simulation and software development.

The Role of Universities

Although as many as 50 U.S. universities are involved in advance computer architecture (ACA) research,[14] significant funding levels are available in only a few major schools. (See table 18.)

University research in advanced computer architecture is characterized by a series of stages of elaboration of a concept including: 1) theoretical paper and pencil work; 2) simulation of ideas on existing computer systems; 3) "breadboard" wiring of designs with off-the-shelf components; and 4) full-scale engineering and construction of prototype machines in which state-of-the-art components, software and peripheral devices can be integrated to test the design on full-scale problems. OTA found that few if any projects currently under-

---

[11]L. M. Thorndyke, "The Cyber 2xx Design Process," presentation at the *Frontiers of Supercomputing Conference*, Los Alamos, Aug. 15, 1983.
[12]B. Smith, "Latency and HEP," presentation at the *Frontiers of Supercomputing Conference*, Los Alamos, Aug. 15, 1983.

[13]"Next-Generation Computing: Research in the United States," *IEEE Spectrum,* November 1983, pp. 62-63.
[14]The OTA workshop on Advanced Computer Architecture concluded that every major Computer Science and Electrical Engineering department has some interest.

Table 18.—1983 DARPA, DOE, and NSF University Funding of Advanced Computer Architecture

Institution	DARPA	DOE	NSF
California Institute of Technology	1,000[a]	550	
Massachusetts Institute of Technology	2,000[a]	250	102
University of California, Berkeley	2,000[a]		
Stanford University	2,000[a]		
New York University		600	150
University of Illinois		155	200
University of Texas		107	120
University of Wisconsin		95	
Duke University			197
Other			570
Totals	7,000[a]	1,757	1,339

[a] Estimate.

SOURCE: DARPA numbers from a personal communication with Duane Adams; DOE numbers from Edward Oliver at the OTA Workshop on Advanced Computer Architecture; NSF numbers from *Summary of Awards: Fiscal Year 1983*, National Science Foundation, Division of Computer Research.

way in universities have funding to carry a design concept through to the final, systems engineering stage. Several projects will produce prototypes, but the elaboration of an idea into a system with software and supporting peripherals to demonstrate the performance and utility of the concept on real problems requires funding on the order of twice what the currently best funded projects receive.

The major distinction between efforts pursued in industry and in universities on ACA, aside from the commercial and product development orientation of industry work, is that more radical and advanced designs are being pursued in universities, whereas evolutionary designs are sought by industry. This is a result of the stake that industry has in the existing base of software and users and the need for upward compatibility of systems. University researchers have a greater ability to pursue revolutionary designs that could require completely new programming approaches and techniques.

Facilities Requirements

The increasing availability and capability of VLSI circuitry and computer-aided design tools are expected to have significant impact on computer design.[15] Prototype production time and cost will decrease. Both general purpose and custom application architectures are implementable in VLSI, opening opportunities for the testing and evaluation of many more computer architecture ideas. However, the initial investment required for VLSI design and fabrication equipment is very costly and will probably remain so. It is unlikely that most universities will be able to afford this equipment.

Other expenses associated with ACA research include computer-based simulation facilities. There may be a need for current generation supercomputers at universities to facilitate and test the design of new architectures. Bell Laboratories currently devotes most of its Cray computer to VLSI circuit design.

Supercomputers are also used by Cray and Control Data for software development, so that software is available when a new hardware design is completed. Universities would benefit from access to these software development tools, giving researchers the chance to test ideas experimentally. But here again, the costs associated with the procurement and operation of these design and computing resources are beyond the means of university project budgets. Some universities are forming consortia to spread the cost of microelectronics design and fabrication facilities across several institutions (see ch. 6). Shared supercomputer facilities are a key element to NSF plans for Advanced Scientific Computing.

---
[15] S. Trimberger, "Reaching for the Million-Transistor Chip," *IEEE Spectrum*, November 1983, p. 100.

Annual operating costs for government supercomputer facilities average more than $10 million.[16] Only three U.S. universities currently operate such facilities and these are utilized at less than 50 percent of capacity. The reason for this low usage is the high cost of computer time on these systems, ranging from $2,000 to $3,000 per hour. University ACA research is therefore usually done on minicomputers which lack the capability of generating sophisticated, high-resolution graphics of importance to the design of integrated circuits.

Critical Areas of Research

Currently, the goal of most advanced computer architecture research and development is parallel computation.

The two major U.S. industrial developers of supercomputers, ETA Systems and Cray Research, and the Japanese manufacturers, Hitachi and Fujitsu, are pursuing parallel architectures in a conservative incremental fashion, contemplating the production of machines with up to 16 parallel processors by the late 1980s. Vector architecture will remain the dominant method for achieving fast numerical processing in these systems.

Universities, by contrast, are pursuing a number of methods of achieving "massively parallel" computation with upwards of 1,000 processors working in concert. One of the basic problems of computing in parallel is the requirement for communication and coordination among the individual processing elements when they are working on pieces of a single problem. Often the results of one process are required for another process to go forward. Several architectural solutions to these difficulties are under study, and extensive evaluation of different approaches must be done before their viability in real-world problems can be assessed. Detailed simulation of concepts and testing of prototypes is required, and present university funding is inadequate to support such work.

There are currently more than 50 concepts for parallel processing architectures under consideration in academic and industrial institutions. However, there are no standard metrics for comparing the performance of different architectural designs or the software to be used on parallel machines. Nor is it likely that any *one* metric could fully measure differences in performance, since different applications place different demands on systems. The development of such metrics and the establishment of suitable test facilities for implementing standard design evaluations are critical issues in advanced computer architecture. The Federal Government may have a role in this area by setting voluntary standards for computer performance measurement, and by providing facilities for testing.

Thus far little attention has been devoted to the problems of *symbolic,* as opposed to numeric processing architectures. In the past, the von Neumann architecture has been used for both kinds of computations; the focus of advanced computer architecture R&D has been on computers for "number crunching" applications, or high precision calculation, simulation and modeling for science and engineering. The increasing importance of artificial intelligence is encouraging the design of special machine architectures, both to ease the programming of artificial intelligence applications, and to speed the processing of symbolic computations. Several companies are now producing machines for artificial intelligence, and the list is expected to grow.[17]

Three other areas of technology are critical to the development of advanced computer architecture systems: integrated circuits, circuit packaging, and algorithm and software design.

Integrated Circuits (IC)

An order of magnitude (10x) increase in computer speed is expected from improvements in IC materials and manufacturing techniques. Silicon will remain the dominant IC substrate material through 1990 because the technology

---

[16]*A National Computing Environment for Academic Research,* op. cit., p. 22.

[17]See the case study on Artificial Intelligence in this chapter.

is well understood and the practical limits of device density, speed and power consumption have yet to be reached. Silicon will be the basis of a growing set of special purpose VLSI architectures. Gallium Arsenide (GaAs) digital logic and memory circuits are growing in importance, and will be used in the Cray-3.[18] University based research in chemistry, physics and microelectronics are expected to make significant contributions to increased integrated circuit capability.

Packaging

Interconnections among the logic elements on some complex chips occupy over half of the useable chip area, and affect the performance speed of chip functions. Currently, three sandwiched layers of interconnection within a chip are typical, and it is expected that as many as 12 layers will be common in a decade.[19]

As chips have become more complex, containing greater numbers of logic elements, the number of "pins," or inputs and outputs, required for communication with them has grown. The connection of sets of chips has thus become more complex, and the difficulty of simultaneously housing and powering chips, and dissipating the waste heat from chip sets is forcing advanced computer designers to find more sophisticated methods of packaging them.[20]

Cryogenic liquid cooling equipment is required for most existing and planned supercomputers. Facilities must be provided for the refrigeration and storage of the coolant. And the size, weight, and reliability of the cooling equipment must be considered in the purchase and use of these systems.

Packaging is also a critical factor in supercomputer manufacturing costs. Cray machines are currently hand wired. In an effort to reduce costs, the Japanese are developing designs that lend themselves to automated manufacturing procedures.

Software and Algorithms

The lack of applications software for supercomputers has been a significant barrier to their adoption and use.

One half of recent Cray Research R&D funds have reportedly been devoted to software development,[21] and the vectorizing FORTRAN compiler, a software program that helps prepare standard FORTRAN code for execution on the Cray vector architecture, has been a major factor in the commercial success of the Cray-1 line.[22] Users of vector computers, including the Cray, are quite pleased to obtain 20 percent of the maximum rated speed of these machines on typical problems.[23] Work is continuing in industry and universities to develop software to make vector machines more effective and easier to use, and this work will be of critical importance through this decade.

The introduction of parallel processing designs and the proliferation of special purpose computer architectures will make software production and design more complicated.[24] The creation of new high-level languages that are more easily understood by users, and other tools and programming support environments that facilitate the expression of logical, symbolic, mathematical, scientific, and engineering concepts in computable form, could greatly

---

[18]L. T. Davis, op. cit.

[19]J. A. Armstrong, "High Performance Technology: Directions and Issues," presentation at the *Frontiers of Supercomputing Conference*, Los Alamos, Aug. 15, 1983.

[20]MCC is devoting some of their initial efforts to packaging technology; and ETA Systems sources estimate that 60 percent of the R&D effort for the GF-10 will be in packaging. ETA is planning to use liquid nitrogen cooling to obtain a doubling in speed from CMOS silicon integrated circuits (L.M. Thorndyke at the Los Alamos Conference).

[21]Rollwagen, op. cit.

[22]Nippon Telephone and Telegraph, the Japanese state telecommunications monopoly, has chosen a Cray-XMP over recently introduced Japanese supercomputers of comparable or superior speed, reportedly because of the software, and the experienced team of field representatives, available from Cray. "NTT Picks Cray Super CPU," *Electronic News*, Oct. 10, 1983, p. 87.

[23]David Kuck, at the OTA workshop on Advanced Computer Architecture, July 14, 1983.

[24]Paul Schneck, at the OTA workshop on Software Engineering, Nov. 17, 1983.

expand the utility and lower the costs of operating advanced computer systems.[25]

In order for the speed potential of advanced computers to be used, problems must either be programmed to take advantage of the computer design, or the architecture must be designed to handle the unique characteristics of the problem. The mediating factor between the problem and the architecture is the algorithm, or the structured procedure for solving the problem. In the future, computer designers will have to be more cognizant of computational algorithms and the effects of computer architecture on programming and problem solution, and thus they will need greater knowledge of applications. Similarly, designers of complex programs, especially scientists, mathematicians, and engineers, will need to have a greater appreciation of the inherent capabilities and limitations of particular computer architectures as they become more dependent on advanced computers in their work. Collaboration between the *users and designers* of future computer systems is critical to both the utility and the commercial success of advanced architecture computers.[26]

Manpower

There is a shortage of people capable of designing software for advanced architecture computer systems. In particular, people skilled in the design of software and software tools for use in sophisticated scientific and mathematical applications are scarce.[27] There is a need for people who understand scientific problems in a range of disciplines, and who can design and implement computer systems to solve those problems.

Attracting talented faculty to train the next generation of computer researchers is a problem. The difficulty results, in large measure, from the uncompetitive salaries and low job mobility offered by universities. The problem is expected to become acute as demand for computer architectures employing symbolic processing and artificial intelligence capabilities increase. (See Artificial Intelligence case study.)

International Efforts
Japan

Two Japanese firms, Fujitsu and Hitachi, have introduced advanced architecture computers whose performance is competitive with the fastest available American supercomputers. Early copies of these machines have been installed in three Japanese universities. A third company, Nippon Electric, has announced plans to introduce a supercomputer in 1985.

The Japanese Government is funding two national efforts in advanced architecture research and development: "High Speed Computing Systems for Science and Technology" and the "Fifth Generation Computer System" program.

The Electrotechnical Laboratory of the Agency of Industrial Science and Technology (AIST), an arm of the Ministry of International Trade and Industry (MITI), is managing a 10 year project (January 1981—March 1990) called "High Speed Computing Systems For Science and Technology." It is focused on microelectronics research and development (GaAs, Josephson Junctions and High Electron Mobility Transistor devices), parallel processing systems with 100 to 1,000 computing elements, and systems components, including mass storage and data transfer devices, to support high-speed scientific and engineering calculations. Total government funding will be on the order of $100 million. A consortium of six major Japanese computer companies (the Technology Research Association) has been formed to conduct much of this work in industrial laboratories on "consignment" from MITI.[28]

---

[25]M. B. Wells, "General Purpose Languages of the Nineties," presentation at the *Frontiers of Supercomputing Conference,* Los Alamos, Aug. 17, 1983.

[26]OTA workshop on Advanced Computer Architecture, July 14, 1983.

[27]This point was emphasized in one applications area in particular, telecommunications (Paul Ritt at the OTA workshop on Advanced Computer Architecture, July 14, 1983).

[28]"Super Computer—High Speed Computing Systems for Science and Technology," *Science & Technology in Japan,* October-November, 1982, p. 16.

The "Fifth Generation Computer System" program is managed by the Institute for New Generation Computer Technology (ICOT). The program is described in more detail on page 105, as part of the artificial intelligence case study.

Great Britain

Great Britain has reacted to the Japanese efforts (in particular the Fifth Generation project) by establishing a national plan for research in advanced computer systems, known as the Alvey Programme for Advanced Information Technology. It is discussed below in the Software Engineering and in Artificial Intelligence Case Studies. Researchers in British universities have made significant contributions to advanced computer architecture research. For example, the University of Manchester has an advanced prototype of a "dataflow" architecture machine.[29] Work is also being pursued in industry.[30] Inmos, Ltd. has developed the Transputer, a device which combines processing and communications functions on a single chip. This device has been specifically designed for the connection of a number of units to achieve concurrent processing.[31]

France

France has considerable interest in advanced computer architecture research and development. Two industrial companies, Cii-Bull and CGE, as well as seven government funded institutions including five universities are pursuing work in this area.[32] Three "supercomputer" projects are expected to produce machines by 1985-88, but these systems are not likely to be speed rivals of American and Japanese systems of similar vintage.[33]

West Germany

West Germany has four universities and six industrial companies working on advanced computer architecture R&D.[34] The government is providing about $4 million per year for research at the universities on parallel processing. A project at the Technical University in West Berlin has received a grant from the Ministry of Research and Technology to develop a full-scale prototype.[35]

The European Community

The Commission of the European Communities (EC) has initiated ESPRIT (European Strategic Program for Research and Development in Information Technology) to pursue information technology R&D on a cooperative basis with industry, universities, and the governments of the EC countries pooling their efforts. Four institutions (three Belgian and one French) have thus far announced plans to study parallel processing with ESPRIT funding.[36] The proposed ESPRIT plan calls for the development and use of computerized facilities to study new computer designs.[37] (For more information on ESPRIT, see ch. 7.)

---

[29] A. L. Davis, "Computer Architecture," *IEEE Spectrum*, November 1983, pp. 98-99.

[30] Five have been identified, see "Next—Generation Computing: Research in Europe," *IEEE Spectrum*, November 1983, pp. 65-66.

[31] "Transputer Does Five or More MIPS Even When Not Used in Parallel," Iann Barron, Peter Cavill, David May and Pete Wilson, *Electronics*, Nov. 17, 1983, p. 109.

[32] "Next—Generation Computing: Research in Europe," *IEEE Spectrum*, November 1983, pp. 64-65.

[33] *Report of the IEEE Super Scientific Computer Committee*, Oct. 11, 1983.

[34] *IEEE Spectrum*, November 1983, op. cit., pp. 67-68.

[35] "Western Europe Looks to Parallel Processing for Future Computers," *Electronics*, June 16, 1983. p. 111.

[36] A. L. Davis, op. cit.

[37] Proposal for a Council Decision adopting the first European Strategic Programme for Research and Development in Information Technologies (ESPRIT), Commission of the European Communities, June 2, 1983, p. 24.

Case Study 2: Fiber Optic Communications

Findings

- Fiber optic communications technology is an important export (e.g., a $3 billion world market projected for 1989), and is a key element in improved productivity and reduced costs in telecommunications systems.
- Fiber optic communications technology is developing rapidly and the potential benefits from continued research are extensive.
- The most significant research is concentrated in only a few large firms and universities, in part because of the expense and the required long term commitment.
- Increased Government funding in this technology—now at a low level—would enlarge university participation and accelerate technological advances.
- The scarcity of trained research and development personnel is a continuing handicap. A large proportion of university researchers in fiber optics are foreign nationals and many return to their native land after completing graduate studies.
- Research conducted in Japan and Europe is among the world's most advanced and exchange of research information internationally among colleagues is critical to scientific advancement.
- Japan is the world's leader in several key aspects of the technology, and is a strong competitor to American firms.

The first successful transmission of voice signals using energy from the Sun was accomplished in 1880 by Alexander Graham Bell and Sumner Tainter using a device called the photophone, but was abandoned because weather made the system unreliable.[38] Since 1970, interest has resumed in using light energy for telecommunications, in the form of fiber optic communications because of two technological advances: the laser and light transmission through low loss silica glass fibers.

---

[38]Report on Research at the University of Arizona, vol. 1, No. 1, fall 1983, p. 11, published by the Research Office, University of Arizona.

Advantages

Fiber optic communication is the transmission of light signals through transparent glass or plastic fibers, where the signals are generated by lasers or light emitting diodes (LEDs) and received by photodetectors, which convert light signals to electrical signals. The major components of fiber optics technology are the fiber cables and connectors, transmitters and receivers, and repeaters, or regenerators,[39] which amplify and reconstitute the signals periodically along the fiber.

There are several properties of fiber optic communications that make them attractive for telecommunications applications:

- large bandwidth, meaning that large amounts of information (voice conversations, computer data, graphics) can be transmitted rapidly. For example, a quarter-inch diameter optical cable with two fibers carries as much data as a 3-inch copper cable with 20,000 wires.[40] (See fig. 9.) Conservatively, the capacity of a single pair of fibers currently available commercially is about 4,000 voice grade circuits in field applications and about 400,000 voice grade circuits under controlled laboratory conditions;
- less susceptibility than copper wire to radio frequency interference, providing less cross-talk, higher quality signal transmission, and immunity from electromagnetic pulse (EMP) effects—characteristics of value for both civilian and military uses;
- lower loss of signal strength, meaning that fewer repeaters are needed;
- resistance to "noninvasive" or covert wiretaps;

---

[39]In standard copper telephone wires, signal regeneration is required at about one-mile intervals. Repeaters add significantly to the installation and maintenance costs of transmission systems.

[40]High Technology, "Fiber Optics: Light at The End of the Tunnel," March 1983, p. 63.

Figure 9.—Optical Fibers Are Small, Lightweight, and Versatile

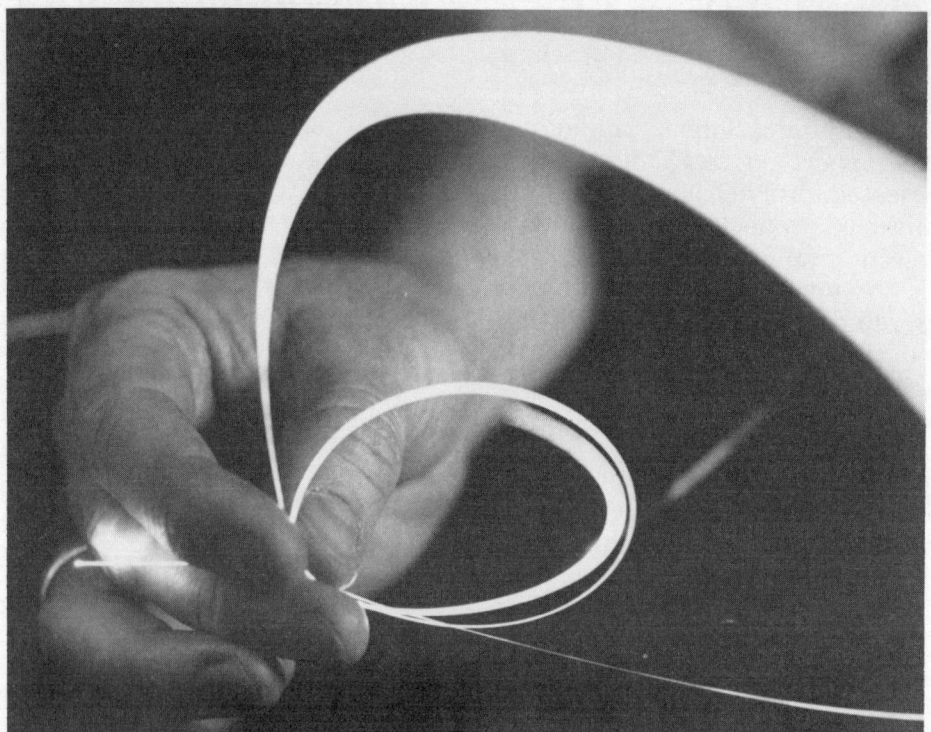

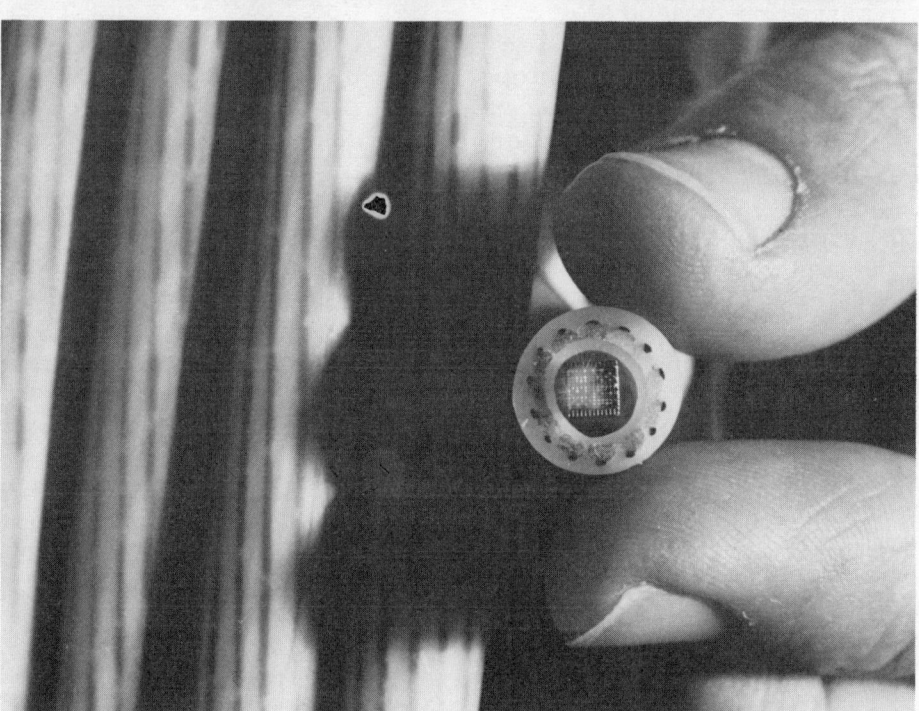

Photo credits: AT&T Bell Laboratories

- small size and low weight, factors that contribute to ease of transport and less need for underground and building duct space;
- declining cost compared to other terrestrial telecommunications technologies.[41]

Commercialization Trends

The technology has progressed rapidly into the commercial marketplace since 1966, when researchers[42] first proposed the possibility of purifying the glass used in optical fibers to reduce losses in signal strength. In 1970, the first low loss fiber was produced by Corning Glass Works, and by 1977 prototype systems were being installed by AT&T and General Telephone and Electronics Corp. in the United States. Today, many developed countries have fiber optic communication systems in operation or plan to install them.

The United States, Canada, Western Europe, and Japan accounted for an estimated 96 percent of a $550 million world market in fiber optics communications equipment in 1983. The world market was approaching $1 billion for 1984,[43] and is projected to expand to $3 billion by 1989,[44] as countries satisfy their telecommunications system expansion and replacement needs with the increasingly cost-competitive fiber optic communication systems rather than with microwave radio, copper twisted wire pair, and coaxial cable.

Applications in the United States

Telecommunications, the major market (85 percent)[45] for fiber optics, can be described in four segments: long distance; interoffice trunks that connect telephone central offices; local feeder lines; and local area networks. Long distance applications are currently the most cost effective for fiber optic communications, and comprise the vast majority of current use in the United States.

Interoffice trunking provides links between intracity telephone facilities. Feeder lines include intracity transmission links between carrier facilities and subscriber distribution points, while local feeder lines extend to subscriber locations. Local area networks (LANs) serve limited communities, for example, within a building or a building complex. They are just emerging and will become an important market for fiber optics.

There are a growing number of installations of fiber optic systems in long distance telecommunications. Among these are AT&T's Northeast Corridor route. In 1983 a line connecting Washington, DC and New York City was inaugurated. In 1984 this line was extended to Cambridge, MA, and Richmond, VA. The total Northeast Corridor line will use 45,000 miles of fiber over the 750 mile route. The first phase of a west coast route, which will eventually extend from Los Angeles to Oakland and Sacramento, has been completed. A trans-Atlantic cable (TAT 8), engineered to carry 40,000 voice circuits at a cost of less than half that of its predecessor, is scheduled for installation in 1988. By March 1983, AT&T had already installed over 100,000 miles of fiber and projections are for another 300,000 miles by 1990.[46]

Other firms planning major systems include United Telecommunications, Inc., with its 23,000 mile, $2 billion lightwave network to be completed by 1987.[47] Southern New England Telephone Co., in a joint venture, will route its system through 20 States along railroad rights of way; MCI, with a 4,000 mile system intended to serve the east coast;[48] and Cable and Wireless, a British company, with

---

[41]This comparison is based on the relative cost per channel-mile, which is the number of voice circuit equivalents (channels) multiplied by the distance of the transmission link.
[42]Kao and Hockman, ITT Standard Telecommunications Laboratories, England.
[43]D. G. Thomas, "Optical Communications," *Research and Development*, June 1984, p. 203.
[44]*Signal*, September 1983.
[45]The remaining 15 percent of the noncommon carrier applications are said to be in vehicular,, industrial control systems, and in CATV. *High Technology*, op. cit.

[46]Optoelectronics Supplement to *Electronic News*, "Fiber Optics Market Still Baffles Suppliers," p. 5, Apr. 4, 1983.
[47]"23,000 Mile Fiber Network Planned by United Telecom," *The Journal of Fiber Optics*, June 1984.
[48]*Fiber Optics Industry Service: Competitive Environment*, Gnostic Concepts, Inc., 1983, pp. 1-2.

a 560 mile network that will link major cities in Texas.

Fiber optics is already an attractive replacement for copper cable in some *local* telecommunications applications: 1) in trunk lines between telephone central (switching) offices where the average 10-mile distance can be spanned by optical cables without repeaters, thus installation and maintenance costs are lower, and 2) in local feeder lines in large cities where crowding in underground utility ducts is a growing problem.

Local area network applications are expected to grow rapidly according to some industry projections, particularly as user requirements for bandwidth increase to the 10 to 100 million bits per second (Mbs) range. The past slow growth of fiber optic applications in LAN systems is due to the variety of technical needs among different customers, and a lack of uniform technical standards. In contrast with long distance communications systems, which have traditionally paid extensive attention to technical standards development, a Federal telecommunications standards committee only recently (July 1984) held its first meeting to develop Federal guidelines for LANs. Once standards issues are settled, growth in the use of fiber optics within buildings and building complexes is expected to be rapid.[49]

Other factors limit the adoption of fiber optic communications technology. The large base of installed copper wire in the AT&T plant (some 827 million miles) is likely to be replaced slowly. The large capacity (up to 100 television channels) of some CATV systems and the fact that this expensive investment in coaxial cable has been made quite recently in many cities, suggests that fiber optics will not be widely used for cable television for some time. Advances in nonoptical transmission techniques are enabling considerable increases in the information carrying capacity of copper wire pairs.

In applications other than communications carrier uses, such as aerospace and military systems, fiber optic technology is already being exploited. These are primarily in command, control, and communications applications including guidance and control systems for aircraft, spacecraft, and missiles; optically multiplexed data bus transmission systems; electronic warfare and sonar applications; and advanced instrumentation systems. The imperviousness of fiber optics to electromagnetic interference, along with light weight, small size, and high information rates, make it of special value in aerospace and military applications.

Foreign Applications

Installation of fiber optic communications systems have been completed, or are planned in a number of countries. A small sample of these includes:

- *West Germany.* By late 1984, 10 broadband integrated fiber optic local area networks will be built in Berlin, Hamburg, Hanover, Düsseldorf, Nuremburg, and Munich, called the BIGFON (Broadband Integrated Fiber Optic Local Network) network. In addition to having access to the public switched telephone network, subscribers will also be able to access the integrated telex and data network and receive radio, television, telephone, and full motion picturephone. The long-term goal is to include all telephone subscribers in the nation.
- *France.* Several fiber optic systems are being installed by the French. The government has decided to upgrade the nation's antiquated telecommunications network by leapfrogging toward the most advanced technology available—especially fiber optics. They also plan to install a submarine cable between France and Corsica in 1985, providing over 7,600 channels operating at 280 Mbs.
- *Japan.* One of several projects being undertaken is an 80 km fiber optic route in the suburbs of Tokyo. The system operates at 400 Mbs, providing video confer-

---

[49]*Aviation Week and Space Technology,* "Promising Future Seen for Optical Fibers," pt 1, Oct. 12, 1983, pp. 44-77.

encing and facsimile services. In addition, the Japanese have installed a broadband network for data communications in Tsukuba to facilitate scientific and technical communications.

An Intelligent Network System (INS) is being developed by Nippon Telephone and Telegraph's Yokosuka Laboratory near Tokyo. Services include voice, data, CATV, still and motion pictures, facsimile, TV conferencing and high resolution TV. The INS is expected to make extensive use of fiber optic technology. Another project involves a 45 km undersea fiber optic cable south of Tokyo, operating at 400 Mbs. The system will be extended over a 1,000 km route between islands.

- *United Kingdom.* British Telecom, the nation's telecommunications authority, has committed itself to using only fiber optics in the trunk network from 1984 on. By 1990, half the trunk network will be fiber optic systems.

Mercury Communications, a communications carrier in limited competition with the government telecommunications authority, has begun installing an intercity fiber optic network using the British rail rights of way.

The British plan to construct a nationwide cable telecommunications system for the delivery of television programming, FM radio, pay television, and text. An experiment with a small number of homes is being conducted using fiber optics technology. This is considered to be the prototype for the national system.

United States R&D

Much fiber optics R&D in the United States is being conducted by a few large companies: AT&T Bell Laboratories; Corning Glass Works; ITT; and, to a lesser extent, GTE; a few universities; and some smaller companies. Many of the commercial products now available are a result of R&D performed by Bell Labs. AT&T began funding optic communications research in 1960 and related laser research in 1958.

There is concern that many U.S. companies have been inclined to undertake research only where the prospective payoff is likely to occur within a very few years. This attitude has the effect of shifting investigation away from promising areas such as research on infrared systems, where another 5 to 10 years of work may be required before commercial products become available. Thus, the importance of stable Federal funds for basic research is underscored by short-term planning within industry.

The expense of research in fiber optics makes it difficult for small firms to play a role in R&D, except in some areas of product commercialization. In addition, there is a tendency for equipment purchasers to prefer vendors of complete lines of components, which works to the detriment of small firms. As a result, small specialty firms often must rely on DOD for research funds, on takeovers by larger firms, or on venture capital in order to remain competitive. Regardless, these firms play an important role in the technology by providing innovative ideas and products, by serving as conduits for the commercialization of university-based research, and by filling niches that might not be attractive to larger firms.

Because of the considerable expense associated with research in fiber optics technology, and the low level of available funding, few universities have major research programs. The importance of cost is illustrated by the $500,000 or higher cost of Molecular Beam Epitaxy equipment (needed for growing alternating epitaxial layers on semiconductor light sources and detectors) and $200,000 for fiber drawing equipment (needed to produce fiber and to experiment with different fiber designs) required to perform research. Very little university research is focused on glass fibers, but instead is directed toward light sources and detectors. The principal universities with major research programs are the California Institute of Technology, the University of Illinois, Stanford, Cornell, Princeton, and the Massachusetts Institute of Technology.

Government Funding

University research has been supported for decades through NSF funding for the support of research and, more recently, training and laboratory equipment. NSF supports several universities, such as the University of Arizona in Tucson, Northeastern University, and Cornell University's Submicron Facility. Although NSF funding levels in this technology are not large—$1.75 million in 1983—they represent a consistent source of funds, often supporting fundamental research with very long term potential payoff. Additional levels of funding would likely accelerate the rate of technological advance.

Between 18 and 20 projects are being funded by NSF in about a dozen universities. Many of these are concerned with advancing theoretical knowledge in areas such as laser technology, the development of pioneering optic and optoelectronic integrated systems and bistable optical switching devices, research into infrared lasers and detectors, and the application of integrated optical interface circuits in local area networks at gigabit (billions of bits) per second data rates. Another $300,000 of NSF funding is available for upgrading university laboratory equipment.

The DOD funds fiber optics research through mission-oriented procurements. Approximately 95 percent of the research is carried out by industry. DOD has some $32.4 million committed to the development of cables and connectors, light sources and detectors, radiation effects exploration, and to sensor and communications applications. An estimated $12.6 million of this is committed to research, principally applied research. In addition, the military departments allocated about $22 million for fiscal year 1984 among seven procurement programs for applications ranging from surveillance, shipboard and long distance communications, and helicopter flight control systems.

Cooperative Research

NSF has several activities directed at encouraging cooperative research between universities and industry, and transferring technology into industry. One of these noted in chapter 2, the Industry/University Cooperative Research Centers program, provides planning grants to aid universities in establishing industry affiliations and support for specific scientific or engineering technologies.

NSF has awarded a $75,000 grant for planning purposes to the University of Arizona at Tucson, Optical Sciences Center. The University held its first meeting with industry in early 1984 to begin determining mutual interest in specific areas of cooperation and industry support. Most of this research is expected to be directed toward long term projects in physics and materials science with potential applications in optical logic circuitry and optical computers, with limited attention to fiber optics.

Another NSF activity funds specific projects where research is undertaken cooperatively by universities and company investigators. Funding is at levels of about $100,000 per year over a 2 to 3 year period, on the average. One of the funded projects is being undertaken jointly by Bell Laboratories and the University of Arizona, Optical Sciences Center. This project's long-term research is in high speed optical, bistable switching devices operating at picosecond (1 trillionth of a second) rates.

The current level of cooperation in research is not extensive, but holds promise for broadening the base of research. Among the problems and issues to be worked out are finding ways for competing firms to share research data and establishing a balance between university investigators' interest in long-term research and companies' desire for short-term payoffs.

Manpower and Industry Support

Fiber optics research requires training in both physics and in electrical engineering. Because universities, in general, do not provide this cross disciplinary training at the bachelor and masters degree levels, companies hiring recent graduates provide supplementary in-house training. Some companies also establish an affiliation with universities. An example is the affiliation between Corning Glass Works and the University of Rochester Institute of Optics, in which the company provides some faculty and funding. Another example is the support from United Technology Research Center to the Rensselaer Polytechnic Institute which is providing real estate for new facilities and adjunct faculty to teach specialized engineering courses.

The University of Rochester is the only school in the United States to offer an undergraduate degree in optics. Only three schools in the nation offer graduate degrees in optics: The University of Arizona in Tucson, the University of Rochester, and Northeastern University.

A factor aggravating the availability of trained Ph.D. graduates in this field is that a large proportion of the students are foreign nationals. Industry argues that immigration laws make it difficult for the student-graduate to remain in the United States after graduation, although many would prefer to stay and perform research.

Directions of U.S. Research

Among the areas of R&D focus identified during the course of this study are:

Fibers

The early fiber optic cables put in use were of the *multimode* type, in which lightrays enter the fiber at a variety of angles and travel through the core of the fiber reflecting from its inner refractive surfaces. However, *single mode* fiber technology, where lightrays follow a single direct path along the fiber core, has important advantages. Single mode fibers have greater information carrying capacity and allow a tenfold increase in the distance between repeaters for regenerating signals.

Today's single mode fiber systems are able to transmit, without repeaters, up to 200 Mbs (million bits per second) over 80 to 100 km. (This information rate is sufficient to carry simultaneously a video channel, high fidelity audio, data, and many telephone calls.) In laboratory tests, this performance has been exceeded by about 10 times, suggesting far greater potential gains from research. Improvements from research are expected to continue in both multimode and single mode fibers.

Improvements have been made in lowering attenuation (losses in signal strength) in both types of fibers by a factor of 100 since 1970, primarily due to development of methods to reduce impurities in the fibers.

Activities are being directed toward further improvements in optical fibers. These include research into different cross sections for fiber cores, such as circular, triangular, and oval, as investigation into new materials such as plastics, and improvements in fiber splicing techniques. Research into plastic materials is about at the stage of 1975 era research in glass fibers, and promises even lower cost, more durable fiber materials for some applications.

Longer wavelength (1.7 and 4.0 micron) material for fibers is also receiving attention, as these show promise of decreased attenuation by a factor of 10 to 100 over that of currently available fibers, with long-term prospects for transcontinental or transoceanic transmission without the need for repeaters.

Light Generators and Detectors

Light generator and detector technologies are important areas of research. Research is continuing to improve the lifetimes of these devices, their spectral stability, the narrowness of spectral emissions, switching speeds, current threshholds, and receiver sensitivity. The most recent advance is the cleave-coupled cavity laser—a device notable for its wavelength stability and capability of changing frequencies rapidly, making it attractive as a multisource generator. It has been demonstrated at 274 Mbs over 100 km of fiber optic cable by Bell Laboratories, and at 1.6 Gbs (billion bits per second) over 40 km by the Japanese.

Coherent detection, a technique to improve receiver sensitivity and to increase the information carrying capacity of fibers, is being pursued in many research laboratories, and may become important if a variety of obstacles can be overcome.

Research is also continuing into ways of integrating light sources, detectors, and the associated circuitry into single chips thus lowering cost and increasing reliability.

Optical Multiplexers

Optical multiplexers (and demultiplexers) are devices that combine (or separate) different signals so they can be sent through the same optical fiber. Wavelength muliplexing is already being used in AT&T's east coast and west coast systems, and a few experimental systems in Japan, Canada, and Europe. Research in wavelength multiplexing techniques should lead to important cost savings for wideband systems.

Connectors and Splicing Techniques

Research is continuing to simplify techniques for splicing together separate segments of optical fiber and to achieve lower losses due to the splice.

Bell Labs recently announced the development of an ultraviolet splicing system that contributes only 0.03 decibels to signal loss, using an optical test signal to assist in the alignment of fibers.

Switches

Switching permits a signal to be routed through specific paths to subscribers. Switching is a bottleneck in optical communications systems because the conversion of signals from light to electronic (current switch technology is electrical) causes delays in moving the signals through the system. Improvements in switching capabilities hold promise for reducing the number of conversions required from optical to electronic and vice versa. Current switches are expensive, limited in applications, and of unpredicted reliability.

Optical switching research is being conducted at Bell Laboratories and the University of Arizona, where experimental, room temperature switching rates, for "turn on," of 50 picoseconds (50 trillionths of a second) have been measured.

Storage

Research is continuing into methods for storing optical signals on fixed and volatile memory devices. Improvements in storage will make possible store and forward and electronic mail features for optical networks.

Amplifiers and Repeaters

Regenerative repeaters detect a signal, then amplify, reshape, and retime it into a replica of the original signal. The regenerated signal then modulates a laser or light emitting diode for transmission along the next span of optical fiber. Decreasing the number of repeaters required along a line depends in part on amplification capabilities.

Integrated Circuits

Research is continuing to improve capabilities for putting optical and optoelectronic light generators and detectors onto single integrated circuits, and to increase the operational bit rates. Recent breakthroughs hold promise for reducing the number of discrete components required in fiber optic systems and expanding bit rate capabilities.

Research in Japan

While research in fiber optics is being actively pursued in the United Kingdom, France, and West Germany, the most advanced foreign research has been undertaken in Japan.

Japan's research is being conducted, at least in part, to support the development of a new nationwide broadband telecommunications network that will make extensive use of fiber optic technology. Research is also being supported for future commercialization and international markets. Fiber optic research supporting this network is performed mainly in private companies, and is supported by the Ministry of International Trade and Industry (MITI) through the Optical Measurement and Control System (OE) project. OE plans to develop optoelectronic integrated circuits, transistors, and GaAs/GaAlAs lasers and detectors. The budget is approximately $100 million for the 1979-87 time period. Half of this amount is to be devoted to a coordinated research facility, information exchange among researchers, and the remainder on projects in six or seven companies, including Hitachi, Nippon Electric Corp., Toshiba, Mitsubishi, Fujitsu, and Matsushita. Japanese investment in infrared laser research is estimated at between $3 million and $4 million.

Case Study 3: Software Engineering

Findings

- Software is an important factor in information technology, exceeding four times the cost of hardware in large systems. The relative decline in hardware costs is shifting the focus of R&D to software. The complexity of new applications and information systems is also forcing the focus of information technology R&D toward software issues.
- R&D in software engineering has produced prototypes of software design tools and programming environments (integrated sets of tools) that promise significant productivity increases. But the cost of retooling, including retraining software manpower, and the uncertainty associated with innovation in software development are retarding adoption of innovative tools and techniques.
- In order to speed the acceptance of software engineering innovations, an applied research base needs to be established to scientifically test and validate new software development techniques, and to disseminate information on their performance in specific applications environments. Such an applied research base would link basic research in universities to applied research and development efforts in industry and government.
- Foreign efforts, particularly those in Japan but also national targeted efforts in Europe, show signs of movement toward such an applied software engineering research base.
- The Federal Government, through the Department of Defense, is making some efforts to create a software engineering applied research base for national defense purposes, but the applicability of this research base to the general problem of software productivity in the American economy is uncertain.
- It is difficult to differentiate software *production* activities from R&D, especially development. Much software production is a creative design effort. There are some aspects and types of programming that are clearly *not* R&D, but the dividing line is difficult to define.

Introduction

The term software refers both to the instructions that direct the operation of computer systems, and the information content, or data, that computer systems manipulate. Software is thus a logical rather than a physical product. An adequate organizing formalism or calculus for software creation has not yet been discovered.[50] Therefore, the development of large, complex software systems depends heavily on the insight and creativity of sys-

---
[50]"We are in a business that is 35 years old... and I invite you to think where civil engineering was when it was 35 years old... they had not discovered the right angle yet." Harlan Mills at the OTA workshop, Nov. 17, 1983.

tems designers and programmers. The methods presently employed to develop and test software are ad hoc, without a strong scientific basis. Thus, software systems are expensive to build and maintain, and can be unreliable in operation. The problems associated with inadequate software methods are growing as information technology uses spread and are relied on for larger, more complex, and more critical applications.

Research and development efforts have produced new methods that show promise for improvement in the productivity and reliability of software creation, testing and maintenance. These include *advanced program editors* and *debuggers*, new *languages, design methodologies* and *integrated programming environments*. However, the introduction of innovative techniques into software production is proving difficult. The adoption of new methods often requires the conversion of large existing program inventories. This is expensive and risky because evidence that one methodology is better then another is not systematically collected. As well, most software development is oriented toward the single project at hand and often relies on antiquated programming habits and attitudes. The high job mobility of programmers and software systems designers perpetuates individualism and fragmentation in software methodology.

The establishment of software engineering then, involves not only the development of superior methodologies, but a transformation of the programming process—from an *art* to a *science* and from a *labor intensive* to a *capital intensive* effort. The pressures on software production for larger, more complex, more cost effective, and more reliable systems, make the present situation untenable.[51] A concerted effort among researchers, educators, data processing managers, systems designers, and programmers, and support from corporate and Government management is required for this transformation to occur.

Software R&D Environments

Varieties of Software and Characteristics of Software Development

Software is classified as being of two general types: *applications software* that is designed to apply computer power to a specific task or tasks, such as computer-aided design of automobiles, or payroll or inventory management in a department store; and *systems software* that is used to manage the components of an information system itself, such as computer operating systems that control input and output operations.

In general, systems software is an integral component of the hardware because its job is to control the hardware, including the peripheral equipment—e.g., disk, printer, and memory usage, and to schedule and accommodate the creation and execution of applications programs. A recent trend, encouraged by the spread of personal computers, has been toward the use of standard systems software so that a large number of applications programs can be made compatable with hardware from different suppliers. The manufacturers of hardware or specialized software vendors write most systems programs, and more of the systems programs are being embedded in hardware—in programmable integrated circuit memory called ROM (Read Only Memory). Thus end-users now generally do not create or alter systems programs.

Much applications programming is done by users. For personal computers in homes and for supercomputers at the National Weather Service, programs must be written to tell the machines how to solve problems and organize

---

[51]"According to a projection made at an early 1981 data processing managers conference, Department of Defense software costs would increase nearly three times as fast as the department's budget, and nearly 20 percent faster than expenditures for computers during the 1980s." B. M. Elson, "Software Update Aids Defense Program," *Aviation Week and Space Technology,* Mar. 14, 1983, p. 209. Just as the explosion in numbers of telephone operators in the 1930s and of bank clerks for check processing in the 1960s forced a move to automated systems, the sheer demand for manpower in computer program-

ming seems to be increasing the pressure for the introduction of less labor intensive software development techniques; see T. C. Jones, "Demographic and Technical Trends in the Computing Industry," *DSSD User's Conference.*

Photo credit: Smithsonian Institution

Like software development is today, telephone switching was once a labor-intensive effort

information. Much of this work is done by highly trained professionals knowledgeable about computer systems and the problems to be solved.

Not all applications programming is software R&D. For example, an economist writing a short program to calculate a unique set of statistics that may never be used again or by others is not engaged in software R&D. Conversely, a physicist developing a program for a supercomputer to calculate formulas used in nuclear reactor design certainly may be involved in R&D. There is a large area in between these examples that is ambiguous, and no hard data is available concerning the time spent creating different catagories of programs. The Internal Revenue Service has faced this difficulty in defining the types of software work that are eligible for the R&D tax credit. Their proposed solution has been to consider the costs of developing computer software as *not* eligible for tax credits, unless the software is "new or significantly improved," or "if the programming itself involves a significant risk that it cannot be written."[52]

Software R&D in Industry

The information processing industry is devoting a large and growing amount of resources to software development. Purchases alone, currently some 12 percent of total spending for software, are expected to exceed $10 billion in 1984. Approximately 10,000 companies of various sizes, from one man operations to divisions of major corporations, are developing software for sale. Estimates of the total number of programmers in industry range from 500,000 to nearly a million,[53] and

---

[52]"Credit for Increasing Research Activity," *Federal Register*, Jan. 21, 1983, pp. 2799-2800. There has been considerable controversy over this issue. See W. Schatz "A Taxing Issue," *Datamation*, June 1983, pp. 58-60.

[53]ADAPSO estimates, and T. C. Jones, op. cit. p. 83.

the distinction between hardware and software developers is becoming increasingly blurred.[54]

Every major computer and telecommunications equipment manufacturer and service provider develops programs and software tools to make their products suited to the needs of users. Some firms such as Hewlett-Packard, reportedly spend nearly two-thirds of their R&D budgets on software.[55] More than 40 percent of the technical people at Bell Labs are involved with software development.[56]

Interest in the improvement of software productivity has led some large corporations to establish formal programs for the development and evaluation of software practices—to introduce scientific and engineering techniques into the evaluation of software development and use. AT&T currently employs approximately 300 Ph.D.s in software research, while IBM has approximately 150 and ITT has about 20 of these researchers developing and using formal experimental methods of evaluating software engineering techniques. Other large companies, including Control Data, Xerox, and Honeywell, are also beginning to use experimental R&D studies as the basis for improvements in software production.[57]

The Federal Role

The National Science Foundation funds university and some corporate research in software engineering. The NSF Software Engineering Program within the Division of Computer Research awarded $2.2 million in grants in fiscal year 1983.[58] Additional research related to software engineering is funded by other programs in the Computer Research Division (e.g., the Software Systems Science, Computer Systems Design, Theoretical Computer Science and Special Projects Programs) bringing the total funding to $5 million to $10 million per year.[59]

The Federal Government is the world's largest user of data processing resources. A recent GAO study found that 95 to 98 percent of the Government's applications software is custom developed.[60] The cost of software for the Department of Defense is estimated to be $4 billion to $8 billion per year.[61] DOD operates a patchwork of incompatable systems and computer languages.[62] The incompatability of software contributes to increased software development costs, through schedule slippages, lengthy testing programs, and problems in contracting for hardware and software services.

DOD has moved toward the development and use of a single standard computer language. The rationale for this is the potential for saving several hundred million dollars a year through lower personnel training costs, increased programmer productivity, and substantial reuse of standard code modules. After competitive development of four separate languages and extensive design evaluation, the Pentagon chose a language developed by the French company Cii Honeywell Bull. The name of the language, *Ada*, is trademarked, and compilers using the Ada name are strictly controlled and validated to assure that the language remains standard. Ada is expected to be the primary DOD computer language by 1987.

There is some resistance to use of Ada. Several years ago, the Air Force developed its own quasi-standard language, *Jovial*. Comparison tests between Ada and Jovial will continue for

---

[54]See, for example, S. B. Newell, A. J. De Geus, and R. A. Rohrer, "Design for Integrated Circuits," *Science*, Apr. 29, 1983, pp. 465-471. See also "The Changing Face of Engineering," *Electronics*, May 31, 1983, pp. 125-148.

[55]W. P. Patterson, "Software Sparks a Gold Rush," *Industry Week*, Oct. 17, 1983, pp. 67, 69-71.

[56]*AT&T: 1982 Annual Report*, p. 19.

[57]OTA workshop on Software Engineering, Nov. 17, 1983.

[58]*Summary of Awards, Fiscal Year 1983*, National Science Foundation, Division of Computer Research.

[59]Estimates by OTA.

[60]"Federal Agencies Could Save Time and Money With Better Computer Software Alternatives," General Accounting Office, GAO/AFMD-83-29, May 20, 1983, p. 1. Even standard applications such as payroll are largely custom designed. This GAO report found that there are at least 78 different Federal civilian payroll systems.

[61]Elson, op. cit., p. 209.

[62]I. Peterson, "Superweapon Software Woes," *Science News*, May 14, 1983, pp. 312-313. Testing of software alone is estimated to account for nearly half of this cost.

the rest of the decade.[63] The Army is more enthusiastic about Ada. The Navy, which has more software already written than the Air Force and Army combined, is interested, but the task of switching the Navy to Ada will be enormous. The Navy has over 450 different systems and subsystems with embedded computers, and the number of Navy computers has been doubling every 2 years.[64]

A limitation of Ada is that a new programming language only addresses about 20 percent of the total software problem. As detailed below, *coding* of computer programs is 20 percent or less of the effort of developing and maintaining software. Government computer systems in particular require an enormous amount of documentation, and Ada has no facilities for automated documentation.[65]

To deal with these problems of software design, production and maintenance, DOD has proposed a new initiative called Advanced Software Technology.[66] This is envisioned as a 10 year program costing $250 million.[67] The administration requested a funding level of $19.3 million in fiscal year 1984, but the Senate Armed Services Committee cut the program to $10.5 million because, "The Committee is not convinced that the necessary planning has been done to justify a budget of nearly $20 million in the first year."[68] Included in the plan, as it has thus far been developed, is a provision for a Software Engineering Institute to help formulate and standardize software engineering techniques and practices.[69]

Content and Conduct of Software Engineering R&D

Software engineering ideally is a set of concepts and tools for transforming descriptions of tasks to be performed by computer systems into digital code that machines can understand. Software engineering research involves the study of methods to understand, improve, implement, and evaluate these concepts and tools, and to embody them in *software development systems* or *programming environments* to facilitate the entire *software lifecycle.*

The Software Lifecycle

As can be seen in figure 10, there are several stages in the life-cycle of a piece of software. Each of these stages is characterized by its particular set of objectives and methods that influence each stage of research and expected improvements. Testing occurs continuously throughout the life of a software and is an integral part of software production and maintenance. Documentation, an activity not depicted in figure 9, is of preeminant importance in every phase of the software lifecycle. Comprehensive records of every activity and software characteristic must be created to aid designers, programmers, maintainers, and users in understanding the structure and operation of the software system.

Requirements Specification

This initial phase of software development involves the description of the system objectives and the tasks that the end users want performed. This description requires a thorough knowledge of the application by the software design project team. It is accomplished by rigorous and continuing communication between the project team and the end users.

OTA advisors and published sources emphasize that requirements specification is the most critical phase of project development, because all of the later stages must build on the foundation laid in this activity. At the same time, it is the most difficult activity in the software lifecycle to develop a rigorous method-

---

[63]J. Fawcette, "Ada Tackles Software Bottleneck," *High Technology*, February 1983, pp. 49-54.
[64]Peterson, op. cit., p. 313. It has been estimated that there are some 50 million unique lines of Navy software code in a variety of languages currently in use. It would cost, it has been reported, some $85 billion and take several years to rewrite this mass of code.
[65]The OTA workshop on Software Engineering, Nov. 17, 1983.
[66]This initiative is known within DOD as STARS, Software Technology for Adaptability, Reliability and Serviceability.
[67]Peterson, op. cit.
[68]*Omnibus Defense Authorization, 1984, Report to Accompany S.675*, Committee on Armed Services, U.S. Senate, p. 131.
[69]OTA workshop on Software Engineering, Nov. 17, 1983.

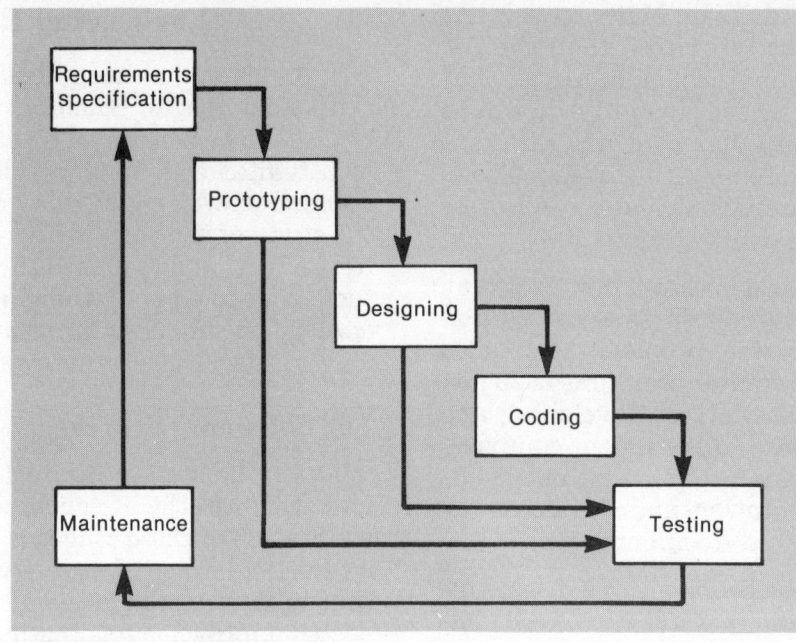

Figure 10.—The Software Life Cycle

SOURCE: *Data Communications*.

ology for. Requirements specification involves the understanding, explicit organization, and integration of what are often idiosyncratic practices of information usage. Often it is not possible to completely specify requirements at the beginning of a project; also, requirements can be expected to change over the course of a long software development project.

Computerized tools now available or under development may offer assistance in the specification process.[70] They are designed to help users describe and specify system properties, functions and performance requirements. Some of these tools allow the specifications to be checked by computer for consistency and correctness; some of them can generate simulations to help the user analyze the operation of a specified system. Thus far these tools have worked well only on a limited range of applications.

A difficult problem is specifying how the knowledge, experience and habits of workers in particular environments can be described and how these abstract specifications can be converted into machine code. Research is proceeding in *knowledge representation* and *knowledge engineering* (see Artificial Intelligence Case Study). Near term prospects are uncertain for identifying core concepts for organizing the different kinds of knowledge found in the variety of environments in which computers are applied, or designing broadly applicable *very-high-level languages* which can automatically render abstract specifications in machine-executable procedures.[71]

The experience now being gained in research and development of "expert systems," and the more fundamental research efforts in knowledge representation, machine learning and human cognition should eventually contribute to the process of computer systems requirements specification. But for the near term, this phase of software development will remain labor intensive and will require special skills (including human relations) and specific knowledge of applications among its practitioners.

---

[70]OTA workshop on Software Engineering, Nov. 17, 1983.

[71]R. Yeh, "Software Engineering," *IEEE Spectrum*, Nov. 1983, p. 92.

Prototyping

Once the project team has a working knowledge of the requirements of the software, a preliminary design of the final system is made so that the team can obtain feedback from the users. Thus, fine adjustments can be made at an early stage.

A software *prototype* can be as simple as a paper and pencil sketch that runs through the workings of the system, or as complex as a large and intricate computer simulation. The choice of prototype complexity is based on the nature of the application, the level of training and the sophistication of the end users, the size of the final software system, and the criticality of the application.[72]

Research and development of the prototyping phase involves the design, development and testing of methods and tools to make prototyping more understandable to systems designers and users, and more automated so that it is a logical and accepted part of software development. Research efforts in universities and industry are focusing on languages that make the quick production of prototypes possible, and on the design of man-machine interfaces to enhance and verify the effectiveness of communication between the system and its users.

The major issue in prototyping involves the acceptance of this activity and the awareness among system designers of its importance. Prototyping is commonly ignored in current software development practice because of its expense and difficulty and the lack of automated support. But experts contend that, in the long run, prototyping can save time and effort because changes to requirements specifications become more costly as each phase of software development proceeds.

Design

The design stage of software development involves the reduction of the software specifications to a set of *procedures* that can be programmed for the computer. The software design team analyzes the application and segments the design problem into subproblems or *modules* that can be programmed by individuals or small groups.

The segmentation or modularization of the software design breaks the problem into manageable pieces to maximize the ease of programming and testing the segments, and to facilitate the interchange or replacement of the modules to simplify maintenance. Proper segmentation is of particular importance because it has been demonstrated that as the size of the programming project team grows, more and more time is spent communicating among team members and coordinating communication among program segments and less in actually writing code. Thus segmentation has a crucial impact on the overall productivity of the software development team.

The design phase of software production relies heavily on the experience and intuition of the design team and is considered to be best learned by apprenticeship. Understanding of fundamental mathematical principles is also important.[73]

Research on the design phase of software engineering is embedded within the larger framework of R&D on "programming environments." The objective of software engineering is to provide as much support as possible for the creative designer. Facilities should be made available to ease the rendering of abstract principles and problems into workable, testable, reliable, and cost-effective solutions. Software design can be made more productive in much the same way that design of complex integrated circuits has improved: by the application of computer-aided-design (CAD) tools based on sophisticated graphics workstations. A number of companies are making significant productivity gains using CAD tools for software design.

---

[72]For example, air traffic control software requires extensive simulation, whereas an inventory system might need only a simple sketch and some text to check against user needs.

[73]*Data Communications,* op. cit. p. 81, and *Mosaic,* op. cit. pp. 4-5.

In the longer term, software design productivity could improve significantly through the expanded development and use of *software libraries,* or systems to store and access standard, reusable software modules that perform functions required in many programs. As now practiced, software design generally segments each program problem in a unique fashion, both to accommodate the unique features of new applications and to make the most efficient use of hardware. Program modules are usually not designed for reuse, and there is no strong incentive to do so because facilities are not provided for storing separate modules or for classifying and finding appropriate segments for new programs, and because the project development team is generally unable to spread the cost of creating reusable modules across a large organization. The result is that designers and programmers are constantly "reinventing the wheel" in software development.

Researchers in computer and information science have identified basic techniques and have designed tools to provide generic programming modules, data structures and algorithms, and to classify and organize them for storage and access. But the software community has been slow in adopting the facilities necessary to make software libraries work because of high initial cost, poor management understanding of such systems, and reluctance among programmers to modify long-established design practices.

Coding

Coding is the stage of software production that makes a procedural description of the system executable by computer. More emphasis has traditionally been placed on this activity than on any other, even though it is estimated to comprise only 15 to 20 percent of the total software development effort.[74] The reason for the traditional emphasis on coding is that it represents the basic mechanism by which programmers control the operation of computer systems.

Many tools are already available to programmers to help produce efficient and reliable code. The most familiar of these are the high-level languages such as FORTRAN, COBOL, and Basic that were designed to aid programmers in coding certain broad types of applications. *Compilers* translate high-level language into machine executable binary digital code. *Editors* and *debuggers* facilitate the entry, testing, and correction of code lines.

Research and development in the improvement of computer code writing continues. Innovations over the last decade include *structured programming* which greatly simplifies the tasks of testing and deciphering code during maintenance, and *new high-level languages* designed to be easy to learn and use or technically sophisticated (no languages yet introduced appear to be both simple and highly flexible).

A recent trend, that has proceeded hand in hand with the introduction of personal computers, has been the development of coding systems or languages that can give end users of computer systems more control—and remove the need for the help of a professional programmer for each application. An example is Visicalc.

Large companies, including manufacturers of mainframe computers, are interested in decentralizing the control of computer programming and use by providing software systems that are responsive to the needs of non-computer professionals. A proposed solution to the software bottleneck dilemma is to farm out some of the work now done by professional programmers to end users. IBM, for example, asserts that up to one-half of computer applications development can and should be handled by the end-users with personal computers.[75]

---

[74]*Data Communications,* op. cit. p. 58, and E. B. Altman, "Software Engineering," *Mini-Micro Systems,* December 1982, p.184.

[75]*Application Development in Practice,* Tech Tran User Survey, Xephon Technology Transfer, Ltd., 1983, pp. 53-54. Some experts consider this solution to be dubious, and believe that it may in fact merely spread software problems.

The proliferation of personal computers in the business world has some other possible implications, both for the process of software development and for employment patterns of professional software development personnel. End-users programming on personal computers could allow central data processing departments to concentrate their efforts on the larger, more complex, and more critical applications. A reduction in the backlog of small projects could also encourage the development of new large-scale applications that heretofor languished because of long waiting times. It is conceivable that the demand for professional programmers will slacken in such industries as financial services which have traditionally employed a large part of the data processing workforce in coding and maintaining applications programs. This could result from trends toward: 1) small-scale applications development by end-users with personal computers using commercially available software packages, and 2) increased use in data processing shops of standardized and automated software development tools, also commercially obtained, for large-scale projects. But increasing demand for innovative, off-the-shelf applications programs and software development tools suggests that demand for the *most talented* software designers will *increase* as competition intensifies in these expanding markets.

There is a secondary impact of the introduction of personal computers on software development. Upper management is becoming familiar with the problems and possibilities of software and computer use through experience with personal computers. Management awareness of and commitment to change in the software development process may be a key factor in introducing and accepting software engineering concepts and innovations.

Large and complex applications will continue to depend on the efforts of professional software designers and programmers. Thus, the introduction of automated tools and techniques such as CAD are imperative. Pressure will continue for more productive and reliable software engineering as the complexity of computer-based systems increases and as more of society's functions are entrusted to computerized systems.

Testing and Validation

An important activity in software production and maintenance is the testing of the products of the various phases of the software lifecycle. Until recently software development budgets included sufficient funds for adequate testing in only a few highly critical projects.

It is impossible, no matter how extensive the testing activities, to *guarantee* large software systems to be error free. A risk assessment based on the cost associated with software defects or breakdown in a given application must be made to determine the level of effort in testing that is justified. A rigorous testing regime can double the cost of software development.

There are many concepts, tools and techniques available and undergoing research or development for testing and validating software. They range from traditional methods such as manual "desk checking" or "walk throughs," to statistical methods to determine the probability of errors in a set of code, to some as yet highly experimental automated *program provers* that verify that properly structured programs perform as specified. The broad applicability of program provers will depend on some fundamental breakthroughs in program theory.[76] Until the requirements specifications and design stages of software development are better understood and supported, manual techniques will be the key testing methods available. Although some automated tools are in use, few exist as integrated packages. They must generally be pieced together by individual projects; and

---

[76]Some experts contend that the pursuit of formal verification methods such as program provers may prove fruitless because of the increasing complexity of software and the rapid changes in software development practices. See R. A. DeMillo, R. J. Lipton and A. J. Perlis, "Social Processes and Proofs of Theorems and Programs," *Communications of the ACM*, May 1979, pp. 271-280.

they themselves can become sources of high cost and errors.[77]

Maintenance

This is the phase of the software engineering lifecycle that is concerned with the revision of software that is in use. Software maintenance consists of two kinds of activities: correction of errors that went undetected in the course of software development and testing but that crop up in the use of the software; and changes in programs resulting from altered or additional requirements specifications. It has been estimated that 50 to 90 percent of current software costs involve maintenance. Some software systems may cost 25 times as much to maintain as to develop.[78] Because of poorly designed, badly written, and inadequately documented code, much of the maintenance programmers' time is spent trying to understand programs rather than changing them.

A solution to the maintenance problem adopted in many cases is to discard old code. This is because experience indicates that the "patches" made in programs when they are fixed or revised often increase the complexity and difficulty of maintaining code and make it inefficient to run. Therefore an average of 10 months worth of programming development effort is thrown away each year by mainframe based data processing organizations. Unfortunately, this old code is often replaced by poorly designed new code which again is difficult and expensive to maintain.

Poor requirements specification and design practices, idiosyncratic coding styles, and poorly organized documentation increase maintenance costs. Because requirements were vaguely specified or have changed, the design proceeded on assumptions that were false or later rendered invalid. Bad design assumptions lead to poor segmentation and structuring of programs which exacerbate the problems of making changes and testing. A change in one part of a poorly designed program will require changes in other parts of the program, multiplying the cost and time for maintenance. Novel coding of standard functions increases the difficulty of predicting the effects of changes. Large and cumbersome, poorly organized and incomplete documentation make it difficult for maintenance programmers to know what the system is supposed to do.[79]

Junior programmers with little experience are generally assigned to maintenance tasks, thus increasing the delays in bringing software back into use, and also perpetuating the knowledge and acceptance of poor programming styles and habits.

The Scientific Basis for Software Engineering

There are some well understood scientific methods that can contribute significantly to the improvement of software engineering tools and practices. The application of scientifically designed, experimentally based statistical methods for the evaluation of the effectiveness of software tools may produce the concepts and methods for at least an order of magnitude increase in software productivity.

In particular, in the critical area of human interaction with computers, a body of research methods have been developed in universities that, if widely and systematically applied, could identify, quantitatively assess, and produce improvements in programs for making computers more responsive and easier for people to program and use. Research in behavioral psychology and psychophysics is being applied to the design of computer systems and software engineering tools on a limited basis in a number of university programs.

The limited scale of commitment to *applied research* in software engineering may be a major reason for lack of dissemination and use of these well understood techniques. Acad-

---

[77]W. R. Adrion, M. A. Branstad, and J. C. Cherniavsky, "Validation, Verification, and Testing for Computer Software," *ACM Computing Survey*, June 1982, p. 183.

[78]Olsen, op. cit. p. 58.

[79]OTA advisors related that program documentation captures, on average, only 60 percent of the information needed to fully understand a program.

emics are generally involved in small-scale, *fundamental research* oriented projects that cannot test large size programs or a large number of possible software development aids. Some researchers suggest that applied research on a massive scale following the model of medical clinical trials is necessary to disseminate and make use of the knowledge embodied in available techniques.

Industry participation is an important ingredient in increasing the scope of experimentation because of its large and diverse software efforts. As a user of innovative tools and systems, industry must also be involved in the research so that essential feedback is provided to tool designers and evaluators. Inadequate appreciation of the gains that can be achieved in software productivity and a concentration on short-term results have made industry management reluctant, until recently, to make a commitment to large scale or long-term experimental software development studies.

As mentioned earlier, some large companies are becoming interested in applied software research and are hiring computer and human factors scientists to develop research programs. However, competitive and proprietary considerations and the uncertainty of software protection by copyright or patent appear to have inhibited an integrated applied research effort *among* companies. Antitrust laws may also have a chilling effect on industry based joint applied research.[80]

An alternative approach is for the Federal Government to use its software development efforts as a test-bed for software engineering research. Some moves in this direction are being discussed within the defense community, and the National Bureau of Standards has a research effort in software engineering in its Institute for Computer Science and Technology.

International Efforts in Software Engineering R&D

Japan

The Japanese have had a software engineering effort since 1970.[81] The Information Technology Promotion Association (IPA), a consortium of private companies and the government, together with long-term credit banks, provided $25 million in 1983 for software R&D and technology transfer. Current projects include: purchase or development of software packages for rent to users; a Software Maintenance Technology Project, to be completed in 1985, which is developing work stations for program analysis, documentation, testing, and production management; and a cooperative effort among users, suppliers, and researchers to develop computer-aided design, computer-aided instruction, and software engineering innovations.

A noteworthy aspect of Japanese software engineering efforts is the establishment of *software factories.* These are consortia, staffed by people from participating companies, which are creating integrated environments for software production, testing, and maintenance. Impressive programmer productivity gains are reported to have resulted from the average reuse of 30 percent of computer code in new applications.[82] Japanese software factories appear to owe their success in raising productivity levels, in part, to the fact that only restricted kinds of applications with fixed and well understood requirements are attempted. It is uncertain how effective these software factories would be on more difficult applications. Nevertheless, these concerted, cooperative efforts provide a test-bed for new software engineering concepts and tools in a well capitalized development and production environment. As well, they train people in the use of advanced software development techniques, serve as a dissemination mechanism

---

[80]Eleven major defense contractor companies recently announced plans to form a consortium for the pooling of efforts in software engineering R&D. The Justice Department has reportedly given the go-ahead for the development of a formal business plan patterned after the Microelectronics and Computer Technologies Corp. (MCC). M. Schrage, "Software Research Group Set," *Washington Post*, Oct. 10, 1984, pp. C1-C2.

[81]*Summary of Major Projects in Japan for R&D of Information Processing Technology,* prepared by Arthur D. Little (Japan), Inc., under contract to OTA, July 1983.

[82]Raymond Yeh at the OTA workshop on Software Engineering, Nov. 17, 1983.

when those people return to their companies, and raise management awareness of the importance and efficacy of software engineering. Thus software factories have potentially significant implications for future Japanese software development efforts on a broad scale, regardless of their impact on individual software systems.

Britain

As a part of the Alvey Programme for R&D in information technologies (see ch. 7), Britain plans to spend approximately $100 million over 5 years (1984-89) on software engineering R&D, which is approximately 20 percent of the total Alvey Programme effort.[83] Britain's traditional strength in software will be built upon, expanded and modernized to minimize dependence on software imports.[84] An initial focus of the Alvey effort will be the measurement of the cost effectiveness of software engineering through analysis of software imports and exports. Also, the program will track the capitalization of software development and analyze the relationship of capital intensity to programmer productivity. Efforts will be made to establish formal output measures for software cost and quality to help evaluate new tools and methods and to establish a system for software warranties.[85]

The software engineering effort will consist of three main thrusts:[86]

1. *Exploitation* of existing tools and methods, the transfer of technology from universities to industry, and increased investment in software production capital and in training.

2. *Integration* of tools and methods for the improvement of hardware and software development which will be focused in an Information Systems Factory.

3. *Innovation* in software engineering through increased levels of R&D aimed at developing new tools and evaluating their effectiveness.

The Information Systems Factory, to be established by 1989, is based on the premise that information systems' functional requirements may be written independently of whether a given function is to be implemented in hardware or software. Therefore, it is reasoned, the trend should be toward the design of modules whose uses are known in relation to other modules, such that the decision of whether to implement a function in hardware or software may be made on the basis of economic, time-scale and other cost-benefit criteria. The Information Systems Factory concept will evolve into the 1990s, by which time advances in fundamental research are expected to make possible a truly intelligent software engineering production environment with fully automated and integrated tools and a large library of standard function modules.[87]

The British consider the understanding of software engineering concepts to be too primitive at this point to make a final determination of a single direction to pursue to produce a fully integrated software engineering environment. Like those in the United States, current British research projects are too small in scale to adequately test software in diverse applications to determine the efficacy of new tools and methods. The Alvey Programme will fund several approaches for full-scale development, both to select useful techniques and to build technology transfer bridges between research, development, and production. In this context, the software engineering effort is expected to contribute to, and to benefit from, the parallel Alvey Programme efforts in computer-aided design for VLSI circuits and knowledge-based systems.[88]

---

[83] *A Programme for Advanced Information Technology: The Report of The Alvey Committee,* Department of Industry, Her Majesty's Stationery Office, p. 47.

[84] *Alvey Software Engineering—A Strategy Overview,* prepared by Alvey Software Engineering, Director D. E. Talbot, Department of Trade and Industry, p. 1.

[85] *Software Reliability and Metrics Programme: Overview,* prepared for the Software Engineering Directorate by the Center for Software Reliability, Alvey Directorate, Department of Trade and Industry, April 1984, p. 4.

[86] *Alvey Software Engineering—A Strategy Overview,* op. cit., p. 3.

[87] Ibid., pp. 5-7.
[88] Ibid., pp. 7-8.

France

Like the British, the French have been noted in the past for the quality of their software.[89] The major French R&D centers for software engineering are run by L'Institute National de Recherche en Informatique et en Automatique (INRIA) and the Centre National d'Etudes Telecommunications (CNET). Together, these laboratories employ approximately 100 researchers in software engineering and related studies.[90] In addition, 11 other French Government and industry labs are pursuing R&D in software engineering.[91]

---

[89]Three significant computer languages, Algol, Prolog, and Ada, were originated in France.

[90]*Research and Development in Electronics USA-France 1982/1983,* French Telecommunications and Electronics Council, March 1984.

[91]*IEEE Spectrum,* November 1983, pp. 64-65.

Case Study 4: Artificial Intelligence

Findings

- Artificial intelligence (AI) research seeks to make computers perform in ways that demonstrate human-like cognitive abilities: perception and action in complex situations and environments; interaction with humans in natural language; and common sense and the ability to learn from experience.
- The capabilities of artificial intelligence are often subject to exaggeration. AI has gone through several waves of optimism and disappointment as new fundamental concepts have been discovered by research, as new computational techniques and equipment have allowed these concepts to be tested, and as the limits of these concepts have been realized when applied to real-world or large-scale problems.
- In the last several years, the first real commercial products of about 25 years of AI research have become available. These systems are of three types:
  - *expert systems* that aid human experts in analyzing complex situations and in making decisions,
  - *natural language processing programs* that serve to make the interaction of humans and computers more natural, and
  - *image or vision processing systems* that can make robots and other automated processes more flexible in operation.
- Presently available AI technology is of value in only a limited range of applications. But the promise and potential have led to several national efforts to push AI technology forward.
- In the United States, AI research has been supported principally by the Department of Defense. Plans for putting artificial intelligence concepts to work in defense applications have recently been announced. These applications are far beyond the capabilities of any present systems.
- Basic AI research is conducted at a relatively small number of the nation's top universities by a small number of researchers. These researchers are under conflicting pressures from companies wishing to capitalize on the production of highly valuable systems, from students demanding training in AI, and from personal desire to pursue their own research interests.
- Only a few universities have the facilities and equipment to compete with industrial AI labs. Therefore some highly motivated researchers are drawn out of academia where they would be available to perform needed fundamental research and to train future generations of researchers.

Introduction

The goal of artificial intelligence (AI) research is to create systems that demonstrate some of the following characteristics: the ability to assimilate unstructured information and to act independently in complex situations; the capability of natural language interaction (e.g., in English) with humans; common sense, and the ability to learn from experience.[92] The possibility that machines may be made capable of such activities has burst into public consciousness as a result of the increasing power of microelectronics-based computers and their application in many new environments, the establishment of national efforts with the aim of creating intelligent computer systems, and the sudden emergence of some commercial products that embody characteristics of artificial intelligence.

Some experts contend that the ultimate aim of computer science is to produce intelligent machines. Just as the industrial revolution was driven by the urge to amplify human and animal muscle power with more efficient mechanical devices, the computer revolution is driven by the desire to amplify human intellectual power with electronic information machines.[93]

An expanding user population and the increasing diversity and complexity of the applications of current and planned information systems, are compelling designers to find ways to build intelligence into computers. Computers are increasingly being required to exchange information among people with diverse interests, backgrounds, and levels of computer sophistication, so they are being designed with software that permits people to interact with them in forms more closely resembling natural language. New varieties of sensors and increasingly diverse sources of information are providing input, thus computer systems must be more flexible to make use of information with varying levels of importance and confidence attached to it. Processing and output facilities are needed that present information in forms that are tailored to the unique needs of individuals, or that can control operations in complex and perhaps unpredictable circumstances.

The complexity of the environment in which the system is to operate is perhaps the most important dimension to be considered in the design of AI computer systems. As the number of environmental variables increases, and the number of possible responses multiplies, automated systems must exhibit increasing degrees of intelligence. Currently, computer systems are being designed for environments in which they will be required to resist confusion and error from ambiguous or contradictory input signals, automatically coordinate diverse activities under changing conditions, and provide logical and understandable explanations of their actions to operators.

The highest degree of machine intelligence might be the ability to automatically adapt to conditions that were not specifically anticipated by the designers. Such ability would require a machine to have "common sense," broad world knowledge from which to infer reasonable courses of action, and also the ability to assimilate new knowledge by learning, through self-organization of experience. Machines with this degree of intelligence are speculative, and attempts to push present AI concepts toward such capabilities illustrate both the difficulty of the problems, and the inadequacy of present concepts as a foundation for machine intelligence on a scale approaching the cognitive abilities of humans.[94]

There have been some notable recent successes in applying AI concepts to real-world problems. The introduction of a number of AI systems into commercial use has elicited a demand in industry for AI software that can make computer systems more responsive and productive. Three types of artificial intelligence products in particular are generating in-

---

[92] D. Waltz, "Artificial Intelligence: An Assessment of The State-of-the-Art and Recommendation for Future Directions," *AI Magazine*, fall 1983, pp. 55-66.

[93] For example, the Japanese 5th Generation Project is motivated by a belief that intelligent computer systems will be one of the cornerstones of a healthy economy and society in the later years of the 20th century and beyond. See T. Moto-oka, "Challenge of Knowledge Information Processing Systems (Preliminary Report on Fifth Generation Computer Systems)," pp. 3-89, and H. Karatsu, "What is Required of The 5th Generation Computer—Social Needs and its Impact," pp. 93-106 in *Fifth Generation Computer Systems,* T. Moto-oka (ed.), JIPDEC-North Holland, 1982, 287 pages.

[94] Some tasks requiring "intelligence" are already performed better by machines than humans, for example long division; other tasks may never be performed by machines. See Waltz, p. 55. See also M. Michael Waldrop, "The Necessity of Knowledge," *Science*, Mar. 23, 1984, pp. 1279-1282.

tense interest among industrial companies. These are: *natural language data base interfaces* that allow users to access information stored in a computer data-bank with English language queries; *expert systems* that aid people in complex tasks that require experience and detailed knowledge to perform; and *robot vision systems* that promise increased flexibility in manufacturing and other robot applications. Industry sees these systems as enhancements or potential replacements for rare and/or expensive human skill.

Similarly, the Department of Defense is interested in artificial intelligence to enhance the power, efficiency and reliability of increasingly automated computer-based weapons and command and control systems. DOD's new "Strategic Computing" program seeks to push the frontiers of AI science and technology for use in battlefield management systems, autonomous (unmanned) tanks and submarines, and automated expert assistants for airplane pilots.

There is concern, among both AI researchers and observers of information technology R&D, that enthusiasm about recent successes and fear of foreign competition are encouraging irrational expectations for artificial intelligence. These forces are drawing limited AI R&D resources toward risky, short-term development work, and away from some of the tough questions that AI research should and could answer. As Arno Penzias, Nobel laureate and Vice President for Research at Bell Laboratories has written about artificial intelligence R&D:

> A crash effort in any one area would inevitably pull talented people away from other areas ... whose payoffs to society might be even greater in the long run. Our challenge is to improve computers and extend their expertise into all the areas where people will need them and want them. We can best do that with a balanced program of research and development ... using knowledge to help create a society that provides a meaningful life for all the people in it.[95]

The sudden discovery of promise in artificial intelligence by society at large raises several questions. Of immediate concern are the questions of whether AI, as it is now understood, can meet industry and military expectations for performance, or whether there will be expensive failures in applying this technology, and by implication a casting of doubt on the entire AI enterprise, because present concepts are immature and limited; and whether the present educational structure, or some reasonable extension of it, can meet the growing demand for trained AI R&D talent. For the longer term, there is a question whether the progress of AI research can be sustained in the face of feverish commercial development, or whether the limited number of researchers will be drawn away from the study of fundamental and difficult problems and the teaching of new AI people. There are also profound questions concerning how artificial intelligence technology might be used, and how these uses might affect society in general, especially in terms of employment and the potential the technology offers to enhance or compete with human intellect.

Artificial Intelligence R&D Environments

The Roots of AI

The idea of automated intelligence has intrigued mankind for more than a century.[96] In the 1950s, two important figures in the early history of electronic computers, John von Neumann and Alan Turing, both expressed confidence that within a short time computing machines would equal or surpass human intellectual capabilities.[97]

---

[95]A. A. Penzias, "Let's Not Outsmart Ourselves in Thinking-Computer Rush," *Wall Street Journal*, Sept. 13, 1983.

[96]E. Charniak, "Artificial Intelligence—An Introduction," presentation at the 1983 Conference of The American Association for Artificial Intelligence, Washington, DC. One can conceive of artificial intelligence as the culmination of the *mechanistic* paradigm of scientific thought that has been dominant since the time of Newton. See *Science and Change, 1500 to 1700* by Hugh Kearney, McGraw Hill, New York, 1971, for a discussion of the emergence of the mechanistic paradigm. Some historians suggest that Man has always sought to represent and embody life and intellect in his artistic and useful creations. See J. David Boulton, *Turing's Man: Western Culture in the Computer Age*, (Chapel Hill) University of North Carolina Press, 1984.

[97]See J. von Neumann, "The General and Logical Theory of Automata," pp. 99 and 109, and A. M. Turing, "Computing

Improvements in the understanding of computation and knowledge organization coupled with advances in computer speed and memory capacity made possible through improvements in electronics, have encouraged intermittent waves of optimism that super electronic "brains" were just a few years in the future. Time and time again, these waves of optimism have ebbed in the face of a common problem. As the systems that researchers contemplate and build are required to deal with more information, and as the situations in which they are required to operate become more realistic (more perceptually complex and unpredictable), the fundamental computational principles and methods they have to work with become less efficient and impossibly slow.[98]

The term "artificial intelligence" was coined by John McCarthy in a grant application in 1956 to describe the subject of a conference that he was organizing.[99] This meeting, held at Dartmouth College, brought together researchers in different fields whose common concern was the study of human and machine cognition. The conference established AI as a distinct discipline, and also served to define the major AI research goals: 1) to design machines that think, and 2) to understand and model the thought processes of humans. Thus AI research is grounded in computer science and electrical engineering and also has its roots in cognitive psychology, linguistics, and philosophy. There is an appreciation among many researchers that AI is an interdisciplinary study born of the interaction of these two goals, and that the intersection of the separate traditions constitute what has come to be a core of concerns that distinguish artificial intelligence from other fields of science and engineering.[100] (See fig. 11.)

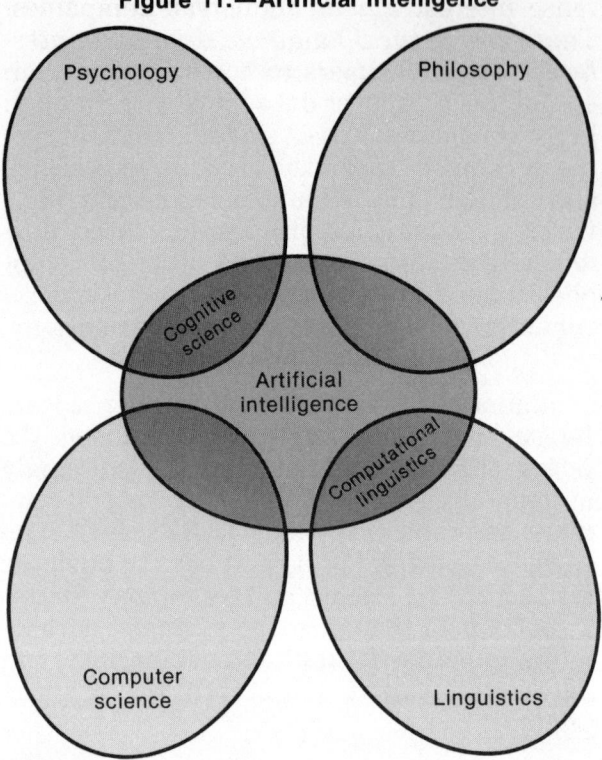

Figure 11.—Artificial Intelligence

SOURCE: Randy Davis and Chuck Rich.

As an esoteric study melding some aspects of computer science, linguistics, psychology, and philosophy, artificial intelligence research has grown up, for the most part, in an exclusive set of universities. Some industry-based research efforts at AT&T Bell Laboratories, Xerox Palo Alto Research Center, Bolt Beranek and Newman, and SRI International span more than a decade, but most of the work has been concentrated at Massachusetts Institute of Technology, Stanford University, and Carnegie-Mellon University, the leading research and academic centers offering a full range of AI subdisciplines. The concentration of effort and expertise in these top tier universities has tended to restrict entry into the field, and to foster a very tightly knit community of researchers.

Some years ago, AI research and training programs began to spread to a wider set of universities, and this expansion of academic programs continues. These schools have programs built around one or two graduates of

---

Machines and Intelligence," p. 245, in *Perspectives on the Computer Revolution*, Z. Pylyshyn, (ed.), Prentice-Hall, Englewood Cliffs, NJ, 1970.

[98] J. T. Schwartz, "Research in Computer Science: Influences, Accomplishments, Goals," *Report of The Information Technology Workshop*, R. Cotellessa, Chairman, National Science Foundation, Oct. 10, 1983, p. 18.

[99] Charniak, op. cit., p. 5.

[100] Nils Nilsson, "Artificial Intelligence Prepares for 2001," Presidential Address given at the Annual Meeting of the American Association for Artificial Intelligence, Aug. 11, 1983.

the established programs, and thus they offer only restricted AI curricula. Also, a number of new industry-based R&D programs are being formed. The newer industrial programs in AI R&D have also tended to center on the ideas of one or two researchers from the top schools. The lifespan of these industrial efforts may be limited if they are unable to draw in new talent from the small available pool and are unable to obtain infusions of new ideas.[101]

The difficulty of establishing and maintaining new AI R&D programs results from the fact that there is only a small base of existing researchers. Second, the nature of AI work is such that an interdisciplinary team is required in most cases to produce programs of useful size and complexity. This "critical mass" of workers knowledgable in AI concepts exists only in a few universities and companies and requires a number of years to pull together before fruitful work can be expected.[102]

OTA found that a major transformation is occurring in AI, resulting in two major directions for the R&D community. On one hand, fundamental research will advance theory. The other direction is taking existing AI concepts and developing their applications. As in other fields, the two directions reflect the divergence of interest between basic scientists and applied scientists or engineers (see fig. 12). However, AI is distinct from other fields that have undergone this transformation in at least four significant ways: 1) AI is a very young (scientifically immature) field, 2) there are few trained AI practitioners, 3) the expectations for the technology are high, and 4) the pace of transformation to an applied study is fast. The divergence of interests is expected to eventually result in the concentration of the traditional "top-tier" university centers of AI research on the fundamental scientific questions, an expansion of industrial R&D efforts to deal with the development of applications, and the establishment of new academic programs for the training of applied AI scientists and engineers.

The growing commercial and military importance of AI is forcing researchers to make difficult choices in how they spend their time. They must balance a number of commitments: to the study of research issues that have long-term significance; to the teaching and supervision of students;[103] to consulting for industry and government; and to startup companies in which they develop personal interests. To be sure, not all of these commitments are mutually exclusive. Long-term research and student supervision can reinforce one another. Consulting and entreprenuerialism can be complimentary. But the wearing of many hats by AI faculty may pose conflicts apart from the overcommitment of time.

First, there is a danger that students may be judged, consciously or unconsciously, on their contribution to the business interests of faculty, rather than on their progress in learning the science of AI.[104] Second, the progress of AI, as well as that of other sciences, is dependent on the free exchange and public dissemination of research results. Yet proprietary interests may inhibit that flow of information.[105] Third, many researchers face a conflict between the objectives of the sponsors of research and their own conception of the best direction for the research. (See ch. 6 of this report on New Roles for Universities.)

This latter conflict may be particularly acute among those in AI research because of the fact that the social implications of artificial intel-

---

[101]The OTA workshop on Artificial Intelligence, held Oct. 31, 1983. There is some controversy on this point, but it is generally agreed that some "critical mass" of AI trained people, working in close proximity where they can exchange ideas, is a critical factor in performing advanced AI work.

[102]Waltz, op. cit., pp. 64-65.

[103]One OTA advisor said that at his university, one quarter of the students now entering computer science and electrical engineering want to study AI. AI faculty across all schools are obliged to supervise, on average, some ten graduate students; in other fields the average ranges from less than one to about four. As well as teaching and advising, faculty must spend time writing proposals and seeking funding and equipment for graduate thesis work.

[104]MIT has developed a policy that prohibits faculty from supervising students that work for companies in which the faculty member has substantial interest. Patrick Winston at the OTA Workshop on Artificial Intelligence, October 31, 1984.

[105]This point was made by advisors at the OTA workshop on Artificial Intelligence, and is discussed by Jordan J. Baruch in an editorial in Science, Apr. 6, 1984.

Figure 12.—Artificial Intelligence Science and Engineering

Research Topics

SCIENCE

Knowledge representation	Expert Systems
Reasoning	Natural language systems
Cognition	Vision (image understanding)
Pattern recognition	Program development tools
Learning	

Motivations

| Challenging intellectual pursuit | Entreprenurialism |
| | Proprietary position/advantage |
| Relevance testing .... University-industry .... Technology |
| cooperation | transfer |
| More sophisticated .... Interdisciplinary .... Fine-tuned |
| concepts | R&D | applications |

Requirements

Peer review; exchange of results	Testing and standardization of tools
	"Critical mass" of trained manpower	Protection of intellectual property
Continuity of effort		Flow of new ideas

ENGINEERING

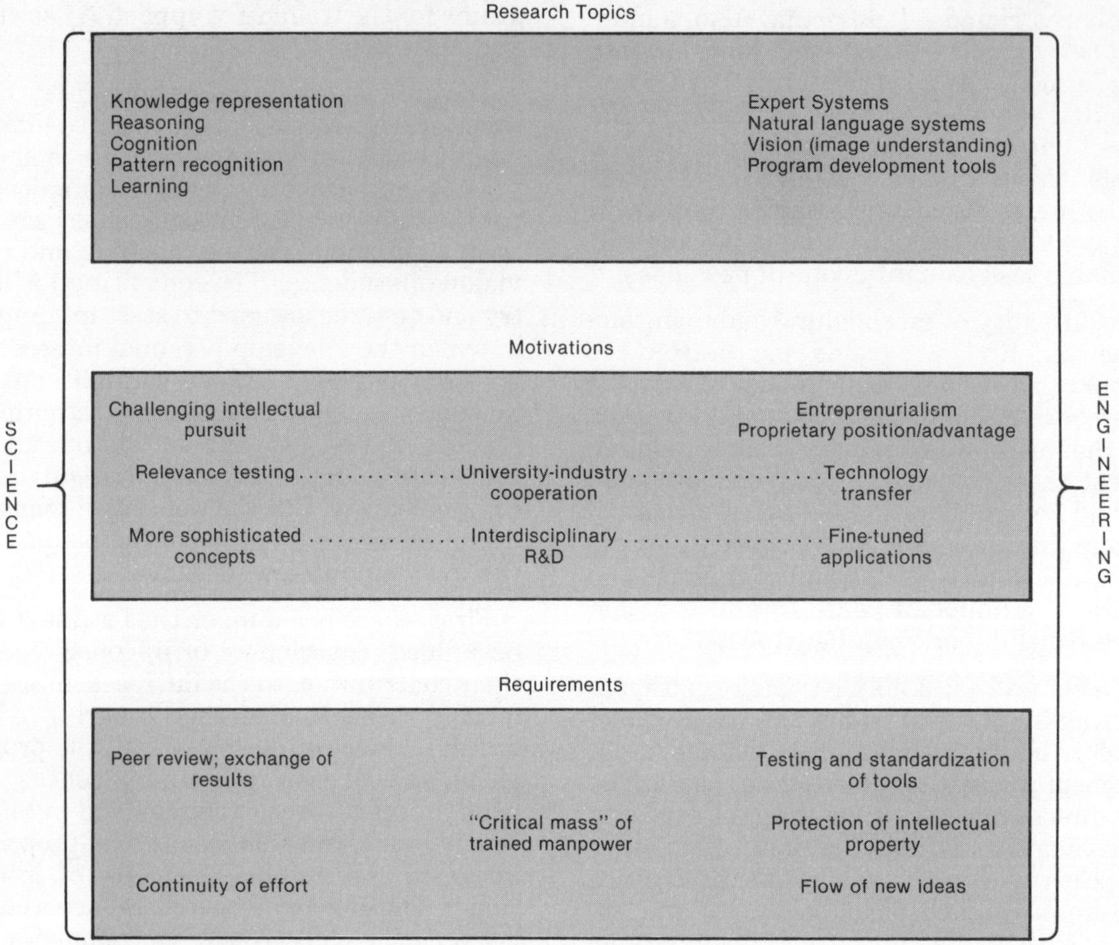

The evolution of the field of artificial intelligence is producing new relationships and new distinctions within the AI science and engineering community.

SOURCE: Office of Technology Assessment.

ligence are so profound. They include the replacement of humans with machines in skilled work, the increased reliance on automated systems and the risk of system failure, and affects on man's perception of himself, and his institutions. These conflicts raise ethical questions such as: how much responsibility do the creators of powerful technologies have for the social impacts of their creations? or, should scientists consider the public interest in deciding what research should be done?[106]

---

[106]The reader is referred to "Relations of Science, Government and Industry: The Case of Recombinant DNA," by Charles Weiner, ch. 4 in *Science, Technology, and the Issues of The Eighties: Policy Outlook*, A. H. Teich and R. Thornton (eds.), Westview Press, Boulder CO, 1980.

Until recently, artificial intelligence research was supported by four Federal agencies, primarily the Defense Advanced Research Projects Agency (DARPA) plus the National Science Foundation, the Air Force Office of Scientific Research, the Office of Naval Research, and a handful of companies. Now, significant levels of work are beginning to be funded in several corporations as the profit potential of AI grows. The Department of Defense plans to expand AI research in universities and defense contractor companies.

Industry Efforts

An increasing number of industrial firms have begun AI R&D efforts in the past few years. Market research sources report that industry spent a total of $66 million to $75 million in 1983 on AI products.[107] As many as 15 or more of the largest U.S. corporations are on the threshold of expanding the development of expert systems.[108] The Microelectronics and Computer Technologies Corp. (MCC) is devoting a fair amount of its early R&D efforts to AI related questions.[109] Three U.S. companies, Xerox, Symbolics, and Lisp Machine, Inc., currently offer computer systems especially designed for AI program development.[110] Four other computer companies, Sperry, Apollo Computer, Data General, Hewlett-Packard and Digital Equipment, are also developing AI computers.[111] Of most significance is the number of startup companies developing AI products, particularly expert systems.[112] At least a dozen firms have been founded in the past few years and they are obtaining people, techniques, and seed ideas from the top universities and from nonuniversity centers such as SRI International.

Government Funding

The Department of Defense is the lead agency funding AI research. The Defense Advanced Research Projects Agency (DARPA) established the three university "centers of excellence" at MIT, Carnegie-Mellon, and Stanford, and has awarded contracts since the early 1960s. The Office of Naval Research (ONR) and the Air Force Office of Scientific Research (AFOSR) have been funding AI work since the 1970s. The Air Force in particular is interested in AI techniques for image understanding. DARPA has proposed a significant expansion in its AI efforts (see "Strategic Computing" below). ONR and AFOSR funding is expected to remain stable in the near term.[113] (See table 19.)

The National Science Foundation has awarded grants for university and some industrial AI projects since the late 1950s. In recent years the NSF AI research budget has remained stable, between $5 million to $6 million annually. (See table 20.) Two NSF directorates, Computer Science and Information Science and Technology, provide the bulk of these funds, and a number of the awards (13 of 80 in 1983) are made jointly between these two divisions, or with the NSF Office of Interdisciplinary Research, or with other programs within NSF.

"STRATEGIC COMPUTING"

DARPA has embarked on a major effort to push the frontiers of computer technology and artificial intelligence for application in future military systems. The "Strategic Computing" program plans to spend $600 million over the next 5 years (see table 21), over and above past levels of funding, and spending will accelerate to unspecified levels as prototype development gets underway in the late 1980s. The project calls for the demonstration of significant mil-

---

[107]T. Manuel, and S. Evanczuk, "Commercial Products Begin to Emerge From Decades of Research," *Electronics,* Nov. 3, 1983, pp. 127-129. It should be noted that these numbers reflect a very broad definition of AI with which many experts would disagree.

[108]J. Johnson, "Expert Systems: For You?," *Datamation,* February 1984, pp. 82, 84, 88.

[109]See ch. 6, in this report.

[110]These so-called "Lisp Machines" (because they use the AI programming language Lisp) represent an estimated market value of $50 million.

[111]These machines are useful in many types of complex program development; nearly one-half of the sales of these machines, by at least one of the current vendors, are to users that are not necessarily developing AI applications. J. M. Verity, "LISP Markets Grow," *Datamation,* October 1983, pp. 92-94, 98,100.

[112]See Verity, op. cit. p. 94, and Kinnucan, P., "Computers That Think Like Experts," *High Technology,* January 1984, p. 42. One OTA advisor believes that venture capital will be a significant source of funding for AI R&D. At least $16 million has thus far been invested in startup companies developing expert systems, J. W. Verity, "Endowing Computers With Expertize," *Venture,* November 1983, p. 49.

[113]Personal communications from Dr. David Fox, Director of Mathematics and Information Science, Air Force Office of Scientific Research, and Paul Schneck, Head, Information Sciences Division, Office of Naval Research.

Table 19.—Major Government Sources of Artificial Intelligence R&D Funding[a]

	Estimates	
	Low	High
National Science Foundation	5.0	6.0
National Institutes of Health	3.5	4.2
Office of Naval Research	1.2	1.4[b]
Air Force Office of Scientific Research	2.5	3.0
Defense Advanced Research Projects Agency[c]	15.0	20.0
Total	27.2	34.6

[a]Sources indicate that these levels have obtained for the past several years, and with the exception of DARPA, are expected to remain stable or increase modestly in the near term.
[b]This *does not* include $900,000 in robotics research, some of which is in artificial intelligence.
[c]This represents the base level of DARPA funding *before* the initiation of the "Strategic Computing" program (began in fiscal year 1984).

SOURCES: NSF numbers from *Summary of Awards* publications of the Division of Computer Research, FY 1982-83, and the Division of Information Science and Technology, FY 1981-82 and 1983, National Science Foundation. NIH numbers from Susan Stimler, Director, Biomedical Research Technology Program, Division of Research Resources, National Institutes of Health. ONR numbers from Paul Schneck, Leader, Information Sciences Division, Office of Naval Research. AFOSR numbers from David Fox, Director, Division of Mathematics and Information Science, Air Force Office of Scientific Research, DARPA numbers from Ronald Ohlander, Program Manager, Defense Advanced Research Projects Agency.

Table 20.—NSF Grant Awards in Artificial Intelligence

	Fiscal year 1982	Fiscal year 1983
Number of institutions	41	38
Number of awards	67	80
Total awards granted ($000)[a]	$6,077	$5,150
Top 12 institutions:	(Dollars in thousands)	
MIT	946	240
Stanford University	485	587
Rutgers University	245	442
University of Maryland	351	317
University of Illinois	478	141
University of Pennsylvania	302	288
SRI International	302	202
New York University	360	130
Yale University	170	301
Carnegie-Mellon University	185	227
University of Massachusetts	87	229
University of Michigan	40	337
Total	3,951	3,441

[a]These numbers reflect the awards in each fiscal year and not the amount of funding during those years. Sixteen of the 67 awards made in 1982 were multi-year grants (most were 2 year grants); 5 of the 80 awards made in 1983 were multi-year grants. Therefore, total funding probably increased somewhat between 1982 and 1983.

SOURCE: Office of Technology Assessment, and the National Science Foundation, Divisions of Information Science and Technology and of Computer Research.

Table 21.—Strategic Computing Cost Summary

	Fiscal year				
	1984	1985	1986	1987[a]	1988[a]
	(Dollars in millions)				
Total military applications	$ 6	$15	$27	TBD	TBD
Total technology base	26	50	83	TBD	TBD
Total infrastructure	16	27	36	TBD	TBD
Total program support	2	3	4	TBD	TBD
Total	$50	$95	$150	TBD	TBD

[a]Out-year funding levels to be determined by program progress.
SOURCE: Defense Advanced Research Projects Agency.

itary capabilities within 10 years (see fig. 13).[114] The major areas of focus are:

- autonomous (unmanned) vehicles,
- pilot's associate systems to aid combat pilots in coping with the complexity of current and planned aircraft, and
- battle management systems to help commanders make decisions under conditions of uncertainty.

To lay the groundwork for the development of such systems, DARPA plans to fund the building of Galium Arsenide integrated circuit pilot production lines for the manufacture of low power and radiation resistant microelectronics. In addition, DARPA is focussing efforts on research and development of advanced computer architectures to meet the computational speed, and physical size and weight requirements of mobile systems (see the case study of Advanced Computer Architecture in this chapter), as well as artificial intelligence R&D in vision, speech, natural language, and expert systems.[115]

Some of the goals of the "Strategic Computing" program, particularly the vision system requirements for autonomous vehicles, have been described as "extremely ambitious."[116] Some describe this program as unprecedented in the history of U.S. Government funding of science and technology.[117] Unlike the Manhat-

---

[114]*Strategic Computing,* "New-Generation Computing Technology: A Strategic Plan for its Development and Application to Critical Problems in Defense," Defense Advanced Research Projects Agency, Oct. 28, 1983, p. vii.

[115]Ibid., app. IV, p. 2.
[116]Ronald Ohlander, at the OTA workshop, Oct. 31, 1983; see also *Strategic Computing,* pp. 22-23.
[117]Mitch Marcus at the OTA workshop, Oct. 31, 1983.

Figure 13.—Strategic Computing Program Structure and Goals

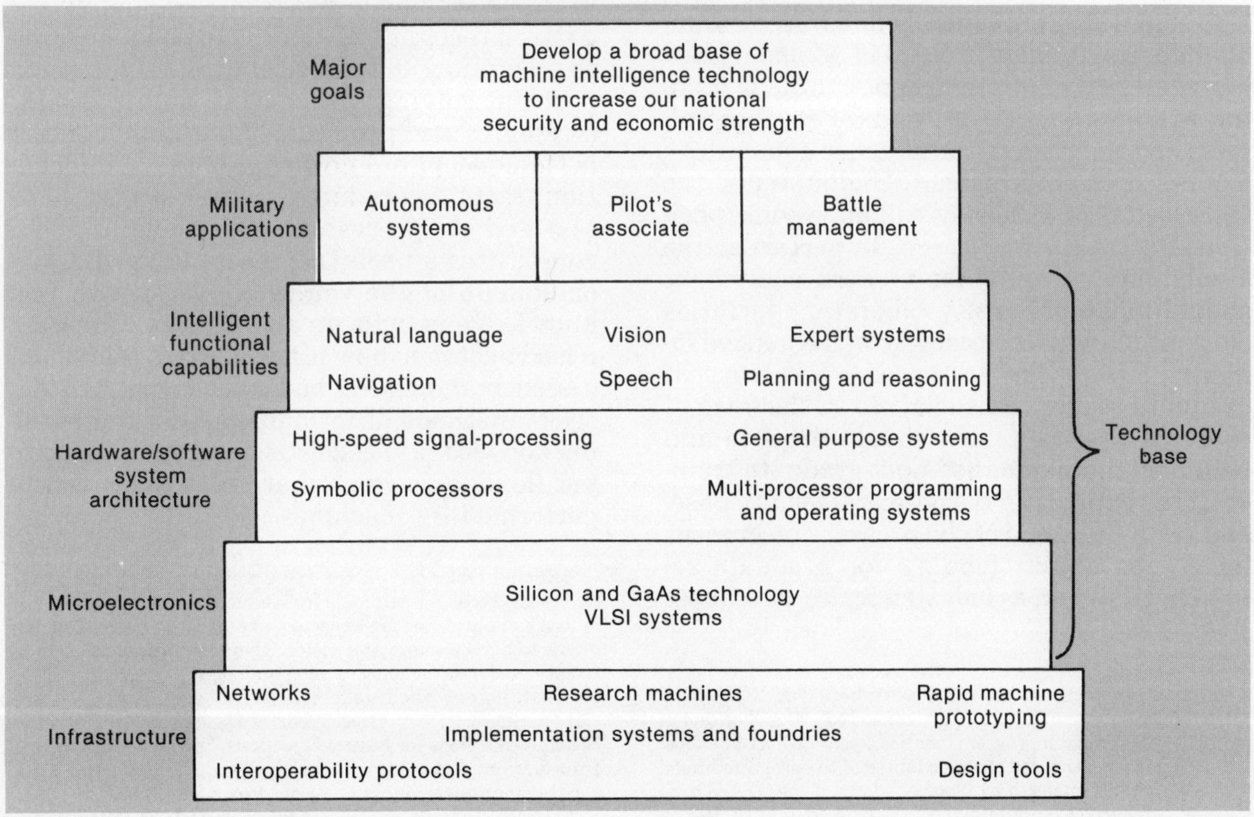

Major goals	Develop a broad base of machine intelligence technology to increase our national security and economic strength
Military applications	Autonomous systems / Pilot's associate / Battle management
Intelligent functional capabilities	Natural language / Vision / Expert systems / Navigation / Speech / Planning and reasoning
Hardware/software system architecture	High-speed signal-processing / General purpose systems / Symbolic processors / Multi-processor programming and operating systems
Microelectronics	Silicon and GaAs technology / VLSI systems
Infrastructure	Networks / Research machines / Rapid machine prototyping / Implementation systems and foundries / Interoperability protocols / Design tools

(Intelligent functional capabilities through Infrastructure = Technology base)

SOURCE: DARPA.

tan Project or the Manned Moon Landing Mission, which were principally engineering problems, the success of the DARPA program requires basic scientific breakthroughs, neither the timing nor nature of which can be predicted.

> The kind of work that is being done now [in AI research] that would support, for instance, an autonomous vehicle system, is primitive in relation to the problems that are to be addressed [by the DARPA project]. Operation in a complex combat environment that may have multiple targets with camouflage, different kinds of obstacles with varying degrees of threat and impedance associated with them, and the integration of various kinds of sensors, for example touch and vision, and the appropriate knowledge representation to deal with them, is an enormous problem that will be solved only by significant strides in basic AI research, and not just development in narrow vehicle applications.[118]

It is expected that the Strategic Computing Program will approximately quadruple the annual Federal funding of R&D in AI and related hardware.[119] This major increase in R&D funding will have significant and far reaching effects on the artificial intelligence community and research environment. Undoubtedly, the increased flow of money will have some positive effects on AI research. In particular the availability of funds for modern equipment should make university laboratory facilities comparable with increasingly well equipped industry labs.[120] The increased availability of graduate student financial aid in the form of research assistantships should draw in and help hold more qualified post-graduate trainees, thus expanding the potential faculty base, and relieving some of the pressure on current faculty to obtain funding for graduate research. However, as industry scales up to meet military requirements, additional pressures on the limited AI manpower resources are expected.[121] Although the expansion of training programs should eventually increase the supply of manpower, the rate of that expansion is limited by the small existing faculty base.[122] The current imbalance in the supply and demand of AI manpower will continue, and likely increase, and may intensify competition among commercial, military and academic AI R&D agendas. Thus some applied research, such as work toward "intelligent library systems" and computer assisted education, and fundamental research that is unlikely to have high immediate commercial or military value, may be neglected.[123]

Content and Conduct of Artificial Intelligence R&D

Artificial intelligence as a field is a set of somewhat loosely related R&D activities that range from the study and implementation of machine sensing (e.g., vision and speech) and pattern recognition algorithms and systems, to theoretical and practical work on automatic problem solving, inferencing and reasoning strategies and programs. Of central concern is the concept of knowledge, a set of information (facts, procedures, patterns) that is integrated and processable as a whole, and thus constitutes a useful representation of a part or domain of the world. AI deals with how knowledge is built up and used in computer-based systems: how it is collected, stored, accessed, manipulated, and transferred. AI R&D seeks methods of formalizing and representing knowledge in consistent and unambiguous, yet flexible ways so that these tasks can be performed by machines.

---

[118]Marvin Denicoff, at the OTA workshop, Oct. 31, 1983.

[119]From about $30 million to approximately $120 million (averaging the $600 million program over its 5 year projection). One DARPA source estimated that one-fourth of the program funds would be spent in universities. (Duane Adams at the OTA Workshop on Advanced Computer Architecture, held July 14, 1983.)

[120]This may be an inducement for researchers to accept research appointments.

[121]Ronald Ohlander, at the OTA workshop, Oct. 31, 1983.

[122]In the three AI subfields from which most commercial and military applications are expected, expert systems, natural language understanding, and vision, there are approximately 60 faculty at the top schools turning out some 30 Ph.D. graduates per year, half of whom take industry jobs. D. Waltz, "Artificial Intelligence: An Assessment of the State-of-the-Art and Recommendations for Future Directions," prepared for the NSF Information Technology workshop, Jan. 5-7, 1983; and a personal communication from Azriel Rosenfeld, Apr. 25, 1984.

[123]David Waltz at the OTA workshop, Oct. 31, 1983. A private funding organization, the Systems Development Foundation, is sponsoring research directed at "intelligent libraries."

Although investigators in a number of fields perform work that contributes to and overlaps with the subject matter of AI, a number of areas are considered the core of AI research.

Symbolic Computation

Since AI is concerned with the processing of knowledge, intelligent machines are required to manipulate symbols that represent objects, concepts, and qualities, as well as symbols that represent numbers or quantities, which are the focus of traditional computation. These qualitative symbols may be represented within a computer as logical relationships or as lists of symbols with pointers linking various objects, concepts, and qualities. The manipulation of symbols provides a mechanical means of achieving inference, in particular deductive inference, in which a problem solution or a conclusion is tested against facts in a *knowledge base* to determine its truth or validity.

A branch of AI research and development, which forms a link with R&D in advanced computer architectures, is the design of computing machines that optimize efficient manipulation of symbols. Some in computer architecture research maintain that this R&D effort has not received sufficient attention.[124]

---

[124]Sidney Fernbach at the OTA workshop on Advanced Computer Architecture, July 17, 1983.

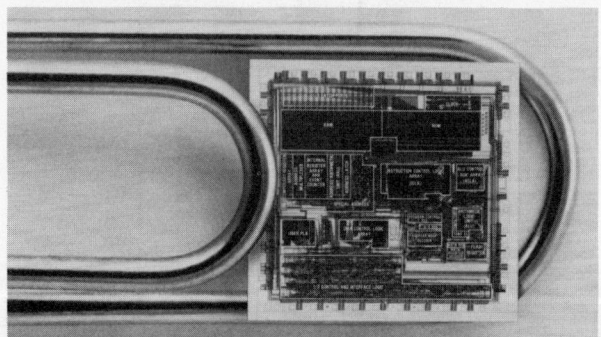

Photo credit: AT&T Bell Laboratories

Specialized microprocessors promise increasing levels of "intelligence" in computer systems

Pattern Recognition

Of particular importance to the branches of AI concerned with sense perception, such as machine vision and speech understanding, is the idea of matching input from the environment with symbolic representations of patterns (e.g., visual objects or speech utterances) stored in the system. Raw sensory input, in the form of electrical signals from a television camera or a microphone, must proceed through several levels of processing to produce patterns that are comparable with stored symbolic representations and recognizable as having unique meaning.

In general, these processing levels include:

- **Formation:** The sound or light signals are digitized and stored as a set of simple physical parameters such as frequency and amplitude.
- **Analysis:** Patterns of variations in the parameters, for example areas of light and dark in pictures or variations in pitch and intensity in an utterance, are detected and measured to produce a detailed physical description of the input.
- **Interpretation:** The patterns, now represented by sets of measurements, can be either directly compared with *templates,* stored descriptions of entire patterns, or further analyzed to extract *features,* which are parts of patterns that are of particular value in defining and identifying the patterns.

Knowledge Representation

This area of research deals with ways of expressing knowledge in computable form and making and exploiting connections among the facts or propositions in a knowledge base. A basic concept in knowledge representation is the *propositional formalism,* which is simply the structured way that facts are expressed so that ambiguities are avoided and processing operations are as efficient as possible.

As well as a formal structure or *syntax,* knowledge representation requires a method of capturing meaning, or *semantics,* in a knowledge base. Meaning in a qualitative sense is expressed by the relationships that are stated to exist among concepts. One method of representing relationships is the *Semantic Network* (see fig. 14).

A knowledge representation scheme that is similar to semantic networks has been developed in which the *attributes* of concepts are expressed and related. *Frames* provide slots to fill to structure knowledge about things, thus they represent expectations about what attributes members of a given frame will possess. These "expectations" can be exploited to imply procedures. For example, a computer can be programmed to inquire about the attributes of a newly introduced object.

Similarly, knowledge representations called *scripts* can represent expectations about a knowledge domain. But instead of representing concepts, scripts describe *situations* and *actions* that are expected in those situations. A classic example is a restaurant script in which one expects people to order from a waiter (or waitress), to eat, and to pay the bill. Thus, invoking the restaraunt script would invoke the entire set of expectations surrounding restaurants that have been programmed.

Another knowledge representation scheme, one that was developed in the mid-1960s, is the *production system.* This essentially consists of a set of *if-then rules* that specify a pattern, for example, "if the temperature is less than 65 degrees" and an action to be taken, "then turn the furnace on." The importance of this scheme is its ability to express *procedural knowledge* and to initiate operations depending on prevailing conditions. Its major weakness is that a fixed rule must be stated for every condition that is to be encountered.

Figure 14.—A Semantic Network

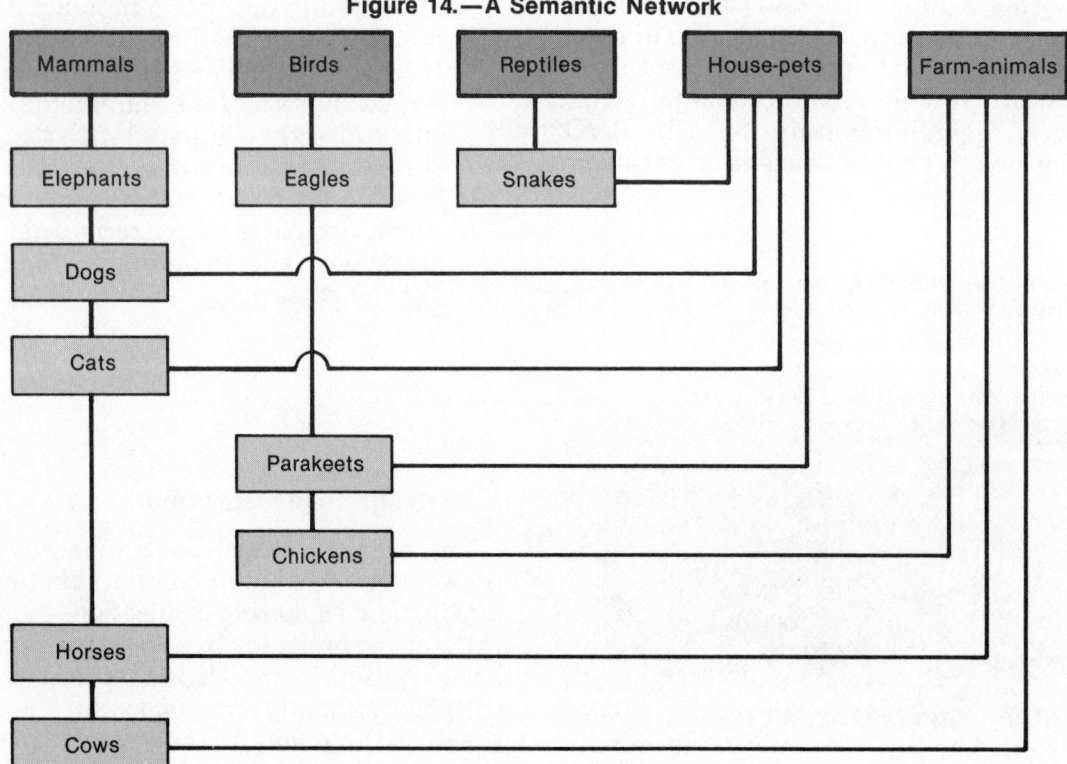

SOURCE: Randy Davis and Chuck Rich.

All of the knowledge representation schemes thus far adopted by AI reseachers use considerable computer memory if they contain a sizable or complex domain of knowledge. Traditionally, researchers and builders of programs have had to "shoe-horn" knowledge into computer systems with limited and expensive memory capacity. The precipitous decline in the cost of computer memory is alleviating some traditional AI problems, making possible for the first time the production of cost-effective systems with enough knowledge to tackle "real-world" problems. Advances in computer architecture design, especially the ability to make customized VLSI processors dedicated to symbolic computation and capable of parallel processing, should have a great impact on the kinds of problems that may be addressed by knowledge-based systems.

Other difficulties inherent in the application of existing knowledge representation schemes will not necessarily be alleviated by lower memory costs and advances in hardware capability because they involve the limitations of the schemes themselves. Existing knowledge representations deal only with *surface knowledge,* which is either explicitly stated in relationships or deductively inferred by the chaining of propositions. *Deep knowledge,* knowledge gained from inductive inference (reasoning from facts to general principles), and *commonsense knowledge* that is routinely learned by children through experience, are not expressable using current knowledge representation systems. Other problems involve the inflexibility of procedural knowledge and the difficulties of programming machines to reason about unforseen occurances.

Given the large collection of facts, relations and patterns in a useful size knowledge base, even the fastest computers can bog down. Therefore, an AI program must concentrate the search of its knowledge base on those portions that are most likely to hold the facts, patterns, or solutions that are needed in a given situation. The problems associated with the search of knowledge bases are ubiquitous in AI. They result from what is termed the "combinatoric explosion": as the size of a knowledge base increases, the number of possible paths to a sought-after piece of information increases exponentially. AI interest was originally in developing *general knowledge* AI systems, but the combinatoric explosion sets a limit on how broad or useful such systems can be. More recent work has focused on specific problem domains where a detailed representation of the world can be built and exploited, and where the search is controlled by *knowledge about the problem domain*, or heuristics.

Machine Learning

The study of *heuristics* ("rules of thumb" or knowledge acquired from experience), how they may be used to process knowledge, and how they may be generated automatically by computer systems are major pursuits of AI research. Ideally, a computer could modify its repertoire of procedures as new facts are added to its knowledge base. Likewise, new procedures should suggest new relations among facts, but current knowledge representation and programming techniques are incapable of supporting changing knowledge and rule bases.

Commonsense Knowledge

Human knowledge is based on a wide range of experience acquired through sense organs. This experience is fed into a cognitive system that can integrate that knowledge in order to cope with a complex, dynamically changing world. Much of what people know involves relationships that are obvious but that depend on explanations beyond the comprehension of most. Representing commonsense knowledge in computer systems is a major challenge to researchers, and is essential for certain kinds of intelligent machine behavior, such as reasoning about the chronology of events in the course of a disease or reasoning about the movement and characteristics of robots.

Pragmatic Knowledge

Current artificial intelligence systems employ syntax (structure) and semantics (meaning) to represent knowledge about the domains in which they operate. Systems of higher intelligence, ones capable of choosing among a range of responses in complex situations, of adapting to changing (and unanticipated) conditions, and of interacting with humans and perhaps other intelligent systems on a high level of understanding, must employ ways of representing and reasoning about the *needs of users* and about *knowledge itself*. Truly intelligent machines would respond to people of different backgrounds and needs in ways that are appropriately tailored to individuals. They would also possess an understanding of the uses and limits of knowledge—a mechanism for judging the appropriateness of information to a given situation. For example, a robot tank would need to be able to distinguish between trees it could run over and those that it would have to avoid.

Current syntax- and semantics-based artificial intelligence systems employ knowledge representations that are inadequate to support *pragmatic* knowledge. Frame- and script-based representations can, in a rudimentary way, deal with expectations about situations, but those situations must be tightly circumscribed and clearly defined at the time of program design. Research has yet to identify knowledge representation schemes that can support the processing of pragmatic knowledge in complex and dynamically changing domains.

Commercially Available Artificial Intelligence

Notwithstanding the fundamental limitations of present artificial intelligence concepts, programs are being developed that are proving useful in a widening array of applications. Two market forecasts[125] describe the commercial potential of AI systems as exploding over the next decade. From the small 1983 sales base of $66 million to $75 million, the market for AI products is expected to rise to $2.5 billion to $8.5 billion by the early 1990s.[126] The changing mix of products and sectors in which they will be used is depicted in figure 15, which shows AI emerging from the laboratory into the home, the factory, and into schools. Three types of AI-based systems in particular are expected to experience rapid growth—vision systems, natural language understanding systems, and expert systems.

COMPUTER VISION SYSTEMS

Vision systems are being designed as input subsystems to enhance the utility and flexibility of computer-based automation. Vision systems are increasingly used in industry for quality control inspection, for product identification, and for robot guidance and control.[127] Machine vision will be a crucial function in many future automated systems, including aspects of the DARPA "Strategic Computing" initiative. For example, an advanced vision system will be an integral component of autonomous vehicles.

Some sources estimate a current annual market for machine vision systems of $35 million. This market is projected to double each year for the next 5 years, and should reach about $1 billion by the end of the decade.[128] More than 250 companies, most of them in the United States, are designing and selling machine vision systems.[129]

Vision systems consist of cameras and computer processors to analyze and interpret the information collected by the cameras. The cameras provide the processor with frames, typically 60 per second, collected by scanning the camera's visual field. A frame forms an image consisting of a matrix of dots, or pixels (picture elements), numbering in current systems 64 X 64 or 256 X 256 pixels. Higher resolution cameras are being developed, but as the resolution (number of pixels per frame) increases, higher speed processors are needed to handle the increased information within rea-

---

[125]International Resource Development, Inc., and DM Data, Inc.
[126]Manuel and Evanczuk, op. cit., pp. 127 and 129.

[127]The reader is referred to the OTA report, *Computerized Manufacturing Automation: Employment, Education, and the Workplace*, April 1984, pp. 89-92, for a discussion of current industrial applications of machine vision systems.
[128]"Machines That Can See: Here Comes a New Generation," *Business Week*, Jan. 9, 1984, pp. 118-120.
[129]Ibid., p. 118.

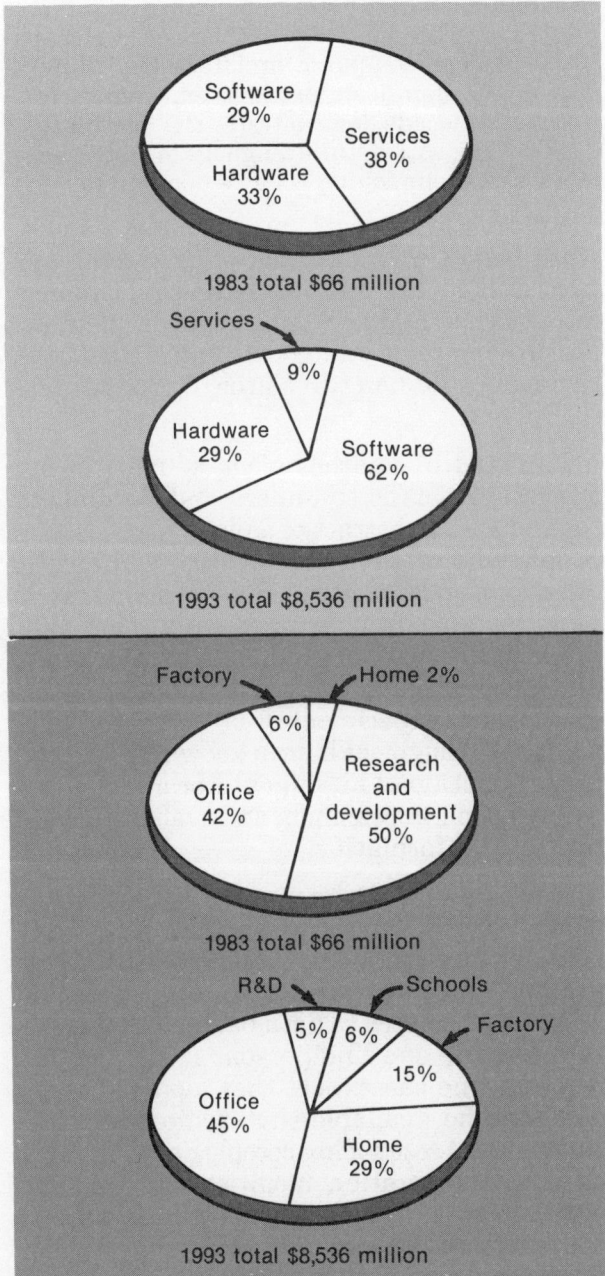

Figure 15.—Markets for Artificial Intelligence

1983 total $66 million
- Software 29%
- Services 38%
- Hardware 33%

1993 total $8,536 million
- Services 9%
- Hardware 29%
- Software 62%

1983 total $66 million
- Factory 6%
- Home 2%
- Office 42%
- Research and development 50%

1993 total $8,536 million
- R&D 5%
- Schools 6%
- Factory 15%
- Home 29%
- Office 45%

SOURCE: International Resource Development Inc.

sonable time limits.[130] Each pixel represents an area of light or dark in the image. Most systems allow a pixel to represent only black or white, though systems are being developed and are in use in which pixels may be one of as many as 64 shades of gray, and color vision systems will soon be available. Gray scale and color systems will be capable of higher acuity, but such systems require much higher processor speed and more sophisticated algorithms to interpret the increased information flow.

The processor analyses the image to extract patterns that may represent edges or textures that can be used to characterize and recognize objects in the visual field. Simpler systems have stored "templates," or representations of entire objects, in memory to which the extracted patterns are compared. More sophisticated systems store "features," or characteristic parts of objects. In these systems, sets of features are extracted from the image and are combined to represent constraints on the list of possible objects that may be present; recognition involves the identification of an object (or objects) that could satisfy those constraints.

A major problem in machine recognition is inferring three-dimensional information from two-dimensional information in an image of the scene.[131] One method that has been adopted to solve this problem is to project "light stripes" on objects in the scene; depth cues and contours can be inferred from distortions in the stripes.

Current vision systems are primitive in comparison to human visual recognition capability. The human retina can perform at least 10 billion operations per second, and the brain is undoubtedly capable of much higher processing speeds.[132] As important, human experience with the visual world provides a store of knowledge with which the eye and brain may make inferences and interpretations to resolve

---

[130] A Stanford University researcher has developed a robot cart that can navigate in a simple environment at a speed of 3 to 5 meters per hour while analyzing one image of its surroundings for each meter of progress using a computer capable of processing a million instructions per second. For such a system to naviagate at walking speed would require a computer capable of from 10^9 to 10^{10} instructions per second. T. Kanade, and R. Reddy, "Computer Vision: The Challage of Imperfect Inputs," *IEEE Spectrum*, November 1983, pp. 88-91. Computers of this speed are being developed, but may require facilities as large as a room just to provide cooling for the hardware.

[131] Azriel Rosenfeld, personal communication, May 25, 1984.

[132] Kanade and Reddy, op. cit., p. 88.

ambiguities caused by shadows and variations in lighting, the orientation of objects, and the presence and often overlap of multiple objects in a scene. Also, subtle variations and movements can be detected and used by the human eye and brain to distinguish superficially similar objects (e.g., the faces of identical twins).

In order to make vision systems based on current processor architectures and algorithms work, the number of environmental variables that may cause ambiguities must be reduced. For example, objects on an assembly line may be arranged so that only one face is presented to the camera or only one object at a time is in the visual field. Lighting may be controlled so that perceived edges can be interpreted as facets of an object and will not be the result of shadows or variations in the reflectance of surfaces of an object; or structured lighting may be used to infer distance and contour.

If vision systems are to operate in less controllable circumstances, such as out-of-doors or in the home, much higher speed processors and more sophisticated algorithms for analyzing and interpreting visual scenes will be needed. Custom designed, massively parallel VLSI-based processors dedicated to visual analysis are being looked to to provide more powerful hardware. Research in vision algorithms is proceeding to provide more powerful concepts and more sophisticated software. The parallel advance of hardware and software solutions, and fundamental advances in AI research, will be required to produce systems capable of the interpretation of complex and unstructured visual scenes.

NATURAL LANGUAGE UNDERSTANDING SYSTEMS

These systems are intended to allow communication with computers in English or other human languages, freeing users from the need to learn a computer language. In the words of one researcher:[133]

> The ultimate goal of creating machines that can interact in a facile manner with humans remains far off, awaiting breakthroughs in basic research, improved information processing algorithms, and perhaps alternative computer architectures. However, the significant progress experienced in the last decade demonstrates the feasibility of dealing with natural language in restricted contexts, employing today's computers.

Automatic natural language understanding work began with the goal of producing systems that could translate one natural language into another. Such systems are in use now, but are proving to be limited to rough translation, requiring a human translator to produce final fluent text.

The goal of another class of natural language systems is to understand documents: to produce an abstract of a piece, perhaps alert people who might be interested, and answer questions on its content. Such systems might be paired with document generators that could produce instruction manuals.[134] Document understanding and generation systems are still largely experimental, but they have the potential to augment human knowledge through the production of intelligent library systems, aiding people in searching and evaluating large bodies of information.

More immediate-term applications are in using natural language systems as "frontends" or interfaces to computer systems. Natural language systems are in operation that serve as interfaces to data bases, for example, to help store and find personnel or inventory records. One can expect that model systems will soon be available that demonstrate the feasibility of controlling complex systems such as power generation facilities and weapons systems with natural language interfaces. In conjunction with expert systems, natural language systems are being developed for computerized medical advisor, trouble-shooting and repair, mineral exploration, and investment analysis applications. Future applications, requiring advanced work to produce, might include use in the creation of graphical displays and in computer-aided education.[135]

---

[133]Waltz, *AI Magazine*, op. cit., p. 56.

[134]Ibid., p. 57.
[135]Ibid.

There is also current work in producing *speech understanding* systems, which would replace keyboards with voice input devices. Primitive systems are available, but true *speaker independent* systems with large vocabularies that can handle *continuous speech,* as opposed to isolated words separated by pauses, are as yet unattainable with present technology. Advanced integrated circuit signal processors should produce some progress over the next decade.[136]

In part, the capabilities of natural language systems have been limited by the cost of computer memory. Natural language systems must have large vocabularies to be "natural" to users. This problem is diminishing because of the fall in computer memory prices.

Two other problems are replacing memory cost as an upper limit to system size and functionality. First is the "combinatoric explosion" problem: as the size of the system vocabulary increases, the time required for presently available computer architectures to process a sentence increases exponentially. Novel machine architectures based on parallel processing promise some relief for this problem. Second, as noted in the previous discussions of commonsense reasoning and pragmatic representation, researchers are finding difficulties in designing systems with broad and deep knowledge of the world, and with pragmatic understanding of situations. In language, this kind of knowledge is crucial to the solution of ambiguities.

EXPERT SYSTEMS

These AI-based programs are designed to serve as consultants in decisionmaking and problem solving tasks that require the application of experience and judgment.[137] Expert systems consist of a set of "if-then" rules which express the knowledge and experience of an expert, and the actions one would take when faced with a set of conditions in the domain of his expertise. They also generally have a separate knowledge base which states facts about the domain, to which the program can refer to make inferences and deductions about given situations and conditions.

Expert system programs are developed from extensive interviews with recognized experts in the field of application. Such interviews often reveal many unwritten (and even unconscious) rules and criteria for judgment that the expert applies in solving problems.[138] The interviewer, called a *knowledge engineer,* then codes the rules and facts in a way that is efficiently processable by computer. Extensive testing and validation must be conducted before a system is considered complete enough to use in actual practice.

This area of AI application is receiving considerable industry and military interest because expert systems may be capable of relieving some of the demand for high-priced experts in the fields in which they are applied. Ironically, because they require man-years of effort from scarce knowledge engineers to develop, expert systems are quite expensive. Therefore they are currently being attempted commercially only in applications that promise a particularly high payoff.[139]

Research in this field has demonstrated that expert systems can rival human expert judgment *if the domain of application is properly*

---

[136]For discussions of the state-of-the-art in voice input computer systems, the reader is referred to: A. Pollack, "Computers Mastering Speech Recognition," *New York Times,* Sept. 6, 1983, pp. C1 and C7; R. D. Preuss, and D. J. Jurenko, "Digital Voice Processing," *Astronautics and Aeronautics,* January 1983, pp. 44-46; and R. J. Godin, "Voice Input Output," *Electronics,* Apr. 21, 1983, pp. 126-143.

[137]Expert systems illustrate an interesting point about human intelligence, "Paradoxically, it has proven much easier to emulate the problem-solving methods of some kinds of specialists than to write programs that approach a child's ability to perceive, to understand language, or to make 'commonsense' deductions," R. O. Duda, and E. H. Shortliffe, "Expert Systems Research," *Science,* Apr. 15, 1983, pp. 261-268.

[138]This fleshing out of unwritten rules is a possible side benefit of the development of an expert system; it can lead to progress in the field of application itself. Conversely, some fear that this codification of knowledge in automated systems could "ossify" and constrain progress in certain fields by foreclosing the possiblity of the unexpected discovery of new solutions through serendipity.

[139]Some of the enthusiasm recently demonstrated by companies for expert systems may be unfounded; OTA advisors were wary of overstated claims for the usefulness and applicability of current generation expert systems.

chosen.[140] This means that the application must have certain characteristics for an expert system to be successfully applied. These include:[141]

- There must be recognized experts in the field;
- The task normally takes the expert a few minutes to a few hours to accomplish;
- The task is primarily cognitive (as opposed to manual);
- The skill is teachable to neophytes;
- The task requires no commonsense.

More generally, the application domain must be restricted enough to be expressable in a finite set of rules, numbering less than 2,000 at present, so that available computers can solve problems in a reasonable amount of time. Even so, most current expert systems take longer to perform a task than a competent human expert.[142]

Table 22 shows a representative sample of current expert systems and their uses. Several companies are forming or expanding efforts in developing expert systems, and venture capital interest in startup companies is reportedly brisk.[143]

Current systems, because of the limitations of the concepts on which they are based, all suffer from several serious weaknesses:[144]

- They are highly customized to specific applications and are useless in other, even closely related fields;
- Since the knowledge on which they are based is collected over a period of time, often from a number of experts, there can be inconsistencies in the programs that are difficult to detect and repair;
- The systems are necessarily based on narrow sets of rules and facts, therefore their judgments and recommendations can be myopic and naive;
- Since all of the current systems contain only surface knowledge from which to make inferences, if knowledge that is critical for a given judgment is missing, their performance is poor;
- Few current systems have natural language interfaces, therefore they can be difficult for the uninitiated to use.

Although many systems can provide explanation for the chain of reasoning that led to a given conclusion, these explanations are often unsatisfactory because they are not tailored to the needs or understanding of individual users. Neither do the explanations usually refer to underlying principles, such as physiology or geology, so human experts find them unconvincing.[145]

---

[140]In fact, one OTA advisor said that the success of current applications depends more on the choice of domain than it does on how well the program is written. Patrick Winston at the OTA workshop, Oct. 31, 1983.

[141]R. Davis, and C. Rich, *Expert Systems: Fundamentals,* Tutorial at the AAAI Conference, Aug. 22, 1983, p. 31.

[142]Waltz, *AI Magazine,* op. cit., p. 61.

[143]See *Electronics,* Nov. 3, 1983, pp.127-131, and *Venture,* November 1983, pp. 48-53.

[144]Waltz, op. cit.

[145]Duda and Shortliffe, op. cit., p. 266. See also G. O. Barnett, "The Computer and Clinical Judgement," editorial in *The New England Journal of Medicine,* Aug. 19, 1982, pp. 493-494.

Table 22.—Representative Expert Systems

Expert system	Domain	Type of evaluation	Routine use
DENDRAL	Mass spectroscopy interpretation	Case studies	Yes
MYCIN	Antimicrobial therapy	Randomized trials	No
INTERNIST-1	Internal medicine diagnosis	Case studies	No
CASNET	Glaucoma assessment and therapy	Case studies	No
PROSPECTOR	Geological exploration	Case studies	No
R1	Computer layout and configuration	Case studies	Yes
Digitalis Advisor	Digitalis dosing advice	Randomized trials	No
PUFF	Pulmonary function test interpretation	Randomized trials	Yes
Microprocessor EXPERT	Protein electrophoresis interpretation	Case studies	Yes
HASP and SIAP	Ocean surveillance (signal processing)	Case studies	No

SOURCE: R. O. Duda and E. H. Shortliffe, "Expert Systems Research," *Science,* Apr. 15, 1983.

Research is underway to help alleviate some of these shortcomings, including the study of improved knowledge representation schemes and inference methods. Novel computer architectures should push back some of the limitations now imposed on system size by computer speed. The most immediate and probably far-reaching problem is the difficulty and expense of building and testing expert systems, including the acquiring and validating of rules and facts. Applied research work is progressing in the development of programming aids (tools, languages, environments) to lower the time and cost of building expert systems. Some current basic research is concerned with the automatic acquisition and structuring of knowledge. Incremental advances can be expected over the next decade, but fundamental breakthroughs will be required to expand the usefulness of expert systems significantly beyond current limits.

Foreign National Efforts in Artificial Intelligence R&D

Artificial intelligence is a key pursuit of recently initiated national, government financed R&D programs in Japan and Great Britain. Britain's effort is in fact a reaction to the Japanese Fifth Generation Project[146] as it was detailed in a conference held in October 1981.[147] The achievements of the objectives of these targeted national programs will require unprecedented fundamental advances in basic research. Their ultimate success is much less certain than were previous national technical efforts, such as the Manhattan Project or the Manned Moon Landing. However, these national AI research commitments are likely to produce advances in AI science, technology, and commercial application.[148]

The Fifth Generation

The Japanese plan to build, from a base of research that is almost exclusively borrowed from the United States and Western Europe, significant artificial intelligence systems with the stated purpose of enhancing productivity in areas of the Japanese economy that thus far have proven resistant to automation.[149] The total funding for the life of the project is not publicly stated, but some sources estimate that up to $1 billion to $1.5 billion may be spent over the next 8 to 10 years.[150]

The Fifth Generation Program is centrally managed by the Institute for New Generation Computer Technology (ICOT), formed by the Ministry of International Trade and Industry (MITI) in 1982.[151] The program will be funded, for the most part, by eight industrial companies. The government has provided seed money and staffing; 42 of the total staff of 52 have come from MITI's Electrotechnical Laboratory.[152] Spending thus far has been $2 million in 1982, $12 million in 1983, and $27 million in 1984.[153]

Overall, the functions that the Japanese see their Fifth Generation system performing include:[154]

1. problem-solving and inference,
2. knowledge-base management, and
3. intelligent interface (with users),

These goals correspond roughly to previously discussed research in:

1. expert systems,
2. knowledge representation, and

---

[146]A British delegation reported that the extent and cohesiveness of the Japanese plan, and the reaction to it that could be expected from American industry, were a "major competitive threat." *A Programme for Advanced Information Technology, The Report of The Alvey Committee,* Department of Industry, Her Majesty's Stationery Office, London, October 1982, see p. 5.

[147]*The International Conference on Fifth Generation Computer Systems,* Tokyo, Japan, Oct. 19-22, 1981.

[148]OTA workshop, Oct. 31, 1983.

[149]These include agriculture and fisheries, the office, and the service industries; applications are expected, as well, in areas that are already highly automated such as electronics and automobile design and manufacturing. *Fifth Generation Computer Systems,* T. Moto-oka (ed.), op. cit., see p. 3.

[150]P. Marsh, "The Race for the Thinking Machine," *New Scientist,* July 8, 1982, p. 85-87. Note, this is the *highest* estimate encountered.

[151]"Fifth Generation Computer System Under Development," *Science & Technology in Japan,* January/March 1983, p. 24-26.

[152]"ICOT: Japan Mobilizes for the New Generation," *IEEE Spectrum,* November 1983, p. 48.

[153]Personal communication from John Riganati, National Bureau of Standards, June 1984.

[154]*Science & Technology in Japan,* op. cit., p. 24.

3. natural language understanding.[155]

The Fifth Generation R&D plan calls for three phases of 3 to 4 years each:[156]

- **Phase I:** Development of "basic technologies" consisting of computer architectures and related software.
- **Phase II:** Development of prototypes of the inferencing and knowledge-base functional components, to correspond to the architecture and software developed in phase I.
- **Phase III:** A "total system" prototype is to be developed in the final phase.

The reactions of experts in this country to the Fifth Generation Program goals and methods have been mixed, ranging from enthusiastic to skeptical. However, there is agreement that the goals the Japanese have established are quite ambitious for the time frame that is set for achieving them, and the program is unlikely to succeed in all of its objectives.

The Alvey Programme

Named for John Alvey, chairman of the committee that developed the plan for a British response to the Japanese Fifth Generation Program, this academia-government-industry cooperative effort will concentrate on four segments of information technology, one of which is artificial intelligence, termed by the British, "Intelligent Knowledge Based" Systems.[157]

The British see a manpower shortfall in AI R&D similar to that in the United States, so their program will initially have a strong educational component, focusing on the expansion of both academic and industrial training facilities in the early part of the proposed 10 year effort. As the program progresses, emphasis will shift first to a broad effort in many aspects of basic AI research, and will later focus on specific demonstration systems to be developed in collaboration between the strengthened university programs and industries interested in particular applications.[158] Expected milestones include:[159]

- The research community (numbered in 1982 at some 150 people) is to grow by 50 percent in 2 to 3 years and double in about 5 years as a result of increases in graduate student funding, and numbers of faculty and research positions;
- Computer equipment and software support are to be expanded into an adequate base for research in 2 to 3 years;
- An increased understanding will be gained of knowledge representation and intelligent computer interface concepts, and knowledge based tasks and domains within 2 to 3 years;
- Within 5 years, there will be substantial progress in understanding the application of knowledge based concepts using logic programming languages and parallel processors, expert systems and natural language understanding systems;
- Over the 10 year time course of the program, progressively more sophisticated demonstration systems will be developed, some early target applications being teaching assistant programs, software production aids, and improved robot systems; later applications might include medical advisor systems, tactical decision aids, full 3-D vision systems, and office management and document production systems.

The government has pledged a total of $310 million for the entire Alvey program, with private industry expected to contribute an additional $230 million.[160] The plan calls for expenditures of about $39 million on Intelligent Knowledge Based Systems in the first 5 years, some $30 million of that going to universi-

---

[155]L. R. Harris, "Fifth Generation Foundations," *Datamation*, July 1983, pp. 148-150, 154, 156.
[156]Ibid., p. 25.
[157]The other areas are Software Engineering, Man/machine Interfaces, and VLSI. *A Programme for Advanced Information Technology*, op. cit., p. 21.

[158]Ibid., p. 35.
[159]Ibid., pp. 38-40.
[160]M. Peltu, "U.K. Eyes 5th Gen.," *Datamation*, July 1983, pp. 67-68, 72.

ties.[161] The Science and Engineering Research Council (SERC), roughly the equivalent of the American NSF, will develop plans and disburse most of these funds.[162]

The United Kingdom has a strong tradition in AI, particularly in the University of Edinburgh and Imperial College, London. But in the years immediately preceding the Alvey initiative, efforts had been scaled back because of an unfavorable government report on the prospects for artificial intelligence, and many researchers emigrated to the United States to continue work in American universities.[163] Alvey Programme funding may reverse these trends, but there is disagreement among experts concerning the ability of European universities, in general, to respond flexibly to the growth of a field such as AI, where interdisciplinary research across traditional academic departmental lines is so crucial.

---

[161] *A Program For Advanced Information Technology*, op. cit., pp. 47 and 49.
[162] Ibid., p. 48.
[163] The OTA workshop, Oct. 31, 1983.

Chapter 4
Effects of Deregulation and Divestiture on Research

Contents

	Page
Findings	111
Antitrust Laws, Deregulation, and Divestiture	113
Divestiture	116
Management of Research at AT&T	120
The Modified Final Judgment and Bell Laboratories	121
Bell Labs After Divestiture	122
Factors Affecting Research	123
Stability of Earnings	123
Allocation of Research and Development Expenditures	125
Basic Research	128
Role of Bell Communications Research, Inc.	129
Availability of Research Results	130
Policy Implications	131
Chapter 4 References	134

Tables

Table No.	Page
23. Regional Bell Operating Companies	119
24. R&D Intensities of Selected Major Telecommunication Firms	125

Figures

Figure No.	Page
16. Pre-Divestiture Bell System	117
17. Post-Divestiture Organization of AT&T	118
18. Bell Operating Companies	119

Chapter 4
Effects of Deregulation and Divestiture on Research

Findings

As a major source of information technology R&D—and as an organization that has recently undergone major legal, regulatory, and institutional changes—AT&T's Bell Laboratories merits special attention. In reviewing the potential effects of the AT&T divestiture and of recent regulatory decisions on Bell Labs, OTA made the following findings:

- Organizational changes within AT&T Technologies and within Bell Labs indicate that AT&T is already preparing to speed the development and marketing of new products. Other firms may also increase their development activities to meet competition from AT&T.
- The effects on the research side are less clear. AT&T has some incentives to continue funding applied and basic research at past levels, but these stand in tension with powerful new forces that could tempt AT&T to direct more resources away from research and into short-term research and development projects. There is little reason to think that AT&T's competitors will perform more basic research now than they have in the past.
- The areas where AT&T will be the most likely to focus its competitive efforts are also the areas where Bell Labs has been responsible for major scientific contributions computer science, solid-state physics, and photonics. Work in those areas, including basic research, is likely to continue into the foreseeable future.
- A significant portion of Bell Labs' research base has been moved to Bell Communications Research, Inc. (Bellcore), a unique new organization owned jointly by the divested Bell operating companies. Bellcore's role in basic research is still unclear.
- It is possible to monitor research activities over the next few years to determine whether the quality or direction of basic research change in a deregulated environment. Because of the long-term nature of the work, however, it may take some years for any changes to become evident.

The AT&T divestiture has been making headlines since January 1982, when AT&T and the Department of Justice announced the settlement of the Department's long-standing antitrust suit. The divestiture marked the end of an era. Before divestiture, AT&T had been the nationwide provider of end-to-end telecommunications services. AT&T's system of Bell operating companies provided local service to 85 percent of the telephones in the United States; the Long Lines division carried the vast majority of long-distance calls; the Western Electric subsidiary manufactured most of the equipment used in the system and leased to end users. With assets of $150 billion and annual revenues of $69 billion, it was the biggest communications company in the world. On January 1, 1984, the size of the corporation was reduced to one-fourth as AT&T spun off the Bell operating companies and gave up local telephone service.

While divestiture is indeed a dramatic event, the concern and publicity associated with it have tended to obscure a related regulatory decision: the Federal Communications Commission's (FCC's) decision in the Second Computer Inquiry (Computer II) detariffed the sale of terminal equipment, deregulated enhanced telecommunication services, and permitted AT&T to sell these to end users through a subsidiary after Jan. 1, 1983.[1] These changes in AT&T's structure and markets have raised some important questions related to research and development in telecommunications. The question addressed here is how divestiture and deregulation will affect the functioning of AT&T's research arm, Bell Laboratories,

---
[1]"Enhanced communications" are services which require adding value to a transmission by altering the message in some way, as explained below.

viewed by some as the star of modern industrial and scientific research.

In 1982, before any of the changes associated with divestiture and compliance with Computer II, Bell Labs had a budget of $2 billion, facilities at 21 locations, and 25,000 employees—3,000 with doctorates and 5,000 with masters degrees. Bell Labs provided nearly all R&D leading to the manufacture of Western Electric's products, as well as systems engineering to support the Bell System generally. While the Labs' principal role is in developing products for sale or use by AT&T, about 10 percent of the budget has been dedicated to scientific research. The research has had fallout applications in a wide variety of fields, from telephony and computer science to astrophysics and health care. The research results and technical standards are widely published in scientific and technical journals. Bell Labs researchers have made many fundamental advances, inventing the transistor and other concepts at the base of the current generation of computer and telecommunication technology. Among Bell Labs' employees and alumni are seven Nobel laureates.

The Labs recently (1983) received its 20,000th patent; this amounts to one patent per day since Bell Labs was incorporated in 1925, and many other of its inventions have not been patented. Traditionally, about 99 percent of AT&T's R&D has been done internally. Very little technology has been bought from outside, although AT&T does enter into cross-

Photo credit: AT&T Bell Laboratories

Bell Labs developed the first 32 bit microprocessor: the dime-sized chip contains nearly 150,000 transistors and has processing power comparable to that of today's minicomputers.

licensing agreements. On the other hand, it had been AT&T's policy since the 1920s, and a legal requirement under the 1956 consent decree described below, to license its own patents to other firms at reasonable cost. There are currently over 400 such licensing agreements outstanding in the United States and 200 more with foreign firms. Arno Penzias, Bell Lab's Vice President, has been quoted as saying that "without Bell Labs there would be no Silicon Valley."[2]

Although that may be hyperbole, it is certainly true that Bell Labs holds the basic patents for the processes and products needed by many United States and foreign firms to get their start in microelectronics, computers, telecommunications, or other fields. The availability of licenses and technical information from Bell Labs greatly speeded development of the microelectronics industry.

Bell Labs' R&D efforts are clearly important to information technology generally. The Labs' budget makes up perhaps 15 percent of the R&D investment by information technology firms.[3] Further, if Bell Labs is producing over 370 patents per year, then it accounts for perhaps 5 percent of U.S. patents in information technology fields.[4] Anything that might reduce the scope or quality of research at Bell Labs alarms observers who see the Labs as a major contributor to the U.S. lead in information technology R&D.

The restructuring of AT&T creates pressures and incentives for Bell Labs that did not exist while AT&T was a regulated, end-to-end monopoly. Because of competitive pressures on AT&T in the deregulated markets, Bell Labs may choose to devote more of its resources to product development and to reduce the number of long-term research projects leading to fundamental scientific discoveries. Such an event could be deleterious to the long-run competitive position of AT&T, and more importantly, might negatively affect the level of U.S. R&D in information technology.

This chapter discusses the problems and opportunities that the new post-divestiture environment offers Bell Labs, and the possible effects that the changes in AT&T's corporate structure may have on research at the Labs, and throughout the telecommunication and computer industry. It focuses specifically on the future stability of AT&T's earnings, its incentives to engage in research, and the possible effects of deregulation on research elsewhere in the telecommunications and computer industry. Finally, it outlines some methods for monitoring the health of research at Bell Labs and possible options for Federal Government action.

Before examining the effects on Bell Labs, it is necessary to briefly review the regulatory and legal decisions leading to deregulation and divestiture and to discuss the technological and market forces that drove them.

---

[2] "Bell Labs, Threatened Star of US Research," *Fortune*, July 5, 1982, p. 47.

[3] See page 316. Investment in information technology by industry in 1983 is estimated to be about $10.8 billion. Bell Labs' R&D budget of $2 billion is about 18 percent of the $10.8 billion invested in IT R&D by large IT companies in 1982. However, the $10.8 billion figure may be too low, as it does not include R&D expenditures of many small firms.

[4] This is an estimate based on approximately 5,180 Bell Labs patents as a fraction of 101,900 US patents in communications equipment and electronic components in 1963-1981. Data on U.S. patents from National Science Board, *Science Indicators, 1982*, U.S. Government Printing Office, 1983, p. 207.

Antitrust Laws, Deregulation, and Divestiture

American Telephone and Telegraph is no stranger to antitrust litigation. In order to avoid a threatened Government suit under the Sherman Antitrust Act in 1913, AT&T entered into negotiations with the U.S. Attorney General that resulted in the Kingsbury commitment. In the commitment, AT&T agreed: 1) to end its policy of aggressive mergers with competing independent telephone companies; 2) to allow the remaining independents to interconnect with its long-distance system; and 3) to get out of the telegraph business by divesting itself of the Western Union telegraph company.[5] It removed AT&T from the telegraphy market and significantly constrained future purchases of competing telephone companies.

However, the actual effect of the Kingsbury commitment was to confirm AT&T as a regulated monopoly and to quell the competition between Bell operating companies and independents which had grown up in the 1895-1913 period. Under terms of the commitment, Bell companies and independents negotiated the borders of their service areas and exchanged telephones where necessary to give each other geographical monopolies. AT&T was acknowledged to control the entire long-distance network, and the independents used that network as noncompeting partners in end-to-end service.

The next major antitrust case against AT&T, in 1949, asked for an end to AT&T's ownership of Western Electric and an end to all restrictive agreements among AT&T, the Bell Operating Companies, and Western Electric. The suit essentially sought the separation of regulated monopoly services from equipment supply.

A negotiated settlement of the 1949 suit led to a consent decree in January 1956. The consent decree imposed two important restrictions on AT&T's future activities. First, AT&T was restrained from entering other lines of business, such as the sale of solid-state components or computers. It was restricted to providing regulated common carrier service, with Western Electric as its captive equipment manufacturer. AT&T was free to develop Bell Labs technology, such as the transistor, for use within its own system, but was forbidden to market these products to the public. Second, AT&T was required to license all patents controlled by the Bell System to any applicant at a "reasonable royalty" and to provide technical information along with patent licenses on payment of reasonable fees. This licensing provision ensured that other firms could use Bell technology outside of regulated telephone markets.[6]

Two major trends, each with a technological and a regulatory component, developed over the ensuing 25 years to make the line of business restriction of the 1956 consent decree increasingly unworkable. First was the development of technological alternatives in transmission and switching that greatly reduced the cost of providing long-distance service and made it economically attractive for competitors to challenge AT&T's dominance of the long-distance market. Second was the advance in computer microelectronics, which has been leading to a convergence and interdependence of communication and computation services. These technological changes, and the market activity that they generated, led to a number of regulatory decisions that eroded AT&T's monopoly position and gradually opened the telecommunication transmission and equipment markets to competition.

The first chink in the long-distance monopoly was FCC's 1959 *Above 890* decision,[7] opening the microwave radio spectrum to private users. This led eventually to FCC's approval, in 1969 and again in 1971, of MCI's application for authorization to offer private line service via microwave. It was also in 1971 that the FCC made its *Specialized Common Carrier* decision,[8] in which it concluded that a general policy in favor of entry by new carriers into specialized communications would serve the public interest. Long-distance service from "other common carriers" became more widely available to the public in 1979 after a series of FCC and court decisions. By the end of 1984, other carriers had captured 15 to 20 per-

---

[5]Gerald W. Brock, *The Telecommunications Industry: The Dynamics of Market Structure* (Cambridge: Harvard University Press, 1981), p. 155.

[6]AT&T had been granting licenses and making available technical information on its inventions before 1956. AT&T had developed cross-licensing agreements with major manufacturers like General Electric over the previous two decades. The policy of licensing patents to smaller firms was in force in the 1940s.

[7]27 FCC (1959).

[8]29 FCC 2nd 8 70 (1971).

cent of the long-distance market, as measured by minutes of calls transmitted.⁹ Other carriers can now claim relatively small numbers of subscribers, but they are principally the high volume users. AT&T estimates that other carriers serve about one-third of the highest volume residential callers (those spending over $25 per month) and one-half of high volume business callers (over $150 per month).*

In the terminal equipment market, the FCC's 1968 decision in the Carterphone case[10] was the first FCC action to allow consumer-owned terminal equipment to be attached to the Bell system network. This decision, together with an equipment registration program authorized by FCC in the 1970s, allowed manufacturers other than Western Electric to enter the U.S. market, giving rise to the "interconnect" market for telephones and other customer equipment.

Meanwhile, the computer industry was growing rapidly and without significant government regulation. In order to determine how best to deal with the policy questions that were already emerging from remote-access data processing, FCC initiated in 1966 its first *Inquiry into Regulatory and Policy Problems Presented by the Interdependence of Computer and Communication Services and Facilities* (Computer I Inquiry). The decision in Computer I, adopted in 1970, divided computer/communications services into two regulated services—pure communications and hybrid communications—and two nonregulated services—hybrid data processing and pure data processing. Under the terms of the 1956 Consent Decree, AT&T could provide pure and hybrid communications but could not provide any service or product that fell into the data processing categories.

Throughout the 1960s and 1970s, AT&T had been manufacturing and selling terminals for access to mainframe computers. These were primarily built by the Teletype Corporation, a subsidiary of Western Electric. Early terminals were clearly communication devices—they were only of use for sending information to a remote computer for processing. As microelectronics advanced, however, more intelligence and power could be placed in terminals. It became increasingly difficult to determine at what point a terminal ceased to be a "hybrid communications" device and became a "hybrid data processing" device.

AT&T's applications to the FCC for permission to market new terminal equipment were sometimes challenged as being in violation of Computer I rules and the consent decree.[11] Further, AT&T was at a competitive disadvantage because it had to go through a (sometimes lengthy) regulatory process before introducing each new product, whereas the unregulated terminal suppliers (computer manufacturers) could introduce new products whenever, at whatever price, they chose. It was clear that the combination of Computer I rules, the consent decree, and the evolution of technology were preventing AT&T from offering state-of-the-art terminal equipment to the public.

FCC initiated its second inquiry, Computer II, in 1976 and issued a decision in 1980. That decision deregulated the sale of terminal equipment, both voice and data, and allowed

---

⁹FAA estimate, private communication, February 1985.

*AT&T Communications briefing to OTA staff, August 17, 1984.

[10]See 13 FCC 2d, 420, 437 (1968). "Terminal equipment" or "customer premises equipment" terminates the telephone wire on the customer's premises. The most common example is the ordinary telephone. The terms are also used to refer to systems of telephones, like the six button "key sets" used by many small businesses, and to switching equipment, like the private branch exchanges (PBX) used to route calls inside large businesses. Modems (modulators-demodulators that convert analog signals to digital signals) interface between the telephone wire and a computer and are considered terminal equipment, as are computer terminals with built-in modems.

[11]For example, AT&T's request for a tariff to sell the Dataspeed 40/4 was denied by FCC's Common Carrier Bureau in December 1976. IBM and others objected that the terminal would be in direct competition with terminals built by computer manufacturers, and the Common Carrier Bureau agreed that the terminal's storage and processing capabilities (designed to allow an operator to correct mistakes before sending data to the computer) violated FCC rules. The full Commission overturned this decision 9 months later. In its decision the Commission noted that the Computer I rules were inadequate to deal with the changing technology and that Computer II Inquiry then beginning would establish a new policy. See FCC Transmittal No. 12449, 1977.

AT&T to offer this equipment for sale to the public through a subsidiary. Computer II also allowed AT&T to offer other enhanced telecommunication services through a subsidiary.[12] AT&T created that subsidiary, AT&T Information Services or ATTIS (originally called American Bell), in June 1982.

Divestiture

Meanwhile, the Department of Justice brought an antitrust suit against AT&T in 1974, seeking many of the same goals as in 1949. The suit alleged that AT&T monopolized the manufacturing, long-distance, and local service markets; that it used its monopoly power in each market to strengthen its power in the other markets; and that it attempted to prevent competing equipment manufacturers and long-distance carriers from gaining access to the local networks. In January 1982, Department of Justice announced that it had reached agreement with AT&T on changes to the 1956 consent decree and in August 1982, Judge Harold H. Greene of the U.S. District Court for the District of Columbia approved the Modified Final Judgment. The Government's case was dismissed upon acceptance of the terms of the Modified Final Judgment by all parties.

Under the Modified Final Judgment, local Bell operating companies providing local exchange telephone services were divested by AT&T, and spun off into seven regional holding companies. AT&T retained ownership of a nationwide intercity network composed of its Long Lines division and the intercity facilities of the Bell operating companies, and continued to own Bell Laboratories and Western Electric. The Modified Final Judgment allowed AT&T to enter computer, computer-related, and information services markets in competition with unregulated firms (although there are still restrictions on AT&T's actions; e.g., AT&T may not provide information services over its own lines for 7 years).

The breakup, according to Judge Greene, reduces AT&T's ability to rely on its monopoly at the local exchange to exact competitive advantage in interexchange (long-distance), terminal equipment, and computer services markets. AT&T's long-distance market is still regulated, but FCC regulation was not viewed by the court as so extensive, nor were barriers to entry seen as so high, that AT&T will be able to use its currently large share in this market to provide a competitive advantage in unregulated segments of the industry.

Figures 16 and 17 compare the predivestiture and post-divestiture organizational structure of AT&T and the Bell operating companies. Before divestiture the entire Bell system existed under a single corporate umbrella and the firm was organized to provide end-to-end telephone service. The Long Lines division provided interstate long-distance services; Western Electric manufactured equipment for use throughout the system; the 22 wholly owned Bell operating companies provided local and intrastate service; a small international division marketed AT&T equipment abroad. Bell Labs provided design and development for Western Electric as well as research and network system engineering for the rest of the system. The AT&T Information Systems subsidiary was created in 1982 in response to the Computer II decision.

As figure 17 shows, AT&T after divestiture is primarily comprised of AT&T Communications, AT&T Technologies, AT&T International, and the subsidiary, AT&T Information Systems. AT&T Communications provides long-distance service between local calling areas.[13] AT&T Technologies includes the functions of Western Electric and Bell Labs. It now provides research and development, man-

---

[12]In its *Second Computer Inquiry* decision, the FCC distinguished between basic and enhanced services. Basic services were defined to be the transmission of information, while enhanced services involved adding value to transmission by changing or acting on the message itself in some way. As an example, in voice traffic, a simple long-distance telephone call constitutes basic service. Enhanced service would be provided if the carrier stores and forwards calls or provides recorded messages for those who are calling. An enhanced data service might be one that provides protocol conversion so that non-compatible computers can communicate.

[13]LATA—Local Access and Transport Area—is the term now used to identify a local calling area.

Figure 16.—Pre-Divestiture Bell System[a]

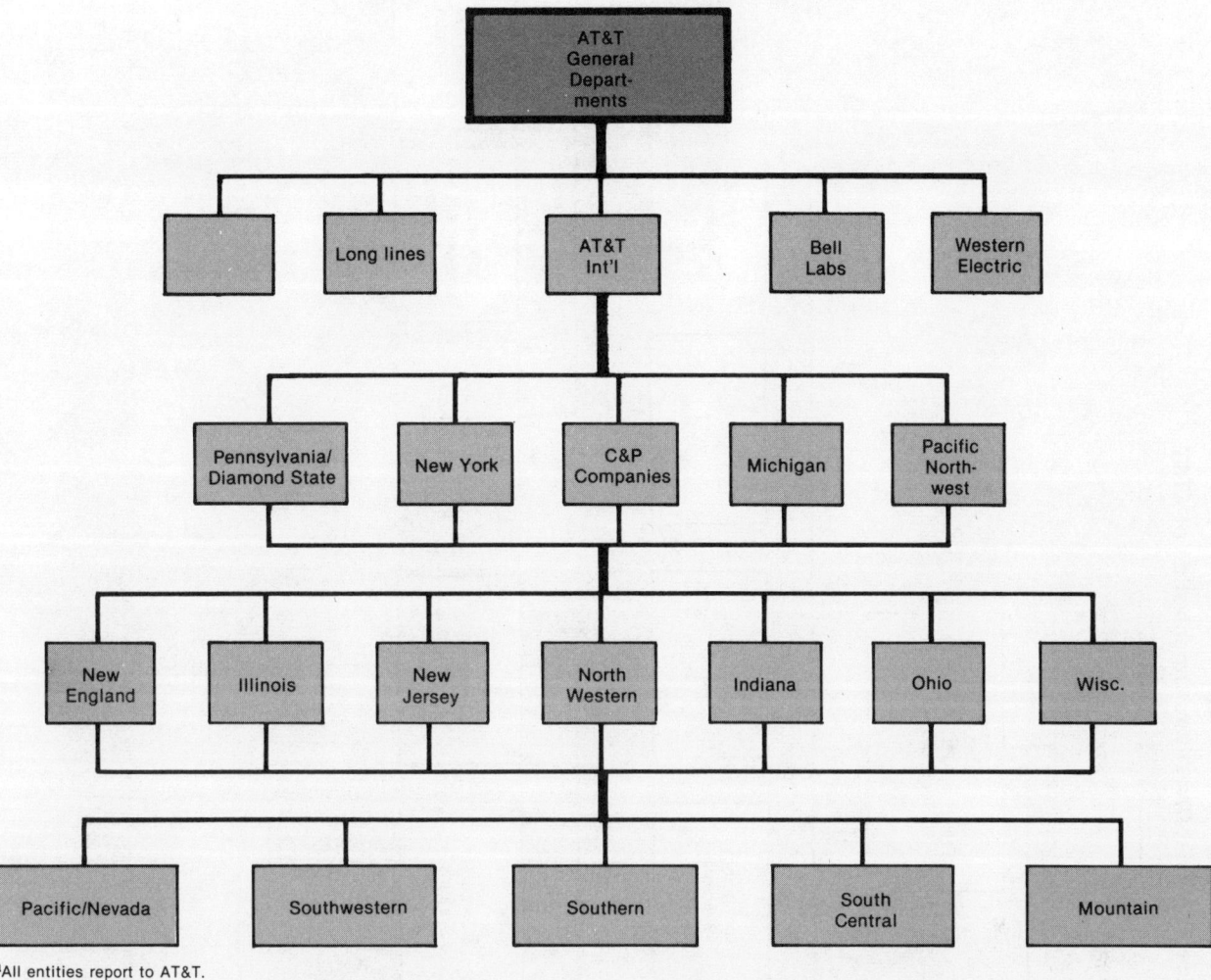

[a]All entities report to AT&T.

ufacturing, and marketing of equipment and services both in the United States and abroad. Western Electric no longer exists as an organizational unit, but AT&T Technologies will continue to use it as a trade name. Bell Labs is the section of AT&T Technologies responsible for R&D.

AT&T Information Systems will market information services, terminal equipment and computers to end users. Dealings between ATTIS and the other AT&T entities, under rules of Computer II, must be at arm's length. Information related to AT&T's customer base, for example, cannot be shared with ATTIS (unless it is also shared with competitors).

As shown in figure 18 and table 23, divestiture places the Bell operating companies into seven regional holding companies, of approximately equal size in terms of assets and customer base. The seven jointly own and operate Bell Communications Research (Bellcore), which provides technical and administrative services.

Judge Greene ruled shortly after the divestiture that the name "Bell" and the familiar

118 • *Information Technology R&D: Critical Trends and Issues*

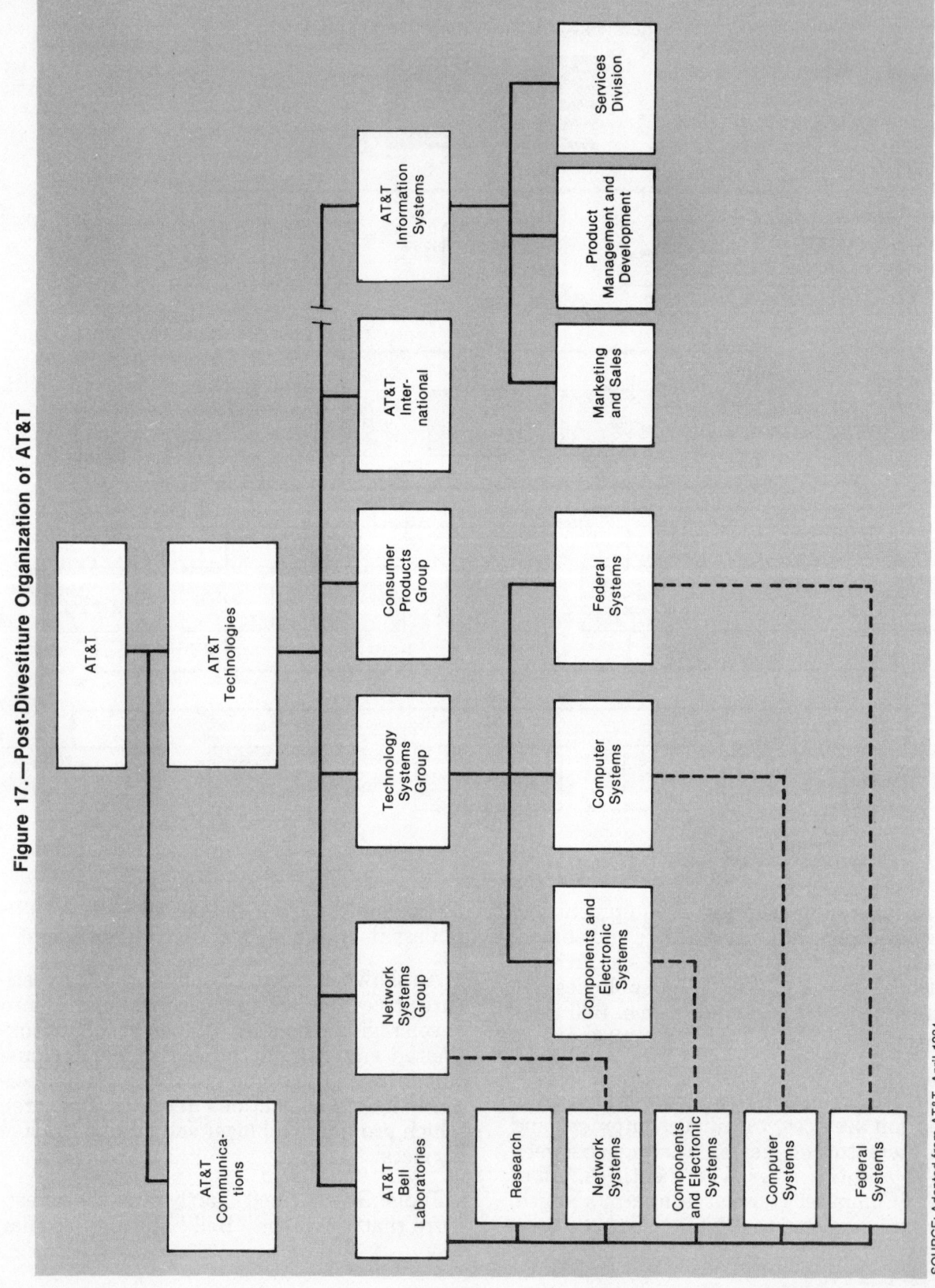

Figure 17.—Post-Divestiture Organization of AT&T

SOURCE: Adapted from AT&T, April 1984.

Figure 18.—Bell Operating Companies[a]

The seven regional Bell operating companies

1 Nynex
New England Telephone
New York Telephone

2 Bell Atlantic
C&P Telephone (4 companies)
Diamond State Telephone
New Jersey Bell
Bell of Pennsylvania

3 Bellsouth
Southern Bell
South Central Bell

4 Ameritech
Illinois Bell
Indiana Bell
Michigan Bell
Ohio Bell
Wisconsin Telephone

5 Southwestern Bell
Southwestern Bell

6 U.S. West
Mountain Bell
Northwestern Bell
Pacific Northwest Bell

7 Pacific Telesis
Pacific Telephone
Nevada Bell

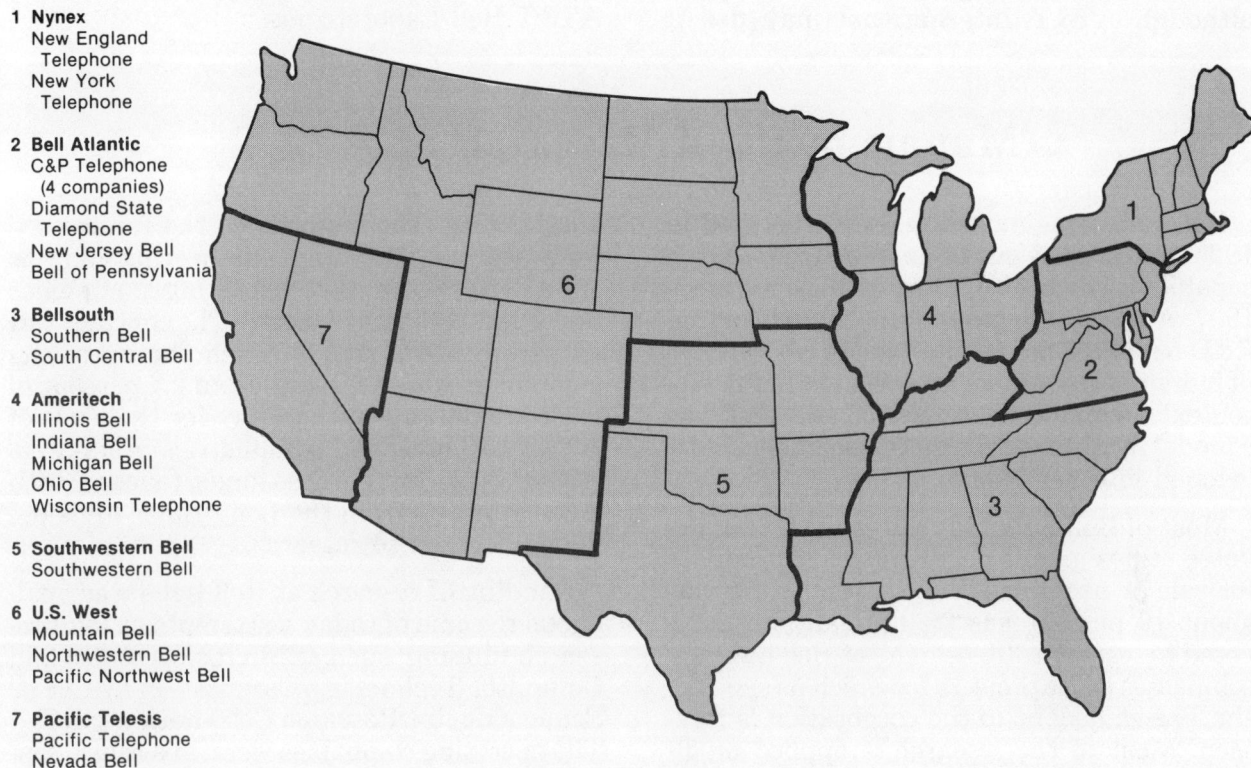

[a] The regional Bell operating companies are holding companies for Bell operating companies that offer service in the States indicated above. Within most States local telephone service is also provided by independent telephone companies.

SOURCE: AT&T.

Table 23.—Regional Bell Operating Companies

Regions	Total operating revenue (millions)	1984 assets (billions)	Net income (millions)	Value of embedded plant (millions)	Access lines (thousands)
Ameritech	8,900	16.26	1,037.1	14,409	13,970
Bell Atlantic	8,732	16.26	1,054.5	14,596	14,011
Bell South	10,512	20.81	1,393.1	19,081	13,367
NYNEX	10,006	17.39	1,029.8	15,186	12,658
Pacific Telesis	7,895	16.19	977.1	14,493	10,717
Southwestern Bell	8,859	15.51	887.9	14,112	10,189
U.S. West	7,596	15.05	910.9	13,767	10,381

SOURCE: Bell Communications Research, Inc., November 1984.

logo are the property of the Bell system—that is, the Bell operating companies. AT&T may not use the name or logo in the United States, although AT&T International may use it abroad. The one exception to this ruling was that the name of Bell Laboratories did not have to be changed, although it is now called AT&T Bell Laboratories.

Management of Research at AT&T

Bell Labs was named and incorporated in 1925, but it grew out of an in-house research capability which AT&T had maintained since 1907. AT&T was a groundbreaker in bringing R&D out of the homes and private laboratories of individual inventors and into the industrial context. In many ways, research at AT&T was a model for the modern industrial lab as it developed in other industries.

Most of Bell Labs' resources have been devoted to design and development of products for sale or use in the Bell system. However, about 10 percent has traditionally been devoted to research. "Research" at Bell Labs encompasses those projects for which no specific, short-term benefit to the corporation is foreseen. Most of the research is applied or directed systematically toward the solution of particular problems, but some resources have been devoted to basic research, sometimes leading to major scientific advances.

Before divestiture, Bell Labs' work was supported by the other AT&T entities. In 1982, and typically in the predivestiture era, about half of the Labs' support (54 percent) came from Western Electric, to cover costs of specific design and development.[14] In addition, Western paid another 3 percent to support work on products being developed under Government contract. Another 11 percent came from Bell operating companies to pay for centralized development of computer information systems.

The remaining 32 percent of Bell Labs budget was paid by AT&T for research and systems engineering. The majority of the funds used for research and system engineering came to AT&T from the Bell operating companies under the "license contract." The contract was an arrangement under which the operating companies were assessed up to 2.5 percent of their annual revenues to pay for their use of AT&T technical and administrative services. About 30 percent of these funds, together with a contribution from the Long Lines division, were allocated to research.

Funding of research at Bell Labs was analogous to some of today's attempts at joint research funding, such as Microelectronics and Computer Technology Corporation (MCC) or Semiconductor Research Corporation (SRC).[15] The operating companies were, in a sense, separate user companies that contributed to the support of a central research facility for mutual benefit. The difference in this case was that the operating companies all existed under a single corporate umbrella, so that they had little control over how their contributions were spent and no option of withdrawing from the joint funding venture or establishing other arrangements.

A number of factors in the "climate" of Bell Labs have been cited as contributing to its achievements in fundamental research. Some have pointed out that Bell Labs scientists had access to state-of-the-art equipment, and were free to focus on their research without the responsibilities of teaching or serving on committees that would be required in a university setting. Because of job security and the stability of funding, there was no need for researchers to spend time pursuing grant support.

---

[14]Figures from Charles River Associates, *Impacts of the AT&T divestiture on Innovative Behavior,* unpublished paper prepared for OTA, 1983, p. 17.

[15]For a description of these joint research ventures, see ch. 6.

There has been a tradition of staff interactions across disciplinary boundaries. Bell Labs maintained an open publication policy—its researchers have published about 2,000 papers per year. With these advantages, Bell Labs was able to attract outstanding scientists and engineers to work in its research organization.[16]

The Modified Final Judgment and Bell Laboratories

In his opinion on the Modified Final Judgment, Judge Greene commented on the proposal that Western Electric and the Bell Laboratories be divested from AT&T. He noted that the success of the Bell Laboratories in basic and applied research (and the beneficial impact of that research on the Nation's economic position) was due to its relationship with the operating companies and the Long Lines division. He argued that continued association of the Labs with the AT&T entities providing manufacturing and long-distance services would supply "the practical experience that would be useful in stimulating the research operations."[17]

The possibility of negative effects on research at Bell Labs was considered in the negotiations leading to divestiture, but was not considered a matter of highest priority. Chessler,[18] in summarizing the position of Government negotiators, indicates that they accepted the possibility that divestiture might lead to a reduction in basic research activities:

> The competitive era in station equipment, interexchange communications, and information services under the [MFJ] will bring forth a great blossoming of progress in those areas of telephony. It was the thought of the framers... that the blossoming will be so great as to more than compensate for the loss of pure research at Bell Telephone Laboratories, and the reduced incentives for innovation at the Bell operating companies.

Judge Greene did not believe that incentives for innovation were being sacrificed or that divestiture per se would hurt the quality of service provided by the operating companies or the research performed by of Bell Laboratories. He noted that the largest potential customers of Western Electric will be the divested operating companies, hence, Western Electric's association with Bell Laboratories should provide an incentive to improve equipment and technology.[19]

The Modified Final Judgment sets aside the 1956 Consent Decree and the requirement that AT&T grant nonexclusive licenses for its patents to any applicant. The elimination of this requirement makes it easier for Bell Labs to appropriate the potential benefit of new breakthroughs, and therefore might be considered an incentive to research. AT&T may now grant or deny licenses as it chooses, and may change whatever royalty it chooses. Before divestiture, when revenues from local exchange ratepayers were supporting Bell Labs' research, it made sense to require AT&T to share the fruits of its monopoly financing with others, according to Judge Greene. With the divestiture of the operating companies and the termination of the license contract fee payments, this rationale for required licensing is eliminated. Judge Greene also believed that the advance of technology and the dispersion of knowledge related to telecommunications technology has reduced the dependence of established domestic firms and foreign competitors on information from Bell Laboratories.[20]

The Modified Final Judgment requires that AT&T grant licenses to the divested operating companies on all existing patents and all patents issued for a period of 5 years following approval of the Modified Final Judgment. AT&T is also required to provide the operating companies with nonpatentable technical information that has been funded by the license contracts. The operating companies will have the right to sublicense AT&T patents and technical information to those providing them with goods and services.

---

[16]OTA, notes on interview with workshop participants.
[17]*Opinion and Order*, Aug. 11, 1982, p. 62.
[18]Cited in "Bell Labs on the Brink," *Science*, Sept. 23, 1983.
[19]Charles River Associates, "Impacts," p. 43.
[20]Ibid.

Bell Labs After Divestiture

The most noticeable change resulting from Computer II and divestiture is a reduction in Bell Labs' size. About 4,000 employees became part of AT&T Information Services (ATTIS). FCC has interpreted the Computer II ruling that ATTIS and Bell Labs deal at arm's length to mean that ATTIS employees must be kept separated from former Bell Labs colleagues, even though they are sometimes located in the same buildings. Another 3,000 Bell Labs employees went to the newly created Bell Communications Research Inc. (Bellcore, formerly the Central Services Organization) of the Bell operating companies. This leaves Bell Labs with about 18,000 employees, returning it to approximately the size it was in 1978.

Organizational changes taking place elsewhere in AT&T Technologies will also affect Bell Labs. In 1983, AT&T Technologies was organized into "line of business" divisions defined by customer and product type. Within Bell Labs, development teams have been reorganized along the same line of business categories in order to facilitate cooperation with manufacturing.[21] Authority for managing design and development of products within Bell Labs was given to executives running each line of business division, as shown by the dotted lines in figure 17.

This is a major departure from previous AT&T policy wherein Bell Labs, Western Electric, and AT&T shared this authority; unlike practice at most firms, the old arrangement gave Bell Labs some control over a product even after it went into production. The new arrangement was chosen to make development more responsive to the needs of marketing and manufacturing, and is a preparation to enter competitive markets. Although the organizational structure is new, it marks the continuation of a trend which began when the market for large private branch exchanges (PBXs)[22] became competitive after 1968. Shortly thereafter, nearly all Bell Labs personnel working on PBXs were collected in one Colorado Lab facility near the Western Electric facility where PBXs were manufactured.

Figure 17 also shows that research at Bell Labs remains independent from the lines of business in AT&T Technologies. However, sources in Bell Labs note that research is undergoing review and changes as a result of deregulation and divestiture. The loss of research personnel to ATTIS and Bellcore caused some realignment of research projects. Some other areas of research—for example, regulatory economics and social psychology—have been judged unproductive or inappropriate and have been cut back. New research topics, such as robotics, are being undertaken.

A major change to Bell Labs' funding since divestiture is the termination of the license contract revenues from the local operating companies, funds that were specifically dedicated to research and system engineering. Under the current funding arrangements, research is supported by AT&T Headquarters with funds provided by the AT&T companies under a "composite allocator." AT&T entities will be assessed for Bell Labs research (as well as administrative functions of AT&T Headquarters) according to their size, number of employees, and revenues. The allocation formula, under the Computer II rules, must be reviewed and approved by FCC to ensure that AT&T allocates a reasonable portion of research costs to the unregulated portion of its business and does not subsidize it from regulated long distance revenues.[23]

Another major change for Bell Labs will be an increase in the work done on military projects. AT&T Technologies is planning to increase the number of defense contracts, and the design and development work will be done in Bell Labs. Although defense contracts were once very important to Bell Labs, they had been reduced to a minor part of the R&D budget during the 1970s. In 1971, Bell Labs derived 30 percent of its income from defense-related

---

[21]Bro Uttal, "Cold New World," *Fortune*, June 27, 1983, p. 83.
[22]Private Branch Exchange is a generic term for the switch used on the customer premises for routing calls within a building or organization.

[23]See FCC 83-600, Dec. 22, 1983 and FCC 83-123, Mar. 31, 1983.

work; by 1976 the share was down to 2 percent and in 1983 about 3 percent.[24]

Growth of defense projects to an expected 10 percent of Bell Labs' budget should not be difficult. Based on its previous work, AT&T has strong ties with the Pentagon and a good reputation for designing and building the kinds of large complex systems that the Department of Defense wants. As Solomon J. Buchsbaum, executive vice president for consumer systems, points out, "The military side of government is a voracious eater of new technology, and we are good at [providing] that."[25]

---
[24]Marilyn A. Harris, "Bell Labs Looks to Military Research," *Electronics*, Feb. 9, 1984.

[25]"Bell Labs: The Threatened Star of U.S. Research," *Business Week*, July 5, 1982, p. 49.

Factors Affecting Research

All the changes taking place in AT&T's mission, markets, and corporate structure cannot but affect the activities of AT&T Bell Labs. The purpose of the Labs has always been to provide research, systems engineering, and product design to support the corporate activities of AT&T. As those activities have evolved, the role of the Labs has also changed. Of particular concern to many observers is the way in which deregulation and divestiture might cause changes in the commitment to *research*, particularly basic research, within Bell Labs.

Several concerns have been voiced. Will AT&T, as a smaller corporation with a narrower revenue base, be able to support research as it has in the past? What incentives does AT&T have to allocate funds to research, and how strong are they compared to incentives to allocate more resources to development of competitive products? How will changes related to divestiture and deregulation affect research at other firms in the telecommunication and computer industries? Could a reduction in the level of research at Bell Labs have a negative effect on U.S. research generally, and if so, what can be done about it? The remainder of this chapter addresses these questions.

Stability of Earnings

The future funding of research at Bell Labs will depend, at least in part, on AT&T's success in the market. The combination of divestiture and deregulation leave AT&T a smaller firm. While the predivestiture AT&T had a book value of $150 billion, the new AT&T has assets of only about $34 billion. However, the new AT&T is expected to have a much more favorable ratio of revenues to assets. Annual revenues are now expected to be on the order of $57 billion, compared with $69 billion for the predivestiture firm. This is largely because AT&T will continue to provide long-distance service, which has traditionally been very profitable and is estimated to provide two-thirds of the corporation's profit base.[26] Also, AT&T will continue to manufacture telecommunications equipment. Further, AT&T now has the opportunity to expand into potentially profitable computer-related markets.

While competitive computer markets are potentially profitable, they are also notable for their volatility over the past few years: new firms and new products have had meteoric successes and catastrophic failures. This kind of market may be dangerous for a firm which is unaccustomed to competition. AT&T has not been particularly successful in markets where it has been open to competition in the past. After 1976, when customers were permitted to purchase their own private branch exchange (PBX) switching equipment from other manufacturers, AT&T's market share fell sharply. Although AT&T is still the largest single manufacturer, it now has 24 percent of U.S. sales,

---
[26]Peter Hall, "AT&T and the Great Divide," *Financial World*, Jan. 10, 1984.

compared to 100 percent 8 years ago. Major competitors, specifically, Northern Telecom, Rolm, and Mitel have shares of 16, 14, and 11 percent, respectively.[27]

This loss of market share is due at least partly to AT&T's higher prices and relative slowness in bringing new products to market. Both these tendencies could be major disadvantages in industries that are noted for rapid introduction of new products and rapid obsolescence of old ones. In part, slowness in bringing products to market was related to the regulatory process—a situation that has been eased since Computer II, but not eliminated.

AT&T has traditionally designed and manufactured its products to extremely high standards; they were expected to be highly reliable with a long useful life. Such a strategy made sense when AT&T was the owner of a huge nationwide network of transmission and terminal equipment that had to be depreciated over 20 to 40 years. The higher costs of conservative design were made up by a long production run. Western Electric maintained a price advantage over some other manufacturers by producing large numbers of standard products over many years.

Western Electric has often been at a cost disadvantage, however, in the case of newer electronic products, the very ones that are the target of the competitive market. Small digital PBXs for example, cost Western about 75 percent more to manufacture than those made by their lowest cost competitor, Mitel.[28]

AT&T has made a concerted effort to streamline its manufacturing and to reduce costs. AT&T Technologies is reducing its work force, and several former Western Electric factories have been closed down or cut back. Although AT&T did not sell integrated circuits and other electronic components to the public, it is the Nation's 12th largest manufacturer. AT&T Technologies is now expanding that manufacturing capability, including construction of a new plant in Florida to make lower cost chips for use in computers and switches.

AT&T Technologies will continue to be a major manufacturer of telecommunication transmission equipment, large central office switches, and terminal equipment. Potential customers include Bell operating companies, independent telephone companies, and telecommunications agencies abroad.[29]

In addition, AT&T is now free to sell products it developed but could not market to the public under the 1956 consent decree. It can now market computers based on the UNIX operating system, the 256 K-byte memory chip, and the 32-bit processor, all developed at Bell Labs. Its 3B computer series will offer a range of computers of varying size and capability.

For the first time, AT&T is acquiring some of its new products, marketing talent, and distribution channels through other firms. For example, AT&T acquired a 25 percent interest in Italy's Olivetti Co. at a cost of about $260 million.[30] Olivetti is Europe's largest word processor and computer manufacturer. The agreement is expected not only to supply AT&T with Olivetti office equipment for the U.S. market, but also to provide a European distribution system for AT&T products. AT&T has also entered a joint venture with a Netherlands electronics firm, Philips, to manufacture central office switching equipment for Europe. AT&T has also made agreements with a number of smaller U.S. office computer manufacturers for development of new office automation equipment.

At the same time, and equally importantly, AT&T is developing its own marketing capability. Before divestiture, Western Electric was strictly a manufacturer and dedicated very few resources to marketing. One observer notes that a competitor, Northern Telecom, spends about 9 percent of manufacturing sales on marketing while Western Electric spent

---

[27]Northern Business Information, Inc., as cited in "ITT's Big Gamble" *Business Week*, Oct. 22, 1984.

[28]Northern Business Information, as quoted in Bro Uttal, "Cold New World," *Fortune*, June 27, 1983, p. 83.

[29]Kathleen K. Wiegner, "Prometheus is Unbound and Seeking His Footing," *Forbes,* Mar. 12, 1984, p. 143.

[30]Ibid.

only 1.2 percent in 1982.[31] Now, AT&T Technologies will be responsible for marketing all products not handled by ATTIS, and a marketing division and all the support functions are being developed.

Allocation of Research and Development Expenditures

As listed in table 24, AT&T and IBM have the largest R&D budgets among the U.S. firms shown. The R&D intensity, that is, R&D as a percent of revenues, is based on total sales, which before divestiture included revenues of the operating companies providing local telephone service. AT&T's R&D intensity is a fairly low 3.3 percent when based on total revenues. Nordhaus cites historical evidence, however, to indicate that as a percent of *manufacturing* sales AT&T spent approximately 9.8 percent of revenues on R&D in the 1970s, as compared with an average of about 2.8 percent for communication firms, and 1.9 percent for manufacturers generally.[32]

On average, Bell Labs has spent about 10 percent of its R&D budget on research. Among the other firms in table 24, both Northern Telecom and IBM also claim to spend about 10 percent on research. While Northern Telecom is a competitive firm, it operates under the corporate umbrella of Bell Canada, and shares the expenses of Bell-Northern Research with the regulated firm.

The general argument expressed by concerned observers is that AT&T may be forced, because of competitive pressures, to invest more of its R&D funds in developing salable

[31]Bro Uttal, "Cold New World," *Fortune*, June 27, 1983, p. 83.

[32]Charles River Associates, op. cit., p. 7.

Table 24.—R&D Intensities of Selected Major Telecommunication Firms (1982)

Company	R&D Expenses (millions of dollars) (1)	Sales (millions of dollars) (2)	R&D intensity (percent) (1)/(2)
AT&T	$2,126[a]	$65,093	3.3%
COMSAT	22.3	410	5.4
GTE	267.0	12,066	2.2
Harris	92.8	1,719	5.4
ROLM	24.4	381	6.4
United Telecommunications	11.2	2,249	0.5
Western Union	11.0	1,025	1.1
Zenith Radio	63.8	1,239	5.1
ITT	519.0	15,958	3.3
Rockwell International	222.0	7,395	3.0
General Dynamics	139.0	6,155	2.3
IBM	2,053.0	34,364	6.0
Motorola	278.0	3,786	7.3
RCA	195.4	8,237	2.4
General Electric	781.0	26,500	2.9
L. M. Ericsson (1980)	231.3	2,779.4	8.3
Northern Telecom	241.4[b]	3,035.5[b]	8.0
Plessey (fiscal year 1982)	241.8	1,723.9	14.0
Siemens (fiscal year 1982)	3,300(DM)	34,600(DM)	9.5
Thomson-CSF (1980)	3,600(FF)	22,300(FF)	16.1
The CIT-Alcatel Group (1981)	1,000(FF)	10,700(FF)	9.3
Hitachi (fiscal year 1981)	609.0	15,996.1	3.8
NEC (1981)	227.8	4,820.2	4.7
Fujitsu	256.1	2,769.9	9.2

[a]Includes $1,515 million spent by Western Electric Co. and other subsidiaries, not reported in AT&T's 10K.
[b]Canadian dollars.

SOURCES: *Business Week*, June 20, 1983; L. M. Ericsson Telephone Co., *Annual Report*, 1980; Plessy, *Report and Accounts*, 1982; Siemens, *Annual Report 1981-82*; *Thomson-CSF in 1980: The Year in Review*; *CIT Alcatel Group Review*; Hitachi, *1981 Annual Report*; NEC Nippon Electric Co., Limited, Annual Report, 1981; and Fujitsu Limited, *Annual Report*, March 1981.

FROM: Charles River Associates, "Impact of the AT&T Divestiture on Innovative Behavior," unpublished report prepared for Office of Technology Assessment, December 1983.

products, and correspondingly less in funding research projects that may lead to future scientific breakthroughs. They note that the license contract fees described above, which provided a steady income source for Bell Labs, will no longer be available, and that research funding will depend on yearly corporate decisions. Any reductions, instability, or even uncertainty about funds could have negative effects on the productivity of research projects that by their nature require long-term attention and investment.

The arguments related to a possible change in AT&T's policy toward research are based on two major effects of the deregulation and divestiture—AT&T will be operating in competitive markets and it will be a smaller corporation.

Neither the theoretical nor the empirical relationships between market structure, firm size, and innovative activity are straightforward or well understood. It is not clear whether innovation is most likely to occur under conditions of competition or of monopoly. In addition, although many support the view that larger firms have more incentives to innovate, there are many examples, especially in the information industries, of small firms that grow large due to extremely successful innovations. Further, most existing theory deals with "innovative behavior" or R&D as a whole, rather than with the specific relationship of market

Photo credit: AT&T Bell Laboratories

A dust-free "clean room" for manufacturing integrated circuits.

structure or firm size with the basic research component of R&D.

One theoretical argument, as proposed by Schumpeter and others, is that innovative behavior is greater in monopolistic industries than in competitive ones because a firm with monopoly power: 1) can prevent imitation and therefore capture more profit from innovation, and 2) is better able to assemble the funds and bear the risks of R&D.[33] On the other hand, critics of this position theorize that firms in competitive industries are more likely to innovate because new products or processes will help them to reduce costs or increase market share. In this view, monopolistic firms would be slow innovators because they can continue to earn profits by continuing to produce the current products. In addition, because the monopolistic firm is under less pressure to operate efficiently, the results of innovative activity would be obtained at excessive cost.[34]

Real-world markets are characterized by varying degrees of concentration rather than extremes of pure competition or monopoly. Attempts to empirically measure the relationship between innovation and degree of industry concentration have had mixed results.[35] For example, Scherer[36] found some evidence that dominant firms in highly concentrated industries are more innovative. However, in a later study[37] he found that the relationship varied greatly depending on the industry, and that there were examples where higher levels of innovation were associated with more competitive industries. In some cases, dominant firms were only moderately productive innovators, but they were able to aggressively take advantage of innovations by other firms. IBM was given as an example of such a firm.[38]

The empirical evidence on the effects of firm size on innovation is less ambiguous than the evidence on market structure. R&D at small firms is sometimes more efficient than at large ones for R&D projects undertaken by both large and small firms.[39] However, some projects are simply beyond the reach of small firms and there may be economies of scale for other projects. It appears that R&D intensity increases with firm size until firms reach annual sales of $250 million to $400 million (1978 prices) and then level off.[40] After reviewing the empirical evidence on firm size and innovation, Scherer concludes that an industry with a moderate degree of concentration and a variety of firms of different sizes is most conducive to innovation.

> All things considered, the most favorable industrial environment for rapid technological progress would appear to be a firm size distribution that includes a preponderance of companies with sales below $500 million, pressed on one side by a horde of small, technology-oriented enterprises bubbling over with bright new ideas and on the other by a few larger corporations with the capacity to undertake exceptionally ambitious developments.[41]

After divestiture, AT&T is still many times the threshold level of size that empirical studies have associated with maximum R&D. It will still be the dominant firm in a telecommunications industry that fits well Scherer's description of the environment most favorable for innovation. Thus, though the details of AT&T's R&D may change, there are no convincing theoretical arguments or empirical evidence related to market structure or firm size that would predict a lessening of its innovative activity.

---

[33] Summarized in Morton I. Kamien and Nancy Schwartz, *Market Structure and Innovation* (New York: Cambridge University Press, 1982), p. 47.

[34] Morris E. Morkre, "Innovation and Market Structure: A Survey," Working Paper No. 82, Bureau of Economics, Federal Trade Commission, 1982, p. vi.

[35] The literature is reviewed in Morkre, "Innovation," p. 11.

[36] F. M. Scherer, "Firm Sizes, Market Structure, Opportunity, and the Output of Patented Inventions," *American Economic Review*, 55:1119.

[37] F. M. Scherer, *Industrial Market Structure and Economic Performance* (New York: Rand McNally, 1980), p. 431-432.

[38] Ibid., p. 432.
[39] Morkre, p. vi.
[40] Charles River Associates, "Impacts," p. 88.
[41] Scherer, *Industrial Market Structure*, p. 422.

Scherer and others have concluded that the important determinant of innovation may not be market structure or firm size but rather the richness of innovative opportunities opened up by the underlying base of scientific knowledge. Advances in science related to semiconductors, computers, software, satellites, microwave transmission, fiber optics, and lasers provide a rich set of technological opportunites upon which to base innovations in telecommunications and information technology.[42]

Basic Research

Economic literature on "innovation," however, does not deal adequately with the effect of firm size or market structure on contributions to the knowledge base that supports innovation. The expected effect of competition, as noted above, is investment in development of new products and services, which will reduce cost or improve market share in the short term. Investments in research, especially basic research, may not pay off until many years after the initial investment is made.

One unique characteristic of Bell Labs is its reputation for doing basic research.[43] In general, only a few firms in the information industries have spent much on in-house basic research. In 1981, out of 110 firms doing R&D in information technology, only seven did any basic research at all, according to the National Science Foundation.[44] Speaking of Bell Labs one observer from Bell-Northern Research noted, "Most other organizations are looking at how to exploit technology, not at how to push it forward."[45]

When AT&T gets more experience as a competitive firm, will it continue to do basic research, or will it begin to behave as it appears other competitive firms do, and dedicate more resources to product-oriented research and development? Some observers, including Nordhaus, believe that AT&T will now "tilt much more toward a conventional equipment manufacturer, and it will therefore have a relatively greater incentive to invest in R&D that will enhance its equipment sales and profits" and relatively less incentive to invest in basic research.[46]

At the present time, AT&T's management has voiced a commitment to continuing fundamental research, recognizing that advances in science are necessary to advances in technology. In testimony before the Senate Commerce Committee, AT&T President Charles L. Brown called Bell Labs the "jewel" of the Bell system, and pointed out that "basic research has been the root of Bell Laboratories success . . . . and will continue to be the root of it. We do not intend to skimp on it . . . . This is something we have as a basic tenet."[47]

It is probably true that more than half a century of reliance on internally developed technology will not be quickly tossed aside. One Bell Labs spokesman said that the "corporate culture" of AT&T is completely oriented toward doing basic research in-house. The forces of habit and tradition may resist some pressures to shift too many resources to development.[48] Most of the technologies that will be commercially important to AT&T in the future—computer science, photonics, and solid-state physics—are the very areas where Bell Labs has made ongoing contributions to basic

---

[42]Charles River Associates, *Impacts*, p. 85.

[43]National Science Foundation, *Research and Development in Industry, 1981,* NSF 83-325 (Washington, DC: U.S. Government Printing Office, 1983), p. 3. The National Science Foundation defines basic research as "original investigations for the advancement of scientific knowledge not having specific commercial objectives, although such investigations may be in fields of present or potential interest to the firm.

[44]Information technologies in this case includes firms in the following categories: office, computing, and accounting machines (SIC 357); communications equipment (SIC 366); electronic components (SIC 367). See "Table B-33—Number of R&D Performing Companies Conducting Basic Research By Industry: 1981," p. 38 in National Science Foundation, *Research and Development in Industry, 1981,* NSF 83-325 (Washington, DC: U.S. Government Printing Office, 1983).

[45]John A. Roth, executive VP, Bell Northern Research, as cited in "Bell Labs the Threatened Star of US Research," *Business Week,* July 5, 1982.

[46]William Nordhaus, cited in "Bell Labs on the Brink," *Science,* Sept. 23, 1983, p. 1267.

[47]Testimony of Charles L. Brown Before the Senate Committee on Commerce, Science and Transportation, March 1982.

[48]Interview, March 1984.

science. It is highly unlikely that AT&T will abandon research in these areas. Further, as was pointed out in the case studies in chapter 3, the boundaries between basic and applied research in these fields are sometimes very fuzzy. Bell Labs' researchers are likely to make some contributions to the advancement of science even in pursuit of commercial ends.

There are some tangible and intangible benefits of performing basic research that are as advantageous to AT&T now as they were before Computer II or divestiture. For example, Nelson[49] points out that research often yields discoveries and inventions in unexpected areas. The wider a firm's scope of activities, the higher the proportion of these unanticipated outcomes it will be able to use. Thus, diversified firms can realize higher rates of return from research, and engage in more of it than firms with narrow product lines. Prior to divestiture, AT&T was a vertically integrated firm which could make use of research results in a large number of areas. Although the size of the firm is now reduced, AT&T is now in a position to diversify in other areas, and will continue to benefit from research results.

An additional benefit to funding basic research is that a reputation for achievements in basic science gives the Labs a certain prestige, credibility, and glamour, even if its chief business is not basic research. Although these benefits are not quantifiable, they are useful in attracting qualified scientists and engineers.

Divestiture and Computer II changed the rules under which AT&T funds research, and there has been speculation that the new rules may bring about a reduction in the amount spent on research over the long term. As a rate-base regulated monopoly, AT&T was able to spread the costs of basic research over many ratepayers. The license contract fee was essentially a "tax" on telephone calls. The revenues generated provided a regular source of income that could be counted on year after year.[50] AT&T was free to use those funds much as a government might use tax revenues, allocating some portion of those revenues to support activities that were for the general good but provided no immediate commercial benefit. While some research eventually paid off in discoveries useful to AT&T, some never paid off at all. Many research results that were not of direct benefit to AT&T were made available to others through licenses of patents or through scientific and technical publication.

As a competitive firm, AT&T must now support its research through a different internal funding mechanism. An important aspect of the deregulation and divestiture rules is that AT&T will be watched closely by FCC to be sure that it allocates a reasonable portion of research costs to the nonregulated portion of its business. Before divestiture, most of the cost of research was paid for by the Bell operating companies and the Long Lines division. Under the new "composite allocator" developed by AT&T and approved by FCC, approximately 50 percent of research costs will be paid by AT&T Communications and 50 percent will be paid by AT&T Technologies and AT&T Information Systems.

Role of Bell Communications Research, Inc.

Another unknown factor in the future of telecommunications research is the role of Bell Communication Research, Inc. (Bellcore), the technical services organization owned by the regional holding companies. The scope and quality of Bellcore's research effort is still unknown. One of Bellcore's jobs will be to test and evaluate products and equipment for the Bell operating companies. In order to do this properly, Bellcore will have to stay ahead of the manufacturers, anticipating the state-of-the-art and doing some basic research. According to Alan G. Chynoweth, Vice President for

---

[49] Richard R. Nelson, "The Simple Economics of Basic Scientific Research," *Journal of Political Economy* 67, 3 (June): pp. 297-306.

[50] AT&T points out that the license contract payments were not completely guaranteed income. Occasionally a State regulatory commission would disallow a portion of a BOC's license contract payment.

Applied Research, "Everything we do will be chosen because of its relevance to the long-term needs of the telephone companies. We're smaller than Bell Labs. We have to be more selective. But in those areas we select to be expert in, we'll dig very deeply."[51] Among the areas where research will be done are mathematics and computer science, materials, solid-state science, fiber optics and photonics, and switches.

Nearly half of Bellcore's technical personnel came from Bell Labs. To the extent that former Bell Labs research personnel will still pursue the same sorts of problems at Bellcore, the value of their research contributions has not been lost to the Nation. It remains to be seen whether the creation of Bellcore will have a positive or negative impact on basic research in areas related to information technology. The research agendas of Bellcore and Bell Labs will naturally overlap in certain areas. It is possible that this duplication of effort will be inefficient and may reduce the quality of U.S. research in information technology overall. On the other hand, it may be that the creation of this new center of initiative will have a stimulating effect on research.

The regional Bell operating companies are the owners of Bellcore and have control over how funds are spent. Under the current arrangement, they all contribute to certain "core" projects, but each is able to limit its investment in "noncore" projects it does not believe to be beneficial to its own business.[52]

Funding priorities for Bellcore will depend partially on actions of State regulatory commissions. Before divestiture, a few State commissions sometimes disallowed part of a Bell operating company's payment for support of Bell Labs on the grounds that research did not benefit the telephone ratepayers of that State. Support of research at Bellcore may face the same sort of problem.

The growing competition among its owners may also affect Bellcore's future. Although they provide regulated telephone service only within their assigned geographic areas, the regional operating companies are creating subsidiaries to enter other lines of business. Among the enterprises already under way are computer sales and repair, computer software sales, office equipment sales, cable television installation, and real estate development. In many cases the regionals are providing goods and services in nationwide markets, in direct competition with one or more of the others. Other ventures are being planned, subject to approval by Judge Greene's court, under terms of the divestiture.

The regional Bell operating companies have many common R&D goals because the majority of their business will continue to be the provision of regulated local and interstate telephone service. However, there are a growing number of areas where their interests diverge or where one company wishes to withhold information from some or all of the others. Bellcore is still developing an organizational structure to deal with this situation. It is possible that the growing competition between the owners could encourage them to jointly fund basic research at Bellcore but to turn to other labs for development of products needed for the competitive market. At this point it is impossible to say what Bellcore's long-term research agenda will be. Bellcore will be an interesting experiment in jointly funded R&D. It remains to be seen how much of Bellcore's resources the regional Bell operating companies will be willing or able to spend on basic research with possible long-term payoffs.

Availability of Research Results

Even if Bell Labs continues to perform research at the current levels, it has fewer incentives to make the results available to others. It has maintained a fairly open policy, encouraging its scientists to publish results, present papers, and consult informally with other researchers. Some of the research results, as well as some of the patents, were of little direct value to AT&T because it was permitted only to provide regulated common carrier service. But some of them were of immense value to firms in related fields and even to AT&T's competitors.

Now, according to Bell Labs Vice President Arno Penzias, AT&T will "have the opportunity and motive to use our own technology."

---

[51]Lee Dembart, "Dividing Bell Labs: Breakup to Put the Best to New Test," *Los Angeles Times,* Sept. 6, 1983, pp. 1,3.

[52]Remarks of Irwin Dorros at seminar "Research at Bell" held Apr. 5, 1984, Massachusetts Institute of Technology, Program on Research in Communications Policy.

Photo credit: AT&T Bell Laboratories

An experimental, interactive computer-based system is helping Bell Labs engineers design integrated circuits.

However, he emphasized that in the area of basic research, Bell Labs is still part of the scientific and technical community where communication and trading of information is vital. In order to benefit from the results of research elsewhere, it will have to continue to share its research results. In order to keep good scientists on the staff, it will have to allow them to publish.

Only a small number of basic research projects lead to results that have an obvious application. In some of those cases AT&T would probably get patent protection before publishing the results. In other cases, the published paper may report a discovery without giving details of how to duplicate it. This type of protection has been used by many labs, including Bell Labs in the past. Penzias noted that at IBM the number of papers published per dollar of research is about the same as Bell Labs, even though IBM is a competitive firm.[53]

A policy of complete openness of research results may be transferred to Bellcore. Its interest is to see that research results are disseminated widely so that manufacturers can use them to produce the best and lowest cost products for use by the Bell operating companies. Bellcore itself, under its current charter, will not be able to manufacture products or otherwise benefit from any discoveries or inventions resulting from its research. Therefore, it may establish a publication and licensing policy even more open than Bell Labs' has been in the past.

[53] Arno Penzias, remarks at a seminar "Research at Bell," held Apr. 5, 1984, Massachusetts Institute of Technology, Program on Research in Communication Policy.

Policy Implications

The recent divestiture and the entry of AT&T into competitive markets poses new challenges for U.S. policy toward the telecommunication and information industries. The 1979-83 period in which the divestiture and Computer II decisions were announced and implemented was also a period of intensive congressional debate about telecommunications. Bills have been introduced to modify the Communications Act of 1934, to deregulate parts of the industry, or to force some version of AT&T divestiture.[54] Many of the policy issues raised in this legislative debate have now been addressed by FCC in Computer II and through settlement of the Department of Justice suit. Speculation over the effects of the new policies have added to the uncertainty and change in the information industry. Several years under the new rules will be necessary before all the effects can be assessed.

Similarly, the full effects of deregulation and divestiture on the quality and direction of research at Bell Labs will only become clear as this "shake-down" period goes on. Neither history nor economic theory seem to be of much help in foreseeing the future of research at Bell Labs. There appear to be only a few things that government can do about major changes in research at Bell Labs. Clearly, in the post-divestiture era, decisions about the funding and nature of research will be in the hands of AT&T management. This is not new. Decisions about research have always been management decisions, in AT&T as throughout U.S. industry.

[54] For example, S. 898, H.R. 5158, as introduced in the 97th Congress, are only two bills which proposed modifying the 1956 consent decree, creating a subsidiary of AT&T to enter new unregulated markets, and stimulating competition in terminal equipment.

It is possible that, in the new climate created by deregulation and divestiture, AT&T management will make decisions about research that will allow the quality or quantity of Bell Labs' research to decline. In that case, there may be a role for limited government action. Some regulatory or funding policies might be developed to stimulate or facilitate research. These policy changes, discussed later in this section, might be aimed at AT&T alone, but might also be applied more generically to raise the quality of research in industry, universities, and government.

However, it would be premature to introduce policy changes without evidence that the current institutional arrangements are inadequate, or that the U.S. research capability is in jeopardy. The first step of government action might be to monitor Bell Labs' research over the next several years to see whether the quality of research actually changes. The monitoring effort might be expanded to include the whole range of industry and university research in information technology. It would not be difficult to develop an analytical framework and a set of criteria for measuring the vigor or quality of research. A number of possible measures are suggested below. While none of them is decisive in isolation, together they might give a picture of the health of research at Bell Labs and at other research organizations.[55]

For example, it would be possible to monitor the funds that AT&T allocates to research over the next few years. Dollar amounts seem very objective and quantifiable, but alone are not a sufficient gauge of the quality or direction of research effort. For example, if all basic science were dropped and the research effort steered toward more applied projects, the total amount spent for "research" might remain the same. This criterion may be useful, but cannot be used in isolation.

Another measure would be the number of papers by Bell Labs scientists published in prestigious scientific and technical journals each year. A decline in the number of papers could be an indication that the amount of research is declining, perhaps, or that AT&T is significantly limiting publication in order to protect possible commercial advantage stemming from certain types of research.

In addition to monitoring the number of papers published, it might also be possible to examine the quality of the journals in which they appear. Although this measure is subjective, it should reflect the quality of Bell Labs work as viewed by other members of the scientific community. Researchers in all fields have a clear idea which of their journals is the "best." To the extent that Bell Labs work continues to be published in the same sorts of journals as now, it may be evidence that the quality of results remains unchanged. A shift to publication in less prestigious journals might indicate a decline in quality.

The vigor of research can also be measured by its usefulness to other researchers. Thus, a possible measure of the continuing value of Bell Labs research would be the number of times their work is cited in papers published by scientists in universities and other labs. In addition, the attitude of the scientific community toward Bell Labs could be monitored by its ability to attract and retain well-qualified research workers.

There is the possibility that, even with a reduction of basic research at Bell Labs, research in the information field generally will not suffer. Scientific research may simply move to other laboratories. Any decline in quality of fundamental research would certainly make it harder for Bell Labs to attract and keep a staff of qualified scientists. Top graduate students would choose to work at other firms or at universities. To the extent that researchers continue to work in the same scientific fields and are equally productive in their new surroundings, there may be no noticeable effect on U.S. basic research.

To get a complete picture of the effects of deregulation and divestiture on the state of information technology basic research in the United States as a whole, it would be necessary to monitor the research performed throughout industry and at university labs as well. Even then, it would be extremely difficult to attribute observed changes in the U.S. research environment to changes occurring at Bell Labs. As noted in chapter 2, the state of information technology research is in flux and changes will occur with or without Bell Labs.

---

[55]Some of the measures listed have actually been used informally by Bell Labs management to monitor the strength of research in the Labs.

It may be possible, however, to trace some causal factors and to, at least, draw reasonable inferences.

One difficulty with the proposed studies is the collection of relevant data over an extended period of time. While the data needed are not extensive, they include items that firms do not currently report to any Federal agency (except that the FCC will continue to be concerned with AT&T's research budget). Some special effort and cooperation on the part of industry and the Federal Government would be needed to collect and analyze the necessary information.

It is difficult to say who might be best suited to carry out the studies mentioned above. One possibility is the FCC, which is responsible for oversight of many aspects of AT&T's business. However, many of the firms and institutions engaging on information technology research are not regulated by the FCC and it may not be appropriate for the Commission to study them. Other possibilities might be the National Telecommunications and Information Administration (NTIA), which has an interest in the health of U.S. information R&D, or the National Science Foundation (NSF), which monitors the state of R&D and basic research in a number of fields. Yet another possibility might be an independent research group outside of government—perhaps one created by a university or industry association. Most of the technical and scientific journals needed for bibliometric studies are already in the database of the Library of Congress. These analyses might be performed by the Congressional Research Service, an independent research group, or one of the agencies mentioned above.

For some of the studies mentioned above data may only be available several years after the actual research has been done, and in many cases meaningful conclusions can be drawn only after data for 5 or 10 years have been analyzed. If there is a reduction in basic research at Bell Labs, the trend might have been under way for several years before the data indicate a change. By that time, it might be difficult to effect any correction in the trend.

If it is determined that changes in basic research at AT&T have had a major effect on the U.S. research capability, and that Government action is warranted, there is a question of what can be done. Basically, it appears that two general approaches might be considered. Regulatory policies might be changed to modify the rules under which AT&T operates, giving it greater incentives to perform basic research or requiring it to do so. More broadly, consideration could be given to implementing funding policies that might stimulate more basic research throughout industry and in university laboratories.

In the regulatory area, for example, it might be possible to allow some subsidy for basic research. At the present time, FCC is working under the terms of the divestiture and Computer II to make sure that AT&T does not use the revenues it earns in the regulated market to support research or development that leads to advantages in the nonregulated market. For this reason FCC must approve the "composite allocator" developed by AT&T to allocate research costs among the various AT&T entities. The economic theory is that a competitive firm should pay its own R&D costs without shifting them to regulated ratepayers.

On the other hand, when AT&T was permitted to use such a cross-funding arrangement, it used the funds to create a highly respected and productive research organization that presumably benefited the Nation as a whole. If experience over the next few years shows that it is impossible for AT&T to maintain Bell Labs' quality without additional funding, and if it is determined to be in the national interest that such an organization be maintained, then additional funds must be provided. They could come from a direct Federal subsidy or from some kind of cross-funding. The former is not likely to be politically acceptable; the later is increasingly complex as the long-distance telecommunication market becomes more competitive. By its own estimate, AT&T now provides only 69 percent of total long-distance capacity.[56] AT&T is rapidly losing the market power it once had

---
[56]AT&T, private communication, Apr. 30, 1984.

to control prices throughout the industry. If it were required to raise the price of long-distance calls to provide greater support for basic research, it would be placed at a competitive disadvantage with respect to other long-distance carriers that do not support research. Development of a mechanism by which all long distance carriers contribute to funding basic research would be difficult in the increasingly competitive long distance market.

An alternative regulatory approach might be to stimulate basic research by allowing more cooperation between ATTIS and Bell Labs. About 4,000 former Bell Labs employees were moved to ATTIS when it was created in 1982. Expertise in some research areas has been lost to Bell Labs through this transfer and through the subsequent transfer of 3,000 employees to Bell Communications Research. The FCC's interpretation of Computer II rules do not allow the exchange of market and network information between ATTIS and Bell Labs and they also prohibit the joint development of certain products, especially computer software.

In the future, easing this requirement to the extent of allowing ATTIS and Bell Labs to cooperate on certain types of research, might allow greater cross-fertilization among the two research organizations.

Policies to stimulate basic research generally might include such incentives as additional grant support from National Science Foundation (for example), direct support of basic research through direct Federal subsidies, or tax incentives for industries that engage in basic research. Such policies might be applied not only to Bell Labs, of course, but to Bellcore or to other university and industry research organizations. Over the next few years, while the health of research is being monitored, it might be possible to structure such programs to stimulate research and to develop "trigger" mechanisms for putting them into place if results indicate that the quality of research is declining.

In conclusion, it is still too early to tell whether the quality or direction of research at Bell Labs will be adversely affected by deregulation and divestiture, or whether any changes in its research would have major repercussions for U.S. research as a whole. There are several possible measures for monitoring the health of basic research at Bell Labs, but evidence of change may not be apparent for several years. While Bell Labs is a major contributor to the sciences related to information technology, it is not the only important player. To gain a true picture of the effects of deregulation and divestiture it would be worthwhile to expand such studies to monitor the state of basic research throughout industry and at university labs as well. It will be important to begin collecting information soon in order to fully document the transition from the pre- to post-deregulation environment.

Chapter 4 References

"Bell Labs on the Brink," *Science,* Sept. 23, 1983, pp. 1267-1269.

"Bell Labs: The Threatened Star of U.S. Research," *Fortune,* July 5, 1982, pp. 46-52.

Brock, Gerald W., *The Telecommunications Industry: The Dynamics of Market Structure* (Cambridge: Harvard University Press, 1981).

"Competing with the New AT&T," *Venture,* January 1984, pp. 54-57.

Charles River Associates, *Impacts of the AT&T Divestiture on Innovative Behavior,* unpublished paper prepared for Office of Technology Assessment, 1983.

Dembart, Lee, "Dividing Bell Labs: Breakup to Put the Best to New Test," *Los Angeles Times,* Sept. 6, 1983, pp. 1,3.

Hall, Peter, "AT&T and the Great Divide," *Financial World,* Jan. 10, 1984, pp. XX.

Harris, Marilyn A., "Bell Labs Looks to Military Research," *Electronics,* Feb. 9, 1984, pp. 102-104.

Kamien, Morton I., and Nancy Schwartz, *Market Structure and Innovation* (New York: Cambridge University Press, 1982).

Morkre, Morris E., "Innovation and Market Structure: A Survey," Working Paper No. 82. Federal Trade Commission, Bureau of Economics, 1982.

National Science Board, *Science Indicators, 1982* (Washington, DC: U.S. Government Printing Office, 1983).

National Science Foundation, *Research and Development in Industry, 1981,* NSF 83-325 (Washington, DC: U.S. Government Printing Office, 1983), p. 3.

Scherer, F. M., "Firm Sizes, Market Structure, Opportunity, and the Output of Patented Inventions," *American Economics Review,* 55:1119.

Scherer, F. M., *Industrial Market Structure and Economic Performance* (New York: Rand McNally, 1980).

Uttal, Bro, "Cold New World," *Fortune,* June 27, 1983, pp. 81-84.

"Why AT&T Will Lose More Long Distance Business," *Business Week,* Feb. 13, 1984, pp. 102-104, 110.

Wiegner, Kathleen K., "Prometheus is Unbound and Seeking His Footing," *Forbes,* Mar. 12, 1984, pp. 141-148.

Chapter 5
Education and Human Resources for Research and Development

Contents

	Page
Findings	139
The Concern About Manpower	139
The Relationship Between Manpower Development and Economic Growth	140
Identifying Particular Manpower Problems and Solutions	141
The Range of Manpower Predictions	145
The Supply of Manpower	149
The Problems in Higher Education	149
Elementary and Secondary Education	154
The Federal Role in Manpower Development	157
The Societal Context for Determining Federal Manpower Policy	161
Chapter 5 References	163

Tables

Table No.	Page
24. Scientists and Engineers Engaged in R&D Per Labor Force Population, By Country: 1963-82	145
25. BLS Manpower Estimates	146

Figures

Figure No.	Page
20. Employed Scientists and Engineers by Field, 1981	143
21. Distribution of Scientists and Engineers by Primary Work Activity, 1981	144
22. Percentage of Firms Reporting Available Jobs for Scientists and Engineers	148
23. Comparison of Growth in Engineering Undergraduate Enrollment and Number of Faculty, 1973-80	150
24. Share of All S/Es Employed in Educational Institutions by Field, 1981	151
25. Educational Gifts by Computer Vendors	153
26. Selected Indicators of the Overall Quality of Mathematics and Science Education in the United States	154
27. America's Science Teacher Shortage	156
28. Selected Indicators of Shifts in Undergraduate Science/Engineering Education	157
29. A Quarter Century of Student Aid	160

Chapter 5

Education and Human Resources for Research and Development

Findings

OTA found that major Federal actions designed to affect the supply of manpower to perform research and development (R&D) in the area of information technology would appear to be unwarranted at this time. Forecasts of future manpower needs in this area are replete with uncertainty. Moreover, developing manpower for the specific areas where potential shortages might tentatively be predicted would be particularly hard to accomplish through broad Federal actions. The educational backgrounds and skills required to meet these potential shortages are at once both too broad and too narrow to be developed at the Federal level. In addition, given the length of time required to develop skills and the rapid changes taking place in the area of information technology, Federal action, taken now, might prove to be inappropriate in the future.

A number of legislative proposals have been made that are designed to increase the future supply of highly qualified scientific and technical manpower. These proposals differ considerably in terms of their goals, their targets, their costs, and their scopes. Given the high levels of uncertainty that surround the present manpower debate and the number of competing uses to which the Nation's limited educational resources might be profitably put, the most prudent course might be to adopt those policies that would provide for the greatest amount of flexibility and the broadest range of skills.

The Concern About Manpower

In the United States today, there is a growing and widespread belief that the Nation's poor economic performance is inextricably linked to the relative decline in the size and the quality of its technical work force. Noting that Japan and West Germany, our major international competitors, have four times as many electrical engineers and computer scientists, per capita, as the United States, many of the people who hold this view fear that, as the economies of the developed world become more technologically intensive, and thus as R&D becomes more critical to their success, the United States will increasingly lose its ability to compete. Typical of this perspective is the statement made by Representative Margaret Heckler during hearings on Engineering Manpower Concerns, when she said:[1]

To maintain its technological edge in world markets the United States must reemphasize science and engineering on our agenda of national priorities. When the Soviets launched Sputnik I, a remarkable engineering accomplishment, the United States rose to the challenge with new dedication to science and technology. Today, our technology lead is again being challenged, not just by the Soviet Union, but by Japan, West Germany, and others.

The negative consequences of having a shortage of manpower in information technology R&D, it is argued, may be particularly severe. Given the speed with which the field is changing, even a temporary shortage might impair the ability of information technology industries to remain at the frontiers of re-

---

[1]Representative Margaret Heckler, Opening Statement, *Hearings On Manpower Concerns,* before the Committee on Science and Technology, House of Representatives, 97th Cong., 1st sess., Oct. 6-7, 1981, p. 4. For a more recent statement of this perspective, see also, *Hearings on Mathematics and Science Education,* before the Committee on Education and Labor, House of Representatives, 98th Cong., 1st sess., Jan. 26-28, 31, 1983; see also, *America's Competitive Challenge,* Report of Business-Higher Education Forum, 1983.

search. And, because the information technology industry represents the fastest growth sector of the economy, failure to keep pace in this industry may have serious consequences for the Nation's economy as a whole.

Concerned about the state of available human resources for high-technology jobs, spokesmen from business, government, and education have called on the Federal Government to undertake a number of significant educational measures and reforms. These measures range widely in terms of goals, targets, costs, and scope. Some of them, for instance, focus on a specific curriculum area, such as math and science; others emphasize educational infrastructure—the training of teachers and the need for equipment; while still others seek to foster new modes of cooperation between business, government, and educational institutions. Given our Nation's limited resources and the growing number of demands and stresses that are being placed on our educational system at all levels, choices and decisions will have to be made about which goals to pursue and about which measures to adopt.

Notwithstanding the widespread discussion and concern about the poor state of the Nation's manpower resources, there has been very little systematic effort to clearly identify and characterize the nature and the extent of the problems. Before making any major policy decisions designed to affect the supply of manpower, therefore, it will be necessary to have a greater understanding of: 1) what we know and don't know about the relationship between manpower development and economic growth; 2) what we know and don't know about this relationship as it relates in particular to R&D in information technologies; 3) the range of projections about the future supply of and demand for manpower in this field; 4) the ability of the present institutional structure to accommodate these manpower needs; 5) the role of the Federal Government in the development of manpower; 6) the societal context in which, today, decisions about education will be made; and 7) the range of Federal alternative strategies and options for meeting future manpower needs in the area of information technology R&D. The following discussion provides a preliminary basis for such an understanding.

The Relationship Between Manpower Development and Economic Growth

The assumption of a positive relationship between the size and quality of a nation's work force and its economic wealth is not a new one. Over 100 years ago, for example, the British Government sponsored a parliamentary committee to investigate the causes of rapid industrial growth in the United States. Like many of our recent studies of economic growth in Japan, the British parliamentary committee attributed much of America's industrial success to the superior education of the American worker.[2]

Indeed, ever since the beginning of the industrial revolution, economists and other social observers have argued that a skilled and educated work force is the most productive. Writing as early as 1776, Adam Smith, for example, pointed out that "the skill, dexterity, and judgment with which it's [the nation's] labor is generally applied," is the primary factor determining the size of "the fund which originally supplies it with all the necessities of life."[3]

---

[2]*Report From the Select Committee on Scientific Instruction,* Parliamentary Papers, 15, (1867-1868) Q 6722, as cited in William Abernathy, Kim B. Clark, and Alan Kantrow, *Industrial Renaissance: Producing a Competitive Future for America* (New York: Basic Books, 1983).

[3]Adam Smith, *The Wealth of Nations* (New York: The Modern Library, 1937), p. lviv.

As modern societies became more technologically advanced, an increasing amount of attention was paid to the development of the labor force. Anticipating the effect that technology would have on society, the German sociologist, Max Weber, pointed out for example, that, in an advanced industrial society, the organization of human relations could no longer be left to chance. Instead, human beings become factors of production—their

Present government policies designed to affect the supply of manpower are also based on this assumption. However, as the following discussion illustrates, while we can identify some general linkages between education, manpower, and economic development, our understanding of causal relationships, or of relationships in specific situations, is extremely limited.

While acknowledging that having qualified manpower is critical to the success of a nation's economy, social and economic analysts are still unable to fully account for, or to completely explain, the nature of the relationship between the size and the skill level of the labor force and economic growth and development. As the economist, Nathan Rosenberg, has noted:[4]

---

relationships to be structured in accordance with the requirements of industrial progress. And the American economist, Thorsten Veblen, writing in the 1930s, went so far in his discussions of technology and society as to suggest that, for technology to develop to its full potential, the technical expert—the engineer—would have to play a key role in society's decisionmaking process. Jay Weinstein, *Sociology/Technology: Foundations of Post Academic Science*, Transaction Books, 1982, p. 32; Thorsten Veblen, *The Theory of the Leisure Class* (New York: The Modern Library, 1934).

[4]Nathan Rosenberg, *Inside the Black Box—Technology and Economics* (Cambridge, MA: Cambridge University Press, 1982), p. 8.

One of the central historical questions concerning technical progress is its extreme variability over time and place. . . . Clearly the reasons for these differences, which are not yet well understood, are tied in numerous complex and subtle ways to the functioning of the larger social systems, their institutions, values, and incentive structures. The explanation of these differences is intimately tied to such even larger questions as why social change occurs and why economic growth proceeds over time and place.

Not only is each piece of the puzzle difficult to solve; the whole problem is subject to the vagaries of external events, well beyond our anticipation and calculation. Nor are the tools of analysis particularly refined. For—although demographers may tell us something about population trends; sociologists something about the institutions and processes in which individuals are recruited, educated, and trained for work; economists something about the point at which, and the rate of exchange by which, the supply and the demand for labor are brought into a state of equilibrium—historians are sure to remind us that it is, more often than not, a unique set of circumstances that has had the most significant effect on a particular outcome.

Identifying Particular Manpower Problems and Solutions

Our limited knowledge of the role of human resources in economic growth and technological change is clearly evident in our efforts to identify and analyze specific manpower problems and solutions. For although manpower specialists might agree that having sufficient qualified manpower is critical to a nation's economy, they do not necessarily agree about the number of people who are required to meet the employment needs of a particular sector; about the kinds of skills and experience that might be required to perform particular kinds of jobs; or about the way in which these skills might best be obtained or developed.[5]

---

[5]National Institute of Education, *Education, Productivity, and the National Economy, A Research Initiative*, December 1981; see also Edwin Mansfield, *Education, R&D, and Productivity Growth*, revised, University of Pennsylvania, Jan. 31, 1982.

To identify future manpower needs in a particular area, policymakers have traditionally relied on economic and other forecasting methodologies. While useful as policymaking tools, these methodologies are subject to a number of problems and weaknesses which stem, among other things, from imperfect data, weak forecasting models, and ill-founded assumptions.[6] To be most useful, forecasting methods need to be flexible and responsive. Acknowledgment should be made of the limitations of these methodologies, and efforts should be undertaken to verify their results by conducting frequent surveys and by performing case studies designed to determine

---

[6]R. H. Bezdek, *Long-Range Forecasting of Manpower Requirements* (New York: Institute of Electrical and Electronics Engineers, 1974).

the changing skill requirements that are linked to the emergence of new technologies.

It should be noted, moreover, that manpower forecasts can themselves produce a pendulum effect, undermining the validity of the projections. This effect results from both the long period of time that it takes for people to prepare for a field of work, and from the fact that, once committed to a career path, people rarely change their plans in midstream to adapt to new circumstances. Upon hearing predictions of an impending manpower shortage in a particular field, for example, an inordinate number of students may seek to pursue such a career, hoping that when they have finished their educations, jobs will be plentiful and competition will be in short supply. The resulting manpower glut will appear only later; but predictions of it may induce a number of students to avoid the field, leading to another shortage in the future.

It should also be remembered that manpower predictions can be interpreted differently by different kinds of people. Economists might describe a shortage, for example, when they see a rapid increase in wages due to a gap between the supply and demand for labor. Businessmen might consider that there is a shortage of manpower when they are dissatisfied with the quality of preparedness of the pool of people from whom they have to select employees. New graduates may interpret a manpower shortage to mean that they face little competition in seeking employment.

The problem of predicting manpower needs in the area of information technology R&D is even more complicated, because the field is new and in a rapid state of flux. There is, for example, very little historical basis for identifying who the people are who might typically perform R&D tasks in the area of information technology; what skills they should possess in order to perform these tasks most effectively; or what their optimum career patterns might be.

It is only very recently that either the National Science Foundation (NSF), the key agency mandated to monitor the supply and demand of engineers and scientists in the United States, or the Bureau of Labor Statistics, have begun to treat computer scientists as a distinct group. NSF, for example, has only recently stopped labeling everyone who works in a computer-related field as working in the area of computer theory, a heading that was itself a subcategory of mathematics. And, even today, NSF does not list a department of computer science under that heading if the department's name appears in a combined form and if the words "computer science" appear second in that combination.[7] Even when the appropriate statistics have been collected, moreover, they have often been subject to a variety of interpretations.[8]

It is also difficult to determine not only who or how many people are working on or with these technologies but also who or how many people are performing specific R&D tasks in this area. NSF estimates that in 1981, 3.1 million scientists and engineers were employed in the United States. Of these, 47 percent were employed as engineers (including engineers doing management jobs), and 13 percent were working as computer specialists (see fig. 20).[9] NSF reports, moreover, that 34 percent of all scientists and engineers are involved in R&D activities[10] (see fig. 21). As table 24 illustrates, compared to other countries, this is a high proportion of R&D scientists and engineers relative to the total labor force. Figures are not available, however, for the percentage of scientists and engineers who specifically perform R&D tasks in the area of information technology.

Use of aggregated data based on broad skill categories or outmoded technologies reduces the value of manpower demand forecasts. A category such as computer programmer, for example, is much too broad to use for forecasting manpower demand in R&D. Further sub-

---

[7]Kent K. Curtis, "Computer Manpower—Is There a Crisis?" (Washington, DC: National Science Foundation, January 1983).
[8]Ibid.
[9]*Science Indicators 1982: An Analysis of the State of U.S. Science, Engineering, and Technology,* National Science Board, 1983, p. 63.
[10]Ibid., p. 66.

Figure 20.—Employed Scientists and Engineers by Field, 1981

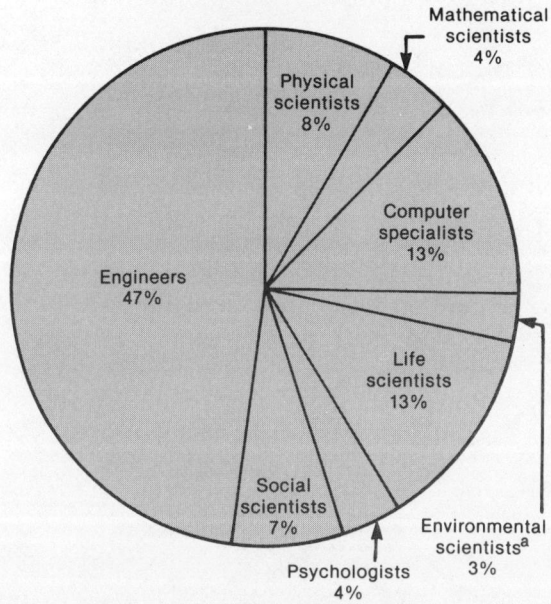

aIncludes earth scientists, oceanographers, and atmospheric scientists.
NOTE: The total number of scientists and engineers in 1981 was 3.1 million.
SOURCE: *Science Indicators*, 1982.

division into types such as entry level, applications, and systems programmers based on existing job specifications, while useful, will probably not suffice for long, since the mix of computer-related skills required for R&D is especially sensitive to technological innovation.[11] Some of the most important skill categories, for example, lie at the frontiers of information technology, and these do not show up in the broad categories based on aggregated data. The problem of identifying these skills, therefore, is not just one of substituting one set of static descriptors for another; it is a problem of gathering information about new skills over time and in response to changing conditions.

The task of identifying research and development workers in the field of information technology is complicated, moreover, by the fact that the traditional distinctions that have always been made between the tasks that are entailed in R&D and those entailed in production are becoming increasingly blurred in this area. This problem is clearly evident in the case of software engineering. Calculations of future manpower needs that focus specifically on R&D activities are, therefore, particularly difficult to make in the area of information technologies.

Questions also arise with respect to how the skilled technical workers, who provide support to the R&D process but who do not perform the most highly skilled tasks, might best be factored into manpower projections. These workers might include, for example, all of those who maintain, troubleshoot, repair, and sometimes fabricate sophisticated equipment, those who build and help develop prototypes of new products, draftsmen and nondegree designers, computer system operators, and technical writers. Since the skills that these workers require may be more easily obtained or may be more easily substituted—either by other workers or by technology—than the skills required for the more highly technical jobs, the manpower projections for this sector of the R&D process, and the policy implications that might be drawn from them, may also be quite distinct. Policies designed to affect the availability of skilled technical workers, for example, might call for some general educational changes at the elementary and/or secondary levels whereas those that are designed to influence the supply of manpower in a highly technical area such as artificial intelligence, or software engineering, might call for targeted incentives at the university or graduate studies level.

Defining R&D manpower and estimating manpower needs for this area becomes even more troublesome the further one looks into the future. Over the long run the future demand for manpower, for example, is likely to depend on the extent to which and the speed at which the new technologies are deployed throughout society. However, the rate and degree of their deployment will depend, in turn, on the kinds of social variables that are most often left out of forecasting models, and that are the most difficult to predict.

---

[11]Abbe Mowshowitz, "On Predicting R&D Skill Requirements for Information Technology," paper prepared for the Office of Technology Assessment, February 1984.

144 • *Information Technology R&D: Critical Trends and Issues*

Figure 21.—Distribution of Scientists and Engineers by Primary Work Activity, 1981

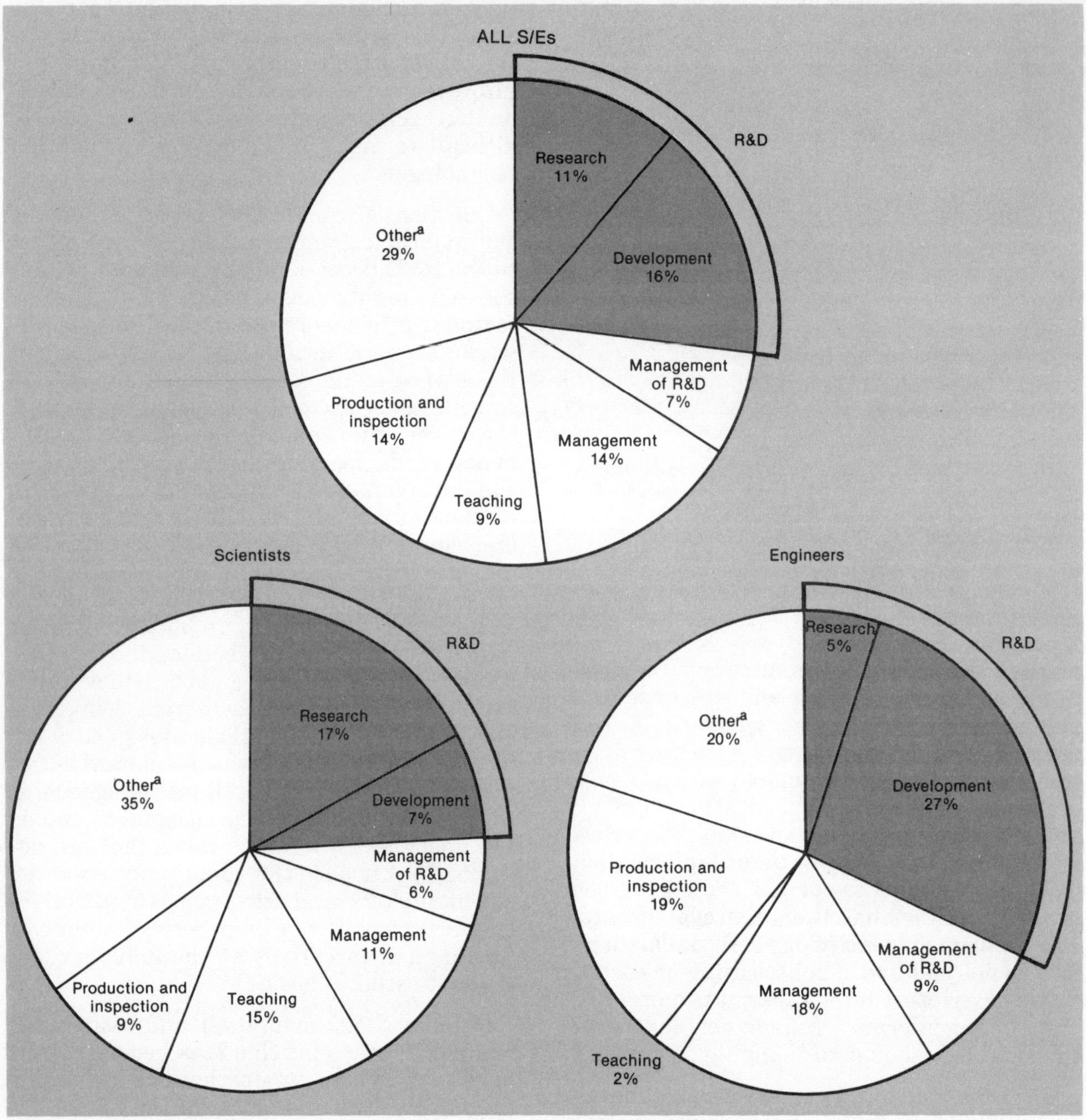

ALL S/Es
- Research 11%
- Development 16%
- Management of R&D 7%
- Management 14%
- Teaching 9%
- Production and inspection 14%
- Other[a] 29%

Scientists
- Research 17%
- Development 7%
- Management of R&D 6%
- Management 11%
- Teaching 15%
- Production and inspection 9%
- Other[a] 35%

Engineers
- Research 5%
- Development 27%
- Management of R&D 9%
- Management 18%
- Teaching 2%
- Production and inspection 19%
- Other[a] 20%

[a]Includes reporting, statistical work and computing, consulting, other, and no report.

SOURCE: *Science Indicators*, 1982.

Table 24.—Scientists and Engineers[a] Engaged in R&D Per Labor Force Population, By Country: 1963-82

Country	1965	1968	1972	1975	1979	1982
S/Es[a] engaged in R&D per 10,000 labor force population						
France	21.0	26.4	28.1	29.3	31.6	NA
West Germany	22.7	26.2	36.0	41.0	47.7	NA
Japan	24.6	31.2	38.1	47.9	50.4	NA
United Kingdom	19.6	20.8	30.4	31.2	33.2[b]	NA
United States	64.1	66.9	57.9	55.5	57.9	63.8
U.S.S.R. (lowest)	44.8	53.5	66.5	78.2	84.4	89.8
U.S.S.R. (highest)	48.2	58.8	73.2	87.5	95.5	102.4
S/Es[a] engaged in R&D (in thousands)						
France	42.8	54.7	61.2	65.3	72.9	NA
West Germany	61.0	68.0	96.0	103.9	122.0	NA
Japan	117.6	157.6	198.1	255.2	281.9	NA
United Kingdom	49.9	52.8	76.7	80.5	87.7[b]	NA
United States	494.5	550.4	518.3	532.7	620.2	716.9
U.S.S.R. (lowest)	521.8	650.8	862.5	1,061.8	1,216.4	1,340.4
U.S.S.R. (highest)	561.4	715.2	950.1	1,187.6	1,377.4	1,340.4
Total labor force (in thousands)						
France	20,381	20,744	21,817	22,310	23,059	NA
West Germany	26,887	25,968	26,655	25,323	25,573	NA
Japan	47,870	50,610	51,940	53,230	55,960	NA
United Kingdom	25,498	25,378	25,195	25,798	26,464	NA
United States	77,178	82,272	89,483	95,955	107,050	112,383
U.S.S.R.	116,494	121,716	129,722	135,767	144,201	149,215

[a]Includes all scientists and engineers engaged in R&D on a full-time equivalent basis (except for Japan whose data include persons primarily employed in R&D excluding social scientists, and the United Kingdom whose data include only the Government and industry sectors).
[b]1978.
NA—Not available.
SOURCE: National Science Foundation, Science Indicators 1982.

Future manpower requirements in software engineering, for example, might be significantly reduced as new software tools are developed and introduced, if new institutional practices are adopted to improve the efficiency of those working in the area, and if more and more applications software are developed on personal computers by end users.[12] Predicting these changes or their future impacts is extremely difficult, given the newness of the field and the fact that they are dependent on a number of social variables—e.g., the willingness of individuals and institutions to both adopt and adapt to technological changes—variables that are themselves notoriously unpredictable.

[12]Ibid.

The Range of Manpower Predictions

Given the problems involved in identifying future manpower requirements, it is not surprising that there has been considerable controversy over and discrepancy between many of the projections that have been made about the need for high-technology manpower. Among those making forecasts, the consensus has been the greatest with respect to projected shortages of Ph.D.s to teach at the university level in the fields of engineering and computer science. To a somewhat lesser degree, manpower experts concur that the future growth in demand for computer scientists will be extraordinary. They disagree, however, about whether or not the educational system, as it exists today, can effectively respond to meet that demand. Agreement is lowest with regard to whether or not there will be a future shortage of engineers.

The following summary provides some sense of the range of projections. Because these forecasts are based on different assumptions, methodologies, baselines, and timeframes, it is impossible to compare and contrast them analytically as a whole. Evaluations about their reliability and accuracy are quite dependent, therefore, on judgments about the validity of their methods and assumptions.

Generally speaking, however, it can be said that manpower forecasts are more reliable the greater the number of and the more refined the underlying analysis.[13] The least sophisticated forecasting methodology, for example, might be one based solely on survey data, or simply extrapolating trends on the basis of the present. A much more comprehensive approach, on the other hand, might be one that takes into account such things as changes in the relative prices of capital and labor, and/or that posits a set of alternative assumptions about the future. The most ambitious forecasts are those that try to factor into their analysis the impact of technological change.[14]

Perhaps the most widely referred to, and among the more sophisticated projections, are those that have been put forward by the **Bureau of Labor Statistics** (BLS). These projections cover a period of 10 to 15 years. They are not only based on a set of alternative economic scenarios, positing different rates of growth; to some extent, they also seek to take technological change into account. Moreover, BLS has consistently sought to improve its methodology by systematically evaluating the accuracy of its own projections. Such evaluations show that BLS has had more success in determining how technology might effect future job growth than it has in identifying at what point such changes in employment patterns might take place. Past projections have,

moreover, tended to exaggerate the growth of technical occupations and underestimate the decline of certain traditional jobs. One useful measure of the accuracy of these projections is the recent finding that 60 percent of the 1980 forecasts fell within a 10 percent range of the actual employment level for that year.[15]

BLS projects the rate of growth and the future demand for manpower in given occupational categories. The Bureau's most recent projections for those categories most relevant to information technology are listed in table 25.[16] For each category, there are three projections—high, medium, and low—each corresponding to one of the three economic scenarios used by BLS in developing their forecasts.

Because it does not make predictions about the future supply of manpower, the Bureau of Labor Statistics does not predict labor shortages or labor surpluses per se. However, review of the recent articles in the BLS publication, *Occupational Outlook Handbook,* suggests that there will be a multi-tiered mar-

---
[13]Henry M. Levin and Russell W. Rumberger, *The Educational Implications of High Technology,* The National Institute of Education Report #83-A4, 1983.
[14]Ibid.
[15]Ibid.
[16]Conversation with Tom Nardone, Manpower Economist, Bureau of Labor Statistics, Department of Commerce, May 15, 1984.

Table 25.—BLS Manpower Estimates

Base year: 1982		1995
Electrical and electronic engineers:		
320,000	Low	531,000
	Moderate	528,000
	High	540,000
Computer specialists:		
Programmers:		
226,000	Low	465,000
	Moderate	471,000
	High	480,000
Systems analysts:		
254,000	Low	469,000
	Moderate	471,000
	High	480,000
Technicians:		
55,000	Low	106,000
	Moderate	108,000
	High	108,000
Computer operators:		
211,000	Low	366,000
	Moderates	371,000
	High	378,000

SOURCE: Tom Nardone, Manpower Economist, Bureau of Labor Statistics, Department of Commerce, personal communication, May 15, 1984.

ket for these job categories, with a shortage of people with some specific skills and a surplus of those with others.

The **National Science Foundation** also makes projections of the supply and demand for scientific, engineering, and technical personnel. These projections are developed using a multi-step model, similar to the one used by BLS. Like the BLS model, for example, the NSF model tries to anticipate how technological change might affect future manpower needs. In one way, however, the NSF model goes further than that of BLS: its alternative scenarios posit different levels of defense spending as well as different levels of economic growth.[17]

In its recent report, *Science Indicators 1982*, NSF pointed out that computer specialists accounted for almost 45 percent of the total growth of scientific employment over the period 1976-81. Matching this growth against the future supply of computer science personnel, it predicted a future shortage in this area. Indicators for the future supply and demand of engineers were more mixed, however. For while these indicators revealed a shortage in 1981, they also suggested that by mid to late 1982, the situation already appeared to be shifting back towards a balance between the supply of and the demand for engineers in general.

A recent survey conducted for NSF raises some questions about the degree to which manpower shortages may in fact materialize in the future, even in the area of computer science. Nearly one-half of the 351 firms surveyed, for example, reported fewer openings for scientists, engineers, and technicians during the 1982-83 recruiting year than in the 1981-82 period. These results are broken down by area in the following figure[18] (fig. 22).

Focusing on manpower needs for defense, the U.S. Air Force, in *The Regional Planning and Evaluations Systems (ROPES)* Project, forecast manpower needs for 30 States and 70 major cities. The States were selected for analysis because they are major centers of defense activity. The ROPES study found that the need for all skill groups involved in "the use, operation and repair of computer equipment will grow at an alarming rate throughout the 1980s and that these skills will be particularly affected by increased expenditures for defense." Although the Air Force study group did not project the supply of manpower for these areas, they concluded, based on the projected rate of growth in demand, that the field of computer science, and perhaps electrical and mechanical engineering, may be areas of potential national shortage.

A 1982 study by Betty M. Vetter of the *Scientific Manpower Commission* summarizes information on the present and future supply and utilization of scientists and engineers in the United States. Vetter concludes that, except in the field of computer science, the supply of scientists appears sufficient to fill near-term demands. For engineers, she notes that the number of new graduates at the baccalaureate level has been rising since 1975, but that "a high level of demand has not only fueled that increase, but has utilized so many engineering graduates at the baccalaureate level that graduate enrollments of U.S. students have not climbed commensurately and shortages of Ph.D. engineers have become serious, at least at academic institutions." She concludes, however, that there is no general agreement about the adequacy of the future supply of engineers, even when considering particular specialties.

Industry projections of future manpower needs are quite inconsistent with one another. Derived, as they are, by stakeholders, their conclusions must be regarded with some degree of caution.

Basing its conclusions on a survey of 815 manufacturing facilities, the American Electronic Association (AEA) predicts that through 1987, the need for technical professionals will grow by 69 percent; while the need for technical paraprofessionals will increase by 60 percent. Respondents to their survey estimate, moreover, that in 5 years they will need to

---
[17]Levin and Rumberger, op. cit., pp. 12-13.
[18]Ibid.

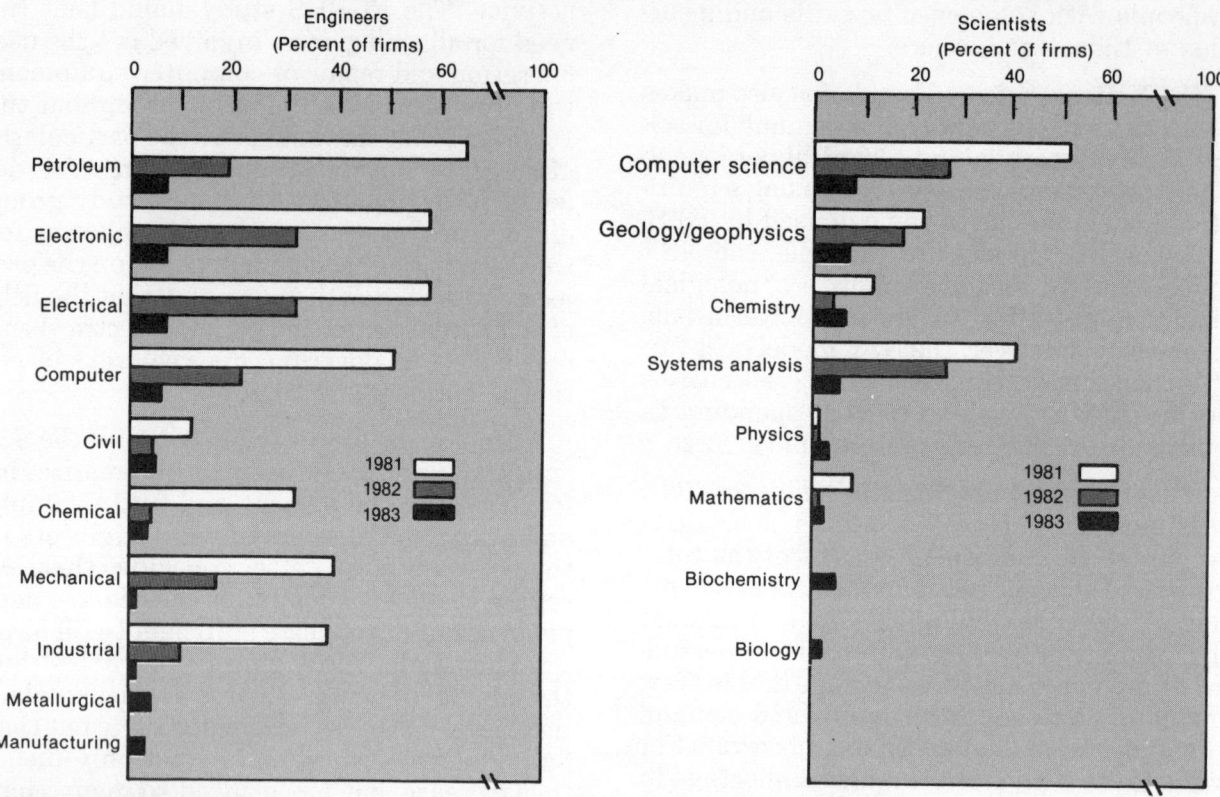

Figure 22.—Percentage of Firms Reporting Available Jobs for Scientists and Engineers

SOURCE: National Science Foundation.

employ more than 100,000 each of new technical professionals and new technical paraprofessionals.[19] The occupational groups for which they foresee a tremendous amount of growth during this period—defined as over 100 percent total increase—are software engineers, electronic engineering technologists, and computer analysts/programmers.[20]

To project the future supply of these key occupational groups, AEA uses data that assume that U.S. colleges will continue to increase the number of Bachelor of Science/Computer Science degrees at the same rate as they have over the past 5 years. Comparing projected supply and demand, the AEA report concludes that by 1987 there will be a shortage of 113,406 computer scientists and electrical engineers. Discounting employment related to defense, the shortage would be 81,780.

More skeptical about the likelihood of an impending shortage of electrical engineers is David Lewis, Council Chairman for the Career Activities Council of the Institute of Electrical and Electronic Engineers, Inc. (IEEE). Noting that the engineering profession is made up of people who are trained in a range of disciplines, projections of shortages, he says, fail to take into account the extent to which electrical engineers can be substituted for by engineers trained in other specialties. He has expressed concern, moreover, that an uncritical acceptance of such predictions might lead to a surplus of electrical engineers, a situation not dissimilar to the one that existed for aeronautical engineers in the early 1970s.[21]

---
[19] AEA, p. 10.
[20] Ibid.

[21] Ibid.

The Supply of Manpower

Although manpower projections tell us something about the number of people who will be needed and who may appear to fill existing high-technology positions, they say very little about the quality of skills and experience that the people who are available might bring to these jobs. To evaluate the quality of our existing and future supply of manpower for R&D in information technologies, we have to look at the major source of this manpower—at the Nation's educational institutions.

Formal educational institutions are, of course, neither the only nor necessarily the most significant institutional setting for manpower training and development. At one point in history, for example, it was the family that dominated in preparing its members for economic roles. Later, as society became more technologically advanced, a somewhat more formal system of apprenticeship emerged. Formal schooling became especially important during the age of industrialization.

Today, as we move towards what has been characterized as a high-technology society, businesses have themselves become involved, both formally and informally, in performing educational tasks. This has been particularly true in the area of information technology, where the larger corporations like IBM, Xerox, and Digital Equipment Corp. have set up their own educational centers. Moreover, informal training takes place and is diffused within the business community as people, trained in large companies, move on to form new companies of their own.

Recognizing that a number of different kinds of institutions are presently involved in the development and training of future manpower, this chapter will nonetheless focus on those that are a part of the formal educational system. For it is chiefly within the context of these institutions that the Federal Government plays out its role in manpower development.

The Problems in Higher Education

While the American university system has always been renowned for the number of scholars and the amount and quality of research that it has generated, today many people are beginning to question whether universities can continue to effectively perform all of their traditional roles. And, although almost all areas of university education have suffered from the problems of increased educational responsibilities and increased educational costs, the problems that universities face appear to be particularly acute in the areas that generate manpower to perform R&D in information technologies. University departments in these areas are having an especially difficult time because, given their limited funding, they are finding it almost impossible to compete for manpower and other resources in what is becoming a rapidly growing and wide-open high-technology market.

The difficulties are well illustrated in the case of engineering and computer science education, where a large proportion of faculty positions are unfilled and where the number of Ph.D.s graduating each year has dropped substantially. The problem in this area is not one of attracting highly qualified undergraduate students.[22] Over the past decade undergraduate enrollments in these areas have grown at a tremendous rate—by 80 percent in the case of engineering[23] and by 20 percent in

---
[22] Jeanne McDermott, "Technical Education: The Quiet Crisis," *High Technology*, November/December 1982, p. 87.
[23] Jerrier A. Haddad, "Key Issues in U.S. Engineering Education," *NAE Bridge*, summer 1983, p. 11.

the area of computer science.[24] And, given the growing popularity of electrical engineering and computer science and the limitations that, in almost all engineering schools and departments of computer science, are now being placed on the number of admissions, the high qualifications of new entrants are without precedent.[25]

Rather, as figure 23 illustrates, the problem at universities has been one of recruiting sufficient faculty members to support this enrollment. According to the American Council on Education, 1,583 teaching positions were vacant in the Nation's 244 accredited departments of engineering during the 1980-81 academic year.[26]

The gap would probably be much greater, moreover, were it not for the sizable number of foreign engineers who teach in American colleges and universities. A recent survey of engineering schools found, for example, that 25 percent of all junior faculty members in engineering received their bachelor's degree outside of the United States.[27]

The shortage of faculty members in the field of engineering and computer science has been attributed to the fact that industry, by offering higher salaries and other, nonmonetary incentives, has been able to draw a number of academics and students away from universities.[28] The extent of the problem is illustrated by figure 24, which shows that, in contrast to other areas of science, only a relatively small proportion of the Nation's engineers and computer scientists are employed in academia.[29]

Discrepancies between the salaries earned by scientists working in industry and academia have, in fact, been quite extensive. It has not been atypical, for example, for an inexperienced electrical engineer with a bachelor's degree to earn more than an assistant professor of engineering with a Ph.D.[30]

---

[24]"As Students Flock to Computer Science Courses, Colleges Scramble To Find Professors," *The Chronicle of Higher Education,* Feb. 9, 1981.
[25]John Horgan, "Technology '84 Education," *IEEE Spectrum,* January 1984. [Data on Admission Illustrations.]

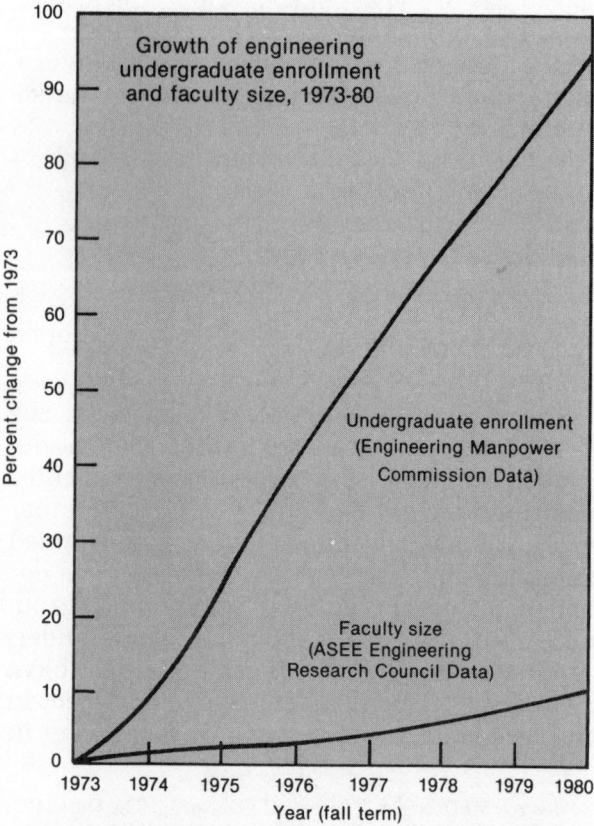

Figure 23.—Comparison of Growth in Engineering Undergraduate Enrollment and Number of Faculty, 1973-80

NOTE: Faculty numbers drawn from ASEE's Research and Graduate Study directory were adjusted on the basis of enrollment data to include the same number of schools as in EMC's enrollment survey.
SOURCE: *Engineering Education,* November 1982.

---

[26]"As Students Flock to Computer Sciences Courses," op. cit.
[27]"As Students Flock to Computer Science Courses," op. cit.
[28]"Supply of Engineering Faculty," *Electronic Market Trends,* January 1982, p. 14:
   It should be noted in this regard that the continued supply of foreign faculty will depend to some extent on the fate of The Immigration Reform and Control Act, a bill that was recently passed by the Senate and that would require foreigners to return home after graduation for at least 2 years. An amendment may be attached to the bill, however, allowing certain students studying in high-technology fields to stay.
[29]*Science Indicators,* op. cit., p. 123.
[30]McDermott, op. cit., p. 47.

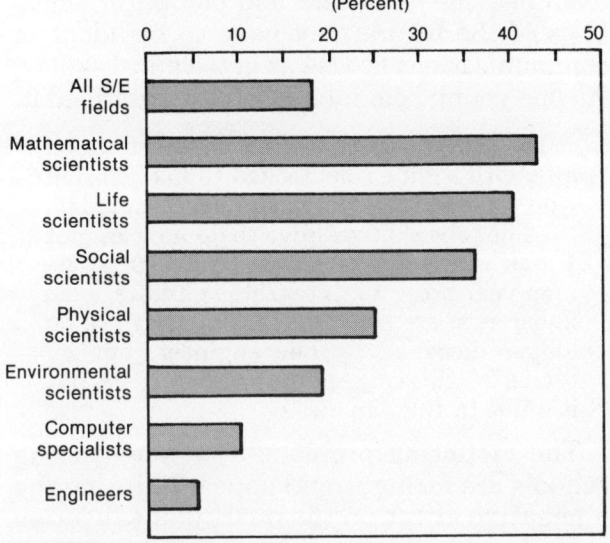

Figure 24.—Share of All S/Es Employed in Educational Institutions by Field, 1981

SOURCE: *Science Indicators,* 1982.

university campuses to industry is the poor condition of most university research facilities. In an effort to reduce costs, for example, many colleges and universities have failed to purchase, maintain, and upgrade their buildings and equipment. As a result of such decisions, university instrumentation inventories are now nearly twice as old as those of leading commercial labs.[31] The cost of adequately improving these facilities in the area of engineering education alone has been estimated to be, at a minimum, between $1¼ billion to $2 billion.[32] This cost, moreover, is rapidly escalating with inflation.

Problems of university instrumentation are particularly serious in those fields where the cost of equipment is especially high and where it plays an essential, if not an integral, part of the educational and research processes themselves. This is the case, for example, in the area of artificial intelligence. Only very few universities can afford the cost or have the space and facilities available to house and support the kinds of sophisticated equipment required to perform R&D at the leading edge of the field.[33]

Other institutional factors that have been cited as reasons for the exodus from academia to industry include uncertainty of tenure, heavy teaching loads, inadequate funds and institutional support for research, and increases in educational fees compounded by diminishing financial aid for students.

It is difficult to assess the extent to which these problems will persist in the future. The number of students studying for Ph.D.s in engineering significantly decreased over the course of the decade 1972-82. Educators of engineering suggest that, as a result, there will not be enough new faculty members to replace even those who die or retire.[34] If this kind of trend continues, there will probably be a faculty shortage in the future. However, there are some indicators that point to a reversal of this trend. In 1982, for example, the number of engineers earning doctorates increased for the first time in 8 years.[35] In 1983, the number increased again—from 2,888 to 3,023.[36]

On the other hand, the academic manpower problem may be more difficult to overcome in the field of computer science where the percentage of faculty leaving for industry is two times that of any other field of engineering.[37] Even in this area, however, there is some anecdotal evidence reported by NSF to suggest that the number of graduate students studying in this area is now increasing.[38]

It is possible, however, that faculty shortages could become even more critical in the future in some specific areas, limiting the amount of research and the amount of teaching that can be done in these fields. This is particularly true, for example, in an area such as artificial intelligence (AI).[39] Because the field

---

[31]John Brademas, "Graduate Education: Signs of Trouble," *Science,* vol. 223, Mar. 2, 1984, p. 881.
[32]Haddad, op. cit.
[33]*OTA Case Study on Artificial Intelligence.*
[34]NAE Bridge, op. cit., p. 121.
[35]*Science Indicators,* op. cit., p. 123.
[36]*Manpower Comments,* vol. 21, No. 3, April 1984, p. 24.
[37]Curtis, op. cit., p. 8.
[38]Conversation with Kent Curtis, National Science Foundation.
[39]*OTA Case Study on Artificial Intelligence.*

of AI is so specialized and because the size of the research community is so small to begin with, the number of qualified faculty members cannot be multiplied rapidly enough to meet the rising number of students who are now beginning to enter the field. The problem is likely to worsen if, as might reasonably be expected, the greater commercialization of AI applications together with enhanced military interest in the field lead to increased competition for those trained in artificial intelligence in the future. The effect of a faculty shortage may be particularly acute in an area such as this where the required skills and knowledge are best taught in an apprenticeship-type situation.

To alleviate the present faculty shortage, more than half of all engineering colleges have had to eliminate courses, and two-thirds are increasingly substituting graduate assistants for full professors for some coursework, a situation that could adversely affect the teaching of advanced technical courses. A number of universities have also increased the teaching load.[40] It has been estimated, for example, that over the past 10 years the teaching burden of the average professor of engineering has increased by 40 percent.[41] While such actions may ameliorate the problem in the short term, in the long term they may—to the extent that they discourage people from pursuing teaching careers—actually exacerbate it.

Compounding their problems of loss of faculty and deterioration of equipment, schools of engineering and departments of computer science will also have to find ways to modernize their curricula to meet the educational needs of a high-technology society undergoing rapid technological change. It has been estimated, for example, that given the speed at which technological change is occurring, today's engineering education, acquired over the course of 4 or 5 years, will be obsolete in about the same amount of time.[42] Up-to-date coursework, moreover, will have to take into account the changing style of doing engineering and computer science. To be effective, for example, the engineers and computer scientists of the future may have to be adept in communications as well as in technical skills.[43] As one young computer scientist described it,

> The old stereotype of an engineer was a guy with a slide rule hooked to his belt and who was not into sports, not into team play. . . . The jobs that we have to do now are not 1-man year projects but are 5- to 10- to 20-man-year projects. Integrated circuits, even linear ICs, are so complex that they are no longer designed by one engineer, but by teams . . . this concept may be new to us, but it's not to the Japanese.

The mounting problems that engineering schools are facing would appear to be having a negative effect on the quality of education that they provide. In the last 3 years, for example, 30 percent fewer engineering schools were given full 6-year accreditation. Moreover, there has been an increase of over 70 percent in the number of institutions that have been asked to show cause why their accreditation should not be revoked.[44] Many university officials agree with this assessment. In a survey of engineering colleges conducted by the American Council of Education, 49 percent of the respondents reported that the quality of education provided by their institutions had either greatly or moderately declined.[45] Concerns about the decline in the quality of engineering education are also echoed in the industrial community, where a number of companies have independently taken steps to improve the pool of engineering manpower.[46]

The current situation is not, however, set in stone. To the contrary, the American educational system is today in the midst of considerable change. In adopting policies to affect the future supply of manpower, therefore, policymakers should be reminded of the "pendulum effect." In making decisions about the fu-

---

[40]McDermott, op. cit., p. 90.
[41]*Infoworld*, May 30, 1983, p. 32.
[42]"The Changing Face of Engineering," *Electronics*, May 31, 1983, p. 127.
[43]Ibid., pp. 127-128.
[44]McDermott, op. cit., p. 90.
[45]*High Technology Manpower in the West: Strategies for Action*, op. cit., p. 12.
[46]For a discussion of many of these efforts see *Chapter 6: New Roles for Universities in Information Technology R&D*.

ture, they need to take into account not only the projections of future manpower needs but also how present reactions to those projections may, in fact, undermine their validity.

Concerned about the present state of high-technology manpower training in the United States, a number of businesses and corporations, for example, have already taken it upon themselves to improve the situation. In particular, they have adopted a number of measures that are designed to keep faculty in academia and to encourage students to pursue academic careers. Bell Labs has recently begun a program that, over time, will provide $2 million to doctoral candidates studying in fields related to telecommunications. The General Electric Co. has donated $2 million to engineering schools to be used primarily by teachers and Ph.D. candidates. IBM has established 150 graduate and postdoctorate fellowships in engineering, computer science, and information systems. And Hewlett-Packard recently initiated a student loan forgiveness program that allows students to write off a part of their loans in accordance with a prearranged schedule for each year that they teach.

Companies are also providing funds for equipment and instrumentation. Digital Equipment Corp. and IBM together have donated $50 million for equipment to MIT. Sizable contributions have also been made to a number of other universities by IBM, Hewlett-Packard, Apple Computer Inc., Wang Laboratories, Inc., NCR Corp., and Honeywell, Inc. (see fig. 25).

In addition, businesses and corporations are, more and more, joining with universities in cooperative ventures to overcome perceived shortages of scientific and technical manpower. The goal of training manpower, for example, was the major reason for establishing the Microelectronics and Information Sciences Center at the University of Minnesota, and the most important inducement in gaining industry support. These cooperative ventures, as well as a number of others, are discussed in some detail below, in chapter 6.

Figure 25.—Educational Gifts by Computer Vendors

IBM	• $50 million in cash and equipment to 20 universities to advance research in CAD/CAM. • Co-donation of $50 million in equipment to MIT to research data transfer. • $15 million pledge to Brown University to establish institute for research in information and scholarship. • $2.4 million in graduate fellowships to science and engineering students.
Digital Equipment Corp.	• $ co-donation of $50 million in equipment to MIT. • $1.6 million to Boston University to fund new computer science programs. • Total of $45 million in fiscal 1982 to higher education.
Apple Computer, Inc.	• $21 million in equipment to California schools grades K-12 for "Kids Can't Wait" Program. Company wants a similar nationwide program, but wants Federal tax deductibility first via so-called "Apple Bill." • $500,000 to Brown University in form of 50 Lisa Computers.
Hewlett-Packard Co.	• Approximately $22 million, mostly in equipment, to universities in fiscal 1983.
Wang Laboratories, Inc.	• Total of $3.7 million in equipment and $458,000 in cash to 23 universities and secondary schools in 1982.
NCR Corp.	• $140,000 in equipment to Michigan State University. • $170,000 in equipment to Cornell University. • Several gifts of companies NCR systems to other universities.
Honeywell, Inc.	• $220,000 to Arizona State University. • $30,000 to United Negro College Fund. • Total of $3 million in education contributions in 1982.

SOURCE: *Computerworld*, July 25, 1983.

The States have also taken steps to improve and foster the development of manpower for a knowledge-intensive society. Not only have they joined in cooperative ventures between industry and the universities, they have also taken steps to enhance the research environment and to improve faculty salaries.

While most State and corporate efforts to improve manpower training have been focused on the most prestigious universities, there have been a number that have sought to improve the education and training provided to less advantaged colleges and universities. Exxon, for example, recently donated $1.8 million to six predominantly black engineering colleges, to be spent during the course of the next 3 years. IBM has lent several of its employees to teach in schools that serve "disadvantaged students."

Elementary and Secondary Education

To determine whether or not there will be enough highly qualified people available to perform R&D in information technology, one must look not only at institutions of higher education, but also at elementary and secondary schools. Generating the pool of students from which university and graduate students are drawn, these institutions have an effect on both the number and the quality of students who desire to pursue fields of study that might lead to work in this area.

A number of reports have been released recently that raise serious questions about the ability of elementary and secondary schools in the United States to adequately prepare the Nation's youth to work in a knowledge-intensive society. While differing in the focus of their concerns, all of these reports find that our schools are inadequately preparing American students for their futures. As evidence, they point to declining test scores, the need for colleges and business to provide remedial education and training programs, the level of functional illiteracy among the general population and the Nation's poor showing in international comparisons of student achievement.[47]

Of particular concern in all of these studies is the overall poor quality of math and science education. A number of indicators give cause for such concern (see fig. 26). Enrollments in math and science courses, for example, are generally low. Only one-third of all U.S. high school graduates have completed 3 years of mathematics, and less than 8 percent have completed a calculus course.[48] Moreover, in grades kindergarten through six, students spent only approximately 20 minutes per day on science lessons. And by 10th grade, only about half of all students study any science

[47]James B. Stedman, *Education in America: Reports on Its Condition and Recommendations for Change,* Issue Brief # IB83106 Congressional Research Service, Library of Congress, Nov. 17, 1983.

[48]Michael Heylin, "High School Science Problems Gain Spotlight," *Chemical & Engineering News,* May 24, 1982, p. 39.

Figure 26.—Selected Indicators of the Overall Quality of Mathematics and Science Education in the United States

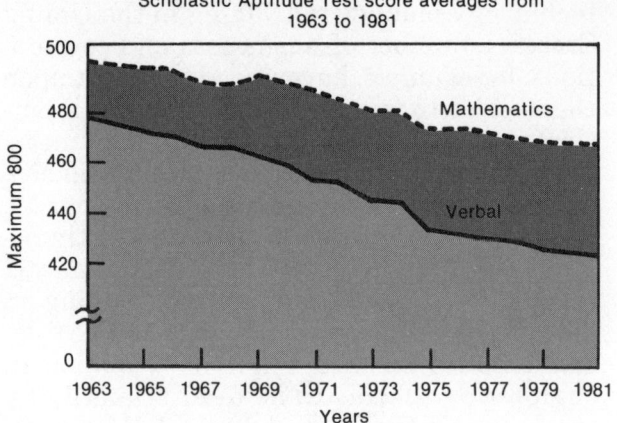

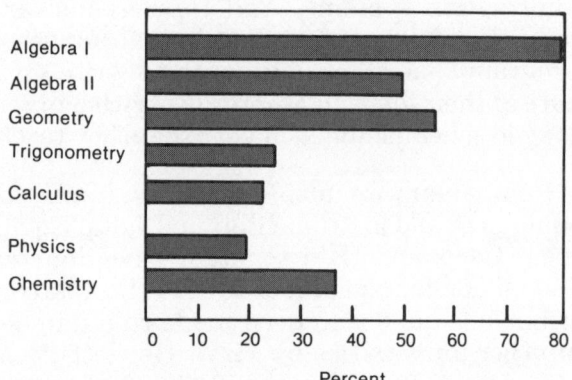

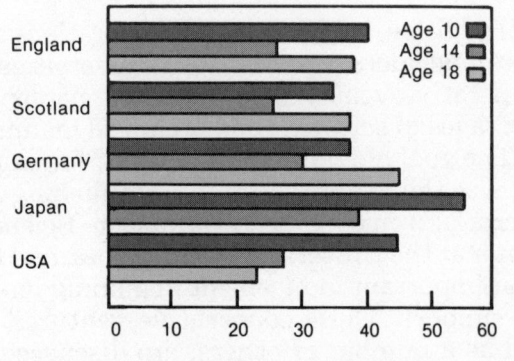

at all.⁴⁹ In contrast, students in many other industrialized countries spend about three times more class time on math and science than the most scientifically oriented American student.⁵⁰

Student attitudes about science and math also reflect problems in the education of these courses at the elementary and secondary school levels. Science, for example, is the subject that is preferred the least by most American students.⁵¹ Moreover, although most children regard scientists themselves as being intelligent and dedicated, they consider the work that scientists do as being "boring, dull, and monotonous."⁵² Mathematics is not much more popular. While it is the favorite subject of 45 percent of students in the third grade, it is rated tops by only 18 percent of those in the 12th.⁵³

Overall, student performance in these areas reflects the lack of interest and low enrollment in these subjects. In the three studies conducted by the National Assessment of Educational Progress, which were designed to assess the achievements of precollege students in a number of areas over the years 1969, 1973, and 1977, all age groups showed significant average declines on mathematical applications which involve the use of mathematical knowledge, skills, and understanding to solve problems.⁵⁴ In the area of science, the results were similar. There was a downward trend for all age groups, from the first to the second assessment, although this decline appeared to be diminishing for 9 and 13 year olds in the third assessment.⁵⁵

As in the case of higher education, many of the problems in precollege math and science education have been attributed to the shortage of high-quality teachers to teach in these areas. According to the Director of the National Science Teachers Association, since 1971 there has been a dramatic decline in the number of people training to teach in these areas—79 percent in the case of math and 64 percent in the case of science (see fig. 27).

The lack of new entrants into the teaching profession is not surprising insofar as there are few incentives to draw well-qualified individuals into the field.⁵⁶ With the financial problems facing schools today, a career in teaching is no longer considered to be secure. And it is considered by many to be less likely to provide the rewards of public status or personal esteem. Since teaching salaries are by no means competitive with those in private industry, many of the most qualified teachers—especially those with training in math and science—are giving up teaching to sell their skills on the open market. Moreover, well-qualified women—a traditional source of high-quality educators—are particularly likely to seek out the wider range of employment opportunities now available to them.⁵⁷

The actual extent of the present shortage of qualified math and science teachers is a matter of some debate, however. A survey of educational placement offices conducted by the National Science Teachers Association found, for example, that no less than one-half of the Nation's math and science teachers were hired on an emergency basis.⁵⁸ The Association for School, College and University Staffing has reported, moreover, that there is a considerable nationwide shortage of teachers in the area of mathematics, physics, and computer programming.⁵⁹ On the other hand, a recent study conducted by the General Accounting Office concluded that the gaps in the available

---

⁴⁹Herbert J. Walberg, "Scientific Literacy and Economic Productivity in International Perspective," *Daedalus*, p. 12.
⁵⁰Heylin, op. cit.
⁵¹Walberg, op. cit.
⁵²Heylin, op. cit.
⁵³Walberg, op. cit.
⁵⁴*Science Indicators,* op. cit., p. 74.
⁵⁵Ibid.

⁵⁶*The New Scientist,* July 14, 1983.
In explaining the shortage of teachers, much of the attention has focused on salary differentials between teaching and industry. While salary levels are no doubt important, one recent study found that internal morale factors, such as the potential for personal growth, are even more so. Edward B. Fiske "Teacher Fulfillment Put Above Pay," *The New York Times,* Oct. 4, 1983, p. C1.
⁵⁷J. Myron Atkin, "Who Will Teach in High School?" *America's Schools: Public and Private,* Daedalus, summer 1981.
⁵⁸*The New Scientist,* op. cit.
⁵⁹*Teacher Supply/Demand 1984,* Association for School, College, and University Staffing.

Figure 27.—America's Science Teacher Shortage

A 1982 survey reveals just how many new science and mathematics teachers in the U.S. do not hold the appropriate qualifications to do their jobs. This is partly a result of a fall in the numbers of those achieving the appropriate qualifications. Another important factor is the far more attractive salaries offered to graduates in the sciences, whether qualified teachers or not.

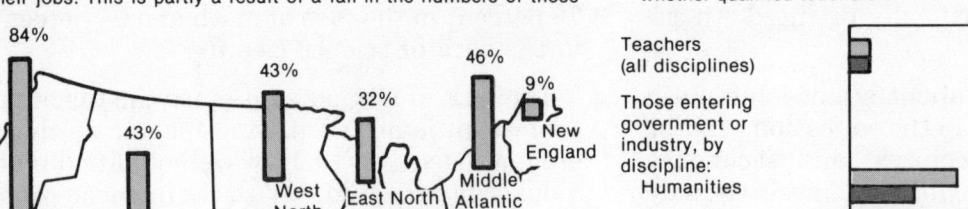

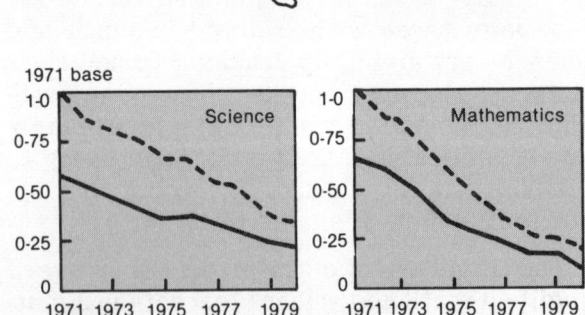

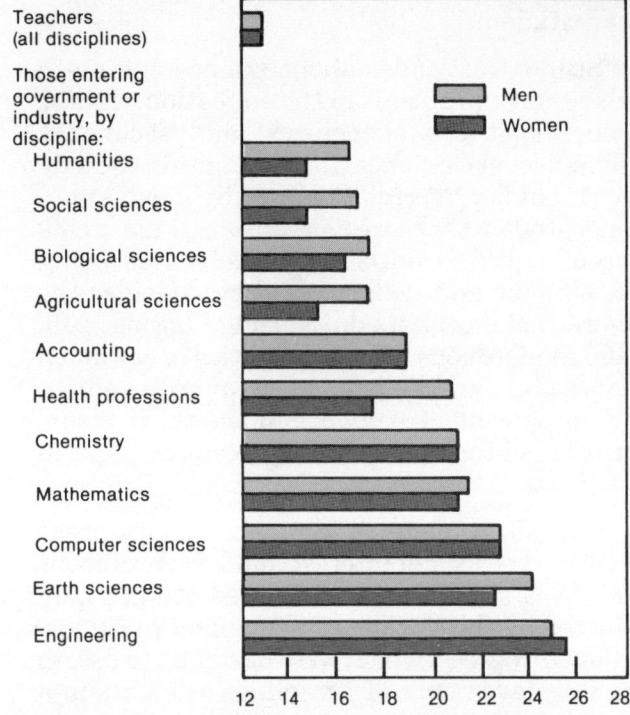

Teachers taken on in 1982 to teach science and math not qualified in those subjects (top left). Decline in number of new teachers between 1971 and 1980 (above left). Starting salaries for new graduates entering careers in government or industry in 1982 (above right).

SOURCE: *New Scientist,* July 14, 1983.

information are so great that whether or not there are shortages of math and science teachers, and whether or not the quality of technical teaching has declined in recent years, cannot be determined.[60]

Since a strong foundation in math and science is, in most cases, essential to a future career in information technology R&D, these findings raise a number of questions about the future supply of manpower in this area. Their answer, however, is not particularly clear or straightforward. For although the data show that the level of math and science understanding and competency for the student population as a whole has declined, it has not declined among those students who are most likely to pursue careers requiring a strong background in math and science.[61] University math and science departments and schools of engineering report, moreover, that they are continuing to recruit high-quality students, many of whom are being drawn from the humanities departments with the idea of having better future job prospects[62] (see, e.g., fig. 28). On the other hand, given the diminishing supply of high-quality educators in these fields and the predicted decline in the school age popula-

---
[60]*New Directions for Federal Programs to Aid Mathematics and Science Teaching,* GAO/PEMD-84-5, Mar. 6, 1984.

[61]*Science Indicators,* op. cit., p. 77.
[62]Frank J. Atelsek, *Student Quality in the Sciences and Engineering: Opinion of Senior Academic Officials,* Higher Education Panel Report No. 58, American Council on Education, February 1984.

Figure 28.—Selected Indicators of Shifts in Undergraduate Science/Engineering Education

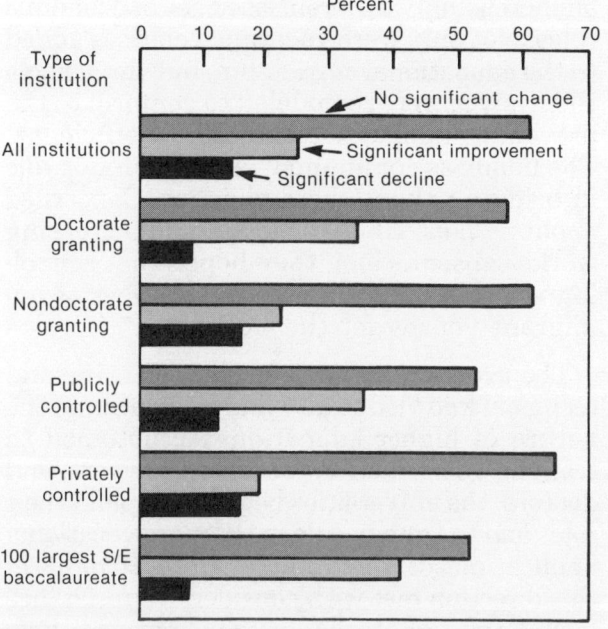
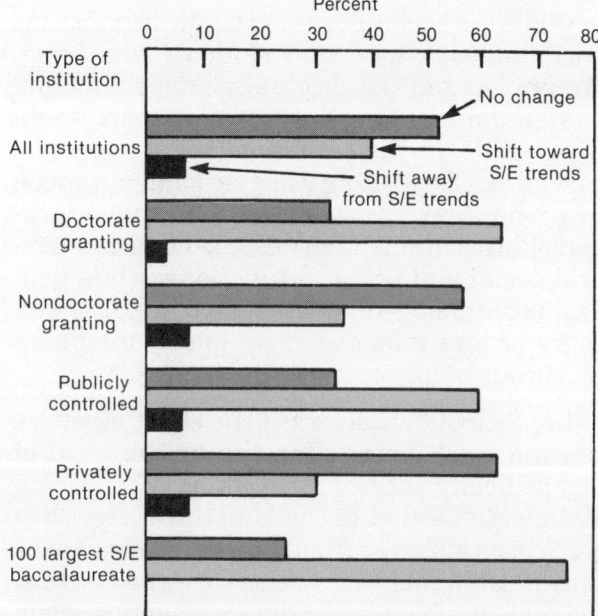

Chart 1. Perceptions of academic officials about change over last five years in quality of undergraduate science/engineering (S/E) students, 1982

Chart 2. Opinions of academic officials about shift in distribution of most able undergraduate students between science/engineering (S/E) and other fields over the last five years, 1982

SOURCE: National Science Foundation and American Council on Education.

tion,[63] a more serious problem may emerge in the future.

Just as the situation in the case of higher education, the situation in elementary and secondary education is not static and changes are taking place that might affect the long-term supply of scientific and technical manpower. The public's response to the numerous reports on the condition of American education has been immediate and widespread, involving parents, teachers, businessmen, and government officials at all levels.

---
[63]The number of Americans graduating from high school is projected to drop from a peak of 3.2 million of 1977 to a low of 2.3 million in 1992, following a roller coaster pattern through the end of the century. *High School Graduates: Projections for the Fifty States* (1982-2000), Western Interstate Commission for Higher Education, Boulder, CO.

The Federal Role in Manpower Development

As the largest employer of scientists and engineers, the Federal Government has a direct interest in whether or not the educational system can provide an adequate supply of technically trained people. Its role in the development of manpower, however, has traditionally been indirect. For it is the States, and not the Federal Government, that have had the primary responsibility for educational policies.

Given the Constitutional limitations on the Federal Government's role in education, the responsibility for developing manpower has always been shared by a number of different social institutions ranging from the family to the business community. As American society has become more technologically advanced, however, the Federal Government has been increasingly called on to play a more significant role. Pressure on it to be more active in this area is particularly strong today, as the Nation seeks to maintain its place in a highly technical and competitive world environment.

While conscious of the economic benefits associated with having a skilled labor force, Americans did not originally adopt a formal system for transmitting vocational and technical skills, in the earliest years of their history, when agriculture was the dominant mode of production.[64] Instead, most formal educational institutions were designed to serve general social and political functions, while general vocational skills were left to be passed on more or less informally, by family members or through apprenticeship systems.[65]

In particular, there was little effort given to, or even much concern for, the development of scientifically trained manpower. When scientists were needed in the United States, they were brought over from Europe. Thus, it was only in 1902 that the Federal Government first became involved in the development of scientific manpower. Concerned at this time about the security dangers entailed in relying almost exclusively on foreigners for scientific expertise, Congress established the Army Corps of Engineers at West Point.[66]

It was only with the rapid industrialization of society, at the end of the century, that education came to be really valued in economic and technical terms.[67] And then, as Americans came to believe that special technical knowledge was the key to prosperity in the modern age, secondary educational institutions were restructured to prepare American youth for an increasingly differentiated set of economic roles. Not only were vocational courses added to the educational curriculum, but the schools themselves were remodeled to conform to the prevailing business standards of efficiency. The business community played a major role in bringing about these changes. Concerned about strikes, labor turnover, and increasing worker absenteeism, they hoped that schooling would socialize a growing number of immigrant youths for the workplace.[68][69]

The growing enthusiasm for scientific and technical knowledge also had an impact on the nature of higher education. Accustomed to training gentlemen as preachers, lawyers, and doctors, the universities began to expand their roles and to train people in the more vocational applications of education.[70] Efforts to move in this direction met with considerable resistance from traditional academics, however, who were disdainful of the study of experimental science and even more so of the teaching of the "useful arts."[71][72]

The transformation of the university system was greatly facilitated by the passage of Federal legislation establishing the land grant colleges. Provided for under the Morrill Act of 1862,[73] these colleges, open to children of all backgrounds, were established to provide education in practical fields such as agriculture, engineering, home economics, and business

---

[64]For a discussion of American education in the preindustrial period, see Bernard Bailyn, *Education in the Forming of American Society* (New York: W. W. North, 1980); Lawrence Cremin, *Traditions in American Education* (New York: Basic Books, Harper, 1976); and Rush Welter, *Popular Education and Democratic Thought in America* (New York: Columbia University Press, 1962).

[65]A. Hunter Dupree, *Science in the Federal Government: History of Policies and Activities to 1940* (Cambridge, MA: Belknap Press of Harvard University Press, 1957).

[66]Ibid. Initially trained in the skills necessary to carry out explorations of the West and to conduct surveys of the eastern coastline, these West Point graduates played a key role in many of the scientific ventures carried out by the Federal Government up until the end of the 19th century.

[67]David K. Cohen and Barbara Newfeld, "The Failure of High Schools and the Progress of Education," *America's Schools: Public and Private,* Daedalus, spring 1981.

[68]David Tyack and Elizabeth Hansot, "Conflict and Consensus in American Education," *America's Schools: Public and Private,* Daedalus, summer 1981.

[69]Ibid.

[70]Ernest L. Boyer and Fred Heckinger, *Higher Education in the Nation's Service* (Washington, DC: Carnegie Foundation for the Advancement of Teaching, 1981); and Edward Shils, "The Order of Learning in the United States From 1865-1920," *Minerva,* vol. 21, No. 2, summer 1978.

[71]David Noble, *America by Design: Science, Technology, and the Rise of Corporate Capitalism* (New York: Alfred A. Knopf, 1977), p. 24.

[72]Boyer and Hechinger, op. cit.; and Shils, op. cit.

[73]This law provided land to the States, the proceeds of which were to be used to teach in the fields of agriculture and mechanical arts. Subsequent legislation provided Federal financial support for research and the operation of the landgrant colleges.

administration. Through their agriculture experiment stations and their service bureaus, their activities were designed to serve the state.[74]

The impact of the Morrill Act on development of scientific and technical manpower is clearly evident in the case of the engineering profession. Before its passage, State legislatures had been reluctant to invest in technical education. Responding to the offer of Federal grants, however, they quickly sought to establish the new types of schools, while private colleges, caught up in the movement, also established departments of engineering.[75] Schools of engineering expanded rapidly, thereafter, numbering 110 by 1886. The number of engineering students similarly increased, from 1,000 in 1890 to 10,000 in 1900.[76] As more and more engineers were educated in formal institutions, there was a greater emphasis in engineering on science. Moreover, with the establishment and growth of these institutions, a profession was developed and with it a means of preserving, transmitting, and increasing an evolving body of engineering knowledge.[77]

The real impetus for manpower development, and for a strong Federal role in it, came, however, after World War II, when advanced technology had proven to be critical not only for the Nation's economic growth, but also for its defense. It was in recognition of this fact, for example, that the National Science Foundation was created in 1950 with the task of improving the Nation's potential in scientific research and in science education.[78]

The philosophical basis for establishing NSF, and the rationale for including the development of scientific manpower within its organizational mission, was explained by Vannevar Bush in *Science—the Endless Frontier,* his report to the President on a program for postwar scientific research. About the need for scientific manpower, he said,[79]

> ... Today, it is truer than ever that basic research is the pacemaker of technological progress. In the 19th century, Yankee mechanical ingenuity, building largely on the basic discoveries of European scientists, could greatly advance the technical arts. Now the situation is different.
>
> A nation which depends on others for its new basic scientific knowledge will be slow in its industrial progress and weak in its competitive position in world trade, regardless of its mechanical skill.

Provoked by the successful launching of the Soviet spacecraft *Sputnik,* defense considerations also motivated the passage of the National Defense Education Act of 1958 (NDEA), which was aimed at improving instruction in mathematics, science, and foreign languages. Under this law, funds were provided on a matching basis to public schools, and as long-term loans to private institutions, for needed equipment in these instructional fields, for curriculum development, for guidance counseling, for vocational education in defense-related fields, and for teacher training in foreign language instruction. The passage of NDEA resulted in substantial increases in Federal aid to education (see fig. 29). Since Federal dollars had to be matched by State and local funds under provisions of the act, the overall investment in NDEA programs was large. Between 1958 and 1961, $163.2 million in Federal funds were dispersed. Approximately 75 percent of these funds were directed to the development of science curricula.

Although the U.S. educational system is organized on a local basis, the Federal Government has, over the years and in response to changing technological developments, come to influence the development of scientific and technical manpower in a number of ways. Particularly in the area of science and mathematics, the Federal Government has, for

---

[74]Clark Kerr, *The Uses of the University* (Cambridge, MA: Harvard University Press, 1972).
[75]Noble, op. cit., pp. 38-39.
[76]Edwin T. Layton, Jr., *The Revolt of the Engineers: Social Responsibility and the American Engineering Profession* (Cleveland, OH: The Press of Case Western Reserve University, 1971).
[77]Ibid.
[78]*The National Science Foundation and Pre-College Science Education: 1950-1975,* report prepared for the Subcommittee on Science and Technology, U.S. House of Representatives, 94th Cong., 2d sess., by the Congressional Research Service, Library of Congress, January 1976.

[79]Ibid., p. 19.

160 • *Information Technology R&D: Critical Trends and Issues*

Figure 29.—A Quarter Century of Student Aid
25 years ago, the National Defense Education Act was signed

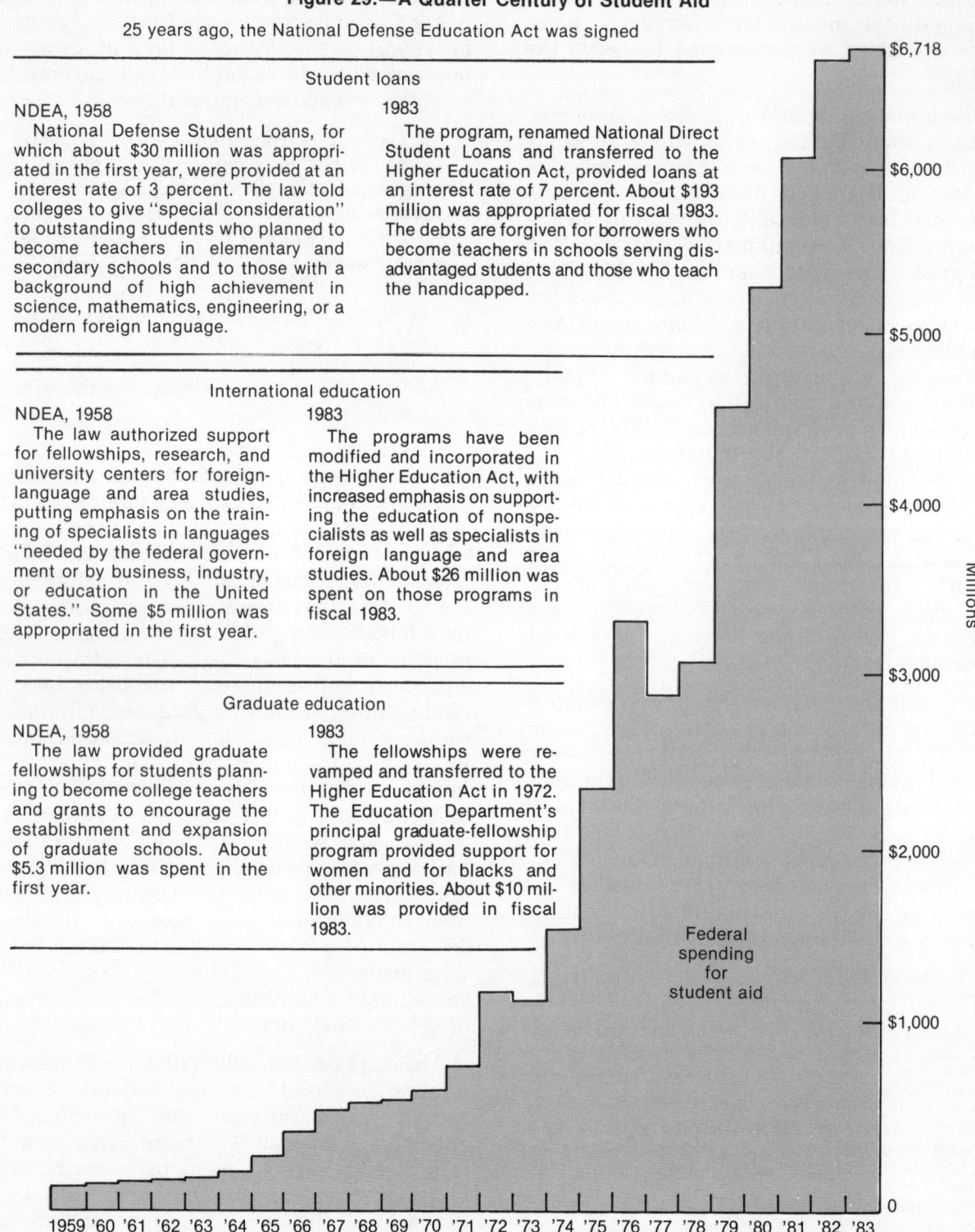

Student loans

NDEA, 1958
National Defense Student Loans, for which about $30 million was appropriated in the first year, were provided at an interest rate of 3 percent. The law told colleges to give "special consideration" to outstanding students who planned to become teachers in elementary and secondary schools and to those with a background of high achievement in science, mathematics, engineering, or a modern foreign language.

1983
The program, renamed National Direct Student Loans and transferred to the Higher Education Act, provided loans at an interest rate of 7 percent. About $193 million was appropriated for fiscal 1983. The debts are forgiven for borrowers who become teachers in schools serving disadvantaged students and those who teach the handicapped.

International education

NDEA, 1958
The law authorized support for fellowships, research, and university centers for foreign-language and area studies, putting emphasis on the training of specialists in languages "needed by the federal government or by business, industry, or education in the United States." Some $5 million was appropriated in the first year.

1983
The programs have been modified and incorporated in the Higher Education Act, with increased emphasis on supporting the education of nonspecialists as well as specialists in foreign language and area studies. About $26 million was spent on those programs in fiscal 1983.

Graduate education

NDEA, 1958
The law provided graduate fellowships for students planning to become college teachers and grants to encourage the establishment and expansion of graduate schools. About $5.3 million was spent in the first year.

1983
The fellowships were revamped and transferred to the Higher Education Act in 1972. The Education Department's principal graduate-fellowship program provided support for women and for blacks and other minorities. About $10 million was provided in fiscal 1983.

SOURCE: Compiled by the American Council on Education, based on data from the U.S. Department of Education. Totals do not include Veterans Education Benefits or Social Security Benefits for college students.

example, provided support for curriculum development and the production of new course materials. In addition, it has also lent considerable institutional support to colleges and universities, in the form of direct grants, research grants and contracts, equipment grants, and the establishment of institutes and specialized instrumentation centers. The Federal Government has, moreover, assisted individuals through training programs and fellowships as well as by providing scholarships and other forms of financial aid.

By targeting scholarships or fellowships for specific fields of study, the Government can also influence the direction of manpower development.[80] This was particularly true, for example, during the years following Sputnik when there was a widespread belief that the normal pool of technically trained graduates could not meet the manpower needs of the civilian space and the military ICBM programs. Where a large number of people have been involved, the Government has tended to provide only generalized incentives. Where the number is much smaller and the area of expertise quite specific, it has sought more to narrowly target its support.

[80]Ibid.

The Societal Context for Determining Federal Manpower Policy

The role of the Federal Government in development of scientific and technical manpower is not only indirect, it is also complicated. It is complicated by the fact that the Nation's educational system—the primary institutional means by which the Federal Government can affect manpower—serves a number of societal goals in addition to, and at times competing with, those that directly relate to manpower development.

Today, given the growing concerns about the United States' declining position in the international economy of high-technology goods and services, the American educational system is being called on to develop the Nation's scientific and technical manpower as a means of gaining for the United States a greater competitive edge. In examining this issue, this chapter has posed a number of questions about: 1) the causal relationships between education and economic performance, and 2) the extent to which there will actually be a critical shortage of manpower in the future to perform R&D in such high-technology areas as information technology. Before policy alternatives can be adopted to address the manpower problem, it is necessary to inquire further and to ask first whether or not Federal efforts to move the educational system more in the direction of manpower development can be achieved without sacrificing other equally, if not perhaps more important, educational and societal goals.

Education has always played a particularly important role in American society. For while educational institutions are publicly supported in many societies, in no other country have they been established with such deliberate purpose and public expectation, or been conceived of as being such an integral part of the political, social, and economic order. Contrasting the attitude of Americans towards education with that of Europeans, for example, Alexis de Tocqueville, the well-known French commentator on American society, noted in 1831:[81]

> Everyone I have met up to now, to whatever rank of society they belong, has seemed incapable of imagining that one could doubt the value of education. They never fail to smile when told that this view is not universally accepted in Europe. They agree in thinking that the diffusion of knowledge, useful for all peoples, is absolutely necessary for a peo-

[81]Alexis de Tocqueville, *Journey to America*, translated by George Lawrence, J.P. Mayer (ed.) Anchor Books, 1971.

ple like their own, where there is not property qualification for voting or for standing for election. That seemed to be an idea taking root in every head.

The goals that Americans have sought to achieve through education have changed over time and in different historical circumstances.[82] In the earliest years of American history, for example, education was considered essential for the survival of the new democratic nation. Later, with the need to acculturate immigrants into society and to unite a divided Nation in the aftermath of the Civil War, it was considered the means for building a nation of citizens. At the turn of the century, education was expected to train and socialize American youths to participate in a modern, industrialized society. In the 1960s, Americans saw in education a way of providing equal access to social and economic opportunity.

Today, much of the national discussion about education has focused on the goal of meeting the manpower needs of a high-technology economy. Unlike earlier periods of American history, however, when the educational system was itself undergoing tremendous expansion and enjoying a period of considerable prosperity, today the educational system is having to take on a multitude of new tasks at a time when it faces the prospect of shrinking economic and human resources. Thus today, given limited social and economic resources for education, the choice to take Federal actions to increase the supply of manpower for R&D in the area of information technology might be made at the expense of addressing other educational problems or of meeting other educational and societal goals.

Some of the most important of the new tasks that educational institutions will have to perform are those that relate to the emergence of an "information society." In the recent OTA study, *Information Technology and Its Impact on American Education,* it was found, for example, that the growing use of information technology throughout society is creating new demands for education and training in the United States and is increasing the potential economic and social penalty for those who do not respond to those demands. Moreover, the study found that the information revolution is creating new stresses on many societal institutions, particularly those such as public schools and libraries that traditionally have borne the major responsibility for providing education and other information services.

New demands will also be placed on the educational system by virtue of the changes that are now taking place in the American economy. Programmable automation, for example, as the recent OTA study, *Computerized Manufacturing Automation: Employment, Education, and the Workplace,* points out, is one of the economic forces that is currently reshaping the roles for and the values being assigned to education, training, retraining, and related services such as career guidance and job counseling. This study concludes, moreover, that the inadequate capacities of the present instructional system may constrain the establishment of strategies to develop adequate skills for programmable automation.

Educational institutions will also be called on to perform a number of cultural tasks. Forecasts of demographic trends suggest, for example, that Hispanics, Asians, and other cultural groups with specialized educational needs will soon comprise a major portion of the school population. Moreover, the increase in the number of school-age children living with a single parent or two working parents will force schools to provide more supervision and socialization. In addition, a growing number of adults are turning to the educational system to fill in the nonvocational, liberal arts gaps in their educational backgrounds.[83] Thus, instead of cutting back on their educational activities, schools and universities will, most likely, have to cater to a growing number and variety of educational needs.

The role of the educational system as a means of providing equitable access to economic and social opportunities could become

---

[82]Welter, op. cit.; Cohen and Newfield, op. cit.; Tyack, op. cit.

[83]"More Adults Return to College to Study the Liberal Arts," *Chronicle of Higher Education,* Apr. 25, 1984, p. 1.

all the more important in an age of high technology. The Bureau of Labor Statistics, for example, has predicted that the number of low-skilled jobs will constitute an increasingly larger proportion of the total work force than the highly technical jobs.[84] Other social observers have suggested, moreover, that the wages earned by low-skilled workers will decline relative to those earned by technical workers.[85] Under such circumstances, the competition for educational credentials may become more intense in the future, and the issue of equitable access may become at least as important as, if not more important than, the issue of manpower development.

[84]BLS, Levin and Rumberger, op. cit.

[85]Bob Kuttner, "The Declining Middle," *The Atlantic Monthly*, July 1983.

Chapter 5 References

"Academic Gap Between High and Low Achievers Narrowing," *Chemical & Engineering News*, Feb. 29, 1983.

America's Competitive Challenge, Report of the Business-Higher Education Forum, 1983.

"Commentary: The Science Education Stampede," *Science & Government Report*, Oct. 1, 1983, pp. 7-8.

"Computer People: Yes, They Really Are Different," *Business Week*, Feb. 20, 1984, pp. 66-77.

Education, Productivity, and the National Economy: A Research Initiative, National Institute of Education, December 1981.

"Education for a High Technology Future: The Debate Over the Best Curriculum," *School Research Forum*, Educational Research Service, May 1983.

"Employment Up in Manufacturing for Scientists, Engineers, Technicians," National Science Foundation, *Mosaic*, March/April 1983.

"Engineers Need More Learning," *Infoworld*, May 30, 1983, p. 32.

Hearings on Mathematics and Science Education, before the Committee on Education and Labor, House of Representatives, 98th Cong., 1st sess., Jan. 26-28, 31, 1983.

"Is Shortage of Engineers a Matter of Definition?" *Science*, vol. 223, p. 800.

"Labor Market Slackens for Science and Engineering Graduates," National Science Foundation, *Mosaic*, January/February 1983.

Manpower Concerns, Hearings, before the Committee on Science and Technology, House of Representatives, 1st sess., Oct. 6-7, 1981.

"Manpower Surveys Continue to Disagree," *Electronics*, July 28, 1983.

"More Foreign Students Enroll, But Only Some Stay to Work," *Physics Today*, October 1983.

New Directions for Federal Programs to Aid Mathematics and Science Teaching (GAO/REMD—84-5, Mar. 6, 1984).

"NSF Survey Shows Academic Employment Gains for Scientists and Engineers," *AFIPS Washington Report*, September 1983, p. 4.

"Recent Reports on Education: A Digest," *Change*, November/December 1983.

Science and Engineering Education for the 1980's and Beyond, National Science Foundation and the Department of Education, October 1980.

Science Indicators 1982: An Analysis of the State of U.S. Science, Engineering and Technology, National Science Board, 1983.

"Supply of Engineering Faculty," *Electronic Market Trends*, January 1982.

"The Changing Face of Engineering," Special Report, *Electronics*, May 31, 1983, pp. 125-148.

The National Science Foundation and Pre-College Science Education: 1950-1975, report prepared for the Subcommittee on Science and Technology, U.S. House of Representatives, 94th Cong., 2d sess., by the Congressional Research Service, Library of Congress, January 1976.

"The Science Education Stampede," *Science & Government Report*, Oct. 1, 1983, p. 6.

"Q and A on Job Market for Science, Engineering," *Science & Government Report*, vol. XII, No. 14, Sept. 1, 1983.

Abernathy, William, Clark, Kim B., and Kantrow, Alan, *Industrial Renaissance: Producing a Competitive Future for America* (New York: Basic Books, 1983).

Adler, Mortimer, "The Reform of Public Schools,"

The Center Magazine, September 1982, pp. 12-33.

Aiken, James N., *Teacher Supply/Demand 1983: A Report Based Upon an Opinion Survey of Teacher Placement Officers,* Association for School, College and University Staffing, 1983.

Atkin, J. Myron, "Who Will Teach in High School?" *America's Schools: Public and Private, Daedalus,* summer 1981.

Bailyn, Bernard, *Education in the Forming of American Society* (New York: W. W. North, 1980).

Bezdek, R. H., *Long Range Forecasting of Manpower Requirements* (New York: Institute of Electrical and Electronics Engineers, 1974).

Blakesless, Sandra, "Teacher Fulfillment Put Above Pay," *New York Times,* Oct. 4, 1983, p. C1.

Botkin, James, Dimancescu, Dan, and Stata, Ray, "High Technology, Higher Education, and High Anxiety," *Technology Review,* October 1982, pp. 49-52.

Boyer, Ernerst L., and Hechinger, Fred, *Higher Education in the Nation's Service,* the Carnegie Foundation for the Advancement of Teaching, Washington, DC, 1981.

Brademas, John, "Graduate Education: Signs of Trouble," *Science,* vol. 223, No. 4639, Mar. 2, 1984, p. 881.

Cohen, David, and Neufeld, Barbara, "The Failure of High Schools and the Progress of Education," *America's Schools: Public and Private, Daedalus,* summer 1981.

Cooper, Edith Fairman, *U.S. Science and Engineering Education and Manpower: Background: Supply and Demand; and Comparison with Japan, the Soviet Union, and West Germany,* Congressional Research Service, Library of Congress, May 24, 1982.

Cooper, Edith Fairman, *United States Supply and Demand of Technology,* Part I, Current Situation and Future Outlook, Congressional Research Service, Library of Congress, Nov. 6, 1981.

Cremin, Lawrence, *Traditions in American Education* (New York: Basic Books, Harper, 1976).

Curtis, Kent K., "Computer Manpower—Is There a Crisis?" National Science Foundation, Jan. 4, 1983.

Dennison, E. F., *Slower Economic Growth* (Washington, DC: Brookings Institution, 1979).

Dollar, Bruce, "What Is Really Going On in Schools," *Social Policy,* fall 1983, pp. 7-19.

Dupree, A. Hunter, *Science in the Federal Government: A History of Policies and Activities to 1940* (Cambridge, MA: The Balknap Press of Harvard University Press, 1957).

Evangelauf, Jean, "Salaries of New Assistant Professors Vary More Than $8,000 Across Disciplines," *The Journal of Higher Education,* Feb. 29, 1984, pp. 15-17.

Evangelauf, Jean, "Top Students Move to Science Studies, Leave Humanities," *Chronical of Higher Education,* Feb. 11, 1984, p. 1.

Finn, Chester F., Jr., "American Education Revives," *Wall Street Journal,* July 7, 1982.

Fox, Jeffrey L., "The Uneven Crisis in Science Education," *Science,* vol. 221, p. 838.

Ginzberg, E., and Voita, G. J., "The Service Sector of the U.S. Economy," *Scientific American,* vol. 299, March 1981, pp. 48-55.

Haddad, Jerrier A., "Key Issues in U.S. Engineering Education," *NAE Bridge,* summer 1983.

Harris, Marilyn A., "Manpower Surveys Continue to Disagree," *Electronics,* July 28, 1983, pp. 108-110.

Herman, Ros, "Science Slops in the Land of Opportunity," *The New Scientist,* July 14, 1983, pp. 110-113.

Heylin, Michael, "High School Science Problems Gain Spotlight," *Chemical and Engineering News,* May 24, 1982, pp. 39-41.

Hubbard, Pat Hill, "Technical Employment Projections: 1983-1987," paper prepared for the Symposium on Labor-Market Conditions for Engineers, National Academy of Sciences, Washington, DC, Feb. 2, 1984.

Irwin, Paul M., "Education in the 98th Congress: Overview," Issue Brief # IB83055, Congressional Research Service, Library of Congress, Oct. 28, 1983.

Jordan, K. Forbis, "Precollege Math and Science Education: Issues and Proposals," Issue Brief # IB82092, Congressional Research Service, Library of Congress, Aug. 1, 1983.

Jordan, K. Forbis, "Teachers for Precollege Mathematics and Science Programs," Congressional Research Service, Library of Congress, July 28, 1982.

Kerr, Clark, "The Uses of the University" (Cambridge, MA: Harvard University Press, 1972).

Kutscher, Ronald E., "Future Labor Market Conditions for Engineers," paper presented to the Symposium of the National Academy of Science, Feb. 2, 1984.

Kuttner, Bob, "The Declining Middle," *The Atlantic Monthly,* July 1983, pp. 60-72.

Layman, John W., "Overview of the Problem," *Physics Today,* September 1983.

Layton, Edwin T., *The Revolt of the Engineers: Social Responsibility and the American Engineering Profession* (Cleveland, OH: The Press of Case Western Reserve University, 1971).

Levin, Henry M., and Rumberger, Russell W., *Forecasting the Impact of New Technologies on the Future of the Job Market,* Project Report #84—A4, National Institute of Education, February 1984.

Levin, Henry M., and Rumberger, Russell W., *The Educational Implications of High Technology,* The National Institute of Education Report # 83-A4, 1983.

McDermott, Jeanne, "Technical Education: The Quiet Crisis," *High Technology,* November/December 1983, pp. 87-92.

McDonald, Kim, "Engineering Deans Ask Congress to Give Their Field Equal Standing With Science in Mission of NSF," *The Chronical of Higher Education,* Feb. 29, 1984, p. 13.

Mansfield, Edwin, *Education, R&D, and Productivity Growth,* revised, University of Pennsylvania, Jan. 31, 1982.

Miller, Harry G., Dean, School of Technical Careers, Southern Illinois University at Carbondale, Carbondale, IL, "Higher Education for Employment: Considerations of Degree Determination for Emerging Technical Careers."

Missimer, William C., Jr., "Business and Industry's Role in Improving the Scientific and Technological Literacy of America's Youth," *T.H.E. Journal,* February 1984, pp. 89-94.

Moshowitz, Abbe, "On Predicting R&D Skill Requirements for Information Technology," unpublished paper prepared for the Office of Technology Assessment, February 1984.

Noble, David, *America by Design: Science, Technology, and the Rise of Corporate Capitalism* (New York: Alfred A. Knopf, 1977).

Olson, Larry, *Future Technical Management Requirements and Availability in Information Technology R&D: United States and Comparison With Japan, France, and the United Kingdom,* unpublished paper prepared for the Office of Technology Assessment, 1983.

Porter, Beverly Fearn, and Czujko, Roman, "Scientific Employment in a Tightening Economy," *Physics Today,* February 1983.

Prewitt, Kenneth, "Scientific Illiteracy and Democratic Theory," *Daedalus,* spring 1983, pp. 49-64.

Richie, Richard W., Hecker, Daniel E., and Burgan, John, "High Technology Today and Tomorrow: A Small Slice of the Employment Pie," *Monthly Labor Review* 106, November 1983, pp. 50-58.

Rosen, S., "Human Capital: A Survey of Empirical Research," *Research in Labor Economics,* (Greenwich, CT: JAI Press, vol. 1, pp. 2-39.

Rosenberg, Nathan, *Inside the Black Box—Technology and Economics* (Cambridge, MA: Cambridge University Press, 1982).

Schultz, T. W., *Investment in Human Capital* (New York: Free Press, 1971).

Setlzer, Richard, J., "Impact of Technology on Employment Probed," *Chemical & Engineering News,* Aug. 1, 1983, pp. 23-24.

Shils, Edward, "The Order of Learning in the United States from 1865 to 1920," *Minerva,* vol. 21, No. 2, summer 1978.

Silverstri, George T, Lukosiewicz, John M., and Einstein, Marcus E., "Occupational Employment Projections Through 1995," *Monthly Labor Review* 106, November 1983, pp. 37-49.

Smith, Adam, *The Wealth of Nations* (New York: The Modern Library, 1937).

Stedman, James B., *Education in America: Reports on Its Condition and Recommendations for Change,* Issue Brief #83106, Congressional Research Service, Library of Congress, Aug. 5, 1983.

Tyack, David, and Hansot, Elizabeth, "Conflict and Consensus in American Education," *America's Schools: Public and Private, Daedalus,* summer 1981.

Upthegrove, William R., "Engineering Manpower and Education: A Report of the Business-Higher Education Forum," paper presented at the Symposium on Labor-Market Conditions for Engineers, National Academy of Science, Feb. 2, 1984.

Vanski, Jeane E., "Projected Labor Market Balance in Engineering and Computer Speciality Occupations: 1982-87," prepared for the Symposium on Labor-Market Conditions for Engineers held at the National Academy of Sciences, Washington, DC, Feb. 2, 1984.

Veblen, Thorsten, *The Theory of the Leisure Class* (New York: The Modern Library, 1934).

Walgerg, Herbert J., "Scientific Literacy and Economic Productivity in International Perspective," *Daedalus,* spring 1983, pp. 1-28.

Weinstein, Jay, *Sociology/Technology: Foundations of Post Academic Science,* Transaction Books, 1982.

Welter, Rush, *Popular Education and Democratic Thought in America* (New York: Columbia University Press, 1962).

Chapter 6
New Roles for Universities in Information Technology R&D

Contents

	Page
Introduction	169
A Conceptual Framework	169
Forces Driving New Relationships	171
Impacts of New University Arrangements	173
Expected Benefits	174
Potential Costs	175
New Roles for Universities: Selected Case Studies	176
Massachusetts Institute of Technology Microsystems Industrial Group	177
Microelectronics and Information Sciences Center University of Minnesota	178
Rensselaer Polytechnic Institute Center for Industrial Innovation	180
Stanford University Center for Integrated Systems	182
Microelectronics Center of North Carolina	184
Semiconductor Research Corporation	189
Microelectronics and Computer Technology Corporation	193
Chapter 6 References	195

Tables

Table No.	Page
26. Stanford University, Center for Integrated Systems Research Topics	185
27. A Distribution of SRC Funding by Region, March 1983	192

Figures

Figure No.	Page
30. A Conceptual Framework: New Roles for Universities in Information Technology R&D	170
31. Stanford University, Center for Integrated Systems Patent Policy	183
32. Communications System Linking MCNC Participating Sites	187
33. MCNC Participating Institutions	187
34. Working Relationships, Microelectronics Center of North Carolina	188

Chapter 6
New Roles for Universities in Information Technology R&D

Introduction

Throughout history, new institutional arrangements have been created to satisfy changing needs. As one of society's major institutions, the university, too, has evolved. Particularly in the case of information technology R&D, new roles for universities are developing. Other major players—industry, State and local governments and the Federal Government—are involved along with the university in the formation of new institutional relationships.

The new institutional arrangements between university and industry, as well as those among university, industry and government, are driven by many factors. These include the need for new knowledge and the application of advancing technologies in new products and processes; the efficient use of high-technology manpower and ensuring a renewable supply of manpower resources; economic survival and future industrial growth; and maintenance of national security and defense.

Since these efforts are essentially in their formative stages, it is difficult to draw conclusions now about their long-term impacts. In establishing a framework for analysis and policy options, OTA developed a series of seven case studies (described later in this chapter) that were selected as examples of the range of new institutional relationships. Taken together, they illustrate several of the key issues in today's debate.

A Conceptual Framework

OTA created a conceptual framework to analyze the changing institutional R&D relationships being played by the Nation's academic institutions—one that emphasizes the pivotal role being played by them. Figure 30 outlines this framework and focuses on the connections among university, industry, and government in terms of education, research, and economic development. At the same time there are forces converging on these institutions that, while creating new opportunities and strengthening connections among university, industry and government, also are creating strains and producing tensions.

While education, research and development, and economic development are separate functions, they, like the institutions that foster them, are becoming increasingly interrelated. For example, concepts in advanced computer architecture taught in a university program or course are directly dependent upon the rapid advances in research and development at both the university and in the industry. Similarly, the development of new industries and subsequent economic growth are directly tied to the products coming from the university—highly trained technical graduates and new knowledge, new processes, and new applications—as well as to the advances and offshoots coming directly from industry.

In examining the institutional players in terms of their relationship to education, research, and economic development, we see that both universities and industry are directly involved in the creation of new knowledge through research, that both universities and State and local governments are directly concerned with the educational process and the provision of a renewable supply of trained graduates, and that both State and local governments and industry are directly concerned with economic health and growth.

Figure 30.—A Conceptual Framework: New Roles for Universities in Information Technology R&D

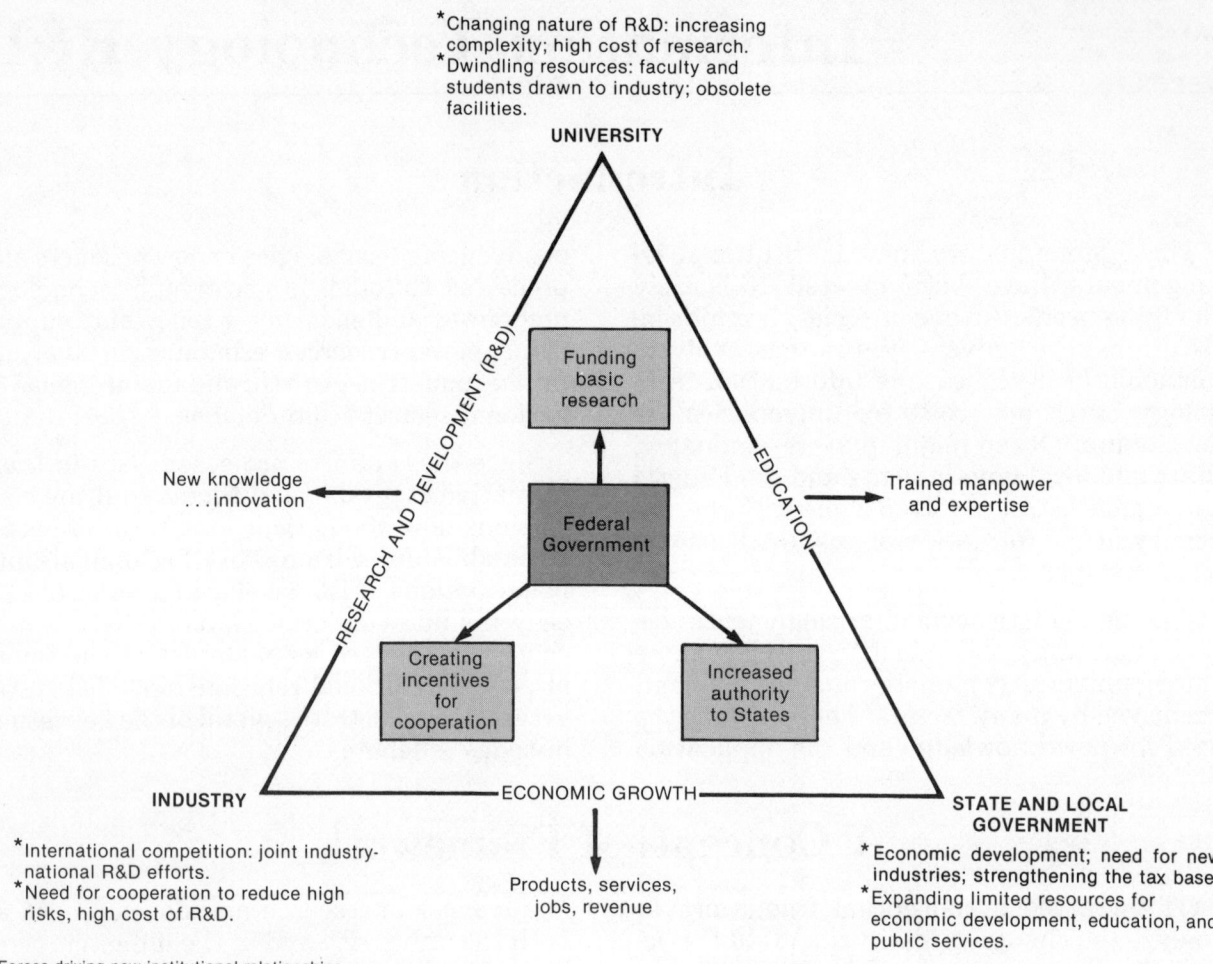

*Forces driving new institutional relationships.
SOURCE: Office of Technology Assessment.

There are also important indirect relationships. The educational program and knowledge resources of the university can have an impact on the economic well-being of the region. Industry is involved in education indirectly through the training and resources it has to offer to the other players. Industry is also a consumer of talent and new ideas, the products of the university. States and localities are finding that they need to be concerned with research not only because the creation of new knowledge can lead to the development of new processes and products by industry, but because the quality and scope of university research efforts can strengthen the educational program and in turn provide the region with a renewable supply of highly trained manpower.

There is also a national dimension to this triad. These relationships and interactions are affected by and in turn affect national issues and the Federal role. The strength and effectiveness of the educational system, the quality of research, and the level of economic growth and industrial innovation and productivity determine, in part, the Nation's national security and economic well-being. The role of the Federal Government has also been both direct and indirect. For example, the passage of the Morrill Act in 1862 fundamentally affected the nature of research and education in the universities, as did the direct collaboration among government, industry and academic researchers during World War II.[1] Recently, the Federal Government's role has become more indirect, increasing authority to State and local government for various discretionary education programs, providing a positive climate for industrial joint ventures, and encouraging joint sponsorship of R&D through tax incentives.[2]

---

[1]See ch. 6, "The Provision of Education in the United States," in *Information Technology and Its Impact on American Education*, OTA, 1982.

[2]See ch. 2, "The Environment for Research and Development in Information Technology in the United States."

Forces Driving New Relationships

One can argue that the institutional framework has been in place a long time, even though the interconnections may not have been sharply defined. Why, then, are the relationships among the university, industry, and State and local government increasing in strength and activity today? Although there are many factors that could be considered, several forces appear to be critical.

One of the principal factors has been the change in the direct and indirect roles played by the four participants shown in figure 30. The changing Federal role in education, research, and economic growth has shifted certain areas of responsibility to State and local governments, academia, and the private sector. While Federal R&D funding has stayed roughly constant in real dollars over the past decade, recent increases have been targeted to specific areas, such as defense. The consolidation of federally funded discretionary programs in education has increased local and State decisionmaking and control.

Universities have been constrained by the resources available for support of research, faculty, students, and facilities.[3] The rapid obsolescence of laboratory and research tools, coupled with the highly complex and sophisticated nature of the equipment now needed for advanced information technology research, results in capital costs beyond the reach of most academic institutions.[4] The retention and attraction of top-quality faculty and the recruitment of advanced-level students, many of whom are being drawn to industry, are critical problems.[5] Further, as information technology R&D advances, multidisciplinary efforts are required to achieve new breakthroughs.[6] Not unexpectedly, universities have had to seek new ways to operate educational and research programs.

Given the resources for R&D within the major information technology corporations,[7] it is logical to ask why industries would initiate or be responsive to new institutional research relationships. The change in the scope of the information technology industry from a national to a global arena has been a critical factor. Competition within the industry has expanded from the U.S. to a new situation where the competition derives from nationally coordinated industry-government efforts worldwide.[8]

---

[3]W. R. Lynn and F. A. Long, "University-Industrial Collaboration in Research," *Technology in Society*, vol. 4, 1982, p. 199.

[4]For example, in 1970 a need for $200 million in new instrumentation in the Nation's university research laboratories was identified; a decade later the accumulated need is estimated to be more than $1 billion. National Research Council, *Revitalizing Laboratory Instrumentation* (Washington, DC, National Academy Press, 1982).

[5]Louis Branscomb, former Chairman of the National Science Board, points to needs for advanced degree training in computer science, electrical engineering, polymer science and materials engineering—a problem which requires both fellowship support and the strengthening of university instructional and research facilities. At the same time, he points out that incentives must be provided to make university research careers as attractive as offers from industry—principally through the provision of research and equipment support. See: L. Branscomb, "The Computer's Debt to Science," *Perspectives in Computing*, vol. 3, No. 3, October 1983, p. 18.

[6]Ibid, pp. 13-15. See also ch. 3, *Case Studies on Advanced Computer Architecture, Fiber Optics, Software Engineering, and Artificial Intelligence*.

[7]See table 23, R&D Intensities of Selected Major U.S. Telecommunications Firms, 1982, ch. 4, *Divestiture*.

[8]See ch. 7. *Information Technology R&D in the United Kingdom, France, and Japan*, for examples of such efforts.

Based on the perception that industrial growth, productivity and competitiveness are dependent on new knowledge and innovation, and a renewable supply of highly trained manpower, industries have turned increasingly to the universities. The increased cost of R&D makes cooperative efforts highly desirable among the industries themselves, and among cosponsored efforts with universities. Such cooperation goes beyond cooperation among large companies. It includes cooperation between large and small companies, and among business, academia, and government.[9] In sum, given the rapid advances in technology, the escalating costs of R&D, and the global intensity of competition, *intranational cooperation* is seen as a means of maintaining *international competitiveness,*[10] and universities are seen as cornerstones of the cooperative effort.

Over the past two decades, several regions of the United States have developed strong local economies based on high-growth, technology-based firms that are engaged in systematic development and commercialization of new products, processes, and services. These firms, and the industries they represent, have provided a major source of new jobs in the manufacturing sector.[11][12] Thus States, as well as local communities have become active competitors in seeking to attract high-technology firms. Just as U.S. industries have had to acknowledge the international change in the competitive forces for their products, so too have State and local governments had to recognize that the competition for high-technology industry is interregional. The intensive State bidding for location of the Microelectronics and Computer Corporation (MCC) is such an example, with some 60 mayors and 27 governors involved. Notes Arizona Governor Bruce Babbitt,

> The great MCC bidding war marks a special chapter in American industrial history. State and local governments across the country have discovered scientific research and technological innovation as the prime force for economic growth and job creation. And local officials have also uncovered a broad base of public interest that can be translated into support for aggressive action programs. With the exception, perhaps, of the post-Sputnik era, such grassroots enthusiasm for science and technology has not been seen since the Gilded Age of the 19th century, when communities vied to finance the transcontinental railroads.*

To attract such industry, incentives such as tax breaks, donations of real estate, venture capital for industry and funding for educational programs have been provided.[13] Not all State and local high-technology initiatives have focused on education, nor does every State or locality have equal resources on which to draw. However, a strong educational base is seen as a way of becoming more competitive. In a survey of 691 high-technology firms, completed for the congressional Joint Economic Committee, "the importance of skilled labor points up the necessity of linking State and local development efforts with a region's universities in order to attract high-technology

---

[9]See for example, testimony by Erich Bloch, Vice President, IBM, and Chairman, Semiconductor Research Corp. "In order to cope with increasing competition in the world market, the semiconductor industry must increase its efforts in research and development. At the same time the research tasks are becoming more complex and more capital-intensive; lead time is increasing and the shortages of sufficiently trained manpower make the staffing of needed projects difficult. For all these reasons, some research efforts are beyond the affordability of individual companies." Hearings Before the Subcommittee on Investigations and Oversight and the Subcommittee on Science, Research and Technology, House of Representatives, 98th Cong., 1st sess., June 29-30, 1983, *Japanese Technological Advances and Possible United States Responses Using Research Joint Ventures,* p. 46.

[10]W. B. Norris, "How to Expand R&D Cooperation." *Business Week,* Apr. 11, 1983, p. 21. *Keynote Address* "Cooperation for Improving Productivity," San Diego, July 20, 1983, IEEE Task Force on Productivity and Innovation.

[11]U.S. Congress, Office of Technology Assessment, *Technology, Innovation, and Regional Economic Development, Census of State Government Initiatives for High Technology Industrial Development—Background Paper* OTA-BP-STI, May 1983; *Encouraging High-Technology Development—Background Paper,* OTA-BP-STI-25, February 1984.

[12]Total employment in the information technology industry experienced considerable growth in the decade between 1972 and 1982, despite economic recessions. See ch. 9.

---

*B. Babbitt, "The States and the Reindustrialization of America," *Issues in Science and Technology,* fall 1984, p. 85.

[13]For examples of such efforts, see the report by the National Governor's Association, *Technology and Growth: State Initiatives in Technological Innovation* (Washington, DC: National Governors' Association, 1983), pp. 23-45.

industries."[14] Moreover, the development of the Route 128 industrial corridor in Massachusetts, the California Silicon Valley, and Research Triangle in North Carolina, provide examples of the critical role played by nearby public and private universities as providers of basic research and suppliers of trained personnel.

[14]*Location of High Technology Firms and Regional Economic Development*, a staff study prepared for the use of the Subcommittee on Monetary and Fiscal Policy, Joint Economic Committee, U.S. Congress, June 1, 1982.

Photo credit: Microelectronics Center of North Carolina

The new MCNC Research Facility, Research Triangle Park, NC

Impacts of New University Arrangements

While we can find examples of State and local high-technology initiatives and numerous examples of long-standing university-industry interactions including industry's support for research through gifts of funds or equipment; cooperative research grants and contracts; the use of university consultants, exchange of personnel between universities and industries and other arrangements,[15] *the university today is in a special position. Universities are being courted by all of the principal actors and many are initiating programs of their own.* Most im-

[15]National Science Foundation, *University-Industry Research Relationships* (Washington, DC: National Science Foundation, 1982).

portantly, they are the linking element in multi-institutional R&D relationships.

The new institutional relationships take many forms; some efforts represent new and largely experimental ways of working together; many efforts that are being developed are not really new, but are evolving from previous efforts and relationships. However, all of the efforts that OTA examined involve a set of agreements whose principal characteristics are multidisciplinary arrangements and commitments to research with long-term objectives. While several of the ventures have been initiated by one or few individuals, the negotiated agreements themselves are made at the institutional level. It is the level of commitment and the extent of the involvement that differs from previous university-industry efforts.

It is too early to know with any certainty the benefits and costs of the new university-centered activities. However, in breaking new ground, the university arrangements, cosponsored efforts, and high-technology State and local initiatives have generated high expectations amid questions of appropriateness.[16] The number of meetings, conferences, hearings, and publications on this subject has been significant.[17] The debates over these relationships have involved university leaders and academicians, governors, congressmen, and corporate executives.

---

[16]This concern has been most focused on biotechnology, where several university-industry agreements have involved large sums of funding, over multiyear periods, and where a major research unit of the university is involved with a single company with varying agreements for industry participation on campus, and on some agreement to delay publication or provide exclusive licensing to processes and products developed during the duration of the research agreement.

[17]"Academe and Industry Debate Partnership," *Science*, vol. 219, No. 4481, January 1983, pp. 150-151; T. W. Langfitt, S. Hackney, A. P. Fishman, et al., Partners in the Research Enterprise, University-Corporate Relations in Science and Technology (Philadelphia: University of Pennsylvania Press, 1983). U.S. House of Representatives, University/Industry Cooperation in Biotechnology. Joint hearings of the Subcommittee on Investigations and Oversight and the Subcommittee on Science, Research, and Technology, June 16-17, 1982.

Expected Benefits

The increased interactions among the university-industry-government triad depicted in figure 30 underlie potentially successful approaches to several critical problem areas:

- *Research and new knowledge:* The coupling between university and industry may match needs of both. Industry gets access to the research and knowledge that resides in the university. Similarly, university researchers can benefit from the pool of industry expertise. The academic community obtains R&D laboratory facilities and research tools, as well as funding to undertake research. With increased interaction, the university has an opportunity for better understanding of the industry's practical concerns, and, conversely, industry may get a closer look at the university's research findings, speeding technology transfer.

- *Education and manpower:* With the increased opportunities for research, and a strengthening of the academic research program, the educational program can also be affected positively. Incentives that would attract and retain top-level faculty and advanced graduate students are derived from higher levels of support of new facilities and research. Moreover, as a result of interacting with industry personnel, students can make more informed decisions about their future employment. The combination of top-level personnel, adequate facilities, and a vigorous research agenda can strengthen the educational program, as new courses are developed and learning opportunities increase. The university products can then feed back into both industry and the community.

- *Economic growth:* New institutional efforts are aimed at a strengthened research base and a renewable source of highly trained manpower, which are needed by industry for its economic growth. This, in turn, can strengthen the regional economic base through new jobs, new spin-off industries, and the continued development of entrepreneurial efforts to fill new niches.[18]

Potential Costs

The increased interactions among academia-industry-government also raise questions of long-term impact:

- *Research and new knowledge:* Closer interaction may lead to subtle changes in the setting of research goals both in terms of the selection of topics to be studied and in the shortening of time horizons for results. Breakthroughs in fundamental research often require decades of study. Thus some problems may be overlooked if the institutional time frames for research are 3, 5, or even 10 years. How will topics *not* of direct interest to industry be covered in such institutional arrangements?

In addition, industry's traditional emphasis on secrecy is in direct conflict with academic practices. The new arrangements have involved extensive negotiation regarding patent and licensing agreements.[19] Thus far, most universities have resisted industry pressure to limit access to research results, maintaining their traditional role "to protect and to foster an environment conducive to free inquiry, the advancement of knowledge and the free exchange of ideas."[20] The conflict between openness and control is of continuing concern,[21] and will require solutions on a case by case basis.

- *Education and manpower:* It is possible that these new, highly visible, exciting ventures will cause competition between research and education, drawing faculty away from teaching, and recruiting students from other areas. There is the danger that these new efforts will skew the balance among programs and capture unequal attention and support from university administration.
- *Economic growth and development:* While there are many other joint industry-university activities involving small and large businesses, a variety of academic institutions, and individual faculty members, the industry sponsors and major participants in both the multidisciplinary university centers and the industry cooperative ventures have mainly been the large information technology corporations. Fewer numbers of smaller companies have joined projects as "associate" (in contrast to fully participating) members. Full membership includes access to research as well as personnel exchanges, and active participation in planning research, selecting proposals for funding and evaluating ongoing programs. Thus, cooperative joint-industry ventures among the information technology giants may put the smallest, entrepreneurial companies at a disadvantage.

The costs of increased interaction come from two directions. First, in coming together, each of the institutions may lose some measure of autonomy and relinquish aspects of their traditional roles. Conflict is inevitable, for example, between the university's need for openness and industry's need for protection of proprietary interests. Another conflict may develop if the traditional distinctions that have separated the use of public funds from private interest and gain are blurred.[22]

Second, there is the "cost" of nonparticipation. Most of the debate has focused solely on

---

[18]For example, in a recent study of the Route 128 High Technology Industrial Corridor, Massachusetts' advantage in attracting and supporting industries has resulted from the rich university environment. "Entrepreneurs in the electronics fields come mainly from the staffs of universities and their research labs, and from other high tech firms (already established)." N. S. Dorfman, "Route 128: The Development of a Regional High Technology Economy," *Research Policy*, 12:6, December 1983, p. 309; see also table 1, p. 301, ibid.

[19]Fowler, "University-Industry Research Relationships: The Research Agreement," *Journal of College and University Law*, 9:4, 1982-83.

[20]A. B. Giametti, "The University, Industry and Cooperative Research," *Science*, vol. 218, December 1982, pp. 1278-1280.

[21]D. Nelkin, "Intellectual Property: The Control of Scientific Information," *Science* 216:14, May 1982, pp. 704-708.

[22]"Weighing the Social Costs of Innovation," *Science*, vol. 223, March 1984, p. 1368. A suit involving the University of California and its research, raises the question of the legality of spending public funds for research that allegedly benefits large agribusiness more than small farmers and laborers.

the generic institution without recognition of the differences within each of the institutional communities. Thus, it has not looked very much at how the establishment of university industry relationships may affect a smaller or less prestigious research institution, nor how joint-industry ventures may affect smaller businesses, nor how local and State initiatives place some other regions or other institutions within the region in an inequitable position.

There is concern that the already existing differences between the Nation's top-tier and second-tier universities may grow even greater as the competition for industrial resources and partnerships accelerates. Thus, there is concern for the needs of the range of the Nation's universities. Even though programs may be less ambitious in scope and scale, the needs for sophisticated equipment, advanced research facilities, highly trained and knowledgeable faculty, and advanced-level students remain critical. Therefore, a diversity of efforts and approaches needs to be explored and supported.

At the State and regional level, the ability to compete for new industry, for research centers of excellence, and for expert manpower may also become equity issues. As noted earlier, while the number of high-technology centers has increased in recent years, the competition among State and regional localities is becoming fierce. The ability of States to assure significant support for new facilities, additional faculty and graduate students, the availability of venture capital, and the cooperative efforts of business and academic leaders are critical factors in attracting new institutional research ventures. Moreover, as a result of successful bids, regions expect to attract other high-technology companies while the universities hope to attract senior faculty and the top graduate students.

New Roles for Universities: Selected Case Studies

University-industry-government information technology R&D efforts demonstrate a variety of approaches which have been only recently implemented. Because these efforts are essentially in formative stages, an assessment of their effectiveness and impact on R&D is premature. Yet it is clear that the efforts examined in this chapter provide important examples of new directions and major commitments. The case studies provide examples of how problems or barriers raised by these new relationships are being addressed, as well as those issues which are not yet resolved. The case studies also provide an understanding of the motives and factors stimulating change, how the institutional players are responding, and the role played by incentives and directions from the Federal Government. Thus, they provide a framework for analysis and the development of policy options.

While each of the case studies is unique, several themes emerge:

- Institutional arrangements involve long-term, multiyear commitments with agreements that include facilities, equipment, and human resources.
- These arrangements bring together multi-disciplines, multi-institutions, and multi-funding resources to support wide-ranging research, educational, and development efforts.
- These arrangements involve leadership and support of individuals at the highest levels of the university, corporations, and government.
- While Federal funds continue to support a significant portion of the research at the university centers, the Federal Government had a limited role in development of the institutional arrangements, influencing them by providing limited funds for startup activities, by creating tax credit incentives, and by its supportive policy towards joint ventures.

Massachusetts Institute of Technology Microsystems Industrial Group

MIT's experience with joint industry arrangements is extensive and reaches virtually every program area in the Institute. More than 300 joint programs are currently sponsored at MIT by industrial firms. Federal sources nonetheless provide the bulk of funding for research. In 1983, only 10 percent of MIT's sponsored research was funded by industry.[23] It is estimated that support from industry will not grow beyond 15 or 20 percent. However, MIT faculty point out that industry involvement is important because it provides exposure to and understanding of industrial concerns, motivations, and needs. This interaction is seen as critical for the future of most students who graduate from the university to work in the information technology field. Equally important, it provides necessary expansion of academic research concerns that would otherwise be guided primarily by the interests of particular Federal funding agencies.[24]

While there have been long and well established industry-university research ties at MIT, the formation of the Microsystems Industrial Group breaks new ground. Increased industrial involvement in the MIT microsystems program was stimulated by the program's need for advanced state-of-the-art equipment and laboratory facilities. A proposal to reach out to industry for help in developing these facilities was made by members of the faculty, who argued that the amount needed (originally estimated at $10 million) could not be supported by any Federal program or by the university itself. The advanced research Very Large Scale Integration (VLSI) laboratory and facilities are supported by industry sponsors; contributions are estimated to be $10 million (half of the actual cost of renovation and operation). The rest of the cost is being recovered through overhead charges on current contract research. In agreements negotiated with industry, full member companies contribute $250,000 annually for 3 years, and associate member companies contribute $50,000 annually for 5 years.

Thus far, 18 companies have joined the group.[25] Full member companies can send one technical staff member to MIT to work in the Microsystems research program annually for 3 years. Each visiting professional submits a plan of proposed research topics, and these are matched with an appropriate faculty member or research group. More than a dozen industry people have participated in the program. The opportunity to work in a new area of interest, "get caught up in the MIT atmosphere" and interact daily with students and faculty members is viewed very positively.[26]

Research projects under way have been developed by faculty and reflect their traditional roles as principal investigators. The director and faculty meet with the industry member advisory group, who provide information and advice. Even more directly, the technical people from industry have contributed to the research efforts, and have broadened the view of faculty and students. The director of the Microsystems Industrial Group explains: "These are smart people with different backgrounds than my University colleagues. It is very important for those of us who do research to have the industrial viewpoint in front of us."[27]

Understanding grows both generally through interaction with the Council of member companies, who offer advice and guidance, and in the process of working out specific visiting relationships. This understanding helps faculty, students, and the academic program. But it is also clear to faculty and administra-

---

[23]Kenneth A. Smith, "Industry-University Research Programs," Physics Today, vol. 37, No. 2, February 1984, p. 24.
[24]Ibid., p. 24.
[25]Full member companies included AT&T Bell labs, Digital Equipment, General Electric, General Motors, GTE, Harris, IBM, Raytheon, and United Technologies. Associate member companies are Analog Devices, GCA, Genrad, NCR, Polaroid, Sanders Associates and Teradyne.
[26]Personal communication, March 1984. According to Paul Penfield, Director, MIG, these experiences provide industry associates unique opportunities for professional growth and development, and appear to be a way for a company to retain highly valued employees.
[27]Personal communication. Paul Penfield, Director, Microsystems Industry Group.

tors who have responsibility for university-industry research that, even though time and competitive pressures are high, the academic integrity of both the research and educational program must not be compromised. Thus, in some cases, decisions are made not to undertake certain projects, for example, when the proprietary stakes are too high, or the timeframes are inappropriate or if scientific exchange is jeopardized.[28] From industry's point of view, the Microsystems Industrial Group, as well as other similar efforts such as the Center for Integrated Systems at Stanford, are working because the research effort is focused.[29]

New institutional relationships can benefit both university and industry if the agreements meet the needs of the partners. In analyzing the aspects of such negotiations at MIT, the Associate Provost and Vice President for Research identifies the fundamental issues to be addressed:

1. *the relevance of a proposed line of inquiry to the essential missions of the university and the industry*—maintaining a balance between the pursuit of research as an integral part of the educational process and industry's need for useful knowledge to be applied in the development of products, processes and services;
2. *the organization of a program that meets the different time constraints of industry and the university*—accommodating the multiyear efforts of graduate students with the shorter time pressures of the marketplace;
3. *the issue of proprietary rights versus openness*—achieving openness and free exchange of research results while protecting the industrial partners' proprietary rights;
4. *the issue of patents and copyrights*—determining licensing agreements that advance scientific and technological discoveries in ways that are most likely to benefit the public and the research participants and institutions; and
5. *the issue of conflict of commitment*—assuring that faculty are primarily committed to the university: its research and its educational programs.[30]

Microelectronics and Information Sciences Center (MEIS) University of Minnesota

The Microelectronics and Information Sciences Center (MEIS) is a joint endeavor between the University of Minnesota's Institute of Technology and Minnesota industry. It was created to establish a center of excellence in these sciences as well as to meet local industry's technical manpower needs. Such joint efforts are not new to Minnesota.[31] The impetus for the Microelectronics and Information Sciences Center came from Minnesota industries—Control Data, Honeywell, 3-M, and Sperry Corp.—who committed $6 million to launch the effort. The Minnesota State legislature allocated an additional $1.2 million. Current operation is at $2.5 million a year matched by $4.0 million in external grants and contracts.

Faculty members, university officials, corporate executives and center administrators have worked together to define the directions for research and educational programs, the center's operation, and the university-industry interface mechanisms. This negotiation took time to work out, and programs were phased in gradually over a several-year period.[32] The

---

[28]Personal communication, George Dummer, MIT, March 1984.

[29]Personal communication, Bill Nelson, GTE, April 1984.

[30]K. A. Smith, "Industry-University Research Programs," op. cit., p. 25.

[31]For example, in the early 1970s such a joint effort initiated the development of the Minnesota Educational Computing Consortium to provide instructional time-sharing capability to the State's colleges and universities, as well as the elementary and secondary schools. See: a case study of "Minnesota Schools and the Minnesota Educational Computing Consortium," *Informational Technology and Its Impact on American Education*, (Washington, DC: U.S. Congress, Office of Technology Assessment, OTA-CIT-187, 1982) pp. 214-221.

[32]The Center's slow start has been criticized by some. However, the benefits of taking the time to work out an arrangement that suited the needs of both the university and the sponsoring industries outweighed the costs of delay. Personal communication, Dr. Martha Russell, March 1984.

results of the negotiations are embodied in the MEIS Center goals:
1. to sponsor and conduct research at the frontiers of microelectronic and information sciences;
2. to strengthen the course offerings of the University of Minnesota in these sciences; and
3. to provide active interplay between university researchers who seek discovery and industrial firms that apply those research results to the development and marketing of innovative products and services.

Research

Through the sponsorship of interdisciplinary research projects, the center links faculty, students, and industry. Proposals for research are submitted by faculty members. MEIS-sponsored research is reviewed annually by technical experts at the university and supporting companies. In 1983, projects in 3-D Integrated-Circuits, Processor Array Concepts for Engineering, Design Automation and Software Engineering, and Ultrasmall Electronic Research received MEIS seed funding, totaling $625,000; additional research funds of $4,312,000, principally from Federal grants, was obtained. In 1984, MEIS has awarded both seed and matching funding to three integrated team efforts in Intelligent Systems Research, III-V Semiconductor Materials and High Speed Devices, and High-Performance Integrated Circuits. Another planned effort will include a project on Artificially Structured Materials.

Renovation and development of laboratory facilities has been directly tied to the research efforts. The University is planning a new Computer Science and Engineering building which will house both offices and laboratories. MEIS co-owns, with Argonne National Laboratory, a Synchrotron X-Ray Beamline Facility, located in Stoughton, WI. In addition, MEIS and the University share the newly remodeled microelectronics laboratory and the VLSI engineering design laboratory.

Education

Strengthening the educational program has focused on increasing the number of faculty members, starting new courses, and attracting top-quality graduate students. Eighteen new graduate and undergraduate courses have been added in computer science, electrical engineering, materials science and chemical engineering; seven new faculty members have already been recruited through a 3-year cost-sharing program with the university, and plans call for hiring an additional four members in Computer Science as well as a director; 54 graduate students and four post-doctoral assistants were supported by MEIS funds in the five departments receiving MEIS research sponsorship; 16 fellowships will be available for 1984-1985.[33]

Technology Transfer

The exchange of knowledge and technology between MEIS member companies and the university community has been a major goal of the Center. Through direct scientist-to-scientist interaction, it is anticipated that the time between discovery and application will be shortened. Faculty, students, and industry technical staff have worked jointly on projects, in some cases using industry's state-of-the-art facilities for design, special fabrication or testing. A major assumption is that graduate students serve a key role in the transfer of technology between industry and university. After the first year of graduate study in the doctoral program, students work in the research laboratories of the industry sponsors, learning what drives industrial use of innovation in science and technology, and bringing their recently acquired knowledge and skills to the task. Research projects developing from these experiences expand the involvement of faculty, students, and the industrial scientists.

Like other joint efforts, the center has fostered the exchange of ideas through confer-

---
[33]Microelectronics and Information Sciences Center, 1983 Annual Report, February 1984.

ences and seminars. MEIS technical reports and newsletters have also been widely disseminated. Center participants from both academia and industry point out that this open exchange has been facilitated by concentrating on long-term research areas conducted over a 5 to 7 year period. The Center has thus far avoided the issues regarding exclusive research and proprietary information.

Continued ability to recruit high-quality graduate students, as well as recruiting and retaining excellent faculty, is critical to the long-term stability and growth of the program. Stable funding and full implementation of programs are anticipated by 1985. In addition, the Center expects to attract additional State and private support.

Rensselaer Polytechnic Institute Center for Industrial Innovation

The RPI Center for Industrial Innovation is the result of a focused University initiative that has involved key participants from academia, industry, and New York State government—including the governor. This initiative was based on the experiences of RPI's three established Centers for Interactive Graphics, for Manufacturing Productivity, and for Microelectronics. With a $30 million interest-free loan from the State and an additional $30 million commitment by RPI, construction of a facility to house these Centers is under way. These Centers involve more than 100 arrangements and agreements with industry, including support for ongoing research through industry affiliates, specific research and problem-solving agreements, continuing education and training, adjunct industry-faculty arrangements, faculty-industry consulting, industry fee payments, and gifts or loans of equipment and software. However, it was not the quest for industrial partnerships, but rather the desire to improve the undergraduate engineering education program, that served as the initial catalyst for these activities.[34]

The effort to improve RPI's educational program was begun in 1975-76 and resulted in several new interrelated directions: expansion of the graduate program (from approximately 500 to a goal of 2,400 graduate students by the year 2000); an institutional commitment to research through the expansion of faculty and facilities as well as of the number of students, and a revision of the undergraduate curriculum to overcome the lack of hands-on engineering experiences.

Center for Interactive Graphics

The first step was the creation of an interactive computer graphics laboratory designed as a service facility for undergraduates. This was based on the belief that an important emerging tool for engineering was the interactive computer graphics terminal. The facility and the applications have grown beyond the original classroom to a Center for Interactive Graphics. The growth was due not only to the increased use in almost all engineering courses, but also to the decision to combine research with practice as the means for keeping up to date with the advancing technology.

The Center for Interactive Graphics was created in 1978, with initial funding from the National Science Foundation. From its inception, it was intended to involve industry, and to share research results with industry. A measure of its success is that the Center has grown from 20 supporting companies with $20,000 annual fees to 35 companies with $40,000 annual fees. An early concern that it would not be possible to keep up with the continually advancing hardware and software has been reduced: companies have been willing to donate their latest equipment. Just recently, for example, the Center received a $3 million equipment grant from IBM.[35]

Center for Manufacturing Productivity

The Center for Manufacturing Productivity and Technology Transfer was the result of a deliberate decision to train students in areas

---

[34]G. M. Low, "The Organization of Industrial Relationships in Universities," *Partners in the Research Enterprise*, T. W. Langfitt et al. (eds.), (Philadelphia: University of Pennsylvania Press, 1983), p. 71.

[35]Personal communication, Dr. Christopher LeMaistre, Director Center for Industrial Innovation and Assistant Dean, School of Engineering, March 1984.

Graduate student and faculty member using a CAD/CAM workstation, in the Center for Interactive Computer Graphics, RPI

that would be needed in the decade of the 1980s and at the same time to meet industry's research needs so that industrial funding would be available. Support from Federal sources was not available. Thus, the Dean of the School of Engineering made initial contacts with executives from General Electric. He and two GE executives traveled to Europe to see how industry and universities were working together. RPI's Center was modeled after one at the University of Aachen in West Germany.

With a commitment from GE, the Center started in May 1979. Presently there are eight founding companies and five affiliate companies who support the operation of the Center and its research.[36] In addition, the Center engages in contract work and involves undergraduates and graduates in "real life, real time" industrial problem solving, all under the direction of faculty and a project manager. The intent is to create experiences that are directly relevant for students' entry into the industrial world. The Center reports to and receives guidance from a board of advisers comprised of founding member company representatives.

Center for Integrated Electronics

The Center for Integrated Electronics also has industrial sponsors, who support research efforts which are fully open with no restrictions on disclosure.[37] The Center is equipped with $8 million in hardware, much of it donated, from companies such as IBM, Calma, and Computervision. RPI also provides "incubator space" for small fledgling companies on campus and provides administrative support to help companies while they find venture capital, develop management capability, and begin to grow.

In addition, RPI has created an industrial park, located 10 miles south of the Institute, on a 1,200-acre parcel of land owned by RPI. With strong leadership from then RPI President George Low the Institute committed $3 million for initial preparation of the site in 1982. National Semiconductor was the first company to move in, with several others following. RPI is currently constructing its own building in the park to provide startup space for companies that are not yet large enough to be on their own.

Center for Industrial Innovation

All of these activities led to the Center for Industrial Innovation. The RPI President and the Chief Executive Officers of GE and Kodak, along with other corporate executives, met with the Governor to push for a State Technology Initiative to be funded through the State legislature. The arguments, as in other industrial States, were that the smokestack industries were dying, new technology industries were locating elsewhere, and that to overcome this, new catalysts were needed. RPI argued that it had the necessary infrastruc-

---

[36]Member companies include General Electric, General Motors, Boeing, Norton, IBM, Alcoa, Digital Equipment Corp., and United Technologies. Affiliate companies include Kodak, Cincinnati Milacron, Fairchild Republic, Fairchild Schlumberger, Altech, and Timex.

[37]Founding members include Harris Corp., Computervision, Digital Equipment Corp., Eastman Kodak, General Electric, Raytheon, Polaroid, GTE, IBM, Phoenix Data Systems, Eaton Corp., and AIR Products. Affiliate members include Sperry, Xerox, Hewlett-Packard, Perkin-Elmer, Fairchild Semiconductor, BTU Corp., Matheson, ITT, and the PEW Memorial Trust.

ture in place and that what was needed was a $30 million interest-free loan.

The ground has been broken for the Center at RPI and the university expects completion of the facility in September 1986. RPI expects to put an additional $30 million into the facilities. In return for the State loan, RPI will provide an outreach program to 2-year colleges and to industry to upgrade the level of technological expertise.

While there has been strong support for these activities and agreement that they have helped the Institute, their industrial orientation does cause concern to some faculty. The Center argument is, however, that there is a healthy balance between uncommitted research support and both focused engineering and applied projects. There is evidence that the program brings together a blend of research and application for students, and that the quality of the instructional program has been significantly improved.[38]

Stanford University Center for Integrated Systems

Like the MIT, RPI, and University of Minnesota efforts, the institutional relationship developed between Stanford University and industry breaks new ground. In May 1983, more than the construction of a $15 million facility to house the Center for Integrated Systems (CIS) was being celebrated. According to participants from the faculty, university administration, and industry, this project and others like it are part of a new willingness by industry and the academic community to become "allies in basic research."[39] According to William Hewlett, "CIS is a clear and distinct answer to three major problems that face the United States—the failure of our national programs of basic research to keep pace with the needs of our universities and industries, the need to strengthen our system of education, and the challenge to U.S. trade and technology posed by foreign countries."[40]

Planning Activities

As early as 1977, Stanford engineering faculty discussed the idea of a center for integrated systems research, a multidisciplinary endeavor involving the interaction of people knowledgeable about integrated circuits with another group knowledgeable about computer and information systems. "From the outset it was clear that a collaboration, more intense than had ever before occurred, between IC types and systems engineers needed to evolve."[41] Furthermore, such a center could vertically integrate the research process, with a state-of-the-art facility for design, fabrication and testing of VLSI chips. This fast-turnaround facility would allow a systems designer, in collaboration with an IC designer, to create experimental devices in a shorter time than ever before.

The faculty took their idea to the Dean of the School of Engineering, and subsequently a formal proposal was submitted to the university. By January 1980, the Center for Integrated Systems was under way with approval from the Board of Trustees. Executives of Hewlett-Packard, TRW, Xerox, and Intel formed a development committee to raise funds. By March 1981, 10 corporations agreed to contribute $750,000 each, spread over a 3-year period. By 1983-84, an additional 10 sponsors brought the total to 20, with each also agreeing to provide $100,000 annually for education, research, and administration of the facility.[42]

Formulating New Policies

Not unexpectedly, the most controversial aspect of the plan was not the facility, but the intention to involve industrial companies as sponsors of the Center and offer them "facilitated access" to the research program. Of con-

---

[38]Low, op. cit.
[39]F. H. Gardner, "Special Report: The Center for Integrated Systems," *Hewlett-Packard Journal,* November 1983, p. 23.
[40]Ibid.

[41]John G. Linvill, Director Industrial Programs, Center for Integrated Systems, Stanford University. Personal communication, April 1984.
[42]Corporate sponsors are General Electric, Hewlett-Packard, TRW, Northrop, Xerox, Texas Instruments, Fairchild, Honeywell, IBM, Tektronix, Digital Equipment Corp., Intel, ITT, GTE, Motorola, United Technologies, Monsanto, Gould/American Microsystems, Inc., North American Philips/Signetics Corp., and Rockwell International.

cern to faculty members and corporate sponsors was how patent ownership, licensing, and intellectual property rights would be determined. The companies' initial posture was insistent on exclusive proprietary rights to inventions which involved their own people. The university, on the other hand, argued that research in the Center was funded principally with Federal support and that the University's legal obligation was to make sure that any resulting patents would be brought into the stream of commerce as quickly as possible, with any company capable of commercialization having the right to bid and obtain a license.

The successful resolution of the issue centered on categorizing the patent in terms of the inventor (see fig. 31, CIS Patent Policy). In addition, if a corporate visiting scholar develops a patentable product jointly with a Stanford faculty member or student, the company may request a 90-day delay of publication to get the patent filed; it also gets free but nonexclusive rights to exploit the product. CIS sponsor companies have also agreed to a cross-licensing plan, sharing any inventions developed at CIS. While intellectual property rights have generated much discussion and have taken time to work out, it appears unlikely that highly commercial applications will result, given the basic nature of the research under way at CIS. Moreover, both sponsors and faculty point out that it is in their interest that the Center produce new basic knowledge as well as students trained as broadly as possible.

Another area of concern focused on the question of research direction: would the nature and direction of basic research be distorted by industrial sponsorship? The answer appears to be that this is unlikely, given the tradition of independent research teams led by principal investigators. At the same time, the investment of industrial sponsors is not insignificant, and there is the sense that faculty will be receptive to good problems posed by industry. There is also the sense that research questions can be shaped to examine fundamental issues likely to be of interest to all.[43] There is additional concern that there will be pressures to keep research secret. Such pressures are likely to be strongly resisted; the number of seminars, publications, and open meetings have demonstrated the University's and the Center's intent to maintain openness.

Finally, there is the question concerning the advantage corporate sponsors have over nonparticipating companies. The questions here

---

[43]John Linvill, Director, CIS, notes, "We gain much more through access with each other. The watchword is not isolation, but interaction." Personal communication, March 1983.

Figure 31.—Stanford University, Center for Integrated Systems Patent Policy

CIS Patent Policy
Disposition of Rights

Inventor	Unsponsored	CIS Annual Gift	U.S. Government Sponsorship	Industrial Sponsorship
Stanford Faculty Staff	Stanford patent policy existing at the time of the invention. Currently, individual inventors retain rights	Public domain (no rights shall be asserted)	Stanford patent policy	Negotiated with research contract
CIS Visiting Scholar			1 or 2 below	
Joint			Stanford policy for staff and 1 below for visiting scholars	
Others			Stanford patent policy	

1. Stanford takes title and inventor receives nonexclusive, fully paid license including right to sublicense.
2. Upon request of inventors, Stanford will authorize a petition by inventor's employers to U.S. Government for greater rights than 1.

SOURCE: Hewlett-Packard Journal, November 1983.

relate not just to this project but to other projects as well. Proponents of the Center argue that the fundamental nature of the university has not been changed, that everything the university does is open to dissemination—a way of life that undergirds every relationship—no matter "whom we get money from."[44] While sponsoring companies have access to graduate students, and may seem to have an advantage in recruiting them, the networks between Stanford faculty and their contacts in hundreds of companies in the Silcon Valley remain strong. In addition, if a CIS research team wishes to include a nonparticipating company on a research project, they can do so. Reaching this agreement, noted several participants, was a hard fight to win.

Nonetheless, the controversy persists, and questions are likely to remain.[45] The negotiated agreements concerning patents, and the disposition of licenses are seen as experiments which may or may not work out and which may need to be revised as research and work progresses. The experimental nature of the center is not limited to intellectual property arrangements, note participants, but includes as well the social and organizational arrangements built around cooperation—both among the various departments and among the corporations.

Center Operation

While the Center itself is still evolving in terms of the agreements for intellectual property rights, the working relationships between corporate sponsors and faculty, and the facilities under construction, the research and involvement of the faculty and students are well under way. CIS research projects, funded principally by the Federal Government, total $12 million a year. (see table 26: CIS Research Topics). Seventy-one faculty members, representing seven departments, are affiliated with the center, and 30 Ph.D. and 100 MS degree candidate students a year are being trained. It is the people who are the most important output of the Center for Integrated Systems: "To the extent that we educate people with the right background, have them do interesting research of significance to the Nation's problems but at a fundamental level, and do this in close collaboration with the industries which need such people, we will significantly modify the nation's productivity and competitiveness."[46]

Microelectronics Center of North Carolina (MCNC)

Universities play a critical role in the Microelectronics Center of North Carolina (MCNC). As a multi-institutional R&D effort, MCNC combines the resources of Duke University, North Carolina A&T State University, North Carolina State University, University of North Carolina at Chapel Hill, and University of North Carolina at Charlotte, as well as the Research Triangle Institute. These institutions, along with the MCNC core organization, the new MCNC research facility, and the communications system linking all the facilities provide a concentration of resources for education, research, technology transfer, and industrial development.

Established in July 1980, MCNC is organized as a private, nonprofit corporation to assist North Carolina's development of modern electronics and related high-technology industry. MCNC has been funded primarily with State grants, as a result of strong leadership from the governor and support from the legislature. Thus far, $43 million has been allocated by the North Carolina General Assembly for constructing, equipping, and operating MCNC. An additional $34 million for new capital facilities at the participating institutions has also been provided.

---

[44]Ibid.

[45]A recent article in the New York Times highlights the continuing questions and controversy. While the Vice Provost notes that CIS is an "innovative setup for Stanford," a professor of history argues, "It's potentially very dangerous for a university to give privileged space and privileged access to information to particular companies. There is a danger that researchers will create relationships that are likely to influence what they study and what they do not study. It is a threat to the autonomy of the university." See: R. Reinhold, "Stanford and Industry Forge New Research Link," *New York Times*, Feb. 10, 1984.

[46]John Linvill, personal communication, April 1984.

Table 26.—Stanford University, Center for Integrated Systems Research Topics

Although its building won't be completed until early 1985, the Center for Integrated Systems is already coordinating a $12-million-a-year basic research program at Stanford, funded largely by the Federal government. Here's a sampler of recent and current topics investigated by CIS affiliated faculty in various existing labs.

Computers
- Research on streamlined-instruction-set microprocessor (featuring partnership of computer and IC engineers)
- Research in VLSI systems
- Knowledge-based VLSI project
- Image understanding
- Intelligent task automation
- Network graphics
- Partitionable computer systems
- Analysis and verification of high-order language programs
- Study of very high-speed integrated circuits (VHSIC-Phase 3)
- Real-time communications systems: design, analysis, and implementation
- Structured design methodology for VLSI systems
- Logical methods for program analysis
- Ultra-concurrent computer systems
- Silicon compilation
- Data base theory
- Computer languages for VLSI fabrication

Information Systems
- Multiple user channels and information theory
- Computational complexity, efficiency, and accountability in large-scale teleprocessing systems
- Multiplexed holographic reconstruction methods for 3D structures
- Information theory and data compression
- Signal processing and compression
- Statistical data processing, system modeling, and reliability
- Algorithms for locating and identifying multiple sources by a distributed sensor network
- Fast algorithms for improved speech coding and recognition
- Dual-energy digital subtraction radiography for noninvasive arteriography

Integrated Circuits
- Computer modeling of complete IC fabrication process
- Integrated electromechanical and optical sensor arrays for Optacon II (a reading aid for the blind)
- BME Center for Integrated Electronics in Medicine (to produce implantable telemetry systems for biomedical research)
- Computer-aided design of IC fabrication processes for VLSI devices
- Submicron device physics and technology
- Development of multichannel electrodes for an auditory prosthesis
- Study of transdermal electronics for an auditory prosthesis
- Multilevel-metal interconnection technology
- Biomedical silicon sensors
- Fast turnaround laboratory for VLSI

Solid State
- Ion implantation and laser annealing in semiconductors and related materials
- Laser and electron beam processing of semiconductors
- Characterization of high-speed semiconductor device materials using advanced analytical techniques
- Ion implantation and laser processing of 3-5 compound conductors
- Defects at electrode-oxide and electrode-silicon interfaces in submicron device structures
- Microsturcture fabrication using electron beams of conventional and very low energies
- Advanced concepts in VLSI metallization
- Advanced packaging concepts for VLSI
- Studies of surfaces and interfaces of 3-5 compounds and Si:silicides
- Silicon photocells in thermophotovoltaic energy conversion
- Investigation of metallic impurities introduced into SiO_2 and Si by various candidate VLSI metallization systems
- Modeling of emitters
- Structural and bonding studies of practical semiconductor layers

Space Telecommunications and Radioscience
- Establishment of a Center for Aeronautics and Space Information Sciences at Stanford University (Funded by the U.S. National Aeronautics and Space Administration. The focus will be on applying VLSI techniques to develop new hardware and firmware for space instrumentation and command and control.)
- Communication satellite planning center

Material Science and Engineering
- Atomic-level physics modeling of the thermal oxidation process
- Fabrication and properties of multilayer structures
- Computer simulation of surface and film processes
- Photoelectronic properties of 2-4 heterojunctions
- Photoelectronic properties of zinc phosphide crystals, films, and heterojunctions
- Photovoltaic heterodiodes based on indium phosphide
- Preparation and properties of CdTe evaporated films compared with single-crystal CdTe

Ginzton Laboratory
- Superconducting thin films, composites, and junctions
- Acoustical scanning of optical images
- Research on nondestructive evaluation
- Evaluation of machining damage in brittle materials
- Optical and acoustic wave research
- High-frequency transducers
- Research on acoustic microscopy with superior resolution
- Study of properties of material by channeling radiation
- Surface acoustic wave MOSFET signal processor

SOURCE: Hewlett Packard Journal, November 1983.

While the extent of State support is significant, such a role is not new for North Carolina. The precedents for government-industry-university cooperation span two decades. The development of the Research Triangle Park, the Research Triangle Institute, the establishment of the North Carolina Board of Science and Technology, and now MCNC, are seen as models of government-industry-university cooperation to develop new technology-based industries.[47]

New Facilities for Education, R&D, and Technology Transfer

The MCNC facility, under construction since May 1982, will house core MCNC staff, visiting engineers and scientists from industry, and visiting faculty and graduate students working on special research projects. The 100,000-square-foot, $30 million facility has capability for performing advanced manufacturing processes, including high-density integrated circuit fabrication, system design, and design tool research.

The MCNC $6.5 million communications system, scheduled for completion by 1985, will put in place a 150-mile microwave network linking the educational and research activities at MCNC, the universities, and the Research Triangle Institute (see fig. 32, MCNC Communications System). In the first phase hookup of the system, computer science students at Duke University in Durham and UNC at Chapel Hill take classes (which originate from Durham) together without leaving their own campuses. Similarly, courses on Computer

---

[47]U.S. Congress, Office of Technology Assessment, *Technology, Innovation, and Regional Economic Development, Census of State Government Initiatives for High Technology Industrial Development—Background Paper*, OTA-BP-STI-21, May 1983, p. 56.

MCNC dual source electron beam/r.f. metal evaporator for next generation integrated circuit manufacturing research

Figure 32.—Communications System Linking MCNC Participating Sites

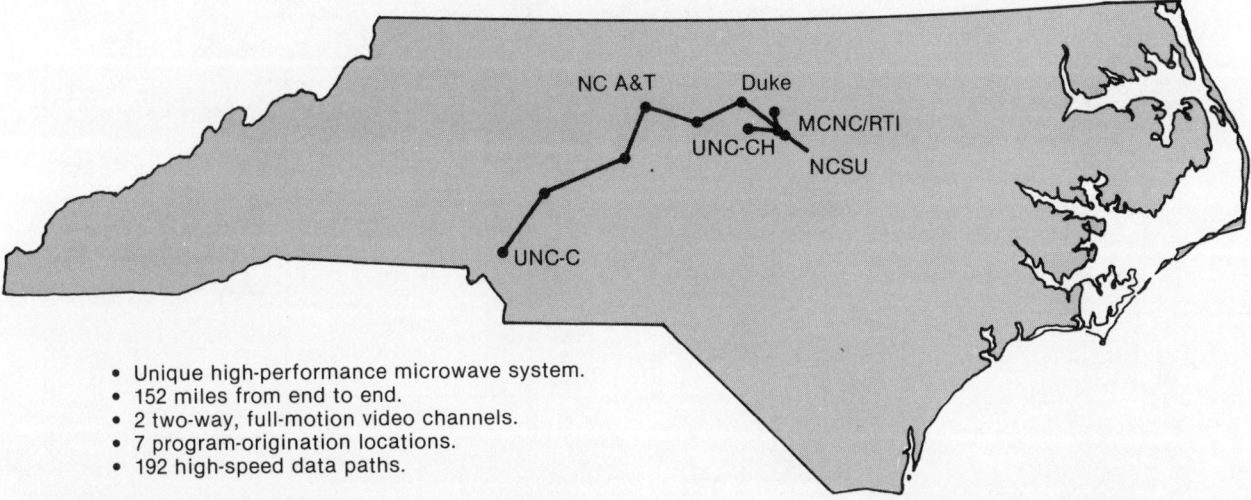

- Unique high-performance microwave system.
- 152 miles from end to end.
- 2 two-way, full-motion video channels.
- 7 program-origination locations.
- 192 high-speed data paths.

SOURCE: Microelectronics Center of North Carolina, Research Triangle Park, NC.

Graphics and VLSI Design originate from Chapel Hill.

Like the MCNC research facility, the development of the telecommunications system required funding beyond the reach of each of the individual institutions. "Before the center was created, each of our participating universities hoped to develop its own major microelectronics program. But the financial realities and the difficulties of attracting talent from the limited talent pool, soon made it apparent that the only way to develop a first class program was to join forces and work together."[48]

MCNC Working Relationships

MCNC is more than a consortium of universities sharing resources and interacting with industry. The participating institutions are linked together by MCNC (see fig. 33, The MCNC Community) and MCNC as an organizational entity and actor bridges the interests and functions of the industry and university communities (see fig. 34, Working Relationships). As members of industry work along with university researchers, the applied re-

[48]D. S. Beilman, President of MCNC, "New Initiatives in Modern Electronics," address before the Materials Research Society Annual Meeting, Boston, Nov. 14, 1983.

Figure 33.—MCNC Participating Institutions

Microelectronics Center of North Carolina
MCNC and the participating institutions

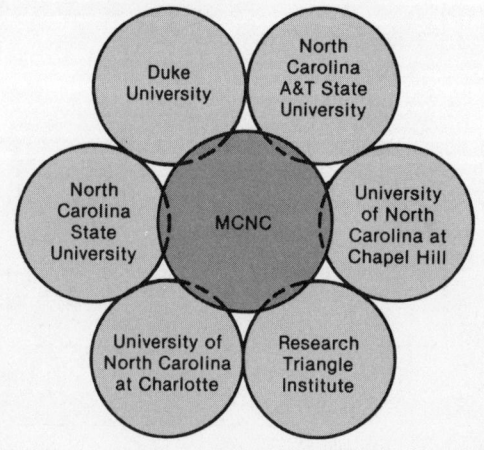

The MCNC community

SOURCE: Microelectronics Center of North Carolina, Research Triangle Park, NC.

search and technology projects tie together the commercial technology activities under way in industry and the basic research being conducted at the universities.

Since 1980, more than 30 new faculty members in microelectronics-related disciplines have been recruited. In contrast to the recent trend of faculty leaving universities for em-

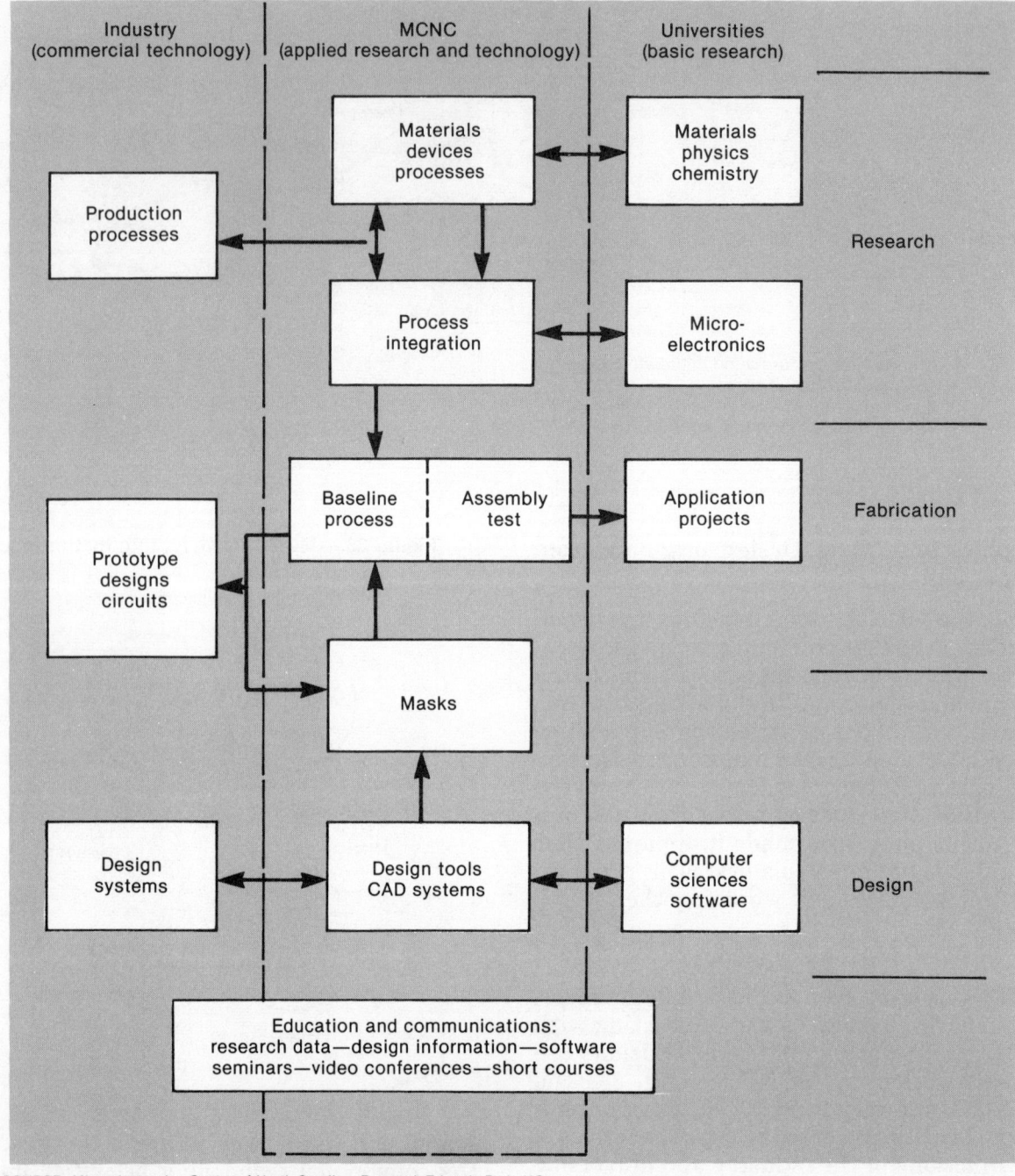

Figure 34.—Working Relationships, Microelectronics Center of North Carolina

SOURCE: Microelectronics Center of North Carolina, Research Triangle Park, NC.

ployment in industry, 20 of the 30 new faculty have come directly from industry.[49] Full-time staff of the Center number more than 70, with 12 having joint institutional appointments. Moreover, the combined microelectronics-related manpower resources at the participating institutions consist of over 150 faculty members and 450 graduate students, a significant pool of talent.

---

[49] It is felt that MCNC was able to compete with industry because it offered industry-level salaries, access to an advanced state-of-the-art research and manufacturing facility, a strong university R&D environment, and a thriving high-technology industrial center.

MCNC spokesmen argue that MCNC's ability to bridge university/industry concerns is enhanced by its structure as a nonprofit "neutral" facility. The Center's permanent staff, specialists with joint university and Center appointments, resident scientists and engineers representing industrial affiliates, visiting scientists from other national centers, and graduate students involved in special projects physically work together in the MCNC microelectronics manufacturing research complex.

In contrast to MCC (see below), a joint venture owned by its corporate companies, MCNC leaders envision this effort as providing technology functions that are not now provided by either MCC, other planned industry joint development programs, or other joint industry-university collaborative efforts in the microelectronics field. "All of the industrial joint development programs or companies are sponsored by the first tier of large electronic companies. The perceived need for these large-company joint efforts to remain competitive greatly amplifies the need for similar support to the larger number of second-tier and evolving smaller companies in the electronics industry."[50] MCNC expects to involve a broader segment of companies, in part because of lower fee levels, and because of substantial, continuing State support. The industrial affiliate program is just getting under way. By 1985, the Center expects to have 20 industry affiliates.[51]

Affiliates can come and use the MCNC facility to develop products, can participate in research and educational programs (tuition and fees are provided for three staff members at a time for each affiliate), are represented on an advisory council, participate in semiannual reviews, and in the process have increased access to faculty and students. Nonexclusive, nontransferable licenses for intellectual property rights are available to affiliates on a preferred royalty basis. It is expected that the majority of cooperative research will be openly disseminated.

The establishment of MCNC appears to be an example of effective university-industry-government collaboration. Some point out that it is an example of how State leadership and initiative can be the driving force in pulling together traditionally independent public and private academic institutions and forging new relationships to attract significant industry participation in education, research, technology transfer, and industrial development. What has made MCNC work? In reflecting on the experiences thus far, the president of MCNC lists three basic requirements:

1. *the need for a long-term strategic approach to substantial funding.* This includes building upon existing programs and investments, as well as obtaining at least a 3-year commitment from all members of the collaborative effort as a dependable commitment to common goals;
2. *the need to structure in-depth interaction among the limited talent available.* Full participation by personnel from industry, universities, and government is necessary for understanding each other's perspective and for crystallizing and mutually accepting responsibility for important common goals; and
3. *the need to plan for and accelerate the transfer of research into technology* and to promote R&D in progressively more scientific endeavors while making use of all basic related investments.[52]

MCNC spokesmen are confident of MCNC's future. Continued support for two-thirds of its operation are expected to come from the State. Industrial and Federal support are anticipated to cover the remaining third.

Semiconductor Research Corporation (SRC)

Under the aegis of the Semiconductor Industries Association, the Semiconductor Research Corp. (SRC) was formed in 1981, to establish

---

[50]D. S. Beilman, personal communication, April 1984.
[51]Each industrial affiliate pays an annual $250,000 fee.

[52]D. S. Beilmen, "New Initiatives in Modern Electronics," op. cit.

a cooperative organization that would sponsor university research needed by the industry. SRC was incorporated in February 1982. As noted by Robert Noyce, of the Intel Corp., "The semiconductor industry is fiercely competitive and that competition has resulted in the vitality and success of the industry."[53] The cooperative institutional arrangement that makes SRC possible represents a change for the semiconductor industry.

In the case of that industry, the forces stimulating cooperation centered around three issues: research, manpower resources, and international competition. There was growing concern that the industry's basic research efforts, the foundation of its future well-being, were increasingly directed towards the solution of near-term problems; that industry research efforts were often duplicative and redundant, as each corporation tried to stay on top of the competition; and that fierce competition and the squeeze for profits, combined with increasing costs of R&D, created disincentives and high risk for long-term industry research efforts.[54]

At the same time, there was growing recognition that the Nation's research universities were underutilized resources that industry could turn to for long-term basic research and creation of new knowledge. There was also concern that the pool of experienced and trained manpower was being "overgrazed" by the industry itself, and that both faculty and advanced graduate students were leaving universities, irresistibly drawn to industry.[55]

In view of the growing competition for semiconductor products, and the increased and coordinated R&D efforts undertaken by its foreign competitors, it was argued that the U.S. semiconductor industry had to increase R&D.[56] Moreover, more complex and more capital-intensive research tasks, coupled with increasing lead time and a perceived shortage of sufficiently trained manpower, created additional difficulties to undertake such research, particularly for a single company.[57] And drawing on the examples of other nations, such as Japan, joint coordinated efforts are seen as ways of assuring long term competitiveness through cooperation.

These factors resulted in four major objectives for SRC:

1. increasing semiconductor research in the United States;
2. sharing research efforts among industry sponsors;
3. strengthening and upgrading research in the universities; and
4. attracting more students to this field of study and improving the quality of education.

Since its formation in 1982, SRC has grown from 10 to 40 companies, of varying size, companies that manufacture or purchase semiconductor devices for manufacturing other products, or companies that manufacture equipment or materials for use by the semiconductor industry.[58] Membership fees are tied to a company's IC sales or purchases worldwide, with annual fees ranging from $60,000 up. All

---

[53]R. Noyce, "Competition and Cooperation—A Prescription for the Eighties," *Research Management*, March 1982, pp. 13-17.

[54]R. M. Burger, and L. W. Summey, "An Update on the Semiconductor Research Corporation", *QIE Conference Proceedings*, 1983, pp. 51-59.

[55]Robert Noyce uses the analogy of the "Tragedy of the Commons", where the commonly held resources, in this case, *research* and *manpower* are exploited by industry self-interest, op. cit., p. 15.

[56]E. Bloch, prepared statement, *Hearings, Japanese Technological Advances and Possible United States Responses Using Joint Research Ventures,* Subcommittee on Investigations and Oversight and the Subcommittee on Science, Research, and Technology, U.S. House of Representatives, June 29-30, 1983.

[57]Ibid., p. 46.

[58]SRC membership, as of September 1984, includes: Advanced Micro Devices, Inc., AT&T Technologies, Inc., Burroughs Corp., Control Data Corp., Digital Equipment Corp., E.I. du Pont de Nemours & Co., Eastman Kodak, Eaton Corp., E-Systems, Inc., GCA Corp., General Electric Co., General Instrument Corp., General Motors Corp., Goodyear Aerospace Corp., GTE Laboratories, Inc., Harris Corp., Hewlett-Packard Co., Honeywell, Inc., IBM Corp., Intel Corp., LSI Logic Corp., Monolithic Memories, Inc., Monsanto, Co., Motorola, Inc., National Semiconductor Corp., Perkin-Elmer Corp., RCA, Rockwell International, Silicon Systems, Inc., Sperry Corp., Texas Instruments, Inc., Union Carbide Corp., Varian Associates, Inc., Westinghouse Electric Corp., Xerox Corp, and Zilog, Inc.. In addition, the following companies are in the Semiconductor Equipment and Materials Institute, Inc.: Micro Mask, Inc.; Pacific Western Systems, Inc.; Probe-Rite, Inc.; Pure Aire Corp.

member companies have equal privileges: access to all sponsored research through seminars, annual meetings, and newsletters and reports, access to research data bases and license rights, as well as an expanded recruiting base.

The SRC 1984 budget is over $15 million, up from $6 million in 1982, and $10 million in 1983. Currently, approximately $12 million is available for university research projects, an amount which "substantially increases total available funding for basic research in semiconductor technology."[59] Spokesmen point out that SRC has promoted research in engineering, mathematics, and the physical sciences underlying semiconductor technology. Major areas of focus established by the industrial board members and the technical advisory board are:

- Microstructure Sciences:
  - Materials, Phenomena, and Device Physics,
  - Microsciences,
  - Device Fabrication Technologies.
- Systems and Design:
  - Design Automation,
  - System Component Interactions.
- Production and Engineering:
  - Reliability, Quality Assurance, and Testing,
  - Packaging,
  - Manufacturing.

Impacts

In planning the research activities to be undertaken, several different levels of funding and effort were envisioned by board members. SRC has awarded individual university research projects, as well as several contracts for major research "centers of excellence" and major research projects. In its initial solicitation for proposals from the universities, SRC received 166 proposals from 63 universities. In the first year of operation, eight universities received research contracts. In 1983, more than 30 universities, involving approximately 100 researchers and 125 graduate students, received $10 million for research through 47 contracts with SRC.[60] By May 1984, 34 universities involving 125 faculty and research staff and 202 graduate students were supported by $12.275 million in SRC research funding.

It has been SRC policy to distribute the contracts for centers and individual research projects on a broad geographic basis among leading research centers as well as to universities whose expertise in these areas is not as well established (see table 27, "Regional Distribution of SRC funding"). Thus, SRC efforts may have an impact that goes beyond the specific research projects: in helping to expand a university's research capabilities, it may help it attract high caliber faculty and graduate students. Moreover, in the long run the SRC support may contribute to additional university-industry cooperation, and new high-technology industrial development.

SRC research "centers of excellence" include Cornell University, University of California at Berkeley and Carnegie Mellon University. Major research programs are supported at the North Carolina consortium (MCNC), Massachusetts Institute of Technology, Clemson, Stanford, Rensselaer, and the University of California at Santa Barbara. Over the next few years, there are plans to support 8 to 10 more of these centers and programs, and to to conduct research into design of microstructures, properties of silicon material, computer-aided design and automation of design, lithography, beam processing, fault tolerance, micropackaging and cooling, three-dimensional silicon structures, and manufacturing systems research.

---

[59]Erich Bloch, Former Chairman of the Board, SRC, estimates that the semiconductor industry allocates 3 to 5 percent of its R&D budget to basic research—approximately $35 million to $50 million annually. He notes that the R&D tax credit was an important factor in the decision to proceed with the formation of SRC. Moreover, if there were a differentially larger tax incentive for industry-sponsored university research, there could be an even broader expansion of industry funding of university research in the future. Testimony before the Subcommittee on Taxation and Debt Management, Senate Committee on Finance, Feb. 24, 1984.

[60]N. Snyderman, "Industry Observer," *Electronic News,* January 1984.

Table 27.—A Distribution of SRC Funding by Region, January 1985

Region/institution	Funding	
New England		$1,377,588
MIT	$ 976,110	
Yale	211,258	
Brown	104,000	
Vermont	86,220	
Middle Atlantic:		$4,441,210
Cornell	$1,776,651	
CMU	1,414,580	
RPI	800,000	
Penn State	126,489	
Rochester	119,000	
Johns Hopkins	114,589	
Columbia	89,901	
North Central:		$1,734,900
Illinois	750,607	
Michigan	337,155	
Minnesota	206,755	
Notre Dame	126,000	
Iowa	118,013	
Purdue	102,870	
Wisconsin	93,500	
South Atlantic:		$1,814,927
MCNC	$ 900,000	
Clemson	215,424	
Georgia Tech	190,553	
Auburn	152,342	
North Carolina	149,744	
Mississippi State	135,000	
Florida	71,864	
Mountain:		$ 738,544
Arizona	$ 503,530	
Arizona State	100,914	
Colorado State	84,000	
Texas A&M	50,100	
Pacific:		$3,510,240
Stanford	$1,511,990	
Berkeley (UC)	$1,350,000	
Santa Barbara	450,000	
Southern California	101,943	
UCLA	96,307	
Total		$13,617,409

SOURCE: Semiconductor Reseach Corp., Reasearch Triangle, NC.

In its short span of operation, SRC provides an example of a joint industry approach in the management and coordination of information technology R&D and in the establishment of new relationships between industry and academia for the conduct of research efforts. Thus far, SRC member companies have been able to agree on research priorities. Ongoing research projects have focused on VLSI circuit processes and Computer-Aided Design, aimed at commercially relevant results over a 3- to 5-year period. In developing a list of potential research topics for longer term research (e.g., research needs in GaAs), SRC workshops have involved both university researchers and industry participants. Beginning with a broad array of potential research needs, the groups were able to reach consensus on research topic priorities and areas for future focus.

There is other evidence that SRC's approach has fostered closer links between industry and academia. In addition to the technical advisory board, composed of member company representatives, SRC has established industrial mentors for each contract. With recommendation from the technical advisory board, an industry engineer or scientist in an SRC member company becomes the direct contact point for each of the SRC contracts. The industrial mentor can help identify important problem areas, and may from time to time be able to provide direct technical assistance to the university research community. Through topical research meetings, additional industry-university contacts are strengthened.

Program reviews of SRC Centers of Excellence cover a wide spectrum of technical interest and are designed to attract a broad representation from the industry and research community. Member companies may also participate in SRC activities by assigning an employee to participate in the management of the SRC program at Research Triangle Park. Industry assignees may also become researchers in residence, spending at least 3 months to a year, working in the university laboratory with one or more of the university researchers. This may foster technology transfer in ways that are not accomplished through the dissemination of reports, newsletters, and conference results.

There is no question that SRC has provided additional research opportunities for the university community and that these opportunities have reached a range of institutions. Research results have been freely disseminated. The ownership rights to the patents are held by the universities. So far, only one patent has resulted from SRC-sponsored research. Several researchers have indicated their appreciation of lack of bureaucratic hassle in the SRC contracting process, and find the yearly reports and reviews helpful.

The eventual impacts of SRC will be seen in how well it meets the needs of both universities and the semiconductor industry. For the member companies, the usefulness of research results, in both the short and long term may become factors in their continued support. For the industry as a whole, new knowledge and new manpower are important, as well as the attraction of additional researchers to new fields of study in the future. How effective is the interface between the university and the industry over the long term? A sign of success, at least interim success, note SRC spokesman, is the increase in the number of member companies and the continued support of the initial companies who have signed on each of the three years of operation.

Microelectronics and Computer Technology Corporation (MCC)

The Microelectronics and Computer Technology Corporation (MCC) is an R&D joint-venture owned and operated by 20 U.S. computer and semiconductor companies.[61] The idea for MCC was conceived by William C. Norris, President of Control Data Corp., and in his view "MCC represents a cooperative effort to develop a broad base of fundamental technologies for use by members who will each add their own value and continue to compete with products and services of individual conception and design."[62] While these companies have traditionally avoided cooperation, "in this period of scarce resources, however, and at a time when this country's leading position in technology is being challenged by foreign competitors, refusal to cooperate is no longer tenable."[63]

Governed by a Board of Directors composed of representatives of each shareholder company, MCC began formal operations in January 1983, with the selection of its chief executive officer and the development of a plan for R&D. A technology Advisory Board of shareholder representatives provides advice in developing the research strategies, in evaluating new program proposals, and in monitoring existing programs.

With a $50 million to $60 million annual budget, four long-range advanced technology programs are expected to cover a 6- to 10- year time span.[64] In defining the areas of research, the shareholder companies "came to concentrate on areas in which they believed accomplishments were necessary to make quantum jumps in the performance of the next generation of computers."[65] The programs include:

- **Packaging:** A 6-year program to advance the state-of-the-art in semiconductor packaging and interconnect technology, with a focus on technologies compatible with automatic assembly at both the circuit and system level.
- **Software Technology:** A 7- to 8-year program to develop new techniques, procedures and tools that can be used to improve the productivity of the software development process by one or two orders of magnitude.
- **Computer-Aided Design and Manufacturing (CAD/CAM):** An 8-year program to improve CAD/CAM technology and to develop an integrated set of tools that will have particular application to complex systems and the complex VLSI chips from which they will be built.
- **Advanced Computer Architecture:** This 10-year effort will focus on artificial intelligence, new techniques for database management, human interface with computers, and parallel processing.

In addition to forming a comprehensive agenda for research, MCC has selected a site for operation and hired staff. While still in tem-

---

[61]Shareholder companies include Advanced Micro Devices, Allied Corp., BMC Industries, Control Data Corp., Digital Equipment Corp., Eastman Kodak, Gould, Harris Corp., Honeywell, Lockheed, Martin Marietta Aerospace, Mostek, Motorola, National Semiconductor, NCR, RCA, Rockwell, Sperry Corp., Boeing, and 3-M.

[62]W. C. Norris, "Cooperation for Improving Productivity," keynote address, Prepatory Meeting for the White House Conference on Productivity, San Diego, CA, July 20, 1983.

[63]W. C. Norris, "How to Expand R&D Cooperation," *Business Week*, Apr. 11, 1983, p. 21.

[64]B. R. Admiral, President, Microelectronics Computer Corp., personal communication, May 1984.

[65]M. A. Fischetti, "MCC: An Industry Response to the Japanese Challenge," *IEEE Spectrum*, November 1983, pp. 55-56.

porary quarters, more than 173 professionals have been brought into the operation. Originally, the staffing plan was to draw senior and highly trained technical professionals from the participating companies, with only about 25 percent expected to come from the outside. In actuality, 40 percent of the professionals have come to MCC from the shareholder companies. There is some concern that MCC will attract senior faculty members from the universities and put a strain on available manpower resouces, particularly in areas such as artificial intelligence.[66] MCC officials recognize that if they hire away the university faculty, they will compromise the universities' ability to produce highly trained top-quality graduates—the very people they need for the future.[67]

So far, the MCC strategy appears to be working; of the talent on board, the majority are from industry, and the remainder from academia and government. Full operation, expected by late 1985, will bring the total number of professionals to 350. At full strength, MCC will be looking for the "brightest graduates," and it is expected that many will come from nearby educational institutions—the University of Texas and Texas A&M University.

Not surprisingly it was these universities, and their promised commitment to develop a major, first-class computer science and microelectronics program, as well as strong support from the State officials and the business community, that led to the decision to locate MCC headquarters in Austin, after conducting a search of 57 cities in 27 States. It has been noted that few cities in Texas—or anywhere else—could put together the incentives that were offered. The University of Texas at Austin promised to construct a $20 million office-laboratory facility, to be leased to MCC. Thirty new faculty positions and 75 new graduate fellowships would be supported. In addition, there was a commitment of at least $1 million a year for maintenance and support for researchers, and $5 million for purchase of laboratory equipment at UT-Austin. After MCC selected the Austin site, an anonymous donor made available $8 million, with the proviso that other private sources match that amount. The university then matched that total, using funds from the Permanent University Fund (derived from revenues from oil leases on land owned by the University). The result is 32 new endowed chairs at the University of Texas, 10 of which are in microelectronics and computer sciences.[68]

The developments in the academic community, the development of MCC, and the developments in the fast-growing high-technology corridor between Austin and San Antonio [69] have drawn national attention. The potential for economic growth, quality education and cutting-edge research are cited as the real cause for excitement.[70] Texas leaders point out that these high-technology initiatives (e.g., MCC, the university programs) are just the beginning of the State's commitment to high technology development. It is recognized that not only the universities, but the entire State educational infrastructure have to be strengthened and supported over the long term. The improvement of the State's elementary and secondary schools has been addressed by the Governor as well as MCC's director, Admiral Bobby Inman and other leaders in industry, who are concerned that without improvement Texas public schools represent a deterrent to recruiting engineers and other highly trained specialists. Among the recommendations of a special panel headed by Texas industry leader, H. Ross Perot, are increased teacher salaries,

---

[66]See the OTA case study on Artificial Intelligence.

[67]In a recent interview, Admiral Inman discussed this issue. "I have a standard rule that I will not recruit from universities. If I am approached by someone on a faculty, my requirement is that they go up the chain and say they are going to leave to go to industry. I can't have it both ways—to encourage the production of additional top-quality graduate students, and to hire away university talent." See: J. A. Turner, "Big-Spending U. of Texas Aims for the Top in Computer Science," Chronicle of Higher Education, Apr. 4, 1984.

[68]All 32 chairs are aimed at strengthening the university's science and engineering programs. Eight disciplines are the focus of this effort: chemistry, mathematics, molecular biology, physics, computer engineering, manufacturing, systems engineering, materials science, and microelectronics.

[69]For examples of recent economic development, see J. R. Linebacker, "Letter from Austin: Texas Cash Fuels Electronics Boom." Electronics, June 15, 1983, pp. 95-96.

[70]J. Kraft, "The Japaning of Texas," Washington Post, Apr. 17, 1984.

State aid to equalize school spending among rich and poor districts, and strengthened curriculum requirements—at a cost estimated at nearly $1 billion in new taxes.

The ultimate test for MCC will be its ability to draw sufficient talent to conduct the R&D necessary to keep its member companies internationally competitive. MCC officials and corporate sponsors are confident that this can be accomplished. Some observers are less confident that MCC will be able to transfer its technology to individual corporate efforts. As noted earlier, MCC originally intended to draw its staff principally from the member companies, thereby speeding technology transfer. Since recruitment has drawn more heavily on outside sources, MCC will have to find other approaches if it is to accomplish this goal.

While it is too soon to assess the impacts of the MCC joint venture, and related activities at the University of Texas and Texas A&M, they do provide an example of how academia, business, and government can join forces to create new institutional arrangements.

Chapter 6 References

"Academe and Industry Debate Partnership," *Science*, vol. 219, No. 4481, January 1983, pp.150-151.

"The Academic-Industrial Complex," *Science*, vol. 216, May 28, 1982, pp. 960-961.

"Artificial Intelligence (I): Into the World," *Science*, vol. 223, February 24, 1984, pp. 802-805.

"Cooperation is the Key: An interview with B. R. Inman," *Communications of the ACM*, vol. 26, No. 9, September 1983, pp. 642-645.

"The Challenges: Designing the Next Generation," *IEEE Spectrum*, November 1983.

Probable Levels of R&D Expenditures in 1984: Forecast and Analysis (Columbus, OH: Battelle Memorial Institute, December 1983).

"Texas Uses Oil to Fuel Research," *Science*, vol. 220, April 22, 1983, pp. 390-391.

"Tomorrow's Computers: The Quest," *IEEE Spectrum*, November 1983.

"Semiconductor Research Co-op Eyes 4 Megabit Memory Chip," *Electronic News*, July 18, 1983.

"Weighing the Social Costs of Innovation," *Science*, vol. 223, Mar. 30, 1984, pp. 1368-1369.

Ashford, N. A., "A Framework for Examining the Effects of Industrial Funding on Academic Freedom and the Integrity of the University," *Science, Technology and Human Values*, vol. 8, Issue 2, spring 1983, pp. 16-23.

Brademas, J., "Graduate Education: Signs of Trouble," *Science*, vol. 223, No. 4639, March 1984, p. 881.

Branscomb, L. M., "The Computer's Debt to Science," *Perspectives in Computing*, vol. 3, No. 3, October 1983.

Brown, T. L. "University—Industry Relations: Is There a Conflict."

Burger, R. M. and Sumney, L. W., "An Update on the Semiconductor Research Corporation," *QIE (Quality in Electronics) Conference Proceedings*, 1983.

David, E. E., "Supporting Research with a Commercial Mission," *Change*, vol. 14, September 1982, pp. 25-29.

David, E. E., "The University-Academic Connection in Research: Corporate Purposes and Social Responsibilities," *Journal of the Patent Office Society*, vol. 64, April 1982, pp. 209-218.

Dineen, G. P., "Why Cooperative Research is a Viable Strategy at Honeywell." Presentation at *Conference on Cooperative Research Ventures*, sponsored by Control Data Executive Forum. Apr. 4-5, 1984, New York City.

Dorfman, Nancy S, "Route 128: The Development of a Regional High-Technology Economy," *Research Policy*, vol. 12, No. 6, December 1983, pp. 299-316.

Fowler, D. R., "University-Industry Research Relationships," *Research Management*, vol. 27, No. 1, January/February 1984, pp. 35-41.

Fowler, D. R. "University-Industry Research Relationships: The Research Agreement," *The Journal of College and University Law*, vol. 9, No. 4, 1982-1983, pp. 515-532.

Giametti, A. B., "The University, Industry and Cooperative Research," *Science*, vol. 218, December 1982, pp. 1278-1280.

Gray, P. E., "The Role of the University in Global Technological Change," In *Global Technologi-*

cal Change: A Strategic Assessment, June 21-23, 1983. Industrial Liaison Program of the Massachusetts Institute of Technology (Cambridge, MA: MIT, 1983).

Hutt, P. B. , "University/Corporate Research Agreements," Technology in Society, vol. 5, 1983, pp. 107-118.

Inman, B. R., "Research and Development Joint Ventures" testimony before the Subcommittee on Monopolies and Commercial Law, House Judiciary Committee, Sept. 28, 1983.

Kraft, J. "The Japaning of Texas," Washington Post, Apr. 17, 1984.

Langfitt, T. W., Hackney, S., Fishman, A. P., et al., Partners in the Research Enterprise, University-Corporate Relations in Science and Technology (Philadelphia: University of Pennsylvania Press, 1983).

Location of High Technology Firms and Regional Economic Development, a staff study prepared for the Joint Economic Committee, Subcommittee on Monetary and Fiscal Policy, U.S. Congress (Washington, DC: U.S. Government Printing Office, 1982).

Lynn, W. R. and Long, F. A., "University-Industrial Collaboration in Research," Technology in Society, vol. 4, 1982, pp. 192-212.

National Research Council, Revitalizing Laboratory Instrumentation, the report of a workshop of the Ad Hoc Working Group on Scientific Instrumentation, Mar. 12-13, 1982 (Washington, D.C.: National Academy Press, 1982).

National Science Foundation, University/industry Research, Relationships: Selected Studies, 14th Annual Report of the National Science Board (Washington DC: U.S. Government Printing Office, 1982).

National Science Foundation, University-Industry Research Relationships: Myths, Realities and Potentials, 14th Annual Report of the National Science Board (Washington D.C.: U.S. Government Printing Office, 1982).

Nelkin, D., "Intellectual Property: The Control of Scientific Information," Science, vol. 216, No. 14, May 1982, pp. 704-708.

Noble, D. F., America By Design: Science, Technology, and the Rise of Corporate Capitalism (New York: Alfred A. Knopf, 1977).

Norris, W.C., "Cooperation for Improving Productivity," Keynote Address, IEEE Task Force on Productivity and Innovation, San Diego, July 20, 1983.

Norris, W. C., "How to Expand R&D Cooperation," Business Week, Apr. ll, 1983, p. 21.

Noyce, R., "Competition and Cooperation—A Prescription for the Eighties," Research Management, vol. , No. , March 1982, pp. 13-16.

Ploch, M. "Micros Flood Campuses," High Technology, vol. 4, No. 3, March 1984, pp. 47-49.

Prager, D. J. and Omenn, G. S., "Research, Innovation, and University-Industry Linkages," Science, vol. 207, No. 254, January 1980, pp. 379-384.

Schmitt, R. W., "Building R&D Policy from Strength," Science, vol.220, June 3, 1983, pp. 1013-1015.

Schmitt, R. W., "National R&D Policy: An Industrial Perspective," Science, vol. 224, June 15, 1984, pp. 1206-1209.

Shils, E., "The order of Learning in the United States from 1865 to 1920: The Ascendancy of the Universities," Minerva, vol. 16, No. 2, summer 1978, pp. 159-195.

Smith, K. A., "Industry-Univeristy Research Programs," Physics Today, vol. 37, No. 2, February 1984, pp. 24-29.

Sproull, R. L., "Protectionism and the Universities," Science, vol. 219, No. 4581, January 1983.

Thomas, L. "The Value of Basic Science," Review Magazine of the University of Rochester.

Turner, J. A., "Big Spending University of Texas Aims for the Top in Computer Science." Chronicle of Higher Education, vol. XXVII, No. 6, Apr. 4, 1984.

U.S. Congress, Committee on Science and Technology, U.S. House of Representatives, Hearings before the Subcommittee on Investigations and Oversight and the Subcommittee on Science, Research, and Technology: Japanese Technological Advances and Possible United States Responses Using Research Joint Ventures, June 29-30, 1983 (Washington, DC: U.S. Government Printing Office, No. 45, 28-377 O, 1983).

U.S. House of Representatives, Hearings on University/Industry Cooperation in Biotechnology, Subcommittee on Investigations and Oversight and Subcommittee on Science and Technology, of the Committee on Science, Research and Technology, June 16-17, 1982.

U.S. Congress, Office of Technology Assessment, Commercial Biotechnology: An International Analysis, OTA-BA-218 (Washington, D.C.: U.S. Government Printing Office, January 1984.

U.S. Congress, Office of Technology Assessment, *Informational Technology and Its Impact on American Education,* OTA-CIT-187 (Washington, D.C.: U.S. Government Printing Office, November 1982).

U.S. Congress, Office of Technology Assessment, *Technology, Innovation, and Regional Economic Development: Census of State Government Initiatives for High-Technology Industrial Development—Background Paper,* OTA-BP-STI-21., (Washington, DC: U.S. Government Printing Office, May 1983).

U.S. Congress, Office of Technology Assessment, *Technology, Innovation, and Regional Economic Development: Encouraging High Technology Development—Background Paper 2,* OTA-BP-STI-25 (Washington, DC: U.S. Government Printing Office, February 1984).

Wilson, K. G., "Science, Industry, and the New Japanese Challenge," *Proceedings of the IEEE,* vol. 72, No. 1, January 1984, pp. 6-18.

Chapter 7
Foreign Information Technology Research and Development

Contents

	Page
International Trends in Information Technology Research and Development	201
International Trade	201
Adapting Technology for International Markets	202
Multinational Corporations	206
Technology Exchange Agreements	207
Patents	210
Scientific and Technical Literature	211
Science and Engineering Students	212
Implications for U.S. Information Technology R&D Policies	214
Science and Technology Policy Goals	215
Government Role in Information Technology Research and Development	216
Government/Industry/University Institutional Arrangements for Information Technology Research and Development	217
Industry Participation in Information Technology Research and Development	219
Conclusions	221
Japan	222
The Size of Japanese Participation in Information Technology Markets	225
Government	226
University	240
Industry	243
France	246
Introduction	246
The Size of French Participation in Information Technology Markets	247
The Political Environment for French Information Technology Research and Development	248
Social Environment for French Information Technology Research and Development	252
Government	252
University	257
Industry	259

The United Kingdom 261
    The Size of U.K. Participation in Information Technology Markets 263
    Government 263
    University... 269
    Industry 270
    European Strategic Program for Research in Information Technology 272

Tables

Table No.	Page
28. Computer Production and Apparent Domestic Consumption of Six Leading Supplier Nations	201
29. U.S. Computer Trade: Origins and Destinations, Flow Value, and Annual Growth	204
30. World Trade in Telecommunications Equipment	204
31. Aggregate Trends in U.S. Telecom Equipment Trade	204
32. Company R&D Performed Abroad by Foreign Affiliates of U.S. Domestic Companies by Selected Industry: 1975 and 1981	207
33. International Technology Agreements	208
34. Number of U.S. Patents Granted to Selected Foreign Countries in All Product Fields and in Communication Equipment and Electronic Components, 1963-81	210
35. Share of Foreign Patenting in the United States for the Three Most Active Countries by Selected Product Fields: 1981	211
36. U.S. Owned and Foreign Owned U.S. Patents in Information Technologies	212
37. Distribution of Foreign Students With Percentage of All Foreign Students by Field of Study, for Selected Years: 1954/55-1981/82	213
38. Doctoral Degrees Awarded to Foreign Students as a Percent of All Doctoral Degrees from U.S. Universities by Field: 1959-81	214
39. Average Annual Growth Rates in the Engineering Industry	218
40. R&D Performed in the Business Enterprise Sector by Source of Funds: 1970, 1975, and 1979	220
41. Percent of Private Industrial R&D in Selected Industries: 1969-79	220
42. R&D Expenditure by Type of Activity	224
43. Japan Development Bank Loans for Development of Technology	240
44. Department of Trade and Industry R&D Programs	266

Figures

Figure No.	Page
35. U.S. Computer Trade Imports by Source; Exports by Destination	203
36. Sources of U.S. Imports and Destinations of U.S. Exports of Telecommunications Equipment	205
37. U.S. Bilateral Trade Position in Telecommunications, With Selected Countries	206
38. Share of Foreign Patenting in the United States for the Three Most Active Countries in 1981	211
39. Index of International Cooperative Research by Country	212
40. Estimated Ratio of Civilian R&D Expenditures to Gross National Product for Selected Countries	217
41. Trends in the Production Composition Ratio of Major Consumer Electronics Equipment	225
42. Japanese Share of World Production of Consumer Electronics Products in 1980	226
43. Japanese Information Technology Industry Sales	227
44. Integrated Circuit Relative Production Share	228
45. Japanese Government Organization for Information Technology Research and Development	229
46. Japanese Government Support for Information Technology	233
47. Cooperation Between Research Participants for the Fifth-Generation Computer Systems Project	234
48. Concept Diagram Showing How Research and Development Are to Progress in the Fifth Generation Computer Systems Project	235
49. Chart Showing the Recommended French Government/Industry/University Cooperation Relationships for Information Technology R&D	251

Chapter 7
Foreign Information Technology Research and Development

International Trends in Information Technology Research and Development

Several trends demonstrate that the United States is experiencing greater international interdependence in the area of information technology research and development. They include: 1) the large and growing world market for computer and communications products; 2) the increasing adaptation of information technology products and standards for international markets; 3) the growing number of multinational information technology firms; 4) the increasing number of international technology exchange agreements; 5) the increasing percentage of U.S. information technology-related patents granted for foreign inventions; 6) the greater utilization of foreign contributions in U.S. scientific and technical journals; 7) and the growing number of foreign students enrolled in technical and scientific programs at U.S. universities.

These trends indicate two significant factors, both of which make foreign organization and activities relevant to U.S. R&D efforts. First, they indicate a growing number of links between other nations' R&D efforts and those of the United States. Second, these trends point to a growing participation of foreign nations in information technology innovation and markets, which has led to a relative decline in the U.S. market share. Thus, the United States, which in the past has developed policies for its internal markets that were largely unaffected by foreign manufacturers, may now need to take greater account of foreign information technology research and development efforts.

International Trade

World trade in computer products is growing rapidly. For each of the major supplier nations, overseas shipments are a steadily rising share of both total output and consumption. Table 28 shows this trend towards a glo-

Table 28.—Computer Production and Apparent Domestic Consumption[a] of Six Leading Supplier Nations

	1982 production ($ million)	Percent change 1981-82	1982 ADC[a] ($ million)	Percent change 1981-82
United States	$33,550[b]	12.3%	$26,888	15.3%
Japan	7,179[c]	21.0	6,276	10.2
France	3,834[d]	−5.0	4,720	8.4
West Germany	3,511	7.5	3,789	5.3
United Kingdom	1,929[d]	11.8	2,898	NA
Italy	1,076	11.0	1,343	3.2
Total	$51,079	10.8%	$45,914	NA
Estimated share of world total (percent)	89		80	

[a]Apparent Domestic Consumption (ADC) is production minus exports plus imports.
[b]Estimated by Bureau of Industrial Economics.
[c]Does not include parts.
[d]Preliminary.
SOURCE: *U.S. Industrial Outlook, 1984,* Bureau of Industrial Economics, U.S. Department of Commerce, 1984.

bal computer market as it has evolved over the last few years, and figure 35 illustrates major sources and destinations. This trend results in part from the rapid rise in demand for computer-related products in the developing world, a steady demand in traditional markets for products that incorporate information technology, and increasing overseas activities of multinational subsidiaries.[1]

For the United States, increased global participation in the information technology market has meant a rapid rise in imports and a decreasing world market share. During the period 1978-82, U.S. imports of computers and computer-related products rose by approximately 30 percent. (See table 29.)

The telecommunications market is also becoming internationalized as equipment manufacturers look beyond maintaining traditional markets (the national telecommunications service monopolies, or PTTs) toward expanding international trade.[2] Table 30 illustrates this trend and summarizes the current positions of the United States, the United Kingdom, France, and Japan.

The internationalization of the telecommunications market, as in the case of the computer market, has weakened the relative U.S. position in telecommunications trade. Although U.S. exports have increased at a rate of 13 to 18 percent per year, a continuing increase in foreign imports (24 to 30 percent a year) has diminished the U.S. trade surplus (table 31). Japan supplied about 50 percent of U.S. imports, resulting in a U.S. trade deficit with Japan of $250 million (figs. 36 and 37).[3]

---

[1]*High Technology Industries: Profiles and Outlooks: The Computer Industry*, U.S. Department of Commerce, International Trade Administration, 1983, p. 22.

[2]*High Technology Industries: Profiles and Outlooks, The Telecommunications Industry*, U.S. Department of Commerce, International Trade Administration, 1983, p. 18.

[3]Although the French, the British, and the Japanese are increasing their participation in information technology markets, particularly in the computers and telecommunications areas, the degree to which this trend is linked to information technology R&D remains unknown. The traditional skills needed for success in the marketplace range from basic research, to applied R&D, to production and distribution, and to marketing skills; it is therefore difficult to attribute success in the marketplace solely to R&D efforts or to any other single factor. See ch. 2 for a more complete discussion.

Adaptations of Technology for International Markets

The growing international trade in information technology products has led to increased efforts to develop international standards for information technology products in order to allow access to foreign markets and to allow interconnections of services. For example, following a recent meeting of the Commission of European PTTs (CEPT), European countries agreed to develop technical standards not only for basic equipment such as telephone handsets, but also for videotex systems and other sophisticated data communications systems. The CEPT program will also suggest other areas where national telecommunications practices might be standardized. This could eventually lead to a unified European network of approximately 400 million subscribers. The European Program for Research and Development in Information Technology (ESPRIT) has a group working on international standards specifically designed to enable various European-manufactured products to communicate with each other.

In markets where standards do not exist, information technology products, such as computer software, must be tailored for international sale. Because personal computer hardware has proliferated worldwide without a parallel growth of indigenous software companies, many American software companies are developing products for the international market.

For example, Lotus Development Corp. has been tailoring its software packages to the language and idioms of other nations. The Lotus International Character Set enables the program to generate different currency signs and different versions of international day and date displays. Although the cost of converting programs for international markets can be quite high, Lotus Corp. reportedly believes that the return on its investment will also be substantial. They expect that international sales will eventually generate between 30 and 40 percent of the company's income.[4]

---

[4]Michael Schrage, "Firms See Boom in Software," *The Washington Post*, Mar. 4, 1984, p. H, 4.

Figure 35.—U.S. Computer Trade (SIC 3573) Imports by Source; Exports by Destination

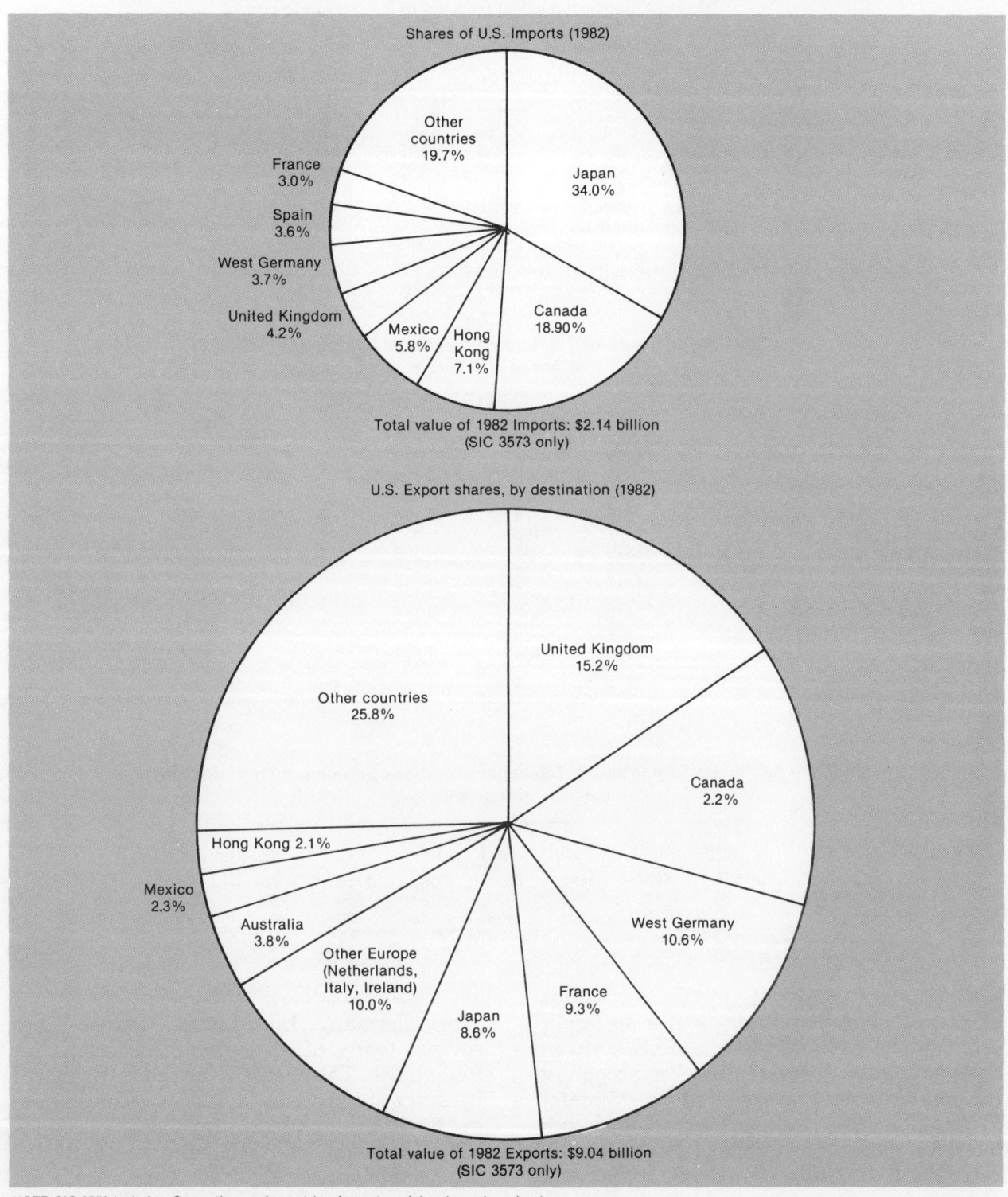

NOTE: SIC 3573 includes: Computing equipment (equipment, peripherals, and services).
SOURCE: *High Technology Industries: Profiles and Outlooks: The Computer Industry,* International Trade Administration, U.S. Department of Commerce, 1983.

Table 29.—U.S. Computer Trade (SIC 3573): Origins and Destinations, Flow Value, and Annual Growth
(1981-82, percent of value) (millions of U.S. dollars)

1982 Imports				United States			1982 Exports		
Japan	$ 729	(+88.2%)					United Kingdom	$1,374	(+15.3%)
Canada	404	(+ 0.0%)			Imports	Exports	Canada	1,103	(−11.2%)
Hong Kong	151	(−21.6%)		1978	$ 755	$4,194	West Germany	958	(− 6.2%)
Mexico	123	(+27.0%)		1981	1,646	8,493	France	841	(+ 7.0%)
United Kingdom	90	(+12.2%)		1982	2,295	8,957	Japan	777	(+ 8.3%)
West Germany	79	(+12.9%)		1983	4,100	10,300	Netherlands	380	(+14.0%)
Spain	78	(+25.3%)		1984	6,470	12,360	Australia	344	(+ 0.0%)
France	64	(− 2.6%)		Growth			Italy	298	(− 4.1%)
Total	$2,140	(+29.9%)		(1978-82)	+29.8%	+21.2%	Total	$9,040	(+ 4.5%)

NOTE: SIC Code 3573 includes: Computing equipment (equipment, peripherals, and services).
SOURCE: *High Technology Industries: Profiles and Outlooks: The Computer Industry,* International Trade Administration, U.S. Department of Commerce, 1983.

Table 30.—World Trade in Telecommunications Equipment (SIC 3661)
(millions of U.S. dollars)

Principal producer countries	1977			1981		
	Imports	Exports	Balance	Imports	Exports	Balance
Japan	$ 24	$ 363	+$ 339	$ 46	$ 911	+$ 865
Sweden	36	458	+422	65	776	+711
West Germany	104	562	+458	128	809	+681
Netherlands	126	228	+102	128	398	+270
France	57	168	+111	86	320	+234
United States	129	257	+128	494	653	+159
Canada	93	80	−13	143	298	+155
United Kingdom	91	247	+156	235	331	+96
Belgium/Luxembourg	76	248	+172	118	262	+144
Italy	50	97	+47	101	143	+42
Total	786	2,708	+1,922	1,544	4,901	+3,357

NOTE: SIC Code 3661 includes: Telephone and telegraph apparatus.
SOURCE: *High Technology Industries: Profiles and Outlooks: The Telecommunications Industry,* International Trade Administration, U.S. Department of Commerce, 1983.

Table 31.—Aggregate Trends in U.S. Telecommunications Equipment Trade (SIC 3661)
(millions of U.S. dollars)

	1972	1977	1979	1980	1981	1982	1893	1977-83 growth rate
Exports	$76	$257	$448	$557	$653	$725	$850	+22.1%
Imports	86	129	319	421	494	635	790	+35.3%
Balance	−10	+128	+128	+136	+159	+90	+60	−11.1%

NOTE: SIC Code 3661 includes: Telephone and telegraph apparatus.
SOURCE: *U.S. Industrial Outlook, 1983,* Bureau of Industrial Economics, U.S. Department of Commerce, 1983.

International marketing is also an important component for Microsoft, a U.S. software company whose overseas market accounted for approximately one-third of its estimated $75 million 1983 revenue. Microsoft already has development operations in Japan and subsidiaries in the United Kingdom, France, and West Germany. Like Lotus, Microsoft has revised many of its software programs for foreign use. The company has closely tailored its software products for the Japanese market by offering phonetic Japanese versions of BASIC, and it has translated its Multiplan program (business applications program) and

Figure 36.—Sources of U.S. Imports (1982) and Destinations of U.S. Exports (1982) of Telecommunications Equipment (SIC 3661)

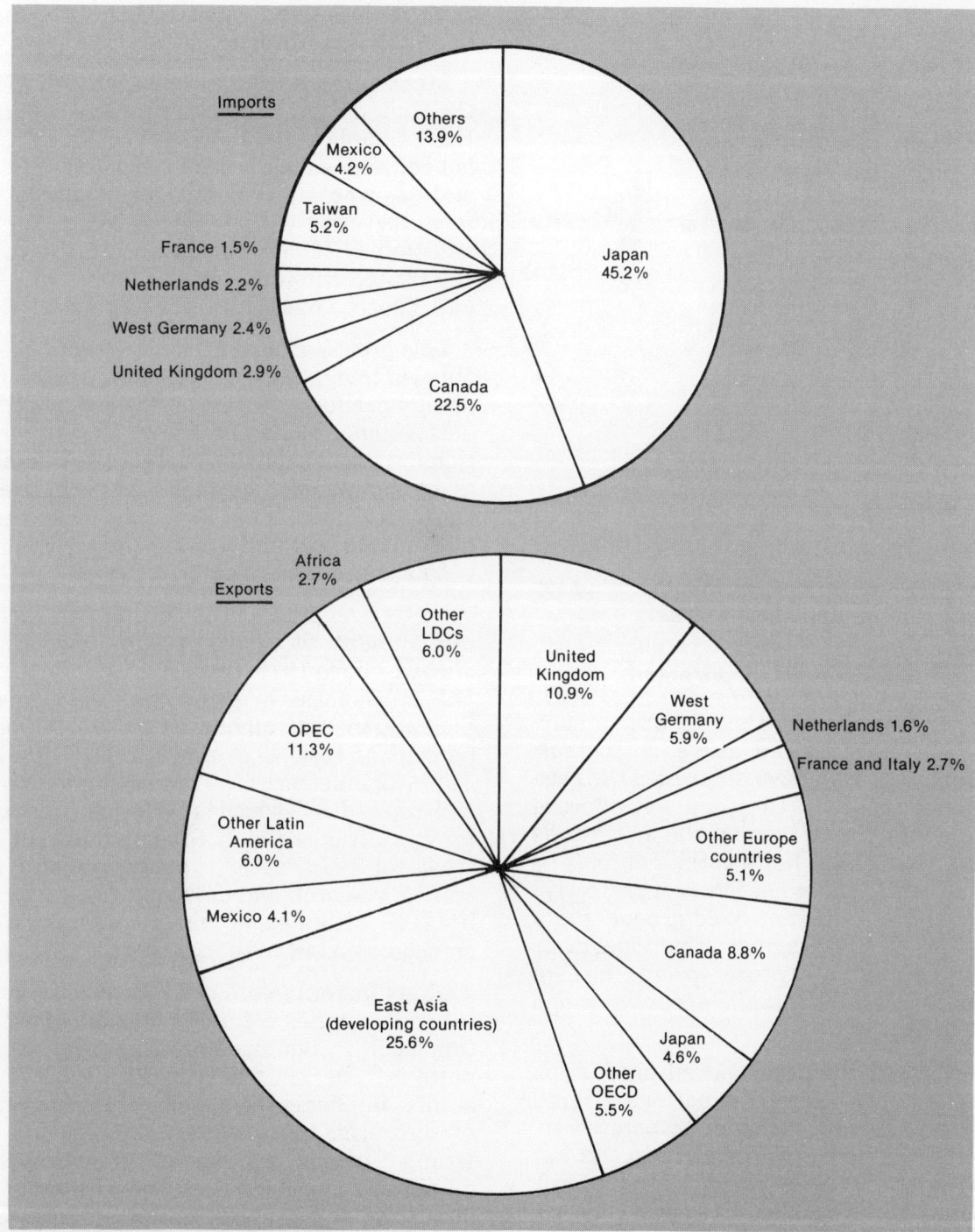

NOTE: SIC 3661 includes: Telephone and telegraph apparatus.
SOURCE: *High Technology Industries: Profiles and Outlooks: The Telecommunications Industry,* International Trade Administration, U.S. Department of Commerce, 1983.

Figure 37.—U.S. Bilateral Trade Position in Telecommunications with Selected Countries (1981)

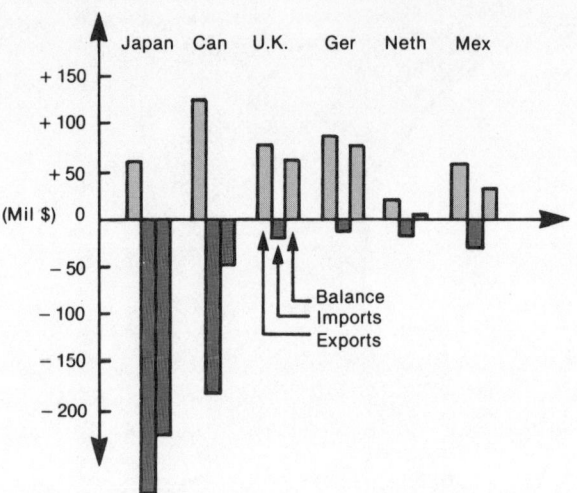

SOURCE: *High Technology Industries: Profiles and Outlooks: The Telecommunications Industry,* International Trade Administration, U.S. Department of Commerce, 1983.

its MSX operating system (home computer program) for the Japanese market.

Multinational Corporations

Rising innovation costs and the accompanying size of financial risks, as well as increasing equipment costs, have intensified the need for expanding production and have forced many manufacturers beyond the limitations of domestic markets. For a variety of reasons including tariffs and other forms of protective legislation that place imported products at a competitive disadvantage, multinational firms have attempted to capture specific foreign markets through the establishment of foreign subsidiaries.

Many U.S. firms have opened production and R&D facilities in foreign nations. Digital Equipment Corp., for instance, operates six plants in Europe and three more in the Far East. Hewlett-Packard, Wang, Data-General, Datapoint, and Texas Instruments are U.S. minicomputer manufacturers that also operate foreign production facilities. Apple Computer has plants in Ireland and Singapore. Amdahl and Trilogy Systems, manufacturers of plug-compatible mainframes, have opened facilities in Ireland, intended in part to supply the Common Market.

Many foreign firms operate subsidiaries in the United States and other foreign countries. For example, Japan's NEC Corp. has established three subsidiaries in the United States and has won major contracts to supply U.S. manufacturers with Japanese technology. In addition, NEC has subsidiaries in Germany, the United Kingdom, and countries in Africa and South America.

This growth of international activity has not only led to increased trade in information technology products, but has also encouraged the performance of R&D by firms in various nations. After establishing foreign subsidiaries, many companies find that R&D is necessary to support local manufacturing when the requirements or standards for the foreign marketplace are significantly different.

U.S. companies are performing an increasing amount of research and development abroad. Since 1975, total R&D conducted by U.S. subsidiaries overseas has more than doubled and in 1981 amounted to $3.2 billion—9 percent of total U.S. private R&D funding. Table 32 illustrates the increasing amount of electronics R&D which is performed abroad by foreign affiliates of U.S companies. In contrast, in 1979, total expenditures for electronics research and development performed by U.S. affiliates of foreign companies increased to $148 million.[5]

Many governments actively encourage foreign subsidiaries not only to establish production facilities, but also to conduct R&D in their nations. The United Kingdom has, for instance, implemented a series of incentives for foreign firms to innovate. In addition to providing financial incentives for establishing manufacturing facilities, the United Kingdom's Support for Innovation Program (SFI)

---
[5]*Science Indicators, 1982,* National Science Board, National Science Foundation, 1983, p. 25.

Table 32.—Industry R&D Performed Abroad by Foreign Affiliates of U.S. Domestic Companies by Selected Industry: 1975 and 1981
(millions of U.S. dollars)

Industry	1975	1981	Percent increase
Food and kindred products...	23	66	187
Chemicals and allied products	269	651	142
Industrial and other chemicals	85	275	124
Drugs and medicines	184	376	104
Stone, clay, and glass products	7	15	114
Primary metals	9	9	—
Fabricated metals...........	(a)	26[b]	NA
Machinery	331	585	77
Electrical equipment	245	455	86
Electronic components	7	47	571
Transportation	412	893	117
Motor vehicles and other transportation equipment .	373	791[b]	112
Aircraft and missiles	39	102[b]	161
Professional and scientific instruments	49	101	106
Other manufacturing industries	105	147	40
Nonmanufacturing industries .	4	12	200
Total	$1,454	$3,157	117

[a]Included in the other manufacturing industries group.
[b]Estimated.
NA—Not available.
SOURCE: *Science Indicators, 1982,* National Science Board, National Science Foundation, 1983.

offers grants of up to 33 1/3 percent towards the cost of significant research and development of high technology products. About 200 information technology firms are located in "Silicon Glen" in Scotland. U.S. firms there include IBM, Honeywell, NCR, Hewlett-Packard, Digital Equipment, and National Semiconductor.

Multinational information technology corporations are also forming cooperative international research and development arrangements. This new type of international arrangement is exemplified by the recent establishment of Europe's first multinational research institution for information technology. Following an agreement made last September, Europe's three largest computer manufacturers, France's Compagnie des Machines Bull SA, Britain's International Computers Ltd. (ICL), and West Germany's Siemens AG, will operate a jointly run and jointly financed European Computer Research Centre (ECRC).

Located in Munich, close to a number of electronics firms, the ECRC will begin operations with an initial capital investment of $655,000 and a staff of four researchers from the three firms. The number of researchers is expected to reach 30 to 35 by 1985, and approximately 50 within 2 years.

Technology Exchange Agreements

Table 33 illustrates some of the recent technology exchange agreements between U.S., European, and Japanese companies. Such technology exchange is seen by firms as a way to spread the risk in large projects, to enter international markets where politics or national market specifications hinder entry into domestic markets, and to allow competitors to pursue a dominant position in a specific market.[6]

An example of a technology exchange agreement is the reciprocal development and marketing agreement for office telecommunications equipment between AT&T and Ing. C. Olivetti & Co., a major European supplier of office automation equipment. In accordance with this agreement, AT&T will increase its stake in Olivetti over the next 4 years to acquire 25 percent ownership in the company. The arrangement gives AT&T access to Olivetti equipment such as workstations, word processors, typewriters, and data processing systems for domestic marketing. In turn, Olivetti will market AT&T communications controllers for voice, data and networking applications, and a variety of micro-computers.[7]

Other technical partnerships include those of LM Ericsson of Sweden with Honeywell, and Atlantic-Richfield in the United States with Thorn EMI in the United Kingdom. In Italy, Italtel is cooperating with Telettra and the U.S. company GTE in the public switching field. The British firm, ICL, has links with Mitel, and Plessey (another U.K. company),

---
[6]"Bulls on Skis," *The Economist,* Feb. 4, 1984, p. 76.
[7]In addition to its technical exchange agreements with Olivetti, AT&T has also made exchange agreements with Philips.

Table 33.—International Technology Agreements

Sector/partners[a]	Date	Technology	Agreement
Communications:			
Hitachi and *Western Electric*	1981	Communication equipment	Patent exchange—technological agreement
Fujitsu and Ungermann-Bass (CA)	—	Local networks	Industrial and commercial agreement
NTT and *Hughes*	—	Telecommunications by satellite	—
Sperry-Univac and Mitsubishi	—	Local networks and communication and data processing system	Technological agreement
Motorola and NEC	1982	Portable paging systems	Agreement for manufacture and commercialization in Japan
Exxon Office Systems and Mitsubishi	—	Telecommunications equipment	Technological agreement
ATT and Philips	1983	PBX	Commercial agreement
Honeywell and *Ericsson*	1983	Telecommunications and office automation	Technological and commercial agreement
GTE and Italtel	1982	PBX	Technological and commercial agreement
Plessey and Stromberg Carlson	1982	PBX	Purchase of Stromberg-Carlson by Plessey
General Instruments and Thomson	1983	Videocommunication and teledistribution by cable	Technological and commercial agreement
Micro V and Jeumont-Schneider	1982	PBX	Technological and commercial agreement with partial acquisition of Micro V and creation of a joint subsidiary
Data processing:			
Honeywell and *NEC*	1984	Main frame computers	Technological agreement
Exxon Office Systems and Toshiba	—	Office automation	Technological agreement
TRW and *Fujitsu*	—	Data processing	Joint venture now controlled 100 percent by Fujitsu
Sperry and Mitsubishi	1982	Office automation	Technological agreement
Vertimag and Teijin (Osaka)	—	High-density magnetic memory	Technological and commercial agreement
Amdhal and Fujitsu	1982	Computers and peripherals	Take-over by Fujitsu
Drexler Technology and Toshiba	—	Smart card	Technological and industrial agreement
Olivetti and Docutel	1982	Office automation	Control of Docutel by Olivetti
Olivetti and Stratus	1982	Minicomputers	Control of Stratus by Olivetti
Nixdorf and Auragem	1983	Minicomputers	Control of Auragem by Nixdorf
Philips and Micom	1977	Office automation	Purchase by Philips
ATT and Olivetti	1983	Data processing, office automation, communications	ATT acquires 25 percent of Olivetti
Fortune and Thomson	1982	Microcomputers	Thomson acquires 17 percent of Fortune
Tandy Corp. and Matra	1982	Microcomputers	Technological and commercial agreement
Matra and Tymshare	1982	Terminals	Commercial joint venture in the United States
Cii Honeywell Bull and *Trilogy*	1980	Main-frame computers	Technological agreement with Cii Honeywell Bull having minor share in Trilogy
Cii Honeywell Bull and *Honeywell*	—	General data processing	Technological and commercial cooperation
AMD and IBM	—	Computer-aided design	Commercialization by IBM of Catia

Table 33.—International Technology Agreements—continued

Sector/partners[a]	Date	Technology	Agreement
Electronics and components:			
Intel and NEC	1982	VLSI microprocessors and circuits	Technological agreement
Texas Instruments and Fujitsu	1979	Integrated circuits	Technological agreement
Hewlett-Packard and Hitachi	—	Integrated circuits	Technological agreement
Western Electric and NTT	—	Integrated circuits	Technological agreement
IBM and NTT	—	Integrated circuits	Technological agreement
Zilog and Toshiba	—	Microprocessors	Technological agreement
Western Digital and Siemens	1982	Integrated circuits	Production and commercial agreement
United Technologies and AEG Telefunken	1982	Custom-made semiconductors	Production and commercial agreement
Philips and Signetics	1975	Components	Purchase by Philips
Philips and Magnavox	1977	Consumer electronics	Take-over by Philips
Philips and Sylvania	1980	Consumer electronics and tubes	Purchase by Philips
GCA and Matra	1982	Microelectronic equipment	Technological and commercial agreement
Harris and Matra	1981	Components and integrated circuits	Technological, industrial, and commercial agreement
Motorola and Thomson	1978	Components and integrated citcuits	Technological, industrial, and commercial agreement
Intel and Matra	1981	Integrated circuits	Technological, industrial, and commercial agreement
Thomson and *RCA*	1971	Color tubes	Technological agreement
Rhone-Poulnec and *Siltec*	1983	Silicon	Joint venture
Rhone-Poulnec and Dysan	—	Magnetic disks	Technological agreement
Sagem and Motorola	—	Bubble memories	Technological agreement
Thomson and Diasonic	1983	Medical instrumentation	Technological and commercial agreement

[a]The technologically dominant partner is italicized.
SOURCE: Office of Technology Assessment. Compiled from *Research and Development In Electronics: USA-France, 1982/1983,* French Telecommunications Council, 1984.

now owns Stromberg-Carlson. In addition, France and the United States have arranged joint ventures whereby American semiconductor firms have exchanged technical know-how for access to the French markets—particularly to the French telecommunications market (normally well protected by the French PTT). These joint ventures in which the French partners hold controlling interests include Thomson and Motorola, Saint-Gobain and National Semiconductor (in a firm named Eurotechnique), and Matra and Harris.

U.S. companies also have technical exchange agreements and other business relationships with Japanese firms. Intel Corp., for example, has a 5-year cross-licensing, cross-compatibility, and technology exchange agreement primarily in the area of controllers and peripheral equipment with NEC Corp. Amdahl Corp. currently uses a semiconductor chip developed and manufactured by Fujitsu in its U.S.-manufactured computers. Moreover, when Amdahl had difficulties raising capital for expansion, Fujitsu bought 40 percent of Amdahl. Although Amdahl might have been sold to another American firm, Amdahl management preferred to sell its stock to Fujitsu in order to facilitate technology exchange agreements, which involve cross-licensing, financing, and information exchange.[8] Fujitsu Ltd. has also recently agreed to supply Texas Instruments with gate array technical knowhow; Texas Instruments will produce the Japanese gate arrays and ship them back to Fujitsu.

Other joint technical agreements between American and Japanese information technology firms include Sperry's high technology cooperative agreement with Mitsubishi, which covers joint activities in manufacturing, re-

[8]Patricia Keefe, "Many U.S. Firms Have Japanese Ties," *ComputerWorld,* May 2, 1983, p. 73.

search and development, and marketing of computer systems. Mitsubishi also has a joint agreement with IPL Systems to develop an IBM-compatible processor. The technical exchange agreement between the two firms combines Mitsubishi's computer-aided design and large scale integration technology with IPL's design expertise. Under the agreement, both firms are granted the right to market the jointly developed products. Mitsubishi and Westinghouse have also arranged a joint venture to design and manufacture integrated circuits. In addition to technical exchange agreements between private firms, the U.S. Department of Defense encourages Japan to transfer defense-related electronics technologies to the United States. In 1981, for example, the U.S. Government asked Japan to provide advanced very large scale integration (VLSI) technology to enhance air and antisubmarine defense capabilities.

Patents

A large number of U.S. patents are granted to foreign individuals and corporations (see table 34). Foreign patenting activity in the United States has been related both to increased foreign inventive activity and to a growing interest in the U.S. information technology market. Moreover, studies have shown that foreign patenting activity in the United States by selected OECD countries correlates significantly with industrial R&D in those countries. This correlation is especially high in the electrical and electronics industries.[9]

Foreign patenting in the communication equipment and electronic components category was as much as 40 percent of the total number of U.S. patents granted during 1979-81, while the percentage of U.S. owned foreign patents in the same category was 13 percent.[10]

[9]Keith Pavitt, "Using Patent Statistics in Science Indicators: Possibilities and Problems," *The Meaning of Patent Statistics*, National Science Foundation, 1979.

[10]The fields that have relatively high percentages of U.S.-owned foreign patents are the areas corresponding to U.S. direct investment and research activity abroad. It is possible that U.S. laboratories abroad supported R&D that resulted in patented innovations. *Science Indicators, 1982*, National Science Board, National Science Foundation, 1983, p. 14.

Table 34.—Number of U.S. Patents Granted to Selected Foreign Countries[a] in All Product Fields and in Communications Equipment and Electronic Components (1963-81)

Country of inventor	All fields	Communications equipment and electronic components
United States	865,124	101,914
Foreign	369,519	41,242
West Germany	91,359	7,850
Japan	77,450	13,013
United Kingdom	51,138	5,976
France	35,244	4,455
Switzerland	21,622	1,258
Canada	20,241	1,773
Sweden	13,368	1,007
Italy	11,958	847
Netherlands	11,103	2,701[b]
U.S.S.R.	5,111	454
Belgium	4,459	360
Austria	4,080	273
Australia	3,585	198
Denmark	2,520	161
Mexico	1,075	21
Other foreign[c]	15,206	895
Total	1,234,643	143,156

[a]Countries were selected on the basis of being in the top 10 of at least one of the Standard Industrial Classifications.
[b]Indicates ranking among the top five foreign countries in this particular product field.
[c]Other foreign includes patents granted to foreign countries not shown separately.

SOURCES: Office of Technology Assessment; compiled from information in Office of Technology Assessment and Forecast, U.S. Patent and Trademark Office, *Indicators of the Patent Output of U.S. Industry IV (1963-81)*, 1982; in *Science Indicators*, 1982, National Science Board, National Science Foundation, 1983.

Table 35 and figure 38 show that Japan has the largest number of foreign U.S. patents in communications equipment and electronic components, although West Germany had been the foreign leader in this field throughout the 1960s and mid-1970s. Since 1970, Japan has doubled its patent activity in communications equipment and electronic components, food and kindred products, primary metals, and professional and scientific instruments.[11] Data for the period 1970-81, presented in table 36, show that the percentage of U.S. patents in information technology areas decreased more than 20 percent while the Japanese share of U.S. patents increased by over 200 percent.[12]

[11]*Science Indicators, 1980*, National Science Board, National Science Foundation, 1981, p. 21.
[12]The Office of Technology Assessment and Forecast, U.S. Patent and Trademark Office.

Table 35.—Share of Foreign Patenting in the United States for the Three Most Active Countries by Selected Product Fields (1981)

Product field	Total foreign	West Germany	Japan	United Kingdom	Other foreign
		Percent of foreign			
Chemicals, except drugs and medicines	100	28	27	11	34
Drugs and medicines	100	23	22	14	40
Nonelectrical machinery	100	26	27	9	38
Electrical equipment, except communications equipment	100	21	37	8	34
Communications equipment and electronic components	100	18	44	9	29
Motor vehicles and other equipment except aircraft	100	26	34	9	31
Aircraft and parts	100	28	42	10	21
Professional and scientific instruments	100	22	43	8	27
		Number of patents			
Chemicals, except drugs and medicines	5,338	1,520	1,452	566	1,800
Drugs and medicines	1,288	300	288	182	518
Nonelectrical machinery	8,166	2,088	2,240	731	3,107
Electrical equipment, except communications equipment	2,541	535	952	202	852
Communications equipment and electronic components	3,027	534	1,338	279	876
Motor vehicles and other transportation equipment except aircraft	1,652	429	563	151	509
Aircraft and parts	777	216	323	75	163
Professional and scientific instruments	4,100	892	1,760	329	1,119

SOURCE: Office of Technology Assessment and Forecast, U.S. Patent and Trademark Office, *Indicators of Patent Output of U.S. Industry (1963-81); in Science Indicators, 1982,* National Science Board, National Science Foundation, 1983.

Figure 38.—Share of Foreign Patenting in the United States for the Three Most Active Countries (1981)

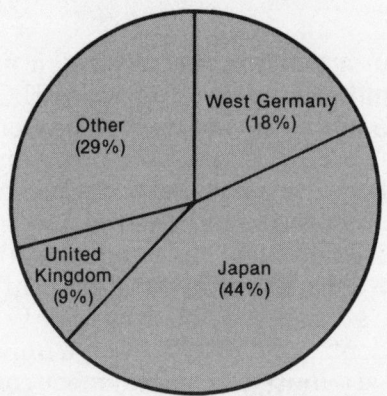

SOURCE: *Science Indicators, 1982,* National Science Board, National Science Foundation, 1983.

While the foreign patenting activity in the United States has been increasing, U.S. patent activity abroad has been decreasing over the past decade. Over the past 10 years, the U.S. proportion of foreign patents decreased from 45 to 37 percent in the United Kingdom and from 32 to 28 percent in France. Overall, from 1971 to 1981, U.S. patenting in Canada, Japan, and in the European Economic Community declined approximately 40 percent.[13]

Scientific and Technical Literature

U.S. utilization of foreign engineering and technical literature is growing. Between 1973 and 1980, U.S. citations of foreign research findings in engineering and technology fields increased by 4 percentage points and by 7 percentage points in the field of mathematics. Although the U.S. utilization of foreign research has grown, U.S. use of foreign research literature is lower than other nations' use of foreign research literature.[14]

The number of jointly authored articles by scientists and engineers from different coun-

---
[13]*Science Indicators, 1982,* National Science Board, National Science Foundation, 1983, p. 15.
[14]Ibid, p. 12.

Table 36.—U.S.-Owned and Foreign-Owned U.S. Patents in Information Technologies[a]

U.S. patent ownership	Percent ownership 1970	Percent ownership 1981	Percent change
United States	76	58	−23.7
Japan	6	19	+216
United Kingdom	4	4	0
France	3	4	+33
West Germany	5	8	+60

[a]Information technologies included here comprise SIC 357—Office computing and accounting machines; and SIC 365-367—communications equipment and electronic components.

SOURCE: The Office of Technology Assessment and Forecast, U.S. Patent and Trademark Office. Information technology numbers were calculated from data developed under the support of the National Science Foundation, Science Indicators Unit.

tries is also increasing. International co-authored engineering and technology-related articles as a percentage of institutionally co-authored articles have risen from 13 percent in 1973 to 16 percent in 1980. In 1980, more than 40 percent of all jointly authored articles in mathematics were international collaborative efforts.[15] Moreover, the United Kingdom, France, and West Germany had a greater percentage of internationally co-authored articles (as a percentage of all institutionally co-authored articles) than the United States. Japan and the United States had the lowest percentages of internationally co-authored articles. (See figure 39.)

Science and Engineering Students

The number of foreign students in scientific and technical fields in U.S. universities is increasing. In mathematics and computer science the number of foreign students enrolled in U.S. universities was 22,620 in 1981-82.[16] (See table 37.) Table 38 illustrates the large proportion of doctoral degrees awarded to foreign students in mathematics and computer science during 1981. In 1982 non-U.S. citizens were awarded 38 percent of the 542 doctorates in electronics and electrical engineering and 54 percent of the 72 doctorates in computer science.[17] Although some of the foreign engineering and mathematics students choose to

---

[15]Ibid, p. 31.
[16]*Science Indicators, 1980,* National Science Board, National Science Foundation, 1981, p. 240.
[17]"Washington Newsletter," *Electronics,* Jan. 12, 1984, p. 70.

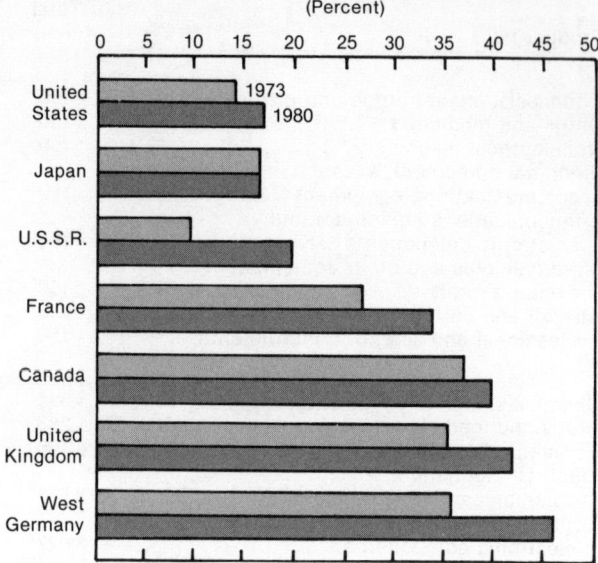

Figure 39.—Index[1] of International Cooperative Research by Country

[1]Obtained by dividing the number of all articles which were written by scientists and engineers from more than one country by the total number of articles jointly written by S/E's from different organizations regardless of the country involved.

NOTE: Based on the articles, notes, and reviews in over 2,100 of the influential journals carried on the 1973 *Science Citation Index* Corporate Tapes of the Institute for Scientific Information.

SOURCE: *Science Indicators, 1982,* National Science Board, National Science Foundation, 1983.

remain in the United States (if permitted), a large number of them return to their native countries.

Although the number of foreign graduate science and technology students in U.S universities has been increasing, the number of U.S. students enrolled in technical programs at foreign universities has been decreasing. The number and percent of U.S. graduate students studying abroad was highest during 1971, but now only constitutes about 1 percent of U.S. graduate students.[18] The decline of U.S. graduate students studying in foreign universities could be attributed to employment considerations and cost of living differences. Currently, as other industrialized nations' technical capabilities improve, the low number of graduate students abroad could inhibit the U.S. ability to keep abreast of the latest foreign research methods and developments.

---

[18]*Science Indicators, 1982,* National Science Board, National Science Foundation, 1983, p. 29.

Table 37.—Distribution of Undergraduate and Graduate Foreign Students by Field of Study in U.S. Universities (1954/55-1981/82)

Field of study	1954/55 Number of students	1954/55 Percent	1959/60 Number of students	1959/60 Percent	1964/65 Number of students	1964/65 percent	1969/70 Number of students	1969/70 Percent	1975/76 Number of students	1975/76 Percent	1978/79 Number of students	1978/79 Percent	1979/80 Number of students	1979/80 Percent	1980/81 Number of students	1980/81 Percent	1981/82 Number of students	1981/82 Percent
Engineering	7,618	22.3	11,279	23.3	18,084	22.0	29,731	22.0	42,000	23.4	76,000	28.8	76,950	26.9	80,470	25.8	75,220	23.1
Business/management	2,953	8.6	4,114	8.5	7,116	8.7	15,587	11.6	28,670	16.0	43,500	16.5	46,960	16.4	54,380	17.4	59,420	18.2
Natural and life sciences	3,681	10.7	6,261	12.9	11,731	14.3	17,006	12.6	23,910	13.3	24,190	9.2	21,880	7.6	23,030	7.4	24,870	7.6
Social sciences	5,041	14.7	6,782	14.0	12,609	15.4	17,272	12.8	20,730	11.6	23,360	8.9	22,530	7.9	24,310	7.8	25,200	7.7
Education	1,457	4.3	2,483	5.1	3,999	4.9	7,779	5.8	9,790	5.5	14,790	5.6	12,340	4.3	11,980	3.8	12,410	3.8
Mathematics and computer science	436	1.3	1,015	2.1	2,670	3.3	4,400	3.3	9,060	5.1	14,740	5.6	15,390	5.4	19,180	6.1	22,620	6.9
Fine and applied arts	1,997	5.8	2,417	5.0	3,946	4.8	6,297	4.7	8,320	4.6	14,120	5.3	14,350	5.0	15,450	5.0	15,190	4.7
Humanities	5,502	16.1	6,829	14.1	12,137	14.8	20,211	14.9	15,030	8.4	14,960	5.7	11,340	4.0	13,070	4.2	12,810	3.9
Health professions	3,184	9.3	3,685	7.6	4,918	6.0	5,969	4.4	7,180	4.0	12,470	4.7	10,950	3.8	11,320	3.6	11,570	3.5
Agriculture	1,199	3.5	1,615	3.3	3,211	3.9	3,667	2.7	5,270	2.9	8,710	3.3	8,750	3.1	8,660	2.8	8,880	2.7
Other	1,164	3.4	2,006	4.1	1,624	1.9	7,040	5.2	9,380	5.2	17,070	6.4	44,900	15.7	50,030	16.1	58,109	17.8
Total	34,232	100.0	48,486	100.0	82,045	100.0	134,959	100.0	179,340	100.0	263,940	100.0	286,340	100.0	311,880	100.0	326,299	100.0

[1] After 1978/79 includes students in a new category called Intensive English Language.
[2] Includes undeclared majors.

SOURCES: *Open Doors 1978/79* (Washington, DC: Institute of International Education, 1980), pp. 18-19. *Open Doors 1980/81*, p. 16, and *Open Doors 1981/82*; in *Science Indicators, 1982*, National Science Board, National Science Foundation, 1983.

Table 38.—Doctoral Degrees[a] Awarded to Foreign Students as a Percent of
All Doctoral Degrees from U.S. Universities by Field (1959-81)[b]

Field	1959	1963	1967	1971	1975	1979	1981
Science and engineering	14.8	15.5	17.5	18.7	22.1	21.1	22.1
Physical sciences	12.6	14.0	15.7	16.7	22.9	21.0	22.0
Physics and astronomy	14.9	14.5	16.9	18.6	27.6	25.7	26.1
Chemistry	10.5	12.2	14.6	15.6	19.8	19.7	21.2
Earth sciences[c]	17.1	19.9	17.2	14.6	22.1	16.6	17.1
Mathematical sciences	13.4	15.2	14.6	17.5	24.3	25.5	30.8
Mathematics	NA	NA	NA	NA	NA	26.7	33.7
Computer sciences	NA	NA	NA	NA	NA	21.3	26.3
Engineering	24.5	20.8	23.7	29.8	42.1	46.8	51.5
Life sciences	17.6	17.5	19.6	18.2	19.5	16.5	19.8
Biological sciences	15.5	16.5	16.2	14.3	14.9	12.1	11.1
Agriculture and forestry	24.9	21.0	32.4	33.6	37.4	35.2	37.6
Social sciences	10.7	11.6	13.5	13.7	13.7	12.9	13.0
Psychology	5.5	4.0	4.4	5.6	5.8	4.0	3.9
Other social sciences	15.5	17.6	19.9	19.3	20.2	22.4	24.0
Nonscience total	6.0	6.5	7.4	8.0	8.7	10.1	11.0
All fields	11.7	12.3	14.0	14.4	16.2	16.1	17.2

[a] Percent of those whose citizenship is known.
[b] Fiscal year of doctorate.
[c] Includes oceanography.
NA—Not available.

SOURCE: *Doctorate Record File, Special Tabulations,* unpublished data; National Science Foundation, *Science Indicators, 1982,* National Science Board, National Science Foundation, 1983.

Implications for U.S. Information Technology R&D Policies

Given the strong links between other nations' information technology research and development activities and those of the United States, and economic competition from countries such as the United Kingdom, France, and Japan in information technology innovation and international markets, foreign R&D initiatives are a concern for the United States. For the U.S. Government to participate in international research and development and, at the same time, successfully compete with these nations' R&D initiatives, the United States will need to understand other nations' economic and social goals for technological development, government, and industry roles in information technology R&D, and the significance of targeted national information technology R&D programs.

Although the philosophy of industrial competition is prevalent in other economies—particularly in the United Kingdom and Japan—these industrialized nations have coordinated their R&D efforts at a national level. Industrial and governmental cooperation is viewed as a means to achieve common national technological objectives and enhance the competitiveness of the entire national information technology industry in global markets. Coordination for R&D includes efforts at the national level to disseminate information on technological developments, share research results, and divide research activities among enterprises. Moreover, in coordinating R&D efforts between government, university, and industry participants, these nations have attempted to link trade competitiveness strategies more closely with R&D policies.[19]

In the United States, competition in technological development among firms is viewed

---

[19] Wilson P. Dizard, "U.S. International Information Trade," *The Information Society,* vol. 2, No. 3/4, 1984, p. 189.

as a variant of other forms of competition, such as competition in production efficiency, product quality, and marketing. Consequently, the United States relies heavily on open market competition and private initiative to spur industrial R&D.[20] Moreover, trade competitiveness factors are not always considered in the formulation of U.S. R&D policy.

Since other industrialized nations target information technology research and development programs at the national level, the question has been raised whether the United States should adopt a similar national industrial strategy for technological development. Although a number of nations that pursue coordinated industrial policies have relatively weaker overall economic performances than the United States, those that target information technology as a national priority may improve their competitiveness.

In response to foreign coordinated national R&D programs, a number of legislative options (several of which are modeled on foreign initiatives) for coordinating and targeting industrial sectors have been proposed in the United States. There is also evidence, presented in this report, that the United States may already be responding in ways particularly suited to its social, governmental, and economic traditions. For instance, the government-industry technology transfer activities stimulated by the Stevenson-Wydler Technology Innovation Act of 1980 (Public Law 96-480) (described in ch. 2) and the recently forming university-industry cooperative joint ventures (described in ch. 6) may be indications that the United States is beginning to develop indigenous mechanisms to pursue common technological objectives.[21]

If, however, the United States is to develop coordinated national industrial strategies in response to other nations' targeted efforts in the area of information technology, the use of other nations' national R&D organizations and activities as models should be carefully considered. As a result of major differences in the historical, cultural, and economic characteristics of each nation, there appear to be differences in their respective approaches to science and technology policies, as well as government and industry participation in information technology R&D. Moreover, the United Kingdom, French, and Japanese national information technology research and development programs differ in overall goals and organization and vary significantly from current U.S. R&D efforts.

Science and Technology Policy Goals

Although the United Kingdom, France, and Japan each developed science and technology policies in part to strengthen and modernize their economies, each of these nations varies in its conception of what technology policy should comprehend and what its objectives should be.[22] In some nations policy is aimed at strengthening the competitiveness of targeted industries. Other nations are concerned with developing information technologies for social needs or national security applications. In other nations, the perception of technology policy is much broader, and constitutes a part of a more general plan of how the economy should be structured in the future. Many of the goals for science and technology policy of the United Kingdom, France, and Japan are rooted in history. At the finish of World War II, each of these nations' societies and economies were severely damaged. These nations' governments therefore perceived a need to actively promote the growth of a high technology industry in order to aid their ailing economies.

Since World War II and particularly in more recent times, science and technology policies have become increasingly politicized. This reflects the view that science and technology is linked to nations' economic well-being (e.g., trade, productivity, and employment) and social welfare (e.g., quality of life, education, and training). Moreover, the widespread belief that

---

[20]Jack Baranson and Harold B. Malmgren, "Technology and Trade Policy: Issues and an Agenda for Action," Bureau of International Labor Affairs, U.S. Department of Labor, and the Office of the U.S. Trade Representative, 1981, p. 5.

[21]See for example, Jan Johnson, "America Answers Back," *Datamation*, May 15, 1984, p. 40-57.

[22]Jack Baranson and Harold Malmgren, op. cit., p. 6.

"the nation that dominates the information processing field will possess the keys to world leadership in the twenty-first century,"[23] has caused nations to look to the development of information technology for their future well-being. Evidence of the movement of science and technology policies into the political arena, for instance, can be found in both the recent Thatcher (United Kingdom) and Mitterand (France) political platforms in which information technology research and development funding and programs were emphasized. However, these two leaders differ in their policies for technological development. These differences are important in understanding and evaluating the roles of these governments in information technology research and development.

The various current approaches to science and technology policy and the different objectives of each nation's research activities underlie the distinct goals of each country's national research program. For example, Japan's concerns lie in developing information technology for improving Japanese society (which entails developing an information-based infrastructure) and improving its world trade position in information technology products. Consequently, Japan's goals for its national information technology research program, the Fifth-Generation Computer Systems Project, is to develop a fifth-generation computer for social applications and to develop a technological knowledge base which will enable Japan to maintain and improve the volume of information technology exports that is so vital to the Japanese economy.

Like Japan, the United Kingdom is also concerned with its economic survival in world markets, as exports also play an important role in the U.K. economy. The basic goal, therefore, for the U.K. Programme for Advanced Information Technology is to improve the competitiveness of the U.K. information technology industries in the world market in order to reverse its negative balance of information technology trade.

French governmental interest and efforts to expand advanced information technology research and production are directed at two major goals: strengthening France's international competitiveness and the development of an information technology-based infrastructure for the preservation and continued development of French culture and society. Reflecting French national goals, France's national information technology research and development program, La Filiere Electronique, has as its long-term goals: to place France on a technological level closer to that of the United States and Japan; create a trade surplus in information technology products; create new jobs; assure a sound technological base; and accelerate the production of information technology products.

The Europeans, through the European Economic Community (EEC), are also concerned about their basic economic survival in world markets. Consequently, Europe's major goal is to establish a strong technological base through collaborative research on various long-range projects that may not be adequately funded within individual nations. The European Strategic Program for Research in Information Technology (ESPRIT), involves the 10 EEC member countries. ESPRIT's major objective is to keep Europe competitive with the United States and Japan in advanced information technology fields.

Government Role in Information Technology Research and Development

The level of government funding for research and development varies widely. The ratios of civilian research and development expenditures to gross national product (GNP) presented in figure 40 show that the United States devotes a lower proportion of its GNP to civilian R&D than Japan, but a higher proportion than the United Kingdom. An examination of the annual growth rates of national research and development expenditures for electrical and electronics industries reveals that the United States lagged behind most of

---
[23]Robert E. Kahn, "A New Generation in Computing," *IEEE Spectrum*, November 1983, p. 36.

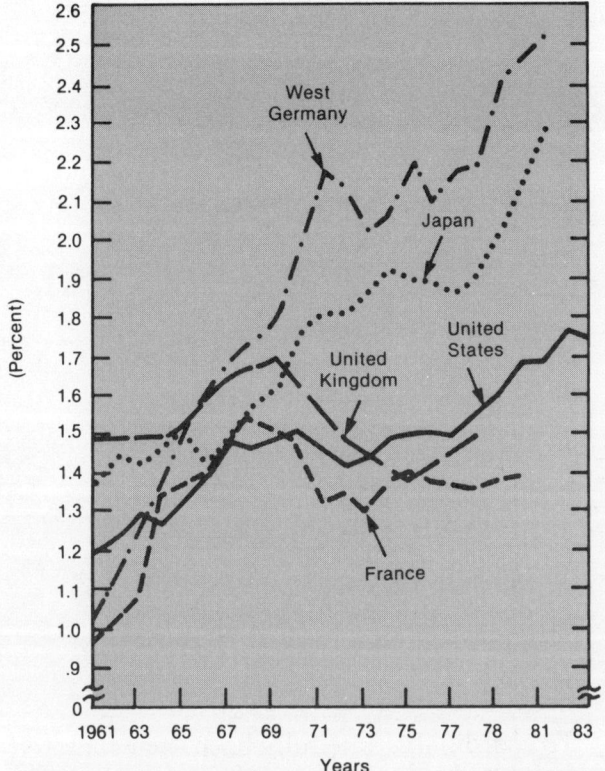

Figure 40.—Estimated Ratio of Civilian R&D Expenditures to Gross National Product (GNP) for Selected Countries[a]

[a]National expenditures excluding Government funds for defense and space R&D.

SOURCE: *Science Indicators, 1982,* National Science Board, National Science Foundation, 1983.

the industrially developed nations during the 1970s.[24]

The United Kingdom, France, and Japan singled out information technology as an area for government promotion and support. This contrasts sharply with the U.S. Government, which at the present time has not singled out or targeted any specific industry or technology for government support. Although in market economies governments use a more or less standard set of policies to support research and development,[25] other nations differ from the United States in the extent to which each coordinates and targets these policies to support information technology research and development. Policy measures for R&D support include low interest loans, direct subsidies, or actual government contracts. Other incentives to stimulate information technology R&D include tax incentives, national development banks which channel funds specifically to information technology industries, public sector procurement, and merger/antitrust policies.

To varying degrees the governments of the United Kingdom, France, and Japan have established institutional mechanisms to facilitate coordinated research and development policymaking. Coordinated government intervention on the part of these industrialized nations is reflected in each of the governments' structure which centralizes the responsibility within one or a few government ministries, and in the establishment of planning councils. Moreover, the coordinated efforts of the British, French, and Japanese extend much further than the U.S. pluralistic and decentralized approach to R&D support, to the coordination of government, industry, and university information technology research and development objectives and activities.

Government/Industry/University Institutional Arrangements for Information Technology Research and Development

A major difference between the institutional arrangements for U.S. information technology research and development and those of the United Kingdom, France, and Japan is the relationship between government and industry. In the United States, government tends to be viewed as a regulator and enforcer of laws and social policies; U.S. industry generally perceives its relationship with government as adversarial. Moreover, the U.S. Government, which traditionally avoids involvement in the private sector, relies largely on private initiatives for risk-taking, innovation, job creation, and the generation of profits and capital.

Although this adversarial relationship between the public and the private sectors ex-

---

[24]Reasons for the relative declining growth rate of U.S. Government R&D funding during this period include major decreases in funding for defense and space research and development, while civilian research and development was held constant. Currently, U.S. budget projections reflect increasing R&D funding for defense purposes.

[25]*International Competitiveness in Electronics* (Washington, DC: U.S. Congress, Office of Technology Assessment, OTA-ISC-200, 1983), p. 381.

Table 39.—Average Annual Growth Rates in the Engineering Industry

	United States	Japan	Germany	France	United Kingdom
	1970-79	1970-79	1971-79	1970-79	1969-78
Research scientists and engineers: [a]					
Aerospace	0.3	—	−5.3	1.1	−2.6
Electrical and electronics	−0.4	6.7	3.2	4.1	0.9
Machinery	5.1	2.5	6.7	3.9	3.6
Transport equipment	3.3	8.5	3.8	1.8	0.2
Total expenditure:					
Aerospace	−1.1	—	−2.3	2.6	−0.5
Electrical and electronics	0.1	5.8	5.8	4.7	3.1
Machinery	5.5	5.2	9.8	0.9	1.5
Transport equipment	5.4	11.0	3.9	7.2	−0.3
Government funds:					
Aerospace	−1.7	—	−1.0	1.8	−3.1
Electrical and electronics	−2.2	—	7.1	0.1	9.9
Machinery	1.0	—	10.0	—	1.1
Transport equipment	3.1	—	10.1	6.9	3.0
Industry and foreign funds:					
Aerospace	0.6	—	4.1	5.0	(b)
Electrical and electronics	2.3	—	4.9	7.7	−0.7
Machinery	6.3	—	8.5	—	−3.4[d]
Transport equipment	5.9	—	3.3	7.4	−1.4

[a] Japan not in Full-Time Equivalents.
[b] Large increases from a very low start.
[c] From abroad 4.91 per annum.
[d] Electrical and electronics. For R&D purposes the following subclasses are identified with this subgroup: ISIC 3832 and ISIC 838 nec.

SOURCE: *OECD Science and Technology Indicators,* OECD, 1984.

ists in most countries, the governments of the United Kingdom, France, and Japan have historically participated to a greater degree in industrial and technological development. For cultural, historical, and political reasons, these industrialized nations often regard government-industry relations as a partnership or perceive government as an institution for guiding and supporting targeted industries. Government-industry coordination has begun in some nations with the establishment of multipartite advisory groups representing government and private industry.[26] Formal and informal advisory councils have become in some nations, particularly in Japan, important forums for government-industry-academic consultations on industry policy and implementation. Particularly in information technology, these councils orchestrate joint research, development, and marketing schemes among information technology firms and government.

To coordinate more fully both their targeted policies and information technology R&D, the United Kingdom, France, and Japan have recently adopted major national programs. These programs, which have no counterpart in the United States,[27] have been established to pursue research projects cooperatively between government, private industry, and universities. The scale of funding for all the national programs is large and roughly comparable, representing a major commitment of between half a billion and several billion dollars over the first 5 years.[28] This funding is magnified because the companies which receive government research funds usually are required to match the funds.

---

[26] Franklin Delano Strier, "On Economic Planning, Japan and West Germany Have a Better Idea," *The Center Magazine,* January/February 1984, p. 36.

[27] Some individuals contend that the Department of Defense (DOD) programs, such as VHSIC, are similar to the national research and development programs of the United Kingdom, France, and Japan. However, there are major differences between DOD programs and these other nations' programs.

[28] Trudy E. Bell, "Tomorrow's Computers-The Teams and The Players," *IEEE Spectrum,* November 1983, p. 46.

Each nation, in structuring its cooperative research program, has looked to successful organizational examples both domestically and in other countries, borrowing organizational concepts and applying them in innovative ways. For example, the Institute for New Generation Computer Technology (ICOT), with its central research center, is unique to Japan. ICOT is organized for close cooperation of research activities among government, industry, and university participants. Japan's customary approach has been to have each participating research institution or company conduct research individually. ICOT is also contracting with outside companies and laboratories for some of the research and development—a technique often used for U.S. defense contracts, but unusual in Japan.

The institutional arrangements for the U.K. Programme for Advanced Information Technology are also unique, although the Alvey Committee closely modeled the program organization on Japan's Ministry of International Trade and Industry (MITI) and the U.S. Defense Advanced Research Projects Agency (DARPA). This new organization is intended in part to stimulate the transfer of basic research from academic environments to industry.

The ESPRIT program shares both similarities and differences with organizations such as ICOT and the Alvey Programme. Like these other new institutional arrangements, ESPRIT research is undertaken by teams of university, government, and industry scientists. In contrast to other nations' cooperative programs, ESPRIT represents a joint venture at the international level in which each project must involve researchers from at least two countries.

The success of these national programs in achieving both national aims and research goals remains undetermined. However, these new institutional arrangements raise some interesting questions for the United States. How will the cooperative research programs of the United Kingdom, France, and Japan alter their traditional research structures and serve as models for future research projects? What are the relative strengths of these new research programs versus traditional U.S. research environments? To what degree will these new national research programs affect U.S. technological development and market share?[29]

Industry Participation in Information Technology Research and Development

Funding of industrial information technology research and development varies from nation to nation. Table 40 represents industrial R&D funding patterns in industrialized nations and shows that industry has been a more dominant contributor in Japan (although the Japanese Government also provides a great deal of support through indirect subsidies) than in any other nation, including the United States.[30][31] The U.S. Government, in contrast, supported approximately half of the U.S. research and development activities in 1970. However, by 1979, U.S. industry had increased its share of industrial funding to 67 percent, approximately as much as the French industry's 71 percent support of its own research.

Table 41 illustrates industrial research and development support for electrical and electronics and computers categories in the industrialized nations. Japan and West Germany had the highest proportion of industrial R&D in the electrical and electronics category. In the computer category, however, the United States had the greatest proportion of industrial R&D followed by the United Kingdom, France, and then Japan.

---

[29]Ibid.
[30]*OECD Science and Technology Indicators,* OECD, 1984, p. 119.
[31]*Science Indicators, 1982,* National Science Board, National Science Foundation, 1983, p. 9.

Table 40.—R&D Performed in the Business Enterprise Sector by Source of Funds (1970, 1975, and 1979)

Country and source	National currency (in millions)			Percent		
	1970	1975	1979	1970	1975	1979
France	8,322.4	15,616.5	26,260.0	100.0	100.0	100.0
Total domestic	8,007.3	14,393.5	24,460.0	96.2	92.2	93.1
Business enterprise	5,310.0	9,965.8	18,723.0	63.8	63.8	71.3
Government	2,689.0	4,376.8	5,674.0	32.3	28.0	21.6
Private nonprofit	4.6	47.2	58.0	.1	.3	.2
Higher education	3.7	3.7	5.0	—	—	—
From abroad	315.1	1,223.0	1,800.0	3.8	7.8	6.9
Japan	895,020.0	1,684,847.0	2,664,913.0	100.0	100.0	100.0
Total domestic	894,193.0	1,683,200.0	2,662,698.0	99.9	99.9	99.9
Business enterprise	876,608.0	1,654,502.0	2,624,843.0	97.9	98.2	98.5
Government	17,585.0	28,698.0	36,807.0	2.0	1.7	1.4
Private nonprofit	NA	NA	935.0	NA	NA	—
Higher education	NA	NA	113.0	NA	NA	—
From abroad	827.0	1,647.0	2,215.0	.1	.1	.1
United Kingdom[a]	680.3	1,340.2	2,324.3	100.0	100.0	100.0
Total domestic	647.7	1,255.5	2,138.8	95.2	93.7	92.0
Business enterprise	431.2	841.4	1,459.0	63.4	62.8	62.8
Government	216.5	414.1	679.7	31.8	30.9	29.2
Private nonprofit	NA	NA	NA	NA	NA	NA
Higher education	NA	NA	NA	NA	NA	NA
From abroad	32.6	84.7	185.5	4.8	6.3	8.0
United States[b]	18,067.0	24,187.0	38,226.0	100.0	100.0	100.0
Total domestic	18,067.0	24,187.0	38,226.0	100.0	100.0	100.0
Business enterprise	10,288.0	15,582.0	25,708.0	56.9	64.4	67.3
Government	7,779.0	8,605.0	12,518.0	43.1	35.6	32.7
Private nonprofit	—	—	—	—	—	—
Higher education	—	—	—	—	—	—
From abroad	—	—	—	—	—	—
West Germany[c]	7,114.0	14,469.0	20,720.0	100.0	100.0	100.0
Total domestic	7,090.0	14,005.0	20,070.0	—	96.8	96.9
Business enterprise	6,146.0	11,397.0	15,650.0	—	78.8	75.5
Government	939.0	2,596.0	4,400.0	—	17.9	21.2
Private nonprofit	5.0	12.0	20.0	—	.1	.1
Higher education	—	—	—	—	—	—
From abroad	24.0	464.0	650.0	—	3.2	3.1

[a]1970 figures for the United Kingdom are from 1969, and 1979 figures are from 1978.
[b]Current expenditures plus depreciation only.
[c]1970 figures for West Germany are from 1969.
NA—Not separately available.
NOTE: Details may not add to totals because of rounding.
SOURCES: OECD Science and Technology Indicators, vol. B OECD, 1982; Research and Development in Industry, National Science Foundation, 1981; in Science Indicators, 1982, National Science Board, National Science Foundation, 1983.

Table 41.—Percent of Industrial R&D in Selected Industries (1969-79)

Industry	United States		Japan		West Germany		United Kingdom		France	
	1970	1979	1970	1979	1969	1979	1969	1978	1970	1979
Six-industry total	71.2	70.2	61.5	55.6	71.1	72.4	58.4	60.7	NA	61.7
Aerospace	11.8	8.6	—	—	.1	.6	1.1	5.4	7.8	8.8
Electrical and electronics	19.5	17.6	24.9	23.4	29.3	26.9	20.4	16.0	16.5	20.2
Instruments	5.3	7.8	2.3	2.9	1.6	2.1	3.1	1.9	NA	1.2
Machinery	}14.3	6.0	8.7	7.0	}7.0	}16.6	8.8	6.6	NA	4.2
Computers		11.5	2.9	2.8			2.9	5.2	NA	3.9
Chemicals group[a]	20.3	18.7	22.7	19.5	33.1	26.2	22.1	25.6	24.2	23.4

[a]Includes chemicals and allied products and petroleum refining industries.

SOURCES: OECD Science and Technology Indicators, vol. B OECD, 1982; Research and Development in Industry, National Science Foundation, 1981; in Science Indicators, 1982, National Science Board, National Science Foundation, 1983.

In addition to direct funding, governments can support or discourage industrial research and development with tax incentives, fiscal and monetary policies which affect interest rates and the availability of capital, regulatory policies, procurement practices, patent policies, and antitrust policies.[32] Moreover, actions of a national government to define the structure of its information technology industry will have profound but unpredictable influence on industrial R&D. For example, France has recently nationalized some major information technology firms, whereas the United Kingdom and Japan currently are moving in the opposite direction by privatizing their telecommunications entities.

[32] Science Indicators, 1982, op. cit., p. 10.

Conclusions

Cultural, social, and institutional differences among nations profoundly influence the way in which technological innovation occurs and underlie the considerable differences in R&D policies in the United Kingdom, France, and Japan. Therefore, many of these nations' successful research and development policies and endeavors may not be easily transferable or applicable to U.S. R&D environments. Nevertheless, cross-cultural comparisons of these individual nations, which have developed different methods of addressing similar public policy issues and technologies, can be useful to an individual society, such as the United States, in devising a conceptual framework for developing information technology domestic and international R&D policies.

International comparisons also provide a useful method for evaluating the status of U.S. information technology research and development activities and expenditures. However, making comparisons is difficult. Differences exist among countries in definitions, concepts, data collection methodologies, and statistical reporting procedures.[33] These problems are particularly prevalent in the area of information technology.[34] Although several international organizations such as OECD and the ITU have initiated the development of uniform definitions and standards for information technology products and facilitated the exchange of information on nations' R&D policies and activities, the U.S. Government currently does not have a designated agency or office within an agency to analyze and monitor foreign information technology R&D policies and practices.

The economic importance of industrial competitiveness and its close reliance on technological development emphasizes the importance of developing a program for periodic mapping of the pattern of technological advantages and disadvantages relative to foreign competitors.[35] Such surveys could help to alert government and industrial representatives to changes in the technological underpinnings of their competitive positions. These surveys could also be broadened to encompass nontechnological factors affecting competitiveness or future technological developments. These could include current or prospective changes in foreign government R&D policies that influence the competitiveness of their pro-

[33] Science Indicators, 1980, National Science Board, National Science Foundation, 1981, p.4.
[34] The U.S. SIC Codes, for example, do not have categories for information technology, but rather information technology products are encompassed within different and separate categories. Moreover, each nation has its own methods for categorizing information technology products and research and development expenditures and activities.
[35] See S. E. Goodman and M. R. Kelly, "We Are Not A A Sample of International Policy Challenges and Issue Information Society, vol. 2, No. 3/4, p. 250-268.

ducers in export markets. Such a broader survey could provide the basis for a more effective assessment of changes in the current and prospective competitiveness of foreign R&D efforts than a narrow focus on technological capabilities alone.[36] As one analyst stated:

> Most governments, and most especially the U.S. Government, are organized to reflect primarily domestic interests and have great difficulty in dealing adequately with one of the consequences of science and technology— the gradual blurring of the distinction between domestic and international affairs . . . .

Perhaps the most important observation [is] . . . that the general character of changes brought about by science and technology tends, overall, to lead to increased international interaction and integration, with correspondingly reduced relevance of national borders. The parallel spread and diffusion of technological competence that is eroding the dominance of one or a few nations in science and technology makes it imperative that we recognize the nature of the underlying changes taking place as we attempt to develop policies to deal with the specific implications of any given technology, or to influence the direction of development of technology itself.[37]

---

[36]Bela Gold, "Technological and other Determinants of the International Competitiveness of U.S. Industries," *IEEE Transactions on Engineering Management*, vol. LM 30, No. 2, May 1983, p. 58.

[37]Report by Eugene Skolnikoff entitled "Impact of Science and Technology on the International System," in "Overview of International Science and Technology Policy" hearings before Committee on Foreign Affairs, House of Representatives, 98th Cong., 1st sess., Aug. 2,3 and Sept. 21, 1983, p. 317.

Japan

Given Japan's minimal domestic natural resource base and its high dependence on other nations for food, energy, and raw materials, the Japanese Government treats science and technology policy as a means of spurring overall economic growth and enhancing Japan's competitive position internationally. Japan's policies focus on maintaining a long-term, high volume of exports in order to gain technological and, thus, market leadership in a broad spectrum of high technology, high value-added products. This perception in Japan has led to a consensus in the nation's government, business, financial, and academic communities to continue strengthening the nation's technological base.

The coordination of science and technology policy to the promotion of economic development is rooted in Japan's postwar recovery efforts. During the postwar recovery period, various science and technology institutions and policies were established on the assumption that they would help stimulate an economy. Another major component of this effort to support and improve technology was the United States and Western Europe. Following the enactment of the law on Foreign Capital in 1950, the Japanese have signed more than 36,000 licensing agreements costing approximately $12 billion.[38] Agreements between Japanese and foreign firms were made under strict government supervision partly to control the outflow of foreign exchange and partly to concentrate technological resources into certain key industries. Products manufactured with these imported technologies initially served to develop the Japanese domestic market, bringing about a GNP growth exceeding 10 percent throughout the 1950s. For example, transistor technology imported and commercialized by the Japanese in the early 1950s provided a foundation for the modern electronics industry.

Although the general trend of importing technologies has been receding, the imports of technologies related to electronic computers increased by 16 percent over fiscal year 1980, with those relating to software accounting for over 166 imports. Broken down into sectors

---

[38]Leonard Lynn, "Japanese Technology: Successes and Strategies," *Current History*, November 1983, p. 366.

of industry, out of a total of 2,142 cases, the number of imports of foreign technologies during fiscal year 1980 in the electrical industry amounted to 413 cases.[39]

In concert with the policy of importing technology, Japan has sought to develop its own indigenous research base. The ratio of national R&D expenditure to national income has risen from less than 1 percent during the first half of the 1950s to 1 percent in 1957, 1.5 percent in 1960, 2 percent in 1971, and 2.36 percent in 1981. According to official plans, this percentage will be increased to 2.5 percent by 1985 and to 3 percent by 1990.[40] According to statistics released by the Japanese Prime Minister's Office, all Japanese R&D, publicly and privately funded, in the area of information processing (which includes software and computer systems development only) totaled ¥ 158.6 billion ($687 million) in 1979 and ¥ 164.6 billion ($713 million) in 1980.[41][42]

In Japan, a far lower percentage of total research funds is provided by government (Japan 27.7 percent, United States 51.1 percent, United Kingdom 51.7 percent) than in other nations.[43] In part, this difference can be attributed to the high level of expenditure on defense research by Western governments (approximately 15 percent of total research funds) relative to the small amount spent by the Japanese Government (0.7 percent). In some areas of information technology R&D such as integrated circuit development, low military R&D expenditure has helped Japanese industry. In general, military areas demand the highest state-of-the-art standards, regardless of costs.

Therefore, these military developments sometimes result in expensive products which are so specialized that civilian or consumer applications can be limited. This is often the case with integrated circuit development in the United States. On the other hand, Japan has succeeded in developing integrated circuit products solely for commercial application.

Taking into account all funds spent on defense, the government of Japan still contributes significantly less to total scientific research expenditure than other countries.[44] More specifically in the area of information processing, the Japanese Government R&D expenditure in 1979 accounted for 8.2 percent in 1979 and 6.2 percent in 1980 of the total Japanese information technology R&D expenditures.[45] In Japan, this government R&D funding is concentrated in the national universities (13.5 percent), national research institutes (13 percent), with as little as 1.5 percent of government funding channelled to private industrial laboratories. Because government R&D funding, which is the major supporter of academic basic research, is relatively limited, reasons for Japan's perceived ineffectiveness in basic research can be clearly understood. As a result, current improvements in the Japanese academic environments for basic research as well as increases in funding levels for overall basic research are high priorities on the Japanese policy agenda.

Because Japanese Government R&D funding is small and for the most part channelled into university and national research institutes, Japanese industry funds constitute approximately 70 percent of R&D activities. Approximately 28 percent of all Japanese industrial R&D funding is devoted to information technology R&D. Although the Japanese Government does not directly make use of the vitality offered by private enterprise, the lack

---

[39]"Import of Foreign Technologies in Japan," *Science and Technology in Japan,* April 1982, p. 27.

[40]"Summary of fiscal year 1981 White Paper on Science and Technology," Science and Technology Agency, Tokyo, Foreign Press Center, 1981.

[41]Barry Hilton, "Government Subsidized Computer, Software, and Integrated Circuit Research and Development by Japanese Private Companies," *Scientific Bulletin,* Office of Naval Research Far-East, U.S. Department of the Navy, vol. 7, No. 4, October-December 1982.

[42]All Japanese yen figures are converted into U.S. dollars according to foreign exchange rates as of June 1, 1984, where ¥ 231 = $1.

[43]"Science in Japan," *Nature,* vol. 305, Sept. 29, 1983, p. 361.

[44]These low expenditures are also the result of the Japanese Governments current large budget deficits.

[45]Barry Hilton, "Government Subsidized Computer Software, and Integrated Circuit Research and Development by Japanese' Private Companies," *Scientific Bulletin,* Office of Naval Research Far-East, vol. 7, No. 4, October-December 1982.

of government funding has intensified competition in the area of information technology research and development. This competitive effort is exemplified in Japan's computer and semiconductor industries which, in order to survive, must develop and efficiently produce high quality products as quickly as possible.

This "privatized" environment for R&D has given Japan advantages and disadvantages in its information technology R&D efforts. One result of the large percentage of privately funded R&D is the lack of basic fundamental research activities. Because the R&D is subsidized mainly by private firms, basic creative research, which is high-risk and long-term, is sometimes ignored in favor of cost-efficient, developmental, applied, commercialized R&D. This continued preoccupation with R&D efforts that bring quick economic results has resulted in a trend which places less importance on basic, innovative studies. The Japanese Science and Technology Agency (STA), for example, published a list of 15 basic discoveries in the fields of recombinant DNA and computer technology (superconductivity, optical fibers, lasers, Josephson junctions, tunnel diodes, and transistors). Japan was responsible for only two of the breakthroughs listed; America for nine; the United Kingdom and the Netherlands for four. This bias in Japan's overall research expenditures toward applied research and prototype development is reflected both in government-supported R&D and private sector research expenditure (see table 42).

On the other hand, in the area of development, the application of basic research results, the Japanese privatized R&D efforts are highly successful. Japan has clearly outstripped most Western nations in processing technologies and incremental engineering—rapidly refining existing designs and ideas by making them smaller, lighter, faster, and cheaper. Japanese engineers, for instance, reengineered the 16 K RAMs with finer features to produce a 64 K RAM within a 2-year period.

Examples of Japanese strengths and weaknesses in information technology R&D are well documented in the area of software development. Software development, currently believed to be crucial for future information technology development, can be classified into various categories. Japan, with its industrial emphasis on applied R&D, has concentrated its efforts in production process-control software which has wide commercial industrial applications and which will reap significant economic benefits, both domestically in terms of the productivity and capacity utilization of industry, as well as internationally, in terms of the benefits of trade and technology transfer. However, in other categories of software development such as computer-aided design (CAD), the United States is technologically more advanced than Japan. Most of this technological lead resulted from billions of dollars that have been allocated for aerospace and defense basic research. As a result of this basic research for U.S. defense purposes, the U.S. computer simulation models and 3-D design programs are among the most sophisticated in the world.

Currently, Japanese industry is beginning to experience some difficulties with its emphasis on applied/borrowed technology. Japan has been slowly catching up to western technological innovations and has less input from foreign basic research patent licenses on which to base its refinements. Furthermore, Western firms are expressing a disinclination to sell patents to Japan, as they see the reengineered Japanese products competing with their own products. Moreover, Japanese firms that have sometimes neglected basic research, have fewer technological innovations worth offering

Table 42.—R&D Expenditure by Type of Activity

	Basic	Applied	Development
1970	18.9	28.2	52.9
1974	15.0	21.7	63.3
1975	14.2	21.5	64.3
1977	16.2	25.1	58.7
1978	16.6	25.1	58.4
1979	15.6	25.9	58.5

SOURCE: Kagaku Gijutsu Hydron (Indicators of Science and Technology), Kagaku Gijutsu-Cho (Science and Technology Agency) 1981. Note: This table covers all R&D, public and private.

Western companies when they wish to inquire about the possibility of cross-licensing. In addition to the fear of the decreasing amount of innovative ideas which Japan can buy and perfect and the fear of being excluded from future U.S. and other Western nations' technical developments, national pride is also forcing Japan to put more effort into basic R&D.

As a result of some of these difficulties, the Japanese Government is beginning to place more emphasis on basic research activities. This movement towards increased basic research is reflected in both government and industrial R&D activities as well as in the current Japanese Government's institutional mechanisms for influencing and funding industrial research. Because the government mechanisms which influence and fund information technology R&D are mostly aimed at promoting R&D in the private sector (and many take the form of informal cooperation), it is difficult at times to disassociate government and private sector initiatives and roles in information technology R&D activities. However, for purposes of clarity and comparison, the role of government, universities, and industry environments for the conduct of information technology R&D will be separately described. Before discussing these environments in detail, it is also important to understand the size of Japanese participation in information technology markets.

The Size of Japanese Participation in Information Technology Markets

Utilizing its basic technology policy which historically dictated that Japan reengineer imported technological innovations, Japanese industry has developed a very strong position in world information technology markets. In many areas where Japan has managed to capture a substantial percentage of the world information technology market, it can largely be attributed to Japanese industry's strong capabilities in product development, marketing strategies, and quality control.

Beginning in the 1950s, Japanese information technology industry efforts focused on microelectronics. Over the last three decades, there have been major shifts in Japanese consumer electronics production. Figure 41 illustrates the shift from the production of radios, to television sets, to audio equipment, and finally to videotape recorders. This production progression is particularly interesting in terms of technology because it not only illustrates the steady restructuring of an industry to higher and more complex technologies, but also illustrates the changing position of Japanese information technology industry in terms of global competition.[46]

In each shift in Japanese consumer electronics production, industry has been dependent on foreign technological innovations. For instance, Bell Laboratories supplied transistor technology, RCA licenses made Japanese color television production possible, and Corning Glass supplied glass tube technology. Perhaps more than any other of Japan's industries, the development of Japan's consumer electronics industry is the result of imported technology that competitive Japanese firms adapted, improved, and drove costs down. Figure 42 illustrates the Japanese share of world consumer electronics productions. The total value of production, second only to that of the United States, reached ¥ 8,683 billion ($37.6 billion) —or approximately 150 times that of 1955— making electronics one of Japan's major industrial sectors.

---

[46]James C. Abegglan, and Akio Etori, "Japanese Technology Today," Scientific American supplement, 1983, p. J, 18.

Figure 41.—Trends in the Production Composition Ratio of Major Consumer Electronics Equipment

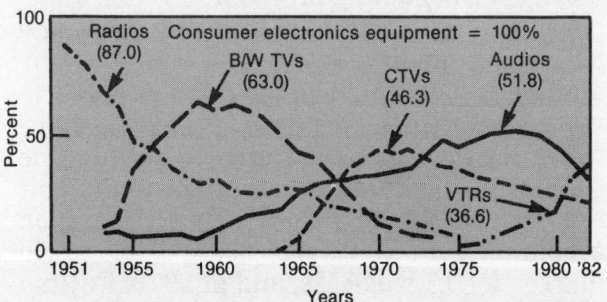

SOURCES: Annual Data on Japan's Electronics Industry, 1983 Edition, Electronics Industry of Japan, Tokyo, 1983; in James C. Abeggian and Akio Etori, "Japanese Technology Today," Scientific American, supplement, 1983.

Figure 42.—Japanese Share of World Production of Consumer Electronics Products (1980)

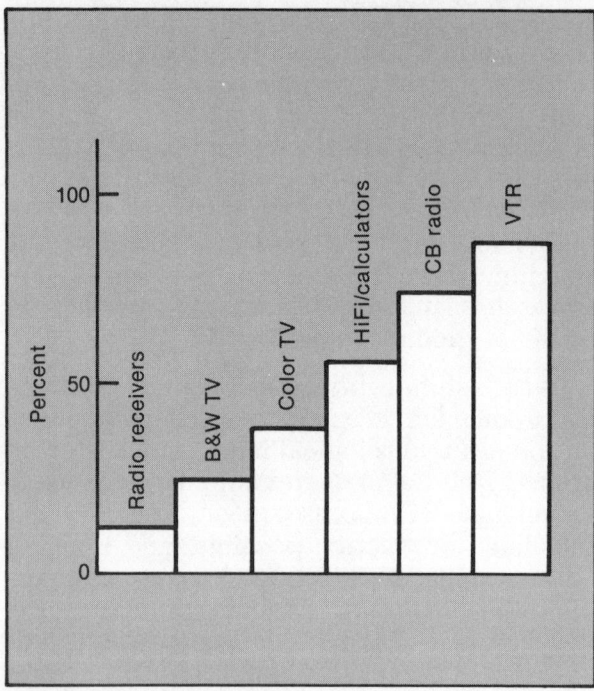

SOURCES: Japan Electronics Industry Development Association; in Gene Adrian Gregory and Akio Etori, "Japanese Technology Today: The Electronic Revolution Continues," *Scientific American*, supplement, 1984.

Recognizing the primacy of computers and telecommunications as growth sectors, as well as conforming to the trend towards more advanced technology production, Japanese industry has focused on a technology key to these areas—integrated circuits. As in the case of consumer electronics, Japan imported basic semiconductor technology and in the early 1970s initiated the production of integrated circuits. Although exports were insignificant during the beginning production years, Japanese industry focused on lowering costs and improving quality. Integrated circuitry production has grown in value terms at approximately 25 percent per year. Figure 43 illustrates the growth in the Japanese information processing, computer, and integrated circuit industries between 1974-81. By 1976, Japan accounted for a 40 percent share of the world market for 16 K RAMs, and in 1978, Fujitsu Ltd. was the first to announce the commercial production of the 64 K RAM. Japanese companies as well as U.S. manufacturers are the first to produce 256 K RAMs which will be available in 1984-85. Figure 44 illustrates Japanese integrated circuit production relative to U.S. production.

Perhaps the most significant step in this technology development sequence is the recent introduction by Japanese firms of one of the fastest supercomputers worldwide. These new computers, manufactured by Fujitsu and Hitachi, represent a major step in Japan's government-sponsored national effort to build fifth-generation computers.[47]

Government

The large percentage of private R&D funding would indicate the tremendous importance of Japanese industry in the Japanese success in world information technology markets. However, it is a mix of government support, a favorable and stable political structure, as well as freedom from national security expenditures, that have combined with the rather unique Japanese sociology to create a period of economic growth in the area of information technology. The nickname for the Japanese economy "Japan Inc.," which was given some years ago, may be said to be a realistic evaluation of the Japanese Government and private corporations during postwar Japan, when Japan sought to catch up with the industrially advanced nations. The term "Japan Inc." is still used today but in most cases this word appears to reflect a misunderstanding of the relationship between the Japanese Government and industry.

The Japanese Government does not control industrial R&D through funding mechanisms or specific policies that must be adhered to, but rather there is a participatory partnership among different segments of government and industry, based on pragmatic decisions, mutual respect, working within a framework of common goals. The councils and industrial associations have long been proposing to the Japanese Government to increase its research

---
[47]Phillip J. Hilts, "Japanese Firms Build Two Fastest Computers," *The Washington Post*, Feb. 7, 1984, p. A,1.

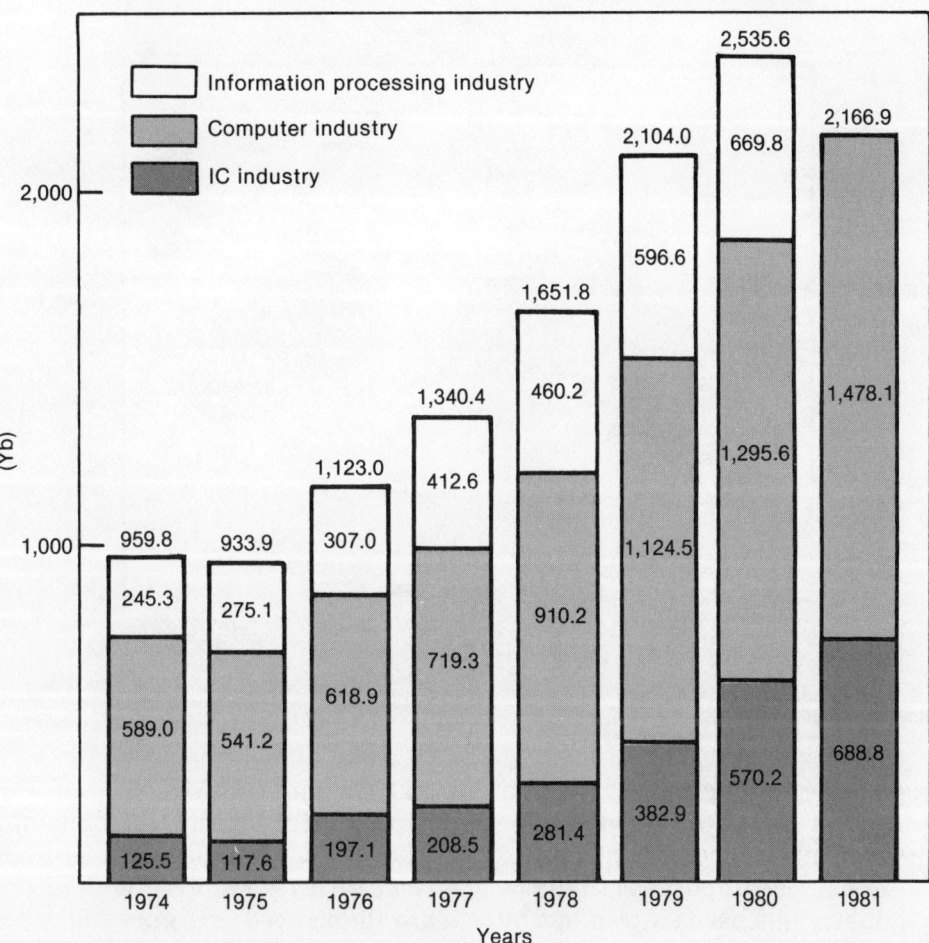

Figure 43.—Japanese Information Technology Industry Sales

NOTE: Information Processing Industry sales figures for 1981 not available.
SOURCE: MITI Survey on Specified Services. MITI Production Statistics in *Computer White Paper 1982 Edition*, Japan Information Processing Center.

and development support, but government funding has only increased 1.4 percent annually over the past 10 years. Although the government does promote some industrial R&D, industry has always been a larger investor. Government-industry relations in Japan have been broadly discussed, and it is often misunderstood that such relations are largely due to the Japanese Government subsidy of industrial R&D.

Japan's information technology firms are fiercely competitive and the government's role is seen as a means for providing an orderly framework for coordinating private industrial development. But when any coordination or intervention is decided on, it is undertaken through the development of a consensus among private enterprise and government. This consensual decisionmaking process between industry and government, frequently accomplished informally as well as through formal institutional structures, is in many ways the most important factor affecting decisions on R&D projects and funding for information technology.

The major function of the Japanese Government is to select, or to guide the selection of technologies to be targeted, to reduce the economic risks normally associated with developing new technologies, and to assist companies

Figure 44.—Integrated Circuit (IC) Relative Production Share

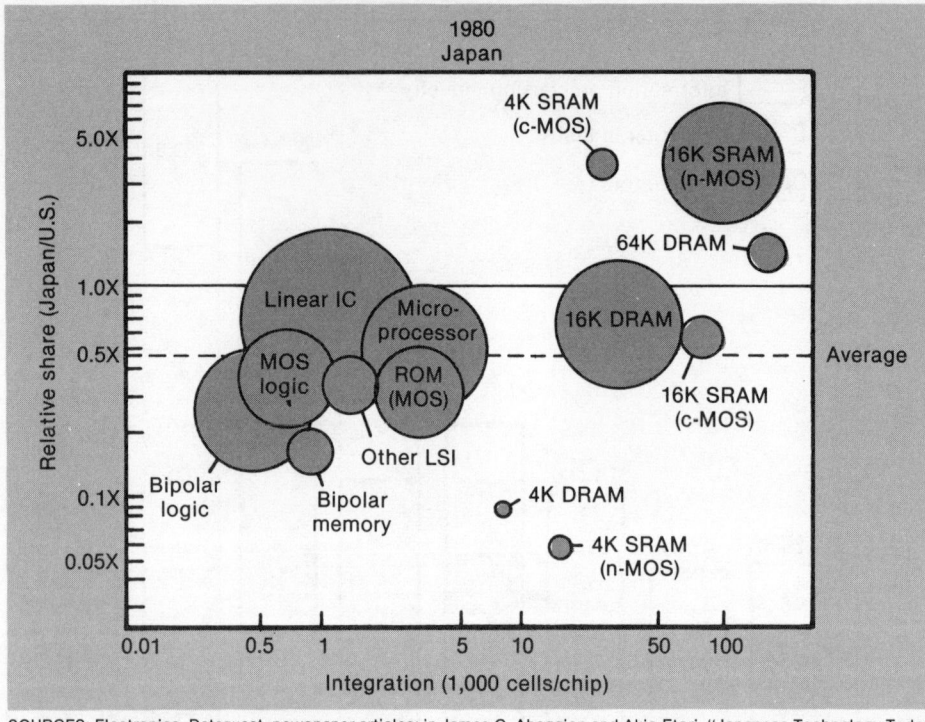

SOURCES: Electronics, Dataquest, newspaper articles; in James C. Abeggien and Akio Etori, "Japanese Technology Today," *Scientific American*, supplement, 1982.

to achieve large scale production. The direct financial support for R&D provided by the Japanese Government to targeted industries is in many instances less important than the fact that the industry has been singled out by the government as a "target" sector. There are tangible and intangible benefits which flow to such industries. A targeted sector gains prestige and public respect. Private banks are more willing to extend credit, customers and suppliers will tend to give preferred treatment, and government officials in various agencies are also likely to be more responsive to the particular needs of target-sector companies.

In addition to the informal consensual decisionmaking, targeting and funding of information technology R&D is accomplished through major formal government institutions: Ministry of International Trade and Industry (MITI), Science and Technology Agency (STA), Ministry of Education, Culture, and Science (MOE), Ministry of Posts and Telecommunications (MPT) which has nominal control over Nippon Telegraph and Telephone (NTT), and the Ministry of Finance (FOC) through the Japan Development Bank (JDB). The major Japanese Government organizations directly involved with information R&D are illustrated in figure 45.

Ministry of International Trade and Industry (MITI)

Perhaps the most misunderstood agency within the Japanese Government, the Ministry of International Trade and Industry (MITI) has been credited by many in the United States as being much more pervasive than it is in reality.[48] Taking into account the scale of the Japanese economy, the complexity of international markets and the rapid changes in technology, MITI alone cannot and does not completely control industry. A case in point is MITI's failed attempt during the 1970s to consolidate the Japanese automobile

---

[48]Toshimasa Tsuruta, "The Myth of Japan Inc.," *Technology Review*, July 1983, p. 43-48, and Robert C. Christopher, "Don't Overestimate Tokyo Industrial Aid," *The New York Times*, Jan. 30, 1984, p. A, 21.

Figure 45.—Japanese Government Organization for Information Technology Research and Development

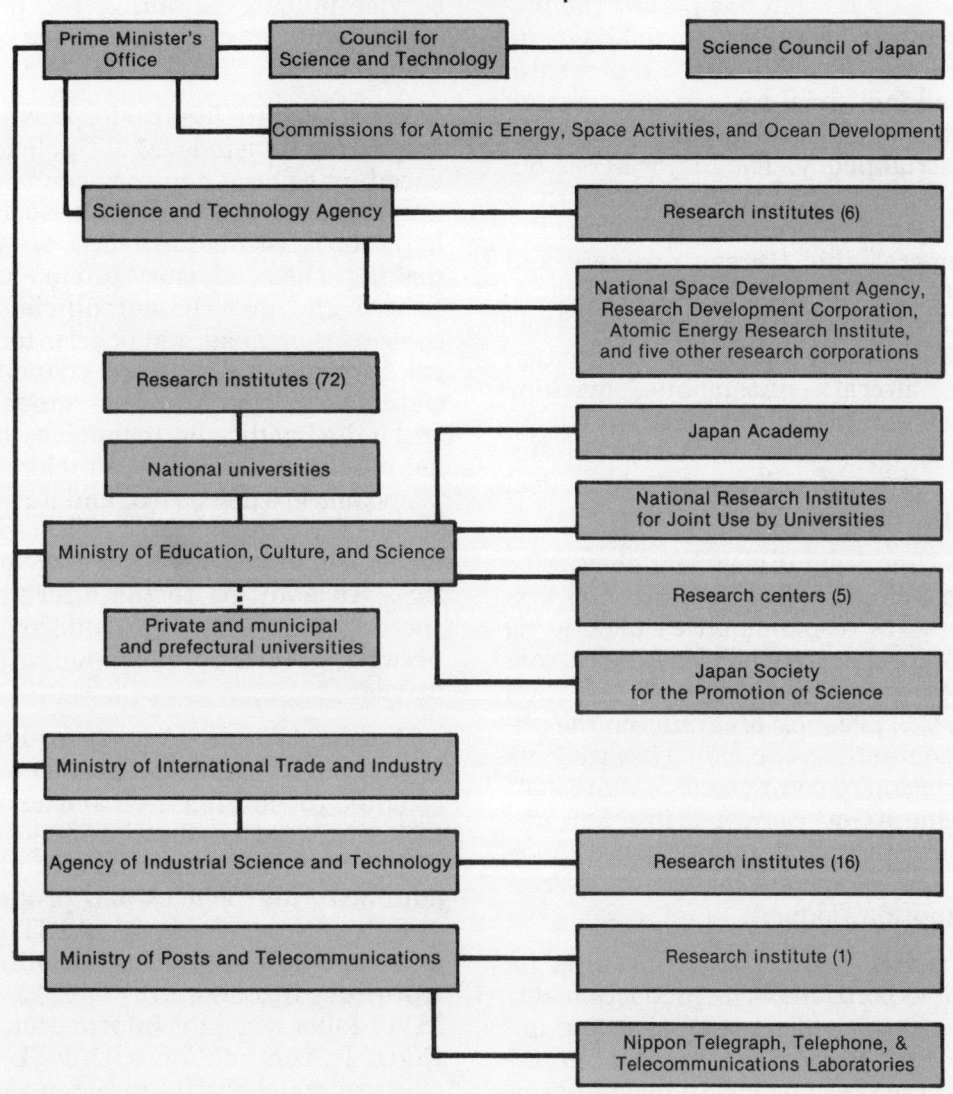

SOURCE: "Science in Japan," Nature, Sept. 29, 1983.

industries into three large groups. Some have claimed that MITI is on paper at least no more influential than the Department of Commerce in the United States.[49]

MITI was established in 1949 with the broad charter of shaping the structure of Japanese industry, managing foreign trade and commercial relations, ensuring adequate raw materials and energy supplies, and managing relationships between particular business and technical industrial sectors and the government. Despite this broad legal mandate, the pervasive MITI practice of "administrative guidance" by which many policies are implemented depends on no statutory authority. Nevertheless, MITI does have the advantage of broad contacts across information technology industries and relies extensively on this informal practice to influence firms and whole industries in the direction it wants them to take.[50]

---

[49]"Science in Japan," Nature, vol. 305, Sept. 29, 1983.

[50]Ira C. Magaziner and Thomas M. Hout, *Japanese Industry Policy* (Berkeley, CA: Institute of International Studies, 1980), pp. 40-41.

Within MITI's bureaucratic structure, the Industrial Policy Bureau has played the major role in guiding overall industrial development. This Bureau consults with representatives from all industrial sectors and through these informal and formal meetings sets Japanese industrial policy. The major MITI bureau involved with information technology is the Machinery and Information Industries Bureau. In general, this Bureau oversees and coordinates export, import, production, distribution and consumption of machinery and mechanical apparatus. In addition to information technology, aircraft, automobile, machine tools, as well as other industries, are within the Bureau's responsibilities. Within the Bureau there are several divisions which deal directly with information technology.

The most significant division involved with information technology is the Electronics Policy Division. Its responsibilities include: 1) planning comprehensive policies for electronics equipment industries; 2) the distribution of computers; 3) planning programs on the utilization of computers; 4) conducting surveys on the utilization of computers; 5) representing the Japanese Government at international organizations concerning information technology matters; and 6) overseeing the Data-Processing Promotion Council.

The Industrial Electronics Division is responsible for exports, imports, production, distribution, promotion of consumption, and improvement and adjustment of communications products. These products include computers, laser application devices, radar, electronic measuring instruments, telephone and telegraph equipment, switchboards, facsimile equipment, broadcasting equipment, fixed multiplex communication devices, and communication wire and cables.

Two other divisions, Data-Processing Promotion and Electrical Machinery and Consumer Electronics, also are directly involved with information technology. As its name suggests, the Data-Processing Promotion Division responsibilities include: 1) the examination and licensing of data processing technicians; 2) the cultivation and promotion of data processing service industries; and 3) the promotion of computer usage and applications programs development.

In addition to these major Bureaus and their respective divisions, MITI policies are influenced by several advisory councils, industry associations, and research associations. Perhaps the most unique aspect of MITI policymaking, these advisory groups are where industry and government officials develop a consensus on goals and policies for technological development. In these councils and associations members from government, academia, and industry discuss technology trends, market potential, and policy. Problems, ideas, and proposals are discussed, and if a general consensus is obtained, it is reflected in government and industrial R&D policies and practices. In addition to these formal channels, there are also a number of informal exchanges between government and industrial representatives.

Within MITI, the Agency for Industrial Science and Technology (AIST) is explicitly oriented toward research and development of technology with industrial applications. In addition to its responsibilities of planning and administering policies and programs for research and development, AIST operates 16 government laboratories, including the Electrotechnical Laboratory (ETL), the major MITI laboratory for information technology R&D. In conjunction with ETL, AIST also oversees collaborative research with affiliated laboratories and private companies—particularly for MITI's targeted national information technology R&D programs. The AIST also administers the industrial standards programs.

Directly under MITI's jurisdiction, the Electrotechnical Laboratory is the largest national research organization in Japan specializing in electronics research. The ETL, with an annual budget of $40 million, employs approximately 730 researchers. ETL's major areas of research include solid state physics and materials, information processing, energy, standards, and measurements. Similar to DOD facilities in the

United States, ETL has in addition to its own internal research, responsibility for advising the government on technology options and monitoring industrial R&D programs. ETL, like other technology in-house research laboratories, does not attempt to compete with industry. As in many U.S. Government research labs, ETL concentrates on identifying research projects and directions (usually high risk) where it could supplement industrial research activities. ETL also oversees the industrial research efforts for MITI's coordinated national R&D projects.[51]

As the Japanese Government began to move into more basic research activities and new state-of-the-art technologies, many of its policymakers felt that its institutions were ill-equipped (e.g., too constrained, rigid) for basic, pioneering research. Consequently, Tsukuba Science City, which was begun in 1966, was planned and built by the government for the purpose of centralizing research and educational activities. In terms of its concentration of high level personnel, it in many ways resembles Silicon Valley in the United States, although in terms of government organization, the North Carolina Research Triangle is perhaps a better comparison. Located within Tsukuba City are 30 of Japan's 98 national research institutes. These 30 research institutes account for approximately 40 percent of the total research budget and 40 percent of the total number of researchers in Japan. In addition to these 30 national research institutes, the Tsukuba Science City accommodates a total of 46 research organizations, including two national universities, six organizations belonging to government-funded special organizations, and eight organizations affiliated with other administrative entities. Approximately 27 research-oriented private corporations have also relocated to Tsukuba Science City.[52]

Photo credit: Embassy of Japan

Tsukuba Science City

National Research and Development Projects

Another effort to stimulate basic long-term research activities by coordinating industry and government research efforts was begun in 1966 with the initiation of National Research and Development Projects. Perhaps the most significant aspect that sets Japanese R&D efforts apart from U.S. R&D, these national projects are directed towards research that is in the Japanese national interest, long-term, high-risk, and precompetitive—research that is not directed towards any specific product, but technology that is useful for an entire industrial sector.

The initiation of a national R&D project is accomplished through a series of steps. First, through meetings with government, academic, and industrial representatives, usually within various councils and associations, MITI officials derive a consensus on areas for national R&D attention. MITI's "Vision of MITI Policies in the 1980s" is an example of the consensual decisions reached among the representatives. Reflected in these "Visions of the 1980s" is Japan's basic national economic philosophy which states that Japan should seek to ensure its economic survival by becoming a technology-based nation and by making maximum use of brain power, which is its greatest resource to develop innovative technology.[53] More specifically, the report suggests

---

[51] George E. Lindamood, "The Rise of the Japanese Computer Industry," *Scientific Bulletin,* Department of the Navy, Office of Naval Research Far-East, vol. 7, No. 4, October-December 1982, p. 61, 62.

[52] For a detailed discussion of Tsukuba Science City see Justin L. Bloom and Shinsuke Asano, "Tskuba Science City: Japan Tries Planned Innovation," *Science,* vol. 212, June 12, 1981, pp. 1239-47 and "Science City in Japan—Tskuba," *Science and Technology in Japan,* January-March 1983, pp. 6-11.

[53] "The Vision of MITI Policies in the 1980s," provisional translation, Ministry of International Trade and Industry, Tokyo, Japan, Mar. 17, 1980.

that Japan should encourage development efforts and a switch-over to "forward-engineering" in the knowledge-intensive or information technologies.

By targeting specific information technology areas for national priority, MITI identifies those areas to receive a combination of direct and indirect project R&D support. This support system for national projects, often termed seed money because of its relatively small amount, initiates basic precompetitive research and leaves to industry detailed product-oriented decisions. Often this seed money is given to various information technology firms in the form of 50-50 matching grants.

Lastly, MITI forms company groups or research associations to work on a specific national project. Sometimes research associations have actually overseen R&D activities (as in the VLSI project); however, these research associations generally coordinate each member's separate research efforts. Staff of these research associations usually include employees on detail from government and industry, as well as retired industry and government officials.

Between 1966 and 1979, the Japanese Government contributed approximately $400 million to 16 different national research projects.[54] A chronological history of Japanese Government support for national information technology research and development projects is presented in figure 46. Since the early projects, typical amounts committed to national research projects appear to be increasing and the scope of the projects is towards more basic research.

The VLSI development project exemplifies one of the better known national information technology R&D projects, largely because of the subsequent market success of the Japanese integrated circuit industry. Begun in 1976, the VLSI project involved the formation of a new VLSI research association with seven participating private companies in addition to Nippon Telephone and Telegraph and the MITI Electrotechnical Laboratory. The project was jointly funded at $150 million from government and $200 million from industry over a 4 year period. The VLSI Research Association and MITI laboratory efforts were largely generic and provided support for already existing industry R&D efforts. The net effect of these efforts was the worldwide introduction of the first 64 K RAM device. The resultant successes of the Japanese information technology industry may signify that efforts across public (MITI), quasi-public (NTT), and private (major corporations) sectors in pursuit of a common national technological goal is in fact one of the strengths of the Japanese national R&D projects system.[55]

The national information technology R&D project which has received the most attention recently is the Fifth-Generation Computer Systems Project. Begun in 1979, the project has become an impetus to the initiation of other major national information technology R&D projects in the United Kingdom, France, and Europe.

In light of the Japanese Government's goal of stimulating basic research efforts, the objective of the fifth-generation computer project is to move Japan to a lead position in information technology areas related to office automation, computer-aided design, computer-aided engineering, robotics, and computer-aided instruction. Moreover, the intent is to direct information technology development in Japan to specific societal needs. These include: coping with an aging society; increasing activity in low productivity areas; increasing energy savings; and assisting the transformation of society into one in which information plays a key role. The goal of the fifth-generation project is to develop basic technology and prototype systems that can perform functions such as inference, association, and learning as well as non-numeric processing of speech, text, graphics, and patterns.

---

[54]Leonard Lynn, "Japanese Technology: Successes and Strategies," *Current History,* November 1983, p. 370.

[55]For an in-depth analysis of the VLSI project, see Kiyanori Sakakibara, "From Imitation to Innovation: The Very Large Scale Integrated (VLSI) Semiconductor Project in Japan," Alfred P. Sloan School of Management, Massachusetts Institute of Technology, 1982-1983.

Figure 46.—Japanese Government Support for Information Technology

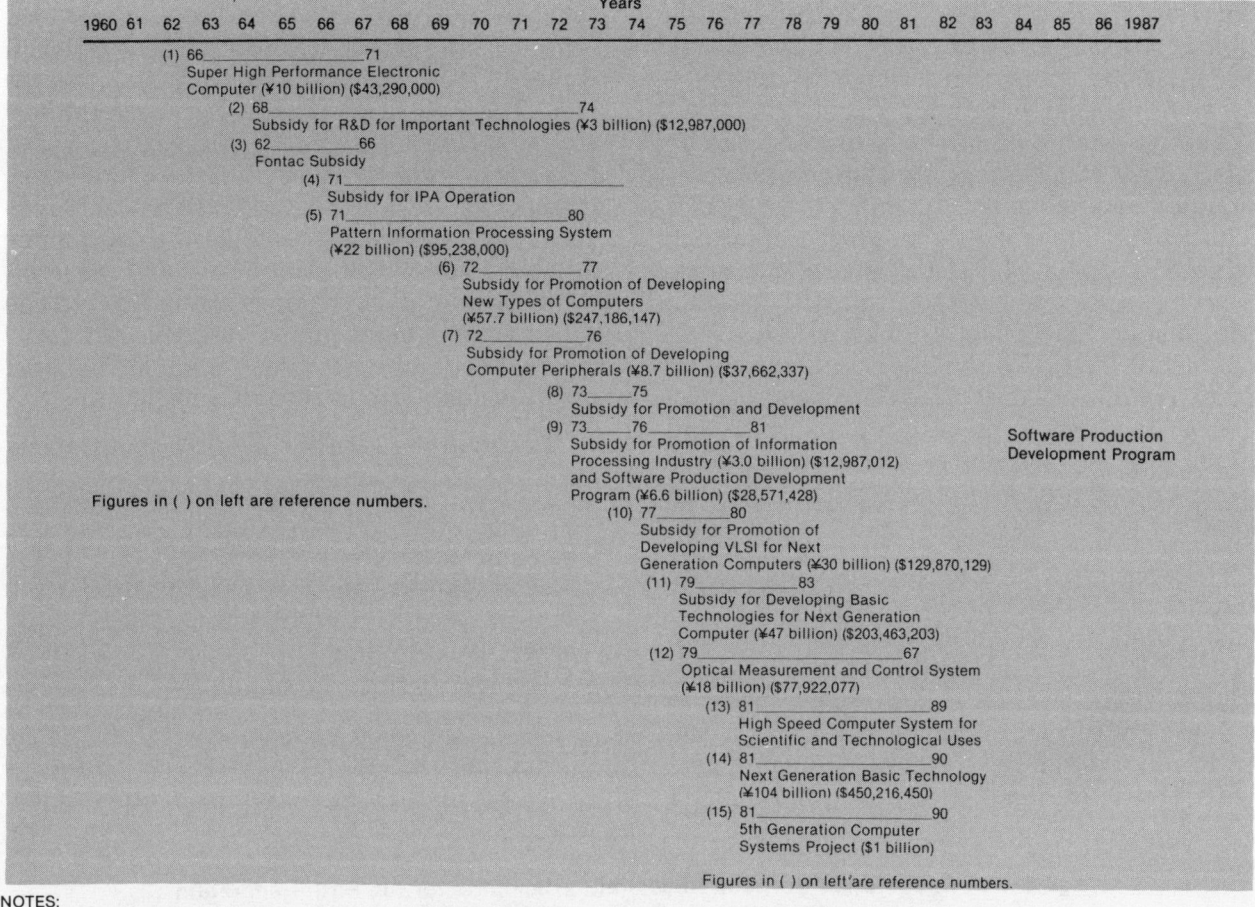

NOTES:
1. *Sponsors:* AIST, Large Scale Project; MITI. *Funding:* All government funding through consignment payments.
2. These are combined because (3) is a continuation of (1). *Sponsors:* AIST, MITI. *Funding:* All government funding through consignment payments.
3. FONTAC was aimed at developing a large size computer competitive with IBM systems. *Corporate participation:* Fujitsu, OKI, NEC.
4. The IPA was established by law in 1970 to encourage the development of software by direct and indirect financing. IPA operations are reviewed by MITI. Three long term credit banks provide loans to software houses and data services through IPA's guarantee fund. Total government support unclear, but subsidies totaled Y14.9 million for FY 1972-1980 (see text for additional material).
5. Continuation of (2). *Sponsors:* AIST and Electrotechnical Laboratory. *Corporate Participation:* Toshiba, Hitachi, Fujitsu, NEC, Mitsubishi Electric, Sanyo, Matsushita Research Institute, Konishiroku and Hoya Glass.
6. Subsidy aimed at developing a new series of computers competitive with IBM's 370 series. *Funding:* a 50 percent subsidy to three computer manufacturer groups. *Corporate Participation:* Fujitsu-Hitachi (produced M series), NEC-Toshiba (produced ACOM), and Mitsubishi-OKI (produced MELCOM).
7. *Sponsor:* MITI; *Participation:* 31 companies; *Funding:* 50/50 (government/private); *Goal:* develop high efficiency input-output units and terminals.
8. *Sponsor:* MITI; *Participation:* unclear; *Funding:* 50/50 (government/private).
9. *Sponsors:* Machinery and Information Bureau and Data Processing Division, MITI; *Corporate Participation:* 17 large Japanese software companies belonging to an IPA subsidiary, the Joint Systems Development Corp., in addition, a number of unspecified smaller firms; *Goal:* to increase the production and use of software programs. This constitutes IPA's most active software development program to date. Results unclear.
10. & 11. because 11 is seen as a continuation of (10); *Sponsors:* Machinery & Information Bureau and Industrial Electronics Division, MITI; *Corporate Participation:* two phases: (I) Fujitsu, Hitachi, Mitsubishi, NEC & Toshiba, OKI, Sharp, Matsushita; (II) above, plus NTT and AIST's Electrotechnical Laboratory staff. *Association Formed:* Phase I: VLSI Research Association formed; Phase II: Electronic Computer Basic Technology Research Association formed (July 1979). *Funding:* (government) conditional loan, repayable if profits are generated from technologies; Phase I: Y30 billion from the government, Y42 billion from the private sector. Phase II: Y22.5 billion from the government; Y24.5 billion from the private sector.
12. *Sponsors:* AIST, National Research and Development Program, MITI; *Corporate Participation:* Fujitsu, Hitachi, NEC, Toshiba, Mitsubishi Denki, Matsushita Furukawa, OKI, Sumitomo Electric; *Association Formed:* Engineering Research Association of Optoelectronics Applied Systems (January 1981); Laboratory Formed by Association: Optoelectronics Joint Research Laboratory within the Fujitsu Kawasaki Plant; *Funding:* all government funding through consignment payments.
13. *Sponsors:* AIST, National Research and Development Program, MITI; *Corporate Participation:* Fujitsu, Hitachi, NEC, Toshiba, Mitsubishi Denki, OKI; *Government Laboratory Assistance:* Electrotechnical Laboratory, AIST; *Association Formed:* the Association for the Development of High Speed Scientific Computers (December 1981), MITI's Electrotechnical Laboratory is also involved, although majority of work will be conducted at companies' own research facilities; *Funding:* all government funding through consignment payments.
14. *Sponsors:* Next Generation Basic Technology Planning Office, AIST, MITI; *Corporate Participation:* 48 companies in 3 areas; numbers in ( ) indicate number of firms; Area I: New Materials (33); Area II: Biotechnology (14); Area III: Semiconductor Function Elements (10); *Association Formed:* five associations formed, 3 for Area I, 1 for Area II, and 1 for Area III; *Funding:* all government funding through consignment payments.
15. *Sponsor:* Machinery and Information Bureau, MITI; *Corporate Participation:* Fujitsu, Hitachi, NEC, Toshiba, Mitsubishi Denki, OKI; *Government Laboratory Assistance:* Electrotechnical Laboratory, AIST; *NTT Personnel Participation:* primarily at preparatory stages; *Association Formed:* The Institute for New Generation Computer Technology, an endowed research foundation (April 1982); *Funding:* total funding yet to be determined.

SOURCE: Jimmy W. Wheeler, Merit E. Janow, Thomas Pepper, and Midori Yamamoto, "Japanese Industrial Development Policies in the 1980's: Implications for U.S. Trade and Investment," Hudson Institute Inc., 1982, for the U.S. Department of State.

The Japanese Government established the Institute for New Generation Computer Technology (ICOT) in April, 1982 as the center organization for coordinating the fifth-generation computer project R&D activities. Although the government is funding the initial 3 year R&D stage, eight manufacturers donated money to establish and run ICOT. The consortium of eight manufacturers which equally support ICOT and share in the research results are: Fujitsu Ltd., Hitachi Ltd., Matsushita Electrical Industrial Co., Mitshubishi Electric Co., NEC Corp., Oki Electric Industry Co., Sharp Co., and Toshiba Co. These companies, in addition to NTT and MITI's Electrotechnical Laboratory, have sent 42 researchers to the ICOT research center.

Beginning with a staff of 52 and a planned budget of $450 million over the first 5 years, the overall research program is scheduled to last for 10 years. In addition to its relatively long-term research, ICOT is unusual because it is a separate neutral organization with a centralized research laboratory. This contrasts with the traditional Japanese approach in which each of the participating research institutions and companies conducts its own research work. In addition to its own internal research, ICOT cooperates with two government laboratories, various Japanese universities, and independent foreign researchers. ICOT also contracts with Japanese industries to make and test prototype software and hardware. The specific universities and companies involved vary with each individual research project and participation is not limited to the consortium of eight major companies sponsoring ICOT. Figure 47 illustrates ICOT's organization for various research projects.

The research plans of the ICOT center focus on seven major areas:

- basic application systems,
- basic software systems,
- distributed function architectures,
- new advanced architectures,
- VLSI technology,
- systematization technology, and
- development supporting technology.

Within these seven areas, 26 research projects are to be conducted by teams of university,

Figure 47.—Cooperation Between Research Participants for the Fifth-Generation Computer Systems Project

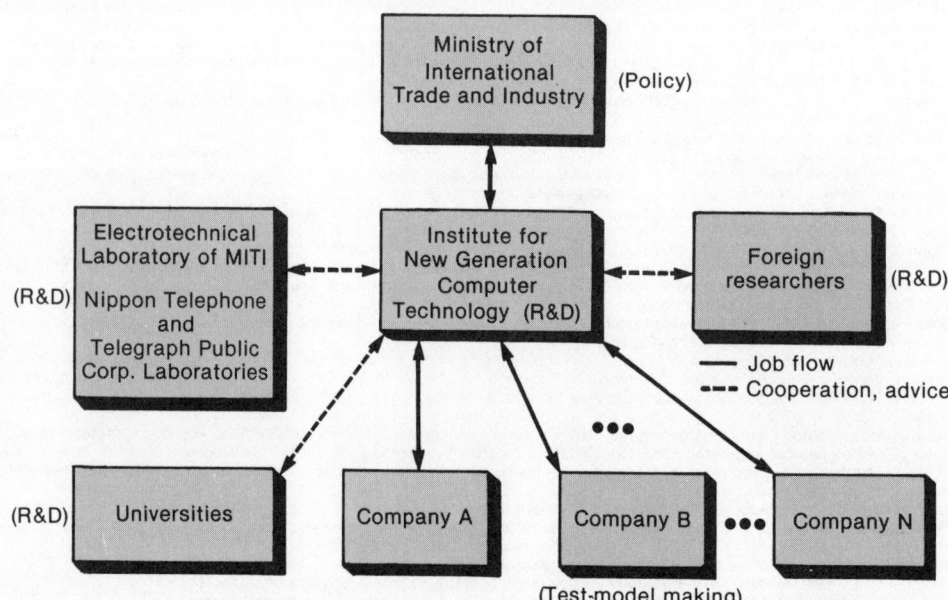

SOURCE: Trudy E. Bell, "Tomorrow's Computers—The Quest," IEEE Spectrum, November 1983.

industry, and government researchers. The 10 year span for these 26 projects is divided into three phases. Begun in 1982, the initial phase involves reviewing and evaluating research on knowledge processing and developing basic technology for the second phase. Hardware and software subsystems such as simulators, prototypes for language processing, and experimental natural language processing systems are being constructed for several experimental systems. The intermediate phase will attempt to develop subsystems for hardware and software as well as algorithms and basic architecture. The final stage will attempt to integrate software subsystems, hardware subsystems, and applications software in order to develop the first fifth-generation computer prototypes. These three phases of research within the seven different areas are illustrated in figure 48.[56]

Science and Technology Agency (STA)

The Science and Technology Agency (STA) is responsible for the overall coordination of social needs-oriented science and technology policy and expenditure in Japan. It is responsible for the planning, formulating and promotion of basic policies pertaining to science and technology, and for coordination of these policies and activities throughout the various

---

[56]See Richard Dolen, "Japan's Fifth-Generation Computer Project," *Scientific Bulletin*, U.S. Department of the Navy, vol. 7, No. 3, July-September 1982, pp. 63-97, and "Research and Development Plans for Fifth Generation Computer Systems," Japanese Embassy, April 1982.

Figure 48.—Concept Diagram Showing How Research and Development Are to Progress in the Fifth Generation Computer Systems Project

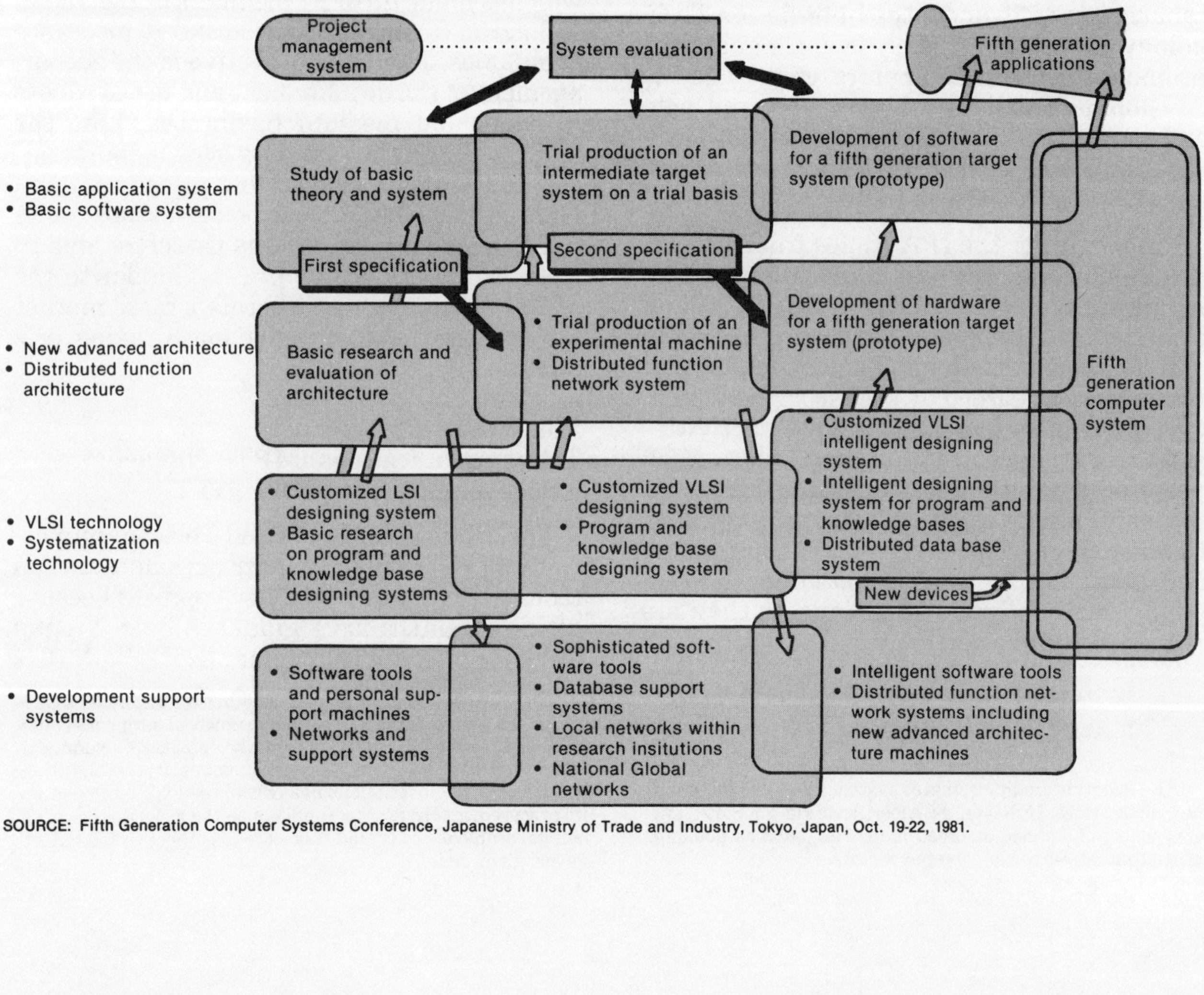

SOURCE: Fifth Generation Computer Systems Conference, Japanese Ministry of Trade and Industry, Tokyo, Japan, Oct. 19-22, 1981.

government ministries. STA has jurisdiction over councils, research institutes and development agencies which mainly concentrate on technological developments in nuclear energy, space and ocean development, aviation technology, and laser technology. Practically none of STA's budget directly supports industrial R&D; therefore, information technology R&D which is categorized as an industrial area, is not widely influenced by STA. However, approximately half of the STA budget indirectly supports information technology R&D through procurement of information and communication technology equipment and facilities for its agencies' activities.

Information Technology Promotion Agency (IPA)

Another government organization aimed at developing and disseminating information and computer systems is the Information Technology Promotion Agency (IPA), which was established in 1970 under the Information Technology Promotion Agency law. Its goal is to promote the use of computers, encourage the development and use of programs, and help software firms. It is the only national organization in the field of software promotion in Japan.

Financing for the IPA comes from government subsidies, private corporations, three long-term credit banks (the Industrial Bank of Japan, the Japanese Development Bank, and the Long-term Credit Bank of Japan), and from revenues earned by the association itself. One of the more important of IPA's activities is its credit guarantee programs. Information processing firms and software houses are often in need of funds to develop software programs, but have limited property that can be used as collateral. The IPA has a system for guaranteeing such obligations, as long as they are registered with the IPA.[57]

Japan Electronic Computer Co. (JECC) and Japan Robot Leasing Co. (JAROL)

Assistance is also provided by the Japan Electronic Computer Co. (JECC), which borrows money from the Japan Development Bank (JDB) and also from private banks. It is a jointly owned firm that purchases computers from participating manufacturers and leases them to customers. In 1980, the Japan Development Bank provided $263 million to the JECC, $218 million in 1981, and approximately $100 million in 1982. When the JECC was first established, it provided major support for the Japanese computer industry; however, as the financial resources of these companies increases, the Japanese computer companies have become less dependent on government subsidy and are establishing their own leasing operations.

The Japanese Government also helped to establish the Japan Robot Lease Co. (JAROL) which is made up of 24 members of the Japan Industrial Robot Association and 10 insurance companies. JAROL's objective is the encouragement of the development and use of robots in small and medium businesses. Like the JECC, JAROL buys robots from manufacturers and leases them at low prices to small businessmen. JAROL also receives most of its funds from the JDB and is therefore able to lease its robots at low prices. Similar to the JECC, JAROL aims to create a mass market for robot technology while encouraging production.

Ministry of Posts and Telecommunications (MPT): Nippon Telegraph and Telephone (NTT)

The Ministry of Posts and Telecommunications (MPT) indirectly influences information technology research and development because of its administrative guidance over Nippon Telegraph and Telephone (NTT).[58] NTT's

---

[57]An IPA-style credit guarantee system is not uncommon in the United States. However, the American credit guarantee systems tend to be aimed at broad industries, such as housing, rather than at narrowly targeted sectors.

[58]There is some contention over whether NTT should be classified as a nongovernmental or governmental entity. Because NTT receives no direct funding from the Japanese Government some argue that NTT is not a government entity. On the other hand, the U.S. Government has encouraged NTT to open up its procurements to foreign suppliers on the grounds that NTT is a government entity and therefore is subject to the GATT government code.

budget, services, tariffs, and overall policies, as well as appointments of top officials, are subject to MPT's review and approval. However, NTT has not received a government subsidy for over 30 years; in fact, over the last 3 years NTT has returned to the Japanese Government on request approximately $2 billion. This contrasts sharply with the idea that the Japanese Government heavily subsidizes information technology R&D.

NTT is the domestic public telecommunications monopoly in Japan, although it does not have any manufacturing capability within the organization. NTT, as the owner of virtually all the telephone lines in Japan, remains the most powerful single entity in Japanese telecommunications. NTT accounts for about three-quarters of the Japanese market for telecommunications and data communications, equipment, and services. As a result, NTT with its demands for new equipment and services has a powerful influence on Japanese information technology research and development—more so than MITI.

Typically, new communications products destined for NTT use are initiated in one of its four Electrical Communications Laboratories (ECL). NTT spends approximately 2 percent of its revenue on R&D (which amounted to more than $350 million in 1980), mainly at ECL labs. This system of labs corresponds to Bell Labs although it is approximately one-fifth of the size of its U.S. counterpart. ECL tends to do more developmental R&D rather than the basic research for which Bell Labs has been so widely acclaimed. Much of the research carried out at NTT's labs is devoted to achieving the extremely detailed and demanding specifications that the company requires when it issues R&D contracts to private firms.

More often, NTT launches research in collaboration with one or more of the four major Japanese electronics firms (NEC, Fujitsu, Hitachi, and Oki Electric), which actually send staff to the NTT labs. The subsidized joint research normally results in NTT's appointment of a preferred supplier from among the researchers when the time comes to purchase the product. Because NTT is one of the largest information technology and telecommunications markets in Japan, most electronics firms cooperate with NTT. Competition often develops between these firms in efforts to be selected as partners in new technologies and systems developments.

NTT divides its procurement procedures practices into three tiers or "tracks" which have been agreed to in the General Agreement on Trade and Tariffs (GATT) and other bilateral trade agreements:[59]

Track I (competitive bidding) is applied to products to be procured based on the Government Procurement Code agreed to by the General Agreement on Trade and Tariffs (GATT). These procurements usually include off-the-shelf products such as PBXs, data terminals, modems, computers, peripherals, facsimile machines, measurement instruments, etc.

Track II is applied to equipment that is not available in the marketplace and which requires some research and development. This track generally refers to products for which a limited amount of collaboration between the supplier and NTT is necessary to tailor applications to NTT's specifications. Track II contracts are normally single-company contracts.

Track III is applied to equipment not available in the marketplace and which requires extensive R&D for NTT use. These are the most highly prized contracts and the most difficult for foreign or small companies to penetrate. NTT seeks a supplier with sufficient research ability to develop a product, or to develop one according to an NTT prototype.

In addition, there are Tracks IIA and IIIA that allow for new producers to take over expired Track II and III contracts.

U.S. and other foreign telecommunications equipment manufacturers have suggested that NTT's close collaborative R&D activities with several Japanese companies prevent them from penetrating the Japanese telecommuni-

---
[59]Jack Osborn, outgoing telegram from the U.S. Embassy in Tokyo, Japan, Oct. 21, 1983, 7 pages.

cations market. With a 20:1 trade deficit in telecommunications equipment and a substantial Japanese penetration of certain U.S. market niches, many U.S. companies would like to balance some of these telecommunications trade deficits.[60] Moreover, other motivations for insisting on participating in the Japanese market relate to the changing balance in American and Japanese research and development. Just as the Japanese presence in the American market has a dual purpose—exports and the transfer of technology—so might American participation in Japanese markets and R&D activities serve two functions.

The issue of NTT's procurement policy can be best viewed within the framework of the plans for liberalization of the entire Japanese telecommunications monopoly. Because a large amount of NTT's profits (last year's profit was $1.6 billion) goes to the Japanese Government ($600 million) which needs revenue in the face of its continuing deficits, NTT cannot make a large profit. Another fiscal constraint is the rapidly decreasing rate of growth in the number of telephone users. More than 90 percent of Japanese households now have telephones, which means that the traditional market (revenue) has leveled off. In addition, NTT is in the process of testing and eventually implementing its ambitious 20-year all-digital Information Network System (INS) program, which is expected to cost up to $120 billion by 1990.

To solve these financial problems, Prime Minister Nakasone is supporting a major four step reform plan recommended last year by a special study group commissioned to study the Japanese Government. The plan, now under discussion, would first convert NTT to an incorporated government-owned entity. NTT would then be free, however, to set its own management and personnel policies. Under the proposed plan, many operations, such as data communications services, would be delegated to spin-off companies operating at a regional level—somewhat like the pattern of the AT&T divestiture in the United States.

Hisashi Shinto, the new chairman of NTT, believes that transforming the massive bureaucratic Japanese telecommunications monopoly into a partly private company will be more profitable, while encouraging greater competition and innovation in the telecommunications and information technologies industries. It is believed that more Japanese companies will be encouraged to vie both for NTT's business and for the private telecommunications market previously controlled by NTT and its selected family of suppliers.

Kokusai Denshin Denwa Ltd. (KDD)

The KDD operates Japan's international telephone, telegraph, and other related communications services.[61] Divided from NTT in 1953, it is 90 percent privately owned, with 10 percent of its stock held by NTT. At the time of the inauguration of KDD, the international telecommunications research group of the Electrical Communication Laboratories of NTT was transferred from NTT and reorganized as KDD's Research Department. By 1969, a development center was created and the department was renamed Research and Development Laboratories. The laboratories, located in Meguro, Tokyo, employ more than 120 R&D personnel and are composed of 12 special purpose laboratories and three divisions.

A new laboratory being built in the Nerima suburb of Tokyo, will be completed in 1985. This R&D reinforcement will permit further research and development concentration in such fields as switching for integrated digital networks, fiber-optic submarine cable transmission, satellite digital transmission, optical-memory disks, system converison techniques, wideband video, etc. To help in this effort, KDD expects to add 50 more engineers to its R&D staff by 1988.

---

[60]In 1982 the Japanese exported more than $408 million in telecommunications equipment to the United States. During this same period, Japan imported less than $88 million of this same equipment from the United States. Peter J. Hann, "Data Communications in Japan," *Data Communications*, August 1983, p. 56.

[61]Yasuo Makino, "Telecommunications in Japan: Changing Policies in a Changing World," *Telecommunications*, October 1983, pp. 139-145.

Defense Agency

Because of Japan's small national market for defense equipment, Japanese defense research and development activities are fairly limited. Overall, Japanese procurement of defense equipment accounts for less than four-tenths of 1 percent of total Japanese industrial production.

Within the Defense Technical Research Institute there are very small-scale development projects on electronics equipment (radar, etc.) with a budget of ¥ 1.3 billion ($5.6 million) in fiscal year 1982, ¥ 0.6 billion ($2.6 million) in fiscal year 1983, and ¥ 3.8 billion ($16.5 million) in fiscal year 1984. These projects are done in cooperation with private firms. In addition, the Defense Agency indirectly supports information technology R&D by purchasing hardware for testing purposes from private electronics firms.

As a result of economic trends in both the United States and Japan, as well as a changing international security environment, there have been growing tensions over trade and defense issues. In general, some Americans believe that the low level of Japanese military expenditures frees funds for civilian research and investment while requiring higher taxes and absorbing resources in the United States which in turn provides defense.[62] As a result, the U.S. Government believes that Japan should increase its military strength as well as information technology R&D expenditures for military applications. Moreover, U.S. companies argue that an inequality exists between United States and Japanese trade: no manufactured U.S. civilian product (with the single exception of airplanes) has captured as much as 10 percent of the Japanese market, while approximately 14 percent of Japanese defense equipment is purchased by the United States.[63]

---

[62]David Denon, "Japan and the U.S.—The Security Agenda," *Current History,* November 1983, p. 355.
[63]Stephen J. Solarz, "A Search for Balance," *Foreign Affairs,* p. 75.

Japan Development Bank (JDB)

The Japan Development Bank (JDB) is another government financial intermediary used to target industrial development. The Japanese Government's Trust Fund Bureau (which is the main organization in its Fiscal Investment Loan Program) provides JDB with its main source of capital, though it can also raise funds by issuing certain types of bonds. JDB's principal responsibility has been the extension of long term, low interest loans for capital investment in new industries. In the years immediately after its formation, JDB concentrated on loans for the reconstruction of basic manufacturing industries.

As a result of the consensus to increase the support for "knowledge-intensive" industries, the JDB began to target support for what it terms "development of technology." The funding categories in area of development of technology are illustrated in table 43. Most of the computer funds, as a matter of policy, have gone to the JECC, although some software firms have also received funding. For the other funding areas for technology development, there are two general JDB loan programs. Both of these loan programs, which resemble MITI's seed money grants, attempt to stimulate private investment in specific areas of information technology R&D. The first loan program, set up under a 1978 law, amounted to ¥ 10 billion ($43.3 million) in 1981. Loans from this program must be directed toward specific project areas designated by cabinet order. Should a designated project area be oversubscribed (as happened with semiconductors), JDB can force larger firms that have better access to private financial markets to utilize those markets, while JDB loans are preserved for the smaller firms.

The other technology development loan program was established by the bank itself and not designated by specific laws, though it still falls within the broad policy guidelines of the government. This part of the JDB budget totaled ¥ 44 billion ($190.5 million) in 1981.

Table 43.—Japan Development Bank Loans for Development of Technology (in billions of yen)

	Fiscal year 1977	Fiscal year 1978	Fiscal year 1979	Fiscal year 1980	
New loans	¥71.2	¥129.0	¥108.5	¥96.4	$457[a]
Development of electronic computers	38.2	55.3	47.1	55.4	262
Domestically-manufactured computers	35.5	53.5	45.0	54.0	256
Computer manufacturing plants	0.4	0.2	0.4	0.6	3
Data processing systems	2.3	1.6	1.7	0.8	3
Use of high technology in certain electronic and machinery industries	8.3	7.8	10.2	14.5	69
Electronic industry	3.8	2.1	7.0	12.0	57
Machinery industry	4.5	5.7	3.2	2.5	12
Development of domestic technology	24.7	65.9	51.2	26.5	126
Development of new technology	20.4	57.4	40.9	22.6	107
Trial manufacturing for commercial use	0.9	4.0	1.2	0.3	2
Development of heavy machinery	3.4	4.5	9.1	3.6	17

[a]In millions of dollars.

SOURCES: *U.S. Facts and Figures About the Japan Development Bank,* Japan Development Bank, 1981, p. 26; and Jimmy W. Wheeler, Merit E. Janow, Thomas Pepper, and Midori Yamamato, "Japanese Industrial Development Policies in the 1980's: Implications for U.S. Trade and Investment," Hudson Institute Inc., 1982, for the U.S. Department of State.

These loans are devoted to new domestic technologies and initial manufacturing efforts for commercialization of these new technologies. Firms that believe that they have developed a process or technology falling within the broad parameters established by the cabinet must apply in order to be considered for loans; JDB does not solicit customers. The firm's proposal is submitted to a council of scientific advisors, which evaluates the proposal. If the technology is approved, the applicant then faces an evaluation of credit worthiness and of the financial characteristics of its loan application. If the applicant is a large company with well established financial links, it must concurrently seek private financing, because JDB will provide only partial funding. If the applicant is small, and has relatively weak financial links, or if the project is large-scale or viewed as a high priority for the nation, then the JDB may take a lead role in putting together a consortium to finance the project. Finally, by general agreement, the JDB only finances the first plant in a new area. Its role is to help launch new technology, not to provide low cost financing for the expansion of industry.

The small size of the JDB loans indicates that the importance of government's financial mediary role "stems not from outright control or from overall size, but rather from socializing risks, coordinating private investments, and processing information."[64]

University

The Ministry of Education, Culture, and Science (MOE) funds research at three research institutes, six National Institutes (for joint use by universities), and 93 national universities.

Among the various national universities in Japan, the big seven are the universities of Tokyo, Kyoto, Osaka, Tohoku, Hokkaido, Nagoya, and Kyushu. In the area of information technology, Tokyo University has activities in several departments: information science (in the Faculty of Science), information engineering and precision engineering (in the Faculty of Engineering), as well as a large central computer center. In most of the other universities, there is just one department (usually in the Faculty of Engineering), as well as a sizeable central computer center. Kyoto University claims to have the oldest information engineering department and is considered a close rival to the University of Tokyo. Other national universities that have significant

---

[64]Eisuke Sakakibara, Robert Feldman, and Yuzo Harada, "The Japanese Financial System in Comparative Perspective," a study prepared for the use of the Joint Economic Committee (Washington, DC: U.S. Congress, U.S. Government Printing Office, Mar. 12, 1982), p. 11.

computer science departments include Tsukuba University and the Tokyo Institute of Technology. Among private institutions, only Keio University and Waseda University are considered to have sizeable computer science programs.

Higher education has become an important social investment in Japan. Between 1960 and 1975, the numbers of students in higher education multiplied by more than three times (to 2.2 million), including students in Japan's junior colleges (post high-school institutions concerned with teacher training, technical education, etc.). Of the 1.73 million undergraduates enrolled at Japanese universities in 1981, approximately 334,000 were enrolled in engineering studies (exactly six times as many students in the natural sciences, including mathematics). Many universities have no science faculty, only engineering departments. These large numbers of engineering students indicate the heavy emphasis placed on engineering in Japan. Consequently, Japan continues to maintain a large engineering manpower base. However, a small percentage of these engineering students continue on to graduate study where they could contribute to basic university research. For instance, in Japan, the proportion of graduate research students to the entire undergraduate student population is 3 percent. In the United Kingdom the proportion is over 19 percent; in France 22 percent; and in the United States 12 percent.[65] Although Japan has more undergraduate students enrolled in electrical and electronics engineering programs than the United States, Japan has approximately one-fourth as many electrical and electronic engineering graduate students as the United States. Because students at the graduate level make a large contribution to basic R&D in university environments, the low number of Japanese graduate engineering and science students has been cited as one reason for such a small amount of university research in Japan. In this context it is also worth noting that Japanese companies, which prefer to train their own development engineers, like to recruit young inexperienced persons—recruiting them before they go on to postgraduate work.

Recently, there has been concern that the environment for information technology basic research has generally not been adequate at Japanese universities. In addition to the inadequate number of graduate students, two other causes for the small amount of information technology basic research activities in Japanese universities have also been cited.

Some researchers believe that the heavy emphasis on rote learning in Japanese schools has helped to suppress creativity in the learning process. Moreover, the importance of severe university entrance examinations has been seen as a deterrence to specially talented or creative students.

Researchers usually cite two indices of success in orginality and successful basic research—the number of Nobel Prize winners and the frequency with which scientists' work is cited by other researchers. Japan has had four Nobel Prize winners. The citation index devised by the Institute of Scientific Information in the United States includes 19 Japanese researchers (and roughly half of those worked in American laboratories) among the 1,000 international scientists accredited with the most frequent citations in the scientific literature.[66]

A second major factor affecting basic research in university environments is the level of government funding. More than 98.8 percent of R&D expenditures at national and public universities was funded by the government and only 1.2 percent by private industry.[67] In 1979, universities spent approximately $3.69 milion for R&D: national and public universities spent $2.459 million, and private universities spent $1.15 million. The funds for research are distributed by the Ministry of

---

[65]*The Economist*, Aug. 6, 1983, p. 65.

[66]The citation system however, does not take into account the fact that very few Western scientists are able to read the Japanese scientific literature that is published in Japanese. See March 1984 hearings held by the House Science and Technology Committee on Japanese science and technology information.

[67]Michiyuki Venohara, Nippon Electric Company, Ltd., "Japanese Social System for Technological Development—Its Merits and Demerits," presented on Dec. 8, 1982 in Endohoven, Netherlands, p. 21.

Education in the form of formula support and project research grants.

Through formula support the government provides each Department Chairman with three posts, two assistant professors and one research assistant or vice versa. In each engineering or information science department or other related department, the chairman is given approximately ¥ 7 million ($28,000) to spend on research. Half of these funds may be kept by the university to cover administration costs. As a result, many departments are left with approximately ¥ 2 million ($8,000).

The research project grants, totaling ¥ 40,000 million ($160 million), also appear to be insufficient because of their short term and small amount. A limitation is that the funds cannot be used for recruiting short-term assistance because most researchers (as well as most Japanese workers) enjoy life-time employment. The Japanese Government began in 1982 to award 3 or 4-year support for research projects, each costing approximately $1 million.

Although funding levels for basic research are sometimes perceived as being inadequate, the equipment in university laboratories has been described as adequate by one recent American visitor to the University of Tokyo labs:

> In general, both in the industrial as well as in the university laboratories, the impression I got was of a lot of equipment, some old, some new, mixed in a somewhat random fashion. In the university laboratories, in particular, space seems to be at a premium. There does not, however, appear to be any shortage of new equipment.[68]

Research and Development Links Between Universities and Industry

Direct cooperation between universities and industries in basic and applied R&D has been relatively limited. Japanese companies do not encourage students to obtain work experience in private industry. Furthermore, most Japanese firms do not generally look to universities for innovative ideas; the larger, more important firms prefer to carry out their own basic research. Some university professors in Japan have accused Japanese firms of suffering from a "not invented here syndrome" and this has caused a great mistrust between industry and university faculty. A further factor is that the Ministry of Education, which is the direct employer of university staff, actively discourages direct links between academics and companies. Professors at state universities are forbidden to consult for private firms because it could lead to nepotism in obtaining appointments.

The most effective channel for university-industry collaboration in Japan is through informal personal links. In comparison with other countries Japanese graduates remain in close contact with each other throughout their professional careers. This leads to valuable cooperation between academics and industrialists, particularly in research. This is reinforced by the role university professors play (as employees of the Ministry of Education) in the establishment and implementation of national research programs, such as the VLSI project and the Fifth-Generation Computer Systems Project. The presence of academics in the controlling bodies of these projects helps to exchange research results between companies and universities more effectively.

Other cases of informal collaboration include exchanges of researchers between companies and industries. For example, the Electronics Department at the University of Tokyo currently has five visiting researchers from well known Japanese electronics companies for periods of 1 or 2 years. Also the department receives grants from at least 10 companies to be used for purchasing equipment. The arrangement for visiting researchers from industry has some similarity to the U.K.'s Teaching Company Scheme, but the emphasis seems to be on the industrialist working in the universities rather than on the academic working in industry environments.

---

[68]Derek L. Lile, "Japanese Laboratory Visits," *Scientific Bulletin,* Department of the Navy, Office of Naval Research, Far East, January—May 1983, p. 48.

Collaboration between companies and university departments is also aided by the practice of using universities as "shop windows" for new equipment that is often given or sold to them at very low prices. Through university use of new equipment, firms receive feedback on the operation of new equipment and often valuable suggestions for modifications and extensions. Instances of this practice can be found in the areas of computers (Fujitsu) and telecommunication receivers (NEC).

Another recent government incentive for industry-university R&D collaboration concerns patents. As government employees, university staff in Japan were not allowed to profit from the commercial exploitation of their ideas. This has created a disincentive to patenting, while promoting dissemination of results through open publications. Currently academic researchers are being encouraged to apply for patents and at least two universities have set up special offices to facilitate the patent application process (Tokyo Institute of Technology and Tohoku University). This could be to make research results more attractive to private firms, which can in turn apply for licenses in order to market the technology.

As the technological level of Japanese industries approaches that of other advanced nations and the innovation of original technologies is more widely demanded by domestic as well as foreign markets, the need has been voiced by Japanese industrial and government circles for much closer cooperation between industry and university researchers. As a result, the Japanese Government is also encouraging closer research links between universities, industrial firms, and government institutions through the development of research parks, such as Tsukuba Science City.

Industry

To compete in global markets, Japanese information technology industries, in general, are large-scale organizations in order to assure maximum economies of scale and to sustain the large amounts of capital necessary for continued innovation. Although there are many smaller electronic firms in Japan, most of them subcontract small-scale production or fill special niches (some in global markets) which require custom or batch labor intensive production technologies. In general, however, major information technology firms are more diversified and highly integrated than other competitor nations' industries. For example, Japanese firms competing in the semiconductor markets are significantly larger in total sales and assets than their U.S. counterparts—approximately two to four times larger than Texas Instruments and Motorola, and much larger than National Semiconductor, Fairchild, and Intel.[69]

In addition to large-scale operations, many of the major Japanese information technology firms are vertically integrated. For example, most computer manufacturers produce semiconductors and several of them are major semiconductor suppliers in the world market. This sharply contrasts with the United States where, although most computer manufacturers have at least some in-house semiconductor development and production capability, only a few firms market both semiconductor chips and computers, and most of them do not

---

[69]Gene Adrian Gregory, and Akio Etori, "Japanese Technology Today, the Electronic Revolution Continues," *Scientific American supplement*, 1983, p. J, 22.

Photo credit: Overseas Public Affairs Office, Electronic Industries Association of Japan

Semiconductor research

sell the large range of products that are available from Japanese companies.

Another type of structural integration that is believed to give the Japanese a competitive advantage is in the area of consumer products. Compared to many American computer manufacturers that specialize in their production capabilities, Japanese firms which manufacture computers are also large producers of consumer electronics products. Because consumer electronics products usually have a large market and generate large sales revenues, Japanese firms can utilize these large profits to fund research and development projects in other information technology areas.

As a result of structural integration, namely, production and development of computers in conjunction with telecommunications equipment, and consumer products coupled with integrated semiconductor development and production capabilities, the Japanese information technology firms may have a strong technological base from which to continue their innovation process. Moreover, because of their vertical integration, Japanese information technology firms can draw on cash flow generated by consumer electronics sales to sustain large capital investments and research and development costs of basic research.

Japanese information technology firms also participate in cooperative joint R&D programs. Because there is relatively low technology transfer between Japanese firms (due to lifetime employment of engineers and fierce competition between firms), they often undertake identical research projects. The efforts of limited numbers of research engineers in each company are therefore spread out across many different areas, making it difficult to concentrate on basic research. In response to these difficulties, the Japanese Government created research associations so that industries could collaborate on research projects centered on different technology areas.[70]

---

[70]See the section on MITI for a description of the industrial participation in the research associations.

Because of the highly competitive nature of the electronics firms, industrial researchers were at first extremely skeptical about these research associations. However, the area of cooperation is limited to very basic research, and development efforts are still necessary to develop commercial products. The basic research efforts generally leave many possible avenues for future product development and allow firms to compete with one another. Because of their wide acceptance and heavy industry participation, these joint R&D programs have been useful to Japanese industry.

NEC Corp.

NEC Corp. is Japan's largest manufacturer of communications equipment with fiscal 1982 sales totaling $4.98 billion and a pretax profit of $204 million. In 1982 sales to NTT and the Japanese Government agencies accounted for $888 million, or 19 percent of NEC's revenues, of which a significant portion was for data communications. Foreign purchasers accounted for 30 percent of NEC's sales. NEC has a strong position in the world market (including several plants in the United States), and it markets over 14,000 products in over 100 countries worldwide. NEC has also produced the distributed information-processing network architecture (DIMA) on which 60 to 70 percent of all networks in Japan are now based. NEC's success in part can be attributed to the fact that it is a vertically integrated supplier with strong shares of the Japanese computer, communications, and semiconductor markets. Internationally, NEC is known for having installed over half of all satellite earth stations and for its microwave technology. NEC's vertical integration activities are best summed up by Michiyuki Uenohara:

> Combining computers and communications (C + C) was conceived as a form of business best suited for our expansion into new areas, making the most of technological resources we have as a company that started out as a communications equipment maker. It was in 1975 that the concept was put into practical business programs, and in 1977, we

came up with a clear-cut expression of C + C. First of all, we achieved the ability to put on the market a digital switching system which can serve as a link between communications and computer networks. Digital switching has made the combination of computers and communications not only possible, but natural.[71]

NEC's central research laboratory, located just outside Tokyo in the city of Kawasaki, houses approximately 700 scientists involved in research on a wide variety of subjects related to computers and communications. Specific research includes projects on GaAs circuit development and semiconductor surface treatment.

Fujitsu Ltd.

Fujitsu is Japan's largest mainframe vendor, and ranks second to NEC in telecommunications equipment sales. Fujitsu is now ranked sixth in the world, ahead of Honeywell (U.S.), CII-Honeywell Bull (France), ICL (U.K.), and Siemens (West Germany). With fiscal 1982 sales of about $3.36 billion, telecommunications equipment accounted for $638 million of Fujitsu's total sales. Sales to NTT accounted for 37 percent and sales to the Japanese commercial market were 27 percent of Fujitsu's total sales. Similar to NEC, Fujitsu is well established in the world information technology market, with a solid history of sales in the United States. Currently, Fujitsu is manufacturing and marketing digital PBXs in a joint venture with American Telecommunications Corp., and microcomputers and terminals in a joint venture with TRW, Inc. Other joint venture partners include Canadian, West German, and Spanish companies. Although Fujitsu ranks second to NEC in microwave equipment, carrier transmission, and automated office equipment, it is a leader in Japan's fiber optics and optoelectronics research.

[71]Gene Adrian Gregory and Akio Etori, "Japanese Technology Today, The Electronic Revolution Continues," *Scientific American, Special Supplement,* 1984, p. J, 44.

The "tsu" in the title Fujitsu means communications and this was the basis of the Fujitsu laboratories. However, because of a perceived saturation of the communications field, Fujitsu decided to diversify and as a result, communications equipment now occupies a minor part of Fujitsu's research operations. Approximately 60 percent of the research activities is currently devoted to computer and computer-related research. The Fujitsu Laboratories, also located in Kawasaki, employ approximately 800 people. The semiconductor division consists of 190 people divided into three main subgroups: GaAs devices and circuits, silicon integration, and materials. Because its research is well advanced in the semiconductor division, Fujitsu is expected to play an important role in the Japanese supercomputer project.

Hitachi Ltd.

Hitachi is Japan's third largest company (after Nippon Steel Corp. and Toyota Ltd.). It entered the computer market in the late 1950s and was one of the first Japanese companies to enter into a technology exchange agreement with a U.S. computer manufacturer (RCA in 1961). Since then, Hitachi has made agreements with Intel. During 1978-80, Hitachi also completed marketing arrangements for its computer systems in Europe with BASF (West Germany), Olivetti (Italy), and St. Gobain (France).

Hitachi generated more than $3.3 billion in fiscal 1982 (out of total sales of $15 billion) from information and communications systems and other electronics devices. Although Hitachi has in the past maintained a strong position in the consumer electronics market, the company is placing more emphasis on industrial electronic equipment. As a result, Hitachi is attempting to evolve into an integrated office systems supplier in the United States. Hitachi is concentrating some of its efforts on the development and marketing of PBXs.

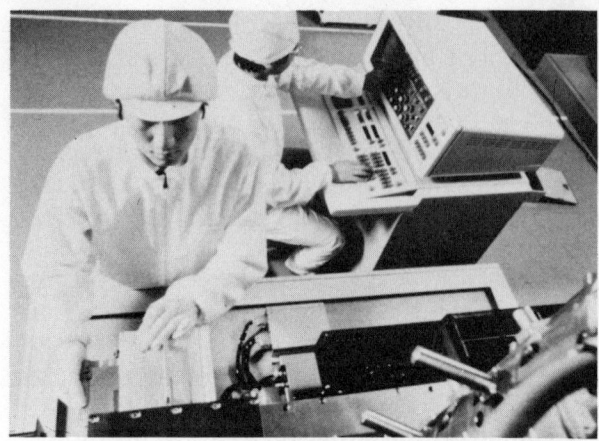

Photo credit: Overseas Public Affairs Office, Electronic Industries Association of Japan

A Hitachi engineer feeds a glass plate into an electron beam lithography device which produces a photomask by drawing LSI patterns on the plate with a sharply focused electron beam under high-precision computer control. The device is also capable of directly writing patterns on silicon wafers.

Hitachi has rapidly increased research and development expenditures. Hitachi's Central Research Laboratory at Kokubunji is one of the five Hitachi research labs and is devoted to the development of new materials and devices as well as new measurement equipment, medical engineering equipment, and communications and information processing systems. The laboratory, established in 1942, employs approximately 1,200 research and support personnel. Their principal integrated circuit research project is aimed at developing a 1K bit static RAM for use in the central processing unit (CPU) and main memory of large computers. Other projects that are also currently underway include the development of GaAs, analog circuits for automobile telephones, and semiconductor material research. There is also research taking place in lasers, light-emitting diodes (LEDs) and light detectors, and some preliminary work in electro-optic integration.

Oki Electric Industry Corp.

Oki Electric Industry Corp. was one of Japan's first entrants into the computer market with its transistorized OKITAC 6020 in 1959. Oki-Univac Company Ltd. was formed in September 1963 to manufacture various Univac-based machines in Japan. Since that time, Oki has not engaged in the development of large computers. However, it remains strong in peripherals and terminals. In 1972, Oki established subsidiaries in the United States to produce and market communications equipment and computer peripherals, terminals, and components, and has subsequently set up similar operations in Germany and Brazil.

Oki Electric Industry Corp. had fiscal 1982 sales of $1.03 billion, of which telecommunications sales to NTT totaled $185 million and those to government entities another $94 million. Oki also exported approximately $120 million in equipment, mainly digital printers, to the United States. In July, the company announced that it will build a plant in Atlanta, Ga., to produce mobile cellular radio telephones for a subsidiary of AT&T. The facility is expected to produce 1.5 million units a year eventually.

France

Introduction

The historically agrarian society of France has changed with tremendous speed since World War II. In 1945 over half of the French population was dependent on agriculture for its income; by 1970 that dependency had been reduced to between 7 and 8 percent.[72] Information technology, particularly telecommunications, has been a major component of this

---

[72]Pierre Aigrain, "Seminar on High Technology in France," Center for Strategic and International Studies, Georgetown University, Feb. 9, 1983.

change. French efforts to expand advanced information technology research and production have been directed toward two major goals: strengthening France's international competitiveness and the development of an information technology-based infrastructure for the preservation and continued development of French culture and society. Coupled with historic French governmental involvement in industry,[73] the comparatively small size of French participation in the world market for information technology, and the unique French social and political contexts for technology, these goals have shaped French information technology research and development into a pattern quite unlike that in the United States.

French information technology research and development activities occur in government laboratories, in industrial settings, and in academic environments. The structure, organization, and direction of R&D activities within these communities are all dissimilar, however, from the American experience. The pervasiveness of government intervention in industrial and academic sectors makes it difficult to differentiate the three areas, but for ease of comparison with the American experience, French government, university, and industry information technology research and development environments are discussed separately below. Before discussing these environments, it is important to understand the size of French participation in information technology, and the social and recent political environments for the conduct of information technology research and development.

The Size of French Participation in Information Technology Markets

In 1982 the French estimated that they controlled about 5 percent of the world market in information technology. This compares with

Photo credit: Scientific Mission, Embassy of France and Ministere des PTT, French Government

Videotex terminal "Minitel"

a United States share of 48 percent in 1982. Moreover, if one were to compute the French share of the world market using information technology goods and services produced exclusively by French-controlled corporations, the share would decline to 4 percent.[74]

Slightly over one-half of the French information market is served by foreign suppliers; the United States holds about 22 percent of the market, Japan and West Germany 7 percent each. The Netherlands holds 6 percent

---

[73]The French Government has traditionally played a large role in the coordination, funding, and direction of the French economy since Jean Baptiste Colbert founded the Academy of Sciences in 1666. French Governments since have changed the scope and nature of that involvement, but the traditional mechanisms used by government in industry, including those of the present French Government, have changed very little.

[74]French telecommunications and Electronics Council, *The Electronics Industry: U.S.A./France 1982*, pp. 10-18.

and Italy, the United Kingdom, Austria and others hold the remainder. Several major subsectors of the French market such as mainframe computers are nearly dominated by U.S. manufacturers. In areas of French strength within the French market (e.g., in telephone terminal and switching equipment, in which the French control about 91 percent of their market), French participation in the United States and/or world markets is often very small. For example, France has less than one-tenth of 1 percent of the U.S. market in telephone terminal and switching equipment. This situation may be more due to the structure of the U.S. telecommunications industry than any French inadequacy. In addition, the future French position in the U.S. telecommunications market may improve as both CIT Alcatel and Thomson CSF have recently established U.S. subsidiaries.[75]

The size of French participation in the markets for information technology affects the level of funds available for R&D. French industrial funding of information technology research and development was reported as $2.2 billion in 1982, some significant portion of which was funded by the government. In addition to information technology research and development in industrial settings, the civilian French governmental funding of information technology conducted in public laboratories was reported to be $0.6 billion in 1982.[76]

The Political Environment for French Information Technology Research and Development

It would be difficult to describe French information technology research and development activities without first considering the context of the present French Government's policy. The last French presidential election (1981) marked the first time science and technology were used as a political issues.[77] Indeed, all candidates had some increased R&D funding planks in their platforms. Before losing to Mr. Mitterrand, Mr. d'Estaing had designed a plan for increasing real government R&D funding 8 percent per year for 5 years beginning in 1980. When Mr. Mitterrand was elected, he more than doubled that goal.

Mr. Mitterrand's emphasis on increasing R&D spending was part of a larger industrial policy for France which included companion employment and education policies as well as planned market programs in several areas of high technology.[78] The overall government policy, designed around the Socialists' principles of decentralization, democratization, humanism, and volunteerism, included several elements.

The first element of the French Government's general policy was the declaration of information technology development as a national priority. Thus a major objective was to bring together universities, government laboratories, and industry to enhance national efforts in technological development.[79] The second element was to convince the French people of the importance of industry, a particularly necessary action in a country that has not yet completely integrated industrial activity among its values and culture. The third element of the French Government's policy was to create conditions for people to accept more readily changes in their work environment and social structure (caused by the introduction of new technologies), basically through a renewed social participation. This was viewed as a necessity for the continuous introduction of new technology. The fourth element consisted of the introduction of mechanisms to increase industrial investment. One of the major mechanisms for attracting investment in major industries has been the nationalization of major French industrial firms.

---

[75]Interview with Mr. Chavance, CIT Alcatel director, June 1983 and *Telephony,* July 25, 1983, p. 24.
[76]*A.F.P. Sciences,* No. 325, Oct. 7, 1982, p. 30.
[77]Pierre Aigrain, "The French Experience in High Technology," Center for Strategic and International Studies, Georgetown University, p. 2.

[78]"French Technology Preparing for the 21st Century," *Scientific American,* November 1982, p. F3.
[79]Robert Chabbal, "The New Investment in Science and Technology in France," in Thomas Langfitt, Sheldon Hackney, Alfred Fishnay, Albert Glowaske (eds.), *Partners in the Research Enterprise, University-Corporate Relations in Science and Technology* (Philadelphia: University of Pennsylvania Press), 1983, p. 138.

The first step taken by the Mitterand government was to establish a ministerial department for research and technology. One year later, the three ministries of research and technology, industry, and energy were combined to create one very large ministry called the Ministere de la Recherche et de l'Industrie. This ministry was created in part to stimulate interactions and exchanges between government and industry.

Another measure taken by the French Government was the nationalization of major industrial firms and most of the banking sector. Nationalism was viewed as a means of controlling investment and ensuring that the government could exert economic leverage to achieve its goals of: expanding employment; transforming the workplace environment; enhancing French productivity and competition; directing research and development into areas of government priority; and recapturing the domestic market by replacing imports with domestically produced products.[80] Moreover, government ownership was seen as means to enable those companies to receive ample funding for innovative, relatively high risk research and development.[81] Nationalization was also viewed as a mechanism to increase cooperation and technology transfer between industry and government.

The nationalization program was implemented in several stages over a period of 2 years.[82] Following several delays, the nationalization program was approved on February 11, 1984, giving the government control of 5 industrial groups, 39 banks, and 2 financial organizations.[83] In the information technology sector, almost every major company has been reorganized to reflect a majority of government ownership. For example, the government took over the central organizations (but not necessarily all the subsidiaries) of the Compagnie Generale d'Electricite, Saint Gobain Pont-a-Mousson, Pechiney-Ugine-Kuhlman, Rhone-Poulnec, and Thomson-Brandt. The government also acquired majority shares in Dassult and Matra, and later negotiated controlling or full ownership of three foreign-owned companies in France, Roussel-Uclaf, Cii-Honeywell-Bull, and I.T.T. France.

The actual effects of nationalization on the information technology industry and on the French economy as a whole are still uncertain. This uncertainty is created in part by the dominant role the French Government has played in the French economy throughout all of the postwar period, and in part by the confusion in the transition to Socialist industrial policy. Moreover, the effects of nationalization have also been obscured by France's economic decline in the first 2½ years of the Socialist government, which in turn has ultimately weakened the nationalization efforts to reshape or control the activities of specific firms or certain sectors of the economy.[84] Nationalization efforts have also been complicated by changes in three different ministers of the Ministere de la Recherche et de l'Industrie within a 2 year period.

Most significant to the general Mitterand strategy for the development of technology was the enactment of the legislation, Law for Programming and Orientation for Research, which established scientific and technological research and development as national priorities. Moreover, the law ensured funding for long-term scientific efforts by stipulating both quantitative and qualitative objectives for the following 5 years. The law stated that between 1981 and 1985 the percentage of the Gross National Product (GNP) devoted to research and development will increase from 1.8 to 2.5 percent, thereby increasing by 40 percent the spending for technological development in 5 years.[85] This process began in 1980 and there

---

[80]Michael H. Harrison, "France Under the Socialists," Current History, April 1984, p. 155.

[81]"Pitfalls in France's Vast R&D Plan," Business Week, Nov. 23, 1981, p. 94.

[82]Companies were actually nationalized on Feb. 11, 1982 (Law 82-155); however, the reorganization plans were not in effect until January 1983.

[83]Michael H. Harrison, "France Under the Socialists," Current History, April 1984, p. 155.

[84]Ibid.

[85]Robert Chabbal, "The New Investment in Science and Technology in France," in Thomas Langfitt, Sheldon Hackney, Alfred Fishnay, Albert Glowaske (eds.), Partners in the Research Enterprise, University—Corporate Relations in Science and Technology (Philadelphia: University of Pennsylvania Press), 1983, p. 140.

have been 12 percent annual increases in each of the three successive budgets.[86] The French Government's contribution will be matched by industry, which calls for industry to increase its expenditure for research and development by 40 percent in the next 5 years.[87]

In addition to meeting broadly the scientific and development needs, these increased expenditures are also for financing national mobilizing programs that are focused on industrial and government targeted priorities, such as information technology. Although there are major programs in biotechnology, new sources of energy, machine tools, etc., the information technology program is perhaps the most ambitious. La Filiere Electronique, implemented by the Mitterand government in 1983, is designed to coordinate and stimulate government, university, and industry information technology research and development efforts in order to move France into the forefront of advanced information technology R&D and production.[88] Figure 49 illustrates some of the coordination efforts between industry and government for La Filiere Electronique program. The 5-year infusion of F 140 billion (approximately $18.7 billion) for R&D is expected to accelerate the production of information technology products by 3 to 9 percent each year, produce a surplus trade balance in information technology products, and create 80,000 new jobs.

Fourteen national projects for research and development are outlined in La Filiere Electronique program:

- large scientific and industrial French computer,
- building blocks of mini- and micro-computing,
- consumer electronics systems,
- display technology,
- ergonomics of computerization,
- computer-assisted instruction,
- multiservice communications,
- widebank communications network,
- design and production assisted by very large scale integrated circuits,
- computer-assisted engineering design and production,
- voice-processing module,
- electrophotographic module,
- electronic editing, and
- computer-aided translation.

In addition to these projects and programs, the plan sets forth mechanisms for state/industrial cooperation and outlines efforts which are aimed at alleviating other constraints on information technology research and development not related to direct R&D funding. These include manpower programs to correct a perceived shortage of engineers and technicians and government-sponsored market promotion efforts.[89]

Because of economic difficulties, there have been some funding problems for the Mitterrand government. Consequently, the plans for an overall increase of 4.5 percent funding for research activities have suffered significantly. For most areas of research, this reduction in funding means that the 1984 research spending will remain at the same level as in 1983. However, the government has stressed that it will maintain its commitment to increase funds for high priority areas, including information technology.[90] Other impediments to La Filiere Electronique program and to French information technology research and develop-

---

[86]This increase occurred after 10 years of decreasing spending for scientific equipment and, therefore, the need was extremely acute.

[87]Robert Chabbal, "The New Investment in Science and Technology in France," in Thomas Langfitt, Sheldon Hackney, Alfred Fishnay, Albert Glowaske (eds.), *Partners in the Research Enterprise, University and Corporate Relations in Science and Technology* (Philadelphia: University of Pennsylvania Press, 1983) p. 140.

[88]A "filiere" in France is a targeted industry grouping or other goal around which a government plan for funding, production, investment, education and dissemination assistance has been developed. There are currently six filieres in France today: robotics, electronics, energy, biotechnology, work environments, and cooperation with developing countries.

[89]For example, the number of people with Level 1 qualifications in information technology (a French Masters degree, approximately equal to an American Ph.D.) is expected to fall short of needs by 70,000 for the period 1981-1990 in France. In the French context, this number is quite large; in 1979 it was estimated that 105,000 scientists and engineers were actively involved in all aspects of French science (energy, pharmaceuticals, mechanics, aeronautics agriculture, etc., as well as information technology). Jean-Pierre Letouzey, Scientific Mission, Embassy of France, *Statement for the American Association for the Advancement of Sciences,* Mar. 24, 1983, p. 9 (unnumbered).

[90]David Dickson, "Hard Times Force France to Cut Back Ambitious Plans to Support Science," *Chronicle of Higher Education,* Apr. 21, 1984, p. 10.

Ch. 7—Foreign Information Technology Research and Development • 251

Figure 49.—Recommended French Government/Industry/University Cooperation Relationships for Information Technology R&D

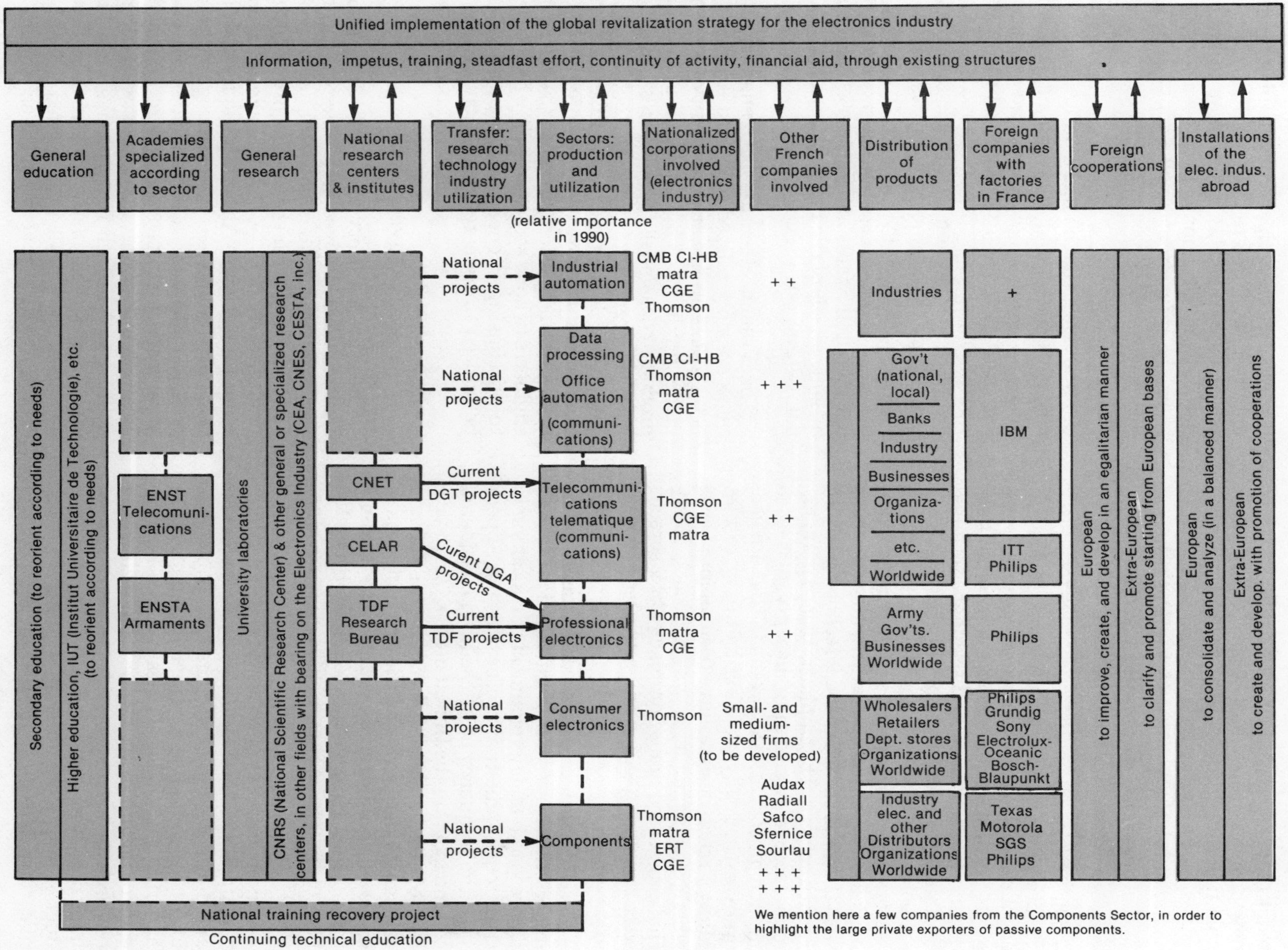

Unified implementation of the global revitalization strategy for the electronics industry

Information, impetus, training, steadfast effort, continuity of activity, financial aid, through existing structures

Categories (with arrows):
- General education
- Academies specialized according to sector
- General research
- National research centers & institutes
- Transfer: research technology industry utilization
- Sectors: production and utilization
- Nationalized corporations involved (electronics industry)
- Other French companies involved
- Distribution of products
- Foreign companies with factories in France
- Foreign cooperations
- Installations of the elec. indus. abroad

Secondary education (to reorient according to needs)

Higher education, IUT (Institut Universitaire de Technologie), etc. (to reorient according to needs)

University laboratories

CNRS (National Scientific Research Center) & other general or specialized research centers, in other fields with bearing on the Electronics Industry (CEA, CNES, CESTA, inc.)

ENST Telecommunications / ENSTA Armaments

CNET — Current DGT projects → Telecommunications telematique (communications)
CELAR — Current DGA projects → Professional electronics
TDF Research Bureau — Current TDF projects → Professional electronics

Sectors (relative importance in 1990):
- Industrial automation — CMB CI-HB matra CGE Thomson — ++
- Data processing / Office automation (communications) — CMB CI-HB Thomson matra CGE — +++
- Telecommunications telematique (communications) — Thomson CGE matra — +++
- Professional electronics — Thomson matra CGE — ++
- Consumer electronics — Thomson — ++
- Components — Thomson matra ERT CGE — +++

National projects (dashed arrows to each sector)

Industries:
- Gov't (national, local), Banks, Industry, Businesses, Organizations, etc. Worldwide — IBM
- ITT, Philips
- Philips
- Army, Gov'ts, Businesses Worldwide — Philips, Grundig, Sony, Electrolux, Oceanic, Bosch-Blaupunkt
- Wholesalers, Retailers, Dept. stores, Organizations Worldwide / Industry, elec. and other Distributors Organizations Worldwide — Texas, Motorola, SGS, Philips

Small- and medium-sized firms (to be developed): Audax, Radiall, Safco, Sternice, Sourlau — +++ / +++

We mention here a few companies from the Components Sector, in order to highlight the large private exporters of passive components.

European — to improve, create, and develop in an egalitarian manner
Extra-European — to clarify and promote starting from European bases
European — to consolidate and analyze (in a balanced manner)
Extra-European — to create and develop with promotion of cooperations

National training recovery project
Continuing technical education

SOURCE: French Government, 1983.

ment may also stem from the proliferation of new projects which may in turn dilute available funds to inconsequential levels.

Social Environment for French Information Technology Research and Development

The French Government's desire to push France into a technologically based future has encouraged information technology research efforts in office automation, microcomputers, consumer electronics, and telephone terminal equipment. In addition, each of these research areas has included a major effort in the human factors aspects of design and interaction, perhaps in recognition of the difficulty expected with the assimilation of these technologies into French society. The emphasis placed upon human factors engineering has given rise to French prototypes and products that are generally esthetically pleasing and easy to use. Many French designs have been adapted elsewhere. For example, it was a French study that suggested amber on black CRT screens were the most pleasing and produced the least eye strain.

Three French characteristics stand out as important with respect to information technology research and development. Risk taking in the French industrial sector does not appear with the frequency or at the level considered commonplace in the United States. One indication of this is the small number of venture capitalists in France and the unwillingness of the traditional banking industry to fund entrepreneurs. However, there are efforts on the part of government and industry to increase the use of venture capital.

For the conduct of information technology research and development, the French risk-avoidance characteristic may be translated into the general lack of leading-edge, often high-risk, technological research. Another possible consequence for information technology research and development is the prevalence of large organizational environments for the conduct of R&D. It is difficult to judge what implications this has for French information technology research and development. It can only be contrasted to the fact that one of the strong aspects of U.S. information technology research and development has been considered to be the infusion of small, innovative firms into the research community.

The second French characteristic which appears to affect the conduct of information technology research and development is the frequency of what might be termed reengineering. Reengineering, or the production from scratch, of French versions of an existing product is very common in French information technology. Reengineering efforts may be attributed to the French attempt to develop domestic production capabilities in order to mitigate United States and Japanese dominance in some niches of the French information technology market.

The French attention to reengineering is quite possibly related to a third French characteristic, strong national loyalty to French-made products. This adherence to French products occasionally provides a serious handicap to French information technology research and development. Because the French do not manufacture all types of state-of-the-art instrumentation, French scientists and engineers (who in some cases may be restricted to purchasing French instrumentation) may be limited in their research activities.

Government

There are a variety of French Government organizations involved in information technology research and development. A few were newly created with the advent of the Mitterrand government, but most have been operating for decades. Although the nationalization of industries and the government provision of research and development under Mitterrand are often thought of as socialist government actions, the link between French politics and French research has been longstanding. Traditionally, France has closely overseen both basic and applied science research through government mechanisms.

Centre National de la Recherche Scientifique (CNRS)

The largest and oldest French Government-funded research organization is the Centre National de La Recherche Scientifique (CNRS), founded in 1939. CNRS supports basic research in chemistry, physics, earth, atmospheric and ocean sciences, life sciences, engineering, social sciences, mathematics, and humanities. In 1984, CNRS had a budget of F 7,735 million (almost 24 percent of the public civil research budget), and employed approximately 25,000 people in 1,350 laboratories or within universities, other government agencies, and industry. CNRS has seven laboratories devoted to basic research in some aspect of information technology. The portion of the 1984 budget applicable to information technology research and development is F 225.2 million, an increase of 13 percent over the 1983 budget. This increase in the budget for the information technology research (in contrast to other CNRS research areas which received less or no increases) is significant and is largely the result of the recognition of the importance of information technology to the French economy and society.[91]

In line with France's new efforts in strengthening its information technology industry, CNRS information technology activities are currently coordinated with the Filiere Electronique program and are becoming largely devoted to applied, industrial research. There are efforts in software development and programming techniques, speech recognition and synthesis, artificial intelligence, and robotics. CNRS draws heavily from the French university system for its personnel, unlike industry or most other government agencies, where the grandes ecoles supply the researchers and administrators.[92]

In the past, CNRS ties with industry have been relatively weak. However, as CNRS increases its applied research activities, ties with industry have also grown. Closer ties between CNRS and industry seem to be important to the Directeur General of CNRS who has recently established several agreements between CNRS and industry.[93]

CNRS has exchange programs and scientific accords with 30 countries, including agreements with the National Science Foundation, the National Institute of Health, Massachusetts Institute of Technology, the University of Chicago, and others.

Ministere des Postes, Telecommunications, et Telediffusion (PTT)

The French Ministere des Postes, Telecommunications, et Telediffusion (PTT), through the Ministere de la Recherche et de l'Industrie, is responsible for the provision of all telecommunications services and equipment, network maintenance, standards development, telecommunications policy, technical assistance to former French colonies and other foreign entities, and research and development. The PTT's jurisdiction over telecommunications policy has resulted in increased PTT involvement in information technology R&D. The PTT often joins the Ministere de la Recherche et de l'Industrie and others in the funding of projects that cross the technological boundaries between telecommunications and computers.[94]

The reach of the PTT through the Ministere de la Rechereche et de l'Industrie into the information technology research and development communities is extensive. The PTT funds the Centre National d'Etudes Telecommunications (CNET) much in the same manner that AT&T funds Bell Labs. The PTT also funds the Institut National des Telecommunications (INT), a portion of the Agence de l'Informatique (ADI), and all of the Ecole Nationale Superieure des Telecommunications

---

[91]Discussion of CNRS based on "French Technology Preparing for the 21st Century," *Scientific American*, November 1982, pp. F4, F11.

[92]Interview with Charles Garriques, President, Agence de l'Informatique, June 24, 1983.

[93]For example, agreements have been signed with Saint-Gobain, Renault, and Roussel-Uclaf. "French Technology Preparing for the 21st Century," *Scientific American*, November 1982, pp. F4-F11.

[94]For example, le Project Pilote NADIR (exploration of new uses of Telecom 1 for data and voice transmission) is funded 50/50 by the PTT and the Ministere de la Recherche et de l'Industrie.

Photo credit: Scientific Mission, Embassy of France and Ministere des PTT, French Government

Videotex terminal "Minitel" with CCP card reader.

States has been a success.[95] In 1974, France averaged 12 main telephone lines per 100 inhabitants; in 1981 the figure was 33.[96] The number of lines in the national network grew from 7 million in 1975 to 20 million in 1982. In 1975 electronic exchanges were virtually nonexistent in France; in 1981, 70 percent of newly installed switching capacity was electronic.[97]

As a result of the recent modernization of the French telephone network, the French have a greater percentage of digital equipment than any other country.[98] This, in turn, has spawned the provision of many sophisticated services such as Transpac (public data packet switching network), Transmic (dedicated data transmission), Teletel, and Videophone (video conferencing). These technological possibilities have pushed PTT-sponsored telecommunications and computer research and development in several directions. The three main directions have been satellite technology (the French launched Telecom 1 in the summer of 1983), an integrated services digital network (ISDN), and optical fibers (a wideband, multiservice optical subscriber network experiment is taking place in 1,500 homes in Biarritz). The major research efforts in all of these areas have taken place at the Centre National d'Etudes des Telecommunications (CNET).

Centre National d'Etudes Telecommunications (CNET)

The CNET was formed in 1944 to provide scientific research and technical assistance to the PTT.[99] The CNET is active in applied mathematics, computer science, solid-state physics, and earth sciences. The total budget in 1982 was about ₣ 1 billion (about $133 million); approximately 55 percent is spent on net-

(ENST). The PTT's terminal equipment, switching and transmission needs are supplied through contracts with CIT Alcatel, Thomson CSF, the French Cable Co., and a host of others. The R&D for the products manufactured by these firms for PTT use is funded by the PTT, generally through cooperative efforts between the industrial entity and the CNET.

The current government-sponsored push in information technology research and development follows upon a recent similar effort in telecommunications implemented by the PTT. By most accounts, the research, development, and implementation programs designed in 1974 and 1975 to transform the French telecommunications system into a technologically advanced network on par with the United

---

[95]"No Hang Ups for French Phones," *Telecom France*, June 1982, p. 10.
[96]Conseil Economique et Social, *La Telematique et L'Amenagement du Territoire*, Apr. 21, 1983, p. 35.
[97]PTT Telecommunications, *Biarritz, The Lightwave Communications World of the Future*, p. 1.
[98]Ibid.
[99]Discussion based on the group of brochures and pamphlets included in the CNET *Dossier Presse*.

work and service engineering, 25 percent on components engineering and 20 percent on basic research.

In 1982 2,600 scientists and engineers worked in six laboratories. Two of the groups are located in Paris. Paris A performs long-term network planning and administers the other five centers. Paris B is the center of basic research for the CNET. Materials and geophysical research are the primary efforts. Applied work in components, transmission, marine cables, and satellites is also performed.

The two centers at Lannion work on local area networks, ISDN, software, human-machine interface, and acoustics (Lannion A) and digital transmission, optical communications, and components (Lannion B). The center at Grenoble is devoted to microelectronics research, while the laboratory at Rennes is shared with the Centre Commun d'Etudes de Television et Telecommunications and studies future telecommunications services and their integration with broadcasting technologies.

Since the advent of the Mitterrand government, the CNET has assumed a significant role in the French national industrial development strategy. Under the plan for the electronics sector (La Filiere Electronique), the CNET laboratory at Grenoble has undertaken projects in CMOS technology for very large scale integrated circuits, gallium arsenide, computer-aided design, and artificial intelligence.

In conjunction with La Filiere Electronique research effort, CNET has introduced a program to improve its transfer of technology to the industrial sector. The CNET owns over 550 patents which it licenses to French and other companies. The licensing is done virtually without regard to the royalty potential; CNET's 550 patents provide approximately F 20 million in revenue per year.

L'Institut National de Recherche en Informatique et Automatique (INRIA)

L'Institut National de Recherche en Informatique et Automatique (INRIA) is one of the newest French Government information technology research agency. It was formed in December 1979 under the d'Estaing Ministry of Industry. INRIA remains under the jurisdiction of the Ministere de la Reserche et de l'Industrie in the Mitterrand government. The name of this ministry has had several evolutions of late. With the advent of the Mitterrand government the Ministere de l'Industrie was changed to the Ministere de la Recherche et de l'Industrie. Currently, the organization is titled the Ministere de l'Industrie et de la Recherche. The first change effected by the Mitterrand government was an effort to combine the mission of the Ministry of Industry with that of the Ministry of Research and Technology. The second change appears to be one of emphasis. INRIA is considered the leading research institute in computer science in France. It has several locations. The main research center is in Rocquencourt (just outside of Paris); another smaller center is located in Sophia-Antipolis. INRIA shares facilities with the CNET at Rennes and Grenoble and has a small group in Toulouse. In 1982, INRIA's budget was F 146 million (about $19.5 million) which funded 409 people, 225 of whom were scientists and engineers. In 1983, the budget was expected to be F 200 million for funding of INRIA contracts with industry.[100]

INRIA has a three part mission: the conduct of research on experimental computer systems; international scientific relations; and the transfer of technology. Each of the missions is guided by industrial needs, at least insofar as those needs are articulated by the Ministere de la Recherche et de l'Industrie. Consequently, the research performed by INRIA is applied and the bulk of the work can be characterized as product development.

INRIA has eight research programs in areas such as system architecture, languages, algorithms, automation, and man-machine interface. Each program conducts three to five projects. In addition, INRIA is responsible for four of six pilot projects to be undertaken in connection with La Filiere Electronique program. Those pilot projects are KAYAK (office

---

[100]INRIA, *Dossier Presse.*

automation), NADIR (applications of Telecom 1 satellite capability), SIRIUS (distributed systems), and SOL (portable software).

Each pilot project has a different configuration of funding, personnel, and industry participation. For example, NADIR is financed 50/50 by the PTT and the Ministere de la Recherche et de l'Industrie. The project's administrative responsibility is shared between the Agence de l'Informatique (ADI) and the Direction des Affaires Industrielles et Internationales, a division of the Direction Generale des Telecommunications within the PTT. The actual research is conducted at INRIA with a mixture of INRIA and CNET personnel. Industry personnel are not research team members, although several industrial representatives are participating through provision of user specifications.[101]

SIRIUS is an older project, and as such, its original funding sources and location have changed. Currently, the project is administered by ADI. The research team includes INRIA, the University of Nancy, several smaller divisions of the Ministere de la Recherche et de l'Industrie and 15 industrial companies including CAP-Sogeti, Cii Honeywell Bull, and SNCF (the French national railroad).[102]

The organization of INRIA is quite different from the CNET and in many aspects provides complementary research support. Unlike the CNET which draws heavily from the grandes ecoles system for its researchers, INRIA recruits from the French university system. Many project directors at INRIA are French university professors who come to INRIA for the duration of a project.

Also unlike the CNET, whose mission is to be the research arm of the state telephone network, INRIA is not responsible to one centrally defined set of research requirements. Rather, the institution generally must respond to a more diffuse set of requirements from industry. The coordination of research projects is nominally the job of the Ministere de la Recherche et de l'Industrie, but most often, such coordination is effected by INRIA research staff members who take ideas forward to the Ministry for funding.

Agence de l'Informatique (ADI)

Like INRIA, the Agence de l'Informatique (ADI) was recently formed. Funded by the Ministere de la Recherche et de l'Industrie (75 percent) and the PTT (25 percent), ADI's 1981 budget was F 300 million ($40 million). Funding in 1982 was F 320 million as was the 1983 budget. A 20 percent cut is expected for 1984. ADI was originally designed to be self sustaining though royalties from its research-derived patents and the sale of its published studies, but as yet, those items account for less than 1 percent of ADI's revenue. ADI has three major areas of activity: research and experimentation, application development and dissemination, and training and education. It also has three support activities: regional programs, international affairs, and economic and legal studies. Sixty professionals manage these programs.[103]

The goal of ADI's training and education program is to produce more computer science graduates and to improve the quality and availability of science and engineering education. Included in the program is a project to put computers in the secondary schools. The application development and dissemination programs provide a forum for users and producers of information products to exchange ideas and develop computer applications tailored to the specific requirements of various business sectors.

ADI's research program funds efforts in computer science in a manner analogous to that of the National Science Foundation; that is, ADI funds but does not conduct the research. This program has approximately F 100 million ($13 million). In addition to the four pilot projects ADI helps fund at INRIA,

---

[101]The Pilot Project NADIR, English Language bulletin, May 1983.
[102]INRIA, *Dossier Presse,* Le Project Pilote SIRIUS.

[103]Agence de l'Informatique, English language brochure, and interview with Charles Garriques, President, ADI, June 24, 1983.

partial funding is provided for the RHIN (system interconnection) and SURF (functional security) projects. These six pilot projects were originally to be undertaken as only a portion of ADI's research mission. Longer-term projects in new architectures, languages and programming, human-machine interface, design aids, automation, computer-aided translation, security, and translation are also planned. Recent budget cuts, however, have limited these research endeavors.

Centre d'Etudes des Systemes et des Technologies Advancees (CESTA)

The Centre d'Etudes des Systemes et des Technologies Advancees (CESTA) is the newest French agency involved in information technology. Founded in January 1982, it is one of two completely new agencies formed by the Mitterrand government in information technology. Under the jurisdiction of the Ministere de la Recherche et de l'Industrie, CESTA's 40 employees have two missions: technology forecasting and identification of employment impacts due to technological advance. The technological scope of CESTA goes beyond information technology (e.g., there are programs in biotechnology) but the majority of its work involves various aspects of information technology. CESTA's forecasting responsibility takes the form of evaluations of market, cultural, and social acceptance of technologically advanced products. When employment impacts can be identified, retraining programs are developed by CESTA personnel. CESTA's major activities undertaken to further these goals are the conduct of seminars and the commission of studies and papers on topics of interest.[104]

Although CESTA resides under the auspices of the Ministere de la Recherche et de l'Industrie, the director described his agency as independent, not administration-linked and drew an analogy between CESTA and the Tennessee Valley Authority. He saw this independence as a necessary ingredient to his ability to gather groups representing divergent interests.

Centre Mondial Informatique et Ressource Humaine

The Centre Mondial Informatique et Ressource Humaine is the other information technology agency created by the Mitterand government. The original mandate of the Center was threefold: research in those areas of information technology applicable to microcomputers; social experimentation in France; and Third World pilot projects designed to explore computer applications for the dissemination of medical and education information.[105] However, the Center's role in information technology research and development has not always been clear. Since its inception in November, 1981, the Center has been racked with political struggles. Exactly what role the Center plays or may play in French information technology research and development, however, still remains uncertain.[106]

University

Two parallel systems of higher education exist in France; one is found in the universities, the other in the grandes ecoles. Both systems produce scientists, engineers and administrators with relatively little training in the applied sciences and/or the business aspects of research such as marketing, management finance, or accounting. Beyond this similarity, the systems have few parallels.

In general, French university training does not usually prepare individuals for careers in government or in the higher levels of industry. University trained scientists are occasionally found in industry and in government research laboratories in instances where the

---

[104]CESTA, *CESTA*, December 1982, and interview with Yves Stourdze, Directeur CESTA, June 20, 1983.

[105]Centre Mondial Informatique et Ressource Humaine, *Fiches D'Information, Statuts et Organisation*.

[106]See for example, Dray and Menosky, "Computers and a New World Order," *Technology Review*, May/June 1983, and Walsh, "Computer Expert Signs Off From World Center," *Science*, vol. 218, Dec. 3, 1982.

work is decidedly theoretical or, as in computer science, the discipline is so new that a grande ecole exclusively for the subject is nonexistent. Although computer science is taught in several of the grandes ecoles, computer scientists, particularly software engineers, in France have emerged from the university community. As a result, several French universities such as the university of Grenoble, have recently become sites for information technology research and development activities around which industry has begun to collect. This may eventually change the nature of French research and development which traditionally has been institutionally split into three components. In general, the universities (and some government organizations) have conducted France's basic research, the government and the grandes ecoles have been the sites of applied research, and industry has been the environment for development activities. Although these various institutions have certainly funded activities in each of the other components, cooperation among them has been minimal.

The highly respected grandes ecoles system, which produces the French cadre of government officials and industrial managers, was formed by Napolean to develop an elite group of French intellectuals who would be responsible for guiding France's cultural, social, economic, and political futures. Today there are about 150 grandes ecoles in France of which approximately 10 produce state engineers. The others produce administrators, economists, sociologists, artists, and a host of other professionals in the sciences, liberal arts, and humanities. All grandes ecoles have entry requirements. One must take a competitive exam which requires between 2 and 3 years of study preparation. Typically, the French high school graduate will prepare for this exam at the university, within the high school setting, or in private preparatory institutions. Based on their test scores, students are generally assigned to specific grandes ecoles.

The Ecole Polytechnique has traditionally produced the highest level of government officials in France. As the name suggests, the curriculum at Ecole Polytechnique is based on a theoretical education in a variety of scientific disciplines. In addition, students who wish to specialize in an area often enter one of the other grandes ecoles for additional training after graduation.

The Ecole Nationale Superieure des Telecommunications (ENST) is the primary grande ecole for the production of researchers and engineers in information technology. The ENST is funded by the Ministere des Postes, Telecommunications, et Telediffusion (PTT), and its curriculum is overseen by the PTT. The school is considered to rank among the top ten of the 150 grandes ecoles in France. The school accepts 70 first year students annually, based on performance on the competitive exam. More students are added during the second and third years of the school's program. Entry into the second year at ENST can be obtained after completion of another grandes ecoles education and/or after graduation with a maitrise (roughly equivalent to a U.S. bachelor of science degree) from the university. These additions result in a total student population of about 540 and the award of 220 degrees annually.[107]

The first and second years of study at ENST involve mathematics, physics, electronics, computer science, economics, foreign language, and humanities. During the third year, a student chooses from eight areas of specialty to study for half of the year. Three months are spent in a work-study project in industry or government or in a foreign study program. These work-study projects are a unique opportunity for students to gain applied or industrial experience. As a result of ENST's emphasis on applied engineering, the proportion of graduates who work in industry is quite high in comparison to other grandes ecoles. Approximately 60 percent of the graduates of ENST go to industry, and the remainder find jobs in the PTT.

The ENST has four laboratories where instructional research is conducted: systems and communications, computer science, electronics

---

[107]Ministere des PTT, *ENST*.

and physics, image and sound, and life sciences. Occasionally research is conducted in collaboration with government research centers and industry; however, the main purpose of the research is to provide student instruction, not to further the state-of-the-art.[108]

The highly theorectical nature of the grandes ecoles training does not always prepare government officials to direct and conduct research for purposes of French industrial growth. Experience in the industrial community does not appear to be an alternative method of developing such preparation for government officials, as the transfer of people from careers in industry to careers in government (or vise versa) is quite rare. However, in conjunction with its goal of strengthening the links between industrial and government research and development, the Mitterand government has implemented several new programs. These include increasing the number of commercially oriented grandes ecoles, the teaching of marketing, accounting, and finance throughout the grandes ecoles system, and encouraging more work-study programs.

Industry

The industrial component of French information technology research and development, just as in the United States, has many members. Similar to the situation in both Japan and the United Kingdom, a few large information technology firms are responsible for the major proportion of research and development efforts. Cii Honeywell Bull, Thomson CSF, CIT Alcatel, and Sogitec, representatives of the spectrum of French industrial experience in information technology research and development, are described below.

Cii Honeywell Bull

When nationalization became operational at Cii Honeywell Bull in January 1983, the firm was completely reorganized. It took on several divisions of Thomson and Alcatel and rearranged its internal divisions into four groups: Bull Systems manufactures mainframes; Bull Sems (purchased from Thomson CSF) manufactures minicomputers; Bull Peripheriques makes disks and printers; Bull Transac (purchased from Alcatel) produces microcomputers and office automation products. The collection of groups is now called Bull. The transfer of the company to state ownership has not only changed the structure of divisions, and their personnel, it has changed the relationships between management and worker to reflect socialist principles. The work week has been shortened, salary differentials between men and women have been eliminated, and the number of upper management personnel and their salaries have been reduced.[109]

Research at Bull has been reorganized into six working groups, each with 30 scientists and engineers: advanced systems research; integrated circuits research and technology; custom design of integrated circuits; standard integrated circuits; interfaces for technology use; and discrete components and subsystems. The integrated circuits research and technology group is mandated to "be a proponent of technology alternatives to our partners" and to "[provide] updated competence for the best choices in integrated circuit technology at the Bull group level." Similarly, the custom integrated circuits group is to "establish knowhow in design of custom VLSI" and "provide support and expertise in our choices of new technologies available outside the company." In addition to the six research groups, additional studies to determine the feasibility of research in languages, artificial intelligence, vector processing, and distributed architecture are underway.[110]

Bull's future position in information technology research and development is unclear. It is important to note, however, that should it not improve, the French efforts in information technology research and development, and indeed in other advanced technology

---

[108]Ibid.

[109]Cii Honeywell Bull, *Bilan Social d'Entreprise, Exercise 1982* and "Avis du Comite Central d'Entreprise sur le Bilan Social, 1982."

[110]Bull, *Corporate Technology*, June 17, 1983.

areas, may be diminished. Much of France's technological future is dependent on the availability of a wide range of sophisticated computers and computer peripherals. As long as the French rely on Bull for these products, a very important link in the information technology research and development chain may remain uncertain.

Thomson CSF

Thomson CSF produces a variety of aeronautic electronics equipment, telecommunications equipment for the public telephone network, medical devices, electronic components, and office automation products. Thomson CSF is partially controlled (40 percent) by Thomson-Brandt, a producer of durable consumer goods, electromechanical capital goods, lamps and lighting fixtures, and engineering and financial services.[111] Thomson CSF produces, sells, and distributes its products through a network of almost 60 domestic and foreign subsidiaries and holding and associated companies.[112] Its revenues are dominated by the sale of electronic equipment followed by telecommunications and medical devices.[113]

In 1981, Thomson CSF spent over F 4 billion ($530 million), approximately 10 percent of Thomson CSF and Thomson-Brandt's combined revenues, on research and development. Seventy-five percent of the effort was internally financed. Thomson CSF performs R&D for both Thomson CSF and Thomson-Brandt, and its spending represents 25 percent of all R&D spending in France. The vast majority (95 percent) of the research is product-related and takes place throughout the company's subsidiary structures. Basic research takes place in the Laboratoire Central de Recherches.[114]

Basic research at Thomson CSF includes programs in gallium arsenide, molecular beam epitaxy, single mode fiber optics, and machine level languages. The basic research effort, while small, is extremely important to Thomson CSF. The basic research effort provides Thomson with entree into the basic research community in France and abroad (Massachusetts Institute of Technology, Stanford University, CNRS and several French universities were mentioned as important research collaborators). Moreover, a credible basic research effort helps with the recruitment of scientists and engineers. Because of the excellent reputation of Thomson CSF's basic research function and the small portion of corporate funds it represents, nationalization is not expected to change the nature of the activities and may even increase funding.

Like Bull, Thomson-Brandt, was nationalized with the passage of legislation in February 1982. The effect on R&D activities at Thomson CSF has been minimal in comparison with the changes at Bull. Product-oriented research has been modified slightly to meet some specifications of La Filiere Electronique program and state management has caused some difficulties, but personnel and directional changes for the company have caused almost insignificant disruption.

CIT Alcatel

CIT Alcatel is a subsidiary of the Compagnie Generale d'Electricite (CGE), the fifth largest company in France. CIT Alcatel (through its 8 French and foreign subsidiaries and affiliates) represents the public telecommunications division of CGE. Another 11 Alcatel Group members produce office automation and professional electronics products and provide computer services. Nationalization has not changed the personnel or the conduct of research at CIT Alcatel. It is anticipated that state ownership will improve the relationships between academia and industrial research and development, although results are not expected for another 10 years.[115]

CIT Alcatel's research and development activities are scattered throughout the company's subsidiaries. In addition, some research

---

[111]Thomson-Brandt, *Principales Filiales et Participations Francaises et Etrangers.*
[112]Ibid.
[113]Thomson-CSF, *Rapport Annual des Activities en 1981.*
[114]Ibid.
[115]Alcatel, *The Alcatel Group.*

activities take place in association with CGE, CNET, and CNRS, and in conjunction with other French (e.g., Thomson CSF) and U.S. companies (e.g., SEMI Processes, Inc.). The company's director estimated that between 10 and 12 percent of the employees (some 17,065 in 1981) were involved in R&D.[116]

Each product division within the CIT Alcatel companies funds the R&D activities it deems needed. Like Thomson CSF, the basic research at CIT Alcatel is performed at a central laboratory that is shared with all members of the CGE Group. Approximately 6 to 8 percent of CIT Alcatel's total research budget is devoted to this central laboratory.[117]

Sogitec, S.A.

Unlike the majority of French information technology firms, Sogitec is not a state-owned corporation and is representative of a small information technology firm. Founded in 1964 by its president, Christian Mons, Sogitec has grown to employ about 550 people in three locations: Paris, Rennes, and Lakewood, California. Sogitec also has sales offices in New York and Washington, D.C. Its sales growth has been impressive; 1978 revenues were doubled by 1979. Customers include General Electric, McDonnell Douglas, Ford, Daussalt, and others in the aircraft, shipbuilding, and automobile industries.[118]

Sogitec has two divisions that are designed to meet individual user needs. The data processing services division provides software packages and the related hardware for full text documentation, storage, and retrieval. The other Sogitec division produces real-time simulators and simulation packages for aircraft, helicopters, land vehicles, and ships. The French military has purchased Sogitec products for combat pilot training in the French Mirage fighter bombers. In addition, Sogitec's simulation expertise is currently being adapted for film production, television commercials, and animation.

Some notion of Sogitec's research intensity can be seen in its distribution of personnel. Over 250 of Sogitec's 550 employees are scientists or engineers involved in research and development (50 are located in the United States). Eighty percent of the researchers come from the grandes ecoles system, the remainder from French universities.[119]

---

[116]Ibid.
[127]Ibid.

[118]Department of State, "WTDR on Sogitec (SIC) Data Systems," Oct. 10, 1983, p. 3.
[119]Ibid.

The United Kingdom

Historically, the United Kingdom has heavily relied upon industrial manufacturing for its economic well-being. As the post-industrial society arrives with the decline of manufacturing as a primary economic activity, the British economy has suffered.[120] The United Kingdom's share of world trade in manufactured goods in the decade 1963-73 fell from 15 to 9 percent. For the first time in history the United Kingdom now appears to be approaching a trade deficit in manufactured products. Moreover, the U.K.'s needs for various information technology products are completely or substantially met by imports. As a result of the importance of exports to the U.K. economy and the increasing importance of information technology to the world economy, both the U.K. Government and industry have concluded:

> Our basic economic situation dictates that we must become a net exporter of high technology, high value-added products; information technology is a prime example of this.

---

[120]Daniel Bell, *The Coming of Post-Industrial Society* (New York: BASIC Books, Inc., 1976).

Moreover, unless our [the United Kingdom] information technology industry achieves a strong world competitive position, then the efficiency of our other industries in the manufacturing services will suffer. Their capacity to be advanced users of information technology has a close synergy with the level of the information technology industry itself.[121]

Traditionally, the United Kingdom has been one of the world's leaders in basic scientific research, particularly in the physical and biological sciences. Britain holds the highest per capita ratio of Nobel Prize winners in the sciences which is more than double those for any of the other industralized nations. Although the United Kingdom has in the past had the largest R&D expenditure percentage of gross national product (GNP) outside of the United States, the United Kingdom has been traditionally weak in converting and applying its basic research efforts to the production and marketing of new products and services.

This difficulty of transferring scientific knowledge to commercial applications has consequently created serious problems in the industrial sector and in the international competitiveness of British-made goods. This failure to capitalize on basic research efforts is documented in a recent publication of the Central Office of Information, London, "British Achievements in Science and Technology":

> ... there have been an array of 'firsts' that apply to the information technology area, including radio navigation, computers, optical fibers, liquid crystal displays, and flat screen televisions, yet in none of these areas is a British manufacturer a principal supplier.[122]

Thus the current challenge in the United Kingdom is to bridge the gap between the creative basic research in information technologies and the relatively weak state of industrial application of these technologies in order to create an environment which is more innovative in pursuing both domestic and international markets. This is particularly important in the area of information technology where the development of user applications of the technologies for the provision of new and innovative services is vital to the marketing of information technology.

Reflecting the need to increase applied research activities, the current U.K. Government has taken measures in the opposite direction of the traditional high level of government intervention in both industry and social programs. The more conservative government's efforts include privatizing the economy and restoring entrepreneurial initiatives, thus attempting to make industry more independent of government and reducing government involvement in the marketplace. Government strategies include privileged credit, deregulation measures, and tax benefits to encourage the growth of small and medium businesses.

Privatization measures also entail exposing state-run monopolies to outside competition. A major example of this introduction of competition is the termination of the monopoly of British Telecom (BT) by granting a license to a major competitor to operate an alternative national telecommunications network. It is hoped that this recently introduced competition into the provision of telecommunications services will stimulate demand for advanced technology transmission and exchange equipment. In conjunction with the privatization measures in the field of information technology, the U.K. Government is also promoting the marketing or applied aspects of research and development by shifting some of its R&D expenditure from government research establishments to the private sector. In Cambridge for example, where a preference for basic research has long prevailed, a new view towards research is emerging:

> What has changed is the idea that money is dirty and that one must do pure science. Now, as in Cambridge, Mass., or in California, people are not adverse to doing research that could be put to commercial use. This change in the work ethic has helped us.[123]

---

[121]The Department of Trade and Industry, "A Programme for Advanced Information Technology," the Report of the Alvey Committee (London: Her Majesty's Stationary Office, 1982), p. 14.

[122]Central Office of Information, London, *British Achievements in Science and Technology,* April 1981, No. 111/RP/81.

[123]Phillip LeFournier, "Is Britain Reviving?" *World Press Review,* September 1983, p. 31.

Because of radical changes in government policy over the past decades in the United Kingdom, the continuity of policy which has, for example, aided Japan in its post-war recovery, has not been there to support industry in its efforts to expand. This complicates any simple characterization of the U.K. Government role in industrial policy and suggests a dynamic situation currently regarding U.K. Government initiatives in information technology. Consequently, it is difficult at times to disassociate government, industry, and university roles in information technology R&D. However for purposes of comparison with United States, Japanese, and French R&D efforts, government, university, and industry R&D environments are described separately below. Before discussing these environments, it is important to understand the size of the U.K. participation in information technology markets.

The Size of U.K. Participation in Information Technology Markets

While the United States and Japan are net information technology exporters, the United Kingdom is a net importer of information technology products by Ł 300 million ($420 million) annually.[124] In 1980, the U.K. industry captured approximately 50 percent of its own Ł 2.1 billion ($2.94 billion) information technology market. Moreover, the U.K. information technology industry captured 3.8 percent of the world information technology market in 1980.[125]

Because of the relatively small size of its national markets, the U.K. information industry has been somewhat inhibited. Moreover, it has had difficulty in generating significant export markets for its information technology products to balance its heavy imports. For example, of the 19 top semiconductor companies in the world, which account for approximately 75 percent of the world market, not one is from the United Kingdom.

Government

The U.K. Government officially recognized the importance of the development of information technology to the British society, industry, and economy by requesting the Advisory Council on Applied Research and Development (ACARD),[126] which advises the Prime Minister and the Cabinet Office on important developments in advanced technology, to address the following questions:

- Should development and application of information technology in the United Kingdom be stimulated?
- Are there constraints on British industry which supplies and applies information technology equipment, software, and systems?

The resultant 1980 ACARD report "Information Technology" has contributed to present policy formulation in relation to information technology, with an emphasis on the application of information technology as a key element in the future industrial and commercial success of the United Kingdom as well as on the potential significance of information technology for both society and individuals.

The ACARD report recommended the following:

1. One minister and one government department should be wholly responsible for information technology.
2. One government department should be responsible for the regulation of communications and broadcasting.
3. There should be a government commitment to information technology.
4. The government should actively promote and publicize British information technology.

---

[124]All U.K. pound figures are converted into U.S. dollars according to foreign exchange rates as of Aug. 1, 1984, where L 1 = $1.4.

[125]"A Strategy for Information Technology," National Enterprise Board, 1981, p. 19.

[126]Probably the nearest United States counterpart to ACARD is the Committee of Advisors, recently created by Dr. Keyworth in the Office of Science and Technology Policy in the White House. ACARD, whose members are experts drawn from industry, government, and academia, offers specific recommendations for government action.

5. Central government, local government, and the nationalized industries should apply information technology vigorously.
6. The Post Office should provide a worldwide network.
7. Education, training, and guidance should be accentuated in information technology.
8. Links between users and suppliers of information technology equipment should be improved.
9. Strong British teams should participate in international fora on regulations and standards.
10. Legislation should be introduced to provide for better protection of data, and other legal reforms will be required.
11. The Post Office monopoly on use of its services should be ended.
12. Public purchasing should be used to "pull through" development of equipment.
13. The Science and Engineering Research Council and the Department of Industry should promote research and development in information technology.
14. All publicly funded information technology research and development should be coordinated. This would involve Department of Trade and Industry, Ministry of Defense, the Post Office, and the Science and Engineering Research Council.

The United Kingdom has taken a wide-scope approach to encourage the development and application of information technology in British industry and society. In response to the ACARD report, Mrs. Thatcher's government has developed an overall strategy for information technology. The main objectives of the U.K. Government's policy for information technology are:

1. The development of a statutory regulatory framework favoring the growth of information technology products and services.
2. The development of new products and techniques through direct research and development support and enlightened public purchasing.
3. Action to make individuals more aware of what information technology offers and so enable them to take advantage of the new information technology products and services.
4. The provision of a national telecommunications network capable of stimulating, and meeting, demands for new services.

For implementation of these goals, 1982 was designated as IT Year in the United Kingdom. A wide range of promotional aids was used to increase the awareness of the general public, industry, and schools, and main procurement agencies. The major force in IT Year, in addition to the information technology awareness campaign, was a major and intensive government-industry initiative to encourage research, development, and application of information technology in order to help strengthen the overall U.K. economy.

Also during 1982, the British Government acknowledged the need to address the field of information technology in a coherent manner and subsequently made significant changes in its policymaking structures. A minister with special responsibilities for information technology was appointed, the first such appointment in any nation. The Minister for Industry and Information Technology has responsibility, under the Secretary of State for Trade and Industry, for all the Department of Trade and Industry's activities concerned with information technology, including those related to research and development. More specifically, the Minister has responsibilities for information technology, telecommunications, computer systems, microelectronics, electronics applications, robotics, and space. He oversees British Telecom and the Post Office public purchasing, research and development (including the industrial research establishments) and the British Technology Group. He is also responsible for sponsorship of the chemical, mechanical and electrical engineering, and paper industries; and for distribution and service trade industries; newspapers, printing and publishing; and for standards and quality assurance and firms. Although the responsibilities of the Minister of Industry and Information Technology are central to the promotion of information technology in the United Kingdom, at times the press coverage of ministry activity tends to be exaggerated.

Department of Trade and Industry (DTI)

As a result of the 1980 ACARD recommendations which suggested increasing coordination between industry and government, the Department of Trade and Industry (DTI) has become the major focus for U.K. initiatives in areas related to information technology. In recent years there has been a shift in U.K. Government support from its own research establishments (which still account for a substantial part of the nation's scientific resource) to the private sector. The DTI total expenditure in 1982-83 was approximately Ł 230 million ($322 million), of which approximately two-thirds was spent in the private sector. DTI allocated approximately Ł 80 million ($112 million) for information technology R&D in 1979-80.[127] This trend is greatly supported by the U.K. Government because it locates research closer to the point of application (which some feel is vital in the area of information technology) and encourages private sector initiatives.

The DTI's decisions on funding priorities for research and development rely on the advice of five Research Requirements Boards (RRBs). Each RRB is chaired by a Senior Industrialist and consists of industralists, scientists, and government representatives. The RRB's are seen as an effective system for monitoring and developing strategies to ensure that research support priorities match the demands of changing technologies and future industrial needs. The DTI, therefore, works closely with industry through the Research Requirement Boards to ensure that research in the national laboratories is directed towards industrial needs. Three of the Research Requirements Boards, Computers, Systems, and Electronics; Mechanical and Engineering; and Metrology and Standards, are involved with information technology R&D support. The Computers, Systems, and Electronics RRB is the major supporter of information technology R&D with 1980-81 expenditures of Ł 6 million ($8.4 million).[128]

In keeping with the current U.K. Government policy, which aims to achieve a profitable, competitive, and adaptable private sector, the DTI has recently implemented a variety of programs that are intended to supplement direct R&D support. Because of the recent recession that has inhibited U.K. companies from investing large resources in R&D activities, these programs are intended to encourage the private sector to research, develop, and use information technology. The DTI's support programs generally comprise three elements:

1. An *awareness* program to stimulate interest in the potential of the new technology.
2. *Consultancy* to explain how a particular technology can be applied to a particular company's needs.
3. *Support* for ensuing projects.

These DTI R&D support programs, categorized by the various applications of information technology, are presented in table 44.

THE ALVEY PROGRAMME FOR ADVANCED INFORMATION TECHNOLOGY

In addition to industrial R&D support schemes, the DTI recently initiated a collaborative national information technology R&D program. One of the catalysts to the formation of the Alvey Programme was the announcement of the plans for Japan's Fifth-Generation Computer Systems Project and Japan's invitation to other countries, including the United Kingdom, to discuss participation in the program. The scale and cohesiveness of this and other Japanese programs were seen by the U.K. representatives to the Japanese conference as a major competitive threat. The British also believed that the U.S. industry's

---

[127] John K. Thompson, "'IT' in Britain," speech given at the British Embassy to the Potomac Chapter of the American Society of Information Scientists, June 9, 1982.

[128] Statement of Kenneth Baker, before the U.K. House of Commons, Dec. 21, 1982.

Table 44.—Department of Trade and Industry R&D Programs

CAD/CAM	— The Computer-aided Design and Computer-aided Manufacture program is designed to promote and accelerate the acceptance and application of CAD/CAM primarily in the mechanical and electrical engineering industries.	± 6 million ($8.4 million) (over 3 years from 1981)
CAD/MAT	— The Computer-aided Design Manufacture and Test Program is designed to encourage the use of CAD/MAT for design testing and production in the electronics industries.	± 9 million ($12.6 million) (over 3 years from 1982)
FMS	— The Flexible Manufacturing Systems Scheme is designed to encourage firms to install flexible manufacturing systems.	± 60 million ($84 million) (over 3 years from 1982)
FOS	— The Fiber Optics and Opto-Electronics Scheme is designed to encourage the development, production, and application of fiber optics and opto-electronics.	± 25 million ($35 million) (over 5 years from 1981)
MAP	— The Microelectronics Application Project is designed to encourage the application of microelectronics in products and processes in manufacturing industries.	± 55 million ($77 million) (commenced 1978)
MISP	— The Microelectronics Industry Support Program is designed to promote the microelectronics components industry, particularly for the manufacture of silicon integrated circuits.	± 55 million ($77 million) (commenced 1978)
ROBOTICS	— The Industrial Robotics Scheme is designed to encourage the development and application of robots in manufacturing industries.	± 10 million ($14 million) (over 3 years from 1981)
SPS	— The Software Products Scheme is designed to encourage the development and application of software products and packages.	
Awareness programs, demonstration projects and other promotional activities		± 80 million ($112 million) (over 4 years commencing 1981)

SOURCE: Office of Technology Assessment.

reaction to the Japanese Fifth Generation Computer Systems Project could also cause an equal if not greater degree of competition for the U.K. industry.

In the light of these factors, the U.K. delegation called for an urgent study into the feasibility for a collaborative R&D program geared to particular strengths and requirements. This study, completed by the Alvey Committee, outlined plans for a national information technology R&D effort to improve the United Kingdom's competitive position in world information technology markets.[129] John Alvey, Chairman of the Committee, comments on the coordination aspects of the program:

> This is the first time in our history that we shall be embarking on a collaborative research project on anything like this scale. Industry, academic researchers, and government will be coming together to achieve major advances in technology which none could achieve on their own. The involvement of industry will ensure that the results as they emerge are fully exploited here in Britain to the advantage of our economy. Information technology is one of the most important industries of the future and therefore one upon which hundreds of thousands of jobs in the future will depend. Collaboration will ensure that the results of the research are widely disseminated particularly to smaller firms which have such an important contribution to make to the industry. No one can guarantee success, but the government is convinced that this program will ensure for British industry secure access to the new technology and to the products and processes on which our future prosperity depends.

The Alvey Program for Advanced Information Technology is a 5 year program funded by three government ministries and industry. Total funding for the program will be approximately $525 million over a 5 year period. The

---
[129]See "A Programme for Advanced Information Technology, The Report of the Alvey Committee," Department of Industry, Her Majesty's Stationary Office, 1982.

Department of Education and Science (DES) through the Science and Education Research Council (SERC) will fund approximately Ł 50 million ($70 million) for promoting advanced research in academic institutions and the training of necessary manpower. The Ministry of Defense (MOD) will fund approximately Ł 40 million ($56 million) for research believed to be important to the defense industry and will contribute its experience in the field of integrated circuits. The Department of Trade and Industry will provide the major portion of the government's funds, approximately Ł 110 million ($154 million), and will have the overall responsibility for management of the program. Industry will fund the remaining Ł 150 ($210 million) in the form of 50 percent matching funds for each R&D project.

The Alvey Program R&D projects are concentrated in four technical areas, known as "enabling technologies." These enabling technologies, seen as crucial to the development and application of information technology in the United Kingdom, include:

- very large scale Integration (VLSI) silicon integrated circuits,
- software engineering,
- intelligent knowledge based systems (IKBS), and
- man/machine interface.

The research projects in these four technical areas will be managed by the Alvey Directorate consisting of staff from industry, DTI, MOD, and SERC. Each of the four technology areas has its own director in addition to a director in charge of networks and communications among the various R&D projects. Each of the research teams will generally be organized in small consortia—e.g., two information technology firms, together with a government research establishment team, and a university team. Unlike the Japanese approach of creating a center for research, research teams will rely on a data network and electronic mailbox service that will allow interactive communication among the R&D program participants.

The United Kingdom will also be a major participant in the European Strategic Program for Research in Information Technology (ESPRIT). Currently, U.K. companies are involved in more than half of ESPRIT's pilot projects. The Alvey program is also designed to complement the ESPRIT program with interlinking communications networks and common parallel research strategies.

THE DEPARTMENT OF TRADE AND INDUSTRY'S NATIONAL LABORATORY FACILITIES

The U.K. national research establishments involved with information technology R&D are the National Physical Laboratory, the National Engineering Laboratory, and the Computed-Aided Design Centre.[130]

The National Physical Laboratory (NPL) has a long distinguished history in computer technology. In 1981-82, NPL R&D expenditures were approximately Ł 22 million ($30 million). Currently, R&D projects are focused on data networks, data security, special input devices, and microprocessor applications. The Laboratory also is developing standard network protocols and evaluating cryptographic methods for data protection. NPL also develops software for solving engineering problems.

The National Engineering Laboratory (NEL) carries out research, development, design, consulting, and testing in automated manufacturing. The 1982 Information Technology Year campaign highlighted the Laboratory's involvement in robotics and automated production systems. NEL R&D expenditures were approximately Ł 16 million ($22.4 million) in 1981-82. Key areas of NEL research include automated assembly, control and optimization of production systems, the development of an advanced turning cell, and other flexible manufacturing systems.

Computer-Aided Design Centre (CADCENTRE) is the primary center in the United Kingdom

---

[130]Discussion of the U.K. National Research Labs, based on "Research and Development Report, 1981-82," Department of Industry, 1982.

for the development of computer techniques in design and engineering. In 1981-82 the CADCENTRE R&D expenditures were approximately Ł 4 million ($5.6 million). The center offers approximately 30 computer software packages in CAD/CAM and provides a comprehensive range of services including software development, consultancy, production services and the provision of hands-on experience in CAD/CAM techniques. Because private sector initiatives were encouraged in DTI sponsored R&D, the DTI agreed to sell the Cambridge-based CADCENTRE to a U.K. consortium led by the U.K. computer firm International Computers, Ltd. (ICL) for approximately Ł 1 million ($1.4 million). The newly privatized CADCENTRE employs ICL staff and DTI management staff. In addition, the DTI has agreed to provide some financial support in order to ease the transition from a government research establishment to a commercially run company. The DTI will be entitled to a royalty based on the CADCENTRE's turnover.[131]

The Ministry of Defense (MOD)

The Ministry of Defense (MOD) is also a major supporter of applied R&D. Almost half of the United Kingdom's R&D budget has been devoted to defense. In the 1970s, defense R&D remained relatively constant although all other areas of R&D decreased by almost 50 percent. In 1978, the Ministry of Defense expenditures for electronics research and development were approximately $900 million.[132]

Beyond the direct support from industrial research funds, the defense sector has potentially the greatest possibility for contributing to civil information technology. There has been a recent shift in emphasis within the MOD away from aircraft and towards electronics research and development. Because the overseas defense electronics market is fairly strong, it is difficult to predict what the long-term consequences of this shift may be. If the market grows for defense electronics, there could be a positive effect on the U.K. supplier industry. On the other hand, because the spin-off effect of U.K. military R&D to commercial products has not been particularly significant, any increase in attention to military needs by the limited U.K. electronics industry might have the effect of further reducing their civilian-oriented work and reducing their market competitiveness.

Department of Education and Science (DES)

Under the advice of the Advisory Board for Research Councils (ABRC), the Department of Education and Science (DES) allocates the science budget to five Research Councils. The Science and Engineering Research Council (SERC) has the primary responsibility for information technology R&D. The SERC budget allocated to information technology R&D was Ł 5 million ($7 million) in 1979-80, Ł 8.5 million ($11.9 million) in 1980-81, and Ł 11 million ($15.4 million) in 1981-82.[133]

SERC, analogous to the U.S. National Science Foundation, accepts competitive bids from universities for special projects. Unlike NSF, SERC provides only half the funds for sponsored projects. The rest of the funding must come from industry, charitable foundations, or other government departments. SERC also provides research establishments with central computing support. The Engineering Board of SERC is most involved with information technology, with funding areas in:

- device-related research,
- skilled manpower training,
- software technology, database utilization, and system reliability,
- distributed computing systems.

SERC operates the Rutherford Appleton Laboratory (RAL). The lab itself has a considerable research program in information technol-

---

[131] Under the royalty arrangements, the U.K. Government will be repaid and could receive a further net amount of L 4.5 million over a 10-year period, assuming forecast revenue levels are achieved by the company.

[132] J. Thyme, "Information Technology in the U.K.: Government Policy," in G.P. Sweeney (ed.), *Information and the Transformation of Society*, North-Holland Publishing Co., 1982, p. 261.

[133] John Thompson, "'IT' in Britain," speech given at the British Embassy to the Potomac Chapter of the American Society of Information Scientists, June 9, 1982.

ogy, with efforts in distributed computing systems, industrial robotics, computing applications in engineering, electron-beam lithography, and image processing.

British Technology Group (BTG)

The British Technology Group is an independent public corporation established to promote the development and application of new technology. The British Technology Group was formed in 1981 and includes the former National Research Development Council (NRDC) and the National Enterprise Board (NEB).

BTG provides funds for technological innovation through:

- joint venture finance under which BTG can provide 50 percent of the funds required for the business in return for a levy on sales of the resulting product or process;
- recirculating loans, which are a form of working capital loan, through which BTG can help a company to meet specific orders for innovative products; and
- equity and loan finance on venture capital terms where a company is set up for the purpose of developing and marketing an invention or new technology; equity may also be provided in the form of redeemable preference shares.

Projects from all sectors of industry are eligible for consideration. The primary consideration for BTG support is that the proposal project must be based on a new invention or a genuine technical innovation.

University

Basic research is supported primarily at the university level (approximately 22 percent of government R&D spending) both by discipline oriented committees of the Science and Engineering Research Council (SERC) and the University Grants Committee (UGC). Recent cuts in university funding have been substantial—15 percent over the last 4 years. In addition, lowered enrollment has caused the universities to become top-heavy with senior, relatively expensive faculty. The steadily rising cost of research equipment has also affected the available funds for university research. Together, these three factors have resulted in substantially less spending for university R&D.[134]

Although university research funding has been decreasing over the last few years there have been marked changes in the distribution of funds—away from basic research towards engineering and applied R&D. This trend towards greater emphasis on industrial application of research results is exemplified in several recently initiated schemes. These schemes, designed to promote high quality research in fields of applied science, are cosponsored by SERC and DTI. In one of the more successful joint SERC/DTI initiatives, the Teaching Company Scheme, DTI pays for engineers to do postgraduate work in industry. Students work on product development, design, and manufacturing processes, but with close attention and support of academic staff who supervise the innovative aspects of the graduates' work. The program so far has attracted great interest from industry, and many firms such as General Electric Co., British Aerospace, Ferranti, and IBM are participating.

Another program aimed at promoting industrial training is the introduction of approximately 150 information technology centers (ITEC centers) throughout the United Kingdom. Funded by DTI, Manpower Services Commission, and industry grants, these centers collaborate with local industries to provide computer training for unemployed high-school age youths. Approximately 70 percent of the students upon leaving the centers find employment in a computer-related field. Other programs that offer technical training include Computers in Schools, through which DTI funds 50 percent of the cost of up to two microcomputers in each U.K. school, and a Manpow-

---

[134]Robin B. Nicholson, "Science and Technology Policy in the United Kingdom," address given at the Nineteenth Annual Meeting of the National Academy of Engineering, Nov. 2-3, 1983.

er Services Commission Program that funds information technology training in computer-related subjects. Approximately half of all the programmers training in the United Kingdom is provided by these programs.

In addition to industrial training programs, the U.K. Government has encouraged greater industrial participation in R&D as well as closer industry-university ties through the initiation of science parks. Similar to the Japanese and U.S. science parks, the U.K. science parks provide an opportunity for industry to locate in the proximity of major research universities.

Industry

Since the late 1960s, the U.K. Government has played an important role in supporting the U.K. computer industry. For example, in 1968 the government encouraged a series of mergers that led to the establishment of International Computers Ltd. (ICL) and then provided funds amounting to approximately $12 million annually until 1976. Moreover, the government encouraged ICL's growth through preferential procurement policies that guaranteed almost all large central government contracts to ICL. ICL became the largest European computer company, with a wide customer base in the United Kingdom as well as overseas, including the United States. ICL became so successful that government assistance was withdrawn in 1976, and in late 1979 the government sold its 25 percent share in the company. However, by 1981, ICL was heavily in debt, and the government (although it encouraged private funding and joint research programs) arranged Ł 270 million ($378 million) in loans for ICL.

In an effort to become profitable again, ICL is currently exploring joint activities with non-U.K. firms. In 1982, ICL and Fujitsu reached a collaborative agreement. The arrangement provides for special access to Fujitsu's advanced microelectronics technology, and provides for purchases of semiconductor chips developed by Fujitsu. ICL will in turn market large Fujitsu computers in Western Europe, thus broadening the ICL product line into more powerful computers. It is hoped to extend this collaboration at a later date to other technology areas, including communications technology. ICL also recently reached an agreement with a small U.S. company, Three Rivers, to manufacture and market worldwide a microcomputer designed by Three Rivers.

In 1979, the U.K. Government also invested $100 million for the creation of a national semiconductor firm, Inmos. Operating as an independent producer, Inmos was established to manufacture a limited range of products (principally high-capacity semiconductor memory chips) to sell to large electrical goods manufacturers. Also, to assure indigenous production of semiconductors, the U.K. Government has convinced several U.S. semiconductor companies to set up production in the United Kingdom by offering them grants up to $33\frac{1}{3}$ percent for R&D costs, under the Support for Innovation Program (SFI).

Currently, more than half of the U.K. industrial electronics R&D expenditure is funded by government. The funding may be in the form of cost-sharing grants, procurements, or any of the multitude of funding schemes. Moreover, the pervasive influence of the U.K. Government is exemplified in the original Alvey proposal which called for the government to fund 90 percent of industrial R&D activities. The proposal, however, was finally amended to the current commitment of 50 percent only after considerable debate, on the grounds that industry would not be committed if it only was required to invest 10 percent of its own resources.

The historically low industrial funding for information technology R&D has been attributed to the U.K. information technology industry's focus on highly specialized markets. Because the U.K. information technology industry in some instances fills small but important market niches, it usually does not capture mass markets; consequently, the U.K. information technology industry has not always had adequate resources for R&D funding.

A case in point is the British semiconductor chip industry. The leading U.K. information technology firms have concentrated on producing specialized chips known as "specials" where the demand is low and the market relatively small. For example, world sales in 1980 of custom-built special chips came to only Ł 100,000 ($140,000) almost one-twentieth of the comparable figure for standard chips.[135] Although the leading British electronic firms' demand for these standard chips are extremely high, U.K. industry has left the manufacturing of these types of chips mainly to companies from the United States and Japan, which together capture approximately 75 percent of the world market. However, the United Kingdom's leading firms—Ferranti, Plessey, and GEC—all plan to expand their manufacturing capability of standard chips for domestic use. This pattern has also been repeated in other information technologies; for example, few British companies produce hardware that directly serves the semiconductor and electronics industry (i.e., for testing and production needs).

There is some indication that U.K. industry may be reassessing its investment policies. Current estimates suggest, for example, that the volume of R&D has been maintained through the recession on a selective basis with substantial advances in areas such as microelectronics and corresponding decreases in metals and traditional engineering. For example, industrial electronics R&D expenditures increased form Ł 279 million ($390.6 million) in 1975 to Ł 442 million ($618.8 million) in 1978.[136]

Similar to the situation in France and Japan, a few large firms are responsible for a large proportion of information technology R&D expenditure in the United Kingdom. Several of these major firms are described below.

Plessey

In 1983, Plessey invested approximately $225 million in R&D, 15 percent of its sales. Approximately $22 million of the R&D expenditures were allocated to basic research activities. Of the 320 researchers in the main Plessey laboratory working on microelectronics, 170 people are working on gallium arsenide and related materials and 150 are working on silicon. Plessey's silicon research is geared towards speciality or custom circuits.

Plessey relies heavily on outside contracts, and approximately 45 percent of its research is done for the MOD and British Telecom. Of the remaining 55 percent, half is conducted for the Plessey operating divisions and half is conducted for the head office. Currently, Plessey is attempting to reduce its reliance on outside R&D funding in favor of more operating division work.[137]

General Electric Co. (GEC)

In 1983, the General Electric Co. (GEC) invested approximately $900 million in research and development, approximately 10 percent of its sales. Unlike Plessey, only 25 percent of GEC's research is for the MOD and British Telecom. Fifty percent of the research is for GEC's 120 operating companies, and 25 percent is for basic, speculative research. Because a large percentage of its R&D is supported by its operating companies, GEC's research activities are more oriented towards commercial product development. GEC's key areas of research include microelectronics, fiber optic devices, software engineering, and custom chip design.[138]

British Telecom (BT)

Previously a public monopoly, the U.K. Government has recently privitized British Telecom (BT). Moreover, the U.K. Government has permitted the licensing of other competitors

---

[135]Peter Marsh, "Britain Faces Up to Information Technology," *New Scientist*, Dec. 23, 1982, p. 637.
[136]Robin Nicholson, "Science and Technology Policy in the United Kingdom," address given at the Nineteenth Annual Meeting of National Academy of Engineering, Nov. 2-3, 1983.

[137]"Profile: GEC and Plessey: Two Approaches to R&D," *The Economist*, Nov. 20, 1982.
[138]"Ibid.

to provide telecommunications services. It is hoped that the introduction of competition into the provision of telecommunications services will stimulate new demand and provision of a vast array of new services. Consequently, U.K. companies with advanced products are expected to be well placed to take advantage of market development and to use the United Kingdom as a springboard for capturing European and other world information technology markets.

The privatization efforts, however, have caused some speculation about the future of BT laboratories in much the same way that divestiture has caused speculation about the future of Bell Labs. Currently, BT Labs research expenditure is approximately Ł 100 million ($140 million) annually. BT has traditionally had strong research programs in four major areas:

- advanced technology (e.g., CAD in large scale integrated circuit design, optical communications systems, gallium arsenide, high speed logic);
- transmission (e.g., digital transmission in LANs, small earth station satellites);
- customer service/apparatus (e.g., Prestel and Viewdata);
- advanced systems (e.g., microprocessor software development, ISDN local connection).

European Strategic Program for Research in Information Technology (ESPRIT)

In an attempt to reverse the decline of Europe's competitiveness, to ensure a stronger technological base, and ultimately to ensure economic and political independence, the Commission of European Communities proposed the European Strategic Program for Research in Information Technology (ESPRIT).[139] Although EEC members hope that ESPRIT will succeed in strengthening Europe's technological base and international competitiveness, there are concerns as to whether research can be effectively undertaken and shared among potential international competitors.

ESPRIT is designed to address three major difficulties that currently face the European information technology industry as it attempts to develop new state-of-the-art technologies: the problem of raising adequate funds for long-term research and development during a period of economic recession and falling sales; a domestic market which, unlike those of the United States and Japan, is fragmented into a number of relatively small national units; and reluctance by some within individual countries to subsidize other nations who have historically been economic and political rivals.[140] Consequently, the ESPRIT program seeks to: increase the size of research teams, optimize the use of human and financial resources, and initiate definition and adoption of European standards for information technology products.[141]

ESPRIT attempts to address the problem of the fragmentation of the European market, as well as the divided efforts of the individual member nations' national R&D support programs, by linking a significant proportion of key European engineers and scientists from government, industry, and universities. In this respect, ESPRIT is similar to other national research and development programs such as Japan's Fifth-Generation Computer Project, the United Kingdom's Programme for Advanced Information Technology, and the U.S. Semiconductor Research Corporation (SRC), which are also partnerships among various companies, academic research laboratories,

---

[139]In 1975, the European Community had a trade surplus in information technology products; however, by 1980, the trade deficit in information technology products reached $5 billion and reached approximately $10 billion in 1982. At present, Europe represents one-third of the world information technology market but accounts for only 10 percent of world information technology production. For example, in the European domestic market, 2 out of every 5 information technology products sold are European; 8 out of 10 personal computers sold in Europe are imported from the United States; 9 out of 10 videotape recorders sold in Europe come from Japan. ESPRIT Proposal, COM(83) 258 final, Commission of the European Communities, June 2, 1983, p. 8.

[140]David Dickson, "Europe Seeks Joint Computer Research Effort," *Science*, Jan. 6, 1984, p. 28.

[141]ESPRIT Proposal, COM(83) 258 final, Commission of the European Communities, June 2, 1983, p. 9.

and government agencies. However, unlike these other research and development programs, ESPRIT also represents an international institutional arrangement.

Unlike the MITI program in Japan, the ESPRIT program is limited to precompetitive research; it does not intend to develop a commercial product as does the Japanese fifth-generation computer effort. At any point in the research, however, the participating companies are free to take the technical results gained from the ESPRIT projects and develop commercial products on their own. Therefore, ESPRIT is not seen to be in competition with national research and development programs or individual companies, but as a reinforcement to make them more effective.

Funding for ESPRIT is approximately $1.3 billion for the next 5 years and approximately 2,000 researchers will take part in research activities.[142] The funding will be equally shared among 12 principle corporate partners and other participating companies with the Commission of European Communities. The 12 main corporations participating in ESPRIT include: General Electric Co. (United Kingdom), Plessey plc. (United Kingdom), International Computers Ltd. (United Kingdom), Compagnie General de L'Electricite (France), CIT-Alcatel (France), Cii Honeywell Bull, (France), Thomson-Brandt (France), AEG-Telefunken AG (West Germany), Nixdorf Computer AG (West Germany), NmbH Phillips Gloeilampen-fabrieken (Netherlands), Olivetti SPA (Italy), and Societa Torinese Esercizi Telefoncini (Italy).

The ESPRIT program consists of five major research areas: advanced microelectronics, software technology, advanced information processing, office automation, and computer integrated manufacturing. The EEC has chosen these five areas of information technology because of their perceived importance for future European industrial competitiveness. The first three of these research areas were selected in part to develop better enabling or core technologies. Office automation and computer integration were selected as specific applications areas where information technology is expected to have a large economic and social impact—automation of the office and the factory.

The advanced microelectronics project's major goal is to develop smaller, more reliable, and more powerful integrated circuit technology so that devices can perform more functions or operations than circuits available today. More specifically, the goal of the advanced microelectronics project is to improve the current state-of-the-art process, which is based on three-to-five micrometer structures, to processes that are based on structures smaller than one micrometer. The Europeans are hopeful that this advanced microelectronics project will improve Europe's current integrated circuit trade deficit.[143]

The major emphasis of the advanced information processing project is on information and knowledge engineering, information storage and usage, signal processing, and external interfaces. The research project's overall goal is to develop technological capabilities that underlie machine intelligence. Advances in the new types of information processing will also entail breakthroughs in advanced computer architecture, further miniaturization in microelectronics, and higher reliability.

The goal of the software technology project is to improve software engineering techniques. More specifically, the project's goals include establishing standardized software interfaces, automating the software engineering process, and disseminating and centralizing software research results in a common data base so that individual modules of software programs can be reused where similar functions are required.

---

[142]Actual funding for ESPRIT is 1,500 million European currency units (ECU). Approximately 1 AU equals 1 U.S. dollar. Of the total European Community countries' research and development expenditures, 1.7 percent is for EEC research and development activities. Nine percent of the EEC R&D budget is reserved for industry of which 20 percent is for ESPRIT funding.

[143]Currently, Europe absorbs 20 percent of the world's integrated circuit market, although Europe produces only 6 percent of the world's integrated circuits.

The office automation project, one of the two specific applications projects, is directed at developing a multimedia interface for all office communication needs, and at developing efficient electronic filing systems for unstructured information (text, voice, graphics, images, etc.). The project will also examine the cross-cultural interaction of human factors, educational, sociological, and industrial effects of office automation systems. Moreover, research on machine translation (which is of great importance to the European Community) and aspects of machine-user interfaces, such as integrated image test speech communication, document creation, and distribution will also be conducted.

The goal of the computer integrated manufacturing project is to develop improved systems for automated factories. These systems will integrate in a common data base computer-aided design, computer-aided manufacturing, computer-aided testing and repair, and assembly. Such integration will require further developments in integrated systems architecture, advanced components, real-time based imaging, and integrated control subsystems mounted on semiconductor chips.

Experts from the 12 main industry partners as well as outside consultants have developed a work plan of specific projects in the five project areas. As these specific projects have been defined, proposals are solicited. Proposals may be submitted by research teams from any industry or university, although the team must be composed of nationals from two or more EEC countries. This arrangement is meant to encourage international cooperation between nations and industries, and therefore prevent duplication of research efforts and make optimal use of limited financial and human resources. The main criteria for evaluating proposals include: technical soundness; contribution to industrial strategy in light of ESPRIT objectives; European Community usefulness; technical, scientific, and managerial capability to undertake the proposed project; and proposed activities that will facilitate the dissemination of research results.

The Commission and the advisory board, which consists of industry representatives (mainly from the 12 contributing industries), review research proposals and approve grants. Two broad types of proposals are considered for the different technical projects. Type A, which represents the strategic long-term research activities of ESPRIT, involves large research establishments and large commitments of resources, both human and financial, as well as clear long-term strategic plans to ensure continuity of research and long-term benefits. Type A projects receive 50 percent funding from the European Community, and the research participant is expected to provide the remaining funds. Type B proposals require relatively smaller resources and account for a significant share of the overall efforts under ESPRIT. Type B projects could range from very long-term, very speculative R&D to shorter-term and more specific R&D. Type B projects receive at least 50 percent of their R&D funds from the European Community, or more if the applicant is from an academic institution or smaller business with limited available finance.

One of the first ESPRIT research proposals to be funded is a project to develop advanced interconnection between very-large-scale integrated circuits. The research project is a joint effort between Plessy and GEC in the United Kingdom, Thomson CSF in France, and Telefunken in West Germany. Another initial project, jointly shared between the Polytechnic in London and the University of Amsterdam, is focusing on the development of 11 different aspects of tools and methods for developing machine intelligence.

The Future of ESPRIT

The initial response to the ESPRIT pilot phase has been favorable; the 1 year pilot phase of ESPRIT, launched in mid-1983 with a budget of $20 million and funded 50 percent by the European Community and 50 percent by industry, attracted over 200 research proposals. However, only 36 could be selected to receive EEC matching funds. EEC officials were quite surprised not only at the scale of response, but also at the apparent willingness of companies to permit their scientists to work together with few restrictions.[144]

Currently, however, there is still some doubt as to whether ESPRIT will further achieve its stated goals. In the past, the EEC has had some difficulties with other joint projects. In the 1960s, Pierre Aigrain, then President Pompidou's chief scientist, proposed a European project to strengthen the technological base of the computer and communications industry. However, the project was never launched because of resistance from the European telecommunications monopolies to the suggestion that their own research was insufficient and the lack of a plan to suggest how a cooperative research program supported by established companies and nationalized industries could be beneficial to all the participants.[145] Moreover, in the early 1970s, Dutch, German, and French computer manufacturers formed a joint venture, Unidata. Each company sent their top engineers to a joint research and development facility. However, the project had many difficulties and some of the participants eventually withdrew from the project.[146]

As in past joint European research efforts, the future of ESPRIT depends as much on the results of political struggles around the restructuring of Europe's economic and industrial base as it does on any judgment of its technical and scientific merits.[147] This is illustrated by the first few unsuccessful attempts in early 1984 for EEC endorsement of ESPRIT, which became intermingled with broader economic issues ranging from the efficiency of French farming practices to the EEC's budget procedures. Moreover, it is still unclear as to how the national information technology research programs will mesh with ESPRIT projects. Consequently, there are debates in each country over whether the results of information technology research and development, as an important key to future political and economic strength, should be shared with potential competitors.

International rivalry is also a large industry concern. The lack of an established legal framework in which companies will be allowed to collaborate may cause difficulties for European information technology industries. Because ESPRIT is concerned primarily with long-term precompetitive research, there may not be any conflict with the EEC antitrust laws which are intended to apply primarily to marketing strategies, rather than product development. However, some companies believe that as the gap between scientific discovery or basic research and commercial application narrows, collaborative precompetitive research will be extremely difficult.[148] It is for this reason that three of Europe's largest mainframe computer manufacturers (Siemens, ICL, and Bull) have established the European Computer Industry Research Center. The Research Center discourages open collaboration by initially excluding participation by other companies because:

> If you recognize the fact that you are in a competitive market, in which companies are fighting against each other, then you must accept that it is not in the interest to offer all research results to everyone who might be interested in them, and that at least some projects will be of character that will forbid the open publication of research results from the beginning.... We do abstract research on an international basis where the balance of cooperation and competition should be determined by the rules of international commerce, and market-like research on a national basis, where individual companies can adopt the most appropriate strategies for their domestic and political environment.[149]

---

[144]David Dickson, "Europe Seeks Joint Computer Research Effort," *Science,* Jan. 6, 1984, p. 28.
[145]"What Hope for ESPRIT?" *Nature,* Feb. 16, 1984, p. 582.
[146]Beth Karlin and George Anders, "Europe Looks Abroad for High Technology It Lags in Developing," *The Wall Street Journal,* Oct. 5, 1983, p. 1.
[147]David Dickson, "Europe Seeks Joint Research Effort," *Science,* Jan. 6, 1984, p. 28.

[148]This problem may be particularly acute in research projects such as office automation and computer-aided manufacturing.
[149]Statement by Mr. Heimann of Siemens, David Dickson, "Europe Seeks Joint Computer Research Effort," *Science,* Jan. 6, 1984, p. 29.

Despite the preliminary difficulties in achieving agreement on the funding for ESPRIT, the establishment of the controversial Siemens-ICL-Bull Research Center, and other underlying political and economic rivalry, ESPRIT may succeed in overcoming these impediments. If ESPRIT does succeed, it is likely to be used as a model for similar cooperative European Community projects in other fields, such as telecommunications and biotechnology.

Chapter 8
Information Technology R&D in the Context of U.S. Science and Technology Policy

Contents

	Page
Findings	279
Introduction	279
Part I: Background	280
General U.S. Science and Technology Policies	280
Information Technology R&D Policies	286
Part II: Key Issue Areas	290
Issue A: Organization of Government	290
Introduction	290
Dimensions of the Issue	291
Options for Addressing the Issue	293
Issue B: Military/Civilian Balance	294
Introduction	294
Dimensions of the Issue	295
Options for Addressing the Issue	297
Issue C: International Competitiveness	298
Introduction	298
Dimensions of the Issue	298
Options for Addressing the Issue	300
Concluding Thoughts	301

Tables

Table No.	Page
45. Policy Tools, Actors, and Goals of Science Policy and Technology Policy	281
46. Tenets of Science and Technology Policy, 1960-84	285
47. Forces Affecting Science and Technology Policy Since 1960	287
48. Federal Government Policies Toward Information Technology R&D	288
49. Department of Defense Funding for Basic Research by Discipline, Fiscal Years 1982, 1983, and 1984	296

Figures

Figure No.	Page
50. Federal R&D Budget Authority for Defense and Nondefense Activities	295
51. Federal R&D Budget Authority for Defense Activities by Character of Work	295

Chapter 8
Information Technology R&D in the Context of U.S. Science and Technology Policy

Findings

- Information technology is one of the most dynamic and controversial areas of U.S. science and technology due to its rapid pace of change, the emphasis placed on this technology for economic growth and for national security, and the pervasive or "core" nature of the technology and its effects.
- In this area there is a growing conflict between policies that emphasize basic research and policies that focus on international competitiveness and applications. These issues are prominent in information technology R&D because the lines between basic and applied research are so uncertain.
- Interest in **coordinating** Federal policy for information technology is intensifying, in part because of foreign government policies, growing costs for R&D, and growing concern for international competitiveness. Although coordination of various aspects of Federal policy has been debated for decades, it is a particularly salient issue in information technology: many Government agencies are involved, but none devote high-level policy attention to this area. The advantages of centralization or coordination are that it could save money and more effectively focus R&D in critical areas; the possible disadvantages include the establishment of a cumbersome bureaucracy and the loss of agency autonomy and flexibility.
- The dominance of the **Department of Defense** in information technology R&D has raised questions: Is military work siphoning off too much talent from civilian applications? Is the military work changing the direction of research in information technology in ways that are disadvantageous for the commercial sector or for the public? And are existing efforts to transfer technology from military to commercial applications adequate? Evidence currently suggests that there are growing problems in this area.
- Current policies and practices toward information technology R&D conflict with the realities of increasing **international competition**. The situation may call for a more sophisticated Government role in monitoring and support of industry and research.

Introduction

Earlier chapters documented the rapid changes occurring in information technology research and development. The technologies themselves continue to change in cost, power, and the variety of functions they can perform. At the same time, institutional structures for

R&D are quickly evolving, international competition is intensifying, and the technology's impact on a wide range of social issues and problems is increasingly prominent. Because information technology is pervasive, its effects cascade through many aspects of society—from science itself to education, business, and defense—and at each point create seemingly independent changes and conflicts.

These changes are bringing increased attention to U.S. policy toward information technology R&D. In particular, Japanese and European policies, as noted in chapter 7, have brought increasing demands for U.S. policy responses.

Because the effects of information technology are so wide-ranging, any policy to respond to this technology must consider not only actions within specific issue areas such as manpower, but also broader issues in science and technology policy, such as the organization of Government and the roles of different agencies in R&D. The purpose of this chapter is to examine these more general frameworks for policy toward information technology R&D.

The chapter is divided into two major sections. The first begins with some brief background on science and technology policy in the United States, and the forces that have affected this policy as it has unfolded over the last few decades. Then, the chapter shows how these broad policies and forces set the context for and are closely tied to policy toward information technology. In the second section of the chapter, OTA discusses three key areas that are central to the science and technology policy issues raised by information technology R&D. The areas are the organization of Government, the balance of military and civilian roles, and policy measures to enhance international competitiveness.

Part I: Background

General U.S. Science and Technology Policies

Historically, science policy has been the term used to describe the actions of Government that affect the funding, organization, performance, and use of science.[1] The term has included policy for technology and engineering as well as for science. More recently, however, as technology has played a more prominent role in society and industry, many experts view "science policy" as inadequate in addressing concerns of technology.[2] The term "technology policy" has been used increasingly to refer to policy measures much more directly related to development and use of technologies, particularly as they relate to international competitiveness. In some recent discussions of industrial policy, technology policy has sometimes been considered an element of, or even a synonym for, industrial policy.

Table 45 sketches some of the actors and policy tools involved in both science and technology policy. The two types of policies have different, yet overlapping, constituencies and goals. In an area such as information technology, where "science" and "technology" are often commingled, the boundary between science policy and technology policy is vague. Recent statements of science policy (box A) illustrate the priorities of various policymakers, and show how science and technology are often mentioned together and blurred in the formation of policy. Note that although executive branch statements of science policy may be the most visible, other actors in the science policymaking arena—particularly Congress

---
[1] Science Policy Research Division, Congressional Research Service, *Science Policy, A Working Glossary* (Washington, DC: U.S. Government Printing Office, 1976).

[2] See, for example, J. J. Baruch, "The Cultures of Science and Technology," *Science*, Apr. 6, 1984. Baruch argues that lumping science and technology policy together is unwise, since the two enterprises have quite different approaches, goals, and needs.

Table 45.—Policy Tools, Actors, and Goals of Science Policy and Technology Policy

Science Policy[a]	Technology Policy[a]
Primary policy tools: Funding of basic research Scientific manpower and education measures Science information dissemination International exchange programs	*Primary policy tools* Mission-oriented R&D funding Engineering manpower and education measures Technology transfer mechanisms Limits on international flow of technology and information R&D tax credits Standards and patent policies University/industry research collaboration
Primary Actors: Office of Science and Technology Policy (The White House) National Science Foundation, National Science Board National Academy of Sciences Agencies conducting basic research, e.g., Department of Defense, National Institutes of Health Congress University science community American Association for the Advancement of Science Professional societies—e.g., American Medical Association, American Chemical Society	*Primary Actors:* Office of Science and Technology Policy National Science Foundation National Academy of Engineering Mission agencies—e.g., Departments of Defense, Energy, the National Aeronautics and Space Administration Congress Industrial R&D community Industry associations—e.g., Information Industry Association Professional societies—e.g., Institute for Electrical and Electronics Engineers, Association for Computing Machinery Department of Commerce—International Trade Administration, National Bureau of Standards, National Telecommunications and Information Administration
Social goals: Quality of life Knowledge for knowledge's sake Equity, education	*Social goals:* Economic well-being National security Technological leadership

[a]"Science policy" and "technology policy" are often difficult to separate. The policy tools, actors, and goals listed under each category are those that tend to be associated with science policy or with technology policy. However, in many practical situations, the issues and actors are intertwined.

SOURCE: Office of Technology Assessment.

and the scientists and engineers themselves—have a strong (some would say dominant) influence over actual policy.

A brief history of U.S. science policy (which, as noted above, has usually been defined to include technology policy) is helpful in order to provide a context for the gradual unfolding of policy toward information technology.[3] U.S. science policy has evolved since the 1940s out of tension between two fundamental premises:

1. that research should be supported in order to push ahead the frontiers of human understanding ("science for the sake of science"), lay the groundwork for technological advances, and train future scientists and engineers; and

---

[3]This chapter's analysis of science and technology policy is a synthesis of published books, articles, statements and legislation; in addition, OTA and its contractor (J. F. Coates, Inc.) conducted interviews with several dozen science policy experts. OTA is indebted to this group (see acknowledgments at the front of this volume) for their insights and assistance, although OTA takes full responsibility for the content of this report. For a fuller elaboration of history and issues in science policy, readers should consult, for example: Harvey Brooks, *The Government of Science* (Cambridge, MA: MIT Press, 1968); W. Henry Lambright, *Governing Science and Technology* (New York: Oxford University Press, 1976); Daniel S. Greenberg, *The Politics of Pure Science* (New York: New American Library, 1971); A. Hunter Dupree, *Science in the Federal Government* (Cambridge, MA: Harvard University Press, 1953); U.S. General Accounting Office, *Major Science and Technology Issues* (Washington, DC: GAO, Jan. 30, 1981); Congressional Budget Office, *Federal Support for R&D and Innovation* (Washington, DC: CBO, April 1984); Science Policy Research Division, Congressional Research Service, *National Science Board: Science Policy and Management for the National Science Foundation, 1968-1980,* January 1983; Frank Press, "Science and Technology in the White House, 1977 to 1980," *Science,* Jan. 9, 1981, pp. 139-145, and Jan. 16, 1981, pp. 249-256; and the annual series of reports on R&D from the American Association for the Advancement of Science. For a comprehensive view of the role of one key player in science policymaking, see *Toward the Endless Frontier: History of the Committee on Science and Technology, 1959-79,* House Science and Technology Committee Print (Washington, DC: U.S. Government Printing Office, 1980).

Box A.—Science Policy Statements

From *Chemical and Engineering News,* January 1982 interview with Science Advisor George Keyworth:

C&EN: What would be the distinguishing feature of this Administration's science policy as you would shape it?

Keyworth: Three things. Concentration on basic research. Second, trying to decrease the federal role in the support in the near term of technology that the private sector can support, like synthetic fuels. And third, and most important, is the requirement to discriminate upon the areas where the return on the federal investment merits the costs in a time of fiscal duress.

What I'm trying to do is define the word, discrimination. In basic research it is relatively simple. What we are trying to do is support those areas where the promise is greatest, where likelihood of major advances in our understanding of nature is greatest, and in other areas, more applied science and technology where federal responsibility is clear and where there is real need.

One example would be microelectronics. The semiconductor industry in this country is a major high-technology industry facing increased competition from other nations. I think it is important that the federal role, in addition to what can be accomplished by tax incentives, maintain support for basic condensed matter science that influences future breakthroughs in our understanding of semiconductor technology. In other words, selecting the areas where you are going to invest your federal R&D dollars as well as investing in the people and the institutions that have the most promise for achieving excellence.

From Public Law 94-282, National Science and Technology Policy, Organization and Priorities Act of 1976:

SEC. 102 (a) Principles.—In view of the foregoing, the Congress declares that the United States shall adhere to a national policy for science and technology which includes the following principles:

(1) The continuing development and implementation of strategies for determining and achieving the appropriate scope, level, direction, and extent of scientific and technological efforts based upon a continuous appraisal of the role of science and technology in achieving goals and formulating policies of the United States, and reflecting the views of State and local governments and representative public groups.

(2) The enlistment of science and technology to foster a healthy economy in which the directions of growth and innovation are compatible with the prudent and frugal use of resources and with the preservation of a benign environment.

(3) The enlistment of science and technology operations so as to serve domestic needs while promoting foreign policy objectives.

(4) the recruitment, education, training, retraining, and beneficial use of adequate numbers of scientists, engineers, and technologists, and the promotion by the Federal Government of the effective and efficient utilization in the national interest of the Nation's human resources in science, engineering, and technology.

(5) The development and maintenance of a solid base for science and technology in the United States, including: (A) strong participation of and cooperative relationships with State and local governments and the private sector; (B) the maintenance and strengthening of diversified scientific and technological capabilities in government, industry, and the universities, and the encouragement of independent initiatives based on such capabilities, together with elimination of needless barriers to scientific and technological innovation; (C) effective management of dissemination of scientific and technological information; (D) establishment of essential scientific, technical and industrial standards and measurement and test methods; and (E) promotion of increased public understanding of science and technology.

(6) The recognition that, as changing circumstances require periodic revision and adaptation of title I of this Act, the Federal Government is responsible for identifying and interpreting the changes in those circumstances as they occur, and for effecting subsequent changes in title I as appropriate.

From President Carter's 1979 message to Congress on Science and Technology:

Yet despite the centrality of science and technology in our lives, the Federal government has rarely articulated a science and technology policy. This message sets forth that policy. The thesis is that new technologies can aid in the solution of many of our Nation's problems. These technologies in turn depend upon a fund of knowledge derived from basic research. The Federal government should therefore increase its support both for basic research and, where appropriate, for the application of new technologies...

The Federal government's support of research and development is critical to the overall advance of science and technology. Federal responsibility lies in three major categories:

1. The largest fraction of Federal investment serves the government's direct needs such as defense, space, and air traffic control...
2. The Federal government undertakes research and development where there is a national need to accelerate the rate of development of new technologies in the private sector.... when the risk is great or the costs are inordinately high....
3. The Federal government supports basic research to meet broad economic and social needs....

The majority of Federal support for basic research is in the mission agencies.

From the White House Office of Science and Technology Policy's 1982 Annual Science and Technology Report to the Congress:

The U.S. science policy is
- to enhance the contribution of science to the two most pressing long-term needs of the United States: national defense and the international competitiveness of U.S. industry.
- To maximize the return on national R&D investments; and
- To ensure the long-term vitality of the U.S. science and technology base.

The strategy to implement U.S. science policy
- Emphasizes excellence—in research results and in people:
- Stresses the importance of scientific relevance to national needs, and more clearly defines the appropriate roles of the Government and the private sector in supporting R&D;
- Facilitates cooperation in scientific research among Government, industry, and academia;
- Seeks to support sufficient basic and long-term applied research to ensure that the United States maintains the world's strongest science and technology enterprise;
- Emphasizes the importance of having the leading research universities in the world and of training the highest quality scientists and engineers to ensure continued U.S. qualitative leadership; and
- Allocates Federal R&D resources to support this strategy.

The U.S. technology policy is to ensure that U.S. scientific leadership results in economic and defense leadership.

The strategy to implement U.S. technology policy
- Provides tax and other incentives to the private sector for commercial R&D;
- Continues to emphasize the different private sector and Government roles in developing new technologies, products, and processes so as not to discourage private sector initiative with the threat of Government intervention and competition;
- Improves the climate of cooperation so that maximum cross-stimuli occur among Government, industry, and academia;
- Improves the ability of Federal laboratories to contribute to U.S. industry, and also takes advantage of foreign research results;
- Encourages the change in industry's outlook to emphasize long-term viability rather than only short-term gain;
- Recognizes that the service sector in the U.S. economy is gaining in importance, and focuses emphasis on R&D accordingly; and
- Recognizes the effect of economic and regulatory policies on U.S. science and technology and, ultimately, on U.S. economic competitiveness.

2. that the investment of public resources in research should be moderated and directed at specified high-priority national needs, to which the private sector is unwilling or unable to respond.

The first principle was embodied in the creation of the National Science Foundation and the National Institutes of Health to manage the distribution of public funds to support basic research. The primary mechanism for this support is research grants, which are made in response to requests by recognized scientists and validated by the judgment of their peers.

The roots of the second principle, which underlies all "mission-oriented" Government-funded research, go far back into our national history. The second principle is evident in the science policy statements of box A, particularly those from the Reagan administration, which emphasize the payoffs of science and technology for the economy and defense.

The accountability and focus indicated by the second premise is often at odds with basic research, which sets its own directions and often leads investigators down blind alleys or toward ends that may have no immediate or foreseeable practical applications.

Until the 1940s, most federally supported research was closely related to well-established Government responsibilities such as defense or exploration and development in the West, or to areas basic to the national economy (agriculture, water, and public health). After World War II, leaders such as Vannevar Bush—realizing that we had entered an era of rapid advancement in scientific knowledge that could create new technologies and industries—forcefully led the Nation to accept increased, systematic, and continuing support for science through funding of basic research and science education.[4]

---

[4]See Vannevar Bush, "Science, the Endless Frontier: A Report to the President on a Program for Postwar Scientific Research," originally published in 1945, reprinted by the National Science Foundation, Washington, DC, 1960.

The clearest landmark event in the post-war era was the Soviet launch of Sputnik in 1957, which had two major kinds of effects. The response to Sputnik—the technological venture to put a man on the Moon, and bring him back, by the end of the decade of the 1960s—was unique for a non-war effort in having a singular clarity of mission and unequivocal criteria for success. This mission galvanized a large portion of the scientific and technological enterprise to a single clear goal. The second, more diffuse consequence was to redirect the Nation's attention, albeit for only a brief period, to science, science education and new scientific opportunities.

The premises of science policy, as described above, have gradually evolved into a set of relatively consistent basic tenets or assumptions that guide Government's actions. OTA derived the science policy statements in table 46 primarily from the practices and behavior of U.S. policymakers and institutions over the past 25 years, as well as from published statements and policies and interviews with science policy analysts. Although these principles have been relatively stable, they may contradict one another and come into conflict in special cases, and exceptions could certainly be found for each item in the list. Furthermore, they have rarely been stated explicitly; instead, they are embodied in a diverse collection of decisions, practices, and legislation. While table 46 is in no way a complete set of the principles which guide U.S. science policy, the essential tenets relevant to information technology are included.

Each of the science policy statements displayed in table 46 has varied in importance and salience in driving programs, projects, and organizational relationships. Often, the processes by which a policy issue is resolved result in an overcorrection of some situation which, in turn, later leads to the recognition that the pendulum has swung too far. For example, the advent of Sputnik was perceived to indicate that support for basic science had been too weak. On the other hand, the Mans-

Table 46.—Tenets of Science and Technology Policy, 1960-84

Basic Research
1. Basic research is a Federal mission.
2. The best model for conduct of the basic scientific enterprise is physical science, and in particular, physics.
3. Peer review will be the primary means for selecting topics for basic research. Management concerns will play a role in more mission oriented research.
4. Manpower for the scientific enterprise will be produced primarily as derivative of, and as an intimate part of, basic research at universities.
5. Social sciences will flourish under the traditional (physical science) model of scientific research. Social and interdisciplinary research are keys to the more effective application of knowledge to many classes of societal problems.

Mission Agency R&D
6. There is a useful and significant distinction between basic and applied research and between research, engineering, and technological applications. These distinctions are of primary value in defining the role of Government in relation to the general economy and the role of Government agencies in relation to their missions and to each other.
7. Mission agencies will define their knowledge needs which may be satisfied through R&D and present their case through the budget process.
8. Federal agencies are expected to undertake research in support of the commercial, business, and private sector insofar as support of that research will yield substantial public benefit, especially to the clients and constituents of that agency. Support is encouraged only in those cases where research to satisfy nongovernmental needs is unlikely to be adequately sustained by private initiative.

Defense R&D
9. Defense research, although a major part of U.S. R&D expenditures, will be treated as an isolated, separate case with the expectation that side benefits will accrue to the larger scientific and industrial community.
10. DOD will have a restricted and limited role in support of basic and social research at universities. This policy, manifested in the Mansfield amendment under the renewed pressures of the Cold War, has been relaxed.

Organization of Government
11. Voluntary coordination, rather than legislative or centralized control and coercion, will be the primary instrument by which programs in and among agencies will be integrated. Coordination will be a primary mechanism for assuring completeness of coverage of essential fields and the primary instrument for reducing overlap and redundant budgets and programs.
12. At the Executive level, the Office of Management and Budget will exercise its statutory role in assuring that mission needs are met and that research and development programs are reasonable and realistic. There is also a role for a White House science policy advice mechanism.
13. In the Congress, oversight, both general and budgetary, will be the primary technique by which quality, completeness, and fullness will be assured.
14. Planning for science and setting the agenda for science and technology are best handled by the mission agencies or the specific disciplines.
15. Public and stakeholder participation in science and technology decisionmaking is appropriate, desirable, and encouraged.

Special Federal Roles
16. The Federal Government will help assure the strength of the research system by collecting, analyzing, and disseminating information on subjects such as science, scientific and engineering manpower, and technological innovation.
17. National laboratories are general assets to the nation, well beyond the particular missions for which they were established.

R&D Funding
18. The scientific community may operate on the assumption that there is a firm long-term implicit commitment to incremental funding increases.
19. To avoid disturbances in the established pattern of support for science, the identification of new problems, issues, and options will be handled primarily by budget augmentation, rather than by reprogramming of existing programs. The primary instrument for effective infusion of money in large quantities for new scientific enterprises will be the establishment of an office, a bureau, an agency, or a division.
20. In most fields, the most appropriate method of support will be funding individual projects by individual investigators.
21. On large expensive basic science projects, the Federal role is to provide large block funding and long-term support. It will stand clear of the programmatic side of those activities.

Nonfederal R&D
22. Both basic and applied research in the commercial sector is best and most effectively handled by individual corporations and will best prosper under competition. To facilitate that development certain public strategies, such as patents, copyrights, tax write-offs, and a variety of other measures are appropriate for Government. American commercial research requires no particular Government intervention, attention, or assistance, since it can cope with any foreign competition.
23. Applied research applicable to the private and nonfederal public sector requires little attention. It will take care of itself.
24. Good relationships between universities and industry are beneficial to both institutions, and Government will act to support such relationships, but not directly intervene.

Utilization of Research
25. The free and open dissemination of research results, except those of a commercial proprietary sort or affecting national security, is the best guarantee of the effective use of new knowledge in the service of the nation.
26. With regard to basic research, technology transfer, that is, the practical use of research results, is best handled by the delivery of scientific information through journals and monographs. Commercial use best occurs through scientific channels, through the employment of university scientists as consultants, and through private sec-

Table 46.—Tenents of Science and Technology Policy, 1960-84—continued

tor organizations assuming responsibility for remaining alert to developments in their own interests.
27. Mission agencies have the primary responsibility for getting the scientific and technical results of research to potential users within their mission areas.
28. It is in the national interest to deprive Iron Curtain countries of the benefits of Western, that is American, science and technology. Consequently, systematic restraints will be placed upon trade and exchange where appropriate, primarily at the discretion and behest of the national security establishment.

Technology
29. Policy toward technology is unnecessary or will be treated as an adjunct to science policy. This policy has, of course, come under some challenge in the last few years.

SOURCE: OTA analysis, interviews with science policy experts, and synthesis of published materials. See footnote 3. Note that these are statements of underlying policies, and there are exceptions and contradictions to each statement.

---

field amendment[5] was a rebuke to DOD for obscuring the distinction between basic and mission-oriented research, but it also swung Government away from the Sputnik-induced changes and back toward accountability and strictly defined applied research.

Nevertheless, most of the principles highlighted in table 46 have remained effective and functional over the past quarter-century. As general science policies they influence research and development in the area of information technology. While many of these influences are subtle or indirect, the principles shown in table 46 can be seen in the current situation. For example, the U.S. Government's position toward the global market, reflecting the propositions above, is that industrial competition will deal effectively with issues of international competition and no special Government policy is required. This is in sharp contrast, of course, to Japanese and European strategies, as noted in chapter 7, and this contrast has intensified the debate about appropriate Federal roles in international competitiveness. While these are largely issues of trade policy, there are strong connections between trade and science policies, especially in information technology.

Other aspects of policy toward information technology R&D that stem directly from these general science policies include the separation of military and civilian research in information technology R&D, and the implicit belief that the market process will take care of the downstream social effects of information technology. The next section of this chapter will set forth policies toward information technology R&D in more detail.

Since 1960, several important trends and forces have affected both general science policy and policies toward information technology R&D in particular. Table 47 highlights some of these forces. As is evident from the second column of table 47, many of the forces affecting science policy generally have been particularly prominent in information technology R&D. In some respects, policy toward information technology R&D is the leading edge of issues in science and technology policy. This is in large part due to the rapid pace of change in information technology, the emphasis placed on information technology for economic growth and for national security, and the pervasive or "core" nature of the technology.

Information Technology R&D Policies

Like general science and technology policies, policies toward information technology R&D are not often explicit or coordinated. Instead there have been many decisions, actions, statements, and organizations, which taken togeth-

---

[5]As described in W. C. Boesman, "U.S. Civilian and Defense Research and Development Funding," Congressional Research Service, Science Policy Research Division, Aug. 29, 1983, p. 23:

Even after the establishment of the National Science Foundation, whose mission is the support of basic and applied research and education in the sciences, DOD continued to fund a significant amount of basic research until, in 1969, the Congress passed the "Mansfield amendment" to the fiscal year 1970 military procurement authorization which prohibited funds authorized by that law from being used to conduct R&D not having "a direct and apparent relationship to a specific military function or operation."

The following year, the Congress passed the "modified Mansfield amendment" to the fiscal year 1971 military procurement authorization which prohibited funds authorized by that "or any other Act" from being used to conduct R&D unless the Secretary of Defense determines the existence "of a potential relationship to a military function or operation."

Table 47.—Forces Affecting Science and Technology Policy Since 1960

Trend or force	Implications for R&D in information technology
1. *Growing pervasiveness of science and technology in society.* This is accompanied by rapid blurring of traditional distinctions between basic and applied research, and between science and technology.	Information technology is one of the most vivid examples of this growing pervasiveness. The intertwined nature of basic and applied work, and of information science and technology, raises questions about appropriate Federal roles, which have traditionally been based on those distinctions.
2. *Integration of the global economy.* This is accompanied by an increase in international competition, a challenge to U.S. supremacy in certain research areas, and a growing consensus that U.S. industries are not invincible and may need help.	Information technology is an area in which these challenges have become quite intense: while we still lead in most areas of R&D, our lead is narrowing, and our ability to use our technological leadership in applications for economic gain is in question. The margin of error for actions in information technology R&D has been dramatically reduced because of international competition.
3. *The shifting role of the Department of Defense.* DOD sponsorship of R&D was dominant in the post war era, then was shifted away from basic research and other agencies played stronger roles. Now DOD is once again dominant in most areas of R&D funding, although the funding is much more directed than it was after World War II.	DOD was an early and strong supporter of many areas of information technology. 70-80 percent of Federal funding for R&D in information technology now comes from DOD. In certain areas (e.g., artificial intelligence, software engineering), DOD continues to be a very strong influence on the directions for R&D.
4. *The side effects of technology.* The public seems to have grown increasingly wary of technology, particularly in the '60s and '70s. At the same time, science and technology are viewed as a way out of our economic malaise.	Though there are concerns about privacy and equity issues, use of information technology seems to be viewed as inevitable, and, in many cases, desirable. R&D in information technology, as the basis for innovations, is viewed as essential to support an economy heavily oriented toward high technology.
5. *Big budgets for R&D.* Demand for accountability has grown as R&D budgets have swelled and agencies have undertaken major projects (e.g., accelerators, weapons systems).	The demand for accountability has just begun in information technology R&D, particularly in major software projects, or use of supercomputers. Universities in particular are squeezed by rapidly rising costs for this research.
6. *Internal upheaval in the science enterprise.* The decade-long search for a more effective science policy apparatus has bounced around government, focusing at various times on agencies such as NSF and OSTP. None have been conspicuously effective in a broad-scale science policy role.	Information technology R&D is acutely affected by the multiplicity of agencies and roles in setting policy. Because of the technology's pervasiveness, more than a dozen agencies set policy for R&D in information technology. None of them have devoted high-level policy attention to information technology; it tends to be viewed as a tool.

SOURCE: OTA analysis, interviews with science and technology policy experts, and synthesis of published material. See footnote 3.

er comprise the de facto U.S. information technology R&D policy. Using techniques similar to those used to develop table 46—i.e., analysis of published material and the actions of policymakers, and discussions with policy experts—OTA produced a list of policies specifically related to information technology R&D, which are displayed in table 48. Each of these, elaborated below, can be seen to stem relatively directly from one or more of the tenets outlined in table 46. Note that the following are statements of the effective principles that appear to underlie Government's actions over the past quarter-century. As in the statements of general science policies, OTA has made no judgment that they are necessarily appropriate at present or in the future.

1. **The Federal Government has operated under the assumption that the United States should not be dependent on foreign information technologies to ensure its national security.**

A primary mission area for information technology R&D is national security. Defense spending dominates Federal support in this area of R&D. The U.S. position as leader of the Western military alliance has led to a commitment to keep the United States at the forefront of information technology developments.

Table 48.—Federal Government Policies Toward Information Technology R&D

1. The Federal Government has operated under the assumption that the United States should not be dependent on foreign technologies to ensure its national security.
2. Information technology R&D has been funded separately for civilian and military applications.
3. R&D priorities have been set in Government by mission agencies, and in commercial application areas by the private sector.
4. The Federal Government has assumed that it should promote continuous innovation in information technology.
5. The market has been assumed to be the best mechanism to bring the civilian benefits of R&D in information technology to society.
6. The market has been the primary means to attend to the consequences and effects of information technologies.
7. Where necessary, the Government has used traditional means for regulating the behavior of firms in information technology industries.
8. The short- and long-term manpower needs of information technology R&D have been addressed through traditional means.
9. Government has followed industry's lead in setting standards except where Government is a dominant purchaser.
10. The Federal Government has assumed that free trade policies benefit the United States in the long term.
11. U.S. Government has restricted the export of sensitive technical information, as well as advanced information technology itself, to Eastern Bloc nations.
12. The primary international role for the U.S. Government in information technology has been to promote equitable use of common global resources.

SOURCE: See text.

2. Information technology R&D has been funded separately for civilian and military applications.

This policy is not unique to information technology R&D. It assumes that a useful distinction can be drawn between civilian and military uses of information technology. It also assumes that there is little overlap between the civilian and military uses in this area, and that where such overlap exists, as in weather forecasting, the results of military R&D will find their way into commercial uses. In a few cases, there are small transfers of funds from military to civilian agencies performing R&D.

3. R&D priorities have been set in Government by mission agencies, and in commercial application areas by the private sector.

Government sees information technology as a tool. Therefore, information technology R&D is decentralized. Each agency sets its own R&D priorities—the National Weather Service, U.S. Postal Service, the Department of the Treasury, the Federal Aviation Administration, the Federal Reserve Board, and so on. This area of R&D has not received high level or coordinated policy attention.

4. The Federal Government has assumed that it should promote continuous growth and change in information technology.

Innovation in information technology is viewed as overwhelmingly beneficial to society. On the military side, Government seeks continual innovation in order to keep ahead or abreast of potential adversaries. On the civil side, the contributions of information technology to productivity argue for continued advances to keep the U.S. economy prosperous. On the other hand, the concentration on innovation tends to shift attention, especially within Federal R&D, to new and glamorous technologies and away from improving or reducing the costs of existing technologies.[6]

5. The market has been assumed to be the best mechanism to bring the civilian benefits of R&D in information technology to society.

For the most part Government policy has assumed that the market will identify and meet the needs of society for information technology and that the market will make the appropriate investments in R&D to meet those needs. Similarly, Government policy has assumed that industry will develop the supporting technologies and infrastructure such as software quality control processes as part of meeting the market's needs.

Government frequently encourages innovation in the private sector through indirect measures such as procurement and tax allowances. In cases where developments are important to the national interest, such as national electronic mail, Government has used R&D

---
[6]See L. Thurow, "The relationship between defense-related and civilian-oriented research and development priorities," in *Priorities and Efficiency in Federal Research and Development*, a compendium of papers submitted to the Subcommittee on Priorities and Economy in Government of the Joint Economic Committee of the Congress, Oct. 29, 1976.

contracts to promote innovation while limiting the risks to industry.

6. **The market has been the primary means to attend to the consequences and effects of information technologies.**

This policy assumes positive impacts will result in new markets, while producers will reduce adverse impacts in order to remove impediments to present and future applications. Protection of individual rights is the major exception to the reliance on the market. The Congress, the executive branch, and the courts have all attempted to cope with the issues of individual privacy, intellectual property, and freedom of access. For the most part, the assumption underlying their deliberations and actions is that traditional legal, regulatory, or organizational mechanisms can handle these issues.

7. **Where necessary, the Government has used traditional means for regulating the behavior of firms in information technology industries.**

Historically, the Government seems to have assumed that there is nothing special about information technology industries. Government has not seen antitrust, patent, tax and other regulatory policies as major impediments to innovation. For the past half-century, Government has assumed that: 1) regulated monopolies such as AT&T are effective performers of R&D; and 2) developments in regulated and unregulated areas of telecommunications and computers are not in conflict.

8. **The short- and long-term manpower needs of information technology R&D have been addressed through traditional means.**

As noted in chapter 5, the Government has relied on the universities to meet the needs of the market for the trained scientists and engineers necessary for innovation in information technology. Support of research in information technology at universities is the primary method by which the Federal Government supports manpower development in the field. Government has also assumed that the universities, assisted by various subsidies, will make the necessary investments in equipment to provide the appropriate training for these future information scientists and engineers.

9. **Government has followed industry's lead in setting standards except where Government is a dominant purchaser.**

Government treats information technology like any other industrial product in terms of standards, relying mostly on voluntary industry standards. When Government does get involved in standards-setting, it is usually at the request of industry. In the computer field, the Institute for Computer Sciences and Technology (ICST) at the National Bureau of Standards is responsible for developing standards for the Federal Government, and it also participates in and coordinates a variety of industry standards efforts. In certain cases such as computer networking standards, ICST has taken a firm leadership role, both domestically and internationally.[7]

10. **The Federal Government has assumed that free trade policies benefit the United States in the long term.**

From transistor radios to microchips, the U.S. Government has maintained a position of free trade in the area of information technology. The assumptions underlying this policy have been: 1) free trade will open up foreign markets for U.S products, 2) the U.S. lead in information technology is largely unassailable, 3) the marginal benefits of lower costs to the consumer outweigh the threat to U.S. industry, and 4) competition promotes innovation.

This openness has included access to R&D through the published literature, licensing, joint ventures, and other commercial routes.

11. **The U.S. Government has restricted the export of sensitive technical information, as well as advanced information technology itself, to Eastern bloc nations.**

The importance of information technologies to U.S. national security has led to Government actions to preserve the superiority of U.S. in-

---
[7]J. H. Young, "Effects of Standards on Information Technology R&D," paper prepared for OTA, Nov. 25, 1983.

formation technology. One way is to prevent its adversaries from getting access to, for example, certain research publications, advanced chip designs or cryptography software. This policy assumes that: 1) the Government can effectively control the international operations of U.S. researchers and firms, 2) these controls will not unduly harm the viability of the U.S. information technology industry, and 3) the advantage of such controls outweighs harm done to the U.S. R&D enterprise through restriction of information flow among researchers.

12. **The primary international role for the U.S. Government in information technology has been to promote equitable use of common global resources.**

U.S. actions regarding international use of information technologies have focused on issues such as spectrum allocation, the use of the geosynchronous orbit, the international use of communications satellites, and access to data from weather and other Earth applications satellites.

Part II: Key Issue Areas

The previous section provided background on the nature of policies related to information technology R&D, and on the connections between those policies and broader science and technology policies. A central conclusion is that information technology R&D has been influenced to a substantial degree by policies applicable across many areas of science and technology. However, factors such as the reliance on information technology for economic growth and national security, and the pervasive, core nature of the technology, are increasingly stressing policy toward information technology R&D, focusing attention upon it, and setting it apart from policy for other areas of science and technology.

This section attempts to build on that foundation by examining three particular areas of policy toward information technology R&D that may be ripe for change or improvement. OTA selected the three issue areas because they are key problems for the future development of information technology R&D. Throughout this report, scores of issues have been identified which, in themselves, merit attention. The three issues discussed in this chapter are overarching, in that they subsume many of the earlier issues. Addressing these three areas could help set the direction for many of the more detailed issues. The first, and most fundamental, topic is the organization of Government to deal with information technology R&D. The second issue area is the balance of civilian and military funding in this area of R&D. The final area is international competitiveness.

ISSUE A: Organization of Government

Demands for coherent Federal policy towards information technology R&D conflict with the traditional system of pluralist decisionmaking by various agencies and the private sector.

Introduction

The search for coherence and effectiveness in science policy of all kinds has been the object of many commissions, proposals, legislative initiatives, and reorganization plans. A hundred years ago the first plan for developing a Department of Science and Technology was introduced in the Congress.[8] Several times in the 1970s and again within the last year, the idea of such a central department has reemerged.[9] The fundamental issue coming out of all such proposals is whether science is better managed through a central organization

---
[8]For a discussion see A. H. Dupree, *Science in the Federal Government,* Harvard University Press, 1953, p. xi.
[9]See, for example, H.R. 481, The National Technology Foundation Act, introduced Jan. 6, 1983, by Rep. George Brown, et al.

or as an adjunct to the missions of the Federal Government as reflected by the mission agencies.

While the proposals for a central Department of Science and Technology have consistently failed, the Nation has reorganized its science and technology apparatus several times to meet new and emerging needs. The Department of Energy, the Environmental Protection Agency (EPA), and the National Oceanic and Atmospheric Administration (NOAA) all resulted from the coalescence or rearrangement of diverse scientific and technical functions.

Nevertheless, the traditional Government organization for science in general is decentralized, pluralistic, and only loosely coordinated. The strong centralizing force on science comes from the annual budget review by the Office of Management and Budget. Even there, concern for scientific issues is for the most part split up along agency lines; for example, NASA is in one area, NOAA in another, and Defense science in still another. This pluralistic system of Federal policymaking has the advantages of allowing mission agencies to tailor R&D to their own needs, which is a basic tenet of science policy as discussed earlier. However, several trends are putting stress upon the ability of the current decentralized system to cope with new and emerging problems:

- Increasing international competition, and the presence of coordinated technology policies among our trading partners, are highlighting our absence of coordination and causing many to call for reexamination and change; and
- The costs of R&D of all kinds have risen. At the same time, there is increased pressure on the Federal budget from entitlements, defense, and the deficit. Some argue that a more coordinated and coherent Federal science and technology apparatus could be more cost-effective and accountable.

There is a broad spectrum of possibilities for coordination of Federal activities in science and technology areas, ranging from complete decentralization and pluralism to a central agency which handles the bulk of R&D funding and science policymaking. Despite the appeal of coordination in principle, it has costs that include decreased flexibility of mission agencies, creation of cumbersome bureaucracies, and potential loss of multiple funding avenues—and hence multiple approaches—for researchers. One report notes:

> Coordination is like motherhood; everyone agrees it must be done but it lacks an operational definition.
> Coordination is not a homogenous activity; but rather an umbrella which encompasses many different activities performed by different people, for similar effect.
> Coordination requires significant effort at all levels of management and, therefore, both horizontal and vertical structures need to be considered.
> A certain amount of coordination is good for the health of Government, but like exercise, too much will cripple or kill.[10]

Consequently, most science policy experts argue that some combination of centralized decisionmaking, ad hoc coordination, and mission autonomy is appropriate.[11]

Dimensions of the Issue

Current responsibilities for information technology are dispersed all over Government—from the Department of Defense to the General Services Administration, from the Department of Justice to the Federal Communications Commission. The ad hoc nature of policy in this area is even more evident than most other types of science policy because agencies tend to see information technology as a tool, not as something warranting significant policy attention in itself. In addition, there are simply more agencies involved because of the pervasive nature of information technology.

---

[10]W. A. Hahn, D. S. Alberts, and J. Lovelace, "Interagency Coordination: Workshop Report," in *The Management of Federal Research and Development: An Analysis of Major Issues and Processes* (McLean, VA: The Mitre Corp., 1977), pp. 93-97.

[11]See, for example, Harvey Brooks, *The Government of Science* (Cambridge, MA: MIT Press, 1968).

More than a dozen agencies fund or affect relevant R&D.[12]

There is, however, some coordination in Federal policy. To the extent that DOD dominates R&D funding, it is the de facto lead agency and informal or formal coordination point. And agencies often coordinate their work on an ad hoc basis. For example, the Defense Advanced Research Projects Agency (DARPA) and NSF brief each other on computer science research programs.[13] And ICST at the National Bureau of Standards has a group of senior officials from major agencies who advise the Institute on its programs.

Several specific factors focus attention on the degree of coordination and coherence in policy toward information technology R&D.[14] Among them:

- In general, there is a lack of high-level policy commitment in this area, which has several kinds of effects. One is that the role of mission agencies in information technology is shifting, uncertain and as divergent as the roles of those agencies themselves. Coordination would be useful in such subjects as database collection, R&D research topics, and compatibility of technology and information.
- Many have argued that there are substantial shortages of manpower. However, as discussed in chapter 5, the evidence for such shortages is inconclusive, except in certain very specific areas. The lack of reliable assessments of manpower and the associated uncertainties hinder policymaking in all areas of the Government that work with information technology.
- The Federal Government has an extensive network of national laboratories, although the quality and relevance of some of these facilities has periodically been in question.[15] Researchers at various national laboratories constitute the largest concentration of expertise in use of supercomputers. The question of how best to use the national labs in this and other fields of information technology R&D cuts across a variety of agencies, in particular the Departments of Defense and Energy.
- Related to use of the national labs, chapter 3 pointed out that researchers are increasingly requiring advanced computers or "supercomputers" to perform a wide variety of research. The question of where to house such machines and how to provide access is of concern to a wide variety of agencies involved with information technology R&D. Committees of the Federal Coordinating Council for Science, Engineering and Technology (FCCSET) at OSTP have attempted to address this issue.
- As discussed in chapters 2 and 3, the emerging shared wisdom in the industry is that software is a key problem in cost and effectiveness of computing systems. Many believe that American industry has failed to give adequate research attention to software problems, preferring for a variety of reasons to emphasize hardware. The reliability and maintainability of software will become an increasingly large issue, raising questions of quality control, standards, manpower, and education policy for many agencies in the Federal Government with large information systems.

---

[12]These include the Department of Defense (itself divided into the Defense Advanced Research Projects Agency, the Office of Naval Research, the Air Force Office of Scientific Research and various other units in the Pentagon and the three services), the National Science Foundation, the Department of Commerce (largely through the National Bureau of Standards, the National Oceanic and Atmospheric Administration, and the National Telecommunications and Information Administration), the National Institutes of Health, the Department of Energy, the National Aeronautics and Space Administration, the Federal Aviation Administration, the Patent and Trademark Office, and the Department of Justice (both in their jurisdiction over antitrust, and in R&D for law enforcement systems).

[13]Elias Schutzman, National Science Foundation, personal communication, Mar. 2, 1984.

[14]For further elaboration of some of these factors and discussion of institutional options, see "Institutional Options for Addressing Information Policy Issues: A Preliminary Framework for Analyzing the Choices," a staff memorandum prepared by the Communication and Information Technologies Program of OTA, Nov. 29, 1983.

[15]See the *Report of the White House Science Council Federal Laboratory Review Panel,* May 1983, sponsored by the Office of Science and Technology Policy. (Also called "The Packard Report," after its chairman, David Packard.)

- In the area of regulation, forcing new technology into old categories is nearly universal because the new is not always seen as new, or the new is seen as a problem, not an opportunity. For example, cable television throughout the country is being treated as a local utility occupying some status resembling, perhaps, electric power. Each local government treats what could be an integrated national information utility on a short-term and somewhat parochial basis. In sharp contrast, Canada and France have adopted policies toward cable that aim to develop a national utility.
- Uncertainties about funding levels for information technology R&D contrast with the needs for stability in budgets or support as a base for long-range research in universities and industry. Examples of such uncertainty include some recent vacillations in funding of certain information technology areas by DOD agencies, particularly DARPA; and the current uncertainties concerning supercomputer research support between DARPA and NSF. (See ch. 3).
- Information technology industries are now combining technologies developed under regulation (as in radio, telephone, and television) with computer technologies basically developed in the market system. The convergence of these two types of technologies creates new regulatory issues dealing with ownership, public versus private control, privacy, and access.

Options for Addressing the Issue

As a core technology, information technology is used by everyone but is not clearly the responsibility of anyone. Yet, given its value to the balance of trade and productivity of U.S. industry, the demands for new, more coherent action have become increasingly strong.[16]

---
[16]See, for example, Science Policy Research Division, Congressional Research Service, *The Information Science and Technology Act of 1981,* June 1982.

Option 1: Maintain the Status Quo. The strongest argument for no major change in Federal activity is that the technologies and their effects are highly fluid, and it may be too early to devise appropriate policy or Government organizations. In addition, some may view coherent, coordinated Federal policy toward information technology R&D as unnecessary or infeasible. The ad hoc coordination currently used has been relatively effective, and attempting more formal coordination or more elaborate national policy could be cumbersome. In addition, pluralistic research funding has the advantage of funding more than one approach to a research topic or problem.

The disadvantage of maintaining the status quo is that we may reduce opportunities to enhance our competitiveness and to use our R&D resources in a more socially productive manner.

Option 2: Improve Monitoring and Coordination. A first step toward coordination of Federal roles would be to provide new mechanisms for the various agencies involved in this area to communicate in a systematic way. Such coordination mechanisms would at least raise the level of attention to information technology R&D issues and provide a forum which could facilitate a common understanding of areas of strength and weakness in Federal support. Congress could designate a formal coordination group with representatives from appropriate agencies involved in information technology R&D. In fact, the first priority of a coordination group could be a report to the Congress, and subsequent hearings, on those areas of strength and weakness. Though DOD would be a major player in such a coordination effort, it is important that it not dominate; the status, needs, and objectives of the civil sector should have an adequate platform.

Other coordination and monitoring steps may also be desirable. To the extent that States play a stronger role in promoting information technology R&D centers, and in using information technology for delivery of services, it may be useful to establish mechanisms whereby States and the Federal Government can cooperate in setting priorities for information technology R&D. Such mechanisms could include a national conference on the intergovernmental research needs in information technology R&D, hearings on State and local information technology R&D needs, and commissioning studies of the needs of State and local governments for improved information technology.

Option 3: Set New National Policy. A more comprehensive alternative is to make a high-level policy commitment to information technology R&D. This could be accomplished by reestablishing an office such as the Office for Telecommunications Policy in the Executive Office of the President, or elevating the responsibilities, status and visibility of the National Telecommunications and Information Administration and the Institute for Computer Science and Technology (ICST) in the Department of Commerce. To complement this action, Congress could establish a lead agency for information technology R&D policy that could devote a substantial amount of high-level attention to the issue. However, the establishment of a lead agency has the disadvantage that that agency's mission may be pursued at the expense of others.[17] Note that in the last several years Congress has been considering various proposals for centralized oversight bodies for information technology policy.[18] Congress may also wish to consider restructuring the basic oversight mechanisms for information technology R&D in the Congress and/or the executive branch.

Finally, it may be an opportune time to take action on several more detailed issues. The one that is most prominent is software, as discussed in the chapter 3 case study of software engineering. Federal standards for supporting, using, testing, updating and documenting software could add much reliability to Government information systems and consistency to relations between the Government and industry. One mechanism for dealing with these issues is to work through ICST.

Option 4: Establish a New Federal Organization. Congress could create a new organization, transferring to it much of the current dispersed responsibility for information technology and adding new functions. These new functions could include compiling and interpreting information on Federal procurement of information technology, civilian vs. military priorities in R&D, regulatory actions with direct or indirect effects on the technology, the U.S. position in domestic and international markets, social impacts of information technology, high priority issues to be resolved, and recommendations for congressional action. The advantage of such a new organization would be that it would assure that the technology would be visible and explicitly addressed; on the other hand, it could diminish the effectiveness of other organizations that pursue information technology R&D as part of their mission. A new organization could be part of a new "National Technology Foundation," or it could be a freestanding "Institute of Information and Communication."

ISSUE B: Military/Civilian Balance

Relying primarily on DOD for funding of information technology R&D may conflict with the pressing demands of international competitiveness and productivity.

Introduction

The Department of Defense (DOD) has been by far the largest supporter of information technology R&D among Federal agencies. With increasing budgets for R&D in the recent past, DOD is sponsoring a higher proportion of many fields of R&D activity. The dominance of DOD in information technology is perhaps the most striking of all, however; estimates of the proportion of DOD funding range from 70 to 80 percent or more of all Federal funding.[19] In some parts of the field, DOD has sponsored pioneering work which established

---

[17]See Brooks, op. cit.
[18]See "Institutional Options for Addressing Information Policy Issues," op. cit.

[19]These estimates are based on W. C. Boesman, "U.S. Civilian and Defense Research and Development Funding," Science Policy Research Division, Congressional Research Service, Aug. 29, 1983. Also see ch. 2 for further discussion.

foundations for both commercial and military applications. However, with tightening budgets and growing concern over international competitiveness, the wisdom of DOD's continued dominance of information technology R&D funding is coming into question. Specifically, three questions have surfaced in the course of OTA's study:

1. Is the military work siphoning off too much talent from civilian applications?
2. Is the military work changing the direction of research in information technology in ways that are disadvantageous for the commercial sector or for the public?
3. Are existing efforts to transfer technology from military to commercial applications adequate?

Dimensions of the Issue

DOD and civilian agency funding of R&D have varied in relative emphasis and roles over the past decades. The issue of DOD vs. civil funding of R&D has received little emphasis since the late 1960s, when DOD R&D was drastically reduced because of a perception that the agency had overstepped its mandate, and because of social concerns about the DOD budget. As shown in figure 50, in the past decade (and particularly during the Reagan administration) DOD funding for R&D of all kinds has risen dramatically faster than civilian agency funding, which has actually dropped in real terms. It can be misleading to use the combined term, R&D, in this discussion; as figure 51 shows, for all fields combined, the dramatic increase has been almost exclusively in development, rather than in basic or applied research.

More specifically, DOD support for work in information technology, particularly through the Defense Advanced Research Projects Agency (DARPA), has remained strong and has grown dramatically. As shown in table 49, support for basic research in mathematics and

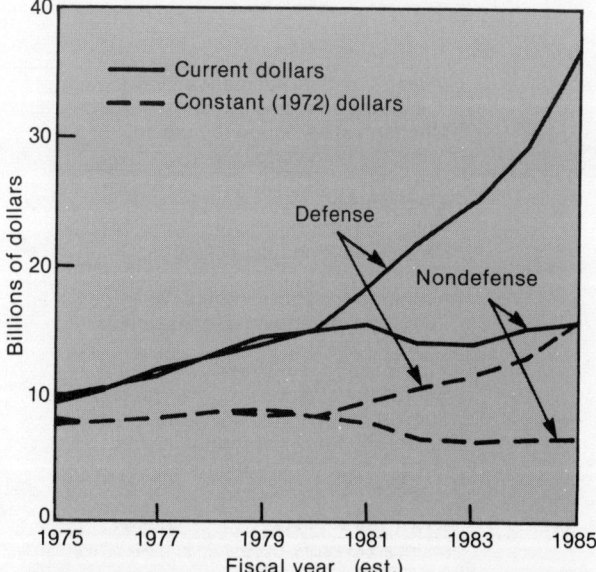

Figure 50.—Federal R&D Budget Authority for Defense and Nondefense Activities

SOURCE: Division of Science Resources Studies, National Science Foundation, "Federal R&D Funding: The 1975-85 Decade," March 1984.

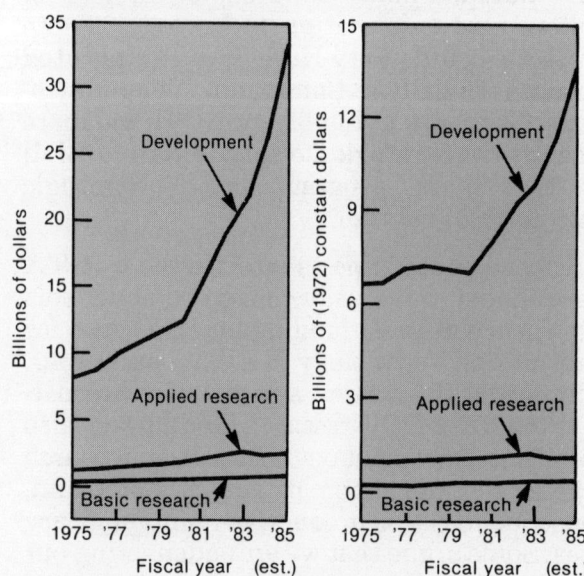

Figure 51.—Federal R&D Budget Authority for Defense Activities by Character of Work

SOURCE: Division of Science Resources Studies, National Science Foundation, "Federal R&D Funding: The 1975-85 Decade," March 1984.

Table 49.—Department of Defense Funding for Basic Research by Discipline, Fiscal Years 1982, 1983, and 1984 (budget authority in millions)

	Fiscal year 1982	Fiscal year 1983	Fiscal year 1984	Fiscal year 1985
Physics, radiation science, astronomy and astrophysics	76.0	80.9	87.2	96.6
Mechanics, aeronautics, and energy conversion	73.1	79.5	86.3	92.2
Materials	71.5	81.0	82.8	87.5
Electronics	90.0	90.5	97.9	93.7
Oceanography	51.1	50.2	53.4	57.5
Biology and medical sciences	64.9	66.3	79.8	86.7
Chemistry	53.1	58.9	62.0	66.3
Mathematics and computer sciences	83.3	98.8	111.7	124.9
Terrestrial sciences, geophysical research	24.3	29.0	30.8	33.9
Atmospheric sciences	20.8	21.8	25.0	28.2
Behavioral sciences, human resources	33.9	33.6	35.2	36.3
Special studies	—	2.0	—	—
University instrumentation	—	30.2	30.0	30.0
In-house laboratory independent research	54.1	57.5	58.4	67.0
Total	696.1	780.0	839.3	899.9

SOURCE: Leo Young, Department of Defense, presentation to AAAS Colloquium on R&D Policy, Mar. 29, 1984.

computer science grew from $83.3 million in fiscal year 1982 to a planned $124.9 million in fiscal year 1985. In applied research and development, several major projects at DOD have pumped many hundreds of millions of dollars into information technology. These projects include Very High Speed Integrated Circuits (VHSIC); Command, Communications, Control, and Intelligence (C^3I); and more recently the Strategic Defense Initiative (SDI) or "Star Wars" program, and the Strategic Computing program.

Science policy experts interviewed by OTA were almost universally concerned about this resurgence of DOD funding for R&D, and for information technology R&D in particular. Comparing the current situation to the post-War era when DOD research funding was also dominant, they point out that current research is generally much more mission-oriented and, consequently, less productive for nonmilitary uses. Some argue that we are endangering our international competitiveness in the long term by monopolizing the information technology R&D community with defense-related projects. Others point out that it is unwise to have a monolithic source of funding for any area—e.g., certain technical approaches may tend to be ignored—and argue that the current situation desperately calls for a civilian balance to DOD's funding. Despite these strong warnings, however, there is inconclusive evidence that these negative results of DOD's funding are occurring.

For example, in artificial intelligence (AI) the pool of researchers is very small and almost all receive DOD funding. As noted in chapter 3, DARPA and ONR have been almost the exclusive funders of artificial intelligence from the start. Yet, some AI researchers noted during OTA's case study that relatively basic research which could lead to nonmilitary applications—such as intelligent libraries—is being neglected. The assumption that AI R&D funded by DOD is equally applicable to both military and civilian applications is, therefore, under question, although more than anecdotal evidence is needed to assess the problem.

Other controversial topics for the science community in general are export and publication restrictions on scientific and technical information. The dominance of DOD funding of information technology R&D raises the danger that the research will be classified too early to allow nonmilitary users to benefit. This danger is particularly prominent in large-scale defense initiatives such as the "Strategic Computing" program. For academic scientists in particular, free information flow is viewed as essential to productivity and to the ethos of science as an international enterprise. Hence, the tension has produced some strong rhetoric. A university association president recently told a gathering of the American Association for the Advancement of Science: "These people feel that any delay or inconvenience for the Russians is worth whatever it costs to us... What we are seeing now is not disagreements among reasonable people; it is ideology without restraint, and it is dangerous to us all."[20]

Again, however, the extent to which restrictions on information flow have actually been onerous or counter-productive has not been carefully examined. More broadly, except for science policy analysts, most people—at universities, in Congress, or in associations or research groups—have not raised DOD funding as an issue. They may be comfortable with the current situation, or they may be uncomfortable alienating a powerful source of funding.

Part of the reason for infrequent questioning of DOD's dominance in this area is that defense applications for computer-related devices are fascinating problems. One computer columnist noted that state-of-the-art equipment, challenging problems, and the mystique of "secrecy" are powerful lures for computer scientists.[21]

[20] R. Rosenzweig, president, Association of American Universities, address to American Association for the Advancement of Science colloquium on R&D policy, Washington, DC, Mar. 30, 1984. This comment was made when the Department of Defense was considering placing restrictions on the publication of "unclassified but sensitive" research. At the time, the presidents of Stanford, California Institute of Technology, and Massachusetts Institute of Technology "warned the Reagan Administration that their institutions may be forced to stop conducting unclassified research for the Pentagon if they are required to give military reviewers the right to restrict publication of some findings." (Kim McDonald, "3 Universities Warn Pentagon on Censorship," *The Chronicle of Higher Education*, Apr. 4, 1984, p. 1.) In part in response to this outcry, the Pentagon rescinded its plan for restrictions. ("White House Decides to Cool Campus Secrecy Issue," *Science and Government Report*, June 15, 1984, p. 1). See also Albert H. Teich and Jill P. Weinberg, American Association for the Advancement of Science, "Issues in Scientific and Technical Information Policy," prepared for Office of Special Projects, National Science Foundation, Dec. 28, 1982.

[21] D. Clapp, "While Japan Builds Computers, We're Making Missiles," *Infoworld*, June 27, 1983.

Options for Addressing the Issue

Option 1: Maintain the Status Quo. While it may be desirable to have a stronger civilian government presence in information technology R&D, some would argue that our national security requirements mandate the current level of DOD involvement, and that it is impractical or unnecessary for civilian agencies to have a balancing involvement.

Potential negative consequences of maintaining the status quo are that we may be compromising international competitiveness, and hence national security, in the long term. The concerns surfacing about DOD's funding of R&D may be early signals of a serious problem, or they could be insubstantial worries. Currently we do not have reliable information to tell the difference.

Option 2: Increase Monitoring and Analysis. The clearest need in addressing the impact of DOD priorities is that it be explicitly addressed and more monitoring and analysis be done. Specific topics in need of monitoring and analysis include:

- Effectiveness and effects of national security restrictions on access to information technology research and devices—especially the exchange of ideas among leading researchers and the ability to use foreign graduate assistants on DOD-related projects.
- Effects of DOD support on the research priorities of leading researchers in the field.
- Transferability of information technology developed for DOD—the ease of transfer, the time lag—compared with primarily commercial development.
- Use of limited manpower in certain fields such as artificial intelligence and software engineering.
- Relation of DOD's requirements for information technology R&D to commercial requirements, and more broadly, the tradeoffs between national security and international competitiveness in this area.

One factor working against explicit consideration of military vs. civilian priorities in

R&D is the fact that Congress is ill-equipped to balance the funding of research among different agencies because the agencies' budgets are independent and handled by different congressional committees. The executive branch is theoretically capable of such considerations, but in practice, as noted above, it also handles agencies' budgets as discrete units. Hence, there may be a need for a new mechanism to weigh R&D goals in information technology from a multiagency perspective. Such mechanisms could include joint congressional hearings, activities of the interagency coordination body discussed in Issue A, and/or a joint study by DOD and a prominent civilian group such as the National Science Board on the relationship of DOD spending to R&D priorities. To be most effective, such a study should probably be tied to subsequent congressional hearings on the issue.

Option 2 does not preclude either of the other options, and hence may be a wise course of action in any case.

Option 3: Bolster Civilian R&D funding. Congress could act to provide a stronger civilian balance to DOD's information technology R&D funding, on the basis of the suggestive evidence of problems, or on the assumption that domination of information technology R&D by one mission agency is unwise. Though such a move would require budgetary increases of several million dollars, many industry and policy experts suggest that the ultimate payoffs in innovation and productivity would be substantial.

Such funding may go beyond some policymakers' notion of appropriate roles for Government. There does seem to be room, however, for more civilian agency funding of "fundamental" (in the sense of being widely applicable and long-term) if not "basic" (in the sense of being disinterested in applications) research in information technology. The funding agency involved would have to be careful that the research community had sufficient manpower to absorb such funds. Some experts have called for a civilian research effort that would mobilize the research community in a way similar to that of the Apollo program—it could be a 5- or 10-year effort toward specific objectives such as uses of computers for education, to aid the handicapped or poor, or other social goals.

ISSUE C: International Competitiveness

U.S. policies and practices are based on an assumption of unassailable U.S. dominance in information technology R&D, which is increasingly inaccurate.

Introduction

Information technology is an important element of global high-technology trade. As discussed in chapter 7, the efforts of the French, Japanese, and other governments to target information technologies as tickets to future international prosperity attest to that fact. Since the advent of information technologies, the United States has had the lead in development and in global market share. That situation is changing as other advanced nations are increasing their patents in international commerce, as the U.S. balance of trade in information technology begins to weaken, and as the industry becomes more global in character and thus less amenable to traditional methods of governmental control.

Dimensions of the Issue

Stresses of global integration and foreign competition on U.S. information technology R&D policies emerge in several areas. One is the effect on policies promoting development of the R&D base of U.S. industry—manpower, facilities, R&D information and R&D behavior. The issues in this area include:

- Foreign versus domestic high-tech manpower. A large percentage of the graduate students in science and engineering are foreign nationals. It has been a matter of significant national pride that the world comes to the United States for training in science; on the other hand, some have argued that we are investing resources in these foreign students which those that

leave then take away to their home country. The value we have placed on science as an international enterprise is under stress as international competition intensifies.
- A related issue is that in those areas that involve national security or commercial secrecy, there are increasing pressures to restrict access of foreign scientists and graduate students. Such restrictions could be a major dislocation in the ethos of the university.
- Restricting the access of foreign scientists to U.S. research may isolate the U.S. research community. Such isolation could reduce the infusion of new approaches and ideas into the R&D process, and thus hinder R&D in the United States.
- Our traditional linguistic chauvinism conflicts with a recognition of the need to translate literature from other countries in this area. Little of the Japanese technical literature, and only somewhat more European literature, is routinely available in English translations.
- Internationalization of the information technology industry is leading to the globalization of R&D. Countries such as Great Britain, the United States, France, and Italy are competing for the location of research centers of the major multinational firms in information technology. Scotland's Silicon Glen is an example. In addition to the competition for multinational R&D facilities, there is growing interest in joint ventures among firms in advanced nations such as Japan, Germany, the United States and France.

Issues also emerge concerning U.S. policies to maintain or improve the current U.S. leadership in information technology R&D and marketing. These include issues related to the structure of the industry, the role of DOD, and the effects of regulation on the industry:

- The individual American corporation in the information technology market may confront foreign government-coordinated, sustained, and supported consortia or consortia of private companies enjoying subsidies and generic research input from their governments.
- The openness of U.S. markets to foreign competition is not met by symmetrical U.S. access to foreign markets. U.S. manufacturers still primarily focus on the U.S. market—the world's largest for information technology. These firms may not be giving adequate attention to developing nations' markets, leaving them largely to other nations. For example, the Japanese are now vigorously pursuing countertrade with the Chinese to exchange mineral resources for Japanese high technology.
- One element of the dominance of DOD in information technology R&D is the potential diversion of talent and resources away from nonmilitary science and technology. The rigid specifications and limited applicability of many DOD-sponsored technologies could skew the development of U.S. information technologies away from those products that are of most use in foreign markets—especially markets in developing nations.
- There is a conflict between the need for free trade and the need to protect sensitive science and technology. The issue is whether U.S. export controls on information technology are unnecessarily excluding U.S. companies from effectively competing for large foreign markets.
- With the development of foreign markets for information technology, concerns arise over the access of small and medium-sized firms to foreign markets. Some feel that where U.S. firms have penetrated foreign markets, the larger firms have dominated trade, to the exclusion of the smaller firms. This is not unusual, since a large majority of manufacturing exports come from large firms. However, with the global integration of the industry, the United States may wish to encourage smaller, innovative firms to seek out foreign trade.
- Promotion of a rational world system for managing the use of information technologies is also important to the long-term leadership of the United States. Though this has long been an area of recognized

importance for U.S. policy, a number of important global standardization issues remain. For example, an increasing issue will be global compatibility of communications systems. The fact that foreign systems are generally run by national governments, while the U.S. system is a market-based system, tends to put the United States in a different, often disadvantageous, position from all the other contenders in international negotiations.

Options for Addressing the Issue

The central issue facing information technology industries is how best to enhance their ability to compete on equal footing with companies from other nations, especially where those companies are strongly supported by government. This problem affects many other industries—from steel to shoes. Continuing debate over the need for an industrial policy flows directly from this issue. As noted in chapter 7, the essential question is not how to imitate the policy strategies of Japan or other countries which appear successful, but to come up with a response that could build on unique U.S. strengths.

Option 1: Maintain the Status Quo. Some would argue that the Federal Government is ill-equipped to become more involved in a fast-paced area such as information technology. The current scheme of activities to promote international competitiveness works well in some respects; the prime role of the Government should be to provide a healthy macroeconomic business climate.

The disadvantage of the status quo is the increasing evidence that the traditional pattern of policies related to international competitiveness does not allow our industries to compete on "a level playing field" with companies from other countries. At present, there is little basis for deciding among options for dealing with foreign competition and its effects on information technology R&D. The relative newness of the threat and the rapid ideological polarization of the industrial policy debate have left the Nation long on conjecture and short on facts.

Option 2: Monitor and Support International Trade in Information Technology, and Related Efforts in R&D. Various measures have been proposed for the support of international trade, and it is beyond the scope of this report to discuss them in detail.[22] A key aspect of trade support is ensuring that foreign markets are open to U.S. industry, and helping U.S. companies to actively seek developing markets for the technology. This could involve increasing the commitment and attention of the U.S. Special Trade Representative, the International Trade Administration, and the Foreign Commercial Service to the needs of information technology firms.

Options more specifically related to R&D include promotion of generic information technology R&D centers in the United States, and close monitoring and evaluation of alternative institutional models—both domestic and foreign—for cooperative research in information technology.

Further, support for international competitiveness in R&D could include establishing mechanisms to monitor foreign technical literature and disseminate translations to American scientists and technologists. Such support could also provide funding for our research personnel to travel overseas for conferences and consultations, and for American students or professors to study overseas. Congress may wish to beef up scientific bilateral agreements and exchange programs.

In addition, it would be appropriate to analyze:

- The amount of foreign purchasing by the Bell Operating Companies that were formerly part of AT&T. As a vast market for information technologies, the behavior of these companies will be critical to the future of the U.S. industry.

---

[22]See the recent OTA report, *International Competitiveness in Electronics.*

- The extent and type of foreign ownership of U.S. information technology firms and the effects of such ownership on the transfer of information science and technology.
- The career paths of foreign computer and electrical engineering graduate students.
- The extent to which major U.S. information technology firms undertake R&D in foreign countries versus in the United States.
- The effects of joint ventures, countertrade agreements, licensing, and other arrangements on the transfer of U.S. information science and technology.

These information gathering activities would be helpful regardless of the path Congress chooses to take in addressing this issue area.

Option 3: Set National Policy. While there is much we need to know, one alternative is to begin setting a long-term policy on the role of information technology in U.S. trade, and to continue the debate on how the United States might restructure its trade policies to respond to those of Japan and other nations. In addition, the United States could assist the international competitiveness of U.S. firms by developing a national position in international standardization which would take into account the needs of Government, the private sector, and the consumers as well as balance short-term needs with the long-term development of foreign markets.

The United States could establish a more coherent policy on the flow of scientific information, and could establish a review and appeal mechanism for DOD's restrictions on the flow of information and technology.

Options 2 and 3 are not mutually exclusive, and probably make best sense in concert with each other.

Concluding Thoughts

As part of the preparation for this chapter, interviews and workshops were conducted with several dozen experts in science policy and information technology R&D. Box B is a sample of their responses to the question, "What single message would you like to get across to the Congress concerning information technology R&D?" The diversity of these responses indicates the multifaceted nature of issues related to information technology R&D. Their responses are reprinted in box B in order to illustrate the wide-ranging priorities of a group of well-informed specialists, and to provide a different perspective on some of the issues discussed earlier in the chapter.

A common theme in these comments, and in many other discussions of policy in this area, is a drive for **perspective**: for a long-range view of technological and social changes, and for policies that work together effectively in a wide range of areas.

Indeed, U.S. policy toward information technolgoy R&D, as in many other areas, is partial and incremental. This lack of long-term perspective may in part be inherent in the policymaking machinery; in other cases, policymakers have explicitly assumed that the Government will be most effective when it responds to a mature issue—an issue that has reached a level of public concern where action is clearly called for, and the background of the issue is well understood.

However, the nature of a "core" technology, facilitating major and pervasive social changes, raises questions about the utility of partial and incremental policies. Many of the issues evolving from a core technology are likely to evolve late rather than early, and are likely to be structural—that is, deeply built into the society, and hence very disruptive and traumatic to correct.

Box B.—Messages to the Congress on Information Technology R&D

During interviews and workshops related to this project, we asked people, "what single message would you like to get across to the Congress concerning information technology R&D?" Some representative messages follow:

We must have long-range planning, and corporations can't do it.

> Organize a U.S. response to MITI. Some government leadership is necessary.

Find ways to encourage young companies and young industries; not save the old ones.

> We desperately need a national effort—a *fifth generation* project but in *software, not hardware.* We have to force software development to leapfrog over where it is now.

Don't let military/industry interests completely drive R&D funding.

> Need some governmental focus to consideration of information technology. Not necessarily a new agency. But FCC cannot do it, NSF does only bits and pieces, NTIA does nothing. There is no institutional infrastructure—we need social assessment of these new technologies, more lead activity of some kind. Repeat, there is no focal point.

Pay attention to the impact in the information revolution on society in terms of lifestyles and institutions. Look at the effects on jobs, working life, social life, and security.

> Our future welfare means establishing some cooperative systems with government and the private sector. We must go past the checks and balances, the hostility, and the adversarial mechanism. Foreign societies with a consensus mechanism have an inherent, not incidental, advantage over us. Let us make a place to decide or organize.

> There is enormous potential in developing a new university-industry-government policy for collaboration in research in information technology which incorporates the individual characteristics of each institution that has made this country a technological leader in the world.

The competitive marketplace has served us well; the government can facilitate the market place but must

> not perturb it without a deep understanding of its effect. In particular, as information technology continues to become more pervasive, the government's role must be targeted to a farther horizon, not merely short-term objectives.
>
> The people and the institutions of this country respond best to challenges when given the latitude to do so. Please do not legislate on matters of information technology R&D except where you absolutely must.
>
> By its inaction, Congress has allowed competitive companies, providing information technology, to be effectively blocked from the world markets. Legislation and administrative efforts are needed to open the world markets to U.S. competitive companies.
>
> Technological progress is dependent on the existence of a strong educational system at all levels. Without adequate Federal support, the educational system is currently seen to be degrading.
>
> Take vigorous action now to enhance science education for people at all levels and all education. Provide strong support for it.
>
> SOURCE: OTA workshops and interviews.

In response to some of these concerns, various interested parties have called for some kind of prestigious national body which could help sort out issues and lay the groundwork for a long-term perspective.[23] Congress may wish to consider such an option. Although one could be skeptical about creating another commission, other countries have tried variations on this theme with some apparent success in developing long-term perspectives.[24] In the United States, this area of research is rather anemic. For example, the National Science Foundation recently reorganized its Policy Research and Analysis Division to address the short-term needs of the executive branch rather than long-term research on social impacts of science and technology.[25]

Given that such little effort is now being undertaken to understand the long-term effects of information technology, it is difficult to say whether development of such a perspective would be possible in the United States. However, such efforts probably entail little risk, in that any insights derived could help inform policymakers on information technology R&D, and on use of the technology itself. An examination and anticipation of the social and cultural impacts of information technology could at a minimum suggest avenues to explore and monitor, possible options to consider promoting, and identification of potential developments that one might wish to thwart or prevent.

---

[23]See, for example, J. L. Kirkley, "Backing into the Future," *Datamation*, February 1982, p. 31; M. R. Wessel and J. L. Kirkley, "For a National Information Committee," *Datamation*, 1982, p. 234; David Burnham, *The Rise of the Computer State* (New York: Random House, 1983). For a discussion also see OTA, "Institutional Options for Addressing Information Policy Issues," op. cit.

[24]See Telecom Australia, *Telecom 2000: An Exploration of the Long-Term Development of Telecommunications in Australia* (Melbourne, Australia: Australian Government Printing Unit, 1975); and Nora, S. and A. Minc, *The Computerization of Society* (Cambridge, MA: MIT Press, 1980).

[25]See National Science Foundation, Division of Policy Research and Analysis, "Program Announcement and Solicitation," January 1984.

Chapter 9
Technology and Industry

Contents

	Page
Importance of Information Technology	307
Findings	307
Composition of Information Technology	308
Functions	308
Examples of System Applications	309
Characteristics of the U.S. Information Technology Industry	316
Employment	317
International Trade	317
Industry Structure	320
Small Entrepreneurial Firms	321
Where the Technology is Heading	323
Microelectronics	324
Silicon Integrated Circuits	324
Gallium Arsenide Integrated Circuits	328
The Convergence of Bio-technology and Information Technology	330
Software	331
The Changing Role of Software in Information Systems	332
The Software Bottleneck	333
Software and Complexity	334
Conclusion	335

Tables

Table No.	Page
50. Functions, Applications, and Technologies	309
51. Characteristics of Human Workers, Robots, and Nonprogrammable Automation Devices	312
52. Comparison of the U.S. Information Technology Industry With Composite Industry Performance, 1978-82	317
53. Employment Levels in the U.S. Information Technology Industries	318
54. U.S. Home Computer Software Sales	320
55. U.S. Office Computer Software Sales	321
56. Percentage of Total Industry Sales and Employment by Size of Small Businesses	322
57. Venture Capital Funding and Information Technology Firms, 1983	323
58. ICs Made With Lithographic Techniques	326
59. Software Sales by Use	332

Figures

Figure No.	Page
52. Direct Broadcasting Satellite System	311
53. The Changing Structure and Growth of the U.S. Information Technology Industry	318
54. Balance of Trade, Information Technology Manufacturing Industry	319
55. U.S. Trade Balance with Selected Nations for R&D Intensive Manufactured Products	319
56. Historical Development of the Complexity of Integrated Circuits	324
57. Read-Only Semiconductor Memory Component Prices by Type	325
58. Median Microprocessor Price v. Time	325
59. Minimum Linewidth for Semiconductor Microlithography	326
60. A Schematic of an Electron Beam Lithography System, and Its Use to Make LSI Logic Circuits	327
61. Trends in Device Speed—Stage Delay per Gate Circuit for Different Technologies	328
62. The Relative Costs of Software and Hardware	332

Chapter 9
Technology and Industry

Importance of Information Technology

Information technology and the industries that advance and use its products are becoming increasingly important to America's economic strength. Information technology is a core technology, contributing broadly to the Nation's trade balance, employment, and national security. The information sector already accounts for between 18 and 25 percent of the gross national products of seven of the member nations of the Organization for Economic Cooperation and Development (OECD) and between 27 and 41 percent of employment in these countries.[1][2]

An important characteristic of this technology is the rapidity with which research results are translated into "advanced" products and from there to the mainstream consumer marketplace. This rapid transfer has been particularly evident in semiconductor research leading to cheaper and more powerful microprocessors.

Given the accelerated movement from the research laboratories to a worldwide marketplace, it is natural that the attention of the trading nations has focused on information technology research and development (R&D). Two basic building blocks of information technology are:
- the microelectronic chip—the large scale integrated circuit that permits the storage, rapid retrieval and manipulation of vast amounts of information, and
- software—the sets of instruction that direct the computer in its tasks.[3]

As noted in chapter 2, there is no consensus on what composes the "information technology industry." Because of the varying definitions and the differing statistical analyses arising from them, it is impossible to pin down the size of the industry. A relatively conservative estimate, discussed later in this chapter, places the annual sales of the U.S. industry at over two hundred billion annually and growing. From another perspective: over one-half million jobs depend on computer industry *exports*.[4]

Findings

In examining the composition of information technology, the characteristics of the U.S. industry, and where the technology is heading, several trends become apparent:

1. The U. S. information technology industry is large and growing rapidly; there is a world market for its products and services as the developed countries increasingly move into the information age.
2. The technology is pervasive, making possible major productivity improvements in other fields, creating new industries, and enlarging the range of services available to the public. The technology diffuses through most facets of life, including business, engineering and science, and government functions.
3. With each level of technological advance in basic information technology, the level of complexity and cost increases for R&D, as does the demand for additional technical training for R&D personnel.

---

[1]*Information Activities, Electronics and Telecommunications Technologies: Impacts on Employment, Growth and Trade* (OECD, Paris, 1981), pp. 22 and 24.
[2]M. R. Rubin, *Information Economics and Policy in the United States,* Libraries Unlimited, Littleton, CO, 1983, pp. 32-44.
[3]Software may also refer to the stored information.

[4]Robert G. Atkins, *The Computer Industry and International Trade: A Summary of the U.S. Role,* Information Processes Group, Institute for Computer Sciences and Technology, National Bureau of Standards, December 1983, p. IX-1. Draft of a report under joint development by ICST and the International Trade Administration, as of February 1985.

4. Domestic and foreign competition for world markets is both intensive and escalating. The stakes for the United States are great in terms of corporate sales and competitiveness in world markets, and employment.

5. There will be continued rapid advances in the capabilities of the industry's underlying basic building blocks, microelectronics and software.

Composition of Information Technology

Individual information technologies have grown explosively in technical sophistication and, at the same time, diminished in cost. That rare combination has propelled the new technologies into the mass marketplace. As the two basic building blocks continue their advances, the parade of new information technology capabilities and applications will go on.

There is a recurrent pattern in which one technological advance makes possible still other advances, often in a "bootstrap" fashion. For example, sophisticated computer-aided design (CAD) equipment is a tool used in development of state-of-the-art random access memories and microprocessors; development of the next generation of super-computers depends on use of today's most advanced computers; "expert" systems— still in their technological infancy—are already employed in configuring complex computer systems and custom-designing integrated circuits.

Functions

For purposes of this report, the term "information technology" has been used to refer to the cluster of technologies that provide the following automated capabilities:

1. **Data Collection.** Examples of automated data collection systems range from large-scale satellite remote-sensing systems such as weather satellites to medical applications such as CAT-scans and electrocardiograms.
2. **Data Input.** Input devices include the familiar keyboard, optical character readers, video cameras, and so on. They are the means by which data are inserted and stored, communicated, or processed.
3. **Information Storage.** The storage media associated with the information industry are the electronic-based devices which store data in a form which can be read by a computer. They include film, magnetic tape, floppy and hard disks, semiconductor memories, and so on. The ability to store increasingly vast amounts of data has been essential to the information technology revolution.
4. **Information Processing.** Information processing is the primary function of a computer. The information stored by a computer can be numeric (used for computations), symbolic (rules of logic used for applications such as "expert" systems), or image (pictorial representations used in applications such as remote mapping). The stored information—in whatever form—is manipulated, or processed, in response to specific instructions (usually encoded in the software). The increasing speed of information processing has been another essential factor in the information technology revolution.
5. **Communications.** Electronic communications utilizes a variety of media—the air waves (for broadcast radio and television), coaxial cable, paired copper wire (used, among other things, for traditional telephony), digital radio, optical fibers, and communications satellites. Communications systems play a major role in broadening the use of other facets of information technology and make possible distributed computing, remote delivery of services, and electronic navigation systems, among many other applications.
6. **Information Presentation.** Once the information has been sent, it must be "pre-

sented" if it is to be useful. This can be accomplished through a variety of output devices. The most common display technology is the cathode ray tube or video display terminal. Hard-copy output devices include the most commonly used impact printers as well as those using non-impact technologies such as ink-jet and xerography. There are also audio systems that permit the computer to "speak"— exemplified by the automobiles that admonish you to fasten your seat belts.

Table 50 shows some of the technologies and application areas that depend on these functions.

Examples of System Applications

A few examples of the many information technology applications are provided below. They have been chosen to illustrate the diversity of applications, and in most cases reflect capabilities that have only become feasible on a significant scale in recent years. The examples include: cellular mobile radio commu-

Table 50.—Functions, Applications, and Technologies[a]

Function	Typical application area[a]	Representative information technology
Data collection	Weather prediction	Radar, infra-red object detection equipment, radiometers
	Medical diagnosis	CAT-scanners, ultrasonic cameras
Data input	Word processing	Keyboards, touch-screens
	Factory automation	Voice recognizers (particularly for quality control)
	Mail sorting	Optical character readers
Storage	Archives	Magnetic bubble devices, magnetic tape
	Accounting systems	Floppy disks
	Scientific computation	Wafer-scale semiconductors (still in research phase), very-high-speed magnetic cores
	Ecological mapping	Charge-coupled semiconductor devices, video disks
	Libraries	Hard disks
Information processing	Social Security payments	General purpose "mainframe" computers, COBOL programs
	Traffic control	Minicomputers
	Distributed inventory control	Multi-user super-micros, application software packages
	Medical diagnoses	"Expert" systems
	Engineering design	Spreadsheet application packages, microcomputers
	Scientific computation	Supercomputers: multiple instruction-multiple data (MIMD) processors, vector processors, data driven processors, FORTRAN programs
	Ecological mapping	Array processors, associative processors
	Factory automation	Robotics, artificial intelligence
Communications	Office systems	Local area networks, private branch exchanges (PBX), editor applications packages
	Teleconferencing	Communications satellites, fiber optics
	Rescue vehicle dispatch	Cellular mobile radios
	International financial transactions	Transport protocols, data encryption, Integrated Services Digital Networks (ISDN)
Data output and presentation	Word processing	Personal computers, printers (impact, ink jet, xerographic)
	Management information	Cathode ray tubes, computer graphics
	Pedestrian traffic control	Voice synthesizers

[a]This list is not exhaustive; any given technology may also be used for some of the other applications mentioned.
SOURCE: Office of Technology Assessment.

nications, direct broadcast satellites, robotics, computer simulation, a biomedical application in heart pacemakers, and financial services.

Cellular Mobile Radio Communications

For decades, use of mobile telephone service has been limited by over-crowding of the electromagnetic spectrum; major cities have had only some few hundred subscribers because of spectrum constraints. Demand for additional mobile voice service has been growing at a 12 percent rate annually for the past 20 years. A new technology—cellular mobile radio communications—holds promise for vastly increasing the number of potential subscribers (to more than 100,000 in particular geographic areas),[5] while providing service of improved quality compared to that available previously. What is most significant about the cellular concept is that it permits conservation of the electromagnetic spectrum —a limited natural resource.

The older technology provided service from a single antenna to the area served. The cellular concept is based on dividing the service area into a number of geometric shapes, or cells, each served with its own antenna. The cell antennas are interconnected with leased telephone lines. When a vehicle leaves a cell, that cell passes control to the next cell, and so on. The number of subscribers is much greater with the cellular concept because the transmission frequencies can be reused repeatedly in nonadjacent cells. Thus the impact of increasing demands on the spectrum is minimized.

According to some estimates, cellular radio will be a $4 billion U.S. industry by 1990 and could reach $6 billion by the mid-1990s. Cellular mobile telephones recently cost about $3,000 but prices are likely to fall rapidly because of competition among vendors.

Other countries are also finding considerable demand for mobile radio services. In Japan, mobile telephone services are now available in Tokyo. In Spain, some 20,000 subscribers are anticipated by 1990. The Netherlands reached approximately 50,000 inhabitants by 1984. Saudi Arabia introduced cellular mobile radio communications in 1981 in three cities; by 1982, there were 19,000 subscribers, and the Saudis have now extended coverage to 32 cities.

Direct Broadcast Satellites

The use of direct broadcast satellites (DBS) has recently become feasible. With DBS, over-the-air signals (e.g., TV, radio) can be received directly by small rooftop antennas (see fig. 52). These new, commercial, geostationary systems may have widespread use in the United States and in other countries, primarily providing entertainment, but also with potential for education, advertising and other business uses. As of early 1985, nine applications had

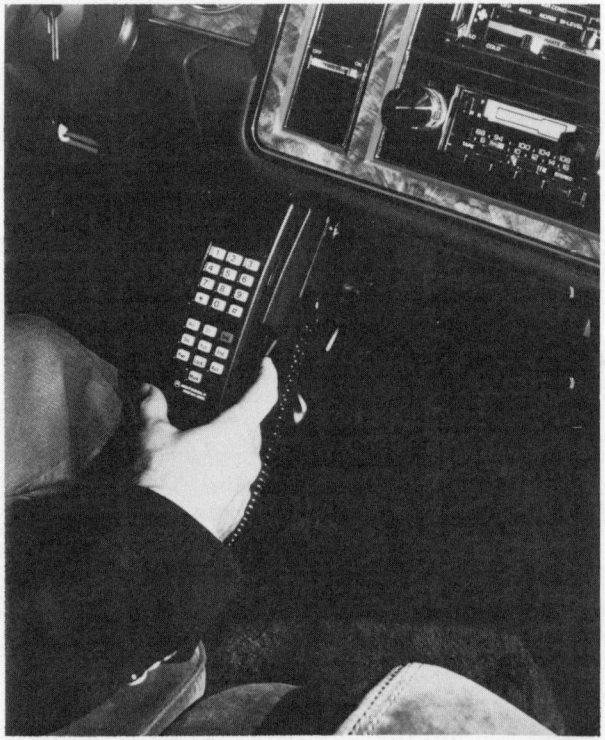

Photo credit: Motorola

Mobile cellular radiotelephone

---

[5]Operation of cellular mobile radio systems in dozens of U.S. cities has been approved by the Federal Communications Commission.

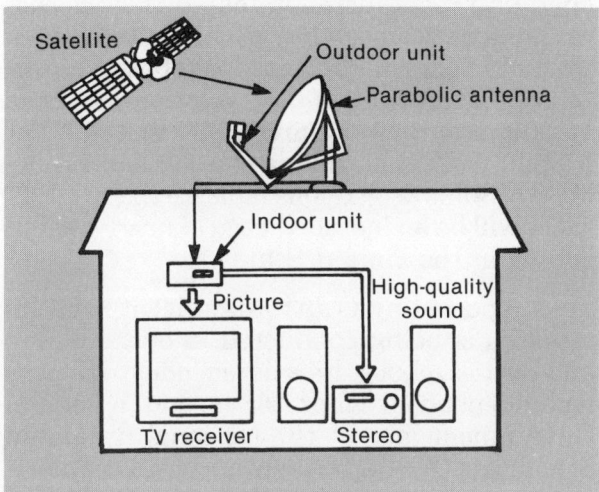

Figure 52.—Direct Broadcasting Satellite System

been approved by the Federal Communications Commission (FCC) for subscription services to the public, some of which may become operational.

DBS services will compete with other media such as multiple distribution systems, STV (subscription TV), and cable TV (CATV) for serving television viewers. DBS services may prove especially valuable for providing service to sparsely populated geographical areas that are not economical to reach by other means, as well as to densely populated cities where new cable installations are prohibitively expensive.

Among the technical improvements that make DBS systems feasible are higher power and more efficient on-board power amplifiers; solar power generation equipment; more accurate satellite station-keeping control; improved ground receiver sensitivity; the use of higher frequencies; and better transmitter downlink beam control. Higher power and higher frequencies also make practical the use of small (about 1 meter or less) rooftop antennas. Some of the early U.S. experimental satellite communications systems, along with parallel advances in solid-state electronics and new materials processing techniques, have contributed significantly to the improvements in components and subsystems available today.

DBS systems had their genesis when NASA's ATS-6 satellite was launched in 1974—a system having a multiplicity of payloads, two of which included TV broadcast capabilities. A number of countries have DBS systems in place or in planning stages. Included among these are: Canada's medium-powered ANIK C-2, which is serving Canadian audiences as well as providing five channels of television entertainment to the Northeastern United States; Japan's modified BS-2 satellite, launched in early 1984; and France's TDF-1 and West Germany's TV-SAT, which are expected to be operational in 1986.

Robotics

Robots are mechanical manipulators which can be programmed to move workpieces or tools along various paths. They are one of the four tools employed in computer-aided manufacturing (i.e., robots, numerically controlled machine tools, flexible manufacturing systems, and automated materials handling systems).[6]

Robotics emerged as a distinct discipline when the century-old industrial engineering automation technologies converged with the more recent disciplines of computer science and artificial intelligence. The convergence produced the growing field of robotics, which has had wide factory applications in areas that include (but are not limited to) materials handling, machine loading/unloading, spray painting, welding, machining, and assembling. The robots are most often used in performing particularly hazardous and monotonous jobs while offering enough flexibility to be easily adapted to changes in product models.

Neither today's robots, nor those likely to be available in the next decade, look like humans nor do they have more than a fraction of the dexterity, flexibility, or intelligence of humans. A simple "pick and place" machine

---
[6]See *Computerized Manufacturing Automation: Employment, Education, and the Workplace* (Washington, DC: U.S. Congress, Office of Technology Assessment, OTA-CIT-235, April 1984.

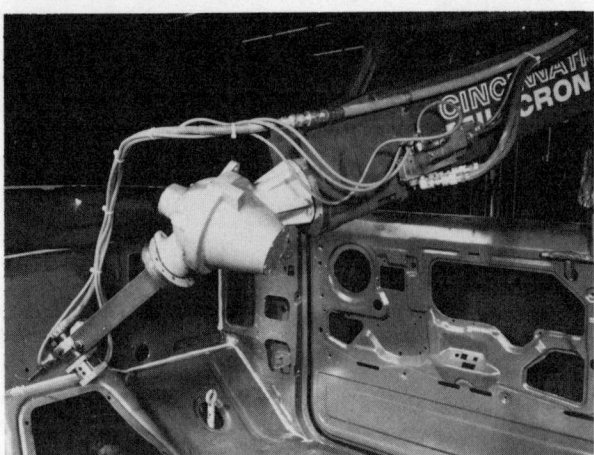

Photo credit: Cincinnati Milacron

Robot

with two or three degrees of freedom may cost roughly between $5,000 and $30,000, while more complex programmable models, often equipped with microcomputers, begin at about $25,000 and may exceed $90,000.

Human workers, robots, and nonprogrammable automation devices each have certain characteristics which offer advantages for the manufacturing process. Table 51 compares some of the salient characteristics.

Table 51.—Characteristics of Human Workers, Robots, and Nonprogrammable Automation Devices[a]

Characteristic	Human Worker	Robot	Nonprogrammable Automation Device
Flexibility	1	2	3
Consistency	3	2	1
Endurance	3	1-2	1-2
Ability to tolerate hostile enviroments	3	1-2	1-2
Cost	n/a	2	1
Speed	2-3	2-3	1
Intelligence/ programmability	1	2	3
Sensing	1	2	3
Judgment	1	2	3
Ability to adapt to change	1	2	3
Dexterity	1	2	3

[a]Numerical ranking indicates relative advantage, with "1" indicating the greatest advantage.

SOURCE: Computerized Manufacturing Automation: Employment, Education, and the Workplace, (Washington, DC: U.S. Congress, Office of Technology Assessment, 1984). This table was derived from the foregoing report.

At the end of 1983 Japan had about 43,000 operating robot installations—by far the largest number in any country. The United States, where the original patents for robots were obtained, had about 9,400 installations (v. about 13,000 in early 1985 and 6,300 in 1982), followed by West Germany (4,800), and France (3,600). Some projections indicate that by 1990 there will be an installed base of nearly 90,000 robots in the United States.*

As reported by OTA[6a], significant robotics research is being conducted in over a dozen universities, about three dozen industrial firms and independent laboratories, and in Federal Government labs at the National Bureau of Standards (NBS), NASA, and DOD. The report further noted that the research was intensively addressing several problem areas: improved positioning and accuracy for the robot's arms; increased grace, dexterity, and speed; sensors, including vision, touch, and force; model-based control systems; software; mobility; voice recognition; artificial intelligence; and interface standards. The interface area is critical to widespread use of automated manufacturing. NBS has created an Automated Manufacturing Research facility in part to perform research on the interfaces between different computerized devices in a factory.

Computer Simulation

"Computer simulation" is a process that employs a computerized model of certain significant features of some physical or logical system which is undergoing dynamic change. We therefore find computers used in applications such as economic modeling and war games where "what if" scenarios can be played out to test suggested social policies or military strategies. As relatively inexpensive computer memories grow in size and integrated circuits grow in speed, increasingly complex operations are being modeled. Software advances have also played a large part in the growing use of computer simulations.

---

*Worldwide Robotics Survey and Directory, 1984, to be published, Robotics Industries Association, Dearborn, MI. This data is based on the RIA's definition for robots which excludes the simpler, nonreprogrammable machines.

[6a]Computerized Manufacturing Automation: Employment, Education and the Workplace, op. cit.

When combined with other information technologies, some startling simulations are possible. In flight simulators, for example, computer-generated imagery techniques are used to create background, images, sounds, and sensations, and to position discrete elements in a scene—elements which have been obtained from video images of real trees, buildings, clouds, aircraft, and other characteristics of the environment to be simulated. The flight simulator is placed in the dynamically changing recreated environment and the pilot then "flies through" in the simulator, which duplicates the performance of the actual airplane. Realistic simulations are made possible by the rapid calculation and implementation of flight characteristics related to the known aerodynamic and engine properties of the craft, air speed, altitude, attitude, and lift. Some systems use 10,000 variables associated with a single-engine jet fighter. In order to achieve visual accuracy, simulator systems calculate the aircraft's position between 25 and 60 times per second.

The Federal Aviation Administration permits 100 percent simulation training for experienced pilots who are upgrading their flight certifications to more advanced aircraft. Simu-

Photo credit: Flight Safety International, Inc.

Flight Simulator

lated dogfight training at Williams Air Force Base is so realistic that some F-4 pilots have become airsick.[7]

Computer simulation is proving effective for improving the quality of training in a variety of jobs—e.g., operating a locomotive, controlling a supertanker, operating a space shuttle—while reducing the cost, time, and risk associated with conventional training.

Heart Pacemakers

Microelectronics and software systems are finding a variety of applications in medical diagnoses and treatment. The heart pacemakers now being used by more than 500,000 patients in the United States are illustrative of the widespread use of these technologies for medical purposes.

The heart muscle contracts in response to electrical impulses generated by a part of the heart itself. The contractions force the blood through the arteries to all parts of the body; but if there is something wrong with the electrical impulses, blood flow is impaired and the heart muscle becomes injured.

Pacemakers are medical devices that can be surgically implanted under a patient's skin with electrode leads fed through the veins into the heart. The two main components of a pacemaker are the pulse generator and the leads. Pulse generators contain a power source and the electrical circuitry for sensing, pulsing, and programming. Some new pacemakers are also capable of telemetry functions, which transmit certain critical measurements of performance of the pacemaker and the patient's condition. Programming changes and telemetry functions require external microprocessors that communicate with the implanted devices in order to monitor performance and to modify the pacemaker's operation.

The first implantable pacemaker was developed in 1958, and the first implantation in a human was performed in 1959. Early pacemakers sent electrical impulses to the heart at fixed intervals. By 1970, the technology for "demand" pacemakers was developed. These pacemakers sense when the heart is not working properly and, when necessary, send out electrical impulses to trigger the contraction of the cardiac muscle. Programmable pacemakers—which are continually being updated with advanced technology— can be reprogrammed without additional surgery, in response to changes in the patient's physiology. This capability reduces the risks of additional surgery for cardiac patients and decreases the costs of their care.[8]

The latest generation of pacemakers is designed to be flexible, enabling updating of the software and external keyboard to accommodate newer technology. The flexibility extends to enabling pacemaker parameter settings to be customized for each patient's special needs, and to the use of the same technology for other medical applications, such as drug dispensers and pain controllers.[9]

---

[7]"The Technology of Illusion," Forbes, Feb. 27, 1984, pp. 158-162.

Photo credit: Medtronic, Inc.

Heart Pacemaker

[8]Special Committee on Aging, U. S. Senate, Fraud, Waste, and Abuse in the Medicare Pacemaker Industry, (Washington, DC: U.S. Government Printing Office, 98-116. September 1982).

[9]Richard M. Powell, "A New Programmer for Implanted Pulse Generators," pp. 678-687, technical paper presented at the 15th Hawaii International Conference on Systems Sciences, January 1982.

Financial Services

The financial service industry would not provide the level of service it does without information technologies.[10] The numbers of checks (over 37 billion annually), credit card drafts (over 3.5 billion annually), and securities trades (over 30 billion shares traded annually) are simply too much for any manual system to handle. In the 1960s, for example, before the financial service industry was substantially automated, there were days when the New York Stock Exchange suspended operations because the broker/dealers were unable to handle the workload.

Both users and providers of financial services have made use of virtually every category of information technology. Banks and other financial service providers have been longtime users of computers. However, an increasing number of retailers—large and small—are installing the hardware and using the telecommunications networks to verify checks and to authorize and complete credit transactions.

Applications software packages for financial services can process market data and generate information used for portfolio management. They can also generate and analyze loan information, and process bank card applications. The spread of remote terminals interconnected with central computers is becoming ubiquitous, and expanding the number of services available to the public.

The video-related technologies—videotex (a two-way information service) and teletext (a one-way information service)—are not yet widely used in the delivery of financial services, but experiments are under way and it is likely that they ultimately will gain acceptance. One videotex system, currently being marketed in Florida, uses an AT&T terminal attached to a television set to link the financial service provider with the customer.

There are also several card technologies. The embossed plastic card with its strip of magnetic tape provides the primary means for accessing credit and debit services that are delivered through both paper-based and electronic systems. Laser cards—not yet used by the financial service industry—can store digital data signifying the bearer's fingerprints. Electron cards combine three encoding technologies—the banking industry's magnetic tape, the retail industry's optical character recognition, and the UPC bar code.

Document and currency readers have had some acceptance, particularly for the reading of checks encoded with magnetic ink. Systems that process credit and debit card transactions already truncate the paper flow at the earliest practical time. The data are recorded on magnetic media and transferred electronically for processing by the card issuer.

Together, these technologies have resulted in a financial service industry that is offering an increasing number of services such as automated redemption of money market funds. At the same time these services are being provided in an increasing number of ways, including the use of automated teller machines and telephone bill payers.

With all this, there is the possibility of redistribution of functions among traditional suppliers as well as potential new entrants. Whereas in the past the payment system has been reserved largely to banks, because they had access to facilities for clearing and settlement, movement of funds electronically makes it possible to avoid the traditional payment system and to settle directly between trading partners. Alternative means of distributing information could diminish the role of brokers for such products as securities, real estate, and insurance. Cash-oriented businesses, such as gas stations and supermarkets, already use onsite automated teller machines to relieve the requirement to cash checks while minimizing the amount of currency that is held at each store location.

---

[10]For detailed discussion, see *Effects of Information Technology on Financial Service Systems*, (Washington, DC: U.S. Congress, Office of Technology Assessment, OTA-CIT-202, September 1984).

Characteristics of the U.S. Information Technology Industry

The information technology industry is a composite of several industries both in manufacturing and services. There is no single, generally accepted definition of the industry. The definitions in use by the Information Industry Association, for example, are too broad for the purposes of this report, while definitions used by the Computer and Business Equipment Manufacturer's Association and by the Association of Data Processing Service Organizations are too restricted.

Despite the ambiguities, this section attempts to characterize the industry in terms of size and structure, growth, employment, investment in R&D, and other areas of special concern. The part of the information technology industry portrayed here includes primarily manufacturers of: electronics; information processing equipment, including computers, office equipment, and peripherals and services; semiconductors; and telecommunications equipment.

Table 52 is a summary of the key indicators for the composite 30 industry categories covered by *Business Week*[11] for the period 1978 to 1982, compared with aggregated data for part of the information technology industry.[12] A point of contrast worth noting is that information technology firms' business performance during the period outpaced the composite industry average significantly as measured by the following criteria:

- growth in sales revenues: 40 percent for the composite industry groups vs. 66 percent for the information technology sector.
- growth in profits: 6.4 percent for the composite vs. 36.4 percent for the information technology sector.
- profits/sales ratios ranging between 4.2 to 5.7 percent for the composite vs. 7.9 to 9.7 percent for the information technology sector.
- growth in the number of employees: a decrease of 7.8 percent for the composite vs. an increase of 11.8 percent for the information technology industry.
- growth in R&D expenditures: 81 percent for the composite vs. 111 percent for the information technology sector. The information technology sector's R&D expenditures per employee were higher than the composite by about 20 percent annually for the period, and both groups increased their R&D investments in spite of a recession.[13]
- investments in R&D as a percentage of sales: averaging 2.1 for the composite vs. 4.2 for the information technology sector; and, as a percentage of profits, 42 vs. 48, respectively.

The above statistics are incomplete because firms whose primary business is *not* information technology do not appear as part of the industry—despite the fact that their information technology activities may be significant. Among the firms not represented are General Electric, Rockwell International, and Westinghouse.

The above data for the information technology manufacturing industry, when combined with related sectors such as the software and computer services, and telephone and telegraph services sectors of the economy, had total revenues of $229 billion for 1982, up from $180 billion in 1980, for a 27 percent increase. Figure 53 illustrates the increasing portion of

---

[11] *Business Week*, R&D Scoreboard, June 20, 1983, pp. 122-153. See also *Business Week*, July 9, 1984, pp. 64-77, which shows a continuation of the trends through 1983.

[12] Data shown by *Business Week* for national composite industry R&D expenditures correlates closely with NSF data in *Science Resources Studies* "Highlights," June 11, 1982.

[13] Of the four sectors—industry, Federal Government, colleges and universities, and other nonprofit organizations—only industry increased its funding for R&D in constant 1972 dollars during the 1978-82 period. *Probable Levels of R&D Expenditures in 1984: Forecast and Analysis*, Battelle, December 1983.

Table 52.—Comparison of the U.S. Information Technology Industry with Composite Industry Performance, 1978-82

	1978	1979	1980	1981	1982	Percent change	
Sales (millions of dollars)	1,085,291	1,277,764	1,421,551	1,586,510	1,520,313	40	Composite
	131,872	149,783	174,449	193,921	218,862	66	Infotech
Profits (millions of dollars)	59,578	72,505	73,493	81,757	63,365	6.4	Composite
	12,780	13,821	15,474	16,056	17,436	36.4	Infotech
Profits/sales (percent)	5.5	5.7	5.2	5.1	4.2		Composite
	9.7	9.2	8.9	8.3	7.9		Infotech
Employees (thousands)	15,133	15,542	15,498	15,045	13,959	−7.8	Composite
	2,952	3,099	3,226	3,252	3,301	11.8	Infotech
R&D (millions of dollars)	20,610	24,674	28,984	33,285	37,179	81	Composite
	4,961	5,885	7,221	8,531	10,473	111	Infotech
R&D $/sales (percent)	1.9	1.9	2.0	2.1	2.5		Composite
	3.8	3.9	4.1	4.4	4.8		Infotech
R&D $/profits (percent)	34.6	34.0	39.4	40.7	59.0		Composite
	38.8	42.6	46.7	53.1	60.1		Infotech
R&D $/employee	1,362	1,588	1,870	2,212	2,667		Composite
	1,680	1,899	2,238	2,623	3,173		Infotech
R&D expenditures per employee Infotech/Composite (percent)	123	120	121	119	120		

Business Week "Scoreboard" Numbers Notes:
A. This is a sample of R&D spending in information technology by U.S. corporations. It is based on total R&D expenditures for those companies that are publicly held, have annual revenues over $35 million, and R&D expenses of $1 million or 1 percent of revenue. Only that spending by companies whose primary business is information technology (electronics, computers, office equipment, computer services and peripherals, semiconductors, and telecommunications) is included.
B. Sales, R&D spending, and R&D spending per employee figures have been adjusted to reflect the numbers from Western Electric and other AT&T subsidiaries that are not included in the "Scoreboard" numbers. This adjustment involves:
  1. addition of revenues received from Western Electric to the total operating revenues figures in the AT&T Annual Reports for the years covered.
  2. use of the total AT&T spending figures for R&D which include spending by Western Electric and other AT&T subsidiaries as provided in Business Week for the years 1980-82 and as estimated from a chart in the 1983 AT&T Annual Report for the years 1978 and 1979.
  3. use of total AT&T employment figures provided in Forbes each May for the years 1978-82.
C. Employment numbers for all sectors have been calculated from the R&D spending per employee and the R&D spending figures provided in Business Week and may reflect rounding errors.
SOURCE: Data obtained, or calculated from Business Week, Scoreboard, June 30, 1983; the U.S. Commerce Department; Forbes, May 1979 through 1983; 10K forms filed by AT&T and Western Electric Corp.

total sales due to services, which are approaching 50 percent of total industry revenues.

Employment

Employment in information technology manufacturing increased significantly between 1972 and 1982 in most segments of the industry (table 53), experiencing employment growth ranging between 9 and 142 percent. Only the consumer products (radio and TV sets) showed a decline (28 percent). Total employment in information technology manufacturing grew by 51 percent, in spite of economic recessions.

Employment in information technology services is about equal to that of the manufacturing segment, with some 1.6 million employees. The employment level in computing services closely matches that of computer manufacturing, both growing by about 140 percent between 1972 and 1982.

International Trade

Technology-intensive products have important implications for the balance of trade. Studies on U.S. trade and the influence of technology have generally concluded that technology serves as an important determinant of comparative advantage in manufactured goods trade.[14][15]

---

[14]C. Michael Aho and Howard F. Rosen, "Trends in Technology-Intensive Trade: With Special Reference to U.S. Competitiveness," Office of Foreign Economic Research, Bureau of International Labor Affairs, U.S. Department of Labor, p. 11.
[15]T. C. Lowinger, "Human Capital and Technological Determinants of U.S. Industries Revealed Comparative Advantage," Quarterly Review of Economics and Business (1974), winter 1977, pp. 91-102, as reported in Aho and Rosen, pp. 11, 12.

Figure 53.—The Changing Structure and Growth of the U.S. Information Technology Industry

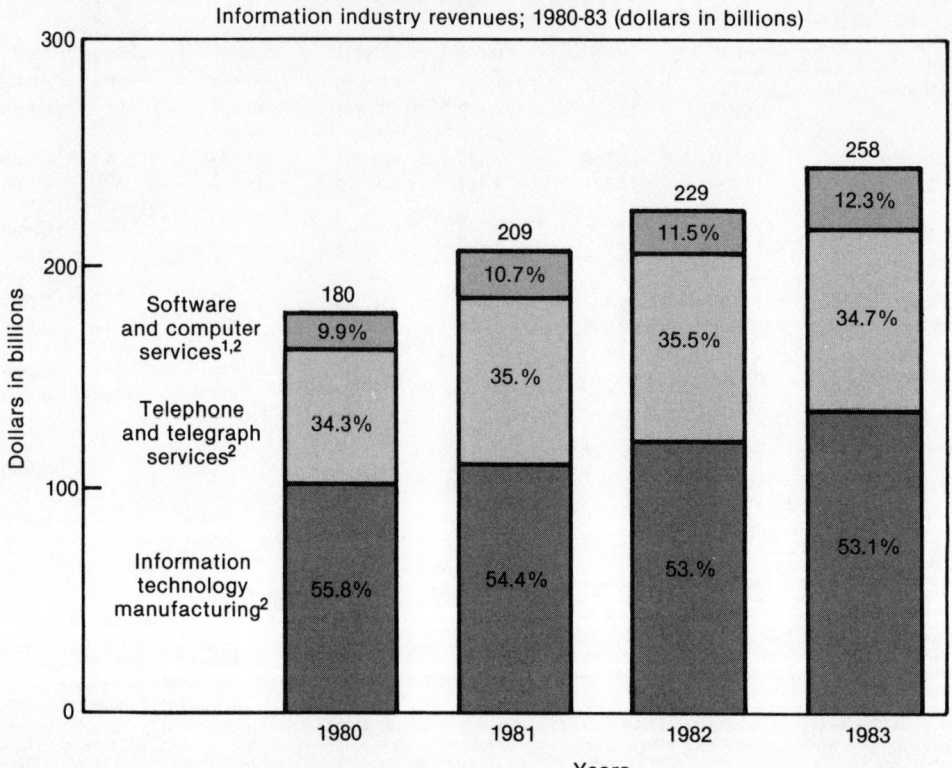

Information industry revenues; 1980-83 (dollars in billions)

SOURCES: [1]ADAPSO; [2]U.S. Industrial Outlook, 1983, 1984.

Table 53.—Employment Levels in the U.S. Information Technology Industries
Employees (in thousands)

	1972	1982	Percent change 1972-1982
Manufacturing[a]			
Computers	145	351	+142
Office equipment	34	51	+50
Radio and television receiving sets	87	63	−28
Telephone and telegraph equipment	134	146	+9
Radio and television communications equipment	319	454	+42
Electronic components	336	528	+57
Totals, manufacturing	1,055	1,593	
Services			
Telephone and telegraph	949	1,131	+11
Computing[b]	149	360	+141
Radio and television broadcast[c]	68	81	+19
Cable television[d]	40	52	+30
Totals, services	1,206	1,624	

[a]Estimates provided by the U.S. Department of Commerce, Bureau of Industrial Economics.
[b]Figures are for 1974 and 1983. Source: *U.S. Industrial Outlook, 1984*.
[c]Figures are for 1979 and 1983. Source: Federal Communication Commission in telephone interview with OTA staff, May 1984.
[d]Figures are for 1981 and 1982. Ibid. (FCC).

The U.S. merchandise trade balance has been negative in recent years: deficits of $42.7 billion in 1982; $69.4 billion in 1983; and over $100 billion in 1984. In 1980, advanced technology products showed a positive trade balance of $31 billion, compared with a deficit of more than $50 billion for all manufactured goods.[16]

Information technology manufactured products[17] usually made positive contributions to the U.S. balance of trade between 1972 and 1982 (fig. 54), led by sales of computer equipment. However, 1983 and 1984 saw trade deficits of $0.8 and 2.3 billion according to Department of Commerce estimates.[18] The deficits would have been much greater without about $6 billion in exports of computer equipment in each of those years (see fig. 55).

---

[16]*International Competitiveness in Advanced Technology: Decisions for America,* National Research Council (Washington, DC: National Academy Press, 1983, pp. 23-24.

[17]The products include: computer equipment, SIC 3573; office equipment, SIC 3579; radio and TV sets, SIC 3651; telephone and telegraph equipment, SIC 3661; radio and TV communications equipment, SIC 3662; and electronic components, SIC 367.

[18]*U.S. Industrial Outlook,* 1978 through 1984.

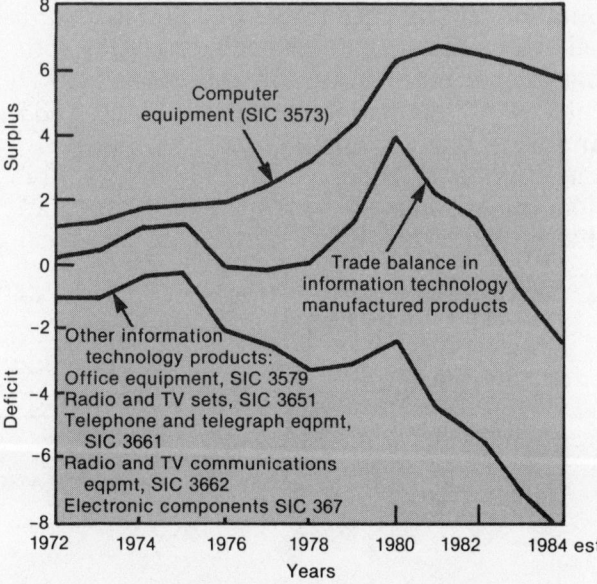

Figure 54.—Balance of Trade, Information Technology Manufacturing Industry
(dollars in billions)

SOURCE: U.S. Industrial Outlook for years 1978 through 1984.

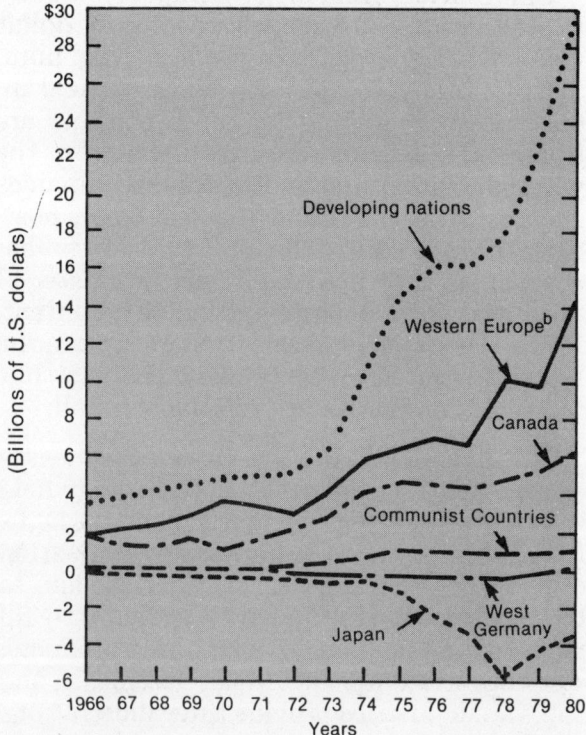

Figure 55.—U.S. Trade Balance[a] With Selected Nations for R&D Intensive Manufactured Products

[a]Exports less imports.
[b]Includes West Germany.

SOURCE: *Science Indicators—1982,* National Science Board, National Science Foundation, 1983.

Although the United States holds the major market share of the industrialized countries' exports of high-technology products, that share has declined from 30 percent in 1962 to 22 percent in 1978, and has increased only marginally since. In absolute terms, the U.S. positive trade balance in high-technology products increased over eightfold from 1962 to 1980. During that same period West Germany, and especially Japan, starting from smaller bases, have had impressive gains in their surpluses of exports over imports—a ninefold increase for West Germany and two-hundredfold increase for Japan.[19]

---

[19]U.S. Department of Commerce, International Trade Administration, as reported in "An Assessment of U.S. Competitiveness in High-Technology Industries," prepared for the Working Group on High Technology Industries of the Cabinet Council on Commerce and Trade, final draft, May 19, 1982.

Industry Structure

Information technology companies in the United States are heterogeneous in dollar value of sales, breadth of product lines, number of employees, and degree of vertical integration. Competing for those markets are thousands of firms ranging in size from the vertically integrated multinational companies such as IBM, ITT, and the still-large, post-divestiture AT&T to the more typical, smaller companies that produce a narrow cluster of products with a large technology content. While the majority of sales dollars are concentrated in the large companies, the vast majority of companies are relatively small.

The diversity in the sizes of the businesses that populate the information technology field is important for reasons that include the benefits of competition; the impetus to innovation due to firms' willingness to take risks and to try new directions; and the tendency to fill niche market demand for specialized products. The U.S. telecommunications, electronics, and software industries provide three illustrations of the contrasts in the breadth of that diversity.

The *telecommunications services* industry is simultaneously both a mature industry dating back to the 19th century and a growing industry marked by limited competition in some markets and diversity in others. While local public telecommunications services are largely dominated by regulated monopolies, long-distance services are now offered in a competitive market. New services, such as paging, cellular mobile radio services, bypass services and direct broadcast satellite services, are not dominated by the established carriers, but are being offered by a variety of firms.

The *telecommunications equipment* providers are exceptionally diverse and competitive. There are hundreds of firms in this field, ranging from a few U.S. and foreign multinational companies manufacturing a full range of equipment to dozens of medium size, and many hundreds of small companies concentrating on a more limited range of products—e.g., speech compression products, multiplexers, modems, data terminals and local area networks.

The *electronics* industry is even more diverse. The thousands of electronic systems and equipment providers, as well as consulting firms, range in size from those with billions of dollars in annual sales to small, start-up ventures such as the Apple Computer's garage operation of a few years ago. For those segments of the industry undergoing rapid technological change, diversity is often accelerated by spin-offs from rapidly growing companies, and other new entries into the field.

The U.S. *microcomputer software* industry is an example of rapid change, growth, and diversity. Future Computing, Inc. estimates that the U.S. market for home computer software grew by 168 percent from 1982 to 1983, and projects an 85 percent growth from 1983 to 1984, with the growth rate declining to 26 percent by 1988 in a projected $5 billion annual market by then (table 54). Software unit sales for office use are projected to enjoy comparable growth. Table 55 indicates growth rates of 87 percent between 1982 and 1983, and 58 percent from 1983 to 1984, gradually tapering off to 24 percent in 1988 in a $6.7 billion annual market.[20] Like the electronics industry, software firms number in the thou-

[20]Future Computing, personal communication, March 1984.

Table 54.—U.S. Home Computer Software Sales[a]

	1981	1982	1983	1984	1985	1986	1987	1988
Software units (millions)	1.1	6.9	19.0	37.0	58.0	82.0	112.0	144.0
Percent growth (units)		486	168	85	52	42	32	26
Revenue (millions of dollars)	48	282	757	1,400	2,100	3,000	4,000	5,000

[a]Data for 1984-88 are estimates by Future Computing.
SOURCE: Future Computing, Richardson, TX, by OTA staff telephone interview, March 1984.

Table 55.—U.S. Office Computer Software Sales[a]

	1981	1982	1983	1984	1985	1986	1987	1988
Software units (millions)	3.2	6.1	11.0	17.0	25.0	35.0	46.0	59.0
Percent growth (units)		111	87	58	44	36	30	24
Revenue (millions of dollars)	343	724	1,351	2,100	3,100	4,200	5,400	6,700

[a]Data for 1984-88 are estimates by Future Computing.
SOURCE: Future Computing, Richardson, TX, by OTA staff telephone interview, March 1984.

sands. Although no hard data are available, it is the impression of industry analysts that the rapid pace of startups in the software industry seen in recent years now appears to be slackening.

An important trend in industry structure is toward concentration in the software and data services industries, where larger firms have acquired hundreds of smaller ones. Among these larger firms are Automatic Data Processing, Electronic Data Systems, and General Electric.

Larger firms are also integrating their product lines—some moving into subsystems and components, and others, such as semiconductor manufacturers, moving into subsystem and computer manufacturing. AT&T, Texas Instruments, Intel, and Northern Telecommunications Corp. are examples of companies recently expanding into computers and related products.

There is also an active trend toward affiliations between information producers and distributors. Among these are publishers of newspapers, books, and magazines and broadcast, cable TV, and interactive computer network companies.

Geographic diversification is taking place at a rapid pace as foreign—primarily European—companies acquire U.S. firms. Among the European firms are: Olivetti, CAP Gemini, Racal Electronics, Schlumberger, Thomson-CSF, and Agfa-Gevaert.

A number of U.S. firms are expanding their markets by establishing joint ventures or by acquiring foreign outlets—e.g., IBM, AT&T, and Datapoint.

Small Entrepreneurial Firms

Small businesses play a central role in U.S. industry in general, accounting for:

- thirty-eight percent of the Nation's gross national product;
- two-thirds of all new jobs;
- two-and-a-half times as many innovations per employee as large firms;[21] and
- a tendency to produce more "leapfrog" creations compared to large companies and to introduce new products more quickly than large firms.[22]

The contributions of small businesses to the information technology industry are significant. Small businesses with less than 500 employees account for 33 percent of sales in electronic components and 34 percent of the Nation's employment in this sector. In the computer services sector, small businesses account for 69 percent of the industry's sales and 67 percent of its employees. These firms also make contributions in sectors where large companies dominate, such as in office computing equipment, consumer electronics, and communications equipment (table 56).

Opportunities for innovation based on advances in information technology have been numerous. Consequently, hundreds of market niche applications have been created that

---

[21]*Advocacy: A Voice for Small Businesses*, Office of Advocacy, U.S. Small Business Administration, 1984. p. 1.
[22]Stroemann, 1977. Karl A. Stroetmann "Innovation in Small and Medium Sized Firms." Working paper presented at Institut Fur Systemchnik und Innovations forschung, Karlsruhe, West Germany, August, 1977. See Vesper (Entrepreneurship).

Table 56.—Percentage of Total Industry Sales and
Employment by Size of Small Businesses

	Companies with under 100 employees		Companies with under 500 employees	
	Sales	Employment	Sales	Employment
Office computing machines and computer auxiliary equipment	2.6	2.6	6.0	6.3
Consumer electronics	5.4	5.9	9.3	10.1
Communications equipment	4.7	5.2	9.9	10.8
Electronic components	18.3	17.2	32.7	33.7
Computer services	51.2	47.7	68.6	67.1

SOURCE: Small Business Administration, 1984.

small firms are quick to fill—niches too narrow or specialized to attract large firms.[23] The development of the computer in the 1940s and the subsequent invention of the transistor led to an explosion of new applications and to opportunities for then small companies whose names are now familiar in the information technology industry: IBM, Fairchild, Intel, Texas Instruments, DEC, Data General, Wang, and Computervision. One market research company's listing of the fastest-growing niche markets shows that about 90 percent of the top 50 entries are in information technology,[24] and many of these technologies are relatively new.

As the successful firms in this industry grow, they tend to generate spin-off companies that often specialize initially in a narrow range of innovative products or processes. Fairchild is such a company, having begun with only eight employees and now accounting for over 80 spin-off enterprises.[25]

Venture capital funding is extremely important to the small entrepreneurial firms. Investments through organized venture capital investment businesses in 1983 amounted to $2.8 billion, up 55 percent from $1.8 billion in 1982.[26] It is improbable that this growth rate will be sustained for very long.[27]

The supply of U.S. venture capital financing has grown at least eightfold since the mid-1970s, helping to fund the more than 5,500 U.S. small startup and expanding firms. These firms tend to operate in innovative market niches where the risks are high and the potential payoffs much higher.

Information technology firms supported by venture capital funds numbered in excess of 1,000 in 1983, and received about $2.1 billion from organized venture capital investment businesses. These funds were used for both startups and expansion of existing companies. The distribution of funds is shown in table 57.

These firms account for a significant number of advances in the information technology field. Among the now-well known information technology firms started or aided by venture capital are: Intel, Apple Computer, Visicalc, DEC, and Data General. R&D limited partnerships also contribute to this process (see ch. 2).

The existence of so many entrepreneurial firms, the current abundance of venture capital to fund their growth, and the strengthening university-industry R&D relationships serve as a powerful source of strength for innovation in the United States. For example,

---

[23]In a July 1981 study, the General Accounting Office found that in concentrated industries, such as the information technology industry, small businesses are likely to perform specialized innovative functions and develop products or processes to be used or marketed by other, usually larger firms in that industry. For example, in the semiconductor industry there are many small companies that manufacture diffusion furnaces, ion implantation machines, epitaxial growth systems, and mask-making systems—all part of a necessary support structure for the semiconductor industry.

[24]21st Century Research, Supergrowth Technology U.S.A., newsletter as published in EDP News Service, Inc., *Computer Age-EDP Weekly*, Feb. 28, 1983, p. 9.

[25]Carl H. Vesper, *Entrepreneurship and National Policy*, Heller Institute for Small Business Policy Papers, p. 27.

[26]Data provided by Venture Economics, Inc., from its database covering organized venture capital investment companies.

[27]"Scramble for Capital at Almost-Public Companies," *Fortune* June 25, 1984, p. 91.

Table 57.—Venture Capital Funding and Information Technology Firms, 1983

	Percentage of 1,000 venture capital firms	Distribution of available venture capital (percent)	Distribution of available venture capital (millions of dollars)
Computer hardware and systems	28	39	819
Software and services	12	7	309
Telecommunications and data communications	9	11	231
Other electronics[a]	10	10	210
Total	59	61	1,569

[a]Includes semiconductor fabrication and test equipment, instrumentation, fiber optics, laser-related devices, etc.
SOURCE: Venture Economics Inc., provided in telephone interview with OTA staff, May 22, 1984.

over 30 new computer chip firms have started operation since the late 1970s. The fastest-growing niche markets noted earlier are heavily populated with products that are new, or radically different from those of only a decade ago. Few of our major competitors now have a comparable combination of factors to spawn the next Silicon Valley. In fact, our West German,[28] French, and Japanese trading partners are now actively seeking ways to emulate the environment that fosters this type of entreprenuership.[29]

Small Businesses and Joint R&D

Congress has passed, and the President signed, legislation that would ease the restrictions of antitrust laws on joint R&D ventures.

Small business may find both new opportunities and impediments. Although small businesses are currently permitted to undertake joint research activities among themselves, the new joint venture legislation may encourage increased opportunities in joint ventures between small and large firms.

This type of cooperation between large companies and small companies has already begun to occur. For example, Control Data Corp. has made its advanced computer design tools available to two small companies, Star Technologies, Inc. and ETA Systems, Inc. (the latter a CDC spin-off). IBM also has a marketing agreement with Floating Point Systems. If the joint venture legislation can stimulate transfers of marketing and technological resources of major U.S. companies to small information technology firms, small companies can realize definite benefits from the encouragement of these new types of arrangements. A potential impediment could occur if technology developed through R&D by large firms is not made available to small firms through licensing or other means.

[28]"The Technological Challenge: Tasks for Economic, Social, Educational, and European Policy in the Years Ahead," speech by Hans-Dieter Genscher, (West German) Federal Minister for Foreign Affairs, Bonn-Bad Godesberg, Federal Republic of Germany, Dec. 13, 1983.
[29]"In This New Age of Entrepreneurs, We're Number One Again," Joel Kotkin, *Washington Post*, Apr. 29, 1984, p. B1.

Where the Technology is Heading

This section looks ahead to prospects for further advances in two building blocks of information technology—microelectronics and software. As discussed later, these technologies are being integrated and are providing important tools for coping with increasing complexity through the use of computer-aided design (CAD) and computer-aided engineering (CAE) systems, and are driving a wide range of applications.

Advances in microelectronics and software are dependent on entirely different underpinnings—e.g., physics, chemistry, materials science and electrical engineering for the former, and computer and information science, psychology, and software engineering, among others, for the latter. Prospects for continuation of the explosive growth of information technology during the past two decades will be paced by advances in microelectronics and software.

Microelectronics[30]

The rate of technological improvement in semiconductors has been phenomenal during the past quarter century, and has sparked new applications and economic advances worldwide. This section reviews the growth of integrated circuit capabilities and seeks to provide insight into future progress, its dependencies and foreseeable limitations, and the likely timeframe of that progress.

Probable trends include:

- Silicon is likely to remain the most important semiconductor material for the next decade and beyond, while gallium arsenide is likely to come into wide use in certain applications where its special properties provide specific advantages. The impact of other innovative materials is likely to be marginal until after the turn of the century, when biotechnology may begin to converge with information technology.
- Prices for the main output of microelectronics technology, logic and memory, can be expected to continue to decline on a per function basis, following the general pattern of the past two decades.
- Continued advances during the next two decades in large-scale integration of silicon and gallium arsenide will require the continued advance of other sciences and technologies, particularly physics, chemistry and materials science, and manufacturing and software engineering.
- The R&D costs for incremental advances in microelectronics technology are expected by industry experts to increase as the complexity of circuits increases and as the theoretical physical limits of microelectronics are approached.

Silicon Integrated Circuits

Transistor Size and Density

Between 1972 and 1981, the number of transistors that could be packed on a chip doubled each year (11,000 in 1972 and 600,000 in 1981) (see fig. 56). Today, integrated circuit technol-

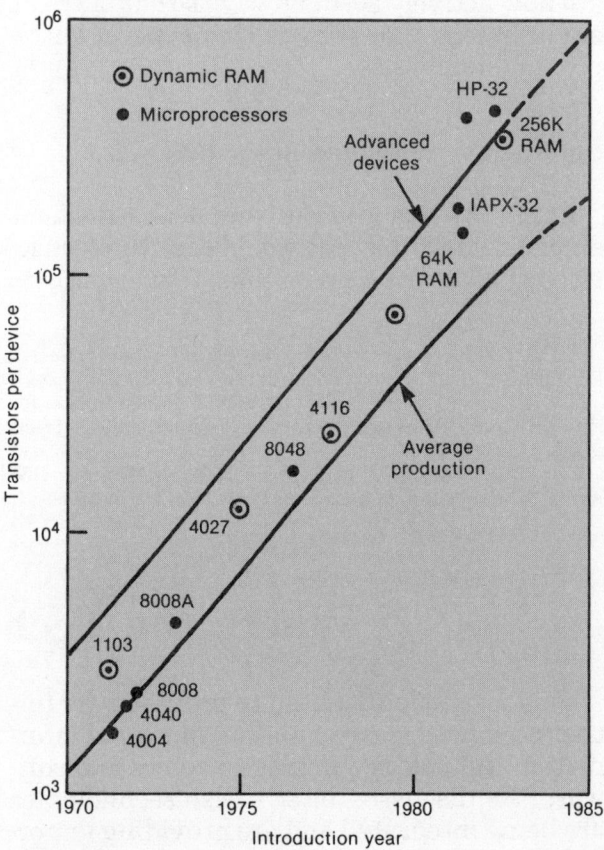

Figure 56.—Historical Development of the Complexity of Integrated Circuits

SOURCE: Arthur D. Little, Inc. estimates.

---
[30] A significant amount of data in this section is taken from, or based on: 1) the Sixth Mountbatten Lecture, *Microelectronics Progress Prospects*, delivered by Ian M. Ross, President, AT&T Bell Laboratories, Nov. 10, 1983, London, England; and 2) J. D. Meindl, *Theoretical, Practical, and Analogical Limits to ULSI*, Technical Digest of the International Electron Devices Meeting, December 1983, pp. 8-13.

ogy is approaching the capability of packing a million components (mostly transistors) on a single silicon chip.[31]

Along with these improvements in density, costs per function have dropped dramatically until now some memory components are less than 0.01 cent per bit, and many microprocessors are under $10 per chip (see figs. 57 and 58). This is the result of a thousand-fold decrease in the cost of manufacturing compared with 20 years ago.

The substantial increases in transistor density have been made possible by reductions in integrated circuit feature size, which in turn have depended on advances in photolithography, the technique by which integrated circuits are manufactured. Minimum line widths have been reduced by a factor of two every 6 or 7 years. Using photolithography with visible light, line widths have been reduced from 25 microns in 1972, or 1/1,000th of an inch, to about 1.5 microns currently, or less than 1/10,000th of an inch.

Optical, or visible light, lithography, which currently remains the leading integrated circuit manufacturing method, is expected to reach the practical limits of its capacity for small feature sizes in the range of 1.0 to 0.5 microns (the wavelength range of visible light). At the same historical rate of progress, these limits will be reached in the 1990-94 period (see fig. 59.).

Most experts believe that advanced lithographic techniques using light of shorter wavelengths, in the X-ray range, and electron-beam (see fig. 60) and ion implantation machines that can directly draw lines and features on semiconductor substrates[32] will be needed in

---

[31]While other technologies (gallium arsenide, indium antimonide, cryogenic superconductors, photonic devices, and potentially biotechnology) with higher switching speeds, lower heat dissipation, or other qualities, will compete in certain special applications, current expert opinion is that silicon will have the major role for the next decade or more in meeting most needs for digital memory and logic.

[32]In current commercial lithographic techniques, the semiconductor substrate is coated with a light-sensitive emulsion, or *photoresist,* and a mask, much like a stencil, is used to expose a pattern in the substrate that is then etched away with a chemical, creating lines and features. Electron beams can be focused and directed to create patterns in the emulsion without a mask, and ion beams can implant materials on the substrate without the need for photoresist or etching.

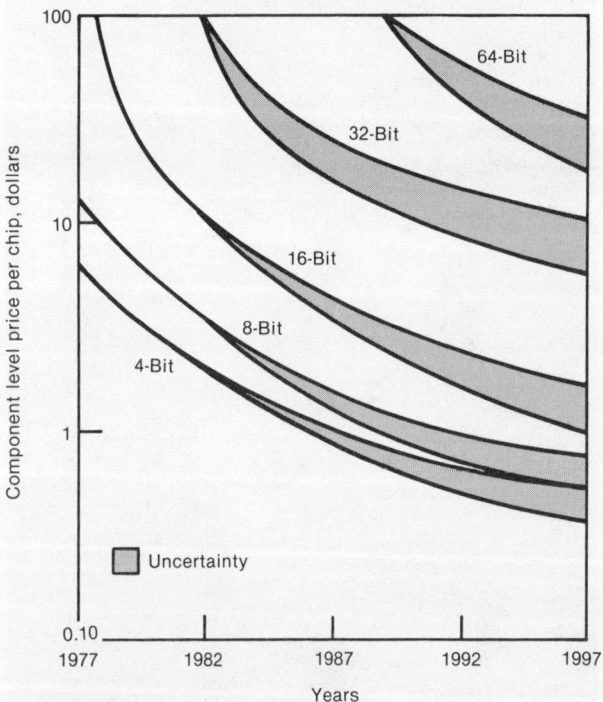

Figure 58.—Median Microprocessor Price v. Time
(1,000 unit purchase)

SOURCE: Arthur D. Little, Inc., estimates.

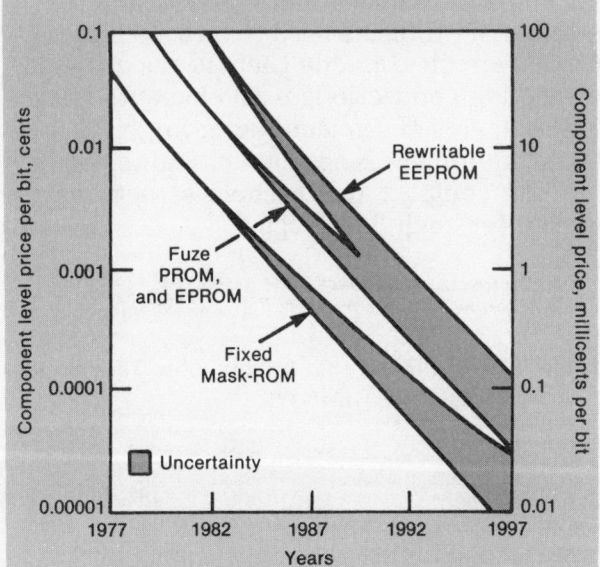

Figure 57.—Read-Only Semiconductor Memory Component Prices (per bit) by Type

SOURCE: Arthur D. Little, Inc., estimates.

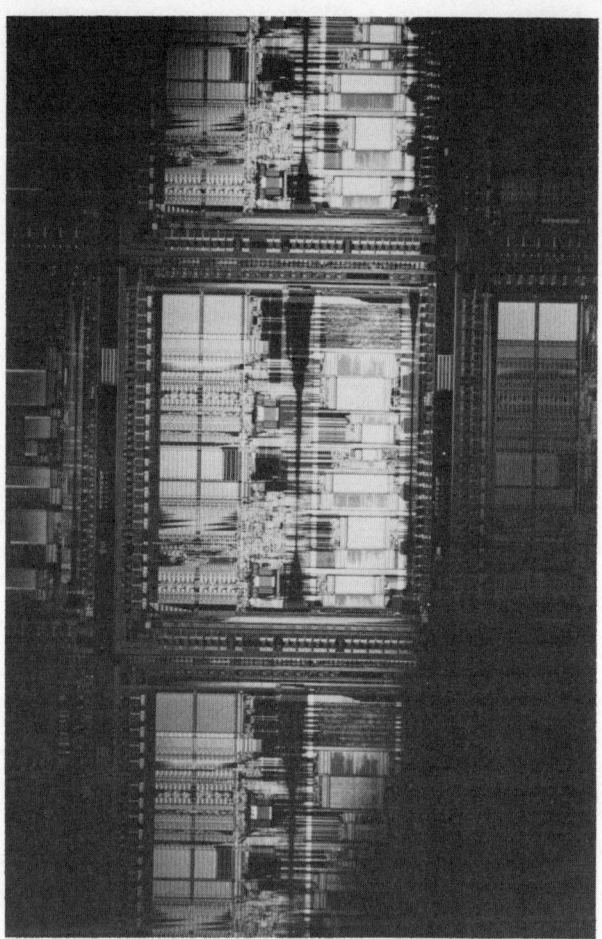

Photo credit: AT&T Bell Laboratories

Microprocessor WE 32100

order to achieve further advances.[33] A number of such machines are in use for experimental purposes and for production of circuits to be used in-house at major companies such as IBM and AT&T.

Electron beam lithography and ion implantation[34] may become the ultimate semiconductor manufacturing techniques, with minimum line widths possible in the range of 0.1 to 0.01 micron. The latter widths are comparable to feature spacing on the order of 20 to 200 atoms. The major drawback of such systems is that they are much slower than mask lithography; they are now used only in producing custom chips of low production volume. Electron-beam and ion implantation technology are expected to be in use on commercial integrated circuit production lines by 1994[35] (see table 58).

Research is under way in the United States and Japan that is striving to achieve more densely packed circuit components by stacking chips into three dimensional structures. A number of problems need to be solved to realize 3-D circuits, among them is the difficulty of making connections with elements buried within layers of semiconductor material. Ion-beam equipment is seen as critical to producing the complex microscopic structures required for such 3-D chips.[36]

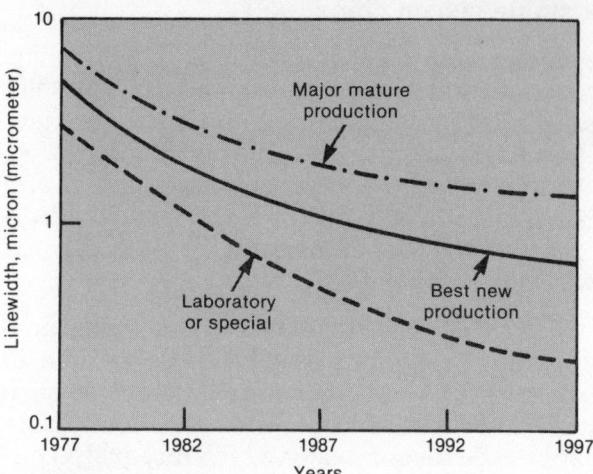

Figure 59.—Minimum Linewidth for Semiconductor Microlithography

SOURCE: Arthur D. Little, Inc., estimates.

---

[33]Some engineers have begun to question the premise that more densely packed circuits are necessary. See "Solid State," *IEEE Spectrum*, January 1984, p. 61.

[34]The Defense Department's Very High Speed Integrated Circuits (VHSIC) program supports research on electron-beam and ion-beam manufacturing techniques. Discussion of both of these can be found in *IEEE Spectrum*, January 1984, pp. 61-63.

[35]*IEEE Spectrum*, January 1984, p. 63.

[36]"3-D Chips," *The Economist*, Feb. 12, 1983, p. 84.

Table 58.—ICs Made with Lithographic Techniques
(percent)

Technique	1983	1985	1987
Optical scanner	85	58	38
Optical stepper	15	40	52
Electron beam	0	1	8
X-ray	0	1	2
Ion beam	0	0	0

SOURCE: *IEEE Spectrum*, January 1984, p. 60.

Figure 60.—A Schematic of an Electron Beam Lithography System, and its Uses to Make LSI Logic Circuits

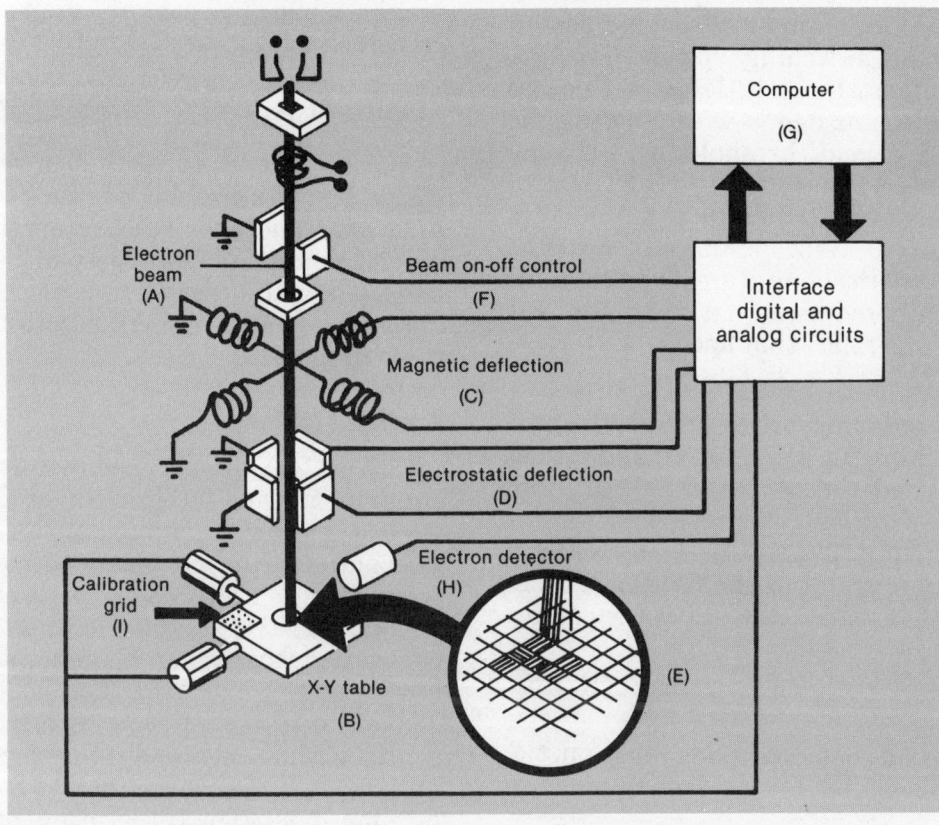

SOURCE: Mosaic, SSI/MSI/LSI/VLSI/ULSI, vol. 15, No. 1, p. 15.

In devices with such subminiature dimensions, other limitations become significant, e.g., the dielectric strength, electronic isolation, and heat dissipation of the silicon material—some of which may represent more severe limitations than the theoretical limits imposed by the most advanced manufacturing techniques. Transistors with critical dimensions of 0.1 micron have been demonstrated to operate by Bell Telephone Laboratories. These dimensions would theoretically lead to some billion components on a square centimeter of silicon. A more realistic, practical limit for silicon may be 100 million components per square centimeter.[37]

Increasing the physical dimensions of the chip may also contribute to increasing the component count per chip. Chip sizes are determined by manufacturing control—the ability to minimize the number of impurities and defects in the semiconductor substrate material and in finished circuits. Today's typical chip size is about 1 square centimeter. There are development efforts under way toward wafer-scale integration[38] which could provide a factor of 100 increase in integrated circuit chip size, to 100 square centimeters or larger. This factor, coupled with component densities of 100 million transistors per square centimeter made possible with the advanced manufacturing techniques noted above, could result in component counts of 1 billion transistors per integrated circuit.[39]

---

[37]Ross, op. cit., p. 6.

[38]Chips are cut from 3 to 6-inch-diameter wafers which are currently manufactured with some 100 separate integrated circuits per wafer.

[39]Ross, op. cit., p. 7.

Integrated Circuit Speed and Reliability

Concurrent with, and largely the result of, decreasing circuit feature size and increasing density, circuit switching speeds have increased significantly. A little more than 20 years ago, switching delays were crossing the millionth of a second threshold; by 1977 the billionth of a second threshold had been passed; by 1990, delays of 1 trillionth of a second (a picosecond, or 10^{-12} second) may be possible (see fig. 61). Practical limits are foreseen, however, that would reduce actual maximum performance to one-tenth that speed, or 10 picoseconds.[40]

As well as reducing circuit delays, the continued shrinking in the size of individual components and the concentration of more functions in each succeeding generation of integrated circuits have reduced computer system chip counts and thus the time used up in computers when signals travel between chips.

---
[40]Ibid.

Figure 61.—Trends in Device Speed—Stage Delay per Gate Circuit for Different Technologies

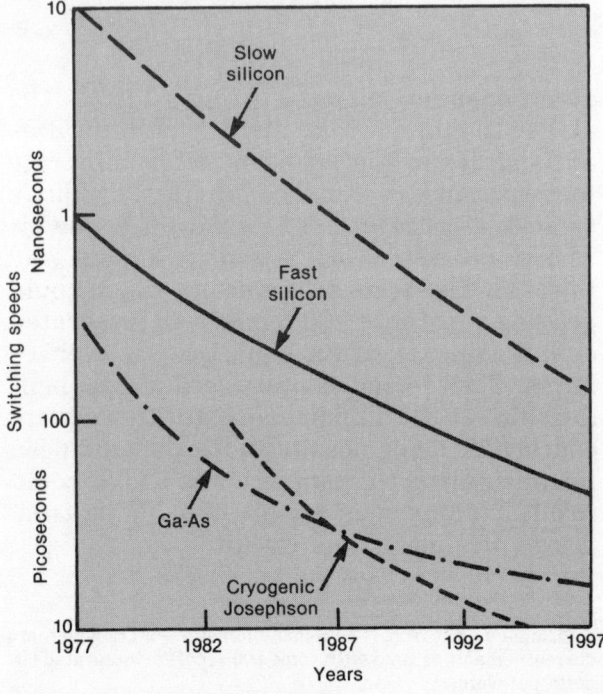

SOURCE: Arthur D. Little, Inc., estimates.

Chip reliability has also improved. It is estimated to have increased by at least a factor of 100, while the scale of integration has increased by a factor of 1,000.[41]

Gallium Arsenide Integrated Circuits

Another compound, gallium arsenide (GaAs), should find an increasing number of applications as a semiconductor substrate because of its special characteristics. These include high frequency operation, low power consumption, radiation resistance and optoelectronic and photonic properties.

Analog Devices

Currently, GaAs is used mainly in discrete component (non-integrated) analog devices such as microwave and millimeter wave radar, telecommunications and electronic warfare transmitters. Electronic signals at these high frequencies (10 to 100 Gigahertz or billion cycles per second) can be generated at much lower power with GaAs than is possible with conventional transmitter technologies. Integrated circuit, or monolithic, microwave and millimeter wave GaAs circuits have recently become available. Integration promises improved performance and lower prices in military systems and private sector microwave communications (local loop bypass and other) applications. Cellular radio is expected to provide a large market for GaAs transmitters, receivers and amplifiers.

Another application that offers a large potential consumer market for analog GaAs integrated circuits is direct broadcast satellite service (DBS). The principal French laboratory of N.V. Philips Co., based in The Netherlands, recently announced development of a GaAs chip that includes all of the functions necessary for the reception of DBS signals.

Optoelectronic and Laser Devices

Gallium arsenide is provoking excitement in another telecommunications technology, fiber optics. It can be fashioned into tiny lasers to

---
[41]Ross, op. cit., p. 2.

function as light sources for fiber optic transmission, into optoelectronic photodetectors to receive optical signals and translate them into electrical signals, and into signal processing components for fiber optic system amplifiers and repeaters (see Fiber Optics Case Study). Recent work at Bell Labs has developed large-scale integrated (LSI) GaAs signal processing circuits that are scheduled for production.[42]

Heretofore, separate devices have been required for fiber optic light generation, reception and signal processing. Communication among these separate devices introduces delays in fiber optic transmission systems. Lasers have been particularly difficult to integrate with the other circuit components on single chips because of their complex structure and the large amount of heat that is generated by their operation.

Fujitsu, the Japanese electronics giant, has conducted GaAs R&D funded by that government as part of a $74 million, 7-year project among a number of Japanese companies. In 1983, it announced development of a process that integrates a laser light source and the signal processing transistors necessary for fiber optic transmission, all on a single GaAs chip that operates at room temperature. A similar integrated optoelectronic photoreceiver is in the works.

American researchers at Honeywell and Rockwell International have also announced the development of integrated GaAs optical transmitters.[43] The Rockwell device in particular is reported to be adaptable to well-known LSI circuit manufacturing techniques, promising low production costs.[44]

Digital Devices

Interest has begun to intensify in the use of GaAs as a replacement for silicon in digital logic and memory devices. High switching speeds and low power consumption make this semiconductor attractive in certain applications. For instance, Cray Research has announced its intention to develop and use GaAs chips in the Cray-3 supercomputer which is scheduled to be available in 1986 (see Advanced Computer Architecture Case Study). But commercial semiconductor firms have thus far been reluctant to move GaAs logic and memory into production. Only low levels of integration (fewer devices per chip than silicon) and low yields (few good chips in a batch) are currently attainable with GaAs. Although 42 U.S. companies conduct laboratory work on GaAs, only two firms have announced plans to sell digital GaAs chips.[45]

The Department of Defense is interested in digital GaAs because, as well as having speed and power consumption advantages, GaAs circuits are highly resistant to radiation effects, making them attractive for military and space applications. Since 1975, DOD, through DARPA, has funded a total of $6 million to $7 million in R&D of digital GaAs integrated circuits. DARPA has announced plans to spend an additional $25 million to set up pilot production lines for GaAs 64K RAM and 6,000 to 10,000 element gate array (programmable logic) chips. The contract has been awarded to a joint venture between Rockwell International, who will develop the gate array chip, and Honeywell, who will design the RAM chip. Each of the two companies will develop production capacity for both the logic and memory chips to provide second sources for each.[46]

---

[42]*Electronics*, Oct. 6, 1983, p. 154.

[43]Honeywell announced an integrated optical transmitter in 1982, but it originally required special cooling. The Honeywell device has since been improved. See C. Cohen, "Optoelectronic chip integrates laser and pair of FETs," *Electronics*, June 30, 1983, pp. 89-90. See also *The Economist*, Feb. 5, 1983, pp. 82-83.

[44]L. Waller, "GaAs Optical IC Integrates Laser, Drive Transistors," *Electronics*, Oct. 6, 1983, pp. 51-52.

[45]W. R. Iversen, "Pentagon Campaigns for GaAs Chips," *Electronics*, July 28, 1983, pp. 97-98.

[46]J. Robertson, "Say Rockwell, Honeywell Get $25M DARPA IC Pact," *Electronic News*, Feb. 30, 1984, p. 4.

The DARPA program has received mixed reviews from the industry. On one hand, Rockwell believes that the DARPA-funded facilities will help make digital GaAs profitable for the entire industry, since the technology is expected to be made available to other defense contractors,[47] but neither of the two companies that have announced plans to develop digital GaAs for the merchant semiconductor market. The companies—Gigabit Logic, which recently entered into a private R&D venture to develop GaAs RAM chips,[48] and Harris Microwave Semiconductors—submitted bids for the DARPA contract. Both cited the DARPA emphasis on low power for portable military systems at the expense of higher speed as the major factor in their decision to forego bidding on the contract.[49] This trade-off is seen as forfeiting the major advantage of GaAs in commercial competition with silicon digital memory and logic devices.

Optical Logic

Another area of applied research in which gallium arsenide is playing a critical role is optical logic. The replacement of computer processors based on electronics with ones based on photonics, which would theoretically be capable of vastly higher speeds, has been considered a possibility for some time. Such optical computers might be capable of trillions of operations per second.[50] With the spread of fiber optic communications technology, optical processing is even more attractive. The large capacity of light-wave transmission demands higher processing speeds to fully exploit the available fiber optic bandwidth. Conversions between optical and electronic signals introduce delays into current fiber optic systems.

Only recently, with the use of GaAs and another new semiconductor material, indium antimonide, has the technology been available to begin to develop optical devices that function like the logic elements that make up microprocessors. Hughes Aircraft Research Laboratories, which is performing R&D work on optical logic under contract from the National Security Agency, has announced the development of a prototype device that is expected to be capable, in about 3 years, of more than 10 times the speed of current electronic logic devices. The device is to be applied in data encryption systems.[51]

The major drawback seen with current approaches to optical computing is that the logic elements are much larger than comparable electronic ones. Barring fundamental theoretical and practical advances, especially in physics and in materials sciences, optical logic systems will probably not see widespread use before the end of the century.

The Convergence of Bio-technology and Information Technology

Advances in the biological sciences and breakthroughs in genetic engineeering have encouraged speculation and some preliminary research on the possibility of designing biocomputers. Devices constructed from biochemical molecules potentially offer greater logic and memory densities, and the possibility of totally novel information processing methods, including the emulation of brain functioning. The first interdisciplinary scientific conference on this subject, sponsored by the National Science Foundation and the University of California, Los Angeles, was held in October 1983.[52] The meeting brought together biologists, chemists, physicists, mathematicians, computer scientists and electrical engineers to discuss the prospects for this technology and to generate questions to guide research.

The field is just beginning to adopt theoretical concepts on how such biochemical-based machines might operate, and on the more dif-

---

[47]Ibid., see also Iversen, op. cit., p. 97.
[48]"Gigabit in $6.1M GaAs static RAM R&D Venture," *Electronic News,* Jan. 9, 1984, p. 66.
[49]Iversen, op. cit., pp. 97-98.
[50]E. Abraham, C. T. Seaton, and S. D. Smith, "The Optical Computer," *Scientific American,* February 1983, pp. 85-88.

[51]L. Waller, "Components for Optical Logic Start to Click," Electronics, Dec. 29, 1982, pp. 31-32.
[52]International Conference on Chemically Based Computing, Santa Monica, CA.

ficult questions of how one might construct a bio-computer and make it work in concert with existing information systems. Lewis Mayfield, head of the Chemical and Process Engineering Division at NSF concluded, "The consensus of the Santa Monica Conference was that a great deal more work will be needed at the fundamental level before development can begin. So although we will accept grant proposals in this area, we have no plans to organize a program to promote it."[53]

Software

Software and hardware are primary elements in information technology systems. The hardware provides the set of generic functions that information systems may perform (input, storage, processing, communications and output), and the software combines and organizes these functions to accomplish specific functions. The two elements are responsible for the burgeoning range of capabilities of information technology, and, increasingly, for advances in the technology itself.

Software is the part of information technology that is most readily modifiable. A major attraction of computer-based systems is that they are programmable—machine functions are fixed, but their sequence may be modified to achieve different ends at different times or to respond to changing conditions. The content of information systems may be changed, expanded and contracted, within limits, to accommodate the changing needs of users. Software is the vehicle for providing the flexibilty of information systems to the users of the technology; software aids users in communicating and managing large bodies of information and in coping with the complexity of large or specialized systems.

Traditionally, the term "software" narrowly referred to programs for large mainframe computers and was of concern only to computer professionals. But as computer power has spread to wider segments of society, the characteristics of software have been modified by the uses to which computer systems are put, and the meaning of software has broadened. Now, software is both the instructions that direct the operations of computer-based systems, and the information content, or data, that computer systems manipulate.

The focus of software production and use is changing from concerns of computer professionals to the concerns of a broad range of *end users* of information technology—i.e., those with no particular interest in the technology, but only its capabilities and results. Because of this and the increasing availability of computer and telecommunications capabilities, future limits on the utility of information technology will depend less on hardware capability and more on the difficulties of defining and accommodating the needs of users.[54]

Possible implications of an expanding number of users of information technology, and a shift in the focus of concern toward the needs of that expanding set of users include:

- The relative importance of software issues in the research and development of information technologies will likely increase.
- Small companies will continue to be important players in software development because of their ability to respond to the specialized needs of small segments of the user population.
- There will be movement toward standardization of software for common applications, such as in accounting, banking, insurance and government.
- There will be continuing pressure to introduce systematic engineering practices into the production of software to lower software development costs and to assure the reliability of software in critical applications. (See Software Engineering Case Study.)
- There will be a demand for higher level, *nonprocedural* computer languages for the development of new and unique appli-

---

[53]J. B. Tucker, "Pioneering Meeting Puts Biochips on the Map," High Technology, February 1984, p. 43.

[54]An analogy can be drawn between computer users and automobile drivers: all want the benefits of the technology but most are indifferent to how it works.

cations; such languages will allow the user to focus on the characteristics of the tasks to be performed and not on how the hardware performs them.
- The search will intensify for powerful and simplifying concepts for the organization of information and knowledge in many fields.
- Computerization will require the users of information systems to more clearly define and organize their habits and operations related to information use.
- There will be more concern among users of information technology with the uses of information and the content of information systems, and less concern with how the technology works.

The production of software has become a major industry in the United States, with estimated expenditures of $40 billion in 1982[55] for software products and for in-house development of programs. Sales of software in the United States doubled between 1982 and 1983 from $5 billion to more than $10 billion, and are expected to increase to more than $24 billion in 1987 (see table 59).

As information technology applications proliferate in the office, factory and home, and in the military, computer software is required to fulfill many new and complex functions. The growing demand for software is causing pressure to make software more useful, reliable and cost effective, and to make software development more productive. Not unexpectedly, software comprises higher and higher proportions of the cost of new information systems. Estimates of the relative cost of software in large systems range to above 80 percent (see fig. 62).

The Changing Role of Software in Information Systems

Computer software is traditionally classified as two general types: *applications software* that is designed to apply computer power to

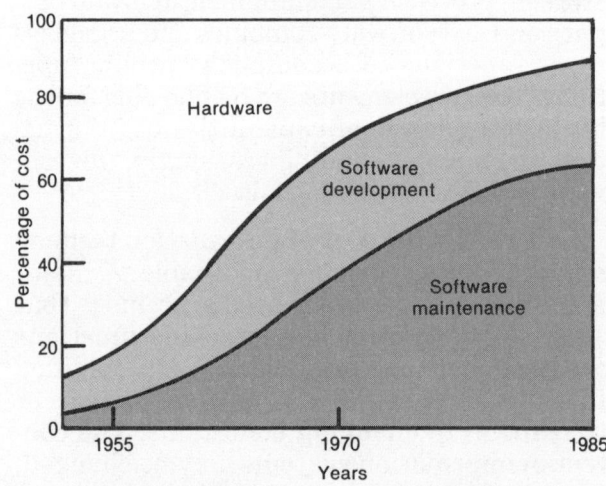

Figure 62.—The Relative Costs of Software and Hardware

SOURCE: Steve Olson, *Pathways of Choice*, Mosaic, July/August 1983, p. 6.

[55]S. Olsen, "Pathways of Choice," *Mosaic*, July/August 1983, p. 3.

Table 59.—Software Sales by Use

	1982	1983	1984	1985
		(millions of dollars)[a]		
Software, total	5,001	10,309	15,017	24,677
Application programs, total	1,997	3,448	5,455	11,100
Computer-aided design, manufacturing and engineering	776	1,126	1,636	3,200
Other applications	1,221	2,320	3,819	7,900
Systems software, total	3,004	6,861	9,562	13,577
Compilers, interpreters, and assemblers ..	541	610	700	932
Data-base management systems	1,100	1,430	1,888	3,500
Diagnostic and performance monitoring ..	493	645	710	945
Operating system	870	4,176	6,264	8,200

[a]All figures in current U.S. dollars.

SOURCE: *Electronics*, Jan. 12, 1984, p. 128.

a specific task or tasks, such as computer-aided design of automobiles or inventory management in a retail store; and *systems software* that is used to manage the operations of information systems themselves, such as computer operating systems or database management systems.

Applications software has come to include a user interface that allows persons other than computer professionals to work with the computer system, while systems software is designed to help computer professionals write and execute programs, make efficient use of system components, diagnose and correct faults, and manage and audit system resources, contents and usage. This distinction, though useful, is beginning to break down with the advent of personal computers, in which operating systems are important tools to help users control the workings of their machines and perform such mundane tasks as copying files. However, the ends to which the software is applied still remain distinct—applications software solves user problems, systems software solves computer problems.

In general, systems software is an integral component of the hardware because its job is to control the hardware and to schedule and accommodate the development and execution of applications programs. The trend has been for the manufacturers of hardware or specialized software vendors to write systems programs, and for more of the systems programs to be embedded in hardware, or ROM (Read Only Memory), making the end user incapable of altering them. There is also a trend toward the standardization of operating systems to increase the *portability* of applications software, or the ability to use identical applications programs on different machines.

The expansion of the computer user population is being fueled by the expanding content of information systems, and is leading to an expanding definition of the term "software." Information systems are increasingly encompassing and integrating many collections of information formerly considered to be separate and segregated, such as the files of corporate divisions or government departments. The technology that has heretofore embodied such large information bases, for the most part paper and print, was not integrated; thus the information contained in those files has not been accessible to single individuals. Now, relatively cheap computer terminals and telephone links are making the enormous amounts of information being stored in digital electronic form (software) accessible by people in their homes and offices.[56] Through such services as videotex, newspapers, periodicals and even entire libraries may eventually be made available "on-line."

Integration of information management on such a large scale will require sophisticated control software to help people find the information that they want; advances in information science and contributions from such fields as artificial intelligence and psychology will be needed for this to occur. The integration of information management will also have profound effects on the way people view and handle information, and on how organizations conduct their business; the social sciences (sociology, political science, anthropology) will increasingly be looked to for understanding of the inevitable organizational and human conflicts that will flow from the changes in information access and use made possible by information technology.

The Software Bottleneck

Demand for computer applications is outstripping the ability of the traditional large data processing organizations (e.g., banks, insurance companies, government agencies) to supply the programs these organizations need in a timely and cost-effective manner. The lag

---

[56]The massive integration of information systems raises a number of public policy issues including questions of the government role in protecting *intellectual property, privacy* and other *civil liberties* assuring *equity of access* to information, and the effect of information technology on the processes of government itself. These and related issues are the subject of two OTA assessments now in progress, "Intellectual Property Rights in an Age of Electronics and Information" and "Federal Government Information Technology: Administrative Process and Civil Liberties."

time between identification of an application and completion of the software in the average data processing department is 2½ years and is increasing, probably discouraging the proposal of many new applications.[57] There are a number of factors that contribute to this "software bottleneck," chief among them that approximately 50 percent of the data processing budgets are spent maintaining old programs—making changes in existing codes because of errors in the design or coding of programs, or because applications requirements were inadequately specified.[58]

Another factor that slows the development of new programs is that software development, as it is practiced now, is *project-oriented.* Each new program is built up from scratch with little systematic reuse of parts of older programs, even though identical functions may be implemented. The knowledge and experience gained in one project are not systematically preserved and transferred to other projects. Innovations in programming techniques tend to be adopted piecemeal as project budgets allow. As a result of this project orientation and lack of standardization, large programs that must rely on the efforts of a number of programmers tend to be patchworks of pieces that reflect different programming styles, and are often nearly incomprehensible to people other than the original authors. These problems are exacerbated by a turnover rate among computer professionals estimated at 15 percent per year.[59]

These difficulties combine to produce the present software development situation in which time is wasted in writing essentially identical parts, testing is laborious and expensive, and maintenance programmers spend most of their time trying to understand programs rather fixing them. The difficulties have grown out of the historical context in computing in which hardware resources were expensive, and the creative aspect of programming was devoted mostly to the efficient use of these resources through the clever compression of code. Now, with the precipitous decline in hardware costs, programming productivity rather than code efficiency is widely recognized as the limiting factor in the use of computing power.

The software development resources now in use appear to be inadequate and too fragmented to keep up with the demand for computing power. These resources include trained manpower and tools (software development tools include workstations, computer-aided-design, coding and testing programs, and documentation) to aid designers, programmers and managers in creating and maintaining cost-effective, reliable software.

Computer manufacturers and software developers, and government, university and industry experts are recognizing the problems associated with the software bottleneck and see the potential for sizable productivity gains by changing the nature of software development. For example, some avenues to alleviating the productivity problems of software development and maintenance lie in the use and reuse of standard function software modules, and the development of software to produce, test, and maintain other software. Research and development efforts in software engineering are seen as essential to this change (see Software Engineering Case Study).

Software and Complexity

Computer software is an important factor in making information technologies useful in a widening array of complex applications—from space vehicles to telecommunications

---

[57] A recent survey of IBM mainframe-based data processing departments found that the average time lag for the initiation of applications programming projects is 2 years and this lag is growing by 3 months per year. Once under development, the average application requires 8 months to complete. At the same time, software representing 10 months of programming effort is discarded yearly by the average data-processing department because of obsolescence. A certain backlog of work is desirable to keep data-processing staff busy, but it is clear that many organizations are falling behind. *Application Development in Practice,* Tech Tran User Survey, Xephon Technology Transfer Ltd., 1983., p. 2.

[58] W. Rauch-Hindin, "Some Answers to the Software Problems of the 1980s," *Data Communications,* May 1981, p. 58. See also the Case Study on Software Engineering.

[59] This figure reflects a recent decline in turnover attributable to the last recession and may well be on the rise. Also, it is believed by experts that the greatest turnover is among those professionals *writing* code, so that this figure understates the effect of turnover on program development productivity.

networks to weapons systems. Software is used to produce *simulations* of complex systems and events, so that scientists and engineers can experiment and analyze without building expensive prototypes, and to control the *operations* of the most complex of man's creations, such as nuclear reactors and the space shuttle.

The need to manage a variety of increasingly complex systems is a major source of the pressure to improve software capability and reliability. For example, a large air traffic control program can consist of more than half a million instructions that must mesh perfectly and be essentially free of errors.[60] The efforts of hundreds of programmers over several years may be required to produce a software system of this size. The complexity of the software makes it virtually impossible to assure that no errors are present in a completed program.[61]

Software written for critical applications such as air traffic control, manned space vehicles, nuclear reactors, weapons systems, or electronic funds transfer, although impossible to guarantee as error-free when completed, must be constructed in such a way that at least the *parts* of programs and their *interconnections* are rigorously designed and adequately tested as they are built up. The complexity of software development is likely to increase dramatically with the advent of *massively parallel* computing systems and the construction of large *knowledge-based* systems.

---

[60]Olsen, op. cit., p. 3.

[61]Every two-choice branch point in a program (where decision is made on what procedure will follow depending on the conditions that are present) doubles the number of possible paths that the program can take, so that a program with 10 branch points will have 1,024 possible paths. A program for a large air traffic control system may have more than 39,000 branch points. If a computer could test a trillion paths per second (a capability far beyond today's most powerful supercomputers) it would require over $10^{11,731}$ *years* (that's the number one followed by 11,731 zeros) to test all possible paths in such a program. See P. E. Olsen, and R. W. Adrion, M. A. Dennis Branstad, and J. C. Cherniavsky, *ACM Computing Surveys*, June 1982, p. 184.

Conclusion

The microelectronic and software building blocks for information technology are likely to advance dramatically in coming decades. The path of progress for microelectronics is reasonably clear into the 1990s as practical and theoretical limits are approached for silicon and as other technologies come into use. For software, the path is less clear, but most likely will include far more standardization, reuse of software modules, and development of software tools to produce, test, and maintain other software. Most importantly, the *integration* of the concepts behind advances in these two building block technologies will shape future capabilities.

Information technology capabilities and their efficient utilization will depend upon the integration of ideas from a variety of disciplines. For example, the acceptance and efficient use of emerging computer and telecommunications resources in organizations require understanding of behavioral and social variables, as well as understanding of computer technology. Similarly, computer-aided-design requires both new software and new hardware for the display and manipulation of complex designs. The integration of hardware and software in new microelectronics and software design tools leads to further advances in information technology itself.

This integrative interaction constitutes a powerful technological engine which is fueling the advance of information technology in many applications—including computers for science, engineering and business, robotics and computer-integrated manufacturing, telecommunications, and artificial intelligence, among many others. These applications in turn will influence opportunities for economic growth and create alternatives for change in society, and thus will have major impacts on some of the policy issues that will become preeminent for legislators.

Index

Index

Alvey, John, 106
American Council on Education, 150
American Electronic Association, 147
AT&T, 14, 16, 78, 111-134

Babbitt, Governor Bruce, Arizona, 172
Battelle Memorial Institute, 32
Bell Laboratories, 11, 14, 16, 74, 113, 120, 153
British Alvey Program, 18
Brown, Charles L., president, AT&T, 128
Buchsbaum, Solomon J., 123
Bureau of Labor Statistics (BLS), 142, 146

California Institute of Technology, 17
case studies, 9
  advanced computer architecture, 9, 55
    changing computer architecture, 56
    computer architecture R&D, 57
    critical areas of research, 63
    international efforts, 65
    manpower, 65
  artificial intelligence, 13, 87
    content and conduct, 96
    foreign national efforts, 105
    R&D environments, 90
  fiber optics, 12, 67
    commercialization trends, 69
    directions of U.S. research, 73
    research in Japan, 74
    United States R&D, 71
  software engineering, 11, 75
    content and conduct of software engineering R&D, 79
    international efforts in software engineering R&D, 85
    software R&D environments, 76
Chynoweth, Alan G., 129
Computer Technology Corp., 36
Congress:
  House Committee on Energy and Commerce, 3
  House Committee on Science and Technology, 3
  Joint Economic Committee, 172
  Senate Commerce Committee, 128
Corning Glass Works, 73

Defense Advanced Research Projects Agency (DARPA), 9, 29, 58, 93, 95, 219
Department of Commerce, 32
Department of Defense (DOD), 5, 11, 13, 20, 29, 41, 58, 75, 78, 89, 93, 279, 294, 329
Department of Energy, 4, 10, 20, 58

Department of Justice, 33, 111, 116
deregulation and divestiture on research, effects of, 111-135
  antitrust laws, deregulation and divestiture, 113
  divestiture, 116
  factors affecting research, 123
    allocation of research and development expenditures, 125
    availability of research results, 130
    basic research, 128
    Bell Communications Research, Inc., role of, 129
    stability of earnings, 123
  policy implications, 131
  research at AT&T, management of, 120
    Bell Labs after divestiture, 122
    modified final judgment and Bell Labs, 121

education and human resources for research and development, 139-166
  concern about manpower, 139
  elementary and secondary education, 154
  Federal role in manpower development, 157
  identifying particular manpower problems and solutions, 141
  problems in higher education, 149
  range of manpower predictions, 145
  relationship between manpower development and economic growth, 140
  societal context for determining Federal manpower policy, 161
  supply of manpower, 149
environment for R&D in information technology, 25-52
  concepts for R&D, 27
  roles of the participants, 28
    conflicts in perspectives, goals, and policies, 42
    Federal Government, 28
    Government funding, 28
    industrial R&D, 34
    other Federal policies, 31
      antitrust policy, 33
      industrial policy, 33
      patent policy, 31
      R&D limited partnership, 33
      tax credits, 32
      technology transfer, 32
    pattern of Government funding, 30
    universities' role in R&D, 37
  measures of the health of U.S. R&D in information technology, 43, 51

information industry profile, 43
U.S. patent activity, 45
European Community (EC), 66
European Economic Community (EEC), 216
European Program for Research and Development in Information Technology, (ESPRIT), 18, 202, 216, 219

Federal Communications Commission, 31, 111, 114, 115
Federal Trade Commission, 33
foreign information technology R&D, 201-276
  conclusions, 221
  international trends, 201
    adapting technology, 202
    international technology agreements, 208
    multinational corporations, 206
    patents, 210
    science and engineering students, 212
    scientific and technical literature, 211
    technology exchange agreement, 207
    trade, 201
    U.S. computer trade, 203
  Japan, 222
    government, 226
      Defense Agency, 239
      Information Technology Promotion Agency (IPA), 236
      Japan Electronic Computer Co., 236
      Japan Development Bank, 239
      Japan Robot Leasing Co., 236
      Kokusai Denshin Denwa Ltd., 238
      Ministry of International Trade and Industry, 228
      Ministry of Posts and Telecommunications: Nippon Telegraph and Telephone, 236
      national R&D projects, 231
      Science and Technology Agency, 235
    industry, 243
      Fujitsu Ltd., 245
      Hitachi Ltd., 245
      NEC Corp., 244
      Oki Electric Industry Corp., 246
    size of Japanese participation in information technology markets, 225
    university, 240
  France, 246
    government, 252
      Agence de l'Informatique, 256
      Centre d'Etudes des Systemes et des Technologies Advances, 257
      Centre Mondial Informatique et Ressource Humaine, 257
      Centre National d'Etudes Telecommunications, 254
      Centre National de la Recherche Scientifique, 253
      L'Institut National de Recherche en Informatique et en Automatique, 255
      Ministere des Postes, Telecommunications, et Telediffusion, 253
    Industry, 259
      CII Honeywell Bull, 259
      CIT Alcatel, 260
      Sogitec, S.A., 261
      Thomson CSF, 260
    political environment, 248
    size of participation in information technology markets, 247
    social environment, 252
    university, 257
  United Kingdom, 261
    ESPRIT, 272
    government, 263
      British Technology Group, 269
      Department of Education and Science, 268
      Department of Trade and Industry, 265
      Ministry of Defense, 268
    industry, 270
      British Telecom, 271
      General Electric Co., 271
      Plessey, 271
    size of participation in information technology markets, 263
    university, 269
  U.S. information technology R&D policies, implications for, 214
    government/industry/university institutional arrangements, 217
    government role, 216
    industry participation, 219
    science and technology policy goals, 215
France, 66, 70, 87, 246
French La Filiere Electronique program, 18

General Accounting Office (GAO), 39, 78, 155
General Electric, 181
Georgia Institute of Technology, 30
goals for Federal R&D policy, 3
Great Britain, 66, 71, 86, 261
Greene, Judge Harold H., U.S. District Court for the District of Columbia, 116

Heckler, Representative Margaret, 139

IBM, 12, 36, 53
information technology R&D, nature of, 6
  close boundary between theory and application, 8
  complexity, 8
  multidisciplinary nature, 7
  software as technology, 7
Inman, Admiral Bobby, 194
Institute of Electrical and Electronic Engineers, 148
issues and strategies, 14
  changing roles of universities, 17
  foreign programs, 18
  science policy, 19
  scientific and technological manpower, 16
  telecommunications deregulation, impacts of, 14

Japan, 65, 70, 74, 85, 222
Japanese Fifth Generation Computer Project, 13, 18, 65, 105
Japan Ministry of International Trade and Industry (MITI), 65, 75, 105, 219, 228

Lawrence Livermore National Lab, 58
legislation:
  Economic Recovery Tax Act, 32
  House Authorization Act of 1984, 41
  Morrill Act of 1862, 158, 159
  National Cooperative Research Act of 1984, 33
  National Defense Education Act of 1958, 159
  Public Law 96-517, 31
  Sherman Antitrust Act, 113
  Stevenson-Wydler Technology Innovation Act of 1980, 32, 215
  Tax Equity and Fiscal Responsibility Act of 1982, 32
Lewis, David, 148
Library of Congress, 133
Los Alamos National Lab, 58
Lotus Development Corp., 202

Massachusetts Institute of Technology (MIT), 17, 177
McCarthy, John, 90
Microelectronics Center of North Carolina, 36, 184, 188
Microelectronics & Computer Technology Corp., 36, 120, 172, 193
Microsoft, Inc., 204

National Aeronautics and Space Administration (NASA), 4, 10, 30, 31
National Bureau of Standards, 37, 85
National Center for Education Statistics, 34
National Oceanic and Atmospheric Administration (NOAA), 4
National Science Foundation (NSF), 8, 9, 27, 29, 30, 40, 41, 58, 94, 142, 147, 159
National Science Teachers Association, 155
National Telecommunications and Information Administration, 133
Nelson, Richard R., 129
new roles for universities in information technology R&D, 169-195
  forces driving new relationships, 171
  impacts of new university arrangements, 173
    expected benefits, 174
    potential costs, 175
  new roles, 176
    Microelectronics Center of North Carolina, 184, 188
    Microelectronics & Computer Technology Corp., 193
    Microelectronics and Information Sciences Center, University of Minnesota, 178
    MIT Microsystems Industrial Group, 177
    Rensselaer Polytechnic Institute for Industrial Innovation, 180
    Semiconductor Research Corp., 189
    Stanford University Center for Integrated Systems, 182, 185
North Carolina State University, 30

Ohio State University, 30

Penzias, Arno, vice president, Bell Labs, 130
Perot, H. Ross, 194
principal findings, 5

Rensselaer Polytechnic Institute, 30, 73, 180
Research Triangle Park, NC, 173, 231

Semiconductor Research Corp., 36, 120, 189
Stanford University, 182, 185

technology and industry, 307
  characteristics of the U.S. information industry, 316
    employment, 317
    industry structure, 320
    international trade, 317
    small entrepreneurial firms, 321
  composition of information technology, 308
    examples of system applications, 309
      cellular mobile radio communications, 310
      computer simulation, 312

      direct broadcast satellites, 310
      financial services, 315
      heart pacemakers, 314
      robotics, 311
   importance of information technology, 307
   where the technology is heading, 323
      convergence of biotechnology and information technology, 330
      gallium arsenide integrated in circuits, 328
      microelectronics, 324
      silicon integrated circuits, 324
      software, 331-334
Texas A&M University, 194
top 15 U.S. companies in R&D spending, 44
Trilogy Ltd., 33
Tsukuba Science City, Japan, 231
Turing, Alan, 90

University of Arizona, 74
University of Minnesota, 178
University of Rhode Island, 30
University of Rochester, 73
University of Texas, 194
U.S. patent activity, 45
U.S. Patent and Trademark Office, 47
U.S. science and technology policy, 279
   background, 280
      general policies, 280
      science policy statements, 282
      tenets of science and technology policy, 285
   information technology R&D policies, 286
   key issue areas, 290
      international competitiveness, 298
      military/civilian balance of R&D funding, 294
      organization of government, 290

Vetter, Betty M., 147
von Neumann, John, 90

West Germany, 66, 70

Office of Technology Assessment

The Office of Technology Assessment (OTA) was created in 1972 as an analytical arm of Congress. OTA's basic function is to help legislative policymakers anticipate and plan for the consequences of technological changes and to examine the many ways, expected and unexpected, in which technology affects people's lives. The assessment of technology calls for exploration of the physical, biological, economic, social, and political impacts that can result from applications of scientific knowledge. OTA provides Congress with independent and timely information about the potential effects—both beneficial and harmful—of technological applications.

Requests for studies are made by chairmen of standing committees of the House of Representatives or Senate; by the Technology Assessment Board, the governing body of OTA; or by the Director of OTA in consultation with the Board.

The Technology Assessment Board is composed of six members of the House, six members of the Senate, and the OTA Director, who is a nonvoting member.

OTA has studies under way in nine program areas: energy and materials; industry, technology, and employment; international security and commerce; biological applications; food and renewable resources; health; communication and information technologies; oceans and environment; and science, transportation, and innovation.

RAYMOND H. FOGLER LIBRARY
DATE DUE

BOOKS ARE SUBJECT TO
RECALL AFTER